◆ *Sixth Edition* ◆

Social Studies and the Elementary School Child

George W. Maxim
West Chester University

Merrill, an imprint of
Prentice Hall
Upper Saddle River, New Jersey   Columbus, Ohio

Library of Congress Cataloging-in-Publication Data

Maxim, George M.
    Social studies and the elementary school child / George W. Maxim.
  — 6th ed.
      p.   cm.
    Includes bibliographical references (p.   ).
    ISBN 0-13-649898-1
    1. Social sciences—Study and teaching (Elementary)—United
States.   2. Interdisciplinary approach in education—United States.
3. Effective teaching—United States.   I. Title.
LB1584.M478   1999
372.83′044—dc21

98-22993

CIP

Cover art: © Melissa Taylor
Editor: Bradley J. Potthoff
Production Editor: Mary M. Irvin
Photo Researcher: Nancy Ritz
Design Coordinator: Diane C. Lorenzo
Text Designer: Custom Editorial Productions, Inc.
Production Manager: Pamela C. Bennett
Director of Marketing: Kevin Flanagan
Advertising/Marketing Coordinator: Krista Groshong
Marketing Manager: Suzanne Stanton
Editorial Production Supervision: Custom Editorial Productions, Inc.

This book was set in Optima by Custom Editorial Productions, Inc., and was printed and bound by R. R. Donnelley & Sons Company. The cover was printed by Phoenix Color Corp.

© 1999, 1995 by Prentice-Hall, Inc.
Simon & Schuster/A Viacom Company
Upper Saddle River, New Jersey 07458

Photo Credits: pp. 4, 50, 93, 154, 199, 409, 585, Barbara Schwartz, Merrill/Prentice Hall; pp. 7, 31, 113, 210, 259, 333, 476, 508, 550, 617, 622, Scott Cunningham, Merrill/Prentice Hall; pp. 12, 274, 293, 384, Anne Vega, Merrill/Prentice Hall; pp. 55, 74, 140, 161, 235, 361, 369, 372, 376, 451, 572, 604, 609, Elizabeth A. Maxim; pp. 67, 103, 122, 521, KS Studios Merrill/Prentice Hall; pp. 144, 179, 193, 245, 286, 303, 336, 415, 464, 504, 564, 580, Anthony Magnacca, Merrill/Prentice Hall; pp. 197, 276, 397, 447, Todd Yarrington, Merrill/Prentice Hall; p. 324, Linda Peterson, Merrill/Prentice Hall; p. 425, Pat McKay; p. 639, Kevin Fitzsimons, Merrill/Prentice Hall.

Printed in the United States of America

10 9 8 7 6 5 4 3 2 1

ISBN

Prentice-Hall International (UK) Limited, *London*
Prentice-Hall of Australia Pty. Limited, *Sydney*
Prentice-Hall of Canada, Inc., *Toronto*
Prentice-Hall Hispanoamericana, S. A., *Mexico*
Prentice-Hall of India Private Limited, *New Delhi*
Prentice-Hall of Japan, Inc., *Tokyo*
Simon & Schuster Asia Pte. Ltd., *Singapore*
Editora Prentice-Hall do Brasil, Ltda., *Rio de Janeiro*

Dedicated with affection to my wife Libby for her
encouragement, support, and patience.

Preface

Social Studies and the Elementary School Child, Sixth Edition, was written with the belief that the most consequential ingredient of a successful social studies program is a good teacher. The physical setting is critical, as are the instructional materials and activities, but a teacher's skills and sensitivities are of utmost importance. A teacher's personality and professional skills combine to set the tone of the environment and make a lasting impact on the students, on their families, and on society in general.

Skilled teachers must exercise the same rigor and calculating precision that the most gifted surgeon or engineer practices in selecting a plan of action. By doing so, their social studies programs become both stimulating and inspiring, capturing the spirit of wonder and imagination young children naturally attach to all the mysteries of their unfolding world. As youngsters actively investigate the fascinating people, places, and events that make up their social environment, they not only continue to grow as active investigators, but also acquire a rich storehouse of content essential for effective decision making.

This book takes the position that no single method of instruction, by itself, can achieve all the important goals and objectives of social studies instruction. The keys to effective teaching are variety and flexibility. Therefore, teachers must be cautious decision makers. Like the best actors, they must take on many roles, each being played with sensitivity and awareness. Sometimes teachers lecture, but not often. Sometimes they place students in committees to accomplish a task; other times they encourage the children to work alone. Sometimes teachers read selections from quality literature; often they will assign a textbook selection. The strong emphasis is on variety. The teacher's biggest job is to concentrate on experiences that allow children to grow to their fullest potential. To that end, this book offers a sound theoretical background and a wealth of appropriate practical applications that prospective teachers need to plan and implement effective social studies programs.

REVISIONS IN THE SIXTH EDITION

This edition maintains the focus of previous editions, but has been comprehensively revised and updated to reflect contemporary thinking in the dynamic field of social studies education. The importance of alternative classroom strategies and of professional decision making establish the focal point of this sixth edition.

The chapters open with "advance organizers" designed to help readers attach their present knowledge of the content to the central themes *(What I Know)*. Students not only log what they already know, but also jot down questions they hope to answer after previewing the chapter headings. Summary sections *(What I Now Know)* at the end of each chapter encourage readers to reflect on the degree to which the chapter has enlarged and enriched professional understandings. Following the "advance organizers," each chapter opens with a "Classroom Sketch" that is designed to offer a practical illustration of the content, and a section called "Classroom Connection" that connects the sketch to the chapter content.

"Technology Samplers" are included within each chapter of this sixth edition. They suggest starting points for exploiting computers as crucial planning and instructional tools. "Afterwords" at the end of each chapter summarize the content just presented and offer the reader something extra to think about.

Four new chapters have been written for this sixth edition. Chapter 2, "Creating a Supportive Environment," examines the characteristics of the rich diversity of students who make up our elementary school population. Chapter 3, "Planning Lessons," offers a comprehensive view of planning responsibilities in the social studies program. Chapter 8, "Promoting Civic Education," probes the question "What kinds of adult citizens do we want our schools to help build?" Chapter 14, "Selecting Instructional Resources," surveys the wide range of stimuli that are needed for effective instruction.

Five chapters from the fifth edition were eliminated—"Small-Group and Individual Learning," "The Language Arts Link," "The Allied Social Sciences," "Supplementary Instructional Content," and "Assessment Strategies." Much of the associated content was infused throughout this sixth edition, however. For example, material in "The Language Arts Link" was expanded and redefined as two separate chapters—"Reading as a Meaning-Making Activity" (Chapter 11) and "Writing to Learn" (Chapter 12). Much of the content in the former "Assessment Strategies" chapter was divided and relocated to the two planning chapters (Chapters 3 and 4).

As readers use this text, they will realize that there is no single correct way to teach social studies. They will learn about old strategies and new ones. Although they may be tempted to look more favorably on new theories because of their contemporary nature, it is important to examine each option carefully, and to select one for use because it is the most likely to achieve a stated instructional goal. Even the most current teaching technique can make the classroom dull and lifeless if it is not carried out expertly by a skilled teacher. Therefore, this sixth edition is designed as a sourcebook and guide to help teachers set learning into motion.

ACKNOWLEDGMENTS

Writing a book is not an individual accomplishment: An author cannot take complete credit for the finished work. This is especially true for this sixth edition. Many people have made important contributions to this book.

First, I must acknowledge the contributions of my wife, Libby. Her patience was pushed to the breaking point a number of times, but she rarely let me know. She willingly helped me out while I was sequestered at the keyboard, and freed up the time I needed to complete the manuscript on time. In addition, Libby's outstanding knowledge of the computer aided me in no small measure in completing the "Technology Samplers." Without her help, I could not have put together this text feature.

Next, I must single out the contributions of my two sons, Mike and Jeff. Although they were not aware of how much they helped, their pride in my work and their exuberance never failed to pick up my spirits whenever the "writing day blues" hit. The only "tough" part of writing this sixth edition was sacrificing the time that could have been spent with my family.

I am also indebted to my parents, Rose and Stanley Maxim. Their honorable work ethic instilled in me the value of persistence in tackling a job as overwhelming as writing a book. Their love of parenthood was an important model and inspiration for me throughout my life and career.

On a more professional level, I am indebted to the distinguished editorial team at Merrill/Prentice Hall. Jeff Johnston, editor-in-chief, must be cited for his faith in the book. Brad Potthoff, Editor for Curriculum and Instruction, made the revision process constructive and rewarding. His insightful and studied knowledge of social studies education offered excellent targets for improvement. Linda McElhiney's extraordinary vision helped concieve the marvelous design of this book. Mary Irvin, production editor, did a wonderful job coordinating the efforts of everyone involved in the production process. And JaNoel Lowe of Custom Editorial Productions was masterful in carrying out her responsibility to manage the production of the book. Her expertise and constructive support were much appreciated. Tom Lewis did a commendable job as copyeditor. I thank him for his talents. And Mary Evangelista, editorial assistant, was not only efficient and thorough, but highly personable as well. I appreciate the skill and friendliness everyone at Merrill/Prentice Hall brought to this project.

My colleagues at West Chester University warrant special consideration for their support and encouragement: Tony Johnson, Dean of the School of Education; Mary Ann Maggitti, Chair of the Department of Childhood Studies and Reading; and faculty involved in teaching elementary social studies courses—A. Scott Dunlap, Martha Drobnak, and Ruby Peters. I am also grateful to Dan Darigan for his inspiration to explore more deeply the literacy–social studies connection.

The form and format of this sixth edition was greatly influenced by the wise suggestions and critical commentary offered by these judicious reviewers: Sally R. Beisser, Iowa State University; Duane M. Giannangelo, The University of Memphis, Thomas B. Goodkind, University of Connecticut; Robert Kizlik, Florida Atlantic University; Denee J. Mattioli, East Tennessee University, and Tony L. Talbert, Sam Houston State University. I am grateful for their expert recommendations.

Brief Contents

Contents

LIST OF ACTIVITIES

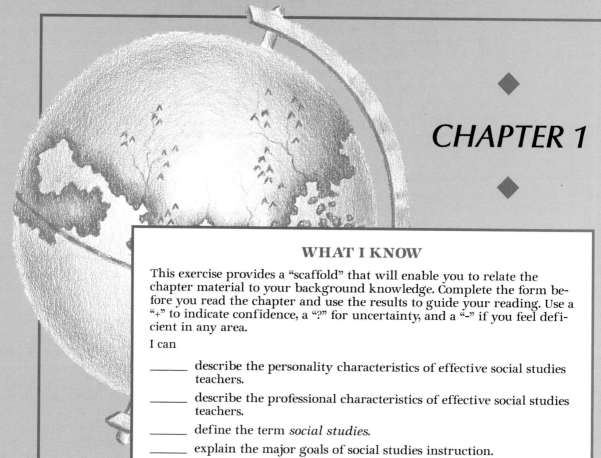

CHAPTER 1

WHAT I KNOW

This exercise provides a "scaffold" that will enable you to relate the chapter material to your background knowledge. Complete the form before you read the chapter and use the results to guide your reading. Use a "+" to indicate confidence, a "?" for uncertainty, and a "-" if you feel deficient in any area.

I can

_____ describe the personality characteristics of effective social studies teachers.

_____ describe the professional characteristics of effective social studies teachers.

_____ define the term *social studies.*

_____ explain the major goals of social studies instruction.

_____ list and describe the major disciplines contributing to social studies instruction.

_____ identify what is meant by the term *powerful social studies.*

_____ identify patterns for organizing social studies content for instruction.

_____ describe the possibilities of connecting social studies to the other school subjects.

_____ discuss the role of the thinking skills in a social studies program.

_____ explain how standards influence social studies instruction.

_____ describe the role of "authentic" assessment in social studies instruction.

_____ analyze the role of a "good citizen."

_____ explain the importance of one's professional preparation for good teaching in social studies.

Using the results as a guide, what questions will you seek to answer as you read?

Connecting Beliefs
to Practices

◆ **CLASSROOM SKETCH**

Students in Mrs. Beck's fifth-grade social studies class were investigating various customs of people around the world. One day, as they were watching a video on cultural traditions, the students became particularly absorbed in the historically popular Islamic greeting of keeping the palm of one's hand open and touching the breast, forehead, and lips, signifying endearment in heart, thoughts, and words. Traditional greetings of various cultures around the world became the rage in Mrs. Beck's class as the students engaged in a spontaneous and productive discussion of the many interesting ways people greet one another: "The people of Japan bow politely when greeting someone." "The French and other continentals 'kiss' one another on both cheeks." "Boy Scouts in America shake lefthanded—the hand nearest the heart—with the three middle fingers extended to the other person's wrist." The greatest reaction surfaced after some students demonstrated the handshaking styles of baseball, basketball, and football players. The main area of interest seemed to be, "Who started all of this?"

Mrs. Beck encouraged her students to pursue their interest by helping them locate and explore various resources that might assist them in arriving at an answer. Some searched the World Wide Web, using *Yahooligans* (http://www.yahooligans.com/) as a starting point. Others examined library offerings for pertinent books and magazines. A few students thought it might be instructive to interview parents, teachers and other adults. They found some fascinating information, discovering that as far back as the sixteenth century the Ashanti of Africa had a handshake and an expression of greeting: "Five must lie within five." The Dutch of old ended business negotiations with a ritualistic handslapping, high and low, which served as a basis for the expression "striking a bargain." As far as identifying the source of these modern "shakin" variations, the students discovered that, although they are rooted in African American culture, the evidence was inconclusive as to who actually started the practices: Basketball player Magic Johnson claimed to have originated the "high five" at Michigan State in 1980; long jumper Ralph Boston argued that the "slap five" began among African American track athletes on the international track circuit prior to 1968; and some insist that revolutionary handshakes started prior to the 1940s when African American musicians greeted each other with a special shake accompanied by the jive phrase, "Gimme a little skin, man."

◆ CLASSROOM CONNECTION

Mrs. Beck allowed her students to pursue this line of study because she believes the most productive learning experiences in social studies happen when children work at what *they* want to know. Her philosophy of education is based on a belief that elementary school students are naturally inclined to dive headlong into whatever excites their curiosity and that teachers should be a little more flexible, a little more spontaneous, and a little more willing to depart from routine plans to help students explore their personal interests. In this case, Mrs. Beck knew that the children's attraction to the topic was very strong and that it was important to take the risk of temporarily departing from from the regular curriculum to help them search for substantive information to resolve the issue at hand. "If teachers are reluctant to take risks, how will they ever inspire these ideals in their students?" she asks. "It is the job of social studies teachers to value, not suppress, the natural curiosity their students bring to the elementary school classroom. The students are often their own best teachers."

When teachers such as Mrs. Beck express strong feelings about how students should be taught, they are stating their *philosophies of education*. Philosophies of education incorporate our beliefs about how children learn; in turn, they help us to determine which activities and materials are most appropriate for achieving instructional goals. Philosophies are important because they provide direction for what teachers do and help explain why learners do what they do. Philosophies are not acquired intuitively; they grow from ideas we gain through experience, as well as those we gather from learning about the theories of respected authorities in the field. As applied to our distinctive social studies focus, the following two questions undergird the development of a philosophy of social studies instruction: What skills, content, and personal values are most critical in helping students learn about the world and participate more fully in society? How can these learning outcomes be attained most effectively in the social studies program? These questions are not shocking or new; they have captivated the thoughts of social studies educators since the early history of our nation's schools. The answers to these questions are still not clear-cut or conclusive, so they are difficult to describe precisely. But they do provide us with insights into current views of what effective social studies teachers do.

EFFECTIVE SOCIAL STUDIES TEACHERS

Examples of superb teachers like Mrs. Beck are everywhere. Many social studies programs are excellent, built by teachers who have a sound knowledge of why they are teaching, whom they are teaching, what they are teaching, and how they are teaching. Becoming an effective teacher is a momentous and rewarding goal. Special people work with children; they understand the long-range implications of their work, not only as it affects children but also as it affects families, communities, and even the nation or world.

Bernard M. Baruch was reported to have once said, "When I die, I hope it will be my good fortune to go where Miss Blake will meet me and lead me to my seat." Obviously, Baruch's teacher made a highly significant impact on his life. And, like Baruch, we all hold precious memories of our own "Miss Blakes," those very special teachers who made the classroom a delightful and rewarding place to be. A group of confident, happy, active children reflects the masterful touch of a Miss Blake, someone who is able to pull together all the essential qualities of an educational program so that every child's special interests and needs are met through a wide range of productive learning experiences.

The "Miss Blakes" of our lives have brought an aura of uniqueness to their social studies classes; they obviously enjoyed their work and the lives they touched. They may have been *entertainers*: free enough to have fun with the children and bring a flair for the dramatic to their work. They may have been *intellectuals*: intensely interested in knowledge and its place in the lives of children. They may have been *directors*: shouting out, "You're in my classroom now and we'll operate by my rules." They may have been *recapitulators*: repeating everything taught until they were sure everyone understood. You may have had one of these teachers, unique individuals who found a special way of becoming successful at what they did.

Whether discussed around the dinner table or debated in a formal educational setting, it is difficult to determine the exact traits that characterize effective teaching in social studies. However, it is generally agreed that effective social studies teachers must display two fundamental qualities: *wholesome personalities* and *sound professional competencies.*

Personal Characteristics

People who choose to become teachers view their professional responsibilities as an extension of their own lives. Many field-experience students, student teachers, and beginning teachers overlook this idea and try to alter their own individual nature by taking on different personalities they consider to be signs of success. They often mimic the behaviors of a great teacher from their past or a wonderful cooperating teacher from a field-experience course or student teaching assignment. Thinking that they have stumbled upon a magical mold from which all excellent teachers emerge, these beginners often try to teach exactly as their model did. As a result, they often flounder until they eventually discover who they *really* are. Some are lucky; they are able to find their true character and emerge as successful teachers:

> When I first began teaching, there was Al Cullum the teacher and Al Cullum the person. I soon discovered that this split personality was not a healthy one for the children nor for me. I realized I had better . . . present Al Cullum the person, or else the school year would become [a disaster]. (Cullum, 1969, p. 19)

It is difficult to describe the ideal personality of an effective social studies teacher, but I often think of a description I once heard of "great social studies teachers"— *people who don't remind you of anyone else.* Effective teachers use every approach at their disposal to bring a young child's world to life. They understand why the social studies program is important. They tap its great promise for helping children reach their fullest potential by using techniques, activities, and strategies that grow from rich knowledge, creativity, and sensitivity. Good social studies teachers never become complacent with the job they do. They always search for new ideas and techniques: "There is so much more for me to know." Good social studies teachers

Good social studies teachers go out of their way to build strong personal bonds with children.

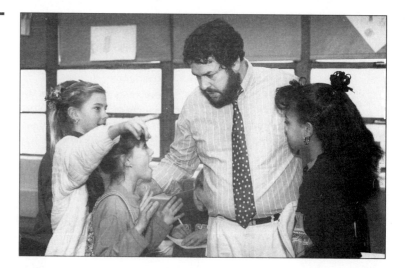

make an intense commitment to teaching; they spend vast amounts of time and energy—physical and emotional—on the job. They might spend the bulk of their summer vacation planning a "very special" thematic unit or take the risk of depleting the family vacation budget to buy a "priceless" candle snuffer, a replica of a British half penny, or an imitation trencher to be included in their lessons the following year. Whatever the circumstance, teachers are never completely off duty. Good social studies teachers earn their status both through their commitment to students and their conviction that teaching is hard work. First-class social studies teachers sacrifice, but they find it's all worth the effort when a child unexpectedly exclaims, "Hey, social studies is awesome. I really like it this year!"

Professional Characteristics

Making sense out of the complicated world of teaching and finding your way as a teacher is a tough job—much tougher than it appears at first. Some people, for example, may be so impressed by an individual's pleasing personality that they categorize him as a "natural teacher." They imply that this individual's disposition and temperament are so extraordinary—he has such a natural talent to reach others—that his personality alone could allow him to achieve the same degree of success in teaching as someone who has received sound professional training. On one hand, it is good that these people understand the value of a teacher's personality; on the other hand, their insight into the significance of professional training is much too narrow. Graham and Persky (1977) provide examples of how the untrained person lacks the critical professional knowledge or skills necessary to maximize learning opportunities for elementary school learners:

> The untrained person, recognizing the importance of establishing rapport and communication with a child, will show a book . . . and ask, ["Do you like the picture?"] She does not realize that a question asked in this way boxes the child into a "yes" or "no" response. The person who understands that there is a relationship between thought and language and that verbal interaction can promote thinking skills will word her comments so that they evoke a more thoughtful and complex response—e.g., ["How is living in a city different from living in a small town?"] This can be the beginning of a conversation and an exchange of ideas rather than a simple question and answer episode. (p. 336)

You will soon hold a very special place in children's lives and be expected to expertly handle with keen insight and skill all the subtle professional tasks of a social studies program. For example, you might find yourself the target of a third grader who eagerly rushes toward you holding up a picture book full of colorful photos of penguins. No intensive professional training is needed to inform you how to respond in this situation; a sensitive person will instinctively want to share in the spirit of the moment—to look at the pictures together for a short time. However, when six more children rush to the scene, craning their necks to see what the fuss is all about, the ability to make informed professional decisions comes into play. Should you thank the child for sharing the book with you and and tell the group that it is time to do something else? Or should you look through the book with *all* of the interested children? Should the first child be asked to describe the book to the others as they look at the pictures? Should everyone simply examine the pictures, or would it be better to read short extracts from the text, too? Maybe it would just be better to sit back and see what develops before you make any response.

There are many different ways you might respond to typical daily encounters with children; some responses can be highly constructive, while others could be ruinous. "Correct" responses are the result of studied professional decisions that are based on a maze of complicated information. Despite this highly sophisticated professional base, we often hear skeptics say, in essence, "Anybody can teach social studies to elementary school children. What do social studies teachers do, anyway—ask the children to take out their textbooks? Read a few pages? Answer the questions at the end of the section? Why, even *I* can conduct a class like that!" When faced with such an accusation, the best way to cope is to admit its validity. Anybody *can* direct children to take out their textbooks and read a few pages, and ask them to answer some questions. The accusation is true, but there is one thing wrong with it—it misses the whole point of elementary school social studies education. Textbooks are not meant to be used that way; if they were, there would be no point in your taking this course.

You, however, will be a well-informed professional who thinks more deeply about what goes into your work. You will understand that there is much more to using the textbook or any other specialized learning tool in the social studies classroom than many would believe. Materials are but the substance of the program. By themselves, they are of little or no benefit; in the hands of a skilled teacher, they are the magical tools for developing active, informed citizens. All the materials we use in the social studies program involve the children in serious work and, with proper guidance, help them acquire important learnings, skills, and sensitivities. A "geographer" bends down to study the effect of sand sifting through her fingers. An "economist" helps determine how the class will obtain the money necessary to buy a sapling for the school playground. A "political scientist" petitions the principal for a new piece of playground equipment. A "historian" listens in awe as a guest speaker describes life of the past. Children will pass through these experiences in unique ways, but they all will have one thing in common—a teacher who integrates much of what is known about effective teaching into her professional persona:

- *Presenter*—not a lecturer, but one who demonstrates, models, and presents activities to groups of children and options to individuals so that direct pupil experiences are encouraged in an ongoing fashion.

- *Observer*—one who works in formal and informal ways to identify children's ideas, to interact appropriately, and to provide learning options.

- *Question Asker and Problem Poser*—one who stimulates idea formation, idea testing, and concept construction by asking questions and posing problems that arise from observation.

- *Environment Organizer*—one who organizes carefully and clearly what children are to do, while allowing sufficient freedom for true exploration; one who organizes from the child's perspective.

- *Public Relations Coordinator*—one who encourages cooperation, development of human relations, and patience with diversity within the class, and who defends this practice and educates others outside the class about the benefits for children of this approach.

- *Documenter of Learning*—one who satisfies the accountability expectations and gauges the impact of these practices on each learner in terms of knowledge construction and . . . skill development.

- *Theory Builder*—one who helps children to form connections between and among their ideas and to construct meaningful patterns that represent their constructed knowledge. (Chaille & Britain, 1991, p. 54)

Good social studies teachers have worked hard to master these specialized professional duties and realize that progress toward good teaching is deliberate. "Good teacher" is a status that takes time and hard work to achieve, much like completing a demanding race. Top-notch teachers know that the race takes years to complete, but realize that once they reach the finish line the greatest rewards of teaching are theirs. Their satisfaction, however, comes not from arriving first at the finish line, but from the race itself. Some teachers train for but never start the race; others begin but eventually determine that it takes more time and energy than they are willing to invest. Still others stride steadily and strongly forward until they break through as superbly talented professionals. Which will you be?

Good social studies teachers challenge children with stimulating classroom learning encounters. Making sure that this stimulation is just right is skilled professional work.

Dash into your studies with total dedication. Only by plunging yourself completely into your work will you fully appreciate the realities, the joys, and the hardships awaiting you. And only by giving your best effort at all times will you develop the sophisticated sensitivities and skills required to assist children through their most delicate years.

By working hard to fulfill your personal and professional dreams, you will be bound for success. For the ambitious, mediocrity has no place. One consistent thread running through the careers of teachers who excelled is not only that they learned, but that they were also willing to take risks. They tried new ideas, spoke out for their beliefs, and tackled assignments with uncertain prospects for success. They demonstrated, without timidity, that they would rather be challenged than safe and bored. It's a good idea to accept as much risk as you can early in your career; succeeding in risky situations helps identify potential greatness more clearly than any other factor. Those who take risks have a high degree of self-confidence, which is a distinctive quality of outstanding social studies teachers. As someone once said, having a positive sense of self-worth is worth 50 IQ points. So work hard, dream a lot, and muster up the grit to establish a point of view. However, risks cannot, and should not, be taken unless your fundamentals are solid. Risks are never taken blindly by outstanding teachers; they are based on a strong foundation of knowledge and skill. Build that foundation in social studies education and take your risks there, for it is the one area of the elementary school curriculum that most openly invites the ideas and dreams of adventurous professionals.

Your teacher certification program will have started you in this direction; ultimately, however, you must gather the desire and persistence to work toward the goal of becoming even more skilled and dedicated. You will be able to draw upon diverse sources of knowledge to meet this challenge—the trials and tribulations of the past, as they were met and conquered by effective teachers, can help you discover links between certain types of teacher behavior and learner achievement. Competent, experienced teachers are only too eager to stretch out a protective wing as they help answer questions or provide instructional ideas and resources to novices. For beginning teachers, this often has more impact and becomes more meaningful than being informed by a "scholarly expert." That's because the experienced teacher has been right on the "firing line" and can speak with more authority: "This is what *I did* in *my classroom.*" At the start of your career, you are more likely to respond to this kind of informal feedback than to be told, by a scholarly authority you have never met, "This is *what you should do* in *your classroom.*" Such "experience sharing" will be a significant source of learning throughout your career.

As helpful as experience sharing can be, you will also eventually begin to value the advice of recognized social studies authorities. Good teachers learn not only from seeing ideas in action, but by looking into the accumulated research and other scholarly works. Reading current articles and books and attending conferences keep teachers busy changing, throwing away, and updating. An unquenchable thirst for more knowledge will keep you well informed. Clark and Cutler (1990) elaborate:

It's interesting to listen to my teachers talk in the lunchroom. One guy has all the answers—too many of them. I suppose that's what happens when people stop learning. In reality, a person ought to become *more* teachable as he learns, not less.

Someone could rightfully hang a "not-interested-in-learning" sign around this guy's neck. Nobody's asking second-grade teachers to become scholars, but surely they can be expected to keep up in their field. Something happens to a teacher when he stays in the trenches all day and never climbs out and looks around. It's too easy to strap your blinders on and rely only on your own experience. It's dangerous.

Not all my teachers are that way. I've got one who's a constant reader. I go into the faculty lounge and she's got her nose in the newspaper; I go into the lunchroom and she's got a book propped open on her lunch tray. Coming in and out of school, she's always got a book under her arm. I mean, that's some kind of example for third-graders! And it's not just novels or current events. She knows the social studies texts, she's read up on computer software, she's always on the lookout for new methods of teaching science. I go to her when I want to know what's going on! Guess how this affects the kids? (p. 452)

Ten Basic Tenets of Instruction

Good teachers realize that effective social studies instruction must be based on the learned recommendations of leading authorities in their field. Toward that goal, I now present ten basic tenets of teaching elementary school social studies. Each tenet is based on the recommendations of recognized authorities and organizations in the field; together, they serve as guidelines for effective social studies instruction.

Tenet 1: Effective Social Studies Teachers Understand That Good Citizenship Has Been and Remains a Fundamental Goal of Social Studies Education.

We are living at an extraordinary moment in history. Few others have been or will be able to match what we will experience—ushering in not only a new century, but a new millennium. To put this tremendous milestone into perspective, read the following thoughts of the Children's Defense Fund (1996):

> A thousand years ago the United States was not even a dream. Copernicus and Galileo had not told us the earth was round or revolved around the sun. Gutenberg's Bible was not printed, Wycliffe had not translated it into English, and Martin Luther had not tacked his theses on the church door. The Magna Carta did not exist, Chaucer's and Shakespeare's tales had not been spun, and Bach's, Beethoven's, and Mozart's miraculous music had not been created to inspire, soothe, and heal our spirits. European serfs struggled in bondage while African empires flourished in independence. Native Americans peopled our land free of slavery's blight, and Hitler's holocaust had yet to show the depths human evil can reach when good women and men remain silent or indifferent.
>
> A thousand years from now, will civilization remain and humankind survive? Will America's dream be alive, be remembered, and be *worth* remembering? Will the United States be a blip or a beacon in history? Can our founding principle "that all men are created equal" and "are endowed by their Creator with certain inalienable rights" withstand the test of time, the tempests of politics, and become deed and not just creed for

every child? Is America's dream big enough for every fifth child who is poor, every sixth child who is Black, every seventh child who is Latino, and every eighth child who is mentally or physically challenged? (p. xi)

The new century and millennium present an incredible transitional period during which social, economic, and political crises in combination with the evolution of a more linguistically and culturally diverse society call for new forms of knowledge and new approaches to teaching. Although the needs of society have changed over the years, our schools are in their usual place of central responsibility to develop future citizens who understand how their actions and values can influence our nation's survival. Will our students be delivered an education that cultivates the moral grit to stand up and cry out for the protection of our nation's future, or one that minimizes civic responsibility and respect for the legacies and principles of our families, neighborhoods, and national communities? How will our future citizens measure the purpose and quality of life in our nation?

These questions are not new; variations have been asked by educators throughout the years. This is because each elementary school subject is a manifestation of a strongly perceived educational need—that need being, in this case, a deep concern about how to place in our children's collective hands the trust and understanding required to protect peace and freedom and help the American dream survive. As a nation, we have placed social studies instruction at the core of this responsibility because we are a proud people—a democratic republic of over 250 million citizens, each of whom is part of a unique political venture. We prize our political processes, our institutions, our shared heritage, and our freedom. To preserve and protect this prized inheritance, we call upon our schools to effectively prepare our youngsters with a wide range of information, skills, and values essential for good citizenship. The primary reason for educating our youth, from the earliest days of schooling in our nation, has been the development of good citizens. And, as our society has evolved over the years, so has our concept of what is meant by "good citizenship."

During the colonial era, for example, citizenship education centered around religious and moral instruction. Early colonists settled in the New World primarily to spread Christianity and seek religious freedom; therefore, a primary emphasis of schooling was on strict discipline, high moral standards, and the creeds and ceremonies of Christianity. The overall purpose of schooling was to mold "saints," since "saints were wiser than other people because they knew God. In one way or another everything done in the schools tied into the overall purpose, which was the development of saints" (Mason, 1960, p. 21). Children were required to memorize the laws of God as well as the laws of the land until they "attained that happy state . . . when they were afraid they should 'go to hell,' and were 'stirred up dreadfully to seek God'" (Ford, 1879, p. 4). Today, "good citizens" are described in quite different fashion. Religion remains an important institution in every community, but doctrines separating church and state have assigned faith education to our homes and places of worship. Pressing social circumstances over the years have transformed the purpose of education in the direction of helping students know and care about the democratic foundations of our nation as a free country with liberty and justice for all, the meaning of our Constitution, and the importance of our democratic institutions. We want students to respect our historical past as a democratic society and recognize the rich contributions of all groups who have made modern America a free and powerful nation. We want students to take active roles as champions of freedom who stand up and cry out for the rights and responsibilities of citizenship. We want students to speak with their voices, actions, and votes for the improvement of the quality of life in our families, neighborhoods, nation, and world. The Curriculum Standards Task Force of the National Council for the Social Studies (1994) recommends that the overriding purpose of social studies should be to provide students with the education required to fulfill these roles—to ready students for the most important post they will be entrusted with in the new millennium—the office of citizen:

> Citizens who take this office seriously are in touch with the cultural heritage of the nation. They possess knowledge of the economic, political, and social factors that make up the human ecosystem in which all must function, and they understand its relationship to natural systems. They understand the principles of rule of law, legal limits to freedom, and majority rule with protection for minority rights. They have informed spatial, temporal, and cultural perspectives. They possess the attitudes and behaviors that support fair play and cooperation. Without a conscious effort to teach these ideals, a free republic will not long endure. (p. xx)

The knowledge, skills, and attitudes gained through an effective social studies program are worthwhile citizenship education goals but, Parker and Jarolimek (1996) advise, "The real test of a social studies program comes in the out-of-school lives of children. If the school has provided them new insights, improved skills, and increased civic-mindedness, such learning should be apparent in their out-of-school behavior now as children and later as adults" (p. 71). Such thinking coincides with the thoughts of today's social commentators who have shown concern for the "disappearance of civic America," lamenting that we have become a nation of "civic couch potatoes" (Tyack, 1997). As trustees of education for the next millennium, how can we find a solution to social indifference by strengthening citizenship education of our youth?

Educators are challenged today with the idea that democracy cannot exist without its citizenry assuming an active role: serving in civic or political life (PTA, town council, etc.), writing letters to the editor, deliberating and debating public policy, working for public interest groups, and voting. Cogan (1989) maintains that such active participation as adult citizens begins in school when "students and their teachers [become] active participants in the society. . . . How else does one ensure active participation as adults if this is not learned naturally in the living laboratory represented by the school?" (p. 341). Gerzon (1997) adds this thought:

> Methods will vary, but the principle behind teaching democracy can remain constant: modeling in the school community the way democracy works. Tolerance, respect, a willingness to learn from one another—these are the values on which democratic nations thrive. They are the values that schools must teach and practice. (p. 11)

Social studies programs help to make society. A classroom for elementary school children should have a uniquely democratic spirit.

As we continue to move from the Industrial Age into the Information Age, our civilization will undergo a massive transformation. Preparing students for the third millennium and a drastically different world requires a forward-looking social studies program with civic education as its heart. A program centering on participatory citizenship must be made a regular part of school life to help students establish the sense of personal responsibility and accountability that forms a solid foundation to participate as adults in civic life.

Tenet 2: Effective Social Studies Teachers Understand the Confusing Nature of Social Studies and the Forces That Affect Curricular Decisions.

What happened between the period of colonization and present-day society to cause such a drastic change in our concept of good citizenship—from that of sainthood to participatory citizenship? A complete explanation is beyond the scope of this text but, in a nutshell, the early religious emphasis remained pervasive until just after the Revolutionary War, when, after the colonists threw off British rule, they found they had very little in common with one another except a flag and a name. Many wondered if the 13 "free and independent states" would ever unite into one nation. Eventually, however, the people began to develop a growing sense of common cause, and an emerging identity of 13 "United States" took form. Throughout the period of unification, one-room public schoolhouses popped up in every part of the countryside as the new nation's desire to educate its citizens became a pervasive concern. Religion remained a central goal of schooling, but new school subjects such as geography and history were targeted to build such shared values as loyalty, unity, and citizenship.

History and geography grew to dominate citizenship education until after the Civil War. At that time, the United States faced one of its most difficult political challenges—pulling together a divided nation. The mission of saving the Union spread to the schools, where the study of our government and the Constitution joined geography and history as the content considered necessary for good citizenship in a strong United States. Therefore, civics, or political science, joined geography and history as the major school subjects responsible for helping youth become useful citizens.

The Civil War had ended slavery, but prejudice remained a serious issue into the twentieth century. Few African Americans felt free or equal, women lacked many rights, and the lives of immigrants were especially grim. Reformers tried hard to change American society, working feverishly to demand that everyone receive equal rights to vote, to be treated equally before the law, and to go to school. In 1916, as part of an effort to make our nation's schools more responsive to prevailing social conditions, the National Education Association (NEA) established various subject area committees to study existing curricula. The Committee on Social Studies was created to determine whether citizenship needs were being adequately addressed by school programs dominated by the separate subjects of geography, history, and civics. The committee concluded that, other than providing the supply of facts that helped students exercise their brains (educational theorists of the time thought the brain was much like a muscle) or pass stringent college entrance examinations, there was little justification for the commanding stature of history, geography, and civics; they simply did not meet the pressing needs of a changing society. Instead, the committee supported educational innovators of the time, such as John Dewey, who proposed that the work of our schools was to guarantee *social efficiency*—training students to understand and resolve social problems; readying students for the job market in a changing world of business and industry; and developing in students practical skills related to health, hygiene, and nutrition. These innovators recommended that school subjects should be practical: What point was there in teaching history and geography when most students would never go to college? The committee considered these concerns and proclaimed a new curricular area—social studies—as the major school experience responsible for promoting "social efficiency." The NEA (1916) envisioned social studies as "the subject matter related directly to the organization and development of human society, and to individuals as members of social groups" (p. 5).

The committee recommended that social studies be molded into a unique subject area by integrating content from among the prevailing social sciences (systematized bodies of knowledge derived from methods of inquiry) of the time: history, geography, and civics. How was this integration to be accomplished? An answer to that question was as difficult to arrive at in 1916 as it is today. Since first addressing the issue, social studies educators have labored to find an answer acceptable to all factions in the field. According to critics, their efforts have come up empty; they have constructed nothing more than an endless maze of ambiguity, inconsistency, and contradiction. Finn (1988) expounds on this point:

> The great dismal swamp of today's school curriculum is not reading or writing, not math or science, not even foreign language study. It is social studies, a field that has been getting slimier and more tangled ever since it changed its name from history around 1916. (p. 16)

Students in social studies methods courses often become confused when informed of the years of deep internal conflict among social studies educators, and wonder aloud, "Why can't social studies educators agree on the nature of this school subject?" To gain some perspective on this question, you must understand that, as with every sensitive educational issue, attempts to reshape the social studies are sparked by experts holding strong opinions about such volatile issues as how students learn best and what learnings are most valuable. Such disagreements are not suddenly resolved; years of controversy, disagreement, and debate are to be expected when societal complexities cause theoreticians and curriculum specialists to examine what is meant by "educating good citizens" (see Figure 1–1). However, patterns of agreement finally seem to be taking shape out of the confusing maze of reform efforts. Barr, Barth, and Shermis (1977) explain:

> It is similar to one of those puzzles found in introductory psychology textbooks. After gazing at length at a hopeless tangle of lines or colors, suddenly the perceptual gears slip into place, and out of the confusion emerge insight and clarity. Out of careful and patient observation of the seemingly incoherent, tangled, and contradictory practices . . . patterns have begun to appear. (p. 57)

Contributing to such budding optimism, the National Council for the Social Studies (1993b) took an official stand on the nature of the social studies and, after a good deal of thoughtful study and deliberation, approved the following definition:

> Social studies is the integrated study of the social sciences and humanities to promote civic competence. Within the school program, social studies provides coordinated, systematic study drawing upon such disciplines as anthropology, archeology, economics, geography, history, law, philosophy, political science, psychology, religion, and sociology, as well as appropriate content from the humanities, mathematics, and natural sciences. The primary purpose of social studies is to help young people develop the ability to make informed and reasoned decisions for the public good as citizens of a culturally diverse, democratic society in an interdependent world. (p. 3)

FIGURE 1–1
What to Include in the Social Studies Curriculum? The Search for Identity

Barth (1996) comments that, "With this [effort], NCSS supported the argument that a nature of the social studies had emerged that could be defined and applied as standards and statements on teaching and learning" (p. 17). Now, social studies has been set apart as a distinctive, complex field of study based upon a well-defined statement of meaning. Clearly, the definition reaffirmed citizenship education as the primary purpose of social studies instruction, presented an argument for integrated content from the social sciences and other disciplines, emphasized the need for higher-order thinking, and identified the essential characteristics that make the social studies a unique field. However, it did not specifically explain *how* social studies should be taught—what teachers should do to help students become good citizens in a culturally diverse, democratic society and in an interdependent world. To that end, the remaining tenets in this chapter identify the key features of effective teaching and learning in the social studies as gathered from key position statements and available research and scholarship in the field.

Tenet 3: Effective Social Studies Teachers Understand That Teaching Is Powerful When It Is Meaningful, Integrative, Value-Based, Challenging, and Active.

After it accomplished the task of defining *social studies,* the NCSS turned its attention to the process of identifying the kinds of learning that could promote citizenship education most effectively. Keeping the NCSS definition foremost in mind, the NCSS Task Force on Standards for Teaching and Learning in the Social Studies (1993a) developed a position statement identifying key features of ideal social studies teaching and learning. The task force labeled its approach "powerful social studies," a concept that comprises five key features: *meaningful, integrative, value-based, challenging,* and *active.* These key features are described in Figure 1–2. The vision of powerful teaching in social studies conceives teaching and learning for understanding, appreciation, and life application in active, creative classrooms where teachers want their students to become competent in solving problems, making decisions, communicating effectively, and collaborating with others.

The sprouts of powerful social studies instruction established their roots during the early part of the twentieth century when educational pioneers such as John Dewey argued for an emphasis on *meaningful* learning:

> In their lives and work and thought, people do not need simply to be able to recall facts or preset procedures in response to specific stimuli. They need to be able to plan courses of action, weigh alternatives, think about problems and issues in new ways, converse with others about what they know and why, and transform and create new knowledge for themselves; they need, in short, to be able "to make sense" and "to learn." (Peterson & Knapp, 1993, p. 136)

Over the years, this "progressive" view of education has swelled and receded according to the urges and impulses of the most influential policymakers of the time. Most often, the cause for deemphasizing "meaningful" education has been a passion for rote learning; that is, treating learning in a stimulus–response manner where the teacher and textbook are considered the primary fountain of knowledge that directly enlightens the learner. The students memorize facts and skills through drill-and-practice exercises, being rewarded for correct answers. Heuwinkel (1996) warns that "[r]ote learning will not suffice in education today; rather, education requires meaningful learning that allows one to manipulate and reflect on knowledge in order to solve unforeseen problems. This view underscores the need for teaching methods that promote *understanding,* not memorization. . . ." (p. 29). This emergent prototype of learning, whether called "powerful" in social studies circles or "constructivist" in more general arenas, is not entirely new. It is derived from the basic "progressive" ideas of Dewey, but transformed to a degree by newer reforms in education. You will learn more about how to become a powerful (or constructivist) social studies teacher in Chapter 4.

FIGURE 1-2
Powerful Social Studies

Five Key Features of Powerful Social Studies Teaching and Learning

Meaningful

The content selected for emphasis is worth learning because it promotes progress toward important social understanding and civic efficacy goals, and it is taught in ways that help students to see how it is related to these goals. As a result, students' learning efforts are motivated by appreciation and interest, not just by accountability and grading systems. Instruction emphasizes depth of development of important ideas within appropriate breadth of content coverage.

Integrative

Powerful social studies cuts across disciplinary boundaries, spans time and space, and integrates knowledge, beliefs, values, and dispositions to action. It also provides opportunities for students to connect to the arts and sciences through inquiry and reflection.

Value-Based

Powerful social studies teaching considers the ethical dimensions of topics, so that it provides an arena for reflective development of concern for the common good and application of social values. The teacher includes diverse points of view, demonstrates respect for well-supported positions, and shows sensitivity and commitment to social responsibility and action.

Challenging

Students are encouraged to function as a learning community, using reflective discussion to work collaboratively to deepen understandings of the meanings and implications of content. They also are expected to come to grips with controversial issues, to participate assertively but respectfully in group discussions, and to work productively with peers in cooperative learning activities.

Active

Powerful social studies is rewarding but demanding. It demands thoughtful preparation and instruction by the teacher, and sustained effort by the students to make sense of and apply what they are learning. Teachers do not mechanically follow rigid guidelines in planning, implementing, and assessing instruction. Instead, they work with the national standards and with state and local guidelines, adapting and supplementing these guidelines and their instructional materials in ways that support their students' social education needs.

The teacher uses a variety of instructional materials, plans field trips and visits by resource people, develops current or local examples to relate to students' lives, plans reflective discussions, and scaffolds students' work in ways that encourage them to gradually take on more responsibility for managing their own learning independently and with their peers. Accountability and grading systems are compatible with these goals and methods.

Students develop new understandings through a process of active construction. They develop a network of connections that link the new content to preexisting knowledge and beliefs anchored in their prior experience. The construction of meaning required to develop important social understanding takes time and is facilitated by interactive discourse. Clear explanations and modeling from the teacher are important, but so are opportunities to answer questions, discuss or debate the meanings and implications of content, or use the content in activities that call for tackling problems or making decisions.

Source: Alleman, J., & Brophy, J. (1995). NCSS social studies standards and the elementary teacher. *Social Studies & The Young Learner, 8,* 4–8. ©National Council for the Social Studies. Reprinted by permission.

Tenet 4: Effective Social Studies Teachers Fuse Content and Processes From the Six Major Social Sciences Into the Elementary School Social Studies Program.

Whenever teachers and curriculum planners pinpoint *what* should be taught in our nation's schools, they are addressing the *scope* of the curriculum: "From which disciplines should social studies draw its content?" As delineated in the NCSS definition, eleven disciplines offer the content foundation for elementary school social studies programs, but the six most commonly associated with elementary school social studies programs are *anthropology, economics, geography, history, civics,* and *sociology.* A brief description of each follows; comprehensive suggestions for instruction appear in later chapters.

Anthropology.   *Anthropologists* study people to find out about their culture—the total pattern of human behavior and its products particular to a special group (language, tools, beliefs, social forms, art, law, customs, traditions, religion, superstitions, morals, occupations, and so on). Anthropologists study how human cultures have changed, from earliest preliterate societies to today's technological environments—gatherers and hunters, nomads, and diverse groups in modern societies. *Archaeology,* a branch of anthropology, is the scientific study of extinct cultures carried out by investigating physical survivors of the past—skeletal remains, fossils, implements, tools, monuments, and other items found in the earth. Because of this immense scope of scientific study, anthropology has often been described as a universal discipline, one that comprehensively studies cultures by looking at all aspects of their existence.

Economics.   *Economics* as a discipline studies the production, distribution, and consumption of goods and services. Economics affects all of our lives. From youngsters who save their allowance for a special toy, to college students who must scrape together enough money for tuition, through newlyweds who apply for a mortgage as they buy their first home, all people face situations where they attempt to satisfy unlimited wants with limited resources. Referred to as the *scarcity* concept, it is from this idea that a family of economics learnings emerges. Because of scarcity, humans have attempted to find ways to produce more in less time with less material, by which *specialization* of labor was developed. From specialization has emerged the idea of *interdependence,* a reliance of people upon one another that necessitates monetary, transportation, and communication systems. From interactions of these factors, a *market* system developed through which buyers and sellers produce and exchange goods or services. Finally, *governments,* responsible for controlling segments of the market system, ensure the welfare of all their citizens. Information about the economy, including the study of taxation, consumer economics, and economic policy, helps one assess pressing issues of the day.

Geography.   *Geography* contributes to the elementary school curriculum by providing the substance through which children learn about people and places, the natural environment, and the capacity of the earth to support life. The Joint Committee on

Geographic Education (1984) elaborates: "As a subject for study in the schools . . . geography provides an effective method for asking questions about places on the earth and their relationship to the people who live in them. It involves a pattern of inquiry that begins with two essential questions: *Why* are such things located in those particular places and *how* do those particular places influence our lives?" (p. 2)

In carrying out programs in the elementary grades, children should have opportunities to explore and understand their own life space as well as the features of other locations of the world. The learnings they accumulate help satisfy our urgent need to become more sensitive toward the quality of life on earth. The Joint Committee on Geographic Education (1984) states:

> The first task in geography is to locate places, describing and explaining their physical (natural) and human characteristics. Geographic inquiry continues by exploring the relationships that develop as people respond to and shape their physical and natural environments. It permits us to compare, contrast, and comprehend the regions of the world and its various physical and human features and patterns. This knowledge helps us to manage the world's resources and to analyze a host of other significant problems in terms of the spaces they occupy and how these spaces interact with each other on the earth's surface. (p. 2)

Although geography is not commonly taught as a separate subject in our elementary schools, its content and processes are vitally important for the preparation of informed citizens.

History.   People deal with the discipline of history as they systematically go about studying the past. *History* deals with the dynamics of change that occur over time. Many people think of school-related history as requiring wearisome memorization of names, dates, and events, but history belongs in the social studies program because of more important reasons. It helps describe the human condition over time and helps students understand how and why some things change and others continue. Realizing that the present is but a link in the continuity of past and future helps students comprehend and deal with change. History provides the temporal context in which students can find their place in the human story.

History is the primary discipline contributing to the social studies but is not itself considered to be a true social science, because the processes of empirical science are not utilized rigorously in historical study. This is not to fault the efforts of historians, but only to indicate that they are handicapped in their abilities to control or reproduce the phenomena they are studying, as scientists do. Instead, historians must reconstruct events of the past from surviving evidence, and resulting interpretations are not always accurate. For example, interpretations change as historians develop more sophisticated techniques of examining evidence and accumulate different kinds of evidence. Consider that, in the 1920s, many historians argued that the first large constructions in the world were the Egyptian pyramids. This contention was disproved in the 1960s with the introduction of the technique of carbon-14 dating, which indicated that northern European monuments such as Stonehenge were constructed earlier than most of the pyramids. As we enter the twenty-first century, powerful new methodologies, many using computers, may offer historians the rigorous processes that a true science demands. But for now, history is treated as a discipline wavering somewhere in the murky region between the sciences and the humanities. This is why you may frequently see references to social studies as "history and the social sciences."

Civics.   Traditionally, *civics* (sometimes called *political science*) has been defined as the discipline associated with the study of society's attempts to maintain order by establishing governing institutions and processes. The emphasis of civic study has been to examine the structure and functions of government—how people get power, what their duties are, and how they carry out their duties. Brody (1989) adds, "Political scientists approach their subject . . . through analyses of the historical development of a political institution or policy, and by means of detailed examinations of the day-to-day workings of contemporary governments. . . . Political scientists take polls, examine the speeches of politicians, study the actions of legislators and judges, and probe the beliefs and personalities of political leaders" (p. 59). Political scientists share strong scholarly interests about the ways human beings think, organize, and act politically.

Law-related education is a component of the study of political systems. It involves the knowledge of laws and legal systems, how legal and justice systems operate, and the importance of systems of law and justice for compatible coexistence. The quality of our everyday lives is inescapably affected by law and politics, so there is a pronounced need to understand politics and the political process in the social studies programs of our nation's schools.

Sociology.   The *sociologist* studies people by examining their interactions with one another in groups or organizations such as the family, government, church, or school. Sociologists analyze the values and norms these groups hold in common to discover how they become organized (or disorganized) or why they behave as they do. They study how groups form, how they operate, and how they change.

Sociologists organize their study of groups around many questions, such as, What kinds of groups of people form in any given society? What are the expectations of each group member? What problems do the group members face? How does the group control its members?

To answer these questions, sociologists may visit a particular group, observe what the people in that group do, interview group members, or even live with a group for a short time to more completely understand its nature. This firsthand information is enough to get sociologists started, but they must check the validity of their information. By studying written material, films, television and radio programs, and a variety of other resources, sociologists determine whether their original descriptions were based on inaccurate observations or sound perceptions.

Organizing Social Studies Content.   When we answer the question, "*What* content from the social science disciplines should be selected for our social studies program?" we have pinpointed the *scope* of the program, what will be taught. This is

TABLE 1–1
*The Expanding
Environment
Approach*

Grade	Social Studies Topic(s)
Kindergarten/Grade One	Home, Family, School
Grade Two	Neighborhoods, Neighborhood Helpers
Grade Three	Communities—Local and Regional
Grade Four	Our State
Grade Five	The United States
Grade Six	The World
Grade Seven	American History and Government
Grade Eight	Greek and Roman History

but one critical question when considering the makeup of the social studies curriculum. The second crucial query is, "*When* is the most developmentally appropriate time to teach the selected content?" Answers to this question create the *sequence* , or order, in which the content is treated.

Traditionally, the elementary school social studies program has sequenced its content according to the *expanding environment* pattern. No one knows exactly how this system first evolved, but sometime during the 1930s an organizational pattern emerged similar to that shown in Table 1–1. This pattern of content organization was a strong attempt to break away from the rigid methods of instruction popularly used prior to the 1930s, memorization of facts that children cared little about. Chief among the educators seeking to break this memorization mold was John Dewey. He attacked memorization strategies as harmful; instead, Dewey argued, teachers should provide many opportunities that enable children to actively experience their environment. Mitchell (1934) seized those sentiments and developed a detailed sketch of how teachers should base children's experiences on the world around them—on the *here and now* of their lives. She suggested that appropriate learning experiences should begin with the home, then widen to the neighborhood, and eventually broaden to the community. Hanna (1963) reaffirmed this concept of expanding environments in an article so influential that his name is today that most closely associated with the idea.

In 1983, the National Council for the Social Studies organized the Task Force on Scope and Sequence to determine if the expanding environment approach has remained suitable for contemporary times, specifically to study whether modern modes of transportation and communication have affected today's children in such ways as to render the approach obsolete. The task force's response is shown in Figure 1–3. It is apparent that recommended topics coincide precisely with the traditional expanding environment format. The Task Force met once more in 1989 to reconsider its proposals in light of perceived relevance for a new century and millennium; it reaffirmed its 1983 recommendations.

FIGURE 1–3
Recommendations of the
Task Force on Scope and
Sequence

Kindergarten—Awareness of Self in a Social Setting
Providing socialization experiences that help children bridge their
home life with the group life of school.

**Grade 1—The Individual in Primary Social
Groups: Understanding School and Family Life**
Continuing the socialization process begun in kindergarten, but
extending to studies of families (variations in the ways families
live, the need for rules and laws).

**Grade 2—Meeting Basic Needs in Nearby
Social Groups: The Neighborhood**
Studying social functions such as education, production, consump-
tion, communication, and transportation in a neighborhood setting.

Grade 3—Sharing Earth-Space With Others: The Community
Focusing on the community in a global setting, stressing social
functions such as production, transportation, communication, distribution, and government.

Grade 4—Human Life in Varied Environments: The Region
Emphasizing the region, an area of the earth defined for a specific reason; the home state is studied as a political region where
state regulations require it.

**Grade 5—People of the Americas:
The United States and Its Close Neighbors**
Centering on the development of the United States as a nation in
the Western Hemisphere, with particular emphasis on developing
affective attachments to the principles on which the nation was
founded; Canada and Mexico also studied.

Gade 6—People and Cultures: The Eastern Hemisphere
Focusing on selected people and cultures of the Eastern
Hemisphere, directed toward an understanding and appreciation
of other people through development of such concepts as language, technology, institutions, and belief systems.

Grade 7—A Changing World of Many Nations: A Global View
Providing an opportunity to broaden the concept of humanity within
a global context; focus is on the world as the home of many different people who strive to deal with the forces that shape their lives.

**Grade 8—Building a Strong and Free
Nation: The United States**
Studying the "epic of America," the development of the United
States as a strong and free nation; emphasis is on social history
and economic development, including cultural and aesthetic
dimensions of the American experience.

Source: Task Force on Scope and Sequence (1984), In search for a scope and
sequence for social studies. *Social Education, 48,* no. 4, 376–385.

Reaction to the report of the Task Force on Scope and Sequence was divided. On one hand, it was heartily commended by educators such Butts (1984), who commented, "It takes seriously the oft-proclaimed social studies goal of education for citizenship. It thus reaffirms a long-held traditional purpose of social studies, but does so by explicit and persuasive attention to the common core of civic values and citizenship in a democratic society" (p. 263). Critics of the report noted that very little was proposed for the elementary grades that was different from the traditional scope and sequence plans originating during the 1930s. Hellman-Rosenthal (1984) commented, "If we really support the goals of the NCSS, we cannot base our scope and sequence on the perceived needs, make-up, and motivations of a client population of 60 to 80 years ago. . . . [W]e require a broader scope and consideration of a more developmentally oriented sequence" (p. 264). Ravitch (1988) circulated the report to leading cognitive psychologists and child development authorities. She reported, "None knew of any research justifying the expanding environments approach; none defended it. All deplored the absence of historical and cultural content in the early grades" (p. 39). Despite its vocal dissenters, the expanding environment approach remains the overwhelming choice for curriculum organization among social studies program developers and textbook publishers today.

Tenet 5: Effective Social Studies Teachers Help Students Make Connections Among the Separate Subject Areas of the Curriculum.

In an effort to make their students' education more authentic and worthwhile, today's elementary school teachers are seriously questioning the traditional practice of teaching each subject separately—spelling, math, science, and social studies are treated in separate blocks of time with very little connection to one another. Social studies teachers have become particularly interested in this arrangement, since the limited number of hours in the school day prevents all subjects from receiving equal treatment. In fact, along with science, social studies has traditionally been one of the disciplines most likely to be shoved to the end of the day and eventually postponed or forgotten about altogether. If social studies is somehow squeezed into the day's schedule, the children are often led through a quick oral reading of a textbook section and a brief question-answer recitation period, "just to get it in." To remedy these lopsided practices, teachers are seeking ways to use themes to integrate the elementary school curriculum. By bringing together the various subject areas and relating the content to a central theme, teachers are not only able to effectively and efficiently use the amount of time during a busy school day, they are also able to create interesting and challenging learning opportunities. To that end, current proposals for instruction in the elementary school call for bringing together, or integrating, the various areas of the school curriculum into a wholly unified program where learning experiences cut across *all* subjects. These proposals stress that real-life learning comes to us in big packages with their contents all scattered about, so it is impossible to assemble the whole by focusing on only a single part; little meaningful learning can come from limiting the content as it might be subsumed under any single subject label. Subject matter is important, for it helps teachers focus on the facts, concepts, or skills to teach; subject matter furnishes the direction for learning. But to say that real meaning can be neatly compartmentalized into rigidly defined subject areas severely limits the range of potential learning that might be possible from any single activity. Hymes (1981) clarifies this contention by describing a kindergarten or first-grade trip to the farm to learn where milk comes from:

> If you make the teacher put one label on the experience, she will probably call it science. . . . But what about the conversation in connection with the trip: before, during, and after? That should be called the language arts. The stories before and after the trip are literature. The singing—"Old McDonald Had a Farm" is fated to be sung!—must be called music. Rules for conduct are developed. This is what civics, government, and politics are all about. The teacher recalls what happened the last time the group took a trip: "You remember how we all crowded around and some people could not see." The lessons of the past are usually labeled history. A child misbehaves; the teacher's response is a lesson in psychology. Someone counts the children to be sure no one is left at the farm: arithmetic. The trip costs money; that is when the four-year-olds take a brief course in economics. The cow is probably pretty, even if the farmer and the highway are not. The presence of beauty and the absence of it are matters of aesthetics. When the teacher soothes a disappointed child—"Things don't always work out the way we want"—the lesson is one in philosophy. And if, on such a trip, the children drink some milk, that experience is labeled nutrition. Yet the whole trip is labeled science [or social studies]! (pp. 80–81)

Elementary schools around the country are moving toward the idea of integrating the various subjects of the curriculum, and social studies appears to be the major area for blending subjects previously taught separately. With timely advice, Berg (1988) answers the question, "How does social studies fit in this resurgence of interest in integration?"

> Right in the middle! A major goal of the social studies is to help students understand the myriad interactions of people on this planet—past, present, and future. Making sense of the world requires using skills that allow one to read about the many people and places that are scattered about the globe; to use literature to understand the richness of past events and the people who are a part of them; to apply math concepts to more fully understand how numbers have enabled people to numerically manage the complexity of their world. The story of humankind well told requires drawing from all areas of the curriculum. (unnumbered pull-out feature)

The National Council for the Social Studies (1993a) has supported the integrative aspect of social studies instruction with this statement from its influential position statement, *A Vision of Powerful Teaching and Learning in the Social Studies*:

> . . . *powerful social studies teaching integrates across the curriculum.* It provides opportunities for students to read and study text materials, appreciate art and literature, communicate orally and in writing, observe and take measurements, develop and display

data, and in various other ways to conduct inquiry and synthesize findings using knowledge and skills taught in all school subjects. . . . Particularly in elementary and middle schools, instruction can feature social studies as the core around which the rest of the curriculum is built. (p. 217)

By integrating subject areas with themes having a social studies focus, students become involved in activities and experiences that are both purposeful and meaningful.

Tenet 6: Effective Teachers Institute "Cultures of Thinking" in Their Classrooms.

What else can teachers do to make their social studies instruction more purposeful and meaningful? They must provide opportunities for students to go beyond the simple acquisition of facts; they must offer situations where students use what they know to reason, to analyze, to create, and to evaluate. The NCSS Task Force on Early Childhood/Elementary Social Studies (1989) suggests:

> For children to develop citizenship skills appropriate to a democracy, they must be capable of thinking critically about complex societal problems and global problems. Teachers must arrange the classroom environment to promote data gathering, discussion, and critical reasoning by students. Another important aspect of citizenship is that of decision maker. Children must acquire the skills of decision making, but also study the process that occurs as groups make decisions. Continually accelerating technology has created and will continue to create rapid changes in society. Children need to be equipped with the skills to cope with change. (p. 16)

Elementary school social studies programs have been ardently concerned with the development of thinking skills—that is, a student's ability to use information to find order in the world, to think critically, and to solve problems. This is proper, because the social studies curriculum possesses the richness of content so basic for effective thinking skills acquisition. *Thinking* and *content* are clearly inseparable in quality elementary social studies programs. By engaging children in positive social studies experiences that offer them opportunities to interact productively with the subject matter and among themselves, we are working toward the fulfillment of our primary responsibility of helping children attain the understandings, skills, and attitudes that will last a lifetime.

A significant responsibility of social studies teachers is to offer a sound program with proper balance. Many professional organizations have issued position statements describing precisely how that might be accomplished, but the "Essentials of Exemplary Social Studies Programs," formulated by the National Council for the Social Studies (1981), appears to present as clearly as any other source the major goals of social studies instruction today. These goals are described in Figure 1–4. The rest of this text will be directed toward helping you acquire skills to carry out each of the four major areas of responsibility: *knowledge, democratic beliefs, thinking skills,* and *participation skills.*

FIGURE 1–4
Essential of Exemplary Social Studies Programs

Citizen participation in public life is essential to the health of our democratic system. Effective social studies programs help prepare young people who can identify, understand, and work to solve the problems that face our increasingly diverse nation and interdependent world.

Knowledge

Students need knowledge of the world at large and the world at hand, the world of individuals and the world of institutions, the world past, the world present and future. An exemplary social studies curriculum links information presented in the classroom with experiences gained by students through social and civic observation, analysis and participation.

From this knowledge base, exemplary programs teach skills, concepts, and generalizations that can help students understand the sweep of human affairs and ways of managing conflict consistent with democratic procedures.

Democratic Beliefs

Fundamental beliefs drawn from the Declaration of Independence and the United States Constitution with its Bill of Rights form the basic principles of our democratic constitutional order. Exemplary school programs do not indoctrinate students to accept these ideas blindly, but present knowledge about their historical derivation and contemporary application essential to understanding our society and its institutions. Not only should such ideas be discussed as they relate to the curriculum and to current affairs, they should also be mirrored by teachers in their classrooms and embodied in the school's daily operations.

These democratic beliefs depend upon such practices as due process, equal protection, and civic participation, and are rooted in the concepts of justice, equality, responsibility, freedom, diversity, and privacy.

Thinking Skills

It is important to that students connect knowledge with beliefs and action. To do that, thinking skills can be developed through constant systematic practice throughout the years of formal schooling. Fundamental to the goals of social studies education are those skills which help ensure rational behavior in social settings.

In addition to strengthening reading and computation, there is a wide variety of thinking skills essential to the social studies which can be grouped into four major categories:

Data-Gathering Skills. Learning to:
  Acquire information by observation
  Locate information from a variety of sources
  Compile, organize, and evaluate information
  Extract and interpret information
  Communicate orally and in writing

Intellectual Skills. Learning to:
  Compare things, ideas, events, and situations
    on the basis of similarities and differences
  Classify or group items in categories
  Ask appropriate and searching questions
  Draw conclusions or inferences from evidence
  Arrive at general ideas
  Make sensible predictions from generalizations

Decision-Making Skills. Learning to:
  Consider alternative solutions
  Consider the consequences of each solution
  Make decisions and justify them in relationship to democratic principles
  Act, based on those decisions

Interpersonal Skills. Learning to:
  See things from the point of view of others
  Understand one's own beliefs, feelings, abilities, and shortcomings and how they affect relations with others
  Use group generalizations without stereotyping and arbitrarily classifying individuals
  Recognize value in individuals different from one's self and groups different from one's own

FIGURE 1–4
(continued)

Work effectively with others as a group member
Give and receive constructive criticism
Accept responsibility and respect the rights
   and property of others

Participation Skills

As a civic participant, the individual uses the knowledge, beliefs, and skills learned in the school, the social studies classroom, the community, and the family as the basis for action.

Connecting the classroom with the community provides many opportunities for students to learn the basic skills of participation, from observation to advocacy. To teach participation, social studies programs need to emphasize the following kinds of skills:

Work effectively in groups—organizing, planning, making decisions, taking action
Form coalitions of interest with other groups
Persuade, compromise, bargain
Practice patience and perseverance in working for one's goal
Develop experience in cross-cultural situations

Source: National Council for the Social Studies (1981). Essentials of the social studies. *Social Education, 45,* no. 3, 163–164.

At the roots of a democracy are knowledgeable and thoughtful citizens constituting a learning and learned society. Of course, they have many other qualities, too, but high on the list of behavior for democratic citizens is *thinking for themselves.* Democracy requires individuals who are able to search for and examine the facts whenever they must make up their minds about important issues. These issues might relate to one's personal life or to complex international concerns; regardless, the protection of our freedoms lies in the hands of rational people. Such skills must be learned during the early years with a flexible social studies curriculum that offers meaningful experiences to all. All youngsters must find something to excite their interest and stimulate their thinking. A one-dimensional approach to social studies instruction cannot do this. We fail our children with our narrowness; if our myopic view of teaching has caused them to feel stupid or to be bored, we have lost. Learning for an informed citizenry is too important to be thought of as something that everyone must be able to do in any single way. The danger to our future is great when we restrict the adventuresome, "can-do" spirit of childhood. Therefore, our social studies program for students who will be adult citizens in a new century must be one that prizes lifelong learning through the use of various teaching strategies that promote functional thinking skills. The probing, wondering mind of childhood must be freed. Our society of tomorrow starts in your classroom today.

Tenet 7: Effective Social Studies Teachers Promote "Social Study" Within a Cooperative, Democratic Classroom Community.

There are two fundamental ways students interact with one another in contemporary social studies classrooms; they can (1) *compete* to see who is "best" or (2) *work cooperatively* with a vested interest in their classmates' learning as well as their own. Of these two, competition appears most dominant. Johnson and Johnson (1988) explain:

> The research indicates that a vast majority of students in the United States view school as a competitive enterprise where you try to do better than the other students. This competitive expectation is already fairly widespread when students enter school and grows stronger as they progress through school. . . . Cooperation among students where they celebrate each other's successes, encourage each other to do homework, and learn to work together regardless of ethnic backgrounds, male or female, bright or struggling, handicapped or not, is rare. (p. 34)

We can deduce, then, that social studies teachers, in their efforts to attain specified learning outcomes, can choose to engage their students in either competitive or cooperative enterprises, but competition seems to be their overwhelming choice. What accounts for this state of affairs? Part of the answer can be traced back to the 1980s, when reports such as *A Nation at Risk* (1983) fired volleys of criticism at our nation's schools with searing commentaries such as, "If an unfriendly foreign power had attempted to impose on America the mediocre instructional performance that exists today, we might well have viewed it as an act of war" (p. 9). In response to such shocking denouncements, parents and educators demanded more stringent academic standards, using a rallying cry of "Bring back the basics!" Their concept of back-to-basics programs had the following general characteristics: (1) an emphasis on acquiring basic content and skills; (2) repetitious drill and practice with paper-and-pencil seatwork; (3) considerable use of quizzes and standardized tests; and (4) elimination of "frills" from the school programs, "frills" being interpreted as anything not actually included in the "basics." Therefore, these programs emphasized the acquisition of facts and skills with little regard for how they were attained or for what purpose (other than scoring well on a standardized test).

Goodlad (1984) examined the resulting state of instruction in our nation's schools, noting that classrooms exhibited a "flatness"—little about them could be described as innovative, exciting, or dynamic. Teachers disliked compromising their learner-centered philosophies with a rigid skills/content approach forced upon them by boards of education. One second-grade teacher shared her disillusionment, saying, "We must get them through workbook after workbook. We must make them produce on paper to be verified by all. We feel guilty doing an art lesson or having a wonderful discussion" (Boyer, 1989, p. 74).

Another teacher added these thoughts:

> In the large, affluent suburb where I teach, the pressure is on the kids and the teachers from kindergarten through high school to get good grades, bring up the test scores, and be the best (on the test). Classroom teachers are locked into curriculum, scheduling, and test preparation that leaves little time for innovation, creativity, or diversity in teaching. . . . Somewhere the meaning of education has been lost. (Boyer, 1989, p. 74)

Because most teachers understood the importance of excellent teaching in the elementary school, they were distressed that the public did not share their views and had placed such competitive pressures on these schools and children. They decried the fact that most children left elementary school less eager and less excited about learning than when they entered. Ayers (1989) suggests a way to begin correcting this confused situation:

> The practical place to begin is to recall that children are whole people, with bodies, minds, cultures, and feelings. Furthermore, we can acknowledge that children want what all human beings long for: love, support, respect, community, meaningful work to do, and real choices to make. . . .
>
> Part of our task is to allow children to be children, to protect childhood, and to create spaces where children can interact productively with each other and with caring adults. This is our abiding responsibility to the development of whole human beings. (p. 72)

Ayers reflects the thoughts of many elementary school educators who deplore trends toward competition and favor more humanistic, process-oriented instruction that encourages children to work together. Specific teaching recommendations for today's social studies classrooms reflect Ayers's philosophy—that cooperative group activities are an integral part of social studies instruction. In other words, effective social studies teaching involves appropriate *social study*. Stahl and Van Sickle (1992) explain:

> *Social* . . . refers to the need to engage in worthwhile, goal-oriented tasks within supportive interpersonal environments. . . . Within such environments individuals must become active, contributing, and integral parts of the social community that benefits from their participation. To be effective within this social environment, students must learn and practice the knowledge, abilities, and attitudes necessary to function effectively within the social group.
>
> . . . By *study* we mean the systematic and focused pursuit of knowledge and the ability to apply that knowledge when needed. (pp. 2-3)

Social study, then, refers to a process through which teachers enable students to acquire new knowledge and abilities within viable groups, or social communities. Johnson and Johnson (1985) talk of the motivational power of such working relationships with other people:

> Motivation to learn is inherently interpersonal. It is through interaction with other people that students learn to value learning for its own sake, enjoy the process of learning, and take pride in their acquisition of knowledge and development of skill. Of the interpersonal relationships available in the classroom, peers may be the most influential on motivation to learn. (p. 250)

We are born into a group (the family), so our initial survival needs, as well as the survival of our species, depends upon group membership. It is within the family group, play group, worship group, educational group, and other various organizations that we grow and become socialized into certain patterns of thinking and behaving. Even our self-perceptions are influenced by the ways we are treated by these groups. So, ultimately, our psychological health is significantly influenced by the interpersonal relationships we experience as we are socialized into groups. Some argue that this human relations aspect of group membership is so crucial to our lives that it ought to be taught in our schools as the "Fourth R." If this is to happen, social studies teachers must carefully define student roles and deliberately structure classroom activities so that youngsters are able to participate together as members of a social community focused on the common task of achieving shared learning goals. Brophy and Alleman (1996) advise that this charge is not as difficult to accomplish in social studies as it is in other subjects, since group-oriented learning techniques fit in so well with the overarching goals of the subject.

Tenet 8: Effective Social Studies Teachers Implement a Social Studies Program That Is Sensitive to and Reflective of Students' Backgrounds and Needs.

Have you ever been involved in a situation where you had more difficulty doing something than anyone else? Dancing? Playing a musical instrument? Dribbling a basketball? Speaking a foreign language? Ice skating? Maybe you were the only one who had problems performing a certain task. How did you feel? How would you have felt if every day when you came to school you were the only one who couldn't perform certain tasks that could be completed by others with relative ease? What kind of "treatment" or "special help" would you need to keep you coming to school each day? On the other hand, have you ever been involved in a situation where you were able to do something more easily and quickly than anyone else? How did you feel then? What could be done in school to keep you from becoming miserably bored? What could be done to best help you work toward fulfilling your unlimited potential?

Like any of us who have been in such situations, all children come to school with varied strengths and limitations to form unique collections of distinctive talents and abilities. Some children stand out because they are exceptional performers; others face certain challenges that require special services to help them reach their potential. Teachers achieve quality in the elementary school social studies program when they deliver the best for each youngster and make the most of their time with everyone in their classrooms. Effective teachers adapt instruction to meet the special needs, talents, and interests of all their students; the quality of their social studies programs is distinguished by a keen awareness and consideration of each youngster as a distinct individual. The foremost ingredient of exemplary social studies classrooms is a respect for the rights and needs of all children, *including those whose backgrounds or exhibited needs are not shared by most others.* These children may exhibit specific developmental disabilities, speak a home language that does not match the school's, come from diverse cultural or ethnic backgrounds, or possess unique gifts and talents; whatever the circumstance, the field of elementary school social studies education should be consistently responsive by offering appropriate experiences to fully develop their native capabilities.

At the heart of this topic is a concern about equity and fair treatment for groups that have traditionally experienced discrimination because of race or ethnicity, language, gender, or exceptionality. Because of the wide range of diversity in contem-

Our social studies programs nurture initiative and drive; all children learn together with classmates of diverse backgrounds.

porary society, all teachers must become instructionally effective with diverse groups of students. There are at least three arguments why this charge is especially meaningful for social studies teachers (Winitzky, 1991):

> The first is that these issues should be of major concern to every citizen, that it is incumbent upon us as citizens to work toward the public good by trying to ameliorate these problems. . . .
> The second argument is that Americans have a strong belief in the power of education as the route to later success in life—economically, politically, and culturally. . . .
> Finally, many believe that we really have no choice. We simply live in a [diverse] world, and our schools should reflect that aspect of modern life. (pp. 126–127)

Children in today's schools come from an enormous range of backgrounds, languages, and abilities. To meet their educational needs, social studies teachers must be able to work effectively with *all* students.

Tenet 9: Effective Social Studies Teachers Use Accepted Professional Standards as Guides for Instruction and Program Development.

A powerful nationwide concern for educational reform arose during the 1980s, and a great deal of attention was directed toward the development of standards that might serve as guides for program planning, instruction, and evaluation. Several subject areas of the school curriculum responded to this concern and developed standards for their fields (the arts, civics and government, economics, English, foreign language, geography, history, mathematics, physical education, science, and vocational education). The NCSS (1994) observed these developments with keen interest, and then expressed its distress: "Congress . . . passed, in 1992, the Goals 2000: Educate America Act, codifying educational goals and sanctioning the development of national educational standards as a means of encouraging and evaluating student achievement. While that act included the disciplines named above, *it omitted social studies*" (emphasis added) (p. viii). However, in 1993 the NCSS successfully argued for the annexation of social studies to the list of national standards and named a task force to define what students should know and when they should know it.

"What will students be taught?" "How will students be taught?" "How will student achievement be evaluated?" These were the central questions that steered the course of action for the NCSS task force. Using the questions as a guide, the task force worked for over one year before publishing *Curriculum Standards for Social Studies: Expectations of Excellence* (NCSS, 1994). The standards consist of ten themes that form the framework of social studies (see Figure 1–5). *Curriculum Standards for Social Studies* treats each theme in separate chapters for the early grades, middle grades, and high school. Within those chapters, each theme is followed by a list of performance expectations and classroom activities. For example, for the early grades, the standard and performance expectations for the first theme, "Culture," are as follows (NCSS, 1994):

> Social studies programs should include experiences that provide for the study of *culture and cultural diversity,* so that the learner can:
>   a. explore and describe similarities and differences in the ways groups, societies, and cultures address similar human needs and concerns;
>   b. give examples of how experiences may be interpreted differently by people from diverse cultural perspectives and frames of reference;
>   c. describe ways in which language, stories, folktales, music, and artistic creations serve as expressions of culture and influence behavior of people living in a particular culture;
>   d. compare ways in which people from different cultures think about and deal with their physical environment and social conditions;
>   e. give examples and describe the importance of cultural unity and diversity within and across groups. (p. xiii)

Following a presentation of the standard and performance expectation, the chapter describes classroom activities to illustrate how the standards are applied. For example, to meet performance expectations a, b, and d, the experiences of Carlene Jackson are recounted. Before the first day of school, Jackson examined her class list and inferred from the children's surnames that her class was a rich mix of cultural backgrounds—Mexican, Vietnamese, Korean, African American, and European American. By the end of the first month of school, Jackson and her students decided to study and compare how families meet their basic needs of food, clothing, and shelter in five places: their community; Juarez, Mexico; Hanoi, Vietnam; Lagos, Nigeria; and Frankfurt, Germany.

FIGURE 1-5
Curriculum Standards for Social Studies

Ten Thematic Strands

Ten themes serve as organizing strands for the social studies curriculum at every school level (early, middle and high school); they are interrelated and draw from all of the social science disciplines and other related disciplines and fields of scholarly study to build a framework for social studies curriculum design.

I Culture
Human beings create, learn, and adapt culture. Human cultures are dynamic systems of beliefs, values, and traditions that exhibit both commonalities and differences. Understanding culture helps us understand ourselves and others.

II Time, Continuity, and Change
Human beings seek to understand their historic roots and to locate themselves in time. Such understanding involves knowing what things were like in the past and how things change and develop—allowing us to develop historic perspective and answer important questions about our current condition.

III People, Places, and Environment
Technological advancements have insured that students are aware of the world beyond their personal locations. As students study content related to this theme, they create their spatial views and geographic perspectives of the world; social, cultural, economic, and civic demands mean that students will need such knowledge, skills, and understandings to make informed and critical decisions about the relationship between human beings and their environment.

IV Individual Development and Identity
Personal identity is shaped by one's culture, by groups and by institutional influences. Examination of various forms of human behavior enhances understanding of the relationships between social norms and emerging personal identities, the social processes which influence identity formation, and the ethical principles underlying individual action.

V Individuals, Groups, and Institutions
Institutions exert enormous influence over us. Institutions are organizational embodiments to further the core social values of those who comprise them. It is important for students to know how institutions are formed, what controls and influences them, how they control and influence individuals and culture, and how institutions can be maintained or changed.

VI Power, Authority, and Governance
Understanding of the historic development of structures of power, authority, and governance and their evolving functions in contemporary society is essential for the emergence of civic competence.

VII Production, Distribution, and Consumption
Decisions about exchange, trade, and economic policy and well-being are global in scope and the role of government in policy making varies over time and from place to place. The systematic study of an interdependent world economy and the role of technology in economic decision making is essential.

VIII Science, Technology, and Society
Technology is as old as the first crude tool invented by prehistoric humans, and modern life as we know it would be impossible without technology and the science which supports it. Today's technology forms the basis for some of our most difficult social choices.

IX Global Connections
The realities of global interdependence require understanding of the increasingly important and diverse global connections among world societies before there can be analysis leading to the development of possible solutions to persisting and emerging global issues.

X Civic Ideals and Practices
All people have a stake in examining civic ideals and practices across time, in diverse societies, as well as in determining how to close the gap between present practices and the ideals upon which our democratic is based. An understanding of civic ideals and practices of citizenship is critical to full participation in society.

Source: Nickell, P. (1995). Pullout feature: Thematically organized social studies. *Social Studies & The Young Learner, 8,* 1–8. © National Council for the Social Studies. Reprinted by permission.

Throughout the unit of study, Jackson and her students read books, looked at photos and slides, watched videos, and talked to speakers from their designated cities. The students honed their reading, writing, speaking, and map-reading skills. They created a chart summarizing the data they collected.

An accompanying booklet has been provided with the current text to provide a more comprehensive list of standards, performance expectations, and classroom activities. This useful resource can enrich your teaching repertoire in several ways:

1. to serve as a framework for social studies program design from kindergarten through grade 12 (K-12);

2. to function as a guide for curriculum decisions by providing student performance expectations in the areas of knowledge, processes, and attitudes and

3. to provide examples of classroom activities that will guide teachers as they design instruction to help their students meet performance expectations. (NCSS, 1994, p. ix)

As with most breaks from precedent, the standards movement has elicited both arguments of support as well as blistering criticisms. In speaking of the benefits of standards, Resnick says that "standards and assessments [will] help bring about better student outcomes—a different quality and higher level of student achievement" (O'Neil, 1993, p. 17). Standards become "images of excellence" to their defenders.

Among the most prevalent criticisms are that (1) there is disagreement among the experts in the field as to what information should be included and what level of performance should be expected; (2) there is dissatisfaction among educators that precisely defined content standards will become translated into rigid, teacher-controlled instructional methodologies with evaluation strategies dominated by paper-and-pencil tests, and judgments of students based solely on the test results; (3) the deep-seated involvement of federal agencies in the standards movement constitutes an intrusion into local control of public education; and (4) there is a lack of understanding of what the specific terminology in the standards documents actually means. These issues have become so volatile that the future of the standards movement is unclear at this time. Eisner (1993) summarizes the thoughts of standards critics:

> The current emphasis on standards will provide no panacea in education. Paying close attention to how we teach and building institutions that make it possible for teachers to continue to grow as professionals may be much more effective educationally than trying to determine through [standards] whether or not our students measure up. (p. 23)

Tenet 10: Effective Social Studies Teachers Employ Authentic Assessment Techniques to Acquire Information About Student Performance.

Teaching involves assessment—making sophisticated judgments about various aspects of the social studies program. Teachers are responsible for obtaining and interpreting a wide range of information about what the children are doing and learning while they are in social studies class: "Should Vera get an 'A' or a 'B' on this project?" "Is my class ready to tackle independent study projects?" "Will Adam do better if I slow down the pace a bit?" "Is this field trip appropriate for my students?" "How does the performance of my students compare with the performance of other students?" Teachers have genuine questions about the degree to which the goals and objectives of the social studies program are being met, so they view assessment as a process concerned not only with evaluating student achievement but also with providing feedback about the appropriateness and effectiveness of their instruction.

The methods of assessment teachers select for their social studies programs send clear messages to parents and children about what is valued in their classrooms. Traditional standardized and textbook paper-and-pencil tests that tend to focus on rote memorization clearly communicate the notion that social studies is merely a collection of factual information and that success in the subject is based on how well students do on the tests. With this outlook, teachers often teach to what is tested rather than test what is taught—the test drives the curriculum.

Assessment in a contemporary, "powerful" social studies classroom requires that teachers collect and organize a more diverse range of evidence than that gathered from a test, including observations, projects, interviews, artwork, and writing samples. While traditional tests are typically administered at the end of lessons or units, newer models become integrally interwoven into the instruction. Teachers often help students develop portfolios that incorporate numerous sources of evaluative information relating to a particular topic of study. This new approach is called *authentic assessment* (or *performance assessment*) because it gives information about what students know or what they can do in actual or applied situations.

Bergen (1993/94) cautions that because authentic assessment is quite complex and requires more time and effort to document student performance than grading a paper-and-pencil test, teachers may judge it to be too cumbersome to use. However, social studies offers an optimal context for authentic assessment, especially since social studies involves process as well as content. In quality social studies programs, teachers gather the maximum possible information about student achievement as well as about the level of teacher performance and program effectiveness. In Chapter 5, you will learn about how to construct your own authentic assessment systems congruent with the process-oriented elementary social studies curriculum.

AFTERWORD

The most vital ingredient of a successful social studies program is a good teacher. The physical setting is important, as are the materials used, but a teacher's professional skills and personality are of primary importance. Your personal and professional behaviors dictate the tone of the environment and make a lasting impact on the students, on their families, and on society. Few individuals are more significant in the lives of elementary school children than their parents, close relatives, and teachers. Teachers are admired and imitated; they are expected to display courage, cleanliness, honesty, openmindedness, scholarship, generosity, faithfulness, fairness, sensitivity, tact, and a host of other qualities. Teachers of elementary school children should be among the finest people we can imagine, but being a fine person does not in itself guarantee success in teaching. A superior teacher must also possess a set of professional skills founded on sound theoretical and research-based principles.

The complexities of the twenty-first century may dictate a quality and quantity of education far more different than we can currently imagine. You must take your emerging view of what social studies is and constantly search for ideas that help construct new roles for teachers in a new century. In addition to what we have considered up to this point, one of the most helpful ways of keeping up with current trends is to review the activities and publications of professional organizations.

The largest and most influential professional organization for social studies educators is the National Council for the Social Studies (NCSS). The council publishes several publications of interest to social studies teachers: *Social Education*, the primary journal, focuses on philosophical, theoretical, and practical classroom-application articles involved with K–12 instruction; *Social Studies and the Young Learner*, a separate journal for elementary teachers, offers articles primarily concerned with teaching strategies. The NCSS also periodically publishes "how-to" pamphlets that offer in-depth suggestions for implementing specific instructional responsibilities (such as using creative dramatics or current affairs strategies) in the social studies classroom. You should also become familiar with *The Social Studies*, a journal not associated with any particular professional organization. It deals with classroom practices on the K–12 level and contains a wealth of articles describing ideas for classroom use and stimulating thought on philosophical issues. The relevant addresses follow.

National Council for the Social Studies
3501 Newark Street, NW
Washington, DC 20016

The Social Studies
1319 Eighteenth Street, NW
Washington, DC 20036

TECHNOLOGY SAMPLER

Some useful sources for general social studies topics include these Internet sites:

NCSS Online Links
http://www.ncss.org/links/webtech.html

History/Social Studies Site for K–12 Teachers
http://www.execpc,com/~dboalsboals.html

Internet Resources for Social Studies Education
http://www.indiana.edu/~ssdc/internet.heml

Social Studies Listserves
http://www.tile.net/tile/LISTSERV/index.html

Social Studies Newsgroups
http://www.coe.ug.edu/~asoucek/newsgroup/social.html

Social Studies
http://www.coe.ug.edu/~vceed009/social studies.html

Social Studies Sources
http://education.indiana.edu/~socialst/

NCSS Online
http://www.ncss.org/

WHAT I *NOW* KNOW

Complete these self-check items once more. Determine for yourself whether it would be useful to take a more in-depth look at any area. Use the same key as you did for the preassessment form ("+", "?", "-").

I can *now*

_____ describe the personality characteristics of effective social studies teachers.

_____ describe the professional characteristics of effective social studies teachers.

_____ define the term *social studies*.

_____ explain the major goals of social studies instruction.

_____ list and describe the major disciplines contributing to social studies instruction.

_____ identify what is meant by the term *powerful social studies*.

_____ identify patterns for organizing social studies content for instruction.

_____ describe the possibilities of connecting social studies to the other school subjects.

_____ discuss the role of the thinking skills in a social studies program.

_____ explain how standards influence social studies instruction.

_____ describe the role of "authentic" assessment in social studies instruction.

_____ analyze the role of a "good citizen."

_____ explain the importance of one's professional preparation for good teaching in the social studies.

REFERENCES

Ayers, W. (1989). Children at risk. *Educational Leadership, 46,* 72.

Barr, R. D., Barth, J. L., & Shermis, S. S. (1977). *Defining the social studies.* Washington, DC: National Council for the Social Studies.

Barth, J. L. (1996). NCSS and the nature of the social studies. In O. L. Davis, Jr. (Ed.), *NCSS in retrospect.* Washington, DC: National Council for the Social Studies.

Berg, M. (1988). Integrating Ideas for social studies. *Social Studies and the Young Learner, 1,* unnumbered pull-out feature.

Bergen, D. (1993/94). Authentic performance assessments. *Childhood Education, 70,* 99–102.

Boyer, E. L. (1989). What teachers say about children in America. *Educational Leadership, 46,* 74.

Brody, R. A. (1989). Why study politics? In *Charting a Course: Social Studies for the 21st Century.* Washington, DC: National Commission on Social Studies in the Schools.

Brophy, J. & Alleman, J. (1996). *Powerful social studies for elementary students.* Fort Worth, TX: Harcourt Brace College Publishers.

Butts, R. F. (1984). Reaction to "In search for a scope and sequence for social studies." *Social Education, 48,* 263–264; 273.

Chaille, C., & Britain, L. (1991). *The young child as scientist.* New York: Harper Collins.

Children's Defense Fund. (1996). *The state of America's children: Yearbook 1996.* Washington, DC: Author.

Clark, D. C., & Cutler, B. C. (1990). *Teaching.* New York: Harcourt Brace Jovanovich.

Cogan, J. J. (1989). The continuing vigil for democracy, part II. *Social Education, 53,* 341.

Cullum, A. (1969). *Push back the desks.* New York: Citation Press.

Eisner, E. (1993). Why standards may not improve schools. *Educational Leadership, 50,* 22–23.

Finn, C. E. (1988). The social studies debacle among the educationaloids. *The American Spectator* (May 1988), 15–16.

Ford, P. L. (1879). *The New England Primer, a history of its origin and development.* New York: Dodd, Mead. In N. B. Smith (1963). *Reading instruction for today's children.* Englewood Cliffs, NJ: Prentice-Hall.

Gerzon, M. (1997). Teaching democracy by doing it! *Educational Leadership, 54,* 6–11.

Goodlad, J. I. (1984). *A place called school.* New York: McGraw-Hill.

Graham, L. B., & Persky, B. A. (1977). Who should work with young children? In L. B. Graham and B. A. Persky (Eds.), *Early Childhood.* Wayne, NJ: Avery.

Hanna, P. R. (1963). Revising the social studies: What is needed? *Social Education, 27,* 190–196.

Hellman-Rosenthal, G. (1984). Reaction to "In search for a scope and sequence for social studies." *Social Education, 48,* 263–264; 273.

Heuwinkel, M. K. (1996). New ways of learning=New ways of teaching. *Childhood Education, 73,* 27–31.

Hymes, J. L. (1981). *Teaching the child under six.* Columbus, OH: Merrill.

Johnson, D., & Johnson, R. (1985). Motivational processes in cooperative, competitive, and individualistic learning situations. In C. Ames & R. Ames (Eds.), *Research on motivation in education, Vol. 2: The classroom milieu* (pp. 249–286). New York: Academic Press.

Johnson, R. T., & Johnson, D. W. (1988). Cooperative learning. *In Context* (Winter 1988), 34.

Joint Committee on Geographic Education. (1984). *Guidelines for geographic education.* Washington, DC: Association of American Geographers.

Mason, R. E. (1960). *Educational ideals in American society.* Boston: Allyn and Bacon.

Mitchell, L. S. (1934). *Young geographers.* New York: John Day.

National Commission on Excellence in Education (1983). *A nation at risk: The imperative for educational reform.* Washington, DC: Author.

National Council for the Social Studies (1993a). A vision of powerful teaching and learning in the social studies: Building social understanding and civic efficacy. *Social Education, 57,* 213–223.

National Council for the Social Studies (1993b). Definition approved. *The Social Studies Professional, 114* (January/February 1993), 3.

National Council for the Social Studies (1994). *Curriculum standards for social studies: Expectations of excellence.* (Bulletin 89). Washington, DC: National Council for the Social Studies.

National Council for the Social Studies Task Force on Early Childhood/Elementary Social Studies (1989).

Social studies for early childhood and elementary school children preparing for the 21st century. *Social Education, 54,* 16.

National Education Association (1916). *The social studies in secondary education.* Report of the Committee on Social Studies, Bulletin 28. Washington, DC: Bureau of Education.

O'Neil, J. (1993). On the new standards project: A conversation with Lauren Resnick and Warren Simmons. *Educational Leadership, 50,* 17–23.

Parker, W. C., & Jarolimek, J. (1996). Social studies in elementary education. Upper Saddle River, NJ: Prentice Hall.

Peterson, P., & Knapp, N. (1993). Inventing and reinventing ideas: Constructivist teaching and learning in mathematics. In G. Cawelti (Ed.), *Challenges and achievements of American education* (pp. 134–157). Alexandria, VA: Association for Supervision and Curriculum Development.

Ravitch, D. (1988). Tot sociology. *American Educator, 12,* 39.

Stahl, R. J., & Van Sickle, R. L. (1992). Cooperative learning as effective social study within the social studies classroom: Introduction and an invitation. In R. J. Stahl and R. L. Van Sickle (Eds.), *Cooperative learning in the social studies classroom,* Bulletin 87. Washington, DC: National Council for the Social Studies.

Tyack, D. (1997). Civic education—What roles for citizens? *Educational Leadership, 54,* 22–24.

Winitzky, N. (1991). Multicultural and mainstreamed classrooms. In R. I. Arends, *Learning to teach* (pp. 125–156). New York: McGraw-Hill.

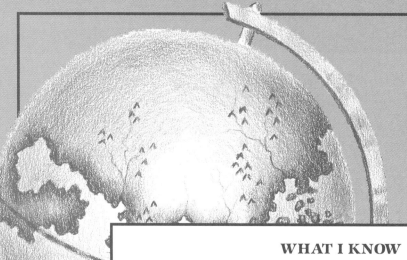

CHAPTER 2

WHAT I KNOW

This exercise provides a "scaffold" that will enable you to relate the chapter material to your background knowledge. Complete the form before you read the chapter and use the results to guide your reading. Use a "+" to indicate confidence, a "?" for uncertainty, and a "-" if you feel deficient in any area.

I can

_____ define what is meant by *multicultural education*.

_____ describe the place of multicultural content in the overall social studies curriculum.

_____ explain what is meant by the term *culture*.

_____ describe some needs that all children share.

_____ identify children with disabilities.

_____ describe the concept of inclusion and how it influences instruction in the social studies classroom.

_____ explain how children exhibit multiple intelligences and talents.

_____ describe the characteristics of gifted children and explain how to adjust instruction to meet their special needs.

_____ identify the characteristics of creative children and analyze their unique educational needs.

_____ explain the importance of gender-fair attitudes and experiences.

_____ give examples of appropriate instruction for low socioeconomic status students.

_____ identify and describe special approaches for dealing with language diversity in the classroom.

Using the results as a guide, what questions will you seek to answer as you read?

Creating a Supportive Environment

◆ CLASSROOM SKETCH

St. Guadalupe:	Knock, knock (pretends to knock on a door).
Rainbow:	Who is it?
St. Guadalupe:	St. Guadalupe.
Rainbow:	What do you want?
St. Guadalupe:	I want a color.
Rainbow:	What color?
St. Guadalupe:	Rojo!

In this game, one child is chosen to be St. Guadalupe and another to be Mother-of-Color, or Rainbow. All of the other children are assigned color names, each one given to them by Rainbow. [You could use English color names only, or create an opportunity to teach their Spanish names: *rojo* (red), *verde* (green), *azul* (blue), *amarillo* (yellow), *negro* (black), *blanco* (white)]. All the colors belong to Rainbow, and they line up behind her—across the play space from St. Guadalupe, whose area is designated as "Home Base." St. Guadalupe then initiates the preceding dialogue. All the children of the color named by St. Guadalupe must attempt to reach "Home Base" without being tagged. If they reach it safely, they are named another color and get ready to go again. Those who are caught help St. Guadalupe tag other players until everyone (including Rainbow) is captured. Then the game is over.

◆   CLASSROOM CONNECTION

The children in this third-grade classroom were playing a game called "Los Colores" ("Colors"), a group game common to Spanish-speaking cultures (Perez, 1993). Their teacher, Ms. Reed, selected it as a way to integrate knowledge about cultures into the regular social studies program. She wanted the children to learn about the uniqueness of various cultures, but in a way that avoided stereotyping—for example, all Spanish-speaking children wear sombreros and break piñatas at birthday parties. The teacher selected games from various cultures because she believed that, despite many fundamental differences, cultures are alike in many ways. In fact, this game is much like the popular childhood game you may have played, "Red Rover."

Ms. Reed includes multicultural experiences as an integral part of her classroom program, establishing an all-inclusive learning environment that nurtures mutual trust and respect for all people. She operates with a strong conviction that children who are equipped with a knowledge of and appreciation for the glorious diversity among people will more likely be wise citizens who respect our nation's rich variety of cultures, heritages, abilities, and interests. She understands that "tourist" approaches to learning about human diversity (Jones & Derman-Sparks, 1992), where classes occasionally visit other people and cultures before returning to the mainstream curriculum, although often carried out with the best of intentions, rarely broaden children's understandings of those people and cultures. "Tourist" approaches are characterized by "special" activities where students do isolated projects, usually associated with a holiday or special situation—such as performing a dragon dance during the Chinese New Year, playing a dreidel game at Hanukkah, or running their fingers over a Braille card in an attempt to understand the conditions of sightlessness. These disconnected experiences might make students a *bit* more aware of the world around them, but genuine understanding comes from *all* that children do during the day. Perez (1994) believes that a "tourist curriculum emphasizes the exotic differences [among people], while ignoring the actual experiences of diverse groups. This way of teaching misrepresents [diversity] and leads to stereotyping" (p. 153). Educators today recommend replacing the tourist approach with strategies like Ms. Reed's—infusing multicultural content into the broad curriculum. The primary goals of infusion are to extend equal recognition for all groups and to help all people achieve equal opportunity in society.

Elementary school programs employing an infusion approach to instruction are popularly referred to as *multicultural programs. Multicultural* was once a term inclined to describe differences, especially cultural and language differences, as "handicaps." Resulting educational programs often pressured culturally and linguistically diverse students to conform to majority standards and mainstream cultural norms. Now, however, multiculturalism accepts cultural and linguistic diversity as a *resource* rather than a handicap, and has been expanded to include groups based on exceptionality, gender, and class, as well as language and culture. Given the diversity of contemporary society, all elementary school teachers must become culturally sensitive and develop instructionally effective strategies to use with widely diverse groups of students.

A rich storehouse of information provides insight into what teachers can do with children in a multicultural program, but before we examine these recommendations, it must be noted that the cultural group categories used to organize this chapter are merely social constructions, which cannot possibly embrace the life of any single individual. For example, a person might be not only "Caucasian," but also French, Southerner, farmer, Roman Catholic, hearing impaired, female, and lower-middle class. This person's group memberships, as we find true for most people, include race, ethnic group, region, occupation, religion, disabled or nondisabled, gender, and social class. Many aspects of one's life are shaped by such groups, making the person described above a much different person than an Asian American male from a large Eastern city who grew up in a crowded high-rise apartment, or a Native American female whose family inhabits a pueblo in the desert Southwest. Groups can be defined along many different lines, but everyone is a member of assorted groups, each of which creates its own culture—knowledge, rules, values, and traditions that guide its members' behavior.

Membership in any specific group may reflect certain tendencies and probabilities of expected behavior; for example, Vietnamese children tend to respect their parents very much, and low socioeconomic status (SES) students demonstrate lower levels of school achievement than high SES students. However, such tendencies do not tell you about *individual* students. Banks (1993) clarifies:

> Although membership in a gender, racial, ethnic, social-class, or religious group can provide us with important clues about an individual's behavior, it cannot enable us to predict behavior. . . . *Membership in a particular group does not determine behavior but makes certain types of behavior more probable.* (pp. 13–14)

All of this is not meant to confuse you, but only to emphasize that the children you teach are not just Puerto Rican, male, or middle class; they are uniquely complex individuals who have become who they are through the interaction of many intricate factors. The labels we choose to describe the groups they belong to are not meant to stereotype, only to provide insight into the best practices for social studies instruction.

CHILDREN WITH SPECIAL LEARNING CHALLENGES

Anyone who has spent time with children knows that there are many ways they are all alike and some ways they stand apart from one another. It is important to keep this perspective in mind, for when you begin to teach you will be entrusted with the crucial responsibility to escort *all* of your students on their remarkable journey through childhood. You have taken this journey earlier in your life, of course, but will be faced with your first appointment as a "tour guide." Certainly, you will have anxieties and fears as you assume this role, but your itinerary for this extraordinary trip is solidly supported by the wealth of knowledge that is understood about children. Using this knowledge is crucial for a rewarding trip. One of the things you will find is that all your travelers are alike in some ways; for instance, they will all have *similar needs* along the way.

Shared Needs

Children with disabilities are similar in many ways to children without disabilities. Wolery and Wilbers (1994) clarify:

> All children share needs for food and shelter, for love and affection, for affiliation with others, for opportunities to play and learn, and for protection from the harsh realities of their environments. All children deserve freedom from violence, abuse, neglect, and suffering. All children deserve interactions and relationships with adults who are safe, predictable, responsive, and nurturing. All children deserve opportunities to interact with peers who are accepting, trustworthy, kind, and industrious. All children deserve. . . educational experiences that are stimulating, interesting, facilitative, and enjoyable. (p. 3)

Despite these commonly shared needs, children with disabilities are different from children without disabilities. Wolery, Strain, and Bailey (1992) explain:

> They need environments that are specifically organized and adjusted to minimize the effects of their disabilities and to promote learning of a broad range of skills. They need professionals who are competent in meeting the general needs of . . . children *and* are competent in promoting learning and use of skills important to the specific needs of children with disabilities. (p. 95)

In addition to sharing a set of basic needs, all children go through similar *stages of development.* Although the timing will not be exactly the same for each, children all around the world move through predictable patterns of *motor development* (they will walk before they run), *language development* (they will babble before they speak in sentences), *cognitive development* (they will want to explore their surroundings with their hands and fingers before they will try to read a book for information), and *social-emotional development* (they will scream to get their own way before they ask permission for things). Chandler (1994) explains that children with special needs may develop at a rate different from that of more typical children, but the sequence of development remains the same:

For example, we know that children learn to sit before they stand, stand before they walk. This sequence is the same whether a child is nine months old or three years old. If three-year-old Amanda is unable to walk, we consider her a child with special needs. However, our knowledge of child development still tells us that she first needs to sit, and then stand, before she can walk, even though her development of these skills is delayed. Again, understanding typical development provides the information needed to teach and care for the child with special needs. (p. 21)

Despite the fact that most children display similarities, some children with developmental disabilities will not be quite like most others. It is estimated that between 10 to 12 percent of all children in the United States fall into the *children with disabilities* category; they deviate far enough from the typical in at least one respect that an individualized school program is required to address their needs. Returning to our "tour guide" analogy, you must understand that these children may not arrive at the point of departure on time; may not demonstrate identical interests and abilities along the way; and may not be able to reach the destination with the others. They may not be expected to travel through the elementary school years with the same means of conveyance—many might be forced to walk through childhood while others will cruise or fly. Who are these *children with disabilities?* Public Law 101–476, the Americans With Disabilities Act of 1990, defines children with disabilities as those:

> A. With mental retardation, hearing impairments including deafness, speech or language impairments, visual impairments, including blindness, serious emotional disturbance, orthopedic impairments, autism, traumatic brain injury, other health impairments, or specific learning disabilities; and
> B. who, by reason thereof, need special education and related services.

The U.S. Office of Education (1994) classifies 51.1 percent of children with disabilities as having specific learning disabilities, 21.6 percent having speech or language impairments, 11.5 percent having mental retardation, 8.7 percent having serious emotional disturbance, 2.2% having multiple disabilities, 1.3 percent having hearing impairments, 1.1 percent having orthopedic impairments, and 2.5 percent having other disabilities. Today, more than 70 percent of children with disabilities are instructed in the regular classroom for at least 40 percent of the school day. Experts believe that this number will continue to increase in the future (Putnam, Spiegel, & Bruininks, 1995). By recognizing and positively valuing their differences, you can provide each child with the opportunity to grow to his or her fullest potential. Understanding those needs helps you plan an overall itinerary for your trip and serves as a general guide for your social studies program. But you must also understand that each child is unique. As an escort, your primary concern should be to discover the most appropriate "mode of transportation" for each child and to make the resulting voyage as productive, purposeful, and happy as possible.

The Concept of Inclusion

Being aware of the most convenient and appropriate "modes of transportation" for children with disabilities is especially important, for there is a growing trend toward *inclusion,* or providing for all children with special needs in the regular classroom. Inclusion is currently popular and receiving attention for a number of reasons. First, state and federal laws mandate, support, and encourage it. Second, some parents of children with special needs are unhappy that their children must attend separate programs. They view these programs as a form of segregation. Third, educators, parents, and children have had rewarding experiences in inclusive environments. Despite these strong points, however, not everyone is sold on the idea of inclusion. First, not all parents want their children with disabilities taken from their special programs. They believe that their children are best served in separate special education facilities. Second, many early childhood teachers feel inadequately prepared to provide for the special disabilities brought to their classrooms. Third, some people think that the great cost of inclusion outweighs its benefits.

Federal Legislation

Despite these opposing positions, inclusion is currently an educational reality and a process in which elementary school teachers find themselves increasingly involved. The trend was initiated with Public Law 94–142 (the Education for All Handicapped Children Act), signed into law in 1975 and implemented in the fall of 1978. It was a valuable outcome of the many social efforts during the early 1970s to prevent the segregation of any child from regular classrooms, whether because of special needs or race. Specifically, Public Law 94–142 made free public education mandatory for all children older than age five who were identified as having special needs. Such education was to take place within a "least restrictive environment." A least restrictive environment was defined as a place where the same opportunities as those available to any other child are offered to children with special needs (those who need special attention to overcome conditions that could delay normal growth and development, distort normal growth and development, or have a severe negative effect on normal growth and development and adjustment to life).

A comprehensive educational, medical, sociocultural, and psychological evaluation by a multidisciplinary team determined the extent of a child's disability. From there, possible remediation strategies were proposed. The school did this by scheduling a meeting with the prospective teacher, the child's parents, a representative from the school district (usually a special educator), and a member of the assessment team. All information was shared and a special education plan, the individualized education program (IEP), resulted.

The IEP is a carefully written plan that includes the following information (U.S. Office of Education, 1977):

1. A statement of the child's present level of performance.
2. A statement of long- and short-term goals.
3. A statement of special services to be provided and the extent to which the child will participate in regular school programs.
4. Dates identifying the duration of services.
5. Evaluation procedures that determine the extent to which the goals are being met.

The process of placing children with special needs into the regular school program may sound time-consuming and replete with paperwork. It is! But when we consider that the intent of P.L. 94–142 was to protect the right of children with special needs to a free public education, the value of a teacher's extra work is certainly apparent.

In 1990, Public Law 101–476 amended Public Law 94–142 in several very important ways. First, the legislation clarified what parents could demand for their children with disabilities. It reinforced the idea that all children with disabilities between the ages of 3 and 21 should receive a free and appropriate public education in a "least restrictive environment (LRE)" with their nondisabled peers. In addition to expanding and clarifying special education services for children with disabilities, the legislation replaced the title of P.L. 94–142 *(Education for All Handicapped Children Act)* with a new one *(Individuals With Disabilities Education Act—IDEA).* Although the change may seem insignificant to some, IDEA communicated a monumental message. By replacing the term *handicapped* with *individuals with disabilities,* Congress declared that professionals should think of children with special needs as *children* first rather than centering on their disabilities. In addition, IDEA was noted for its use of "person-first" language; this means that the person is emphasized first, the disability second. Examples of appropriate person-first usage appear in Table 2–1.

To extend this idea of appropriate terminology, persons without disabilities should be referred to as *nondisabled* rather than *normal* or *able-bodied.* The word *handicap* should be used only in reference to a condition or physical barrier ("The stairs are a *handicap* for Nina," or "Larry is *handicapped* by the inaccessible bus").

TABLE 2–1
Examples of Person-First Language

Use . . .	Do not use . . .
• person with a disability	• disabled or handicapped person
• individual without speech	• mute, dumb
• child who is blind or visually impaired	• blind girl or "the blind"
• student who is deaf or hearing impaired	• deaf student or "the deaf"
• boy with paraplegia	• paraplegic
• girl who is paralyzed	• paralyzed student
• individual with epilepsy	• epileptic
• student who has a learning disability or specific learning disability	• slow learner, retarded, learning disabled
• person with a mental disability, cognitive impairment	• crazy, demented, insane
• child with a developmental disability	• mentally retarded
• congenital disability	• birth defect
• child who uses a wheelchair	• wheelchair-bound child

Teaching Children With Disabilities

Although an awareness of appropriate terminology helps, our desire to include children with disabilities in all aspects of classroom life must also be based on our own feelings toward and understandings of children with disabilities. How would you feel, and what would you do, for example, in each of the following situations?

- Sarah has a convulsion and you are the only adult around.
- David becomes lost and cannot hear you calling him.
- Armand seems unable to sit still; he constantly interrupts other children in class.

Deiner (1983) comments that the way most people choose to "deal" with problems like these is to avoid them. How many of us tend to steer clear of children with disabilities because we feel inadequate or insecure around them? You cannot take this approach as a teacher of elementary school children today. You must replace your feelings of inadequacy by confronting your uncertainties and replacing them with confidence based upon accurate knowledge. To effectively implement the spirit of *inclusion*, all professionals must learn something about how it operates; doing so may alleviate many fears and make those involved in the process feel more secure. The following suggestions are general and should be adjusted in consideration of each unique situation.

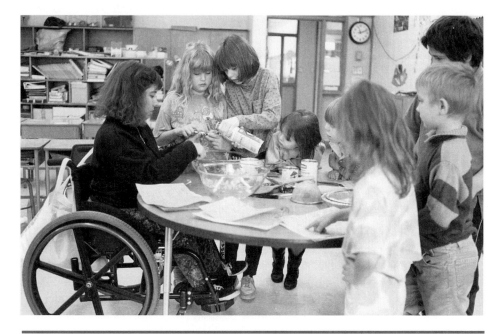

It is important that we use the exceptional sincerity of the elementary school years to start building the best possible interpersonal relationships.

1.   *Learn something about each specific disability.* You have a good start on understanding children with disabilities if you know about child development. After all, children with disabilities are, first of all, children. It is important to know that children with disabilities are more like other children than they are different from them. So your first step in working with children with disabilities is to establish a framework with a solid understanding of child development.

When a child with developmental disabilities is accepted into your program, take time to meet and get to know something about him or her. You might invite the family to visit your classroom, or find it worthwhile to visit the child at home. Whatever the choice, you will need a great deal of background information about the child. Other sources of background information include past teachers or other specialists who have been previously responsible for the child.

Certainly, it is not possible to know everything about each exceptional need you will face during your teaching career, but you will have to learn much about each disability as you encounter it. That is why the relevant public laws stipulate that a team of specialists be involved in the formulation of each IEP. However, you should become familiar with the ways one can accept, understand, and become sensitive to the needs of every child. To help in this regard, search through many professional journals, books, and videotapes available through professional organizations or publishers of special education materials. Get to know each child well.

Once you gather basic information about a specific disability, you have taken the first step in working with a child. Solit (1993) uses the case of Marie to describe how this knowledge background fits into the total scheme of planning a program for children with disabilities:

> The teacher learns that Marie has a moderate hearing loss, with no developmental or cognitive delays. Marie wears hearing aids. The audiologist taught the teacher how to check the hearing aid to ensure it is working. The teacher learns that the hearing aid will make sounds louder, but it will not necessarily clarify speech. The parents explain that Marie uses American Sign Language to communicate. The [principal] decides to find a volunteer who can sign to Marie, communicate with the teacher, and also be a role model for Marie. The teacher also receives release time to attend sign language classes.
>
> The audiologist explains how to adapt the classroom environment so there are less auditory distractions for Marie. The teacher learns that many aspects of the program do not need to change because Marie will benefit from the high quality . . . classroom that is already in place. (p. 133)

2.   *Maximize interactions between children with disabilities and nondisabled children.* Give simple explanations about a child's disability when needed. Youngsters are curious; they want to know about a new child and will be satisfied with an open, honest explanation. ("Russell's legs don't work well, so he needs a wheelchair.") Encourage the children with disabilities to share their strengths. For example, Russell can help another child in a project that involves the use of his hands (such as building a diorama or drawing a picture) while nondisabled learners may assist Russell in special

areas of need. In one classroom, Russell regularly joined his classmates on the playground for recess. One of their favorite activities was playing kickball. To play, Russell selected a "designated kicker" to kick the ball for him; after it was kicked, he wheeled around from base to base in his wheelchair. Social acceptance and cooperation help support students with diverse abilities.

3.   *Individualize your program.* Start where the child is and plan a sequential program to encourage her to build one skill upon another. Visit classrooms where children with disabilities have been successfully included. Look for ways teachers individualize their instruction. How is peer interaction stimulated? Are parents involved in the classroom activities? Are peer questions about a child's disability answered openly and honestly?

4.   *Assess your classroom environment.* Helping children with special needs feel comfortable in the regular classroom involves some very critical considerations. Overall, the inclusive classroom should contain the same materials and activities suggested for general social studies programs, but enhance these offerings with opportunities to meet the needs of children with disabilities. It helps to include photographs or pictures of people with disabilities participating with nondisabled people on the job or in a variety of other activities. Be sure the learning materials are accessible to all the children. Some children will need Braille labels to help them locate things while others may require ramps to move from one area to another. Whatever the case, be sure to explain to the other children why these special adaptations have been made: "This ramp helps Francine get to the top level when she is in her wheelchair." Invite adults with disabilities to share their special talents and interests with your children. In short, the classroom should offer a safe environment where all children feel accepted, whatever their capabilities or limitations. Despite the fact that some adjustments must be made, each child should be enabled to gain skills and understandings in all areas and to reach his or her full potential.

5.   *Choose books that help children learn about and appreciate diversity.* In recent years, many good children's books have offered information about disabilities, explained difficulties youngsters with disabilities often encounter, and told stories about people who serve as positive role models for children with disabilities. Marc Brown's *Arthur's Eyes* (Little, Brown), for example, tells of how a little boy learns to cope with teasing about his new eyeglasses. Ada B. Litchfield's *A Button in Her Ear* (Whitman) explains deafness and how hearing aids help children with hearing losses. Lucille Clifton's *My Friend Jacob* portrays a relationship between a young boy and his older friend with a learning disability. Maxine B. Rosenberg's *My Friend Leslie* (Lothrop) is a photographic essay of a young girl with multiple disabilities. Literature can be one very important path to understanding and acceptance. Keep many types of stories available and use them to promote questions, conversations, and empathy for children with developmental disabilities.

Inclusion involves changes in attitudes, behaviors, and teaching styles. Plan your inclusive social studies program to fit your children's needs. No single chapter in a textbook can hope to give you a complete idea of the responsibilities involved in doing so, but if you truly want to be a standout teacher, you must begin with a sensitivity to the world of all children.

MULTIPLE INTELLIGENCES AND TALENTS

Historically, explanations of how children learn elementary school social studies, much as all other subjects, were based on popular theories of general intelligence. These theories defined "intelligent" students as those who excelled in such areas as reading and verbal comprehension, number operations skills, and the ability to recall vast amounts of information (behaviors easily measurable on standardized achievement or intelligence tests). Because these general elements of cognitive functioning became highly valued in school, teaching practices were logically directed toward developing such areas as reading and language skills, mathematics operations, and the ability to recall specific information. The vast content of social studies contained virtually unlimited quantities of dates, places, and names just waiting to be memorized, so it was considered an especially valuable school subject that could help meet the goal of recalling specific information. During the early part of this century, for example, social studies teachers were advised to "[d]rill thoroughly on the emphasized points. Decide what is important and then assure yourself that your students will carry it with them to their grave" (Moorehouse, 1921, p. 119). In more contemporary times, educators such as Hirsch (1987) proposed the concept of "cultural literacy" to set forth a common core content that all children should master in order to be considered informed citizens. Compiling a list of 4,662 names, places, historical events, and other facts, Hirsch argued that students cannot meaningfully interpret what they are being asked to learn in school unless this core content is mastered. Therefore, he described the responsibility of our nation's schools to fill in these crucial gaps with direct, fact-centered instruction.

Although good elementary school teachers through the years have gone beyond the facts to rouse their students' minds, many transmitted knowledge in such rigid ways that that children with the strength to master information excelled in school while children who did not were doomed to flounder. In more recent years, however, the concept of *intelligence* has been expanded to include much more than this single or general phenomenon; it is now perceived as a collection of several abilities that help individuals carry out various cognitive tasks. Most people are, in fact, exceptional in at least one area. With such a view of multiple intelligences or talents, teachers are free to encourage learning in ways that respect the individual intellectual strengths of each child.

Multiple Intelligences

The idea of multiple intelligences is fairly new; it has grown out of psychological research on how individuals take in and systematize knowledge from the world around them. One of the most recognizable theories growing from this research has been Howard Gardner's *theory of multiple intelligences.* According to Gardner

(1983), intelligence is defined as the capacity to solve problems or make things that are valued in a culture. Under this definition, the ability to work with other people or to produce songs is as "intelligent" as recalling information or solving a math problem. Gardner postulates that intelligence has more to do with an individual's preferred ways of approaching cognitively oriented tasks than it does with simply defining terms such as *veni, vidi, vici* or *manifest destiny*. Gardner proposes that there are at least seven different categories of intelligence; any individual may have strengths and weaknesses in one or several areas. Gardner's seven categories of intelligence are described below.

1.   *Logical-mathematical intelligence.* Children with this strength are good problem solvers. They quickly discover logical patterns and enjoy numbers and counting. They appreciate principles of cause and effect. These students are very curious, enjoy making predictions, and ask endless streams of questions.

2.   *Verbal-linguistic intelligence.* Children with this strength love the sound and rhythm of words. They enjoy listening to, reading, and making up stories, jokes, and riddles. They learn new vocabulary or a second language easily. These children are good at expressing themselves with words and are sensitive to the different functions of language.

3.   *Musical-rhythmic intelligence.* Children with this strength enjoy producing or listening to music. They appreciate various forms of musical expressiveness. You will find them singing, humming, and moving with a constant stream of musical gestures.

4.   *Visual-spatial intelligence.* Children with this strength are able to perceive the visual/spatial world accurately. They are able to draw and paint superbly, enjoy building things with a variety of construction materials, and have an easy time interpreting and constructing maps and models.

5.   *Bodily-kinesthetic intelligence.* Children with this strength are able to control their movements and handle objects skillfully. They dance, run, jump, throw, catch, and climb better than their age-mates. They enjoy making things with their hands and manipulate objects with great dexterity. These children want to move all the time.

6.   *Interpersonal intelligence.* Children with this strength are outgoing and very tuned into other people's feelings. They can recognize the moods and feelings of others, empathize with them, and respond appropriately. They understand other people and work effectively with them. These children appear to be "natural leaders."

7.   *Intrapersonal intelligence.* Children with this strength are inner-directed. They understand things about themselves—their own strengths, weaknesses, and desires. These children appear quiet and often prefer working alone; they have great confidence in their own ability to get things done.

Children need the chance to pursue activities that allow them to experience individual success. Which "intelligence" has this child been encouraged to put to use?

Elementary school social studies teachers attempt to make use of as many of these intelligences as possible in the activities they select for their students. By doing so, it is possible for each child to experience success in ways that build on individual strengths and also encourage strengths in new areas. These goals are achieved when teachers offer learning activities that require children to (1) solve problems, question and reason, or work with numbers *(logical-mathematical intelligence)*; (2) read a story, write down ideas in a journal, or dramatize a historical event *(verbal-linguistic intelligence);* (3) sing a folk tune, listen to music from various cultures, or play a musical instrument *(musical-rhythmic intelligence);* (4) examine pictures and study prints, paint a diorama, or map the classroom *(visual-spatial intelligence);* (5) dance and move in other creative ways to music, make a model of something with their hands, or play physically active games *(bodily-kinesthetic intelligence);* (6) work together in cooperative groups, solve problems together, or share ideas freely *(interpersonal intelligence);* and, (7) express their own unique ideas and emotions, spend time alone planning how to approach a specific learning situation, or pursue their personal interests through individualized learning experiences *(intrapersonal intelligence).*

Multiple Talents

Calvin W. Taylor (1968) is a second proponent of the concept of multiple abilities. He suggests that there are seven basic categories of intellectual functioning, or multiple-talents, that characterize the intelligence of all individuals. Taylor recommends that teachers conduct "talent searches" in their classrooms because each student is considered talented in at least one of seven important areas, as shown in Figure 2–1. The categories are based on "world-of-school" skills, including *academic talents* and six

FIGURE 2–1
Taylor's Multiple-talent Totem Pole

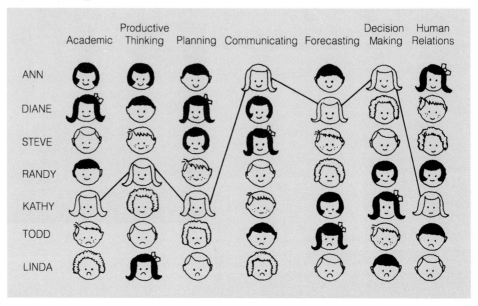

Source: Adapted from Taylor, C. W. (1968). "Be talent developers... as well as knowledge dispensers." *Today's Education, 57,* no. 9, 69. Reprinted with permission.

other talents that are especially significant in the social studies classroom: *productive thinking, planning, communicating, forecasting, decision making,* and *human relations.*

Examining Figure 2–1, you will see that a child named Kathy is placed toward the bottom of the *academic totem pole* because she consistently gets lower grades than her classmates and performs at a "below average" level on standardized achievement tests. You will also find that she has some trouble in activities where *productive thinking* is required. Traditionally, Kathy would be labeled a "borderline student" or a "failure" in social studies because she is not able to do what is valued by some teachers—assume command of the content. If you extend Kathy's profile by following the line in Figure 2–1, however, you will see that she has many strengths that a sensitive teacher could bring out—making *sound decisions, communicating ideas,* and *forecasting.* Instead of losing interest or confidence in her work, Kathy can become more self-assured as instruction is tailored to her strengths. Select any of the other children on the figure and plot the pattern of talents. Each, like Kathy, will certainly have at least one talent strength and some weakness.

Teachers must watch children carefully to ascertain the kinds of talents or intelligences they favor as they work and play. Students often excel in one area and have no striking ability in the others. As areas of strength are discovered, build on them in a sensitive and supportive way. Naturally, every daily social studies activity will not lend itself to the utilization of each talent or intelligence, but all should be in plain sight regularly throughout the school year. All children should be given many opportunities to flaunt their intelligence, whether approaching and solving problems, participating in hands-on activities, taking part in individual or group projects, or uncovering and recalling information. Each child has special strengths and deserves the opportunity to use them in a nurturing, supportive environment. Well-rounded social studies instruction requires the selection of activities that work across a great number of children's intelligences and talents.

Gifted Children

Exceptionally talented or intelligent children were given little special attention in our elementary schools prior to the 1970s. The general consensus was that these youngsters could make good with very little or no help; their superior intelligence and advanced skills guaranteed success in whatever they chose to do. Sparse information, at best, described the specific needs of gifted students. To single out and offer special planning for these youngsters was considered by many to be elitist: "Why," people wondered, "should we channel extra money and resources into education for the gifted when they can learn so well on their own?" However, educators have now begun to realize the importance of accommodating gifted children's needs. Wolfle (1989) underscores this awareness effectively: "Every child deserves a developmentally appropriate education, not just 'average' children and children who are behind" (p. 42).

How do you know when you have an exceptionally gifted or talented youngster in your class? Originally, giftedness was defined primarily in terms of results from intelligence tests: Those with scores of 120 or more were labeled as gifted because they made up only 10 percent of the population. Others suggested a 130 IQ score because only 2.27 percent had scores that high. Still others suggested a score of 140 or over because it would restrict giftedness to only 0.5 percent of the total population. Although IQ scores offer a relatively stable, direct source of evidence for giftedness, there are many other traits that separate the intellectually gifted preschooler from others. What are some of the gifts and talents that characterize this unique population? One way to begin answering this question is to examine your children for exceptional characteristics:

1. *Verbal skills.* Uses advanced vocabulary; spontaneously creates stories; modifies language to the level of person being spoken to; explains complex processes; influences the behavior of others; exchanges ideas and information fluently.

2. *Abstractions.* Retains easily what he or she has heard or read.

3. *Power of concentration.* Attentive to features of a new environment or experience; becomes totally absorbed in an activity; is alert, observant, and responds quickly.

4. *Intellect.* Carries out complex instructions; focuses on problems and deliberately seeks solutions; stores and recalls information easily; memorizes well and learns rapidly; explains ideas in novel ways; is curious; asks questions; masters academics

at an earlier age; has multiple interests; knows about many things of which other children are unaware.

5. *Behavior.* Sensitive to the needs and feelings of other children and adults; has strong feelings of self-confidence; influences others.

Identifying gifted students through formal procedures such as standardized intelligence tests yields valuable information about children's needs, but it must be stressed that elementary school children can display giftedness in many ways. It makes sense for teachers of gifted children to follow the guidelines for establishing a personalized curriculum as described for children with disabilities. No single method will work with all gifted children; individual strengths and interests dictate varieties of approaches. As we consider special approaches, however, above all else, we must not remove childhood from the lives of gifted elementary school youngsters. The gifted youngster is a child first and should be treated like other children. Most eight-year-olds, for example, have similar areas of interest whether they are gifted or not, but gifted children often show greater interest in learning *more* about a topic or material. So, like their peers, gifted first graders will enjoy playing with airplanes and trucks but, while their peers may stop there, gifted youngsters will want to investigate them in more detail (how high airplanes fly or how diesel engines differ from gasoline engines, for example).

The goal of working with gifted students is not to isolate them with the materials and activities only they can use; rather, it is to provide enrichment and acceleration experiences within the classroom for all children. We must allow gifted students to grow to their fullest by building on their interests and talents in developmentally appropriate ways. Some general suggestions follow:

1. Gifted students require faster-paced instruction for skills- and content-based learning so they can move more rapidly through the curriculum.

2. Gifted students require more frequent use of inquiry and independent research projects that encourage independent learning.

3. Gifted students require more advanced materials—higher-level reading materials, computers, self-directed learning packets, and other more highly complex sources that allow students to explore topics in depth.

4. Gifted students require the reorganization of subject matter content so it allows them to explore issues across curricular areas and promotes higher-order thinking skills.

Creative Students

Not all authorities think of giftedness in terms of intelligence—the ability to learn rapidly or to display advanced ability in a specific domain such as math or reading. Clark (1988), for example, considers creativity, rather than intelligence, as "the highest expression of giftedness" (p. 45); others accept creativity as one *type* of intellectual giftedness (Davis & Rimm, 1994). Who is the creative student? If you asked a random sample of people that question, most would probably describe a creative person in terms of having a special talent to produce something, such as composing a poem, playing a violin, or painting a picture. However, classroom observations of creative children indicate that they are not only talented in areas such as these, but display unique *intellectual* and *emotional* characteristics as well. Intellectually, a creative student (1) generates large quantities of ideas as possible solutions to problems (The child who responds to the question, "What things are red?" with "apple, book, car, beet, crayon, and shoes," is more fluent than a child who says, "fire engine and candy"); (2) offers a variety of different categories of responses (The child who indicates that a pencil may be used for such diverse purposes as writing, holding up a window, tapping on a drum, or conducting an orchestra is more flexible than a child who suggests it might be used to draw pictures, write numbers, or compose a story); (3) proposes highly original or clever responses to a problem (A child who finishes the incomplete sentence, "He opened the bag and found" with "a giant, black-and-orange, spotted butterfly" is more original than a child who says, "an apple"); and (4) adds on to or expands simple ideas to make them more "elaborate" (A child who responds to a teacher's request to add more information to the sentence, "The cat sat on the porch" with "The lazy black-and-white alley cat sat on the rotten old porch" is more creative than the child who says, "The black cat sat on the old porch").

Emotionally, creative children are *risk takers* (they have the courage to take wild guesses and expose themselves to criticism or failure, are strong willed, and are secure enough to defend their ideas); *complex thinkers* (they enjoy looking at the way things are and thinking about the way they should be, delving into intricate problems and seeking many alternatives so that order might be brought to chaos); *curious* (they are inquisitive and full of wonder, solving puzzling problems and pondering the mysteries of life); *dreamers* (they fantasize about things, often appearing "lost in their thoughts" while visualizing and building mental images that reach beyond the realm of reality); and *witty* (they laugh at things not normally perceived by children of the same age, and love to listen to and tell jokes).

After examining the characteristics of creative students, the logical follow-up question becomes, "How do we know which students in our classrooms are the most creative?" Several answers have been proposed, but the two most prevalent appear to be using *paper-and-pencil tests of creativity* and *teachers' judgments of creativity.* The most widely accepted paper-and-pencil tests of creativity have been developed by E. Paul Torrance (1972). Tasks call for students to think up responses related to the intellectual characteristics of creativity outlined above: fluency, flexibility, originality, and elaboration. A complex scoring system helps distinguish the highly creative youngsters from the rest. Can creativity tests really delineate the creative thinker? Bjorklund (1989) responds, "The answer would seem to be that they do, but far from perfectly. . . . Creativity is an elusive concept and one not easily measured by paper-and-pencil tests" (p. 279). Woolfolk (1995) asks a follow-up question and offers a response: "If test scores are not reliable indicators of creativity, what about teachers' opinions? Teachers are not always the best judges of creativity" (p. 306), and goes on to recommend that, "Even though creative students may be difficult to identify (and sometimes difficult to handle), creativity is worth fostering" (p. 306). Some authorities, however, believe that schools do more to discourage creative thinking than to promote it:

> Creative imagination. . . seems to reach a peak between four and four-and-a-half years, and is followed by a drop at about age five when the child enters school for the first time. This drop has generally been regarded as the inevitable phenomenon in nature. There are now indications, however, that this drop in five-year-olds is a man-made rather than a natural phenomenon. (Torrance, 1963, p. 79)

Some argue that this phenomenon occurs because schools fail to encourage or appreciate creative thought. "You're acting like a first grader" or "Stop being so silly" and similar sarcastic putdowns often accompany original, adventuresome attempts at self-expression. Highly creative individuals such as Einstein and Edison were forced to leave elementary school because they would not (or could not) conform to the rigid academic expectations of their teachers. As an adult, Einstein expressed his regard for creativity when he commented, "The gift of fantasy has meant more to me than my talent for absorbing positive knowledge." John Lennon, one of our great modern composers, was viewed by the headmaster at the Quarry Bank Comprehensive School in England as a boy who was "up to all sorts of tricks, and didn't make life easy for the staff. I caned him once and he had been caned many times by my predecessor" (Popjoy, 1980). Edison, Einstein, and Lennon had the persistence to fulfill their talents. But what has happened to the thousands of youngsters who surrendered their creative urges to conformity and were never encouraged or allowed to make significant creative contributions?

Teachers must promote creative thinking in the social studies program, for without it the invention of new ideas, new solutions to problems, and the invention of new implements would stagnate. Woolfolk (1995) offers these suggestions:

1. *Accept and encourage divergent thinking.* Teachers can ask, "Does anyone have a different way of looking at this problem?" Teachers should also support unusual solutions to problems, even if the final products are not perfect.

2. *Tolerate dissent.* Encourage all students to support dissenting opinions, and distribute rewards and privileges fairly among conforming and nonconforming students.

3. *Encourage students to trust their own judgment.* Give ungraded assignments periodically and encourage students to have confidence in their ability to answer questions or solve their problems.

4. *Emphasize that everyone is capable of creativity in some form.* Avoid describing the contributions of great artists, musicians, or thinkers as if they were superhuman feats. Recognize creativity (original thinking) as well as conformity (right answers) in students' work. Have a separate grade for originality on some assignments.

5. *Be a stimulus for creative thinking.* Use brainstorming sessions whenever possible and model creative problem solving by suggesting unusual solutions for classroom problems.

MULTICULTURALISM

As a nation, we pride ourselves on our cultural, ethnic, and religious diversity. We are of many colors, speak many languages, and observe many traditions. All of us contribute to our nation's diversity, whether our backgrounds are Ukrainian, Polish, German, African, Swedish, Inuit, Sioux, Jewish, Korean, English, Puerto Rican, Mexican, Irish, Algonquin, French, Brazilian, Japanese, Italian, Russian, Cuban, Seminole, Lithuanian, Spanish, Scottish, Australian, or Chinese. In the past, the term *melting pot* (or crucible) was popularly used to characterize how to deal with this diversity, especially as it was applied to "Americanizing" European immigrants.

The Melting Pot

The term *melting pot* was a metaphor that characterized how many groups should be blended together into a new American culture:

> America is God's great Crucible, a great Melting Pot where all races of Europe are melting and reforming! . . . Germans and Frenchmen, Irishmen and Englishmen, Jews and Russians—into the Crucible with you all! God is making the American . . . The real American has not yet arrived. He is only in the Crucible, I tell you—he will be the fusion of all races, the coming superman. (Zangwell, 1909, p. 37)

Proponents of the melting pot believed that all ethnic groups possessed strengths and that, as the "Crucible of America" amalgamated them into a single mass, a new, superior culture would be cast. The melting pot, then, was not meant to destroy cultural diversity per se, but to combine the strengths of many cultures into something new and unique:

> [The proponents] believed that the new emerging American culture must be built not on the destruction of the cultural values and mores of the various immigrant groups but on their fusion with the existing American civilization. . . . In the burning fires of the melting pot, all races were equal—all were reshaped, and molded into a new entity. (Krug, 1976, p. 12)

The public school system of the time was reasonably tolerant of students from diverse backgrounds, but mirrored the melting pot ideals to the extent that diversity in the educational process was not tolerated. Stearns (1996) comments:

> It remains true that the American educational tradition . . . opted largely for a single cultural standard, to which all minority groups were expected to bow. The standard did not embrace all beliefs; religious diversity, most obviously, was still tolerated and to some degree honored. Yet growing emphasis on political conformity, . . . increasingly detailed rules about sex and hygiene (amid germ theories and residual Victorianism), and pervasive assumptions about proper economic discipline drove the single standard home. (p. 23)

A student cast as a singular mold of middle-class values was was the overriding goal of the educational tradition. Immigrants as well as members of the working class were instilled with "appropriate American middle-class standards" about such habits as personal grooming, punctuality and diligence at work, and political correctness.

Cultural Pluralism

Today, our nation as well as its schools reject the idea of a single "American" culture emerging from a great melting pot. *Cultural pluralism* is the philosophy that now describes how all the parts of society contribute to an American whole; the United States is viewed as a multitude of cultures, each with unique characteristics that contribute to the larger culture. Instead of a melting pot, our society has been likened to a salad bowl, pizza, mosaic, or patchwork quilt where each culture retains its own distinctiveness and value but still contributes to the design of the whole. According to Arends (1991), "Cultural pluralism, while acknowledging the existence of a dominant American culture, also recognizes the strength and permanence of its subcultures" (p. 127). The foundation of social studies instruction is based on this idea of cultural pluralism—becoming sensitive to and respecting the contributions of each group to society in general.

Ethnic Minorities

Although a majority of Americans are of European descent, since 1980 the number of Americans identified as *ethnic minorities* (a term frequently used to refer to people receiving unequal or discriminatory treatment) has been steadily increasing (see Table 2–2). As we examine the statistics, this might be a good place to think about the terms used to identify these ethnic minority groups, because labels assigned to minority groups are constantly changing.

Campbell (1996) has traced their evolution. *African American* has replaced the out-of-date *Negro* and diminishing *Black* designations. *Latino* has changed from *Latin American* to *Mexican American* to *Hispanic* to *Chicano*. It should also be noted that *Chicano* is still used to identify U.S.- born individuals who are descendants of Mexican culture, and *Hispanic* is more often used than *Latino* in the eastern half of the United States. *Asian Americans* were once known as *Orientals,* and *Native Americans* were commonly called *Indians* or *American Indians* (although some members of this ethnic group do not accept the label "Native American," preferring to be called by their tribal name only). To add to the condition, the U.S. Bureau of the Census still uses the labels *White, Black,* and *American Indian* in its figures. If our goals of responding positively to cultural diversity are to be met, we must recognize the terms that the ethnic leaders and the community itself prefer.

Campbell (1996) adds that a new majority is emerging in our urban areas—a majority of people of color. It has been estimated that by the year 2000, 38 percent of children under 18 will be minorities (NASBE, *Right from the Start,* 1988). Woolfolk (1995) suggests that by the year 2020, almost half the population of the United States will come from African American, Asian American, Native American, and Latino ethnic minority groups. As this trend continues to develop, it is obvious that signifi-

TABLE 2–2
Growth of Ethnic Minori-
ties—1990 Census

Group	Total Number	Increase Since 1980
African American	30.0 million	13.2%
Asian	7.3 million	107.8%
Native American	2.0 million	37.9%
Hispanic	22.4 million	53.0%
Other	9.8 million	

cant changes in the makeup of our school population will follow. Our population's growing diversity has important ramifications for all educators, but should be of special significance for those concerned with social studies; that is where the foundation of tolerance and understanding begins.

Cultural Identification (Ethnicity)

All individuals belonging to a group—whether an ethnic group, religion, peer group, or family—have a culture, or a system of behaviors, beliefs, customs, and attitudes. Culture is reflected in the group's artwork, literature, language, inventions, and traditions. Cultural differences are widespread, in both the overt (clothing, hairstyle, language, naming ceremonies) and the more subtle (such as how one greets an elder). According to Brown (1963), culture consists of:

> all the accepted and patterned ways of behavior of a given people. It is a body of common understandings. It is the sum total and the organization or arrangement of all the group's ways of thinking, feeling, and acting. It also includes the physical manifestations of the group as exhibited in the objects they make—the clothing, shelter, tools, weapons, implements, utensils, and so on. (p. 3)

Cultures manifest similar needs, too, but commonly choose to satisy them in different ways. Gollnick and Chinn (1986) illustrate this fact by looking into a need shared by all cultures—food. All groups must obtain food in order to survive; that is one of the many features all cultures have in common. However, different cultures have different ideas of just what items might be used as food:

> Many Americans reject foods, such as horses, dogs, cats, rice, mice, snakes, snails, grasshoppers, caterpillars, and numerous insects, consumed by other cultural groups in different areas of the world. At the same time, other cultural groups reject foods that are normal to many Americans. Muslims and Orthodox Jews do not eat pork. Hindus do not eat beef, some East Africans find eggs impalatable, and some Chinese do not drink milk. Do you remember the foods included on the . . . charts learned in elementary school? Often we find it difficult to believe that not everyone has a diet that includes the basic . . . food groups seen on those charts. (p. 6)

Whether we choose to examine food, religion, holiday customs, clothing styles, or any other of the array of cultural traits, the unique beliefs and behaviors of any distinct culture provide its members with a feeling of ethnic identity (ethnicity) and offer a sense of continuity—belonging—that gives meaning to the life of an individual. DeVos (1975) states that:

> Ethnicity . . . is in its narrowest sense a feeling of continuity with the past, a feeling that is maintained as an essential part of one's self-definition. Ethnicity is intimately related to the individual need for collective continuity. The individual senses to some degree a threat to his own survival if his group or lineage is threatened with extinction. Ethnicity. . . includes a sense of personal survival in the historical continuity of the group. (p. 17)

Gollnick and Chinn (1986) believe that feelings of ethnicity may have both a positive and a negative consequence:

> It is an asset for the culture to be viewed by its members as the natural and correct way of thinking, acting, and behaving. At the same time it often solicits feelings of superiority over any other culture. The inability to view another culture through its cultural lens ("filter") prevents an understanding of the second culture. This inability usually makes it impossible to function effectively in a second culture. (p. 13)

Thinking back to the use of food as an example of a universal cultural need, Kluckhohn (1949) offers this vivid example of how people from one culture reacted to the unfamiliar diet of another through their existing *cultural lens*:

> Guests who came her way were often served delicious sandwiches filled with a meat that seemed to be neither chicken nor tuna fish yet was reminiscent of both. To queries she gave no reply until each had eaten his fill. She then explained that what they had eaten was not chicken, nor tuna fish, but the rich white flesh of freshly killed rattlesnakes. The response was instantaneous—vomiting, often violent vomiting. A biological process caught in a cultural web. (p. 19)

When cultural differences bump into each other like this, misunderstandings often surface and members of one culture may misperceive others as "crude," "strange," or "foolish." Those who ridicule a culture because its members eat different foods, for example, often ignore the basis of that culture's customs and practices. If those connections are not made, individuals often regard unfamiliar cultural practices as "weird." They often become a bit frightened by or apprehensive of new things or ideas, and may resent challenges to their own long-held beliefs and values. This is not an uncommon reaction; all groups appear instinctively to safeguard what they deeply value. If this protective instinct runs so deep, however, that a group becomes hostile toward any departure from its long-held beliefs, then the danger of excluding and alienating other groups grows. Cultural insularity can result, a condition especially worrisome today in light of the need for interdependence among countries and the importance of establishing positive ties among all cultural groups. For this reason, an essential ingredient of effective teaching in social studies is to

FIGURE 2-2
Cultural Diversity

Source: Turner, M. (1980). In *Social Studies and the Young Learner,* 5, 2. ©National Council for the Social Studies. Reprinted by permission.

regard all children and their families with dignity and respect, regardless of ethnic, racial, or religious differences.

Teaching in a Multicultural Setting

In the not-too-distant past, many elementary schools attempted to meet the goals of multicultural education by interspersing the study of various holiday customs, separate from the regular social studies curriculum. This was certainly an honest attempt to understand other cultures, but our current professional responsibilities go far beyond that. Hendrick (1992) contrasts the "holiday" approach to multicultural education with a more comprehensive approach:

> Many teachers seem to think [the study of holidays] is all there is to multicultural education, whereas it is actually only the beginning. We must realize that the basic purpose of providing multicultural experiences is not to teach the children facts about Puerto Rico or Japan, or to prove to the community that the teacher is not prejudiced. The purpose of a multicultural curriculum is to attach positive feelings to multicultural experiences so that each child will feel included and valued, and will also feel friendly and respectful toward people from other ethnic and cultural groups. (p. 283)

Clark, DeWolf, and Clark (1992) warn that narrowly focused approaches to multicultural programs can often become *culturally assaultive*. To explain the nature of culturally assaultive programs, the authors ask you to pretend you are a young child, the only "non-Indian" child in your classroom, who will be learning some very interesting things about non-Indians during Thanksgiving time. As you timidly come into the room and seat yourself in the circle with the others, your teacher leads the following discussion:

"Who knows what kind of houses non-Indians live in? Yes, that's right. They live in square houses with red tile roofs. Who lives in these houses? Mother and father and sister and brother. Yes, that's right. Grandmother? No; they don't live with their grandmothers, like we do. They send their grandmothers away to special places called retirement homes. Why? I don't know.

"Next week, during Thanksgiving, we'll have a unit on non-Indians. We'll all make a non-Indian town out of clay. It's called a 'suburb.' Can you say 'suburb?' Non-Indians sleep in separate rooms, and they have little houses to keep their cars in.

"Now this is a non-Indian hat." The teacher pulls out a Pilgrim's hat. "Non-Indians wore these when they first came to our land." (p. 5)

Clark, DeWolf, and Clark (1992) go on to explain that culturally assaultive classrooms perpetuate biases and stereotypes, usually incorporating the following elements into their practices:

- discussion of cultures only as they existed in the past, such as that of the "Indians" who helped the Pilgrims on the first Thanksgiving Day
- an incorrect or stereotypical version of how those people live or lived, such as characterizing "Indians" as wearing next to nothing and scalping people
- emphasis on differences from rather than similarities to other groups; for example, focusing on the kinds of houses "Indians" lived in rather than the fact that in the Indian cultures, as in other cultures, grandmothers tell stories
- use of songs, stories, and other devices that objectify the group and emphasize the group characteristics, ignoring the fact that individuals exist within the group; for example, using the song "Ten Little Indians" [Do not present any cultures as objects to count] instead of having an "Indian" from the community come in and tell a story from his particular tribe or nation
- token representations of the group in the classroom; for example, one Asian-looking doll among many White-looking ones
- "holiday units" on minority groups instead of saturation of the year-round curriculum with cultural diversity; for example, a unit on Mexican-Americans on Cinco de Mayo and exclusion of that culture on all of the other . . . days of the year (p. 6)

Multicultural education, then, is not something we limit to special events or celebrations—observing African American history only during the month of February, playing the dreidel game only during Hanukkah, tasting pork fried rice only during the Chinese New Year, or breaking a piñata only on Los Pasados to learn about Mexico. Certainly, those events are important and should be rendered a special place in our social studies programs, but limiting a multicultural program to such singular, isolated events does not make the issue of ethnicity an important segment of the entire program. We must explore more deeply the likenesses and differences among cultures so that children learn ways to be more tolerant of people unlike themselves, and to recognize that it is healthier to accept difference rather than to steer clear of it. Teachers who believe that cultural awareness should be part of the child's education must plan to incorporate multicultural activities into the regular social studies routine.

Social studies classrooms must be among the most honorable of all places to live in—a small society filled with understanding of and appreciation for all.

Approaches to Teaching Multicultural Content

To incorporate a multicultural approach to social studies education, a "cultural connectiveness" approach is necessary. What this means is that instruction is focused on developing students' cultural sensitivity and cultural literacy by infusing cultural diversity into their daily learning experiences. Banks (1989) has identified four approaches that have been popularly used to integrate multicultural content into the regular curriculum:

1. *The contributions approach.* Perhaps the most frequently used, this approach is characterized by tacking on the study of ethnic heroes, holidays, and cultural elements to the curriculum while the regular curriculum remains unchanged. Although it is the easiest approach for teachers to use, it does have serious limitations. Mainly, students do not attain a comprehensive view of ethnic groups in U.S. society, but see issues and events as an appendage to the main story of our nation's development.

2. *The additive approach.* Again, the basic structure of the social studies curriculum remains unchanged, but the story of diverse ethnic groups is handled by adding a book or a unit to the curriculum without changing it substantially. The additive approach can be the first phase of a more radical effort to integrate the total curriculum with ethnic content and perspectives. However, this approach shares its shortcomings with the contributions approach.

3. *The transformation approach.* This approach changes the structure of the curriculum by infusing various perspectives, frames of reference, and content from different ethnic groups into the study of the nature and complexity of U.S. society.

4.   *The social action approach.* This approach includes the elements of the transformation approach, but requires students to work toward a society that is more equitable by critically examining concepts, issues, or problems related to social conditions and taking action to relieve them.

These four approaches for integrating ethnic content into the regular social studies curriculum are often mixed in actual teaching situations. Regardless of how they are implemented, the overall goal of any multicultural approach is to gradually and cumulatively move toward a program that empowers students with the knowledge, skills, and attitudes needed to understand and appreciate racial, cultural, and ethnic diversity.

The following steps are suggested as ways to infuse multicultural education into existing social studies programs:

1.   *Know your community.* If you plan to turn your classroom into a place where diversity is a goal, start with a focus on the cultural groups represented by school enrollment. The students, community, and families your school is serving should be the primary starting point for culturally relevant programming, but this is a daunting prospect for many teachers—it is no easy task to incorporate cultural knowledge into one's teaching. However, Gollnick and Chinn (1994) explain that the first step is to know your students' cultural backgrounds:

> You should approach teaching multiculturally as an enthusiastic learner with much to learn from students and community members who have cultural backgrounds different from your own. You may need to remind yourself that your way of looking at the world evolved from the personal experiences you've lived through, which may vary greatly from the experiences of the students in your school. You will need to listen to the histories and experiences of students and their families and integrate them into your teaching. You will need to validate students' values within both school and their out-of-school realities—a process that is not authentic if you have feelings of superiority. . . . To make our classrooms multicultural we need to learn the cultures of our students, especially when the students are members of oppressed groups. (p. 296)

2.   *Seek family support.* A prerequisite for meeting the needs of all families is the belief in their dignity and worth. Researchers have found that "to the extent that the home culture's practices and values are not acknowledged or incorporated by the school, parents may find that they are not able to support children in their academic pursuits even when it is their fervent wish to do so" (Florio-Ruane, 1989, p. 169). Be especially willing to listen as well as talk to the parents of your students—make sure that they understand your program's goals. Find out what they would like their children to learn about their own culture and other cultures. Gollnick and Chinn (1994) stress that "[t]o teach multiculturally requires starting *where students are*" (p. 310). They go on to explain:

> Educators must know the . . . families in [a] community. In a school . . . Islamic parents may be upset with the attire that their daughters are expected to wear in physical education classes, and they would not approve of coed physical education courses. Jewish

students might wonder why the school celebrates Christian holidays and never Jewish holidays. (p. 310)

You may find that the values and expectations of some families may differ markedly from your own. But rather than insist that the children mimic the behaviors and beliefs of your culture, gain a better understanding of the families making up the school culture. Although families may resist some of the content and activities you plan for your social studies curriculum, it does not rule out a multicultural approach to teaching. Celebrate diversity by incorporating appropriate content into the curriculum, but first know the viewpoints of the families served by the school.

3.   *Assign equal recognition for all groups.* Social studies classrooms must reflect the diversity of cultures, whether or not the school population itself is diverse. Instructionally, the curriculum must incorporate information about many cultures and about intergroup relations. Gollnick and Chinn (1994) advise:

The amount of specific content about various microcultures will vary . . . but an awareness and recognition of the culturally pluralistic nature of the nation can be reflected in all classroom experiences. No matter how assimilated students in a classroom are, it is the teacher's responsibility to ensure that they understand cultural diversity, know the contributions of members of oppressed as well as dominant groups, and have heard the voices of individuals and groups who are from a different cultural background than that of the majority of students. (p. 309)

Teachers with a multicultural perspective know that, because they cannot possibly offer equal treatment to the hundreds of microcultures in this country, they must begin planning by developing an understanding of and sensitivity and respect for the various cultures of the children in their school community. In urban Chicago, a teacher would include activities and information from African American culture, and in Lancaster County, Pennsylvania, a teacher should address the Amish culture. In other areas of the country, schools should focus on the character of the groups represented in the community. These cultures should become an integral part of social studies, expanding the standard curriculum with diversity and multiple perspectives. As the students begin to realize that they are important members of the school and that diversity is valued, the curriculum can examine sensitive issues and topics from the perspective of various ethnic and cultural groups—Chinese Americans, Irish Americans, African Americans, Puerto Ricans, Catholics, Southern Baptists, white males, or Jewish women. Cultural diversity must be infused into the social studies program and become the lens through which the pluralistic nature of our nation can be focused.

4.   *Fill your room with fascinating things.* Think about all the curriculum materials in your room. Multiethnic dolls, pictures, and study prints from different parts of the world, crayons that match in degree of skin tone, examples of Japanese calligraphy, tortilla presses, kimonos, cowboy boots, nesting dolls, chopsticks, bongo drums, serapes, and tie-dyed cloth from Africa fascinate children and encourage interest in people.

5.   *Invite visitors into your room.* Having people from the community who are willing to come to your room and share something of themselves is a tremendous addition to a multicultural program. Resource people can demonstrate a special craft or talent, read or tell a story, display and talk about an interesting artifact or process of doing something, share a special food or recipe, teach a simple song or dance, or help children count or speak in another language. If you arrange for visits from different people throughout the year, then your children will begin to respect and value all cultures.

6.   *Draw from the vast resources of the arts.* King (1971) believes that the arts offer one of the most valuable sources from which to draw suitable multicultural experiences. She writes:

> Music, art, and literature know no . . . cultural boundaries. The common expressions of human feeling found in these forms can be used effectively by the teacher to develop children's capacities to identify with other groups and other societies—indeed, the totality of [humankind]. . . .
>   Aesthetic experiences, embodied in the arts and humanities, provide ways of giving the individual an opportunity to try on a situation—to know the logic and feeling of theirs—even though these others [are remote to the lives of the school population]. (pp. 5–6)

It is never too early to introduce young children to the arts of various cultures. Songs, rhymes, chants, and fingerplays evoke pleasure and enthusiasm from the very young in kindergarten and first-grade classrooms. Stories, pictures, books, arts and crafts, stage plays, puppets, dance, and other forms of creative expression add zest to the early grades. Younger children as well as middle- and upper-graders can visit museums or displays, especially those associated with specific ethnic groups. Seeing the beautiful handmade crafts (pottery, silver and turquoise jewelry, baskets, and pottery) of the Hopi and Zuni, for example, helps students understand important aspects of these cultures. Take your children to musical events having distinct cultural characteristics—African chants, Yiddish folk tunes, sailor chanteys, Scottish bagpipe music, or Eastern European polkas. Invite guest speakers to demonstrate special arts techniques—Amish quiltmaking, Inuit soapstone carving, Cajun music, or Ukrainian Easter eggs. Read, tell, or dramatize stories of various cultures. For instance, *The Miracle of the Potato Latkes* by Malka Penn (Holiday House), *The Angel of Olvera Street* by Leo Politi (Scribner's), *The Gifts of Kwanzaa* by Synthia Saint James (Albert Whitman and Company), and *Christmas Around the World* by Emily Kelly (Carolrhoda Books) provide outstanding examples of the many ways people from various cultures celebrate December holidays. Children should be helped to understand that the arts reflect culture, and that one cannot fully appreciate the value of any art without some understanding of the cultural matrix from which it grew. Conversely, one cannot fully appreciate a culture unless one values the creative efforts of its members.

All social studies programs have the responsibility to provide quality educational experiences that help children become compassionate individuals who feel comfortable with their identities and sense their unity with other people. We must create positive environments where children learn to accept others with cultural differences and begin to develop the skills of living cooperatively in a culturally diverse nation.

GENDER-FAIR PROGRAMS

The image each of us acquires about our masculine or feminine characteristics and the various behaviors and attitudes normally associated them is called *gender identity*, or *gender typing*. Like most other aspects of child development, gender identity emerges from dynamic interactions of biological and environmental forces. There is no question, for example, that there are basic genetic differences between males and females; biology sets the stage for gender identification. However, biology alone does not determine gender-specific behavior. From birth, our families begin to show us in subtle ways exactly what it means to be masculine or feminine. For example, little girls are most often dressed in something pink and frilly, whereas boys are routinely clothed in blue. Boy babies are commonly referred to by such terms as "big" or "strong," whereas girls are quite often described as "pretty" or "sweet." From these early days on, choices of toys, clothing, and hairstyles supplement verbal messages to influence gender identity.

Through such environmental influences, children unconsciously form a gender *schema*, or frame of reference, delineating what it means to be a boy or girl. This happens at about the age of two; from that point on, children work hard to fit into their gender roles. By age five or six, they have already learned much of the stereotypical behavior of their gender (Bernard, 1981). Kolhberg (1992) describes this process of gender role identity as evolving through three developmental levels:

1. *Gender identity* describes the initial stage where the infant recognizes simply that he is a boy or she is a girl.

2. *Gender stability* refers to the realization that gender is permanent and unchangeable.

3. *Gender constancy* reflects the child's eventual understanding that superficial changes [in ways of behaving or dressing, for example] are irrelevant to one's basic gender. (p. 403)

"Appropriate" behaviors are reinforced throughout the early years of life by internalizing the attitudes and responses of such environmental influences as family, relatives, peers, and the media. So, little girls who are rewarded for playing with dolls, read books about girls playing with dolls, and see girls playing with dolls on television will be more likely to play with dolls than with trucks. Likewise, little boys who have similar experiences with trucks will be more likely to play with trucks than with dolls. It would seem, then, that if gender-specific behaviors are influenced by such environmental phenomena, children raised in bias-free environments would not exhibit a preference for sterotypically gender-specific toys. However, a phenomenon referred to as "developmental sexism" seems to occur despite our most systematic attempts to shape a nonsexist environment. This means that young children grow to be enormously sexist in their perception of gender roles and choice of play activities—most boys choose to play firefighter and girls play house—even if they have been brought up in a nonbiased environment.

This concept of "developmental sexism" is supported by Kohlberg's idea of "gender constancy." That is, children soon learn that they permanently belong to a category called "boy" or "girl"—their gender cannot change. Once children grasp the concept that they cannot be transformed from girl to boy and back again, they organize the world into "girl" or "boy" categories and become powerfully attached to their gender. (I remember watching one warm spring day as Teddy, a kindergartner, proudly skidded around the playground on his sister's outgrown pink roller skates. "You're a-a gir-l! You're a-a gir-l!" chanted his friend Johnny repeatedly. Each time Johnny finished his melodic rhyme, Teddy angrily retorted, "No, I'm not! No, I'm not!" but Johnny persisted: "You're a girl 'cause you have pink roller skates. You're a-a gir-l!" Johnny continued his taunts until Teddy was reduced to tears.) Such a strong attachment to one's gender continues to grow through the early elementary grades, cementing the peer solidarity that influences behaviors compatible with society's expectations for males and females. Gollnick and Chinn (1994) explain that as boys and girls become socialized, they "internalize the social norms considered appropriate for [their] gender, including gender-appropriate behavior, personality characteristics, emotional responses, attitudes, and beliefs. These characteristics become so much a part of [their] self-identification that we forget they are learned and not innate characteristics" (p. 121).

Although stereotyped gender roles are changing, some characteristics continue to be viewed in the traditional categories of masculine and feminine: Women are perceived as being primarily responsible for child rearing while men fight the wars; nursing and teaching continue to be thought of as female professions while males are more closely identified with construction work and engineering. Gender-role stereotypes seem to be decreasing in our elementary schools, too, but they continue to be a problem. Klein (1985) concludes that females are less likely to be studied in history and read about in literature, and math and science problems are more likely to be framed in masculine terms. And although books appear to be more fair and inclusive than in the past, many children's books suffer from sexist stereotypes (males continue to be active and brave while females are passive and nurturing). Sadker, Sadker, and Klein (1991) believe that although new books are indeed more gender fair, teachers prefer to read the books they grew up with; many of these older books represent highly traditional gender roles. So, even today, the influence of sexist books is pervasive in many classrooms. Sadker and Sadker (1986) add that girls are shortchanged during classroom interactions. Elementary school teachers ask boys more questions, give them more precise feedback, criticize them more frequently, and give them more time to respond. The teachers' reaction may be positive, negative, or neutral, but the golden rule appears to be that boys get most attention from teachers in elementary school classrooms. Sadker, Sadker, and Steindam (1989) suggest that a contradiction exists between standardized test scores, where boys score higher than girls by the secondary school level, and report card grades, where girls outperform boys. The authors interpret these contradictory results as being gender biased, believing that the report card grades are awarded as much for compliance (a traditionally feminine trait) as for achievement. Additionally, the American Association of University Women (AAUW) has reported that

[t]here is clear evidence that the educational system is not meeting girls' needs. Girls and boys enter school roughly equal in measured ability. In some measures of school readiness, such as fine motor control, girls are ahead of boys. Twelve years later, girls have fallen behind their male classmates in key areas such as higher-level mathematics and measures of self-esteem. (1992, p. 2)

Although most of the research into gender bias in schools has been centered on the unfair treatment of girls, Campbell (1996) cautions that:

[i]t is boys who lack role models for the first six years of schooling, particularly African American, Latino, and Asian boys. While young, European American girls benefit from their female-centered primary school experience [the positive experiences of girls begin to change in adolescence], children of color—particularly boys—fail. It is boys who encounter the most conflicts and receive the most punishments in school and most often get placed in special education and remedial programs. (p. 113)

Gender stereotyping can be tied to many influences, but teachers must take a positive role in recognizing bias and replacing it with equitable expectations for all children. This means eliminating one's own biased perceptions of gender-associated behavior and stereotyped notions about gender roles. This can be done by providing males and females with appropriate instruction and by avoiding gender-role stereotyping. Some guidelines to avoid sexism in teaching follow.

1. *Avoid stereotyping masculine and feminine roles.* Examine ways you might be limiting the options open to boys and girls. During class discussions, for example, many teachers attempt to reason with young children in order to create more objective attitudes about gender roles. When a child says, "Only boys can grow up to be truck drivers," teachers are tempted to reply, "That's not true. Women are truck drivers, too." This approach often fails. The young child's way of classifying the world into male and female is new and not open to exceptions. A child may even become upset that the teacher fails to see the world in the same light and defend his case even more strongly. We can compound the problem, therefore, by trying to reason with a child. This presents us with an interesting dilemma: We want children to experience a nonsexist world, but they tend to resist our efforts of objectivity. What can we do?

First, let the children know you understand and accept their unique system of trying to make sense of the world. Their willingness to come to you and share their excitement about new discoveries should always be accepted with openness and sincerity. You do, however, have a responsibility to help them understand that choices should be open to each person, regardless of gender. In responding to the "truck driver" comment, you might say, "I know you've never seen a woman truck driver before, so it's hard to understand that women can drive large trucks, too." On the other hand, trying to reason with a child with comments such as, "It's okay for women to be truck drivers, too. Many women are very good at driving large trucks," often elicits a response such as, "Well, they shouldn't be!"

Good social studies programs seek to build a "can-do" spirit, proclaiming to both boys and girls that they are free to pursue their dreams free of gender bias.

Stereotyping should be avoided at all costs. This advice extends not only into how females are featured, but also into whether men are depicted in traditionally male roles and careers.

2.   *Use gender-free language whenever possible.* Through words and actions, teachers assume the position of a positive role model. Be sensitive to your choice of masculine terms to refer to all people; for example, *police officer* replaces *policeman*, *firefighter* replaces *fireman*, and *mail carrier* replaces *mailman*. If labels such as *fireman* are used frequently by your children, begin a discussion with a comment such as, "Saying the word *fireman* makes it sound like only men fight fires. Do you think that's true?" Then introduce the word *firefighter* and point out that men and women (and boys and girls) can do the same kinds of jobs. Additionally, be aware of how actions can convey ideas of gender-role coequality. For example, the children may learn to interpret gender roles less rigidly if they see their teachers, male and female, displaying characteristics typically associated as either masculine or feminine—being assertive and forceful, sensitive and warm, depending on the situation.

3.   *Make sure your classroom materials present an honest view of males and females.* Just as you lead young children toward understanding the idea of equality through your words and actions, the activities and materials you choose for your classroom should resist gender stereotyping. Books like *Heather Hits Her First Home*

Run by Phyllis Hacken Johnson (Lollipop Power Books) and Charlotte Zolotow's *William's Doll* (Harper & Row) are sensitive books that address stereotypes. *William's Doll* takes a look at a situation many little boys face:

> William would like a doll so he could play with it like his friend Nancy does with her doll. At the very thought of a little boy with a doll, his brother and friend call him creep and sissy. William's father buys him a basketball and a train, instead of a doll. William becomes a very good basketball player and he enjoys the train set, but he still longs for a doll. Finally, when William's grandmother comes for a visit, she buys him a doll and explains to his father that having a doll will be good practice for him when he grows up and has a real baby to love. (Raines & Canady, 1989, p. 50)

Teachers who wish to build a good classroom collection of gender-fair books will need to look for books that show children and other people engaged in a variety of activities, regardless of gender.

A program offering opportunities for both sexes to participate in positive class-room experiences should transcend obsolete sex-role expectations such as boys taking the lead when mathematics skills are required, and girls when sewing or cooking are needed for a project. Encourage the boys to wash the art table after completing a salt-and-flour relief map and the girls to hammer the nails needed to hold together a model clipper ship. If this doesn't happen freely, discuss the situation with your children. Say, "I notice that in most social studies projects the boys build the model. This seems to exclude the girls. Why do you think that is happening?" Invite equal access to activities by encouraging children to engage in a wide range of experiences that are free of gender stereotypes.

4.   *Balance the contributions of men and women in the social studies program.* All students should be exposed to the contributions of women as well as men throughout history. Gollnick and Chinn (1994) point out that social studies courses that "focus primarily on wars and political power will almost totally focus on men; . . . courses that focus on the family and the arts will more equitably include both genders . . . . Students are being cheated of a wealth of information about the majority of the world's population when women are not included as an integral part of the curriculum" (p. 139). Banks (1994) suggests that women can be virtually ignored in written history. Citing the Montgomery, Alabama, bus boycott of 1955 as an example, Banks maintains that most textbook accounts emphasize the work of men such as Martin Luther King, Jr., and Ralph D. Abernathy, or organizations headed by men, but virtually ignore the work of women. He uses the memoirs of Jo Ann Gibson Robinson, president of the Women's Political Council of Montgomery, as an example. The Council was started in 1946 to "provide leadership, support, and improvement in the black community and to work for voting rights for African Americans" (Banks, 1994, p. 6). The Council received numerous complaints concerning bus driver offenses against African Americans who were asked to give up their seats on crowded buses to whites. On December 1, 1955, Rosa Parks was arrested for refusing to give up her seat. Disgusted by such hostile encounters with bus drivers, the Council distributed leaflets that called for a boycott of city buses. Referring to Rosa Parks, Robinson's leaflet read in part:

This woman's case will come up on Monday. We are, therefore, asking every Negro to stay off the buses Monday in protest of the arrest and trial. Don't ride the buses to work, to town, to school, or anywhere else on Monday. (Garrow, 1987)

Although most textbook accounts credit King and Abernathy for the Montgomery bus boycott, plans to end bus segregation with a boycott were actually instituted two years earlier, in 1953, by Robinson's Council. The Parks case in 1955 just happened to be the "right time" to implement the boycott. The situation seems to be improving in recent years, but the work of historically significant females such as Jo Ann Gibson Robinson still must find its way into our nation's textbooks. This does not mean we must sit back and wait for that day; it will take a great deal of scholarly effort to uncover their stories, but the experiences of women from all walks of life must be highlighted in the social studies curriculum.

Schools that foster positive gender roles will help children value the likenesses and differences in themselves, thereby taking an important step toward alleviating the damage resulting from long-ingrained patterns of sexism in our society. It is this unconditional positive regard for children that lies at the heart of social studies education.

SOCIAL CLASS

The term used by the U.S. Bureau of the Census and by sociologists to describe the variations of wealth and power among individuals and families is *socioeconomic status,* or *SES.* SES is normally determined by studying such economic factors as occupation, income, and level of education. Of all the forms of inequality affecting our children's education, SES could be the most powerful; it frequently surmounts the effects of race and gender. For example, although upper-SES Hispanics share customs and traditions with low-SES Hispanic families, they will be more likely to interact with upper-SES families of other ethnic groups than they will with Hispanic families at other class levels.

According to DeParle (1994), families of four living in urban areas and earning an annual income of less than about $15,000 are considered to be living in poverty. It is estimated that about 40 million families live in poverty, over 15 percent of the total population. Research over the past 20 years has indicated a number of strong relationships between SES and school performance. A consistent connection is that low-SES students of all ethnic groups exhibit lower average standardized test scores, receive lower grades in school, and leave school earlier than high-SES students (Alwin & Thornton, 1984; Goleman, 1988; White, 1982). Woolfolk (1995) identifies several factors that explain the lower school achievement of low-SES students: poor health care for mother and child, limited resources, family stress, interruptions in schooling, and discrimination. Garcia (1991) cautions that research in this area is meager, but lists other explanations for lower achievement among low-SES children:

1.   *Low expectations—low self-esteem.* Low-SES students often speak ungrammatically, come to school in old or dirty clothing, frequently are ungroomed and malodorous, are unfamiliar with the themes of mainstream children's literature, and are confused by the punishment and reward systems of the school. Since most

teachers find it difficult to identify with these conditions, they often conclude that low-SES students are not very good at schoolwork. They have reduced expectations for low-SES students, thereby contributing to phenomena called the *self-fulfilling prophecy* (tending to behave as others expect) and the *looking-glass self* ("I am what I think you think I am"). When teachers associate such reduced expectancies with socioeconomic status, discriminatory practices surface and low-SES students are denied access to equal educational opportunity.

2.   *Learned helplessness.* Some children from low-SES homes come to school from communities where dropout rates of 50 percent are not uncommon. Since their relatives and friends leave school early, many low-SES students are not motivated to go on. However, poor but stable families often value education and prepare their students well for school, viewing school as the best place to end their cycle of poverty. Teachers must understand that poverty is not the fault of the child and to think of teaching not in a negative or indifferent way, but as a challenge to help low-SES students overcome the effects of poverty.

3.   *Resistance cultures.* Teachers, especially in inner-city schools serving poor Hispanic-American, African American, or Native American families, will find that some children come to school as part of a "resistance culture," members of which oppose upper- and middle-SES values, including school. This opposition can take the form of willfully breaking school rules, minimizing the value of achievement, and attaching more importance to manual rather than mental work. Students who accept any characteristics considered "middle class" or "white," including behaviors that would make them successful in school, are thought of as "selling out" their minority or peer group. To address this challenge, teachers must interact with the minority groups represented in the school population to determine the most effective instructional experiences for their children.

4.   *Tracking.* A significant factor contributing to poor academic performance among low-SES students is that they are usually placed in low-ability groups or classes, where they are taught differently. Teachers see these children as less able academically and often use teacher-dominated strategies calling for lots of worksheets, rote memorization, and passivity. Additionally, less experienced or less successful teachers are generally assigned to the low-ability groups. After reviewing the research on the effects of tracking, Gamoran (1992) has concluded that "grouping and tracking rarely add to overall achievement in a school, but they often contribute to inequality. . . . Typically, it means that high-track students are gaining and low-track students are falling further behind" (p. 13). What can be done? Slavin (1987) suggests that tracking in elementary schools must be stopped because teachers often fail to match students' needs with instruction. Tracking will continue to have no positive effect on achievement until teachers use it to provide specialized instruction to children having specific needs: "For ability grouping to be effective at the elementary level, it must create true homogeneity on the specific skill being taught, and instruction must be closely tailored to students' levels of performance" (Slavin, 1987, p. 323).

Therefore, since ability grouping rarely contributes to positive academic achievement, it should be eliminated or curtailed. If it is used, students should be grouped according to skills need, and, when instruction is completed, the group should be disbanded.

LANGUAGE DIVERSITY

Hand-in-hand with the rich diversity of cultures enjoyed in the United States is a grand assortment of languages and dialects. Changing populations and an influx of immigrants from Asian and Hispanic nations have produced a situation where there are now over 200 languages spoken in the United States (Arends, 1991). Although this condition has created a fascinating cultural state of affairs, it has resulted in significant challenges for the education of our nation's youth. These challenges, however, are not new. Concerns about the goals and purposes of educating non-English speaking students date back to the Revolutionary War, when school was taught in any of 18 languages spoken by the colonists—English, German, Scotch, Irish, Dutch, French, Swedish, Spanish, Portuguese, and others (Castellanos, 1985). As the colonies eventually blended into a new nation, however, English became the dominant language in public education. The freedom to use other languages has become a matter of unrelenting conflict since that time (Grant & Gomez, 1996).

Although there has been evidence of the sporadic use of languages other than English in our nation's schools, the widespread use of bilingualism (teaching in two languages) did not occur until the 1960s. The civil rights movement called attention to discrimination in many segments of society, including the educational rights of children whose first language was not English. From the 1960s into the 1980s, federal court decisions have insisted that schools offer quality programs to enable students to participate successfully in all-English classrooms.

Currently, our nation's changing demographics require a new look at the needs of children from homes where English is not the first language. Campbell (1996) reports that since 1970 the United States has experienced massive immigration similar to the levels that occurred from 1890 to 1910. At least 10 million immigrants have come to live in this country during the past three decades. Well over 70 percent of these new immigrants are Latinos—from Mexico, El Salvador, Guatemala, Nicaragua, and Honduras—and a great number are Southeast Asians—from Vietnam, Cambodia, Laos, Korea, Japan, and China. Settlement patterns indicate that 80 percent of these immigrants settled mainly in ten states, primarily California, Texas, and Florida. As teachers, we must be aware of how these changing demographics will influence the student composition of our classrooms into the next millennium:

> By the year 2050, the present percentage of Latinos in the U.S. population will almost triple; the Asian population will more than triple; African Americans will increase about 3 percent; the non-Hispanic white population will drop from 76 percent to 53 percent. (U.S. Census Bureau)

Students coming to school speaking a main language other than English are referred to as *English as a Second Language (ESL)* students, and children who are not yet fluent enough in English to perform school tasks successfully are sometimes called *Limited English Proficiency (LEP)* students. Some educators have argued that because many people connect negative attitudes about linguistically diverse students with the term *LEP*, a more positive term such as *Potentially English Proficient (PEP)* should be used (Freeman & Freeman, 1993). Children who speak fluently in English at school and a native language at home are called *bilingual.*

Bilingual education is one of the most fiercely debated topics in education today: Is it better to teach social studies to LEP (or PEP) students in the primary (home) language until the children are fluent in English, or do these children need lessons in English before social studies instruction can be effective? Educators have attempted to answer that question in two primary ways. One proposed solution is *submersion,* in which students are assimilated into the English-speaking classroom and exposed only to English. In their haste to become "Americanized," submersed students quickly learn to value English, often avoiding the use of their native language, even at home.

Proponents of this approach advise teachers to introduce English as early as possible, to speak only in English, and to ask students to give up their family's language. They argue that valuable learning time is lost if children are taught in their native language. Woolfolk (1995) cites three important issues raised by critics of this approach. First, children who are forced to learn a subject in an unfamiliar language are bound to have trouble. Think of how successful you would have been if you had been asked to learn American history or economics using a language that you had studied for only a few short months. Second, students may get the message that their native language (and therefore their culture) is inferior and less important. This influences both language acquisition and self-esteem:

> To devalue a minority child's language is to devalue the child—at least, that's how it feels on the receiving end. The longtime policy of punishing Chicano students for speaking Spanish is an obvious example. While such practices are now frowned upon, more subtle stigmas remain. Children are quick to read the messages in adult behavior, such as a preference for English on ceremonial occasions or a failure to stock the school library with books in Chinese. . . . Whatever the cause, minority students frequently exhibit an alienation from both worlds. Joe Cummins calls it bicultural ambivalence: hostility toward the dominant culture and shame toward one's own. (Crawford, 1992, pp. 212–213)

Third, ironically, is that students who master standard English and let their home language deteriorate are often encouraged to learn a second language when they reach middle school. Had their native language been allowed to flourish in the first place, they would already be fluent in two languages without having to take Spanish I or similar introductory courses.

An alternative to submersion is *bilingual teaching;* that is, "the use of two languages as media of instruction" (Baca & Cervantes, 1989, p. 24). The primary goal of bilingual programs is not to offer direct instruction in English per se, but to teach children in the language they know best and to reinforce their learnings through the use of English (Baca & Cervantes, 1989). Grant and Gomez (1996) explain:

The core curriculum in public school bilingual classrooms is the same as that for any other classroom. The only significant curricular difference is the focus on language development (ESL and the appropriate native language) and attention to the cultural heritage of the targeted language minority group. Besides teaching language, science, math, social studies, art, and music, bilingual teachers must facilitate language learning in everything they do. They are concerned with how best to teach non-English speaking students the full range of subjects while developing native and [English language] skills. (p. 118)

If you visited an elementary school social studies classroom with a bilingual program, you would likely see an English-speaking teacher and another teacher or aide fluent in a native language using language experience or whole language approaches to literature-based instruction. Their preferred teaching approach follows Scarcella's (1990) preview/teach/review format. In this design, the content of the lesson is previewed in English, the body of the lesson is taught in the student's native language, and then the lesson is reviewed in English. Tompkins and Hoskisson (1995) suggest that this approach is often used when two teachers—one English-speaking teacher and one fluent in the native language—collaborate in a team teaching effort. In addition to Scarcella's preview/teach/review format, Freeman and Freeman (1993) recommend the following guidelines for bilingual instruction:

1.   *Environmental print.* Children learn to recognize words written in both English and their native language when they see print in a number of environmental contexts—magazines, newspapers, telephone books, menus, food packages, street signs, days of the week, classroom posters, labels, nametags, charts, bulletin boards, and other interesting sources. Words should be printed both in English and the children's native language.

2.   *Culturally conscious literature.* Classroom use of multicultural literature written in the students' native language helps strengthen cultural values and beliefs. Quality books are now being written for children in a number of languages and are becoming increasingly available throughout the United States. For example, Carmen Lomas Garza's bilingual book *Family Pictures: Cuadros de Familia* (Children's Book Press) is an authentic portrayal of what it is like to grow up in a Mexican American family in South Texas (Rosalma Zubizerreta authored the Spanish version). If you cannot afford to purchase a number of like books, parents or other members of the community might be willing to lend books written in the children's native language. Having a parent or other volunteer come to school and read from these books adds respect and appreciation for the native language.

3.   *Literacy instruction.* Traditional models of literacy instruction that are teacher dominated and skills driven—a lot of teacher talk and student listening—are not very effective in helping ESL students acquire literacy skills. To replace such "hands-off" learning, advocates for changing the nature of literacy instruction in the content areas such as social studies recommend constructivist practices: "Construc-

tivist models of instruction assume that students will learn literacy by engaging in the full processes of reading and writing in a purposeful, largely self-directed manner" (Au, 1993, p. 42). In other words, the best method for teaching reading and writing to English language learners is through the natural use of these skills throughout the entire school curriculum. The strategies suggested to achieve this goal are fully discussed in chapters 11 and 12; they include shared reading, experience charts, literature circles, interactive journals, cooperative learning, and writers workshops.

4.   *Language buddies.* Learning a second language is enhanced greatly when students are paired up with English-speaking classmates who speak the native language fluently. English proficiency is promoted by the classmate's careful explanations, modeling, and assistance with new words.

Bilingual education, like all dimensions of multicultural education, is based on a commitment to school success for all of our nation's children. A bilingual curriculum should provide students with educational opportunities that are meaningful, compassionate, and challenging—to develop the full range of oral and written language necessary to function in school and as a citizen in our democratic society.

AFTERWORD

Good social studies teachers always impress me with the affection they associate with the special moments they experience with all of their students: the expressions on children's faces when they learn something new; the excitement shown by parents as their children make progress during the year; just being with children and knowing that there is a common bond of affection; the children's unspoiled enthusiasm—such experiences revitalize teachers and can strengthen their commitment to the profession. Many teachers find great joy in the candid individual expressions that mark each child's uniqueness: "Henry came up to me holding his finger as if it were hurt. When I asked him what the matter was, he replied, 'An elephant bit my finger,' and then turned and walked away!"

These are the special sources of satisfaction awaiting a teacher of elementary school children. You will find extraordinary joy, affection, excitement, and personal satisfaction as you meet challenges each day.

Children thrive under the leadership of teachers who delight in being who they are—teachers who adapt the social studies classroom to meet every child's cultural, linguistic, and individual needs. This includes providing the child with the time, opportunities, resources, understanding, and affection to achieve important goals of social studies education. To affirm individual differences, teachers must eliminate bias from the elementary school environment. Every child must know she is appreciated and respected by the teacher and needs experiences that reflect an understanding and appreciation for individual and cultural differences. These experiences are not only memorable and pleasurable, but they also last a lifetime—they help make our world.

TECHNOLOGY SAMPLER

Some useful source for related social studies topics inlcude these Internet sites:

Internet Sites

1990 Census
http://www.census.gov/

African American History (sample lessons and activities)
http://www.fi.edu/tfi/hotlists/blackhistory.html

ARC (committed to the welfare of children with learning disabilities)
http://TheArc.org/misc/dislnkin.html

Assistive Technology Home Page (helping children with developmental disabilities)
http://cosmos.ot.buffalo.edu/astech.html

Black History Hotlist (educational site on African American History compiled by the Franklin Institute in Philadelphia)
http://www.fi.edu/hotlists/blackhistory.html

History Channel (one of America's great native nations—the Sioux—comes to the web)
http://www.historychannel.com/sioux/

Intercultural E-mail Classroom Connection
http://www.stolaf.edu/network/iecc

Internet Resources for Special Children
http://w3.one.net/~julio_c/

National Council for Bilingual Education (resources for bilingual education, including comprehensive links to lessons)
http://www.ncbe.gwu.edu

Special Ed Resources on the Internet
http://www.nhgs.tec.va.us/SpecialEd/sped_resources.html

University of Kansas SPED OnLine
http://www.sped.ukans.edu/spedadmin/welcome.html

WHAT I *NOW* KNOW

Complete these self-check items once more. Determine for yourself whether it would be useful to take a more in-depth look at any area. Use the same key as you did for the preassessment form ("+", "?", "-").

I can *now*

_____ define what is meant by *multicultural education.*

_____ describe the place of multicultural content in the overall social studies curriculum.

_____ explain what is meant by the term *culture.*

_____ describe some needs that all children share.

_____ identify children with disabilities.

_____ describe the concept of inclusion and how it influences instruction in the social studies classroom.

_____ explain how children exhibit multiple intelligences and talents.

_____ describe the characteristics of gifted children and explain how to adjust instruction to meet their special needs.

_____ identify the characteristics of creative children and analyze their unique educational needs.

_____ explain the importance of gender-fair attitudes and experiences.

_____ give examples of appropriate instruction for low socioeconomic status students.

_____ identify and describe special approaches for dealing with language diversity in the classroom.

REFERENCES

Alwin, D., & Thornton, A. (1984). Family origins and schooling processes: Early versus late influence of parental characteristics. *American Sociological Review, 49,* 784–802.

American Association of University Women. (1992). *How schools shortchange girls.* Washington, DC: Author.

Arends, R. I. (1991). *Learning to teach.* New York: McGraw-Hill.

Au, K. (1993). *Literacy instruction in multicultural settings.* Fort Worth: Harcourt Brace Jovanovich College Publishers.

Baca, L. M., & Cervantes, H. T. (1989). *The bilingual special education interface.* New York: Merrill/Macmillan.

Banks, J. A. (1989). Education for survival in a multicultural world. *Social Studies and the Young Learner, 1,* 3–5.

Banks, J. A. (1993). Multicultural education: Characteristics and goals. In J. Banks & C. McGee Banks (Eds.), *Multicultural education: Issues and perspectives* (pp. 2–26). Boston: Allyn and Bacon.

Banks, J. A. (1994). Transforming the mainstream curriculum. *Educational Leadership, 51,* 4–8.

Bernard, J. (1981). *The female world.* New York: Free Press.

Bjorklund, D. F. (1989). *Children's thinking: Developmental function and individual differences.* Pacific Grove, CA: Brooks/Cole.

Brown, I. C. (1963). *Understanding other cultures.* Englewood Cliff, NJ: Prentice-Hall.

Campbell, D. E. (1996). *Choosing democracy: A practical guide to multicultural education.* Englewood Cliffs, NJ: Merrill/Prentice Hall.

Castellanos, D. (1985). *The best of two worlds.* Trenton, NJ: New Jersey State Department of Education.

Chandler, P. A. (1994). *A place for me: Including children with special needs in early care and education settings.* Washington, DC: National Association for the Education of Young Children, 1994.

Clark, B. (1988). *Growing up gifted.* Columbus, OH: Merrill Publishing.

Clark, L., DeWolf, S., & Clark, C. (1992). Teaching teachers to avoid having culturally assaultive classrooms. *Young Children, 47,* 5.

Crawford, J. (1992). *Hold your tongue: Bilingualism and the politics of English only.* Reading, MA: Addison-Wesley.

Davis, G. A., & Rimm, S. B. (1994). *Education of the gifted and talented.* Boston, MA: Allyn and Bacon.

Deiner, P. L. (1983). *Resources for teaching young children with special needs.* New York: Harcourt Brace Jovanovich.

DeParle, J. (1994, March 31). Sharp increases along borders of poverty. *New York Times,* A–18.

DeVos, G. (1975). Ethnic pluralism: Conflict and accommodation. In G. DeVos and L. Romanucci-Ross (Eds.), *Ethnic identity: Cultural continuities and change.* Palo Alto, CA: Manfield.

Florio-Ruane, S. (1989). Social organization of classes and schools. In M. Reynolds (Ed.), *Knowledge base for beginning teachers* (pp. 163–172). Oxford: Pergamon.

Freeman, D. E., & Freeman, Y. S. (1993). Strategies for promoting the primary languages of all students. *The Reading Teacher, 46,* 552–558.

Gamoran, A. (1992). Is ability grouping equitable? *Education Leadership, 50,* 11–17.

Garcia, R. L. (1991). *Teaching in a pluralistic society: Concepts, models, and strategies.* New York: HarperCollins.

Gardner, H. (1983). *Frames of mind: The theory of multiple intelligences.* New York: Basic Books.

Garrow, D. J. (1987). *The Montgomery bus boycott and the women who started it: The memoir of Jo Ann Gibson Robinson.* Knoxville: The University of Tennessee Press.

Goleman, D. (1988, April 10). An emerging theory on blacks' IQ scores. *New York Times* (Education Life Section), 22–24.

Gollnick, D. M., & Chinn, P. C. (1986). *Multicultural education in a pluralistic society.* New York: Merrill/Macmillan.

Gollnick, D. M., & Chinn, P. C. (1994). *Multicultural education in a pluralistic society.* New York: Macmillan.

Grant, C. A., & Gomez, M. L. (1996). *Making schooling multicultural: Campus and classroom.* Englewood Cliffs, NJ: Prentice Hall.

Hendrick, J. (1992). *The whole child.* Columbus, OH: Merrill/Macmillan.

Hirsch, E. D., Jr. (1987). *Cultural literacy: What every American needs to know.* Boston: Houghton Mifflin.

Jones, E., & Derman-Sparks, L. (1992). Meeting the challenge of diversity. *Young Children, 47,* 12–17.

King, E. W. (1971). *The world: Context for teaching in the elementary school.* Dubuque, IA: William C. Brown.

Klein, S. (1985). *Handbook for achieving sex equity through education.* Baltimore: The Johns Hopkins University Press.

Kluckhohn, C. (1949). *Mirror for man: The relation of anthropology to modern life.* New York: McGraw-Hill.

Kohlberg, L. In Lefrancois, G. R. (1992) *Of children.* Belmont, CA: Wadsworth.

Krug, M. (1976). *The melting of the ethnics.* Bloomington, Ill: Phi Delta Kappa.

Moorehouse, F. M. (1921). Syllabus for ninth grade study in American history, part III. *The Historical Outlook,* p. 119.

National Association of State Boards of Education (1988). *Right from the start.* Alexandria, VA: Author.

Perez, J. (1993). Viva la differencia. *First Teacher, 14,* 24–25.

Perez, S. A. (1994). Responding differently to diversity. *Childhood Education, 70,* 151–153.

Popjoy, W. (1980). comments made during an interview shortly after Lennon's death in December 1980.

Public Law 101–476, October 30, 1990, Stat. 1103.

Raines, S. C., & Canady, R. J. (1992). *Story s-t-r-e-t-c-h-e-r-s: Activities to expand children's favorite books.* Mt. Ranier, MD: Gryphon House.

Sadker, D., & Sadker, M. (1986). Sexism in the classroom: From grade school to graduate school. *Phi Delta Kappan, 68,* 512.

Sadker, M., Sadker, D., & Klein, S. (1991). The issue of gender in elementary and secondary education. In G. Grant (Ed.), *Review of research in education.* Washington, DC: American Educational Research Association.

Sadker, M., Sadker, D., & Steindam, S. (1989). Gender equity and educational reform. *Educational Leadership, 46,* 44–47.

Scarcella, R. (1990). *Teaching language minority students in the multicultural classroom.* Englewood Cliffs, NJ: Prentice Hall.

Slavin, R. E. (1987). Ability grouping and achievement in elementary schools: A best-evidence synthesis. *Review of Educational Research, 57,* 293–336.

Solit, G. A place for Marie: Guidelines for the integration process. In K. M. Paciorek, (Ed.), *Early childhood education 94/95.* Guilford, CT: Dushkin Publishing, 1994.

Stearns, P. N. (1996). Multiculturalism and the American educational tradition. In C. A. Grant & M. L. Gomez (Eds.), *Making schooling multicultural: Campus and classroom* (pp. 17–33). Englewood Cliffs, NJ: Merrill.

Taylor, C. W. (1968). Be talent developers . . . as well as knowledge dispensers. *Today's Education, 75f,* 68–70.

Tompkins, G. E., & Hoskisson, K. (1995). *Language arts: Content and teaching strategies.* Englewood Cliffs, NJ: Prentice-Hall.

Torrance, E. P. (1963). Adventuring in creativity. *Childhood Edcuation, 40,* 78–81.

Torrance, E. P. (1972). Predictive validity of the Torrance tests of creative thinking. *Journal of Creative Behavior, 6,* 236–262.

U.S. Bureau of the Census (1990). Current Population Reports. Series P-20. Washington, DC: U.S. Government Printing Office.

U.S. Office of Education. (1977). Education of handicapped children. *Federal Register (part 2)* Washington, DC: Department of Health, Education and Welfare, 1977.

White, K. R. (1982). The relation between socioeconomic status and academic achievement. *Psychological Bulletin, 91,* 461–481.

Wolery, M., Strain, P. S., & Bailey, D. B. (1992). Reaching potentials of children with special needs. In S. Bredekamp & T. Rosegrant, *Reaching potentials: Appropriate curriculum and assessment for young children, Vol. 1.* Washington, DC: National Association for the Education of Young Children.

Wolery, M., & Wilbers, J. S. (Eds.) (1994). *Including children with special needs in early childhood programs.* Washington, DC: National Association for the Education of Young Children.

Wolfle, J. (1989). The gifted preschooler: Developmentally different but still 3 or 4 years old. *Young Children, 44,* 42.

Woolfolk, A. E. (1995). *Educational psychology.* Boston: Allyn and Bacon.

Zangwell, I. (1909). *The melting pot* (A Play). Quoted in D. M. Gollnick & P. C. Chinn (1983), *Multicultural education in a pluralistic society.* St. Louis: Mosby.

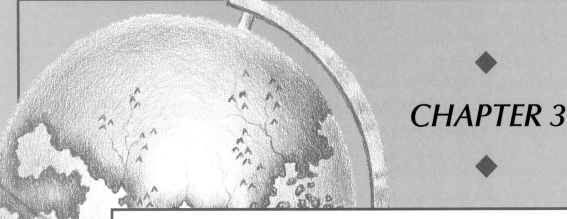

CHAPTER 3

WHAT I KNOW

This exercise provides a "scaffold" that will enable you to relate the chapter material to your background knowledge. Complete the form before you read the chapter and use the results to guide your reading. Use a "+" to indicate confidence, a "?" for uncertainty, and a "-" if you feel deficient in any area.

I can

_____ explain the factors involved in planning an effective social studies lesson.

_____ describe the values of deliberate planning in social studies.

_____ outline the critical components of lesson plans.

_____ distinguish between goals and objectives.

_____ detail the importance of clearly stated instructional objectives.

_____ write clearly stated behavioral and nonbehavioral objectives.

_____ account for varied skills and abilities in the way I state instructional objectives.

_____ select methods and materials appropriate for carrying out the stated objectives.

_____ understand the need to exercise flexibility in selecting instructional procedures.

_____ distinguish between expository and problem-solving procedures.

_____ logically organize and communicate the procedures component of a lesson plan.

_____ utilize appropriate assessment strategies while evaluating the outcomes of a lesson.

Using the results as a guide, what questions will you seek to answer as you read?

Planning Lessons

◆ CLASSROOM SKETCH

Denise Warren, a student teacher impatient to spread her teaching wings, had spent her first two weeks in Mr. Pederson's third-grade classroom observing the daily routine, correcting papers, taking lunch count, assisting individuals in need of special help, and getting to know the children. Finally, the day she had been longing for arrived; her cooperating teacher assigned her to teach her first lesson—a social studies lesson! The class had been involved in a cross-curricular study of Russia, and the students were having a wonderful time discovering some of the unique aspects of Russian culture. To enrich their understandings, Denise's job was to prepare a lesson about Russian money. In a twinkling of an eye, her eager anticipation turned to sudden alarm. "Russian money?" Denise's mind shrieked silently. "Why, I don't know anything about Russian money. How does Mr. Pederson expect me to teach something I don't know anything about? Even worse, what kind of activity can I possibly use to teach information I know nothing about?" Trying to maintain a coolness that wouldn't betray her inner panic, Denise swallowed hard and choked out the words, "I'd love to teach tomorrow's lesson about Russian money!"

Denise was jolted into a sudden realization that elementary school social studies teachers need a lot of information —much more than they can store in their minds. She learned that to be an effective social studies teacher, she must be ready to say many times a day, "I don't know. I'll look it up." So Denise went back to her college library, sat down at a computer, and searched through a CD-ROM encyclopedia for the information she needed for her lesson.

After Denise became familiar with the content that would serve as the focus of her lesson, she needed to select a specific instructional strategy. Knowing she had only 30 minutes for the lesson, Denise needed a time-efficient model. Therefore, she selected a learner-involving expository strategy in which a short explanation of the Russian monetary system would be followed by a challenging activity designed to apply the concept.

Because Mr. Pederson required his student teachers to write very detailed daily plans, Denise now needed to spend time outlining the content as well as the specific steps and activities she planned to carry out. Her final plan of action is shown in Activity 3–1.

"It worked!" Denise whooped as she returned from school the next day. "The lesson actually went well. It wasn't perfect, but it went well. I lost my train of thought once or twice, but the lesson plan kept me on track. I told the children about the Russian monetary system and they listened. We played the Kopek/Ruble game and they loved it. When they got excited and I told them to calm down, they actually did. I feel like a bona fide adult, like I'm ready to be a real teacher. After all the college classwork and all the worries and all the dreaming, it sure feels good."

Activity 3–1

Lesson Plan

Theme: Russia

Grade: Three

Teacher: Denise Warren

General Objective

The children will understand the Russian monetary system.

Specific Objectives

1. The student will identify Russian coins and state their value.

2. The student will solve problems that require the regrouping of kopeks into rubles.

Materials

1. Duplicate for each of five groups: 1 game card; ten 1- kopek coins, ten 10-kopek coins, and one ruble.
2. One die for each group.
3. A set of four small toys such as a plastic car, box of crayons, ball, and spinning top.

Procedure

1. Divide the class into five groups of four students each.
2. Give each group an envelope containing Russian coins and ask them to empty the contents on their table.
3. Ask: "Does anyone know the country these coins came from?" "What are they called?" Have them examine the coins, calling special attention to the Cyrillic letters.
4. Explain that the coins are from Russia and that a ruble is much like the dollar in the United States, a 10-kopek coin is like a dime, and a 1-kopek coin is like a penny. (There are also 2-, 3-, 5-, 15-, 20-, and 50-kopek coins and 3-, 5-, 10-, 25-, and 100-ruble bills.)

5. Allow the students to play freely with the money. Then invite them to play the Kopek/Ruble Game. In each group:
   a. players take turns rolling the dice;
   b. count the sum of the dice and ask for the amount in kopeks;
   c. take the designated amount of kopeks and place them on the kopek section of the game board;
   d. When a group has 10 kopeks in the first column, it must exchange them for a 10-kopek coin and place it in the second column. When a group has ten 10-kopek coins, it exchanges them for a ruble.
   e. see which team can be first to trade ten 10- kopek coins for a ruble.

6. To bring closure, tell the students that you will show them a small toy and the price of the toy in Russian money. Each child in the group numbers off from one to four. Assign each child a toy and ask him or her to select the duplicated coins necessary to buy the assigned toy. Ask, "What are the important Russian coins and bills?"

Assessment

1. Observe the students during the game to see if they are selecting the appropriate coins and whether the coins have been correctly regrouped.
2. Check to see if each student has selected the correct Russian coins to pay for his or her toy.
3. Students write in their journals about Russian money.

Kopeks/Rubles

100	10	1
	Must trade ten 10-kopek coins for 1 ruble	must trade ten 1-kopek coins for one 10-kopek coin

◆ CLASSROOM CONNECTION

Can you imagine a lawyer going to court without preparing a legal summary (brief) of the case? How about about a football coach going into the Super Bowl without a game plan? Would you allow a builder to construct your house without the help of a complete set of blueprints? I think you would agree that the results in each case would be catastrophic. Yet whenever the topic of lesson planning comes up in methods courses, students are likely to emit a collective groan: "Do we *have to* write a lesson plan for everything we teach?"

One of the reasons why so many inexperienced teachers underestimate the value of careful planning is that a great portion of their lives has been spent in classrooms. Lortie (1975) has determined that "the average student has spent 13,000 hours in direct contact with classroom teachers by the time he graduates from high school" (p. 62). These long hours cause many pre-service teachers to feel that they have completed an "apprenticeship by participation"; their life experiences alone have readied them to take over the classroom. But Lortie (1975) cautions these doubters that this contention is based on a set of erroneous beliefs:

> The student is the "target" of the teacher's efforts and sees the teacher front stage and center like an audience viewing a play. Students do not receive invitations to watch the teacher's performance from the wings; they are not privy to the teacher's private intentions. . . . [T]hey are not pressed to place the teacher's action in a pedagogically oriented framework [lesson plan]. They are witnesses from their own student-oriented perspectives. (p. 61)

From these student-oriented perspectives, then, teaching usually appears so spontaneous and unrehearsed that no planning is evident. However, effective teaching is not a haphazard process; in most cases teachers plan ahead—formally or informally—to create an environment that sets learning in motion. Careful planning brings about such a command of content and methodology that a teacher's delivery appears natural, spontaneous, and full of confidence. This message comes across clearly to skeptics who stand in front of the classroom for the first time. They are often shocked to realize that the spotlight is on them, that the initiative is in their hands, that they suddenly have the responsibility for what happens. The classroom, which they saw previously as an orderly domain, suddenly becomes bewildering and problematic, brimming with difficulties at every turn.

Luckily, Denise Warren realized that an important part of successful social studies teaching is that of a deliberate planning. Although planning can be carried out in several ways, the lesson plan receives most attention in field experience–based courses or student teaching. Lesson plans are required in all of these situations, not because college professors and cooperating teachers enjoy loading down students with work, but because daily plans organize learning events that are favorable to student learning. The following statements explain how beginning teachers benefit from writing detailed lesson plans.

1.   *Lesson plans provide important instructional guides for teachers.* They help keep you on course by serving as a roadmap or guide, plotting out the logical flow of instruction.

2.   *Lesson plans encourage teachers to make important pedagogical decisions.* They help you avoid the pitfalls of blindly following the teacher's guide and encourage you to think about alternative strategies and methods that could be employed

in addressing unique student interests and needs. These decisions are based on three major considerations: (a) the students' prior background of experiences, (b) the content to be taught, and (c) the conditions under which the instruction will take place.

3.   *Lesson plans serve as important resources for the next time the lesson will be taught.* They provide a record of what should be retained for the future, as well as a framework into which improvements can be made.

4.   *Lesson plans help your cooperating teacher and college instructor know what you are doing and how you plan to do it.* Both may require a lesson plan prior to observing your lesson. The plan not only lays out what you intend to do, but gives the instructor and cooperating teacher a concrete source on which to provide evaluative feedback both before and after the lesson.

5.   *Lesson plans communicate to all that you are committed to your profession.* Although lesson planning in itself does not guarantee success, it does communicate to others that you are willing to invest the time and effort needed to develop your thinking about developmentally appropriate social studies instruction.

In its standards for the preparation of social studies teachers, the National Council for the Social Studies (1984) emphasized the need for deliberate planning:

> . . . courses in social studies methods should prepare prospective teachers to select, integrate, and translate knowledge and methodology from history and social science disciplines in ways appropriate to students in the school level they will teach and give attention to the goals unique to the social studies and those shared jointly with other areas of the school curriculum. Students should also be able to teach social studies utilizing a variety of curriculum approaches and in different types of settings. (p. 11)

Planning can be a challenging and time-consuming process, but all good social studies teachers plan their daily lessons. Although highly experienced teachers will not spend the time and energy writing out step-by-step, formal plans that you will, they nevertheless understand the importance of planning the strategies and methods they will use with their children. Experienced teachers think deeply about what needs to be done; they might jot down their ideas on a note-pad or in the small squares of large weekly planning books. They can record their lesson plans with such brief notes because their experience has helped them sense what methods and materials might work best in certain situations. You do not yet have this background of first-hand experiences; therefore, you must be much more deliberate in outlining step-by-step descriptions of just how you expect your lessons to proceed.

Lesson plans can take many forms. Some cooperating teachers have a preferred style that they will require of you, while your college professor may feel strongly about a slightly different one. To add to your chagrin, I will present still another suggested format for planning social studies lessons. Although there is nothing magical or extraordinary about any of our approaches, your first efforts at planning should emerge from a "preferred" framework that has worked for experienced educators.

A great deal of time and effort must be spent planning how learnings might emerge in social studies classrooms.

These models will give you an intelligible base from which to operate until you eventually develop one more suited to your personal preferences.

In general, lesson plans contain the following component parts: (1) descriptive data, (2) goals and objectives, (3) materials and equipment, (4) procedure, and (5) assessment.

DESCRIPTIVE DATA

A clearly written lesson plan starts out with background information detailing such things as the topic or theme into which the separate lessons flow, the grade level, and the name of the person who has written (or will be teaching) it. Although *you* know all of this information, your cooperating teacher and college professor will find it useful.

GOALS AND OBJECTIVES

When I started planning this chapter, I needed to have a good idea of what I wanted to write about. Certainly, I knew that the general topic involved "planning lessons," but I was not yet sure exactly I wanted to say. Being aware that volumes have been published on the process of instructional planning, I surveyed the research very carefully in an effort to determine what information might serve as the best guide. This marked the beginning of my plan of action.

After thoughtful study, I decided to weed out everything else and focus this chapter on four interrelated components of lesson planning—goals and objectives, materials and equipment, instructional procedures, and assessment. In other words, my *goal* for Chapter 3 was to help you understand how to design short-term teaching plans that center on these four interrelated components. Goals, therefore, served as my guide for action. Without them, my efforts would have been as directionless as a feather in the breeze.

Goals

Likewise, teachers use various instructional goals to give direction to what they do in their social studies classrooms. Unfortunately, some simply look for anything that might keep their class busy for the period while others strive for something more noble, such as looking into a problem that has captured the interest of a class. Every teacher has in mind some kind of goal for instruction, but the goals selected by various teachers often differ in their value to social studies education. Because of this global nature of goals, teachers have often had a great deal of difficulty pinpointing specifically what it is that they do. Postman and Weingartner (1974) explain:

> Teachers have always been somewhat [wishy-washy] about what it is they do. . . . For example, there is the type of teacher who believes he is in the lighting business. We may call him the Lamplighter. When he is asked what he is trying to do with his students, his reply is something like this: "I want to illuminate their minds, to allow some light to penetrate the darkness." Then there is the Gardener. He says, "I want to cultivate their minds, to fertilize them, so that the seeds I plant will flourish." . . . The Muscle Builder wants to strengthen flabby minds, and the Bucket Filler wants to fill them up. (p. 57)

What general goals do you find significant for social studies instruction? Should we mold the child, as a sculptor would? Perhaps we are much like carpenters who construct a solid foundation and erect a sturdy framework. It is not my intention to poke fun at goal setting with these metaphors, but think how often we hear statements such as these in response to the question, "What are schools for?"

Goals, then, describe the cumulative effect of the educational process. They are normally written as general statements of instructional intent: "What do I want students to know, feel, or be able to do as a result of participating in the social studies program?" For example:

- The students will understand the importance of the national park system.
- The students will understand how national symbols remind us of important beliefs about our country.

- The students will appreciate the many kinds of people who made this country great.
- The students will apply word processing skills to the composing process in social studies classrooms.

Notice that the verbs in each of these statements—*understand, appreciate, apply*—are unspecific; they are not stated in directly observable, measurable terms. But that is the nature of instructional goals; they are meant only to offer a general direction of instruction—an initial step. Goals provide overall guidance for the planning process and are not meant to be achieved at the end of a single lesson. They may take several days, weeks, months, or even the entire school year to accomplish, depending on the complexity of the topic. Such longer-range plans in social studies are called *unit plans* or *thematic plans*; they will be discussed in Chapter 4.

Once teachers set a general direction for instruction, they must identify the specifics related to each goal. I have written one specific statement for each of the goals above:

- Given a map of the United States, the students will identify and locate three national parks.
- The students will explain what each symbol on the flag of the United States stands for.
- After interviewing a parent, students will describe at least one important contribution made by their ethnic or racial group to the culture of the United States.
- The students will select one incident leading to the Revolutionary War and use the computer to write about the incident as a period news article.

Objectives

Did you notice that, although these statements were written in different formats, each described specific behaviors that indicate how the students will reach each goal? That is the purpose of objectives; verbs signal specific performance expectancies—words such as *identify, explain, describe,* and *select.* The written form of these four objectives is patterned after two models that have been especially influential in social studies planning—*Mager's Behavioral Objectives* and *Gronlund's Instructional Objectives.*

Mager's Behavioral Objectives

Perhaps the most hotly debated approach to preparing instructional objectives is that of Robert Mager. Mager (1962) proposes that teachers plan their lessons around specific statements that describe "what the student will be doing when demonstrating his achievement and how you will know he is doing it" (p. 53). He calls these statements *behavioral objectives* (or performance objectives) because they single out the observable, measurable behaviors learners should be able to demonstrate after successfully completing the learning experience.

Mager explains that behavioral objectives can be distinguished from all other types of objectives in that they are written as statements consisting of three parts: (1) the conditions under which the learning will take place, (2) the actions or behaviors expected of the students, and (3) the criteria for success.

Let us suppose that an overall instructional *goal* for a unit under study is "The students will understand the characteristics of the world's oceans." The following is a component behavioral objective written in the Mager format: "After viewing a video about oceans *(learning condition),* students shall be able to identify and locate *(specific behavior)* two oceans bordering the United States *(criterion for success).*"

As you can see, Mager's system requires a high degree of specifity. To help you understand how to write behavioral objectives, let us examine the three components of a complete objective more deliberately.

The Conditions Under Which the Learning Will Take Place.
By designating the acceptable learning condition, you pinpoint exactly how you will deliver the intended information to your students. This decision requires you to examine the wide variety of experiences available for a particular lesson and select one that appears to have the greatest potential for student success. Looking back at our sample behavioral objective, there is no question what the students will be doing—viewing a video. The condition under which the learning is to take place is communicated clearly.

By contrast, vague statements of instructional conditions such as "After learning about . . ." or "Given exposure to . . ." are meaningless; in no way do they clarify how student learning will be carried out. Statements of appropriate learning conditions must precisely designate instructional procedures:

- After examining a jar full of beach sand . . .
- Given a CD-ROM encyclopedia . . .
- After studying a map of the United States . . .
- After listening to a member of Greenpeace . . .

Many educators believe that objectives should always begin with phrases that set forth the strategy to be employed to lead students toward the intended learning outcomes.

The Actions or Behaviors Expected of the Students.
Our original sample behavioral objective not only informed us that the students will be viewing a video but also specified a single observable behavior, or performance, that we expect the students to demonstrate after participating in the learning experience. The key feature is that the student action is observable by the teacher: *Students shall be able to identify and locate.* All behavioral objectives must be written with a clearly stated student performance in mind.

Action verbs signal the behavioral outcomes of a lesson: *locate, recall, describe, construct, select, gather, define, draw, distinguish between, label, outline, compute, write, alphabetize, identify, memorize.* They pinpoint the specific actions students must exhibit in order to demonstrate their understandings. Of course, there are dozens of other possibilities, but the important point is that you must communicate what is to be done by the students in observable, measurable terms. Let us continue the four performance objectives we started above by adding statements of observable performance:

- After examining a jar full of beach sand, *the students will select* . . .
- Given a CD-ROM encyclopedia, *the students will write* . . .
- After studying a map of the United States, *the students will orally state* . . .
- After listening to a member of Greenpeace, *the students will identify* . . .

Selecting the most appropriate action verb is critical, since it spots the exact behaviors that will be assessed as an indication of the degree of student performance.

The Criteria for Success.   When teachers assess the degree to which a student has demonstrated a targeted behavior, they are defining the evaluative *criteria*. Often called the "criterion measure" or "level of minimum acceptable performance," this third component of behavioral objectives designates the *lowest level* of acceptable performance. In our original sample behavioral objective, the following criterion measure culminated with the statement *two oceans bordering the United States.* This is a well-defined standard toward which a teacher's efforts will be directed. It is also reasonable, in the sense that all students have a high probability of achieving it. Establishing reasonable criteria is one of the most difficult of all decisions teachers face when constructing behavioral objectives: "Am I expecting too little from my students?" "Are the standards too high or impossible to reach?" Reasonable criteria are most potently based on a teacher's keen awareness of the level at which their students are working. Criteria vary greatly and depend on the professional judgment of the teacher.
    Examples of criteria selected to complete our emerging behavioral objectives follow:

- After examining a jar full of beach sand, the students will select *three grains that came from rocks and three grains that came from shells.*
- Given a CD-ROM encyclopedia, the students will write a paragraph *containing five accurate facts about oceans.*
- After studying a map of the United States, the students will orally state *three cities that are ocean ports.*
- After listening to a member of Greenpeace, the students will identify *three statements of fact and three statements of opinion.*

    Establishing the criteria for acceptable performance is the final dimension in developing behavioral objectives. Test your developing knowledge of behavioral objectives identifying which of the following objectives are correctly written (my objective for this exercise is "Given a list of five objectives, the students will select each behavioral objective."):

1. The students will really understand the concept of "ocean" after they have read five pages from their textbook.
2. Given a random list of oceans and rivers, the students will circle the names of all five oceans.
3. Given an outline map of the world, the students will label each of the world's five oceans.
4. Each student will think of three or four words to describe an ocean.
5. Given a map of the United States, students will identify the ocean nearest them.

I have selected statements 2, 3, and 5 as behavioral objectives. Do you agree with me? Try rewriting each nonbehavioral objective as a behavioral objective.

Should objectives for social studies lesson plans be written in behavioral terms? Jarolimek and Foster (1997) offer arguments on both sides of the issue. Advocates of behavioral objectives believe strongly that learner outcomes must be directly observable immediately following the instructional experience. They advise that when teachers plan instruction around behavioral objectives, they know exactly which outcomes are to be expected and determine whether or not learning has occurred. It is only when teachers are able to measure clearly defined, observable behaviors that they can determine the amount of learning that has taken place.

On the other hand, many teachers oppose the use of behavioral objectives because they believe they are an expression of *behaviorism.* They insist that such specific statements unfairly restrict learning to that which can be observed and measured. Higher-order thinking and the sensitivities that apply to the arts and aesthetics are likely to be eliminated because they do not lend themselves to precise measurement. Opponents of behavioral objectives argue that there are more subtle forms of learning that stem from feelings and appreciations than from precisely defined, knowledge-based learning. It is easy, for example, to observe a student select the symbol for a railroad on a community map and determine whether the choice is correct. It is not quite as easy to observe how a student determines whether or not the federal government should subsidize railroads so they can be used for mass transit in cities. Even more problematic is judging which decision is "correct."

The position taken in this text is that learning is such a complex process that it may or may not be accounted for solely as a change of observable behavior. Some social studies objectives, certainly, seek an observable change in behavior, but others deal with global responses associated with feelings, attitudes, likes, and dislikes—areas where student comments are likely to please or displease a teacher. Social studies educators don't think of personal feelings as being accepted or rejected in terms of a precisely defined objective, but they are primarily important in terms of what they mean to each individual. Eisner (1985) observes that when specific skills or competencies are targeted for instruction, behavioral objectives can serve as appropriate ways of organizing the instructional plan. When specific outcomes cannot be singled out, when possible outcomes are open-ended, then instructional plans should use other types of objectives: "One must be able to swim four lengths of the pool to be able to swim in the deep end," Eisner (1985) explains in describing the need for specificity, but "one should not feel compelled to abandon educational aims that cannot be reduced to measurable forms of predictable performance" (p. 114). Therefore, because objectives are intended only to set a course of action, the nature of the expected learning outcome should determine the type of instructional objective employed for a lesson plan.

Gronlund's Instructional Objectives

Norman Gronlund (1991) has developed an alternative to the behavioral objective style championed by Mager. His approach is to first write a global objective using such general terms as we described as appropriate for instructional goals—*understand, know, appreciate, synthesize, create, evaluate,* or *apply.* Then specific behaviors are listed to clarify what the students should be taught and what they are expected to learn. An example follows:

General Objective (Goal)

The students shall understand how corporations grew during the late 1800s.

Specific Objectives

1. The student will define the term *corporation.*
2. The student will describe the relationship between *public investments* and *corporations.*
3. The student will identify reasons why people buy stock in certain corporations.
4. The student will explain why large corporations first grew in the Northeast.

Upon detailed inspection of Gronlund's instructional objectives, we can see that the objective is stated in terms of student outcomes rather than teacher performance. Therefore, an objective that begins, "Teach how corporations grew during the 1800s," is inappropriate. It describes a teacher behavior, not a student outcome. Educators today are united in their belief that objectives should be stated in terms of student outcomes. We also see that the general objective is unspecific and, by itself, not very helpful in guiding the lesson. However, it does communicate the overall intent of the lesson. The purpose of the specific objectives is to clarify the general objective.

Gronlund's approach, or adaptations of it, is perhaps the most popular among curriculum writers and teachers today. Jacobsen, Eggen, and Kauchak (1993) explain that its primary advantage is one of economy; content requiring literally thousands of objectives written according to Mager's approach could be expressed in less than one hundred using Gronlund's. "The compromise Gronlund makes is in terms of specificity. He doesn't identify either the conditions for acceptable performance or the criteria . . . " (p. 71).

In this text, I have chosen to use nonbehavioral objectives—an adaptation of Gronlund's approach. Although they are not stated with the precision of behavioral objectives, the form used in this text will be specific enough to target precisely what the children are supposed to learn. Two examples follow:

- The students will develop an awareness of how George Washington Carver devoted himself to helping our nation's farmers.
- The students will identify how George Washington Carver was the victim of racial prejudice.

The Objectives—Professional Standards Connection

Regardless of the format you are required to use while preparing instructional objectives, you must realize that objectives are a vital part of the "real world" of teaching today. The labels we have discussed may be different, but objectives-driven guides for instruction are certainly a part of the educational scene.

For example, the development of clearly stated curriculum standards began in the 1990s in response to a public demand for identifying precisely what students should be taught, how they should be taught, and how their learning should be assessed. Several disciplines, buoyed by the endorsement of the federal government, developed statements of desired outcomes; the social studies standards emerged in 1994 (see Chapter 1). If you examine the social studies standards carefully, you will note that their format corresponds quite closely with Gronlund's scheme. Each of the ten general standards functions much as a general objective. For each standard, a set of precise student performance expectations is specified. These performance expectations correspond very closely to Gronlund's specific objectives. Consider the following excerpt taken from the *Curriculum Standards for Social Studies* (National Council for the Social Studies, 1994):

> STANDARD III
> Social studies programs should include experiences that provide for the study of *people, places, and environments* so that the learner can:
> Early Grades
> a. construct and use mental maps of locales, regions, and the world that demonstrate understanding of relative location, direction, size, and shape;
> b. interpret, use, and distinguish various representations of the earth, such as maps, globes, and photographs;
> c. use appropriate resources, and geographic tools such as atlases, data bases, grid systems, charts, graphs, and maps to generate, manipulate, and interpret information . . . (p. 35)

You need to understand how objectives are written. Even if you do not encounter them while writing lesson plans, you will certainly experience similar statements in the context of *curriculum standards.*

Classifying Objectives

So far, we have focused on one primary goal—understanding the form and use of instructional objectives. Another very important function of instructional objectives is targeting the specific outcomes we wish to derive from the instructional experience.

Two teachers, for example, were about to teach a lesson using an identical reading assignment about China. The only educational outcome one teacher targeted for the lesson was for her students to recall a number of specific facts about the country. The other teacher's objective, by contrast, was for separate groups to create a dramatic skit, each characterizing a different major event from the country's history. It is clear that the expected outcome from an identical source of information was very different for each teacher. How are these assorted outcomes accounted for in lesson planning?

Bloom's Taxonomy

Some lessons are purposely designed to develop critical or creative thinking while others are designed to draw out specific knowledge or skills. For that reason, objectives describe a variety of outcomes—the *information* or *knowledge* the students should know and use, the *skills* or *abilities* they should master or demonstrate, or the *attitudes* or *values* they hold dear. A wide variety of outcomes are possible from any social studies learning experience. How do we use objectives to describe the outcomes of our planned instruction? A majority of educators recommend the use of *Bloom's Taxonomy of Educational Objectives* (Bloom et al., 1956) as the basis for writing objectives that encourage a variety of thought and action. The term *Bloom's Taxonomy* is heard in every social studies methods class, so much so that it has become synonymous with conscientious planning in social studies.

Taxonomies are classification systems that describe different learning outcomes, ordering them from simple to complex. Bloom's Taxonomy was the first system developed in the United States and, because Bloom's Taxonomy has far eclipsed the popularity of all others, it will serve as the focus for our discussion. The fact that it is moving through its fourth decade of popularity is testimony to its value for helping teachers decide what to teach, how to teach, and how to assess the value of the learning experience.

Bloom's Taxonomy classifies cognitive behaviors into six categories, ranging from the simple to the most highly complex. The classifications are considered *hierarchical,* meaning that thinking abilities at lower levels are prerequisite to and serve to support the higher level abilities; the simplest behavior becomes subsumed into the next level, those behaviors combine and become integrated into the next, and so on until the most complex cognitive behavior blooms as a combination of all behaviors below it.

Knowledge.   This is the first level of Bloom's Taxonomy, and the lowest category of cognitive functioning. It encompasses the functions of memory and recall. Students may be expected to memorize specific facts ("What are the major crops of Georgia?"), recall specific terminology or definitions ("What is a dory?"), or remember conventions or rules of usage ("Where would the North Pole be found on a globe?").

Although the knowledge level involves the lowest level of cognitive functioning, objectives in this category are important for the social studies classroom. Remember that Bloom's Taxonomy is hierarchical, so knowledge forms the foundation for all higher-order thinking. Thus, in organizing coherent, connected learning experiences, teachers begin by focusing on the necessary background information before moving on to higher levels of thought. For example, before we can expect students to respond meaningfully to the question, "Who do you think were braver, the Pilgrims at Plymouth or the pioneers settling the West?" they must first know something about the challenges faced by both groups of settlers. Certainly, the students would not be able to respond intelligibly without a background of applicable knowledge.

The problem with knowledge objectives is that some teachers have a tendency to overemphasize them, thereby sending a message to students that social studies is little more than a storehouse of facts to be memorized. Could this be a major reason why some children find social studies flat, boring, and monotonous?

In deciding whether or not to include knowledge objectives in your lesson plan, ask yourself this question: "How can this knowledge be used by the student as background information for higher-level thinking?" If the answer is fuzzy, you should carefully reconsider keeping it in your plan. To learn more about how knowledge buttresses Bloom's next level of cognitive functioning—comprehension—turn to Chapter 5.

Using Gronlund's format, a specific objective in the knowledge category can be written like this: "The student shall recall the names of the five oceans of the world."

Comprehension.   In this level of cognitive functioning, students take information and concepts and use them appropriately in new situations. Merely parroting back what has been taught does not reveal true understanding. Meaning emerges as the students grasp the information and transform it into forms that are understandable to them. An example of this process would be the difference between requiring children to memorize Lincoln's Gettysburg Address (knowledge) and asking them to tell in their own words the message Lincoln was trying to communicate (comprehension).

The idea behind comprehension is to encourage students to do more with information than simply memorize facts. The student who draws an original map of the major battles at Gettysburg demonstrates comprehension, while the student who has memorized the battles and dates does not. To learn more about comprehension as a cognitive strategy, turn to Chapter 5.

Using Gronlund's format, a specific objective in the comprehension category can be written like this: "The students shall differentiate between rivers and oceans."

Application.   As its names implies, this level of cognition requires students to apply knowledge, concepts, and skills appropriately in new situations to solve problems. For a learning experience to be considered at the application level, the problem must be in a context different from that in which the information was originally learned; otherwise, the task involves mere recall. For example, if students are studying about the assembly line process within the context of the growth of the automobile industry in the United States, they would not be offered a problem-solving scenario such as, "Design a process by which automobiles could be produced quickly and inexpensively." Students might simply recall specific information related to Henry Ford's assembly line and be operating only in the knowledge category; if they draw a diagram of the process, they would be in the comprehension category because they are putting together specific information and expressing it in a personal way. For true application to occur, the class would be divided into two groups. In one group, each child would individually make as many peanut butter and jelly sandwiches as he or she could in an alloted time. In the second group, students would be asked to design a system that would allow them to produce more sand-wiches than the first group in the same amount of time. If they were able to *apply* the concept of assembly lines, the students should organize their efforts as an assembly line to perform different tasks—take out two slices of bread, spread the peanut butter on one slice, add jelly to the other, put one slice on top of the other, and put it on a paper plate. The students would then explain why the assembly line was more effi-cient. To learn more about application (problem solving) as a cognitive strategy, turn to Chapter 6.

Using Gronlund's format, a specific objective in the application category can be written like this: "The students will suggest how individuals and communities can help protect our oceans."

Teachers make good use of captivating learning experiences to build in-depth concepts of people, places, events, and ideas.

Analysis.   This category involves the sophisticated processes involved in taking the whole and breaking it down into its separate components so it can be better understood. The "whole" we are talking about includes any source of information— speeches, newspaper editorials, textbook selections, television programs, and lectures—anything that can be taken apart and examined carefully. For example, students might be asked to explore a map of the United States and divide the country into five different regions. Or they might break down the South American continent into its constituent countries. Analysis-level objectives are usually signaled by such verbs as *select, break down, subdivide,* or *separate.*

In many instances, social studies teachers call upon their students to analyze various forms of communication. For example, students might collect a number of magazine ads. These ads would be examined closely to determine the most common types of persuasive techniques employed.

One of the most common types of analysis activities in social studies classrooms is to examine value-laden sources. For example, a portion of an old slave song goes

> Rabbit in the briar patch,
> Squirrel in the tree,
> Wish I could go hunting,
> But I ain't free.

In this particular instance, students could be asked, "What do these lines tell you about the lives of slaves?"

Also, social studies teachers often employ the processes of analysis when they ask their students to identify reasons for certain behaviors: "What were some real motives behind the founding of the missions in the Southwest?" To learn more about analysis as a cognitive strategy, turn to Chapter 8.

Using Gronlund's format, a specific objective in the analysis category can be written like this: "The students shall determine Aleksandr Aleksandrov's motives when he spoke the words, 'We are all Earth's children and we should treat her as our Mother.'

Synthesis.   This process involves the ability to combine ideas to come up with uniquely creative solutions to problems. A solution need not be new to humankind, but unique to the student. For example, at a critical point in the study of the Mexican War, the teacher assigned the following problem to the class: "What might President James K. Polk do to prevent the Mexican War?" If Alex predicted possible alternatives without prior knowledge of Polk's actual decision, she would be operating at the synthesis level. However, if she simply reviewed what is already known, Alex would be working at the comprehension level. A response could belong to either of two or three categories, depending on the degree of originality expected.

Often, educators associate the process of creative problem solving with the synthesis category. This is because these processes encourage students to solve problems with plans or products that are unique to individual experiences. To learn more about creative problem solving as a cognitive strategy, turn to Chapter 6.

Using Gronlund's format, a specific objective in the synthesis category can be written like this: "The students shall compose a short jingle for use in their campaign to clean up dirty beaches."

Evaluation.   This is the most complex level of cognitive functioning—the process of making judgments about ideas and substantiating one's decisions with sound reasons. In the evaluation category, students are asked to share their thoughts and opinions on varied issues, as well as the criteria on which their ideas are based. For example, the children might be asked, "If you were living in the late 1800s, would you rather be a factory worker or a miner?" A response such as, "A miner," would be insufficient because there is no intellectual support in defense of the judgment. To employ evaluative processes, the students must think about the attributes of both occupations and weigh their advantages and disadvantages before making the decision. Feelings are important, but they must be backed up with sound, logical reasoning. To learn more about evaluation as a cognitive strategy, turn to Chapter 8.

Using Gronlund's format, a specific objective in the evaluation category can be written like this: "The students shall decide whether or not garbage should be disposed of in oceans."

As we conclude this discussion of objectives, you should keep in mind that the exact format you use to write your objectives is not critical to the success of your lesson. What is important is that you clearly communicate the exact instructional intent. When you go on a vacation, for example, you tell others much more about your destination when you say, "I'm going to Acapulco, Mexico," rather than, "I'm going to Mexico."

Likewise, instructional objectives specify teaching intent—they target exactly where you are going with the planned instruction. Objectives help you clarify what the students must be able to know or do as a result of a well-planned learning experience.

MATERIALS AND EQUIPMENT

This section of the lesson plan itemizes the special materials you will need to carry out the lesson. These include items such as transparancies, overhead projectors, maps, books, art supplies, construction materials, videotapes, computer software, models, realia, games, globes, maps, puzzles, newspapers, diagrams, tools, and recordings. For a lesson on the first space shuttle, for example, one teacher listed the following special materials: *model space shuttle, photos depicting duties of astronauts, crayons,* and *drawing paper.* She did not include textbooks, even though they were going to be used as the source of information for the lesson. That is because the textbook was regularly used in her social studies program, so it wasn't necessary to list it as a special resource. The other items, however, were listed because they weren't used most of the time. The model and photos were going to be used to establish an experiential background in advance of the reading assignment. The crayons and drawing paper would be used by the children to draw a picture of what the earth looks like from the perspective of astronauts in a space shuttle. By listing these special materials in a separate section of the lesson plan, teachers can always remember the items necessary to complete the lesson successfully.

The effective social studies teacher is one who confronts children with abundant materials, stretching their minds and deepening their social awareness. He is convinced that children must be offered something that immerses them in learning, or they are better off staying at home. College professors help open new vistas of learning with inspiring lectures and first-class readings. These can provoke learning in elementary school children, too, but effective social studies teachers start with reality. The well-equipped social studies classroom is filled with challenging, inviting realia. Good, richly detailed poster-size photos or prints refresh and deepen children's concepts of people and places, too. They stir the children's memory of past experiences and motivate them to seek new information. Textbooks and trade books offer exciting new adventures and challenges. Videotapes and movies bring children close to real-life adventures. Computers are true information generators, stimulants for learning, and sound reinforcers.

Everything selected for a social studies lesson must meet demanding standards. Learning materials are not picked simply because they are "cute." Each item is chosen because it does something well. No musical tape is chosen just because it sounds "cool." It must have relevance to learning. Each picture communicates an important message; each book says something meaningful. Only the most educationally sound materials have a place in quality social studies programs. Materials for the social studies classroom must motivate, not excite the students. They must challenge young learners, not confuse them. Careful balance is the key.

PROCEDURE

The first task of our planning model was to specify the goals and objectives for the lesson. After listing the materials necessary to achieve these goals and objectives, the next logical step is to decide how we will teach toward their acquisition. This is often the section that creates the most confusion in the minds of pre-service teachers. Some instructional models (called *expository* or *teacher-centered*) require the teacher to guide all students through the same experiences at the same time. Other models (called *problem solving/inquiry* or *student-centered*) invite students to actively pursue their own learnings. Which model works best? That is a question that has captivated educators since the onset of formal education, and one that has not yet been convincingly answered. After examining the pros and cons of the alternative models, however, Jarolimek and Foster (1997) offer some wise advice on this issue: "The act of teaching is so complex that it is nearly impossible to demonstrate that a specific way of teaching is superior to other ways for all purposes, with all teachers, with all children, for all times, and in all circumstances. . . . We are forced to conclude that there are many good ways to teach" (p. 146).

The nature of social studies as a school subject calls for flexible, adaptable teachers—informed professionals who eagerly anticipate the challenge of selecting instructional procedures that are most appropriate for any specified learning outcome. But responsive teachers realize that instructional decisions are highly complex and make decisions only after thoughtfully considering a number of factors. Orlich and his associates (1990) identify these factors as: (1) the teacher, (2) the students, (3) the goals and objectives, and (4) the physical environment.

As we discussed in Chapter 1, every *teacher* has a unique set of personal and professional strengths that serve as a firm basis of instruction. It takes some time to discover how these strengths can be transformed into a "teaching personality," however, so new teachers often benefit by beginning their professional careers using an expository mode. In this mode, classroom management challenges are minimized because children are not placed into potentially disruptive situations. This does not mean; however, that you should shy away from the more permissive, student-centered strategies; once you have developed a sense of confidence in the classroom, it is important to try new things in an effort to continually expand your teaching repertoire.

The mode of instruction must also match the *students'* experiences and backgrounds. Just as every teacher's special combination of likes, dislikes, abilities, strengths, and needs contributes to a teaching personality, so do student preferences and unique skills influence "student personality" (see Chapter 2). Some students interact freely with peers while others are shy and withdrawn. Some students prefer to be "turned loose" to attack a problem of personal interest while others would rather sit and listen to an interesting presentation by the teacher. Some students require direct help with specific subskills before attempting a certain task while others readily achieve success if left to their own devices. The effective social studies teacher uses key information about students to make appropriate adjustments to classroom instructional procedures.

Additionally, all procedures must have a purpose; these purposes, the desired outcomes of the learning experience, are specified in the *goals and objectives* portion of the lesson plan. Obviously, procedures must correspond to the goals and objectives of the lesson, so I like to encourage students to make this connection by using the logic required to complete *If-Then Statements.* For example:

- *If* we want to model the correct procedure for using latitude and longitude to locate places, *then* the teacher would explain the concept with the aid of a large classroom globe.
- *If* we want students to investigate their town's interesting past as a social scientist would, *then* they should conduct interviews and search town records to create a "living history" of their community.

Objectives and procedures are brought together with a logical link formed by If-Then Statements.

The final consideration influencing the choice of instructional procedures is the *physical environment.* The procedure you select for any lesson will depend on where the learning will take place. Because procedures depend on where the learning will take place, you must ask the question, "Is the environment the best one to ensure learning with the procedure I've chosen?" A classroom in which student desks are arranged in rows will not enhance cooperative learning; a school located near a large museum should schedule at least one field trip there. Both in-class and out-of-class environments must accommodate the selected procedures.

Expository Procedures

The expository mode involves the teacher controlling and directing the presentation of specific learnings to the whole class with varied instructional resources including textbooks, media presentations, and quality children's literature. Although the teacher's role in exposition has been popularly characterized as "telling," "demonstrating," or "lecturing," it involves much more than that. Nevertheless, when most people hear or read about exposition, they visualize children as passive receivers of teacher-delivered facts. Because of such exaggerated misrepresentations, the expository procedure is often considered unsuited to the developmental needs of elementary school students. Properly used, however, the expository mode can hold an important place in social studies instruction.

Teachers commonly employ expository strategies in social studies classrooms for two major purposes: (1) to help develop specific skills and (2) to facilitate the acquisition of information and ideas. For example, this experience from Mr. Mabry's first-grade social studies program demonstrates how his expository procedure not only helped children create and interpret charts (skills), but also stimulated a variety of high-order thinking.

Today, Mr. Mabry read to his class *The Little Red Hen* by Paul Galdone (Seabury Press). The book was selected to help the children think about the concept of *helping.* After he read the story, Mr. Mabry led a discussion about the story's ending and the hen's decision not to share the bread with the animals who refused to help her. Did the children think the hen made the right decision? Mr. Mabry encouraged the class to think about how the other animals felt about the hen's decision and the other choices she might have made. Finally, he displayed a chart divided into three columns: (1) the child's name, (2) a "yes" column, and (3) a "no" column. Mr. Mabry explained the chart to the children and asked them to predict whether there would be more "yes" or "no" votes in response to the question, "Did the Little Red Hen do the right thing?" The children were invited to write their names and mark their votes answering the question (see Figure 3–1). Afterward, the class discussed the results.

Constructing and interpreting charts is but one skills area of the social studies program where exposition is often used. It is also employed when teachers help children acquire and refine dozens of other skills, including using the computer, composing a journal entry, reading a map, constructing a table or graph, creating a model, checking out reference books related to a topic of instruction, planning an interview, learning the steps of an ethnic dance, or outlining an informational paragraph from an encyclopedia.

In addition to teaching specific social studies skills, expository procedures help to effectively achieve instructional objectives that range from simple information recall to the evaluation of ideas and actions. In the expository mode, the teacher directs,

FIGURE 3-1
Little Red Hen Graph

Did the Little Red Hen do the right thing?

Name	Yes	No
Connie	X	
Robert		X
MarthA		X
Jud		X
DarriN	X	
Anita	X	
Amiram	X	

but learner involvement must be high. The reason expository teaching has received strong criticism is that some teachers tend to do *too much* talking and explaining. However, dynamic teachers with a variety of interesting approaches can make expository teaching a valuable instructional procedure.

General Expository Procedures

To succeed, the procedures employed for expository lessons must be well structured. Toward that goal, it helps to plan this section of your lesson as an organized whole having an *introduction, middle,* and *ending.* The introduction prepares the students for the activity and encourages participation. Any good lesson needs a good beginning because it arouses curiosity, stimulates the imagination, relates new content to past experiences, and creates enthusiasm for what is to follow. The middle, often called the *lesson development phase,* entails the primary learning experience intended to achieve your objectives. The ending helps bind together what happened in the middle phase. It brings closure to the lesson and reinforces the main points. The following lesson plan procedures were written for this objective: The students shall describe how beach sand is created.

Procedure

1. Begin by calling the children's attention to a study print of a beach scene. Discuss what the children see and encourage them to talk about any times they have visited the beach. Encourage them to consider the vastness of the beach. Ask, "Who would care to guess how many grains of sand are on the beach?"

2. Hold up a large plastic jar filled with sand. Ask, "How many grains of sand are in this jar?" Add, "We may never know the answers to these questions, but we do know one thing—how sand is made."

3. Help students generate a list of all they know about how sand is made on a "Knowledge" chart. Write everything they know (or think they know) in an "I Know" column. Then ask them to listen to a story about oceans to check the information on the chart.

4. Read the book *Oceans* by Seymour Simon (Morrow).

5. Students record in the "Now I Know" column all they learned about how sand is made. In addition, any inaccurate information listed in the first column will be corrected.

6. To bring closure, ask students to make an entry in their social studies learning logs summarizing what they have learned about beach sand.

In expository instruction, then, teachers are in control as they demonstrate, model, tell, and teach a specific concept or skill to be learned. It is the teacher's control of the instructional episode that defines the procedure.

The Hunter Approach to Mastery Learning

Very similar to the general expository procedure is the planning method designed by Madeline Hunter (1982). Hunter's model is widely used in many school districts, and is considered to be *the* instructional strategy expected of all teachers in those districts. The model is so popular in some areas that applicants for teaching positions are denied interviews unless they are familiar with Hunter's seven components.

The following lesson cycle is used to implement the Hunter model:

1.   *Anticipatory Set.* The suggested opening of a Hunter-based lesson is an "anticipatory set" that creates a bridge between what the student already knows or can do with the new content or skill to be taught. This bridge can be a statement ("Yesterday, we read about how railroads linked the east and west coasts of the United States. Today, we will listen to a recording of 'John Henry,' a song based on the life of a real railroad worker. Listen to see what the song tells about the contributions of early railroad workers."), a demonstration, or a display of some appealing materials. This communicates to the students that you have an excitement and interest in the material to be learned; it is designed to raise the children's degree of interest to that same level. In contrast, teachers who begin a lesson with, "Take out your books and turn to page 43," convey the message that the social studies lesson is just something that everyone has to get through whether they like it or not. Consequently, the children's interest will be lowered to the level communicated by the teacher.

How do teachers communicate genuine interest in what they are about to teach? Eby (1997) suggests that "[a]nimation is the outward sign of a teacher's interest in the students and the subject. . . . Outwardly, the teacher displays enthusiasm by using a bright, lively voice; open, expansive gestures; and facial expressions that show [fascination with the item on display (manipulative material, realia, study print, etc.) or interest and pleasure in what is about to ensue]. Salespeople who use animated, enthusiastic behavior could sell beach umbrellas in the Yukon in January. Why shouldn't teachers employ these techniques well?" (p. 182). You can "sell" the Great Wall of China better with an enthusiastic voice; you can convince children that the topic of the presidency is important with a look of commitment on your face; you can encourage discussions with welcoming gestures and an accepting smile.

Practice using these skills with your classmates before attempting a lesson with elementary school children. Ask for honest feedback: "How can I improve the delivery of the anticipatory set?" Teaching, just like shooting a basketball, playing the trumpet, or weaving an afghan, requires much practice. Keep striving to improve. You might want to videotape your presentations in the field. As you watch the replay, search for ways you can improve your presentation skills. Some people are their own best critics.

2.   *Statement of purpose.* The introduction to the actual learning activity culminates with the teacher clearly informing the students about what they will know or be able to do at the end of the lesson. For example, after creating an anticipatory set on the topic of "national symbols" with a short discussion about a small replica of the Liberty Bell, one teacher announced, "Today we are going to read about the reasons why three national symbols—the eagle, flag, and Liberty Bell—were selected to stand for something special about our country." Actually, the purpose is an abbreviated version of the objective, but it is restated in terms the students can understand.

Eby (1997) emphasizes that the clarity of a teacher's purpose-setting statement is a critical factor in the lesson's success. Vague statements interspersed with "listen up," "okay," "uh," "ya-know," and "you guys" detract from the lesson (vague terms are in italics): "Listen up, you guys, this Liberty Bell is, uh, ya-know, a national symbol. *Maybe* you have seen it before. This, uh, lesson will *hopefully* help you understand *a little bit more* about *some other,* uh, national symbols. Okay?"

It doesn't require a graduate degree to see that this purpose-setting statement is unlikely to focus the students' attention on the topic of instruction. Clarity can be improved by substituting specific terms for the vague ones, resulting in a simple, straightforward statement: "Today we are going to read about the reasons why three national symbols—the eagle, flag, and Liberty Bell—were selected to stand for something special about our country."

The anticipatory set and statement of purpose constitute the lesson's introduction.

3.   *Instructional input.* Effective expository teachers engage their students in active learning. Consider a teacher planning to teach about our national anthem while employing the traditional strategies of lecturing and reading from the text followed by a whole-class question-answer session. Boring! Students are likely to "go through the motions" with as little effort as required. Add replicas of several national symbols, a poster, or study prints. Students wake up and crane their necks a little more. Now turn off the lights and shine a flashlight on the flag of the United States. Turn on a tape recorder and have the students stand as you play "The Star-Spangled Banner." Describe how Francis Scott Key saw the flag flying over a fort "in the dawn's early light" after surviving a terrible battle. Explain key terms of the national anthem that describe how Key felt about the flag and our country. Now several senses are involved in the learning activity, and students are more likely to "sink their teeth" into the content. The secret to effective social studies instruction is inviting your students to become as directly involved in the learning experience as possible.

4.   *Modeling.* Modeling means directly showing or talking to students about what they should strive for in terms of a *finished product* (story, poem, model, diagram, information web, graph) or *process* (how to replicate early Egyptian artwork, write with Chinese characters, or identify the main idea of a paragraph).

Teachers often use "talk-alouds" to model steps to apply a strategy or a skill to complete a task (Baumann & Schmitt, 1986). For example, before assigning a passage from a book, a teacher might say, "Before I begin to read, I like to look at the pictures and main headings to give me a clue about what information the author might include in the story about South American folk traditions. Here is a picture of a brightly colored, handmade Ecuadorian star with a caption that says it is used as a Christmas tree ornament. I thought it looked real interesting, so I decided to read the page to find out how to make one." Then the teacher asked her students to skim the pages to notice other interesting folk traditions to look for. Using this "talk-aloud," the teacher demonstrated the process for skimming an informational selection in preparation for reading. Following the reading assignment, the teacher may use the "talk-aloud" once more to demonstrate and explain the steps involved in making "Stars of Ecuador" so the children can see a model before attempting one of their own.

In the modeling portion of a Hunter plan, then, the teacher performs the task in front of the students, reflecting on her thoughts and showing what students must do to perform a task.

Expository procedures place the teacher in the role of helping children relate one observation to another, to move from fact to concept and toward broader meaning.

5.   *Checking for understanding.* Teachers must constantly observe students to determine whether or not they understand or exhibit the skills targeted in the lesson objectives. Hunter believes that teachers waste a great deal of time with poor attempts at judging students' performance. The most common wasted effort is the teacher's ubiquitous "Okay?" assuming that a resulting silence indicates understanding: "The Himalayan and Hindu Kush mountain ranges separate India from the rest of Asia. That is why geographers call India a subcontinent, okay?" Such misguided attempts to check on student understanding often result in a teacher marching blissfully through the lesson unaware that some students are lost. To more effectively check on student progress, Hunter recommends that teachers employ (1) *signaled answers* ("Thumbs up if you understand what I've said, down if you don't." "Raise your hand if you know the answer to the question." "Hold up a question mark card if you do not understand."); (2) *choral responses* ("Tell me the name of the country geographers refer to as a subcontinent."); (3) *sample individual responses* (if a "bright" student does not understand, the rest of the class is likely to be confused, too; conversely, if a "slower" student responds correctly, the rest of the class is probably ready to move on); and (4) *sample written or oral responses* (brief statements in which students explain what they have been learning).

Such feedback offers teachers immediate information about whether instruction must be adjusted or whether the material needs to be retaught.

6.   *Guided practice.* During this phase of a Hunter lesson, teachers must circulate among the children to make sure that their instruction has "taken." The student must demonstrate a minimum level of performance (see Objectives); otherwise, clarification or remediation is offered. In this way, teachers are assured that students understand the

material or can perform a task satisfactorily before working by themselves. For example, a teacher demonstrates the use of a map scale while computing distances between points on a map *(modeling)*. After three examples, he asks, "What have I done to figure out the distance between two points on our map?" *(checking for understanding)*. Satisfied that his students are ready to move on, the teacher writes three pairs of locations on the chalkboard and instructs the students to figure out the distances between them. The students practice at their desks as the teacher circulates among them *(guided practice)*. As he circulates, the teacher asks questions and makes comments such as, "How did you get this answer?" "Tell me how you figured out the distance." "It looks like you understand how to use the map scale."

7.   *Independent practice.* Once students demonstrate that they can perform without major errors or confusion, they are ready to strive for fluency by practicing by themselves. To carry our example above one step further, the teacher would assign additional problems to be done as independent practice. In this way, students are free from the control of the teacher as they try out what they have been learning.

Slavin (1987) has examined the Hunter model and comments that, despite its widespread popularity, there is little originality in her approach:

> Certainly, these elements of lesson design are hardly unique to Madeline Hunter. Many learning theorists call for a comparable sequence of activities. Besides, good teachers have used similar lessons ever since the first teacher had to teach more than one student at a time! That is, if asked, *What do you think you should do in an outstanding lesson?,* most teachers would give these steps never having heard of Madeline Hunter. (p. 57)

Slavin's comments help us understand that successful teachers follow established frameworks of instructional design, but that "teachers should be free to use their own creativity. Creative people have tremendous specific knowledge [and build] that specific knowledge into a professional launching pad from which creativity can really soar" (Slavin, 1987, p. 60).

Simply "knowing" the seven steps in planning for effective instruction will not guarantee that you will be able to "artfully" implement the Hunter strategy. Conversely, simply having an artful knack of working with children will not ensure that the elements of sound, professional planning will be carried out in the classroom. Both the "science" and the "art" of teaching are essential for effective social studies instruction. If that occurs, students and teachers are involved in learning together, and the learning-teaching process is action based.

Inquiry Procedures

While operating in the expository mode, teachers direct the children's learning, making sure that a prescribed curriculum is covered and that the children have mastered it. The problem solving/inquiry mode, on the other hand, involves the children in establishing the direction for their learning—asking questions and searching for information. Problem solving and inquiry can take many forms, but the most commonly used format is the five-step process introduced by John Dewey (1933) nearly a century ago:

1. Define the problem.
2. Propose a tentative explanation, or hypothesis.
3. Collect data.
4. Evaluate the data.
5. Form conclusions.

The overall goal of discovery/inquiry learning continues to be that of helping students learn how to ask questions, seek answers or solutions independently, and build their own ideas about the world. Problem solving and inquiry are dealt with comprehensively in Chapter 6, so we will not explore the topic in depth at this point. However, for sake of illustration, this sample "procedure" section from a lesson plan for second graders is offered:

> *Background:* Show the children a stone. Ask them, "Do you think someone can make soup from a stone?" Read the book *Stone Soup* by Marcia Brown (Scribner). The students will enjoy finding out how the stone helped make a pot of delicious soup. Encourage conversation about soup.
>
> 1. *Pose the question/problem:* Invite the children to name some of their favorite soups and describe what they taste like. Then ask, "I wonder what our class's favorite soup might be."
> 2. *Hypothesize.* Invite the children to offer "hunches" or "educated guesses" in response to the question. Record an appropriate number of choices on a graph, as shown in Figure 3–2.
> 3. *Gather data.* Invite the children to color in squares on the graph, indicating which soup they prefer most.
> 4. *Analyze the data.* Total the results and determine which soup was the most popular, least popular, and so on.
> 5. *Form conclusions.* Discuss reasons why a particular soup was voted most popular by the class. Would these results hold up in another second-grade classroom?

The sample procedure section of a problem-solving lesson plan that you have just read demonstrates how the problem-solving process might be approached systematically. The goals of such early experiences are to offer practice in using problem-solving processes and to heighten the children's awareness of the possibilities for conducting inquiries into spontaneous problems that intrigue the class (see Chapter 6 for a discussion of this sophisticated process, which is not always guided by a lesson plan). All in all, the major purpose for problem solving/inquiry is learning how to learn—an indispensable component of lifelong learning.

Which form of instruction is most appropriate for social studies education? Jarolimek and Foster (1997) offer this sage advice:

FIGURE 3-2
"Our Favorite Soup" Graph

Because of the overuse of expository strategies, serious efforts have been made to redress the balance in favor of inquiry. In this process, the contrast between the two
modes of teaching is often overdrawn. Exposition is associated with the worst practices
in teaching: an unimaginative use of textbooks, rigidity, an emphasis on factual learning
and memorization, the misuse of lecture methods, and so on. In contrast, inquiry is

associated with all that is good in teaching: a warm and friendly teacher, flexibility, a concern about higher-level thought processes, and highly motivated learners searching out data to test hypotheses that they themselves have proposed. Such exaggerated criticisms of exposition and acclaim for inquiry actually misrepresent both modes of teaching. The expository mode is often not as bad as is suggested. Similarly, the inquiry mode is not necessarily as productive in terms of measured student achievement as its most enthusiastic supporters would have us believe. (p. 148)

Teaching in the expository mode can engage children in highly productive learning experiences; likewise, problem solving/inquiry is a valued strategy because it encourages students to explore broadly while searching for their own information. There appears to be no clear-cut superiority of one mode over the other; each has its own strengths and limitations. Furthermore, if we consider exposition and problem solving/inquiry strategies at opposite ends of a methodology curriculum, there are dozens of points in between that represent acceptable variations. In actual practice, then, you will be able to choose from a multitude of teaching strategies, selecting the one best suited to students with wide ranges of backgrounds, abilities, and learning styles. Flexibility is the key to successful instruction; keep working throughout your career to expand your methodology arsenal. Dig into the knowledge and past experiences of your professor for interesting ideas; solicit suggestions from your cooperating teacher in the field for activities and materials that worked for him or her; search through professional magazines and journals for current suggestions (photocopy or clip out the best ideas). Work toward developing a style that opens new vistas for all your students, changing the way they view themselves and the world.

ASSESSMENT

Was the lesson successful? How well did the students accomplish what I had planned for them to learn? Is there a system by which I can judge the effectiveness of a lesson? This section of the lesson plan addresses these questions; the assessment component deals with how well the students are learning and how well the teacher is teaching. As Kellough (1997) states, "To learn effectively, students need to know how they are doing. Similarly, to be an effective teacher, you must be informed about what the student knows, feels, and can do so that you can help the student build on her or his skills, knowledge, and attitudes" (p. 421).

Before we enter into a discussion of judging whether students are achieving satisfactorily, we must clarify two terms associated with that process—*assessment* and *evaluation*. Although these terms are used interchangeably by many educators today while referring to the extent to which targeted objectives have been reached, there is a distinction some insist must be made. In the exacting sense, *assessment* refers to the *process* of gathering data that will be used to make judgments about instruction, whereas *evaluation* is concerned with *using* the data to make the judgment. The data you gather from the assessment process helps you make evaluative decisions. Because this distinction is quite trivial, except to those who are closely aligned with the field, and because most authors use the terms interchangeably, I will use the terms *assessment* and *evaluation* synonymously in this text.

Teachers must constantly evaluate their children's work in order to determine whether or not they are advancing toward the intended instructional objectives. Such feedback assists them in planning and monitoring instruction. To accomplish this crucial responsibility, teachers commonly employ two preferred assessment strategies: (1) formative assessment and (2) summative assessment. *Formative assessment* is an ongoing process designed to guide the teacher in planning and to determine whether learning problems are emerging; *summative assessment* occurs at the end of instruction to show the teacher the level of student accomplishment. Because formative assessment occurs daily, teachers are able to quickly identify and correct problems. As deficiencies are noted, remedial work is planned; if students demonstrate effortless proficiency, the pace can be adjusted. In the elementary school, formative assessment is based on such evidence as homework, seatwork, and classroom projects.

Summative assessment occurs at the end of a unit of instruction. It is designed to summarize student achievement for grading purposes. Although most people think of testing in connection with summative assessment, social studies teachers today have many other options. In answering the question, "Is this assessment formative or summative?" Woolfolk (1995) offers this response: "The answer depends on what is done with the results. If the teacher uses the outcome to shape future teaching and 'form' instruction, then the assessment is formative. But if the results are used to determine how much the student has learned and to assign a grade or other final evaluation, then the assessment is summative because it provides a 'summary' of the student's learning" (p. 551).

Although identical assessment procedures can be used for either purpose, formative assessment normally focuses on homework, seatwork, projects, and the results of other lesson assignments. On the other hand, summative assessment is based on such cumulative devices as tests and portfolios. Because formative assessment is more closely aligned with the results of lesson activities, it will be discussed in this chapter. Summative assessment will be discussed in Chapter 4.

Authentic Formative Assessment

Although many alternative measures can be used to provide evaluative feedback, traditional decisions in elementary school classrooms have been based on tests. One type of test, the standardized achievement test, has become a particularly important index of instructional effectiveness. Standardized tests are those official-looking booklets purchased by school districts and administered to students to obtain a score that can be compared to the scores of students who will be taking the same test in school systems across the country. (Standardized achievement tests commonly administered in elementary school classrooms include the Stanford Achievement Test, California Achievement Test, Metropolitan Achievement Test, and Iowa Test of Basic Skills.) These tests are meant to measure how much the student has learned in specific content areas, including social studies. Results help teachers ascertain a student's overall strengths and weaknesses, and thus serve as a catalyst to determine what alterations, if any, should be made in the learning/teaching process.

Despite this potential for improving the educational process, standardized tests have been widely misused. For example, Livingston, Castle, and Nations (1989) describe the extraordinary pressures that have affected elementary school programs because of standardized tests:

> State-mandated standardized tests have a profound influence on the curriculum. . . . As one teacher put it, "Getting kids to perform well on the test is *the* top priority. In Georgia, test scores are published and schools and systems are compared by their scores. The message from the public, policy-makers, and the central administration has been to raise test scores. In short, the test actually is the foundation of our curriculum." (p. 24)

Lee (1992) adds that "students develop resentment, anxiety and mistrust of standardized achievement tests. In addition, low achievers reduce test anxiety and protect self-esteem by not making a serious effort to succeed on the test" (p. 72). Similar criticism of standardized achievement testing has mushroomed massively throughout the 1990s. The National Association for the Education of Young Children (NAEYC, 1988) has forcefully denounced the use of standardized tests with children through the primary grades. Other professional organizations have followed suit, including The Association for Childhood Education International (1991), which has published a position paper disapproving the use of standardized tests in the early grades. Lee (1992) summarizes the most common criticisms of standardized achievement tests expressed by various professional groups:

- Test items tend to focus on rote memorization.
- Tests do not accurately reflect students' abilities.
- Test items are not associated with real-life experience.
- Tests do not measure higher-order thinking skills. (p. 72)

Despite the fact that some groups are working to increase the role of standardized testing, even to the point of developing a national examination, most are advocating a cutback in their use (Madaus & Kellaghan, 1993). In their search for alternatives, educators now advocate the use of "authentic assessment." Proponents of authentic assessment suggest that children's learning must be demonstrated in situations that address three criteria (Stiggins, 1994): (1) students must apply knowledge they have acquired, (2) students must complete a clearly specified task within the context of either a real or simulated exercise, and (3) the task or completed product must be observed and rated in accordance with specified criteria. Instead of recalling information from rote memory, authentic assessment is based on major sources of information: real-life tasks and teachers' observation. Because we are considering formative assessment in this chapter, I will use the term *authentic formative assessment* to describe the process by which teachers obtain feedback about how well the children are learning.

Authentic formative assessment places students into situations where they must do something, make something, offer solutions to problems, or compose a critical response to an issue. It assumes that there is much more to learning than being good at recalling facts; students must try to become good at personalizing the information. Wiggins (1992) explains:

> Most tests, most forms of assessment, are not authentic representations of subject matter challenges. They are more like checkup test and quizzes and drills. An "authentic" assessment is one that would be much more a simulation or representation or replication of the kinds of challenges that face professionals or citizens when they need to do something with their knowledge. Most people, once they leave school, never have anything to do with multiple-choice tests in history. Their use of history has to do with doing research and making a presentation to the board or the Rotary or their firm. The whole idea of secret, secure tests in which you try to figure out what's going to be on the test and then you hope you guess right—all of that is quite unauthentic. We've come to use tests simply as an expedient to check up on whether kids mastered some facts, but it has nothing to do with the authentic act of mastering historical analysis and information. (p. 92)

The use of authentic formative assessment should not suggest that students need not master basic component knowledge or skills; these are necessary, but as integral aspects of an experience rather than as memorized, isolated facts. For this reason, the assessment exercise closely resembles the behavior targeted in the objective as the desired learning outcome. Authentic assessment can often be carried out while using typical learning tasks—written products, demonstrations, group projects, integrated art and music activities, construction projects, dramatizations, museum displays, and so on.

In current practice, authentic formative assessment might involve analyzing essential and nonessential items to take westward in a covered wagon, on a simulated trip along the Oregon Trail. Content comes in as the students dig deeply into their task, and teachers accept answers the children are able to substantiate. Suppose, for example, a child selects these five items to take westward on the simulated trip: food, water, animal feed, guns, and blankets. She justifies her choices by writing that without food and water, people would die. Without animal feed, the pack animals would perish. Travelers would need guns for protection and for hunting animals, and would need blankets for warmth at night. You would consider her response to be appropriate, even though other students' answers differ; they may have selected axes to clear the trees, pots and pans to cook the food, extra wagon wheels in case of an accident, or other things. Their choices are appropriate, too, because they indicate basic knowledge of the items typically taken in a covered wagon. To limit our evaluation by asking for one specific list decontextualizes the learning. Instead, we must connect the content to the complexities of the time or place—to have the students interpret and assess the available knowledge for the purpose of defending a choice. Herman (1992) refers to authentic formative assessment as *good assessment*. She elaborates:

> According to cognitive researchers, meaningful learning is reflective, constructive, and self-regulated. . . . To *know* something is not just to have received information but to have interpreted it and related it to knowledge one already has. . . . For example,

research suggests that poor thinkers and problem solvers differ from good ones not so much in the skills they possess as in their failure to use them in certain tasks. Competent thinkers or problem solvers also possess the disposition to use the skills and strategies as well as the knowledge of when to apply them. (p. 75)

Social studies educators frequently argue that the primary mission of social studies instruction—producing students who are able to think for themselves—is contradicted by standard fill-in-the-blank, multiple-choice, or true-false tests requiring specific answers. A major goal of authentic formative assessment is to better assess what social studies educators value.

Perceived mismatches between information asked for on tests and the kinds of learnings we strive for in social studies classrooms have presented problems for teachers. Some agonize, "I really want my students to be active learners, but they have to do well on the test. There's so little time left for creative teaching." Some see performance assessment as a solution to this problem because the assessment procedures replicate classroom activities.

Contexts for Authentic Formative Assessment

The first step of planning authentic formative assessment tasks is to specify specific objectives for instruction. This means being very clear about the skills, behaviors, understandings, and attitudes the students are to learn and you are to teach ("What do we want students to know and be able to do?").

Once you have determined the instructional objectives and carried through the learning experience, you must devise a context for assessment. For example, the way to find out if Lamont can meet the targeted behavior of reciting by heart the Pledge of Allegiance is to have him recite it. So, if a lesson objective is to teach children to recite the Pledge of Allegiance, then asking them to recite it is an appropriate assessment strategy. On the other hand, if you want to determine whether Belinda understands what life as an early pioneer would have been like, it may be appropriate to have her write a creative piece about challenges facing the early pioneers—perhaps a letter to a friend in England telling what she usually does during the day.

Much authentic formative assessment is, at least in part, similar to regular classroom activities; games, oral reports, creative dramatics, debates, art projects, or writing tasks. By gathering evaluative information from situations and contexts similar to those in which students normally learn, their assessment may be more meaningful to you, to them, and to their families.

Criteria for Authentic Formative Assessment

The second step of authentic formative assessment is to determine precisely what criteria you will consider acceptable. Suppose you create this context for performance: "Imagine that you were a Pilgrim who sailed to Plymouth on the *Mayflower*. Write a letter to a friend in England describing the special challenges you faced during your first year in the new homeland." The goal of this assessment situation is to measure the students' understanding of the hardships of the Pilgrims' first winter in

Authentic assessment is based on evidence teachers gather from the actual learning experience. This child, dressed as an endangered animal, displays the results of her research.

Plymouth, so you must first establish criteria for measuring that understanding. That is, you would expect students to express in the letter ideas similar to the following:

- As the Pilgrims arrived in Plymouth, winter began.
- They did not have enough stored food.
- There were few animals to hunt in the winter.
- The cold weather destroyed any wild berries or other edible plants that grew in the area.
- The Pilgrims had no time to build comfortable shelters.

This task is important because the criteria form your basis for assessment—your expectations may be that every student must address in their letters the five main ideas listed. With such definitive guidance, you can be more consistent when judging the relative effectiveness of students' efforts. Otherwise, for example, you could become so engrossed with a student's sensitive description of the hardships associated with the Pilgrims' lack of food that you fail to notice that he failed to include anything about shelters or the weather. Criterion lists furnish you with a set of standards that help focus assessment on the entire response rather than on any particular components. But, because authentic formative assessment requires students to personalize the way they present the information, end results must not all look alike, as they normally do on traditional tests. This does not mean, however, that students need not include accurate facts and information as they formulate their product. Should a student's letter, for example, discuss the presence of refrigeration or telephones, it would reveal problematical links to the historical period. In contrast, references to preserving meats by salting or smoking and grinding corn into meal would indicate a student's correct historical perspective.

Documents such as the *Curriculum Standards for Social Studies: Expectations of Excellence* (NCSS, 1994) serve as highly useful sources of criteria for authentic assessment. For example, Maria Foseide's sixth-grade students were engaged in a unit designed to promote the following performance expectations:

> Standard V: Individuals, Groups, & Institutions
>   Social studies programs should include experiences that provide for the study of *interactions among individuals, groups, and institutions,* so that the learner can:
>   Performance Expectations
>   a. demonstrate an understanding of concepts such as role, status, and social class in describing the interactions of individuals and social groups;
>   b. analyze group and institutional influences on people, events, and elements of culture; . . .
>   f. describe the role of institutions in furthering both continuity and change. (p. 91)

To achieve these expectations, Foseide's class had been examining current events with respect to the roles various institutions (religious, social, and political) play in the decisions and actions of individuals, groups, and nations. Having familiarized her students with political cartoons throughout the school year, Foseide had her students create political cartoons that reflected the role that any institution played in the decision of a selected individual, group, or nation. Ability to accurately identify the role of the institution in the event and the quality of presentation in the cartoon format served as the criteria for assessing understanding.

What to Do With the Results

The third step of authentic formative assessment deals with the issue of what to do with the results. As Wassermann (1991) advises, "Diagnosis goes beyond the simple determination of value (good/bad, right/wrong) to point out how the performance meets or fails to meet each criterion. A teacher's diagnosis points to what the student must do to improve his/her subsequent learning" (p. 93). In contrast to testing techniques that often seem to search for deficiencies in learning, diagnosis helps determine the students' areas of strength, as well as what must be done to improve subsequent learning. For example, assessment may indicate that Eugenia has difficulty keeping events in proper chronological perspective; therefore, to boost this skill, you could ask her to use a timeline to summarize the Pilgrims' experiences in the first year at Plymouth.

Wassermann (1991, p. 96) presents this outline to summarize how diagnosis fits into the entire authentic formative assessment process:

- be clear about the criteria used to make the judgments
- make the criteria clear to the learner

- use the criteria to write clear and specific comments to the learner that point out how different facets of the work meet or fail to meet the criteria
- think about ways of suggesting how the learner might take the next steps to improve his/her work on the task and be specific about those suggestions
- be selective in pointing out what is more important, rather than overwhelming the learner by attempting to deal with every aspect of the performance that requires improvement.

The skills to carry out authentic formative assessment are not easy to acquire. They involve a great deal of time, effort, and mental processing. And, because related evaluative judgments are deeply personal, you must be careful to be fair—it is important to establish specific criteria and clear standards of expectation. But, like any other sophisticated professional ability, experience and effort will combine to improve your skills in this complicated process. As you find your teaching style in the social studies, you will also need to key in these new evaluative strategies used to assess student learning. Today's teachers are learning to look more and more at student performance while making decisions about educational growth and needs. To use the process effectively, they must be convinced that authentic and enabling evaluation is an important part of social studies education. Otherwise, authentic formative assessment will join the long parade of educational fads that march off into the night.

Teacher Observations

Some contexts for authentic formative assessment, then, entail the student's actual work samples, but another major category includes *observations of students at work*. Teachers who use authentic formative assessment consistently observe students as they interact with curriculum materials, other students, and adults. They observe, but realize that their observations cannot be done in a hit-or-miss fashion. To get the most from an observational experience, teachers must know specifically what they are looking for and then organize their observations systematically.

Descriptive Reports

The most widely used observational technique in elementary school classrooms is the descriptive report, in which teachers target a specific behavior and record specific episodes in which a student demonstrates that behavior. Specifically, the observer's role is to do the following:

- Record all basic information (child's name, age, and gender).
- Describe the setting.
- Observe the behavior of the child and the behaviors of those who interact with the child.
- Report only the facts. Stay away from interpretive judgments ("Arnie's home life will cause him problems in the future") and evaluative terms such as *angry, sad, smart,* or *slow.*

- Organize all events in chronological order.
- Limit observations to brief episodes, usually five to ten minutes.

Writing a descriptive report may look easy, but observers making their first attempt soon learn otherwise. They are frequently tempted by interpretive statements as they describe their observations: "The child is a disinterested learner," "The teacher was insensitive," or "The child thought . . ." While these explanations may be accurate, they do not reflect *observable behaviors*. Good observers learn to separate behaviors (the child identified 50 percent of the state capitals) from the inference (Carl didn't study for the quiz). A sample descriptive report is shown in Figure 3–3. Notice how it avoids inferences and provides clear, concise behavioral descriptions. The descriptive report is an excellent assessment tool, but it takes great concentration and repeated practice before it can be mastered.

Your observations start with questions. Suppose that Brit is a highly inquisitive youngster who pursues learning for the pleasure it brings. You need to know what his interests are, how long he attends to tasks, and other key information. Therefore, you write down your observations for several days and then summarize your impressions: "I believe Brit learns best when he finds things out for himself. I will have to take time to help Brit ask questions and search for information." Such careful observations provide solid guidance as you attempt to determine where the child is and what learning experiences might be most appropriate. A critical professional challenge is to know how to interpret what you are watching. Phinney (1982) explains:

> The ability to understand children through observation might be compared to the ability to judge fine art. We all respond to art—positively, negatively, indifferently—but the person with experience and training can better assess the aesthetic value of a work of art. Similarly, we all form impressions of children, but for the inexperienced observer, the impressions may

FIGURE 3–3
A Descriptive Report

October 23

Brit (boy, age 7) is sitting alone looking intently at a globe. He spins the globe a few times and points to water and land masses each time the globe stops. He gets a toy airplane and "flies" it from land mass to land mass, not naming any of the places he stopped. Brit appears to have developed a budding interest in learning about maps.

be inaccurate, biased, or limited in scope. As we gain more skills and experience, we know better how to look at children, what to look for, and how to interpret what we see. (p. 18)

Your impressions of student achievement are important, but they must be based on solid evidence; observations are part of the evidence that helps you interpret behaviors that guide your decisions about classroom instruction.

Checklists

Because of time constraints, many teachers find it more convenient to use checklists for observational purposes. Checklists are particularly helpful when you wish to assess the degree to which students have demonstrated specific skills, behaviors, or competencies. To determine these, you must first enumerate the specific characteristics to be observed, and then record the occurrence of each. A sample checklist of behaviors considered important for cooperative learning is shown in Figure 3–4.

Rubrics

Some authentic assessment systems contain very specific, detailed descriptions of the criteria for student performance. Teachers evaluate students with these systems by comparing their work to a set of guidelines called *rubrics*. For example, a teacher reads a written report and assigns it a score from 0 to 3. The following scale (rubric) may give you a sense of how this system is used to assess the written reports.

3   The written report is complete. It clearly communicates the content, provides accurate and relevant details, and allows the reader to grasp the writer's message easily.

FIGURE 3–4
Checklist of Cooperative Learning Skills

	Sometimes Present	Mastered
Assists co-workers when needed		
Follows group-established rules		
Does fair share of group work		
Respects group decisions		
Shares materials willingly		

Directions:

( )   Place a check in the "Sometimes Present" column if the characteristic is occasionally observed.

(+)   Place a plus in the "Mastered" column if the characteristic occurs habitually.

( )   Make no mark if the characteristic is observed seldom or not at all.

2   The written report is partial, but is fairly well organized. Although the information selected includes mostly accurate details and ideas, some confusion is encountered from time to time.

1   The written report is sketchy, inconsistent, and incomplete. It includes many random details not organized into cohesive statements, or contains a number of irrelevant or erroneous ideas. The reader has no idea about what the writer is trying to say.

0   There is little or no written material, or it is illegible.

The assessment section closes our discussion of lesson planning in social studies. You should reread this chapter carefully, for all beginning teachers must be able to write considerably detailed, carefully structured lesson plans. A completed sample is illustrated in Activity 3–2. Naturally, writing lesson plans will require a great deal of effort. You will dream of raiding the file cabinets of more experienced colleagues whose lessons seem to be so exciting and motivational; they just seem to inspire students to learn. But even experienced teachers need fresh ideas that incorporate new trends in education.

Activity 3–2

Lesson Plan

Theme: The Pharaohs of Egypt
Grade: Five
Teacher: Alex Virdon

General Objective
The students will research the lives of Egyptian pharaohs.

Specific Objectives
1. The students shall locate information about a pharaoh's life and achievements.
2. The students shall prepare a first-person report and group presentation about a pharaoh's life.
3. The students shall arrange pharaohs chronologically along a class timeline.

Materials
1. Multiple copies of the following trade books:
   • Allan, Tony. *The Time Traveler Book of Pharaohs and Pyramids*
   • Carter, Dorothy. *His Majesty, Queen Hatshepsut*

- Courtalon, Corinne. *On the Banks of the Pharaoh's Nile*
- Harris, Geraldine. *Gods and Pharaohs From Egyptian Mythology.*
- Lauber, Patricia. *Tales Mummies Tell.*
- McGraw, Eloise. *Mara, Daughter of the Nile*
- Sethus, Michael. *The Days of the Pharaohs*

2. Research outline (see attached sample).
3. Class time line.

Procedure

1. Display a small model of a pharaoh's coffin. Ask the students to speculate on the purpose of this elaborate coffin.
2. Explain that ancient Egyptians devised elaborate burial rituals and built huge pyramids to house and protect the remains of pharaohs. The pharaohs were very important; worshipped as gods, these mighty rulers waged wars, made alliances, and regulated the economy.
3. Divide the class into six groups of four students each.
4. Give each group a different book, making sure that each student in a group has a copy of the assigned book.
5. Students read their books to find information about a pharaoh's life and achievements.
6. Students use the research outline to summarize the information from their books.
7. Using the research outline, students prepare a group written report on their pharaoh's life.
8. Each group makes props to represent important milestones in its pharaoh's life.
9. Start with the earliest ruler and, in chronological order, have each group present its pharaoh's life story to the class.
10. Add each ruler to a class timeline.

Assessment

1. Observe the students during the research phase to see if any special help is required.
2. Check to see if each research outline has been completed accurately.
3. Use a scoring rubric to assess the quality of the written reports.
4. Observe the group presentations to assess whether the life stories were presented accurately and creatively.
5. Examine the timelines for accuracy and appeal.

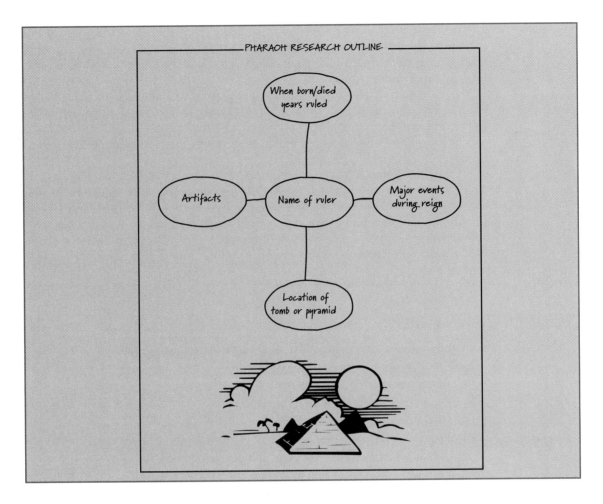

Lesson planning, either formal or informal, is a continual process for everyone, for there is a constant need to keep materials, activities, and techniques up to date. You will work hard to develop a rich teaching repertoire and will find it difficult to wait ten years to fill a drawer in your file cabinet. Inspiration can be found in magazines and journals, but ready-made file cabinets—virtual file cabinets—are out there on the Internet, free for the taking. So, as you dive into the planning process, examine the many planning sites that are popping up regularly. See the Technology Sampler to explore some of the virtual file cabinets and links available at the time of this writing.

AFTERWORD

A good social studies teacher has an album full of clear professional portraits in her mind. Each illustrates a teacher involved in a different mode of instruction. Some modes are new and revolutionary; others are old and time-tested. The skilled social studies teacher is in command of all of these methods and understands that the key to effective instruction is balance and flexibility. She or he also realizes that not everyone can teach elementary school social studies; those who can possess a set of sophisticated skills that stretch each child's mind with meaningful and purposeful learning experiences.

The most important ingredient of a good social studies program is a skilled teacher. The physical setting is important, of course, and so are all the arresting activities and materials. However, a poor teacher exploits these for minimal stimulation and response while the outstanding teacher sets the classroom on fire (figuratively!).

Harriet Paul Jonquiere, former New York State Teacher of the Year, emphasized the need for every beginning teacher to create the teaching skills needed to "set the classroom on fire" by formulating a personalized approach to instruction replete with appropriate and purposeful experiences for all children. To that end, Ms. Jonquiere penned a letter she hoped would be read by every new teacher (see Figure 3–5). Please read it and use it as encouragement for professional growth throughout your career.

TECHNOLOGY SAMPLER

Some useful sources for lesson planning include these Internet sites:

AskERIC Virtual Library of Lesson Plans
http://ericir.syr.edu/Virtual/Lessons/

Busy Teacher's Web Site K–12
http://www.ceismc.gatech.edu/BUSYT

CNN Newsroom Daily Lesson Plans
http://snow-white.gac.peachnet.edu/gather/curric/cnndaily.html

Pitsco's Launch to Lesson Plans
http://www.pitsco.com/p/lesson.html

Tools for teachers: lessons, advice, and great links
http://www.teachnet.com/lesson.html

FIGURE 3–5
Advice for New Teachers

Dear New Colleague:

Congratulations on your appointment! I know your first year of teaching will be wonderful. You have my best wishes for a long and exciting career in education.

I do not want your classroom to look like mine. I do not want to tell you to order certain materials because new and better things come on the market every day. I do not want you to copy my lesson plans. Research continually informs us of more effective ways to enable students' learning. You bring your own special talents and personality to enrich the lives of children.

I do want you to look back. Revisit those special moments in your own education that gave you hope or encouragement or insight. Use them as starting points in developing your own ways of relating to youngsters.

Look around you. Watch your students. Listen to them. Let them teach you what helps them grow. Watch your fellow teachers. Never be afraid to ask a question. Children benefit from our pooled strengths.

Finally, look within yourself. Give yourself time and opportunity to pull together and integrate all you know and feel about teaching and learning. Develop your own personal philosophy of education. Then, you will be a blessing to your students and their families, and you will be a guide and source of inspiration for the rest of us in the field.

Sincerely yours,

Harriet Paul Jonquiere

Source: Jonquiere, H.P. (1990), My beliefs about teaching. *Childhood Education, 66,* 291–292. Used with permission.

WHAT I *NOW* KNOW

Complete these self-check items once more. Determine for yourself whether it would be useful to take a more in-depth look at any area. Use the same key as you did for the preassessment form ("+", "?", "-").

I can *now*

_____ explain the factors involved in planning an effective social studies lesson.

_____ describe the values of deliberate planning in social studies.

_____ outline the critical components of lesson plans.

_____ distinguish between goals and objectives.

_____ detail the importance of clearly stated instructional objectives.

_____ write clearly stated behavioral and nonbehavioral objectives.

_____ account for varied skills and abilities in the way I state instructional objectives.

_____ select methods and materials appropriate for carrying out the stated objectives.

_____ understand the need to exercise flexibility in selecting instructional procedures.

_____ distinguish between expository and problem-solving procedures.

_____ logically organize and communicate the procedures component of a lesson plan.

_____ utilize appropriate assessment strategies while evaluating the outcomes of a lesson.

REFERENCES

Association for Childhood Education International (1991). On standardized testing. *Childhood Education, 67,* 131–142.

Baumann, J. F., & Schmitt, M. C. (1986). The what, why, how, and when of comprehension instruction. *The Reading Teacher, 39,* 640–647.

Bloom, B. S., Engelhart, M. D., Furst, E. J., Hill, W. H., & Krathwohl, D. R. (1956). *Taxonomy of educational objectives: Cognitive domain.* New York: Longman.

Dewey, J. (1933). *How we think.* Lexington, MA: D. C. Heath.

Eby, J. W. (1997). *Reflective planning, teaching, and evaluation for the elementary school.* Upper Saddle River, NJ: Prentice Hall.

Eisner, E. (1985). *Educational imagination.* Upper Saddle River, NJ: Prentice Hall.

Gronlund, N. (1991). *How to write and use instructional objectives.* New York: Macmillan.

Herman, J. L. (1992). What research tells us about good assessment. *Educational Leadership, 49,* 75.

Hunter, M. (1982). *Mastery teaching.* El Segundo, CA: TIP Publications.

Jacobsen, D., Eggen, P., & Kauchak, D. (1993). *Methods for teaching: A skills approach.* Upper Saddle River, NJ: Prentice Hall.

Jarolimek, J., & Foster, C. D., Sr. (1997). *Teaching and learning in the elementary school.* Upper Saddle River, NJ: Prentice Hall.

Jonquiere, H. P. (1990). My beliefs about teaching. *Childhood Education, 66,* 291–292.

Kellough, R. D. (1997). *A resource guide for teaching: K–12.* Upper Saddle River, NJ: Prentice Hall.

Lee, F. Y. (1992). Alternative assessments. *Childhood Education, 69,* 72–73.

Livingston, C., Castle, S., & Nations, J. (1989). Testing and curriculum reform: One school's experience. *Educational Leadership, 46,* 24.

Lortie, D. (1975). *Schoolteacher.* Chicago: University of Chicago Press.

Madaus, G. F., & Kellaghan, T. (1993). Testing as a mechanism of public policy: A brief history. *Measurement and Evaluation in Counseling and Development, 26,* 6–10.

Mager, R. (1962). *Preparing instructional objectives.* Belmont, CA: Fearon.

National Association for the Education of Young Children (1988). Position statement on standardized testing of young children 3 through 8 years of age. *Young Children, 43,* 42–47.

National Council for the Social Studies (1984). Standards for the preparation of social studies teachers. *Social Education, 52,* 11.

National Council for the Social Studies (1994). *Curriculum standards for social studies: Expectations of excellence.* (Bulletin 89). Washington, DC: National Council for the Social Studies.

Orlich, D. C., Harder, R. J., Callahan, R.C., Kauchak, D. P., Pendergrass, R. A., Keogh, A. J., & Gibson, H. (1990). *Teaching strategies: A guide to better instruction.* Lexington, MA: D. C. Heath.

Phinney, J. S. (1982). Observing children: Ideas for teachers. *Young Children, 37,* 16–24.

Postman, N., & Weingartner, C. (1974). In N. Harmin & T. Gregory (Eds.), *Teaching is.* . . . Chicago: Science Research Associates.

Slavin, R. (1987). The Hunterization of America's schools. *Instructor, 35,* 57–60.

Stiggins, R. J. (1994). *Student-centered classroom assessment.* New York: Merrill/Macmillan, 1994.

Wasserman, S. (1991). What's evaluation for? *Childhood Education, 68,* 93–96.

Wiggins, G. (1992). Doing the stuff of social studies: A conversation with Grant Wiggins. *Social Education, 56,* 92.

Woolfolk, A. E. (1995). *Educational Psychology.* Needham Heights, MA: Allyn & Bacon.

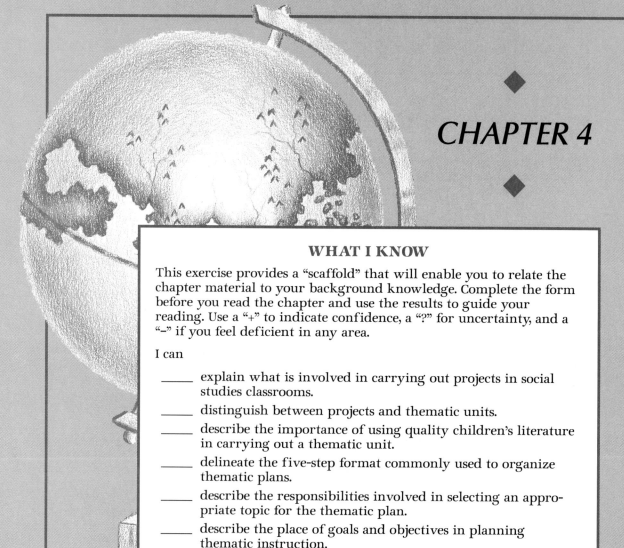

CHAPTER 4

WHAT I KNOW

This exercise provides a "scaffold" that will enable you to relate the chapter material to your background knowledge. Complete the form before you read the chapter and use the results to guide your reading. Use a "+" to indicate confidence, a "?" for uncertainty, and a "–" if you feel deficient in any area.

I can

_____ explain what is involved in carrying out projects in social studies classrooms.

_____ distinguish between projects and thematic units.

_____ describe the importance of using quality children's literature in carrying out a thematic unit.

_____ delineate the five-step format commonly used to organize thematic plans.

_____ describe the responsibilities involved in selecting an appropriate topic for the thematic plan.

_____ describe the place of goals and objectives in planning thematic instruction.

_____ explain how the content is selected and organized in thematic plans.

_____ explain how to choose and sequence learning experiences within the framework of a thematic plan.

_____ select assessment strategies appropriate for evaluating teaching and learning.

Using the results as a guide, what questions will you seek to answer as you read?

CHAPTER 4
Planning Themes and Projects

◆ **CLASSROOM SKETCH**

Mr. Grant put together a classroom interest center, above which hung a large banner bearing the word *Kwanzaa*. The table was covered by a green tablecloth, one of the colors of the African American flag (the others are red and black). On the tablecloth was placed a *mkeke* (m-KAY-kah), or mat of straw used in Kwanzaa celebrations; a *kinara* (kee-NAH-rah), or candleholder supporting the *mishumaa saba* (mee-shoo-MAH-ah SAH-bah), or seven candles representing the seven Kwanzaa principles; a *mazao* (mah-ZAH-oh), or fruits of the harvest—corn, grapes, bananas, apples, and pears—usually placed in a basket; a *dashiki* (de-SHE-ke), or traditional shirt for African men; a *gele* (GAY-lay), or woman's traditional headwrap; a *kikombe cha umoja* (kee-KOOM-bay CHA oo-MO-jah), a communal unity cup; and a thumb piano (a musical instrument popular in many African nations). After exploring the items on the table, Mr. Grant brought the children together and read the book *The Gifts of Kwanzaa* by Synthia Saint James

(Albert Whitman). Afterward, he led a discussion of the story, focusing on the relationship between the items on the table and the experiences of the people in the book, as well as on similarities and differences between Kwanzaa and other traditional winter celebrations.

On succeeding days, Mr. Grant offered these learning experiences:

• Mr. Grant arranged candles on a kinara so that a black candle was in the middle, red candles on the left, and green on the right. Each day, he lit a candle and discussed with the children the associated principle of Kwanzaa: *umoja* (oo-MO-juh), unity; *kugichagulia* (koo-jee-chah-goo-LEE-ah), self-determination; *ujima* (oo-JEE-mah), collective work; *ujamaa* (oo-jah-MAH-ah), cooperative economics; *nia* (NEE-ah), purpose; *kuumba* (koo-OOM-bah), creativity; and *imani* (ee-MAH-nee), faith. The candles were lit in this order: black, red, green, red, green, red, green.

• Mr. Grant invited parents, grandparents, and members of the community into the classroom to share a family photo album or some valued articles that were passed down from generation to generation. And, since music, song, and dance are important to the celebration of Kwanzaa, some guests were able to demonstrate a thumb piano, conga drum, and other instruments with African or African American roots.

• Mr. Grant showed the children examples of beads that were worn by Africans for decoration, ceremonies, and religious purposes. Mr. Grant explained that in some tribes, the patterns or colors of strings of beads could carry very special meaning. White often meant love, red represented anger, yellow indicated wealth, blue denoted going away, and pink symbolized poverty. The children strung their own colored wooden beads that were worn during Kwanzaa week and others that were to be given as gifts during the classroom's Kwanzaa festival.

• The class played the West African tag game called "Snake" *(Da Ga)*. To play the game, Mr. Grant marked off an area about 10 feet square, which served as the *Home of the Snake.* A student was selected to be the Snake. The Snake started out from "Home" to catch another child by tagging him or her. When that child was caught, the two held hands and went about catching other children, using their two free hands. The snake gradually got longer and longer as more and more children were caught. Whenever the snake broke, it was to return to "Home," and a new Snake started out to catch its victims. (If children became frustrated by this rule, Mr. Grant simply had them reattach themselves.) The game ended when all players were caught and became part of the Snake.

- Mr. Grant taught the children songs from West Africa with a recording called *Multicultural Rhythm Stick Fun* (Kimbo). The children listened to the rhythmic melody and responded to the simple directions with rhythm sticks.

- The class tried the traditional African art of tie-dye. Among the many ways to tie-dye, Mr. Grant selected the simplest—he took cotton fabric, had the children use rubber bands and string to bind sections of the fabric, and immersed it in dye. (Gathering fabric around small objects—pebbles, beans, corks, marbles, or beads, for example—and then binding it with string will create yet another effect.) The girls tie-dyed a *gele,* a piece of cloth about 2 yards long and 15 inches wide that is wrapped and draped around a girl's head. The boys designed a *dashiki,* a long, loose, shirt worn by African men. Parent volunteers helped sew each dashiki.

- In keeping with the spirit of Kwanzaa, the children created a simple but natural "gift of the heart" for the animals near their school. (Simple but meaningful gifts are called *zawadi*—zah-WAH-dee.) They threaded popcorn and fresh cranberries on long strands of string. Then they draped the food-covered strings on a tree or bush as a holiday treat for the animals.

- The children created their own woven *mkekas.* Each child was given two 9" × 12" sheets of construction paper (red, green, or black would be most appropriate) and created a weaving sheet by folding the paper in half widthwise and, starting at the folded edge, cutting a straight line every inch, stopping about an inch before reaching the open ends of the paper. When the paper was opened up, there was a 1 inch border around it. Next, the children made weaving strips by cutting sheets of red, green, and black construction paper into 1" × 9" strips. To weave, they slid a strip *over* and then *under* the slats on the weaving sheet; then they began a second strip starting *under* and then going *over* the slats. The children kept alternating in this manner until the entire weaving sheet was filled. Then they pasted the ends to the weaving sheet (see Figure 4–1).

Mr. Grant chose to hold a Kwanzaa celebration in order to pull all the activities together, inviting the children's families to join them at school. Two large tables were placed in the center of the room and covered with the mkekas that were woven by the children. All was in place for the *karamu* (kah-RAH-mu), or feast. The boys were dressed in their dashikis; the girls were splendidly adorned in their geles.

Since the mazao is an important element of the Kwanzaa table, each child was asked to bring to school two pieces of fresh fruit and join together with their families to create a nutritious "First Fruits" salad. An unlighted kinara, a

FIGURE 4-1
Creating a Mkeka

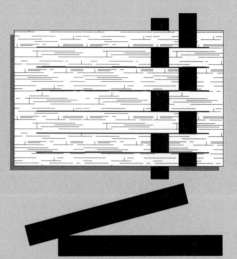

"First Fruits" salad, and one dozen ears of corn (one for each child in the home or, in our case, the classroom) were placed on each table with the mkekas. On a smaller table, the children arranged their Kwanzaa gifts—beads for a family member in attendance and the popcorn string for the birds.

The celebration began with a welcome to all and a brief explanation of Kwanzaa. Everyone received a booklet explaining the seven Kwanzaa principles; adults in attendance read the seven principles and meanings together. Then, the "First Fruits" salad and other nutritious treats were enjoyed. Following the celebration, the children performed their rhythm stick activity and played a game of Da Ga.

Sometimes a celebration of cultural diversity can bring about some very unexpected but precious outcomes. For example, while attending a Kwanzaa celebration, two African American parents found the experience to be both exciting and peaceful. After the festivities had ended and groups began to leave the school, the parents approached Mr. Grant and thanked him for the opportunity to participate in the Kwanzaa celebration. They admitted knowing very little about Kwanzaa before this experience, but that having the opportunity to join in such a meaningful way convinced them to begin celebrating Kwanzaa in their own home as a family and cultural holiday. Since the school calendar forced the class to celebrate Kwanzaa prior its normal dates, the parents had enough time to prepare for the celebration that year. Certainly, the major goal of this learning experience was to help children understand holiday traditions and be respectful of all people's customs and beliefs, but it also encouraged quality lifelong practices. Meaningful activities go far beyond the limits imposed by time and space.

◆ CLASSROOM CONNECTION

Mr. Grant is sensitive to the fact that as children's interest in their world expands, a wealth of stimulating learning experiences can be employed to heighten their discoveries. Therefore, he has found that planning a unit around a particular theme is an effective way to activate children to explore a specific topic in social studies. "Kwanzaa" is the third thematic plan employed by Mr. Grant this school year; the others were "Keepers of the Earth" and "Our Land and People." Mr. Grant has other units based on famous adventurers, pioneer life, historical figures, and countries around the world. Many experiences cut across subject lines and are comfortably integrated with other subjects—growing crunchy bean sprouts (science) for a healthy taste of Chinese nutrition, making a calendar with symbols depicting numbers (math) the ancient Egyptian way, and mastering the Mexican hat dance or Highland fling (music and movement). Other experiences are much more specific to social studies—taking a trip to a natural-habitat zoo, using a map to locate the land where buffalo herds roamed in 1600, or defining the nature of sharecropping.

Whether integrated or more social studies-specific, Mr. Grant believes that the key to effective instruction is planning. In Chapter 3, we discussed the components of authentic learning as applied to planning short-term lessons; now we need to examine how authentic learning is incorporated into long-term instructional plans.

The process of long-term planning is a very delicate, precise process. But many school districts have become obsessed with thematic teaching and try to force teachers to make artificial connections. As a result, social studies themes end up with "cutesy" activities that dilute the focus of the unit. For example, in a unit on famous artists, is it really necessary to measure the area of their paintings? Forced connections run the risk of glossing over important concepts with flimsy activities that result in little or no meaningful learning. Rather than focus on the learning outcomes, teachers judge the elegance of an activity—a nice, sparkling presentation.

Such an outlook is often called a "cookbook" approach, where commercially produced teacher idea books seem to be a common planning source, often suggesting shallow activities that dilute the focus of a theme. In fact, idea books frequently serve as the only curriculum guide. As in planning a meal, however, the individual recipes may be appetizing and flavorful, but pulled together into one menu, the combination could be offensive. Rather than limit themes to "cookbook recipes," it is important to know what makes themes work. How to bring about productive learning is a much tougher task than simply leafing through the pages of a single resource.

PROJECTS

What are the components of a "full-flavored meal"? Some teachers believe that the answer is in the spontaneous happenings that grow from the probing, wondering minds of the children. They view the social studies program as a source for nurturing the the natural responsiveness of children to the world around them. For that reason, social studies is considered a subject that allows children to throw themselves into whatever interests them. This view is supported by the contention that when children love what they are doing, when they do it out of intense personal drive, they will likely work their hardest, and the learning process will become part of them. The teacher's goal is to encourage children to ask questions: "What is that?" "What is it for?" "Where did it come from?" "Who is that?" "Why did that happen?" The answers must not come from the teacher alone, but from the children passionately searching for their own anwers.

Thematic units and projects are designed to help children learn about their world in developmentally and culturally appropriate ways.

Such classroom experiences represent one of the hottest trends among elementary school educators today—engaging children in projects. Some suggest that projects are the most productive way to immerse children in real learning (Katz & Chard, 1989). Hartman and Eckerty (1995) define projects as "children's in-depth investigations of topics that interest them" (p. 141). How do projects differ from Mr. Grant's thematic approach? Borgia (1996) points out a very important distinction between themes and projects:

> What distinguishes project work from theme-based curriculum? . . . thematic planning is teacher-directed.
>
> In project work, the children are included in—and even negotiate—the planning. You don't know in advance where the project will take your class or how long it will go on. You and your children make discoveries together and shape the project as it evolves. The resources you use are generated by the topic and vary with each project. (p. 24)

The important distinction between themes and projects, then, is that projects arise from the interests of the children; themes are more teacher-regulated. Although the project approach is currently receiving significant attention from social studies educators, the idea is hardly new. For almost a century now, the value of projects has been debated in professional journals and books. It all started with John Dewey and his work at the famous experimental school at the University of Chicago. Dewey's philosophy was based on answers he constructed for this critical question: "How can teachers bring the school into closer relationship with the home and neighborhood life, instead of the school being a place where the child comes solely to learn certain lessons?" Dewey's new methods included projects that encouraged students to investigate their own interests through meaningful dialogue and collaborative problem solving. To illustrate, let us suppose that some real-life experience has charged your children with an intense interest in birds. Subsequent learning would involve the study of birds. Dewey believed that in-depth investigations could occur in any combination of four kinds of projects:

1. *Producer's project.* Children make a model, draw a picture, dramatize a scene, or represent ideas about birds in a variety of different modes.

2. *Consumer's project.* Children examine someone else's product, such as looking at a book on birds, watching a video or CD-ROM presentation, going to a bird sanctuary, or examining a painting of birds.

3. *Problem project.* Children solve a problem of deep personal interest, such as, "How can we encourage birds to stay near our school during the winter?" by building a bird sanctuary.

4. *Specific learning project.* Children learn specific facts and skills only when the need arises (e.g., making graphs of the most popular birds in the schoolyard, dictating a story to an adult, or finding out what certain birds like to eat).

Over the years, Dewey's project method has been reincarnated in various forms, taking on such identities as "discovery learning," "inquiry model," "holistic learning," "spontaneous curriculum," "open education," and others. Some even use the term interchangeably with thematic learning. Even though some authorities on the project approach (Katz & Chard, 1989) might disagree, Hartman and Eckerty (1995) advise us that between "[t]eachers or children can initiate a project" (p. 141), and Deborah Diffily (1996) suggests that "[s]ometimes teachers suggest projects . . ." (p. 72). Without getting into a needless discussion of who initiates what, the bona fide focus of a project is on the children's own interests.

How to Carry Out Projects

To initiate a project, motivation often arises from a common reaction to events in the environment. When children think that something is worth finding out about, they will approach learning with much enthusiasm and energy. For example, Mrs. Small sensed her first graders' growing interest in a construction site near the school. On their way to school or as they romped on the playground during recess, the children regularly watched the workers and machinery. Excited conversations took place each day as the children talked about the sounds and sights associated with the project ("Oooh, look at that big bulldozer!"). Recognizing their growing interest in the site, Mrs. Small opened the door to discovery.

The first thing Mrs. Small needed to do was to find out what the children already knew about the construction project. Most were aware that it was going to be a new seafood restaurant like the one on the opposite side of town, which most of the children had visited. Next, she probed into what the children were most interested in. The children generated a whole list of questions, which were written on a large sheet of paper: "What's the name going to be?" "What kind of food will it have?" "How do you order food?" "How do you pay for it?" "Where do they cook the food?" "Who cooks it?" "What does the sign (logo) look like?" The process involved the children in collaborative planning and gave Mrs. Small direction about what to focus on and how to facilitate subsequent learning.

Mrs. Small collected books from the library and gathered related resources such as ads, posters, and flyers from the restaurant. She encouraged the children to explore the materials and to discuss what they found. Mrs. Small called the manager of the restaurant to ask if the children could visit. After gaining approval, the children dictated a letter to their parents explaining the project's goals and activities and requested volunteers to accompany them on their trip. The children thought it might be a good idea to create a seafood restaurant in their classroom when they returned so, in consultation with Mrs. Small, they cleared a space and waited for the trip so they could model their physical layout after the actual restaurant. The children decided to photograph the restaurant and draw a map during the trip so they would have a guide for their classroom model.

Now it was time for the big event itself—the trip to the seafood restaurant. Each child was equipped with a clipboard and pencil and assigned to a group with one adult and two classmates. Each group was to gather information related to the questions the class had generated. Because these were first graders, only some of the children could write, using key words and invented spelling to summarize what they had found. Others drew pictures or dictated their information to an adult. A few were assigned to take photographs, assisted by the adults.

When they returned to the classroom, Mrs. Small helped the children summarize their experiences. She pulled together all of the drawings and dictations and made a book, which was displayed with the other materials in the book center, and exhibited the photographs so the children could use them for reference as they completed their projects. Menus, placemats, napkins, and other materials brought back to the classroom were displayed in a separate center.

After the field trip and follow-up experiences, the children were ready to transform their targeted space into their own restaurant, but decided they would rather serve pizza than seafood. Their initial interest in setting up the restaurant seemed to focus on arranging the tables and chairs for the customers and making sure the "kitchen" was ready to begin producing pizzas. Once that was done, others thought some special touches were needed: flowers for the tables, pictures on the walls, a telephone for reservations, and even wallpaper. Crews went to work on each project, taping up their own artwork for pictures, getting the play telephone from the kindergarten room, using sponge printing to create several sheets of patterned "wallpaper," finding out from Mrs. Small how to make flowers from pipe cleaners and tissue paper, and selecting easy-listening music for the diners.

Next, the children focused on a name for the restaurant as well as signs, menus, a logo, and order taking. They decided that "Pizza Pie" would be a fine name for their restaurant. Mrs. Small provided paint and a long sheet of butcher paper for the children to make a large sign. They decided to use a pizza slice as a logo and painted one next to the name. Other groups made restroom, no smoking, exit, open/closed, and please wait to be seated signs.

After examining the sample menu from the seafood restaurant, the children decided to use it as a model for their pizza menu. They looked through old magazines for pictures, but ended up drawing their own and putting the prices next to an illustration of each food and drink item. Mrs. Small cut some sponges into the shape of their logo, and the children stamped the logo onto the menu, plain white napkins, take-out boxes, place mats, and order pads.

Now the children used their pizza restaurant to dramatize the roles of producers and consumers. Some were customers and sat at the table ("Do you take credit cards?"). Others put on aprons to take orders ("Hello. My name is Christopher. What can I get for you?"). No one seemed to notice that most of the orders were taken down in scribble writing. Two children donned chef's hats and pretended to flip and spin pizza crusts.

The pizza restaurant was only one example of a spontaneous project in Mrs. Small's first-grade social studies classroom. As a matter of fact, Mrs. Small's children began another project immediately after their interest shifted from the restaurant to Gerald, who came to school with a new pair of eyeglasses. You guessed it—a trip to the ophthalmologist and the construction of an eye care facility was next, complete with pipe cleaner "designer frames." The following process was used to implement the project approach in Mrs. Small's room: (1) select the topic, (2) spur interest and involvement, (3) explore resources, and (4) represent the experiences.

Projects help foster the probing, wondering mind by offering situations in which children become actively involved.

One of the questions most frequently asked by teachers who have never tried the project approach is, "How much of my program should I devote to projects?" Katz (1996) suggests that it is only a single component of all that goes on daily and should not permeate everything that is done in the classroom: "Any topic, no matter how fascinating it is in the beginning, will become deadly if everything you do all day relates to it" (p. 20).

This example is of only one first-grade class. Yet the restaurant was one area that the children came back to visit over and over again. As they continued to add to the restaurant, eye care center, and other stores, they took great pride in giving tours to parents, other classes, and building visitors. It became the catalyst and context for the study of neighborhoods and communities throughout the year.

Katz (1996) summarizes the current interest in projects as emerging from increased absorption in the integrated curriculum. At the same time, we are much more sensitive to the very special ways children learn: the capacity to solve problems, raise questions, hypothesize, and theorize—these are the natural dispositions of childhood that are nurtured through projects. Remember, though, that two major features make a project unique: (1) the investigation is planned with the children rather than just by the teacher and (2) project topics arise from various experiences—the most common being real-life experiences.

THEMATIC UNITS

Although spontaneous projects work for some teachers, many are not comfortable with the approach. They insist that projects are too difficult to manage; not knowing in advance where the project will take the class or how long it will go on concerns those who need more structure in their lives. In effect, they often throw up their hands in despair, wondering when children will become provoked to investigate something or while helping shape the project as it evolves. They say in frustration that "I have so many curriculum requirements that I don't have time for projects." These teachers feel it is unreasonable for any teacher (especially beginning teachers) to "have a bagful of tricks on hand at all times to skillfully capitalize on any new interest a . . . child may evidence" (Goetz, 1985, p. 12). Hendrick (1992) echoes this concern and warns that an overreliance on spontaneous activities may result in some real pedagogical problems:

> The real problem with spontaneity, or excessive reliance on spur-of-the-moment curriculum, is that the children may gain only small pepperings of factual knowledge on a multitude of subjects and lack an overall sense of integration and direction in what they learn. In addition, it may mean that some valuable opportunities for practice of more specific reasoning abilities are not provided, since the fortuitous nature of these curriculum "happenings" makes advance planning impossible. (p. 463)

Teachers uncomfortable with the spontaneous activity associated with projects maintain that a lack of advance planning jeopardizes their ability to center instruction on areas considered critical to understanding our world: "What happens if my children never develop a spontaneous interest in China? Does that mean they will miss out on all the interesting discoveries associated with this rich land and glorious civilization?" Certainly not, mediators maintain; the motivation might not be as high as when children discover something by themselves, but if they are allowed to actively pursue what the teacher brings to them, students will become interested in it and be eager to learn.

Despite this apparent turmoil, I contend that concepts worth knowing about should be developed in a variety of ways. Departing from his strong recommendations for spontaneous activity, Jean Piaget (1990) has clearly stated that it is wrong to imply that children should be left with unlimited freedom to work on their own: "It is important that teachers present children with materials and situations and occasions that allow them to move forward. It is not a matter of just allowing children to do anything. It is a matter of presenting to the children situations which offer new problems, problems that follow on from one another. You need a mixture of direction and freedom" (p. 36). Additionally, Moll and Whitmore (1993) sum up the role of a Vygotskian teacher by viewing the teacher as a facilitator, one who consciously plans an environment and the curriculum and selects materials that foster children's learning. The teacher carefully monitors the children's learning, constantly reformulating learning experiences to fit children's constantly changing learning needs.

Piaget and Vygotsky clearly believe that a learner's spontaneity should be encouraged and exploited, but emphasize that teachers must also organize materials and situations to provide functional learning opportunities for their students. In short, I must remind you once more that good social studies teachers must be *flexible.* There are times when you will find it most constructive to base a lesson or series of lessons on textbooks and other times when you will seize upon the spontaneous interests of children. Teachers should try different approaches when they are excited about what they are teaching and about what their students are doing.

One currently popular technique for planning deliberate long-term social studies instruction is the thematic plan, or thematic unit. *Thematic plans* are extended designs of instruction created by teachers around a central idea; they contain an orderly sequence of lessons that provide a sense of cohesiveness, or unity, to classroom instruction. The actual form of a thematic unit varies from teacher to teacher; for some a thematic unit may be fundamentally a chapter from the textbook augmented with a few additional activities, whereas for others it may be a comprehensive plan that incorporates content and strategies across subject lines—from math, science, literature, creative writing, music, art, and others. Although the terms *thematic unit* and *interdisciplinary approach* are fairly new, the concept of connecting separate subjects from a traditionally disjoined subject-oriented curriculum has existed for years; many experienced teachers learned about it in their social studies methods courses when it was called the *unit method.* The popularity of planning social studies instruction in ways that subject boundaries are truly blurred has ebbed and flowed throughout the years; over time the concept has had various labels—*progressive education* and *open education* are two of the most familiar. Without delving into the history of thematic planning, suffice it to say that integration is the call in elementary schools today, with "thematic units" being the rallying cry to bring different content areas together.

Thematic units and the traditional unit method hold much in common, but one major influence that seems to have inspired the *new* philosophy is a system of beliefs associated with the literature-based movement in social studies instruction.

Strickland (1994–1995) emphasizes the importance of literature: "textbooks continue to be important classroom resources, but they are no longer the dominant materials" (p. 295) for learning in social studies. She recommends that students be given many opportunities to read and respond to tradebooks, a process popularly referred to as "literature across the curriculum." Berg (1989) expands on this point:

> A major goal of the social studies is to help students understand the myriad interactions of people on this planet—past, present, and future. Making sense of the world requires using skills that allow one to read about the many people and places that are scattered about the globe; to use literature to understand the richness of past events and the people who are a part of them; to apply math concepts to more fully understand how numbers have enabled people to . . . manage the complexity of their world. The story of humankind well told requires drawing from all areas of the curriculum. (p. 1 of pull-out feature)

Integrating other subjects into the development of social studies themes makes sense to young children; it is an idea that centers education in a true "child's world." A literature-based thematic unit offers a variety of "doings" designed to satisfy and extend a child's natural sense of wonder; it is not fragmented into discretely dispensed subject areas. Subject lines may be critical for adults' administrative and organizational purposes, but the child's world is not bound by such thinking.

A five-step format provides the structure upon which thematic units are built:

1. Select a topic for study.
2. Formulate goals and objectives.
3. Organize the content.
4. Choose a rich variety of learning experiences.
5. Assess to what degree the goals and objectives have been met.

Selecting the Theme

Although it may appear deceptively uncomplicated on the surface, topic selection is one of the most difficult of all responsibilities associated with planning a thematic unit. Among the many factors contributing to this formidable task is the school district's regular curriculum. The amount of expected conformity to established curriculum guides varies among districts, so it is possible to experience any of a number of freedoms or constraints. Consider the following examples:

- School district A has developed a districtwide social studies curriculum based on a textbook series. It expects every teacher to follow the teacher's guide so closely that all teachers must be on the same page of the book at the same date; at times a subject area supervisor may check plan books to see that this is being done. There is very little room for individual planning; the textbook exclusively determines the direction of the program.

- School district B supplies a curriculum guide and textbook program for each teacher. It expects all teachers to plan their instruction around topics found in these sources. Teachers are permitted to extend and enrich the specified topics as long as the basic subject matter and sequence of topics do not change.

- School district C furnishes a curriculum guide and textbook program, but considers these more as references for obtaining broad goals and objectives than as "the final word." The coverage of some topics is expected, but the formality associated with a text-based program is missing. Topics and instructional strategies may be modified as growing interests and needs dictate. This is a middle-of-the-road approach; moving away from teacher-centered planning, but not yet child-centered.

- School district D has developed a philosophy that the social studies curriculum should be planned by the teacher in response to student interests and backgrounds. Teachers formulate their own goals and objectives, learning activities, and assessment procedures. A great deal of emphasis is placed on integrating the curriculum and on the use of a variety of instructional resources, including individualized instruction, learning centers, self-paced materials, learning packets, and research projects.

It is apparent that the responsibility for topic selection varies greatly among school districts. Thus, the freedom delegated to each teacher significantly influences the topics they are able to select. Rarely, though, will principals risk damaging the enthusiasm of teachers who want to try something new. Key to capturing an empathetic ear is to offer a sound rationale for change. Cullum (1967) explains:

> A teacher need not be a professional actor, musical artist, or scientist to present greatness to his students. He need only be aware of the creativity and excitement of the outside world and strive to bring that world into his classroom. If a teacher can show a principal the possible structure of a new project and the rules and regulations that will govern it, most administrators will agree to let him try the program. It will be a rewarding experience and not as difficult as it may sound. (p. 18)

Should you find yourself fortunate enough to have the freedom to create personalized thematic units, it is important to consider some vital ingredients of sound social studies themes. Baskwill (1988) suggests the following:

> Two of the criteria for a good theme are that it be rich in literature, both fiction and nonfiction, and that it have natural links to other areas of the curriculum. A third criterion is time. A theme needs time to unfold and develop. . . . It is impossible to pinpoint precisely how much time you'll need for a given theme the interests of your children serve as the best guide. (p. 80)

A lot of a teacher's energy and time go into selecting a theme; much more than first meets the eye. But the value of a personalized social studies program is obvious: It is chosen with *your* children in mind. And who knows *your* children better—you or the developers of a textbook series or curriculum guide?

Consider the following sources as you review themes for your social studies program:

- *Curriculum guides.* What topics lend themselves to in-depth study?
- *Textbooks.* How can practices be augmented so that children learn by doing rather than just by reading?
- *Colleagues.* What themes worked best for them?
- *Children's interests.* What are they excited about? What are some of their favorite stories, movies, television shows, things to talk about? What questions do they ask?
- *Your interests.* What fascinates you? What trips have you taken? What are you enthusiastic about?

For illustration, Mr. Arroyo developed a representative fifth-grade thematic unit, "Customs and Traditions of Japan." He had five good reasons for choosing this theme: (1) "Japan" was a mandatory topic of study in his school district's third-grade curriculum; (2) the textbook treatment of Japan was limited; (3) he recently visited Japan and became fascinated with the land and its people; (4) he had collected assorted souvenirs, photos, videotapes, and slides during his stay; and (5) his children were enthusiastic learners and very interested in studying cultures from around the world.

Formulating Goals and Objectives

One helpful way to think of actual unit construction is to imagine yourself as a tour guide and your students as your passengers. You are about to escort this group as they embark on a most thrilling journey—a delightful excursion to exciting new worlds.

Choosing a topic for a thematic unit answers the question, "Where are we going?" It provides you and your learners with a general direction, preventing you from wandering aimlessly while searching for direction or hoping for inspiration. But a tour guide cannot expect to launch a satisfying trip without having a deeper understanding of the trip's intent: "Why are we going there?" Likewise, you must consider the many reasons why it is important to carry out a particular theme (or go on your tour); without such careful examination you could flit about from activity to activity without getting much out of any of them, or could devote so much time to a single activity that you run out of interest, time, or energy for the others. Listing a series of learning goals helps you identify what you want to achieve from the thematic unit, and helps prevent the instructional sequence from wandering aimlessly or from becoming stalled in one place too long.

Identifying Goals

Social studies programs have always been planned with the idea of accomplishing multiple outcomes. This means that many important learnings should be expected of any sequence of instruction. As we read in Chapter 1, social studies goals may be efficiently grouped into the following three categories:

1. *Concept development.* The formation of key mental structures that help learners derive meaning from the subject matter.
2. *Skills acquisition and refinement.* The attainment of social skills, study skills and work habits, group work skills, and intellectual skills.
3. *Affective outcomes.* The feelings, attitudes, and values that can be associated with the human condition.

Each of these categories is important to the development of any social studies thematic unit, and different units will accentuate different categories. For example, skills outcomes would be sure to dominate a theme such as "Using Maps and Globes," and concept outcomes would be central to "The Roman Empire." Some units, then, naturally lend themselves to certain goals, but most should incorporate a balance taken from all categories.

The selection of instructional goals is a matter of choice made by individual teachers after careful consideration of the following important information:

1. *Children.* What are their needs and interests? How do they learn most effectively? Can they perform the responsibilities they are likely to encounter?
2. *Nature of the subject.* What types of learning can arise from the subject? What contributions can the subject make in the lives of young children?

3. *Previous experiences.* What has worked in the past? What relation does this new topic have to the children's backgrounds, to previous units, or to other subjects?

It takes much time and practice to conceptualize goals to the point where they can be effectively used to provide direction for subsequent instructional choices. Think of making broad statements of intended learning outcomes and then writing down your ideas, keeping these three considerations in mind:

1.   *State what you want the children to accomplish.* An appropriate goal is, "The children will understand the hardships that were common to frontier families." An inappropriate goal would be, "The teacher will furnish children with information about the hardships that were common to frontier families."

2.   *State the intended outcome, not the activity in which the children will be engaged.* This is an appropriate goal of instruction because it effectively communicates the overall learning outcome: "The children will understand the positions on the French Revolution of the Republicans and the Federalists." On the other hand, the following is inappropriate because it describes an activity; the learning outcome is not recognizable: "The children will draw a campaign poster for either the Republican or Federalist party." Goals must identify the intended knowledge, conceptual skill, or behavioral outcomes, not the actual learning activities or products.

3.   *Limit the number of goals.* One purpose of composing goals is to confine the content to that which is manageable for a three- to four-week span of instruction. Certainly, any theme involves limitless possibilities; a crucial role in unit development is to separate the desirable from the unnecessary so that a major direction can be established. It is appropriate to limit the number of overall goals for any unit of study to three to five.

The following goals will provide purpose and guidance for our thematic unit, "Customs and Traditions of Japan":

1. The students shall understand that the culture in which a person lives influences thoughts, values, and actions.
2. The students shall understand that human beings throughout the world are more alike than different.
3. The students shall value the diversity of cultures around the world.
4. The students shall understand how geography affects the lives of the people in different locations.

Composing Specific Objectives

The goals you have just read are stated broadly and communicate a general direction of study. Goals describe desirable outcomes and yet allow enough room for interpretation, room to make necessary adjustments for individual differences should special needs arise after the unit has begun to move. These give us a general direction, but to pinpoint exactly what outcomes we intend to strive for, more highly detailed information is required. This is done by stating specific objectives. As you learned in Chapter 3, specific objectives target the precise behaviors children will demonstrate as they progress through the learning activities. Teachers frequently use specific objectives to clarify the intent of the general goals. Using Gronlund's approach, one of our goals could be expanded as shown below:

Goal

The students shall understand how geography affects the lives of the people in different locations.

Specific Objectives

1. The students shall locate Japan on a map and on a globe.
2. The students shall identify the major landforms such as islands, mountains, and major bodies of water of Japan from a map.
3. The students shall describe the seasons, climate, and weather of Japan.
4. The students shall identify the major cities and regions of Japan from a map.
5. The students shall compare the size of Japan and their state.
6. The students shall explain how living on a Pacific island affects the way the people of Japan design homes, use the land, build cities, deal with environmental phenomena such as earthquakes and tsunami, and use natural resources.

Space prevents me from breaking down the other general goals in the same way; an identical process would be used to pinpoint the specific behaviors associated with each goal. Although this process is extremely time-consuming, you need to begin your thematic plan with carefully selected and clearly worded educational goals and objectives. They describe what students will be able to do as a result of their educational program and become translated into learning experiences designed to produce those targeted results. Goals and objectives serve as useful guides for planning because they help teachers focus on the outcomes of their instruction.

Organizing the Content

Following the statement of objectives, you must conduct a thorough search for the content required to deepen the children's understandings and skills as well as to provide substance for their affective responses. For that reason, you must be tuned in to subject matter. You must be broadly educated, well informed, and have an insatiable thirst for learning. When you teach, you teach with all you know and can find out about the topic. "Smart" teachers are needed in social studies classrooms every bit as much as college classrooms need informed professors.

Teacher as Scholar

To be sure that their students are building meaningful and accurate concepts, teachers need information. Each concept related to a topic under study has its own body of facts; each has a precise set of data used by social science scholars. Teachers must be in command of this knowledge and use it to support and deepen their children's learning. To appreciate how important it is that a teacher truly understand the concept being taught, let us imagine that you are teaching a lesson dealing with the concept of *igloo* as it pertains to the lives of the native Arctic people commonly referred to as Eskimos, but more accurately identified as Inuit (IN-oo-eet). We shall assume that you have already helped the children establish a meaningful background of information about the Inuit through meaningful classroom experiences: There are many Inuit nations; each has its own language and traditions; most Inuit live in the Arctic—the area around the North Pole—but many live in the northern part of Alaska. The purpose of the current lesson is to help students deepen their understandings of the Alaskan Inuit by learning about their igloos. Focus for a minute on the image that appears in your mind: Is it a domed snow house sitting on a frigid, treeless, barren blanket of snow and ice? If you are like most teachers, this concept of "igloo" is quite clear and would probably guide your instruction, perhaps to the point of having your students construct tabletop models from sugar cubes. With such a clear idea of igloos, is there any need to dig up additional information? You bet there is! If you had been responsible enough to have done an information search, you would have discovered that today's Alaskan Inuit generally use snow igloos only as temporary hunting shelters. Actually, *igloo* is the Inuit word for "house," and Inuit now live in modern houses, or split-level, colonial, condo, or apartment igloos, very similar to those in the rest of the United States and Canada.

What would children learn about the Alaskan Inuit if we limited their exposure to information based solely on what we think we know? In this case, the result certainly would be unfair, stereotypical, and incorrect. In any lesson, we *must* uncover and verify considerable information so that students acquire a genuine image of the culture, period of time, or phenomenon being studied. One experienced teacher's recollection highlights the need for a spirit of continuous learning:

> The biggest surprise of teaching, for me, was that I didn't know my subject matter. That was the one thing I had been most confident about. I had almost an "A" average in my major and felt really on top of my field. When I began teaching and had to explain concepts, I found that I had only a very superficial understanding of them. I knew stuff in kind of a rote way and when I had to explain it to someone else I kind of just fell on my face. I learned more about my subject in my first four months of teaching than I did in my four years of college. (Ryan, Burkholder, & Phillips, 1983, p. 177)

You must continually strive to deepen the background knowledge you bring to teaching; your goal will be to offer a social studies program that encourages inquisitive minds. Inspire your children to examine their world and prod them not only to learn subject matter but to think for themselves.

Factstorming

A useful process for organizing the content selected to address your goals and objectives is called *factstorming*. Virtually any theme can be factstormed by a group or individual. All that is required is to create a web of potential ideas for the study (see Figure 4–2). First, write the word or words describing your theme in the middle of a large sheet of paper and draw a circle around it. Then, by asking probing questions (for example, "What would it be like to go to school in Japan?"), identify related subtopics as appropriate for study. Write them on the paper, too, and draw lines to connect them to the theme statement. Repeat the process with each identified subtopic. This chart is only the beginning. Most teachers do not know enough at this initial stage of the unit planning process to identify all the necessary content, but are only brainstorming "starters," or ideas to help judge whether the chosen theme has sufficient possibilities. If the theme seems too broad or too narrow in focus, it should either be adjusted or discarded altogether. If the theme seems appropriate, you will need to move on and select the ideas you wish to expand upon.

FIGURE 4–2
Factstorming Web for "Customs and Traditions of Japan"

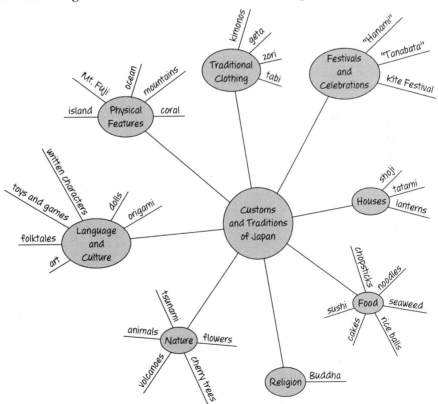

Expand the Content

Should you decide to continue with the theme, the next step is to expand the content. As a teacher of elementary school social studies, you must have much information at your fingertips, and must also have access to resources to supplement that knowledge—the computer and a wide variety of print sources are the places to start. Check with your school or public librarian for references on a theme you wish to pursue. Constantly search for information to bolster what you already know; you should find yourself saying, "I'll look it up," many times a day. Books and the computer will provide most of the needed information, but you will also want additional resources. Consult specialists either in person or by telephone, visit museums and other sites, view films or filmstrips, listen to audiotapes, and seek other opportunities to broaden your background. You will need to spend a great deal of time uncovering and organizing information: What is the key information necessary for a satisfactory understanding of this theme? What are the concepts, skills, and big ideas that might emerge? Do not be satisfied only with accumulating a mass of information: Be sure the information is accurate. You must pass on true understandings, not careless misinformation.

The background material you uncover should be comprehensive; you must be "tuned in" to knowledge. When you teach elementary school children you teach with all you can find out about, learning more than you can ever expect to cover in the unit. The children will ask many questions requiring information on specific points. It certainly is permissible for a teacher to reply, "I don't know. Let's find out

To build sound learnings, teachers have to have a lot of information. As adult scholars, they look at all of life around them with a sense of wonder.

together," to children's questions each day, but the teacher who can answer a great many questions is the one who communicates greater preparation. Study the key facts related to the theme; think about the concepts that should emerge. Constantly seek the major learnings that can arise from the planned instruction. This important background material should be outlined at the beginning of your unit. The outline is usually preceded by a short summary paragraph, like the one in Activity 4–1.

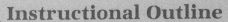

Activity 4-1
Instructional Outline

Summary Paragraph

Japan is an island nation located off the coast of China about 5,000 miles from the United States. It consists of four major islands and many small islands. Of the major islands, the largest is Honshu, the furthest north is Hokkaido, and the remaining two are Shikoku and Kyushu. Tokyo is Japan's largest city. There are many mountains sprinkled with thick green forests in Japan; Mount Fuji is the highest. Some of the mountains, including Mount Fuji, are inactive volcanoes.

Japan is a very old country, with customs and traditions that go back thousands of years. Japanese customs, traditions, and family life will be the focus of this unit, with added emphasis on its climate and geographic features.

Content Outline

Concept: Geophysical Features

1. Japan consists of nearly 3,000 islands.
2. Japan has four major islands: Honshu (the largest), Hokkaido, Shikoku, and Kyushu.
3. If all the islands were put together, they would constitute an area about the size of California.
4. Japan is located 5,000 miles from the United States, off the coast of China.
5. Tokyo is the capital of Japan and is its largest city.
6. Japan's climate is much like that of the Middle Atlantic States.
7. The tallest mountain is Mount Fuji, nearly 12,500 feet high. It is an inactive volcano.

8. Many other high mountains make up the island; several are inactive volcanoes.

9. Thick green forests cover the mountains.

10. In the summer, Japan may experience *typhoons*, very strong storms with high winds and heavy rains.

11. Japan has a great deal of rain during the *tyusu* (rainy season) that comes in early summer.

12. Rain is good for the rice crops, a favorite food in Japan.

Concept: Clothing

1. Contemporary Japanese wear clothes that are just like the clothing worn in the United States.

2. Japanese people traditionally wore layered robes called *kimonos*. Today some do so only on special occasions.

3. A long piece of cloth is tied around the waist of the kimono. It is called an *obi*.

4. Japanese children may wear brightly colored kimonos. Women's silk kimonos and obis may be blue, red, or green, often made with colorful designs. Men's kimonos are not as fancy. The cloth is usually cotton and the color is brown, black, or gray.

5. Japanese wear shoes, but some like wearing *getas*, slippers with high wooden soles and a strap going between the big toe and the next toe. *Zori* are similar, but often have straw soles.

6. Geta and zori are worn over *tabi*, or split-toe cotton slippers that allow the straps to slip between the first and second toe.

7. Many people of Japan have fancy silk umbrellas called *kasa* because it rains so much in Japan.

8. Some children in Japan wear uniforms to school. Each school has a different uniform.

Following the drafting of a summary paragraph, you will normally prepare an outline of the content. It helps to begin by designating the primary concepts that will be highlighted throughout the unit and then recording the key information beneath them. Activity 4–1 displays the content outline for two concepts central to our unit, "Customs and Traditions of Japan": geophysical features and clothing. If space permitted, this outline would continue for each targeted concept: possibilities include houses, festivals, typhoons and earthquakes, school, meals, music, art, religion, pets or animals, games, industry, fishing, language, and so on. Once this content designation aspect of planning is completed, you face the next big challenge: "How can this knowledge be most effectively conveyed to my students?" Now you have reached another point of transition in the process of constructing thematic unit plans: the learning experiences phase.

Selecting the Learning Experiences

Learning experiences are the instructional activities we employ to achieve the stated goals and objectives—the actual experiences that involve children in puzzling, wondering, exploring, experimenting, finding out, and thinking. Not all learning experiences need to be new or unique; highest priority should be placed on balance and variety. Do not choose activities because they are "cute" or gimmicky; choose them because they stand the best chance of accomplishing your goals and objectives. The point of a theme is to explore a social studies topic in depth, and we defeat the whole purpose when we underplay the content by using shallow activities. You may be surprised that not all contemporary methods are original; most are adaptations or reworked versions of older, more traditional methods. The crux of successful teaching lies in the realization that any single method of instruction should be used sparingly in the social studies classroom; the younger the children, the greater the variety should be. As a person of many roles, you should consider these fundamental assumptions as you plan your program:

- Sometimes you will lecture to your children, but rarely; the younger the child, the less you talk.
- Sometimes you will hold discussion sessions with the entire class, using good questioning and discussion techniques.
- Sometimes you will lead whole-group learning experiences from the textbook or another common source of information; such experiences offer balance and proportion to the program.
- Sometimes you will bring to class objects such as jewelry, clothing, dolls, toys, books, catalogs, containers, tools, and other realia. These items help to form classroom connections to other people, times, and places.
- Sometimes you will choose books, computer applications, videos, slides, tapes, filmstrips, records, pictures, bulletin boards, and other learning aids—providing a variety of learning materials is essential.
- Sometimes you will encourage children to solve problems and search for answers to their own questions; an independent quest for information is a lifelong asset.
- Sometimes children will work alone; meeting personal interests and needs must assume high priority in all classrooms. At other times you will encourage children to work together cooperatively; children learn a great deal from one another.

Recall from Chapter 3 that deciding on which of these general forms of instruction to use for any stated purpose is a process greatly supported by the use of "If-Then" connections. For example:

- *If* you want the students to gain insight into life in a Japanese school, *then* simulate a typical day in a third-grade classroom.
- *If* you want the students to understand traditional Japanese culture, *then* have them read folklore such as Yoshiko Uchida's *Samurai of Gold Hill*.
- *If* you want the students to experience music as a universal medium of communication, then sing together the "Japanese Rain Song".

Phases of Planning the Learning Experiences

There are many ways to structure the activities chosen for thematic units; the organized outline that follows is only a rough guide. It should be adapted or restyled to suit your personal preferences and the needs of your students.

Phase 1: Introductory Activities.   Establishing classroom conditions that enhance motivation to learn is a major enterprise during this portion of the thematic unit. What conditions can you create that will enable students to develop a positive attitude toward what they will be learning? Essentially, you must incorporate activities that arouse the curiosity of students or demonstrate to them that they will have an opportunity to explore and discover some unknown. You must also deliver each introductory activity with enthusiasm and intensity, realizing that the teacher's enthusiasm for teaching affects a student's motivation to learn.

Usually encompassing the first day or two of instruction, the process of kicking off a thematic unit can be carried out in a number of ways:

- *Discussion.* You could ask a series of questions about the theme and have the children brainstorm their ideas as you record them on a chart such as a K–W–L chart (see Chapter 5). The K stands for what we *know,* the W for what we *want* to know, and the L for what we *learned.* The chart is a good way to draw from the students what they would like to learn about a topic.
- *The arts.* You might play music that suits the theme, read a poem, share a book, or display arts and crafts items.
- *Audiovisual resources.* A slide presentation, travel posters, recordings, videotape, documents, models, costumes, study prints, photographs, postcards, products, newspapers, magazines, books, and the like serve well to arouse curiosity and stimulate the imagination.
- *Creative dramatics.* The students imagine boarding an airplane or a boat to visit a special city, state, or country. They might also enter a time capsule and imagine being transported back to a historical era or into the future.
- *Arranged environment.* Arrange learning centers, library tables, and bulletin board displays with items to stimulate questions and interest.

There are many good introductory experiences—field trips, community visitors, videos, realia, and the like—but one of the most important ingredients is a good book. Whenever you plan a theme's learning experiences, you must inevitably choose good books. I call books that are used during the introductory phases of thematic units *literature launchers*. Their purpose is to propel children into a realm of experience that motivates interest to pursue the activities that follow. Good books should not be limited solely to the introductory activities, however. They should also be used at strategic points throughout the unit. A good theme is always rich in literature, both fiction and nonfiction. Be careful, though, not to limit your choices only to familiar titles. Carefully analyze additional books and choose them for their relevance to the unit, for their artistry, and for their style.

Phase 2: Developmental Experiences.   Following the introductory activities, you enter into what is often described as the "brass tacks" of the unit. Activities may be done independently, in small groups, or by the whole class, but what really matters is that you stay within the periphery of the children's interests. You must choose worthwhile experiences that are not mere entertainment or busywork but are rich in potential learning. You must be constantly ready and eager to reach out and seize the most gripping experiences available. As you set phase 2 in motion, the students go to work; you may retreat a bit. Your initial teaching responsibilities as a stimulator and arranger are now complete; you will now have more teaching to do, but in other ways. You must now analyze the unit objectives and ask, "What learning experiences will most effectively help me achieve this objective?" Your choice could come from among the following possibilities:

- *Community resources.* Bring real-life action to the children. *Field trips* are important, whether around the school or in the community. Wherever they go, however, children should be active participants, not mere onlookers. *Visitors* to the classroom, if the children cannot go to them, are important sources of knowledge and stimulation. As with field trips, be sure the children are active, not a captive audience for someone's lecture.

- *Instructional media.* Children should have a variety of experiences with vehicles of instruction commonly categorized as *instructional media*, or *audiovisual media*: clothing, tools, documents, household items, toys, models or replicas, maps, globes, computers, videotapes, motion pictures, slides, filmstrips, recordings, pictures, study prints, and graphic materials.

- *Language involvement.* We examined the language arts–social studies connection earlier in this chapter. This connection should be maintained and reinforced throughout the unit through such activities as reading good fiction and nonfiction books, listening to stories, writing reports, transcribing journals, creating written or oral stories, participating in a dramatic skit, delivering an oral report, taking part in oral discussions or debates, and listening to records, CDs, or audiotapes.

- *The arts.* You may use many arts and crafts activities throughout the unit, either as sources of information or as projects to illustrate important learnings. Paintings, sculptures, drawings, paper crafts, models (such as dioramas), songs, games, musical instruments, and dance all foster creativity as well as active involvement in learning.

- *Social relationships.* Sometimes it will be appropriate to work with the whole class; at other times objectives can be more easily achieved in small groups. Many times, special interests touch children deeply—these occurrences must be approached individually. The right steps cannot be prescribed on paper. The direction to go is toward whatever you sense to be the assessed needs of your own group of students.

- *Commitment to evidence.* If students are deeply motivated to learn (and most will be), they eagerly seek out evidence to clarify what puzzles them. "Does air ever freeze solid?" "How did the continents get their names?" Elementary school youngsters are not satisfied with surface explanations; they want to be absolutely sure. We push them into a detective's role whenever we encourage scholarly inquisitiveness. We build a commitment to scholarship when we arrange a variety of learning resources for the children to collect evidence, take opportunities to write down information and record phenomena, and relate observations to one another in an effort to search for deeper meaning.

The developmental experiences, then, offer students opportunities to wrestle with real problems. The whole point is to help them comprehend the interrelationships among phenomena that can make this nation and the world better places to live. We do this not only from the social studies alone, but by utilizing experiences that cut across all subject lines.

Phase 3: Culminating Activity.

While the preceding phases of the unit were content or process specific, the culminating activity allows students to review, summarize, or bring closure to the topic. This concluding portion of the unit usually takes the form of a whole-class project that gives students an opportunity to use what they have learned. The culmination might be a time during which group projects are shared; a festival where dance performances, creative skits, and cultural meals are enjoyed; a "readers forum" where written reports are read; or a construction project such as a model community, where children represent the major concepts learned. Not all units need to end with a culminating activity. Sometimes the unit that follows is such a natural transition that neither a culminating activity for the first unit nor an introductory experience for the second is necessary. If one unit deals with "The First Americans" (Native Americans), for example, and is followed by "Settling the Land" (early settlers), continuity from one unit to the next need not be broken.

You must carefully arrange the three major phases of activities, because each activity flows from preceding experiences and furnishes the foundation for those that

Children need real-life adventures; they learn best through firsthand sources.

follow. Arranging a meaningful sequence is like putting together the pieces of a puzzle.

Thematic Blueprints and Daily Lesson Plans

Thematic unit plans help you teach creatively with a sense of direction. Teachers usually organize the specific learning activities within the unit using either or a combination of two formats: thematic blueprints and daily lesson plans. A *thematic blueprint* contains brief descriptions, in paragraph form, of all the daily activities a teacher intends to offer throughout the unit. *Daily lesson plans,* by contrast, are much more detailed; they elaborate on the blueprint's brief description by clearly detailing the methods and materials. Activity 4–2 presents a sample thematic blueprint for our unit on Japan. Any of the descriptive paragraphs can be expanded into a lesson plan.

Activity 4–2

Instructional Outline

Thematic Blueprint for "Customs and Traditions of Japan"

Phase One: Introductory Activities

Day One

- Arrange a classroom display of pictures, objects, books, travel posters, magazine articles, travel brochures, art reproductions, national flag, examples of Japanese writing, and other items representative of Japan. Have some traditional Japanese music playing in the background as the children enter the room.

- At a conspicuous spot within the display, post a notice that the children have won an imaginary trip to Japan from a local travel agency.

- Respond to the children's comments and record any questions that come up. Using the display material, discuss what the class might expect to find upon arrival, in terms of people, products, landscape, lifestyle, and so on.

- Help the children to prepare for their imaginary trip to Japan in a way that will not only be able to answer their questions, but will help them find out even more about the country and its people. Tell them that they will be pretending to be families on the eve of a tour to Japan. Assign random family units—all families will have three members (for sake of working convenience), but actual family composition will vary from group to group. For example, one family may consist of a single parent and two children; another may have two parents and one child. The students will assume the roles of their fictitious family members within the group.

- Begin to learn about Japan the way real travelers do. Use maps and a globe to determine its location, its distance relative to the United States, and its terrain, climate, and any special physical features. Use the travel brochures and other materials from the display to help determine which locations to visit and whether air travel will be the most convenient mode of transportation.

Day Two

- Have the students prepare for their trip by completing passports (you may use real forms, available at local post offices) and receiving airline tickets. Study Japanese currency, examining exchange rates (if developmentally appropriate).

- Discuss the different expenses to be encountered: airfare, hotels, food, other travel expenses, guide and exhibit fees, tips, souvenirs, and so on.

- Give the students materials from which to construct journals they will complete during the trip. The students will record their adventures daily in these journals with their own words and pictures. Advise the class that their flight to Japan is scheduled for social studies class tomorrow.

- Prepare a travel itinerary as shown:

Travel Itinerary

Names of Travelers: 1.   2.

3.

City and state we will be departing from:

City and county of our destination:

The oceans or seas we will travel over:

The continents we will travel over:

The locations we plan to visit during our stay:
How we will travel to these locations:

Each family can bring only one suitcase. Think about what you will pack in it. What clothes will you pack? What others items do you need? What items can be shared among family members? What others items are important to you? Make a list of all that you wish to pack, and tell why you chose each item.

A gift we would bring to our Japanese host is:

Day Three

- Arrange the students' chairs in sections of three to resemble the interior of an airplane. Process the students through "customs," checking their passports. Assign plane seats by families. After everyone is safely on board, the flight attendant (you, the teacher) offers a greeting and explains critical preflight and in-flight information.

- Play a sound-effects tape or CD of a jetliner taking off. As the simulated flight levels off, explain how long the flight will take and that a movie (*Rim of Fire*) will be shown. Darken the room and start the film projector (or videotape). After watching the film, lead a comprehension activity (see Chapter 3) and invite the "families" to fill in the first page of their journals.

Literature Launcher

Day Four

- The *kamishibai* person, a Japanese storyteller (you, the teacher, in costume), is the first person the children meet. He greets the children, pounds his wooden sticks together, and everyone knows it is storytime. The *kamishibai* is dressed in traditional Japanese garb (kimono and geta) and explains the purpose and function of each part, as well as the fact that these items were worn as everyday garb in the past but are used primarily for special occasions today. The storyteller uses gaily colored pictures to tell a folktale, *The Crane Maiden* by Miyoko Matsutani, illustrated by Chihiro Iwasaki (Parents' Magazine Press).

- As a follow-up, the *kamishibai* shows the children how to make an origami crane out of folded paper, explaining that this is a centuries-old Japanese art form. The children then make their own cranes.

Phase Two: Developmental Experiences

Day Five

Simulate a day in the lives of Japanese schoolchildren. Pretend to be a teacher (*sensei*) who will be teaching the children some basic school-related information—Japanese writing characters and number characters. (Activities 4–3 and 4–4 present the comprehensive lesson plans for this learning experience.)

Day Six

Remaining in the simulated classroom setting, write the word *custom* on the chalkboard. Explain that a custom is a group's special way of doing something. Read aloud excerpts from the book *The Rooster Who Understood Japanese* by Yoshiko Uchida (Charles Scribner's Sons). Discuss the characters and customs portrayed in the story. Help students discover connections among related concepts by completing an information summary chart.

Days Seven to Ten

Write the word *tradition* on the chalkboard and remind the students that a special activity becomes a tradition when it is repeated year after year. Many families in Japan practice traditions passed on to them by their ancestors. Explain that the "classroom families" will now function as cooperative investigation teams to prepare a presentation or project on traditions of Japan. Ask the librarian to help locate books, CDs, tapes, study prints, and other sources to help the students uncover information associated with these topics: (1) folk dances, (2) Kabuki theater, (3) holidays—such as Children's Day, (4) music, (5) folk tales, (6) religion, and (7) food.

Phase Three: Culminating Activities

Days Eleven and Twelve

Celebrate the customs and traditions of Japan by engaging the children in the following activities:

- Display the journals summarizing each family's tour through Japan.
- Share the results of the cooperative investigation. Have the students act as *kamishibai* as they show how Japanese families carry out various customs and traditions.

Thematic blueprints set the general flow of the unit activities; the lesson plans shed light on the explicit way those activities will be carried out. Lesson plans were comprehensively discussed in Chapter 3; two models (Activities 4–3 and 4–4) illustrate a specific plan to carry out Days 5 through 6, a visit to a Japanese classroom. Placing these lessons in sequence should be an orderly process where learning experiences are placed in a logical flow. Many teachers prefer to begin a unit with a motivating activity; once curiosity is aroused, the next several lessons are frequently planned to promote the knowledge and comprehension levels of Bloom's taxonomy. Once the basic knowledge and concepts are built, that base can be used for lessons designed at the application, analysis, synthesis, and evaluation levels. Although this model does not exist everywhere, it is probably used by more teachers than any other.

Activity 4–3

Lesson Plan

Theme: Customs and Traditions of Japan
Grade: Five
Teacher: Luis Arroyo

General Objective

The students shall understand the kinds of experiences their counterparts might undergo in a Japanese classroom.

Specific Objectives

1. The students shall demonstrate how Japanese students greet their teacher.
2. The students shall reproduce the Japanese ideographs representing the numbers 1–4.
3. The students shall learn to count from one to four in Japanese.

Materials

1. A chart depicting the Japanese ideographs representing the numbers 1–4.
2. One thick-bristled paintbrush per child.
3. Black tempera paint.
4. One sheet of manila drawing paper per child.
5. Photos of children in Japanese elementary schools.
6. Chart displaying rules of a Japanese classroom.

Procedure

1. Show photos of children in Japanese elementary schools. Discuss the children's observations.
2. Inform the students that they will be simulating a visit to a Japanese elementary school. Begin by instructing them to stand behind their chairs; demonstrate how the children bow to the teacher (*sensei*) and offer the greeting, "O-hayo gozaimasu," which means, "Good morning." Practice this routine several times and then leave the room. Upon return, the children should stand and extend the greeting.
3. Read and discuss the rules of a Japanese classroom (displayed on a class chart):

- When the teacher enters, rise and bow. Greet the teacher in unison.
- Come to school prepared with pencils, erasers, pens, paper, and text-books.
- Raise your hand to answer questions. Stand before answering.
- Be quiet during class.
- Keep to the right in the hall. No running.
- Help clean the classroom, hall, and yard. Pick up trash, sweep floors and yard, and stack chairs before anyone leaves.

4. Discuss how these rules are like or unlike their classroom rules.

5. Bring the students' attention to the display where Japanese numerals from one through four are illustrated. Ask, "What do you see?"

6. Inform the children that they are going to learn to count in Japanese from one to four. Pronounce each number name and encourage the children to recite them.

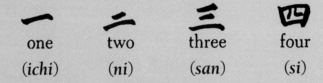

one   two   three   four

(*ichi*)   (*ni*)   (*san*)   (*si*)

7. Give each child one container of black tempera paint. Show the children how to lightly tear the edges of their drawing paper to resemble handmade rice paper. Demonstrate the *suni-e* style of painting: Hold the brush between the thumb and fingertips in a vertical position and move the arm to make the basic two strokes. To create *gung* (wide strokes), apply more pressure; for shey (finer strokes), slant the brush slightly and ease up on the pressure. Have students write the numerals on their drawing paper.

8. Arrange the students' ideographs in a classroom display.

9. Ask the students to think about how their school is similar to a Japanese school and how it is different. Complete a Venn diagram to help organize their responses, recording the unique features of Japanese schools in one circle, the unique features of their school in the other, and features common to both where the circles intersect.

Assessment

1. Observe students during the simulated classroom activity to judge whether they have made progress toward the desired behaviors.
2. Examine the ideographs to check the accuracy of the numeral forms.
3. Determine whether student journal entries incorporate accurately and completely the information shared in the lesson.

Activity 4-4

Lesson Plan

Theme: Customs and Traditions of Japan
Grade: Five
Teacher: Luis Arroyo

General Objective

The students shall understand the kinds of experiences their counterparts might undergo in a Japanese classroom.

Specific Objective

The students shall create a traditional Daruma-san doll as a representation of a traditional Japanese custom.

Materials

1. Souvenir Daruma-san dolls from Japan.
2. One blown egg with an enlarged hole for each child.
3. One small lead fishing sinker for each child.
4. Masking tape.
5. Papier-mâché strips.
6. Paper towels.
7. Various colors of tempera paint.

Procedure

1. Review the previous lesson by having the students greet the teacher in traditional Japanese style.

2. Review the Japanese "math" lesson from the previous day. Inform the students that they will experience a sample craft lesson today; they will be making a toy that has been appreciated for generations in Japan. Discuss some of their favorite toys. Are any of their toys like the ones their parents enjoyed as children?

3. Display the souvenir Daruma-san dolls. Explain that legend has it that these dolls are named for a Buddhist priest (*san* means "mister," a title of respect) who sat in a red robe with his arms and legs crossed for nine years while contemplating serious problems. Daruma-san is represented by a roly-poly doll that, no matter how it is tipped, bobs back upright. Traditional Daruma-san dolls (popularly called "roly-polies" in the United States) are painted red with a face having no eyes. The dolls are given to someone who is trying something new. When that person sets a goal, one eye is painted in; when the goal is accomplished, the other eye is completed.

4. Help the students make their own Daruma-san dolls. To make them, give each student a blown egg with an enlarged hole. The children put a small fishing sinker through the hole and cover the hole with masking tape. Next, they coat their eggs with four layers of overlapping papier-mache strips. After they dry, the students can paint on a face, leaving off the eyes. The clothes could be painted in many colors, but the most traditional is red (symbolizing a red robe).

5. Encourage the students to set a goal for the remainder of the school year. Once this is done, they should add one eye. When the goal is accomplished, the remaining eye should be colored.

6. Discuss the patience and determination it takes to reach an important goal.

Assessment

1. Check the completed dolls to see if they accurately represent the characteristics of Daruma-san dolls.
2. Read student journals to see how students summarized what they learned.

Assessment

You read in Chapter 3 that assessment is carried out in two ways. *Formative assessment* occurs during instruction for the purpose of informing the teacher about the children's current performance. Formative assessment guides the teacher's planning, providing the data that leads the way to appropriate instructional adjustments. This method relies on such day-to-day information as teacher observations and demonstrated performance on specific learning tasks. Good assessment begins with formative assessment—the teacher's evaluation of what students are gaining from instruction every day. Such feedback helps teachers make informed decisions about student progress and about any adjustments that need to be made in the curriculum.

Summative assessment, on the other hand, is carried out at the end of a unit of instruction. It is considered a summary of what the student has accomplished and, because instruction has been completed, is more useful for assessing final achievement (usually for assigning a grade) than for initiating changes in instruction.

Standardized Tests

One of the most hotly debated summative assessment strategies is called the *standardized test.* Standardized tests are commercially prepared, machine-scored, "norm-referenced" instruments. Norm-referencing means that the test is administered to a sampling of students selected according to such factors as age, gender, race, grade, or socioeconomic status. Their average scores then serve as "norm scores" and become the basis for comparing the performance of all the students who will subsequently take the test.

How do we use the results of standardized achievement tests in social studies? What do they offer that we can't get without them? Worthen and Spandel (1991) respond:

> Comparability, for one thing. Comparability in the context of the "big picture," that is. It isn't very useful, usually, for one teacher to compare his or her students' performance with that of the students one room down and then to make decisions about instruction based on that comparison. It's too limited. We have to back away to get perspective. This is what standardized test results enable us to do—to back off a bit and get the big, overall view on how we can answer global questions. (p. 67)

Global questions are those such as, "*In general*, are my fourth graders learning basic social studies content as well as other fourth graders in our school district?" "Compared to sixth graders throughout the United States, how well are those in our school district able to read maps and globes?" "How does our district's social studies curriculum compare with others in the state?" Despite the fact that standardized tests can determine only a small fraction of any student's total achievement in social studies, the public assigns standardized test scores great weight: "Are our students making 'normal' progress?" "Is their overall achievement above or below average?" Shepard (1989) explains what happens when such sharp public interest becomes focused on the results of standardized tests:

> When the scores have serious consequences—and they often do—teachers will teach to the test. Indeed, it is often the explicit intention of policymakers to force teachers to address essential skills. But teaching to the test cheapens instruction and undermines the authenticity of scores as measures of what children really know, because tests are imperfect proxies even for the knowledge domains nominally covered by the tests; and they also omit important learning goals beyond the boundaries of the test domain. (p. 5)

One major concern about standardized testing, then, is that teachers will over-react to the tested areas at the expense of the "real world" of social studies. Seldom in the "real world" is one limited to using memorized information from social studies; applying knowledge to the construction of concepts, the solution of problems, and the formation of attitudes or personal beliefs are required much more of active citizens. "Test-generated" instruction, however, often leads to repeated drill and practice on decontextualized skills and content because teachers are pressured to prove that what they are doing produces desired outcomes. Challenging activities such as problem solving and creative thinking are deemphasized; learning centers, literature, art, and music are eliminated to make more time for daily drill and practice. One first-year teacher described the stress produced by such pressure:

> I was petrified that my class would do so poorly that I wouldn't be back next year. So I taught what the other teachers recommended to get them ready for the test. After the test I started teaching, good teaching. The class enjoyed it, and I think they learned more the last three weeks of school than they did the first six months, because I was more relaxed, the students were more relaxed, and I was able to hone in on those areas where they needed help. (Livingston, Castle, & Nations, 1989, p. 24)

Another teacher commented, "Testing makes me want to get out of the classroom. If they had started this ten years ago, I might have quit and substituted full-time just so I wouldn't have to teach to these tests" (Livingston, Castle, & Nations, 1989, p. 24). Many teachers are opposed to tests that lock them into inflexible roles; they either find a way to resist teaching to the test, capitulate, or get out of the profession. Rote learning has its effects on students, too. Students become bored with such instruction, fail to sense its relevance, and often develop negative attitudes toward social studies and other subjects.

With all this criticism, you may want to ask, "Can standardized testing be a good thing for the social studies program?" The answer is a qualified yes—if the tests are not asked to do too much. They can show differences among groups in a school or district, reveal how students in a school or district compare to other students across the country, indicate whether a school is increasing or decreasing in general social studies achievement, provide support for grouping and placement decisions, help identify students in need of special services, and aid teachers in making curricular decisions. However, school administrators must resist all temptation to view the test as a "district report card," thereby forcing teachers to resort to methods having only one overriding goal—raising the test scores.

Teacher-Made Tests

Of all the sit-down, paper-and-pencil types of tests, teacher-made tests have traditionally been the most common form of assessment for units of instruction in social studies. The reason for their popularity is obvious: When teachers expend the great time and energy needed to originate a comprehensive thematic plan, they want to know if their efforts have resulted in positive student growth.

Constructing Teacher-Made Tests.   Teacher-made tests are referred to as *criterion-referenced tests* and are used to measure the mastery of specific instructional objectives. So, rather than comparing a student's score to a norming sample as we found with norm-referenced tests, criterion-referenced tests measure student performance against a specific guidepost, or criterion. Students are not compared to anyone else, they are judged only by what they can or cannot do. Criterion-referenced tests, then, are used to describe individual performance. Besides this immediate feedback, teacher-made tests also serve other functions:

1. They support information on which grades can be based.
2. They support diagnostic decisions about student needs—their strengths and weaknesses in social studies.
3. They help determine a student's progress.
4. They allow teachers to modify course objectives in accordance with student needs
5. They suggest ways teachers might alter instructional strategies, techniques, and resources.

Teacher-made, criterion-referenced tests are used to measure minimum competence in achieving targeted instructional objectives. If mastery has been achieved, instruction proceeds; if not, the objective will need further attention. Thus, the results of criterion-referenced tests offer teachers meaningful information that they can use in planning classroom instruction. These tests, however, must not encourage the kind of narrowly focused instruction that norm-referenced tests often invite. If the students are evaluated only on their ability to recall information and fall short of the mark, teachers should not be tempted to "right the ship" with a preponderance of one-right-answer drill and practice. To keep this from happening, teachers of elementary school social studies need to be much more informed about teacher-made, criterion-referenced tests.

The Link to Objectives.   To serve as legitimate data sources for social studies instruction, items on teacher-made tests must be directly linked to unit objectives. This is the only way we can effectively assess the degree to which students have benefited from classroom instruction. And, although teachers do not have the test construction expertise that developers of standardized tests have, they must still be aware of the basic steps in designing test items.

The first step in constructing a teacher-made test is reviewing the stated instructional objectives. Whether they originated as part of a textbook series, school district guide, state-mandated curriculum guide, or statement of national standards, or were collected from various sources, these objectives set the course for the unit by clearly communicating what the students are expected to do after the unit has been completed. Before any outcome can be measured by a teacher-made test, then, there must be a clearly stated objective pinpointing the desired performance.

Once the teacher has carefully examined the instructional objectives, she must determine the format of the test items. When testing for knowledge outcomes, images of multiple-choice or true-false questions often dance through our minds. These types of questions continue to dominate testing in social studies classrooms. Multiple-choice, true-false, matching, and fill-in-the-blanks are the most popular of all forms of teacher-made test items.

Multiple Choice.   Multiple-choice items consist of two major components: the stem and three or four alternatives. The *stem* is the part that asks the question; the *alternatives* are the choices available to the student. (The wrong alternatives are called *distractors*.) Students must read the stem carefully and select the best alternative. Here is where the real skill of test construction emerges: You must state the question so that the correct answer is the *only* or *best* alternative available. Although they are useful for older learners, multiple-choice questions are usually very confusing for elementary school children; they respond better to questions with fewer alternatives.

True-False.   True-false items require students to select from among only two alternatives. Figure 4–3 presents true-false items that show common faults. See if you can pick them out before reading my explanations. Sometimes, upper-grade teachers request justification for responses. For example, students might be asked to alter false statements to make them true or support true or false responses with confirming data.

Matching.   Matching items consist of a problem column and a response column. Students must select an item from the response column that correctly matches a problem item. Look at the two formats for writing matching items in Figures 4–4 and 4–5. Which do you think is the most appropriate?

FIGURE 4–3
Guidelines for Constructing
True-False Test Items

1. "Cooperstown is the home of the Baseball Hall of Fame and the Farmer's Museum."
   Fault: The truth of falsity should center on only one point.
   Improvement: "Cooperstown is the home of the Baseball Hall of Fame.

2. "Christy Mathewson was not a pitcher."
   Fault: Negatives should not be used; they are confusing to elementary school youngsters.

3. "Players inducted into the Hall of Fame were deserving the honor."
   Fault: This is a value judgment. Values are not appropriate for true-false items.

4. "The annual Hall of Fame game at Doubleday Field is always a sellout."
   Fault: Words like "usually," "always," or "all" are usually signals that a statement is false.

5. "Lou Gehrig was one of the first ten players enshrined in the Hall of Fame in 1936."
   Fault: The statement contains three facts, two of which are false. Lou Gehrig was not in the first group; there were only five players enshrined that year. Do not mix true and false information in the same statement.

6. Avoid a pattern of responses; students discover patterns quickly. Your goal is to evaluate the students' knowledge and skills, not their ability to solve a pattern puzzle.

In Figure 4–4 the first and most obvious problem is that items are heterogeneous; four items involve names (two in each column), one involves a song title (easily associated by a process of elimination), one refers to a city, and yet another to an object. We limit the range of potential responses with such a distribution. Another common error is to offer an equal number of items in each column. Again, students use the process of elimination to arrive at the last answer or two. Contrast the items in Figure 4–4 with those in Figure 4–5.

Fill-in-the-Blank.   Fill-in items involve simple recall of important names, dates, places, and other discrete information. The test items are usually presented as statements with key words missing. See if you can detect the weaknesses in the samples in Figure 4–6.

FIGURE 4–4
Guidelines for Constructing Matching Test Items

Directions: Select an item in Column B that goes with an item in Column A. Put the letter of your choice in the blank.

Column A

_____ 1. *Take Me Out to the Ball Game*

_____ 2. "The Splendid Splinter"

_____ 3. created the game of baseball

_____ 4. Cooperstown, New York

_____ 5. Babe Ruth

_____ 6. baseball's oldest known artifact

_____ 7. Henry Aaron

Column B

A. Abner Doubleday

B. home of the Baseball of Fame

C. the "Doubleday Ball"

D. song played at first enshrinement

E. holds all-time home run record

F. Ted Williams

G. elected as one of the first five players to be enshrined in the Hall of Fame

FIGURE 4–5
Further Matching Test Guidelines

Directions: Select an item in Column B that goes with an item in Column A. Put the letter of your choice in the blank.

Column A

_____ 1. Amelia Earhart

_____ 2. Sandra Day O'Connor

_____ 3. Clara Burton

_____ 4. Elizabeth Blackwell

_____ 5. Phillis Wheatley

_____ 6. Virginia Dare

_____ 7. Harriet Beecher Stowe

Column B

A. first woman Supreme Court Justice of U.S.

B. earliest known black female poet

C. first English child to be born in America

D. author of *Uncle Tom's Cabin*

E. first woman to make solo Atlantic flight

F. first woman doctor in United States

G. Civil War nurse—Red Cross organizer

H. Underground Railroad organizer

I. Founder of the Girl Scouts of America

FIGURE 4–6
Guidelines for Constructing Fill-in Test Items

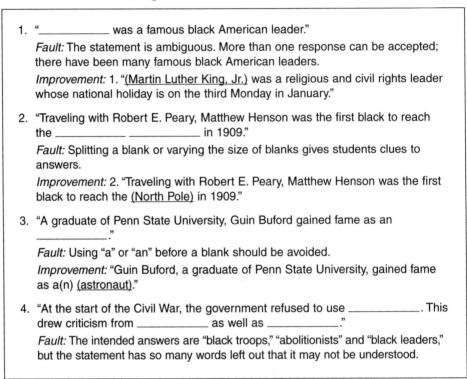

1. "_____ was a famous black American leader."

   Fault: The statement is ambiguous. More than one response can be accepted; there have been many famous black American leaders.

   Improvement: 1. "(Martin Luther King, Jr.) was a religious and civil rights leader whose national holiday is on the third Monday in January."

2. "Traveling with Robert E. Peary, Matthew Henson was the first black to reach the _____ _____ in 1909."

   Fault: Splitting a blank or varying the size of blanks gives students clues to answers.

   Improvement: 2. "Traveling with Robert E. Peary, Matthew Henson was the first black to reach the (North Pole) in 1909."

3. "A graduate of Penn State University, Guin Buford gained fame as an _____."

   Fault: Using "a" or "an" before a blank should be avoided.

   Improvement: "Guin Buford, a graduate of Penn State University, gained fame as a(n) (astronaut)."

4. "At the start of the Civil War, the government refused to use _____. This drew criticism from _____ as well as _____."

   Fault: The intended answers are "black troops," "abolitionists" and "black leaders," but the statement has so many words left out that it may not be understood.

Essay Items. The question formats discussed to this point are especially applicable to lower levels of thinking, such as Bloom's knowledge level. However, you also need to evaluate students on their abilities to think and reason at higher levels—to apply, analyze, synthesize, and evaluate information. For this reason, you must give students opportunities to write responses to questions that involve more complex thought than simple recall. As with the previous items, though, essay questions are prone to problems in construction. Consider the examples in Figure 4–7.

A major concern when grading essay tests is to maintain objectivity; evaluation of essay questions is often influenced by teacher bias. Rubrics (see Chapter 3) can help you maintain objectivity.

Although these formats may remind you of test questions that have been used on teacher-made tests for generations, a "new breed" of assessment items has captured the attention of social studies educators. In these items, students are asked to respond to questions that require a higher level of thinking than simple information recall.

FIGURE 4–7
Guidelines for Constructing Essay Tests

---

1. "Describe how the contributions of Josiah T. Henson helped to improve the quality of life in America."

   Fault: The question is too ambiguous and general; the student may resort to recalling specific events.

   Improvement: "Josiah T. Henson was the inspiration for Harriet Beecher Stowe's *Uncle Tom's Cabin*. Give three examples of how the story of Josiah Henson converted many to abolitionism."

2. What was the Underground Railroad?"

   Fault: The question requires only lower-level recall. Such information is more easily tested with objective items.

   Improvement: "Born as a slave in Maryland, Harriet Tubman ran away in 1849 to Philadelphia, using a series of safe houses called the Underground Railroad. Later she led more than 300 slaves to their freedom, despite rewards offered for her capture. Why did Tubman return to the South time and time again to rescue as many slaves as she could?"

Should an instructional objective pinpoint "comprehension" as a targeted outcome, for example, the resulting test item should assess whether or not students can distinguish relationships among data. In this case, you might consider giving the students lists of words and asking them to circle the word in each set that does not belong. For example, the students would examine the list below and circle the words in each row that are not conceptually related to the other words; then they must justify their choices:

boll weevil	cotton	sharecropper	butter
cattle drive	roundup	stampede	railroad
Sputnik	John Glenn	Neil Armstrong	Sally Ride

Still another strategy is Simpson's (1987) paired-word sentence generation strategy. In this method, the students are given two related words or phrases and demonstrate their understanding by generating one sentence illustrating the relationship of the words/phrases to each other. For example, the names "Thomas Jefferson" and "University of Virginia" might result in a sentence like this: "Thomas Jefferson designed the buildings for the University of Virginia." The words "rock" and "volcano" might be related to each other like this: "Rock is formed when hot lava from a volcano cools and hardens."

Along the same line, questions at the highest level of Bloom's taxonomy (evaluation) would require students to make judgments about the information. One simple way to do this is to ask students to complete an unfinished sentence, such as, "Our unit of work has changed (or reinforced) my ideas about. . . ." Another is to offer students several choices and ask them to select one that most closely approximates their feelings on a topic. For example, here are three reactions to Lincoln's Gettysburg Address:

A. "It is a flat failure and the people are disappointed." (Lincoln).
B. ". . . silly, flat and dishwatery" *(Chicago Times).*
C. ". . . will live among the annals of man" *(Chicago Tribune).*

The students must select the statement they believe most closely describes Lincoln's Gettysburg Address and give reasons to support their belief.

In like manner, when the instructional objective is at any other level of Bloom's taxonomy—application, analysis, synthesis—students should be engaged in test items that indicate mastery not only of the content, but also of the thinking processes involved in those levels.

Testing Primary-Grade Children

So far, you have learned about standardized and teacher-made tests for the social studies program. Most educators agree that if these tests are used *only* for the purposes for which they were designed, teachers could have valuable sources of information about their children and the curriculum. However, there is a great deal of concern about abuses of testing, especially in kindergarten, first grade, and second grade. The National Association for the Education of Young Children (1988), a highly influential professional organization for early childhood educators, recently inquired into the issue of whether we gain any useful information about children by testing. Their summation was emphatic: "[T]esting seldom provides information beyond what teachers and parents already know. The systematic observations of trained teachers and other professionals, in conjunction with information obtained from parents and other family members, are the best sources of information. *Most teachers and parents know that paper-and-pencil tests are not accurate measures of young children's development and learning*" [italics mine].

A developmentally appropriate social studies program, then, should assess K–2 children's learning through ongoing formative assessment strategies rather than by summative tests; many of the important outcomes of early primary-grade social studies programs involve important skills and attitudes that are not easily measured on tests—self-esteem, social competence, self-discipline, and motivation for learning. As a result, social, emotional, and moral development are assigned minor importance in schools with formalized testing programs. Young children are not driven to conform to "right answers," as adults are. Don't rush them; the rest of their lives will be filled with tests. Certainly, they must be taught about the real world and their mistakes must be corrected, but there should be no undue rush to get them through this marvelous period of life. It is a natural stage of development, one that is rich in enthusiasm and desire. Be careful not to squelch this incomparable spirit by placing them in situations that damage their delicate self-concept or their perceptions about how others see them.

Good social studies programs center around student needs. Through sound assessment techniques, we can discover these needs, make adjustments to the program, and judge the success of our efforts. The continuous and informed judgments of teachers can provide information required to discover the conditions that best promote learning for each individual in the elementary school social studies program.

Portfolios

Portfolios have recently come to the forefront as an alternative technique of summative assessment. Because portfolios differ so markedly from conventional methods of assessment, considerable disagreement exists about what exactly they are. The Association for Supervision and Curriculum Development (1993) informs us:

> At present, experts say, there is no common definition of "portfolio" and little data describing how extensive their use may be. In some classrooms, portfolios are little more than folders containing students' assignments; in others, considerable attention is given to what pieces ought to be included in the portfolio, how the assembled pieces form a composite picture of student growth, and against what standards the work is to be evaluated. Some teachers evaluate each piece of work in the portfolio and rate the portfolio as a whole; others eschew portfolio grades altogether. "There's virtually no standard practice that we can find," says Robert Calfee, professor of education and psychology at Stanford University, who recently completed a study of teachers and schools using portfolios. (p. 3)

Teachers need much information to assess the learning that goes on during a theme or project. Portfolios exhibit student achievement throughout the sequence of instruction.

Despite such variation, individuals unfamiliar with portfolios need a somewhat better definition. To that end, I quote Paulson, Paulson, and Meyer (1991):

> A portfolio is a purposeful collection of student work that exhibits the student's efforts, progress, and achievements in one or more areas. The collection must include student participation in selecting contents, the criteria for selection, the criteria for judging merit, and evidence of student self-reflection. (p. 60)

There is no single list of items recommended for all portfolios; Stiggins (1994) advises that what is included should be determined by the following considerations:

- *Purpose*—As the reason for assessment varies, so will the story to be told and the audience. For example, a portfolio intended to document a student's improvement over a semester for motivational purposes will contain different ingredients from a portfolio to be evaluated for [progress during a thematic unit].
- *Nature of the outcome(s)*—The knowledge, reasoning, skills, products, and/or effect to be described in the portfolio will dictate the student work samples to be collected.
- *Focus of the evidence*—The portfolio can either show change in student performance over time or status at one point in time. This factor is an issue in grading as well as in designing portfolios.
- *Time span*—If student improvement is the focus, over what time period—a month, a term—should work be collected?
- *Nature of the evidence*—What kind of evidence will be used to show student proficiency—tests, work samples, observations? (p. 422)

Portfolios may include such items as student writings, art products, photographs, independent research reports, projects, favorite books, and other work samples from the social studies. One teacher's approach to initiating a portfolio program is chronicled in Activity 4–5.

Activity 4-5

 **Case Study**

Personal Portfolios

Mr. Clough went to the chalkboard and wrote the word *portfolio*. He asked how many of his fifth graders might have an idea about what a portfolio is. Anticipating that the idea was foreign to his class, Mr. Clough brought out a box containing items that were important to him. The box contained things that, in effect, created a biographical sketch of Mr.

Clough. He informed his students that portfolios tell a story and he chose objects that helped tell about him as a person.

The first item in Mr. Clough's portfolio was a photograph of his family. "I love my family," he declared proudly. Next came a diploma from college. "I was the only member of my family to have ever gone to college," he announced. Several ribbons followed—they were awarded at college for success in swimming. Mr. Clough then held up a book and explained, "In my spare time, I enjoy reading a good book." The most fascinating item came next—a photo of Mr. Clough taken as a fifth grader. The following item was his report card from fifth grade. "I wanted to show you the best report card I ever received." The last article he removed from the box was a children's book, *The Little Engine That Could*. "This is one of the favorite stories my parents read to me as a child. It taught me that a person could accomplish almost anything if he or she tried hard enough."

Next, Mr. Clough asked the class what should be included in a social studies portfolio. What would show their effort and learning in social studies? He noted suggestions: daily assignments, drawings, illustrated maps, their best writings and those reflecting problems, group projects, individual projects, journal entries, audiotapes of oral reports, and so on. The class then discussed the format of a good portfolio. They decided it should be housed in a suitable container—boxes, file folders, folded sheets of construction paper, binders, and so on. The class also decided it should be neat and should include a table of contents. Furthermore, each article should have with it a short personal statement about why it was important to the learner. Following this discussion, Mr. Clough gave his class one week to organize their portfolios.

There are countless ways to organize portfolios; the important consideration is that the students take an active role in selecting material for and maintaining their portfolios. Of course, the portfolios must address instructional priorities.

When students create their portfolios, their exhibits become a means through which you may provide evaluative feedback and monitor progress. You should hold individual conferences with the students during which you guide portfolio review with such questions as the following:

- "How has your work in social studies changed since last year (or last month)?"
- "What do you now know about _____ that you didn't know before?"
- "What are the special items in your portfolio?"
- "What would you most like me to understand about your portfolio?"

- "How did you organize the items?"
- "What are the strengths as displayed in the portfolio? What needs improvement?"

The conference should focus not just on subject-matter accomplishments, but also on planning strategies, personal reflections, and evidence of progress. Adams and Hamm (1992) address this important aspect of portfolio use:

> Learning requires communication—with self, peers, and knowledgeable authorities. It also requires effort and meaningful assessments of these efforts. Since students need to be involved actively in evaluating and providing examples of their own learning, they must document the probing questions they are asking, identify what they are thinking, and reflect on their understandings. In this way students can create, evaluate, and act upon material that they and others value. Assuming active roles in the learning process and taking responsibility for what students are learning goes beyond simply recognizing that they have made a mistake to imagining why, getting feedback from others, and finding practical ways to do something about it.
>
> Portfolios provide a powerful way to link learning with assessment. They can provide evidence of performance that goes far beyond factual knowledge and offers a clear and understandable picture of student achievement. (p. 105)

Portfolios are a rich source for individual assessment in the social studies. They yield much concrete evidence that allows teachers to evaluate the progress their students are making. While this is important, however, the greatest asset of portfolios may be in self-evaluation. Portfolio assessment offers students the opportunity to set individual goals, select the items for evaluation, and reflect on their work. In this way it encourages pride in learning and helps students develop motivation to improve.

An important point to remember is that no single instrument or technique can adequately assess the range of performances and behaviors in the social studies. For this reason, educators today strongly favor using portfolios containing a variety of measures. Despite these popular endorsements, some teachers have been slow to use portfolios in their classrooms. They are skeptical of whether the results justify the time required to evaluate multiple measures. Administrators must provide teachers with the time and support required to effectively evaluate student portfolios. School district and building administrators hold the key to helping teachers endorse this form of assessment. If teachers can see portfolios as manageable and rewarding, they will be inclined to add them to their already full workload and to evaluate them with enthusiasm.

Because this sample unit is based on multiple objectives, several summative measures will be employed: (1) anecdotal records and checklists that summarize each student's attentiveness, involvement in class activities, and responses to special challenges; (2) student portfolios that serve as a collection of journal writings, assignment sheets, reports, artwork, literature response sheets, creative writing, and other evidence of what was learned; and (3) a written test for summative information and diagnostic purposes.

AFTERWORD

Creative teachers clearly demonstrate a key ingredient of first-rate instruction—a characteristic I call "stick-with-itness." This is a persistent, intense devotion to what they are doing. Teachers with stick-with-itness are thrilled with their professional responsibilities. Teaching is not only their job, it is their obsession. It leaves them virtually starry-eyed and eager to devise experiences that activate children for learning. All children must believe that their teachers are captivated by what they are doing in the classroom. In social studies, this means that teachers view their world with fascination and inspire their children to accept theirs as a neverending mystery. To do this, teachers must plan significant learning situations in which there is a little mystery, a bit of magic, and a dash of magnificence to confront the children. Elementary school children respond to these things; that is what makes their classrooms different from those for any other age.

Teachers achieve magic in the elementary school social studies program when they help *each child* become challenged by the activities and emotionally involved in the subject matter; they deliver the best for each youngster and make the most of their time every day. Teachers adapt instruction to meet the special needs and interests of all their students; they fully understand and are willing to work toward fulfilling the principles and assumptions that underlie learning carried out by small groups or individuals. Teachers use a large variety of learning tasks to meet their students' needs. Although thematic planning has become extremely popular in recent years, many elementary school social studies teachers continue to use a number of techniques that have been a part of the educational scene for years. We will learn more about these techniques and about the kinds of activities most appropriate for individual pursuits throughout the rest of this book.

TECHNOLOGY SAMPLER

Some useful sources for related social studies topics include these Internet sites:

AskERIC: ERIC Document Retrieval Service (EDRS)
http://www.edrs.com/cgi-bin/askERIC (or try http://ericir.syr.edu/)

Global SchoolNet Foundation
http://www.gsn.org/

Kathy Schrock's Guide for Educators
http://www.why-n-not.com/

Scholastic Network
http://scholastic.com/Network/indes.html

WHAT I *NOW* KNOW

Complete these self-check items once more. Determine for yourself whether it would be useful to take a more in-depth look at any area. Use the same key as you did for the preassessment form ("+", "?", "–").

I can *now*

_____ explain what is involved in carrying out projects in social studies classrooms.

_____ distinguish between projects and thematic units.

_____ describe the importance of using quality children's literature in carrying out a thematic unit.

_____ delineate the five-step format commonly used to organize thematic plans.

_____ describe the responsibilities involved in selecting an appropriate topic for the thematic plan.

_____ describe the place of goals and objectives in planning thematic instruction.

_____ explain how the content is selected and organized in thematic plans.

_____ explain how to choose and sequence learning experiences within the framework of a thematic plan.

_____ select assessment strategies appropriate for evaluating teaching and learning.

REFERENCES

Adams, D. M., & Hamm, M. E. (1992). Portfolio assessment and social studies: Collecting, selecting, and reflecting on what is significant. *Social Education, 56,* 105.

Association for Supervision and Curriculum Development (1993). Portfolio assessment bears the burden of popularity. *ASCD Update, 35,* 3.

Baskwill, J. (1988). Themestorming. *Teaching K–8,* August–September 1988), 80.

Berg, M. (1989). Integrating ideas for social studies. *Social Studies and the Young Learner, 1,* 1 (pull-out feature).

Borgia, E. (1996). Learning through projects. *Scholastic Early Childhood Today, 10,* 22–29.

Cullum, A. (1967). *Push back the desks.* New York: Citation.

Diffily, D. (1996). The project approach: A museum exhibit created by kindergartners. *Young Children, 51,* 72–75.

Goetz, E. M. (1985). In defense of curriculum themes, *Day Care and Early Education, 13,* 12.

Hartman, J. A., & Eckerty, C. (1995). Projects in the early years. *Childhood Education, 71,* 141–148.

Hendrick, J. (1992). *The whole child: Developmental education for the early years.* New York: Merrill/Macmillan.

Katz, L. G. (1990). Impressions of Reggio Emilia preschools. *Young Children, 45,* 11–14.

Katz, L. G. (1996). Lilian Katz on the project approach. *Scholastic Early Childhood Today, 10,* 20–21.

Katz, L. G., & Chard, S. C. (1989). *Engaging children's minds: The project approach.* Norwood, NJ: Ablex.

Livington, C., Castle, S., & Nations, J. (1989). Testing and curriculum reform: One school's experience. *Educational Leadership, 46,* 24.

Moll, L. C., & Whitmore, K. F. (1993). Vygotsky in classroom practice: Moving from individual transmission to social transaction. In E. A. Forman, N. Minnick, & C. A. Stone, *Contexts for learning.* New York: Oxford University Press.

National Association for the Education of Young Children (1988). *Testing of young children: Concerns and cautions* (Brochure #582). Washington, DC: Author.

Paulson, F. L., Paulson, P. R., & Meyer, C. A. (1991). What makes a portfolio a portfolio? *Educational Leadership, 48,* 60.

Piaget, J. (1990). Quoted in R. De Vries & L. Kohlberg, *Constructivist early education.* Washington, DC: National Association for the Education of Young Children.

Ryan, K., Burkholder, S., & Phillips, D. H. (1983). *The workbook.* Columbus, OH: Merrill.

Shepard, L. A. (1989). Why we need better assessment. *Educational Leadership, 46,* 5.

Simpson, M. (1987). Alternative formats for evaluating content area vocabulary understanding. *Journal of Reading, 31,* 20–27.

Stiggins, R. J. (1994). *Student-centered classroom assessment.* New York: Merrill/Macmillan, p. 422.

Strickland, D. S. (1994–1995). Reinventing our literacy programs: Books, basics, balance. *The Reading Teacher, 48,* 294–301.

Tompkins, G. E. (1997). *Literacy for the 21st century: A balanced approach.* Upper Saddle River, NJ: Prentice Hall.

Worthen, B. R., & Spandel, V. (1991). Putting the standardized test debate in perspective. *Educational Leadership, 48,* 67.

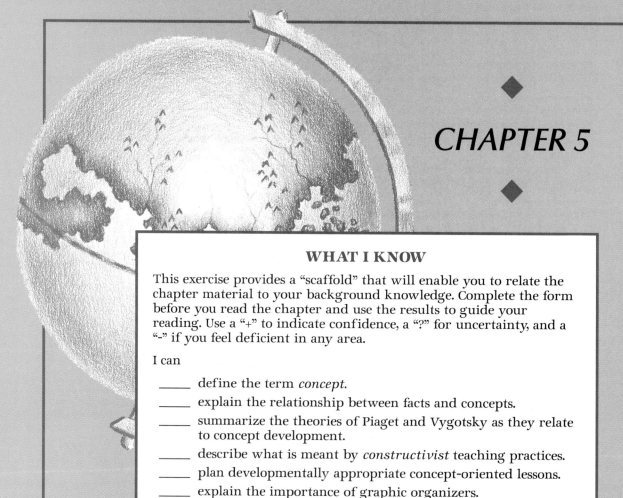

CHAPTER 5

WHAT I KNOW

This exercise provides a "scaffold" that will enable you to relate the chapter material to your background knowledge. Complete the form before you read the chapter and use the results to guide your reading. Use a "+" to indicate confidence, a "?" for uncertainty, and a "-" if you feel deficient in any area.

I can

_____ define the term *concept*.

_____ explain the relationship between facts and concepts.

_____ summarize the theories of Piaget and Vygotsky as they relate to concept development.

_____ describe what is meant by *constructivist* teaching practices.

_____ plan developmentally appropriate concept-oriented lessons.

_____ explain the importance of graphic organizers.

_____ plan a lesson centering on concept development.

Using the results as a guide, what questions will you seek to answer as you read?

Constructing Meaning

◆ **CLASSROOM SKETCH**

M s. Wood's third-grade class has been studying different groups of people who first lived in North America. They have read books, listened to stories, viewed videos, and participated in various other learning experiences intended to deepen related understandings. Ms. Wood begins today's lesson with a reading activity about the Cheyenne, an indigenous Plains Indian group. After facilitating a discussion of study prints depicting the early Cheyenne in their natural environment, she calls the children's attention to a large chart in front of the room. Ms. Wood writes the word *Buffalo* on the chart and circles it. She chooses to highlight the word because it is the central concept of the day's reading selection and will, in the course of the lesson, help students organize information about the animal, which was very important to the Cheyenne. Next, Ms. Wood generates categories related to the buffalo, writing the words *Food, Clothing, Shelter, Tools,* and *Toys* around the central concept. She circles each category and, to indicate a relationship, draws a line from each category to the central concept. Then she activates the students' background knowledge of the many ways the Cheyenne used the buffalo by asking them to offer any details or examples related to the categories on the chart. Within the category of "Shelter," for example, the students suggest "tepees;" for the category "Food," they offer "buffalo meat." All volunteered terms are written below the category circles (see Figure 5–1). Then Ms. Wood leads a discussion about the terms and their relationships. These categories not only help draw information from the students' past experiences, but furnish them with "mental file folders" that help attract and organize new information as it will be encountered in the reading assignment.

Once the selection is read, the students will add to and modify the chart to reflect new information or ideas about the importance of the buffalo to the Cheyenne. Additionally, any any inaccurate information listed before the reading will be corrected.

FIGURE 5–1

What We Know About the Uses of the Buffalo

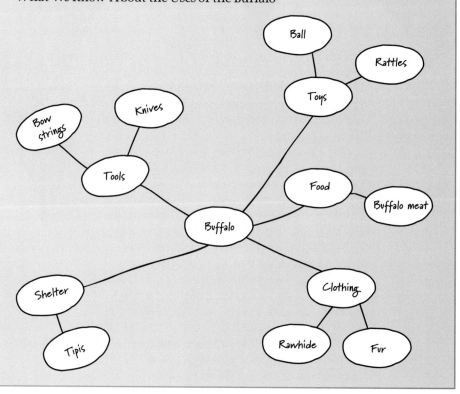

◆ CLASSROOM CONNECTION

Ms. Wood realized that established notions of how children learn play a decisive role in how we teach social studies. Her professional preparation taught her that for centuries philosophers have written endless volumes detailing their observations and have proposed explanations of the learning process, but that today's predominant view is based on the notion of *constructivism*. Constructivists reject the traditional "toss-and-catch" approach to instruction, where teachers cast out knowledge to the children and expect them to snare it and commit it to memory. Instead, constructivists suggest that knowledge must be constructed by learners—what children learn is not a result of copying or repeating what others want them to know, but is rather a result of actively building relationships between old knowledge and new knowledge. That is why Ms. Wood began her lesson with a discussion of study prints, helping students connect previously constructed information related to the topic at hand. Brooks and Brooks (1993) elaborate:

> Constructivism stands in contrast to the more deeply rooted ways of teaching that have long typified American classrooms. Traditionally, learning has been thought to be a "mimetic" activity, a process that involves students repeating, or miming, newly presented information. . . . Constructivist teaching practices, on the other hand, help learners to internalize and reshape, or transform, new information. (p. 15)

Constructivist teachers such as Ms. Wood consider students to be active participants on a journey of discovery. Her constructivist philosophy, as advocated in this textbook, couples the cognitive dimension of learning deeply rooted in the works of Jean Piaget with the social interaction theories proposed by Lev Vygotsky. This combination emphasizes the significance of a cognitive and social partnership in social studies education.

THE COGNITIVE DIMENSION OF CONSTRUCTIVISM

Whenever we consider the topic of "cognitive skills," we refer not to what the children know, but to the ways they order and organize knowledge in their minds. We have learned a great deal about how this happens from the work of Jean Piaget (1952), who described the process of cognitive development as the act of constructing concepts *(schemata)*. Piaget described concepts much as mental file folders into which we all organize and store the information gained from any life experience. Our minds are always acting during these life experiences, whether we are reading a book, taking a dip in the ocean, watching a television program, listening to a lecture, or gazing at a work of art. The mind perceives and makes meaning of whatever information it receives, deciding into which "file folder" any new information should be stored (or constructing a new one if an appropriate folder does not already exist).

The Nature of Concepts

According to constructivists, the mind can be depicted as a huge filing system of concept folders that develops and evolves as one engages in a variety of life experiences. Concept "folders" are most often labeled with single- or multiword titles. We cannot get through a day without hearing some reference to a *concept* or one of its synonyms. A few examples follow.

- "He has no *idea* what a deltiologist does."
- "The candidate offered a new *view* of city government."
- "The explorer's *understanding* of dengue was vague until she visited a tropical rainforest in Africa."

Can you distinguish the major concepts in each of the sentences above? They are *deltiologist, candidate, city government, dengue, explorer,* and *tropical rainforest.* Each of these concepts refers to a mental "file folder" into which you may have accumulated and sorted an extensive array of information. Most concepts were familiar to you (*candidate* and *explorer*), but some may have been quite vague (*deltiologist* and *dengue*). You grasped the meaning of the terms *candidate* and *explorer,* for example, because these words touched off a mental picture formed after participating in repeated life experiences. You have accumulated a background of knowledge about candidates and explorers, so your ideas of these people are fairly clear. But what learning experiences have you had to help you understand the concepts *deltiologist* and *dengue?* Probably none. Therefore, your file folder for these concepts was empty (or nonexistent), and you were unable even to begin sketching a mental picture of them.

Concepts grow from facts; they are firmly rooted in the learners experiences. But what happens when school requirements focus on facts with little or no regard for deeper understanding? Read the short passage that follows.

Diakinesis is defined as the final stage of the meiotic prophase immediately preceding formation of the metaphase plate and distinguished by marked contraction of the bivalents.

As with *deltiologist* and *dengue,* lack of background experiences may have blocked your ability to conceptualize the sentence. Now suppose you were required to know that information for a forthcoming test. Like most people, you would probably repeat the sentence to yourself many times over, committing it to memory and hopefully recalling it for the test—a process often described as *rote memorization.*

This does not imply that facts are unimportant in elementary school social studies. Facts are indeed important; they serve as building blocks, furnishing the details necessary to develop meaningful concepts. Concepts do not appear magically; their form is gradually built by the learner as knowledge accumulates through varied learning experiences. Without a system of organizing the wealth of information about our world, though, each fact becomes isolated and students have very few options other than to memorize it—and to complain that "social studies is boring!"

Facts are highly significant. They help learners distinguish *continents* from *countries, glaciers* from *icebergs,* and *Christianity* from *Judaism.* Because facts provide the defining qualities that make a concept what it is, they must be selected carefully. For example, details of George Washington's $60-a-set dentures (made from ivory, wild animal teeth, or lead covered with gold), as interesting as they may be, would not contribute much to enhancing the concept of our *presidency.* However, they could provide engaging facts to support an understanding of *health care* during colonial times. Concepts are superb organizational devices, but they can be formed accurately only when learners gather meaningful information through sound, developmentally appropriate activities.

Since each schema, or concept, grows and becomes more highly refined as new knowledge is accumulated, young children's schemata (plural for schema) are much different from ours. A young child who has encountered only ducks and geese during her brief lifetime, for example, will use the concept labels *goosey* and *ducky* to stand for large birds living near the water; consequently, all birds that share these attributes are labeled *goosey* or *ducky*. I recall a time at the seashore watching as a three-year-old rushed up to her mother, pointing at a number of large sea birds. She called excitedly, "Mommy, mommy! Look at all the goosies!" It was the first time she had ever seen large sea birds, but they shared enough common attributes with geese (large, feathers, flew, lived near the water) that the child filed them into the "goosey" folder. After continued life experiences with all kinds of birds, however, she will gradually arrange information in new ways to help make sense of her world. Therefore, her schema will become more highly differentiated, and large birds living near the water will be sorted into ducks, geese, sea gulls, pelicans, and so on.

The Process of Equilibration

Piaget labels the complex mental process through which learners add new information to existing schemata *equilibration*. He explains that this is accomplished through an action called *adaptation*. Adaptation consists of the combined effects of two processes—assimilation and accommodation. *Assimilation* is the process of integrating information from the environment into existing schemata to enhance one's picture of the world. *Accommodation* is the process of structuring new schemata or modifying existing schemata to form a new picture of the world.

To illustrate the idea of equilibration, let us examine the strategy employed by Mr. Hernandez as he helped his third graders unlock the idea of "communication" as a system common to all cultures. Mr. Hernandez opened his lesson by gathering the children together in a circle and asking them to sit cross-legged on the floor. Then he chose one child to stand alone in a corner of the room and asked the others to think about techniques they might use to direct the lone child to come from the corner of the classroom to where they were seated. The children offered obvious solutions such as using their voices to call their classmate, gesturing, or printing a command on a large sheet of paper (assimilation). To extend their thinking, Mr. Hernandez showed the children a drum, explaining that drums are among the oldest tools cultures have used to relay messages over distances. He told the children they were to think of ways the drum might be used to send a message to the child standing alone in the corner. After a brief period of discussion, the class invented separate drum rhythms to communicate different ways the lone student might move from the corner to their circle. Taking turns, the children tapped out fast rhythms to represent running, steady rhythms to encourage marching, light taps to suggest tiptoeing, and so on. The children had participated in rhythm and movement activities in music and physical education classes, and they only needed to apply those experiences to solve this new problem (accommodation). The children learned through this active, direct experience that people can communicate without using words (adaptation).

Seeking equilibrium, then, is the process through which constructivist learning takes place. Teachers facilitate the process by creating a situation where cognitive conflict arises—a situation where the child is challenged to assimilate something new into existing schemata. If the child applies an existing schema to the situation and the new data fits, then equilibration exists. If the attempt does not produce harmony, however, it will disturb the child and provoke her to seek equilibrium, or a balance between her present understanding of the world and the new data provided by the situation. That is why children who are confronted with incongruent information will be intrinsically motivated to make sense of it. If the child can accommodate the new information, her thinking changes and learning moves ahead. However, if the information is too difficult and the child cannot accommodate it to existing schemata, she will become frustrated, probably ignore it, and fail to learn.

To learn effectively in social studies, then, children must be helped to associate new knowledge to existing schemata for the purpose of moving to higher levels of understanding. What this means in practical terms is that, if you are considering "Dairy Farms" as a topic of instruction, for example, you must first determine the degree to which your children have developed the concept of *dairy farm* before you begin to select associated learning experiences. Some children, especially those from urban areas, may have had few experiences with dairy farms. They will, in all likelihood, associate the milk they buy in stores with cows and pastures, but may never have actually seen a real cow and heard it moo, smelled a pasture or barn, watched a cow being milked, or patted its big, wet nose. Because the world of cows or dairy farms is quite limited for these children, an attempt to organize the world of dairy farming into concept categories would be quite difficult without a highly direct, concrete learning experience such as a field trip to a dairy farm. If such a trip cannot be arranged, the children will need at least a quality video or a combination of other multisensory experiences before they will be motivated to examine the topic of dairy farming more extensively.

On the other hand, if you find that the children's life experiences with dairy farming are more extensive, it would be unproductive for them to have such basic introductory encounters. Rural children who live on or near dairy farms or have easy access to them, for example, may not need intensive, direct experiences. Instead, they would probably be able to begin with systematic investigations of more complex understandings, such as economic issues facing dairy farmers or the future of dairy farms in our increasingly technological society.

Effective social studies instruction employs learning situations that are familiar to the students, so that they are able to assimilate what is to be learned with existing schemata. This linkage helps learners make better sense of the new information and makes it more meaningful. Smith (1982) contends that if learners are not helped to make this assimilative connection, they often resort to one of these coping tactics:

1. *Rejecting the information.* When the incoming content does not register and we cannot connect it to what we already know, we tend to discard or ignore it.

A skilled social studies teacher offers hands-on experiences to help make concepts grow. In this classroom, the children's readings will be enriched by the artifacts on display.

2. *Miscategorizing the information.* If we choose not to throw out the unperceived information, we may make some attempt to comprehend it. However, the tendency is to misfile it. We may place it into a wrong file folder or simply allow it to float "unattached," thinking that it must belong there someplace and will eventually "settle."

For example, consider the case of young Jeff, an extremely bright and curious second grader. "That is our hummingbird feeder," he announced, "We attract them with *nectarine!*" Although Jeff had a strong foundational knowledge of birds and habitats, his great enthusiasm for learning resulted in occasionally fallible connections. Yet Jeff displayed an inborn penchant for seeing, feeling, thinking, and being that is part of the nature of all young learners.

Although initial concepts may be somewhat inaccurate, such honest attempts at explaining the workings of the world indicate a strong desire to learn. As children accumulate learning experiences and acquire more information, their concepts grow and become more precise. You must provide them with opportunities to add to their existing knowledge; whenever possible, these opportunities should entail first-hand experiences that encourage students to exercise their observation and thinking skills.

Teachers employ systematic procedures to guide and facilitate concept formation, but the act of concept formation itself is performed by the learner. Remy (1990) maintains, "One of the most important attributes of competent citizens in a complex society is the ability to connect things that seem superficially to be discrete. Such an ability is a clear sign of higher order cognition . . . and is a highly prized goal of social studies education" (p. 204). Van Doren (1982) supports Remy's view of the importance of making connections, stating that "[t]he student who can begin early in life to think of things as connected, even if he revises his view with every succeeding year, has begun a life of learning" (p. 384).

Smith (1975) asserts that learning should be considered a process of making sense of the world; he says that we do this best by relating the unfamiliar to the already known. Ausubel (1961) defends this critical idea: "If I had to reduce educational psychology to just one principle, I would say this: The most important single factor influencing learnings is what the learner already knows" (p. 16). Ausubel refers to the techniques that mentally prepare students to assimilate new information into existing concepts as *advance organizers*. There are many ways to present new information with advance organizers; a number will be explained later in this chapter. For a quick example, however, the "What I Know" openers for each chapter of this textbook are examples of advance organizers.

THE SOCIAL DIMENSION OF CONSTRUCTIVISM

Lev Vygotsky (1978) has studied the early works of Jean Piaget and has been strongly influenced by Piaget's belief that children should be active as they acquire knowledge. However, Vygotsky's theory differs from Piaget's primarily on the role that culture plays in helping form intelligence. While Piaget describes children as solitary explorers constructing knowledge of the world through their actions, Vygotsky suggests that most learning takes place in a social context; Piaget emphasizes interactions with physical objects while Vygotsky focuses on interactions with people. McGee and Richgels (1996) provide a vivid contrast of the two views by using an example of a child pulling and stretching a lump of modeling clay, changing its shape. In Piaget's scheme, we can say that the child learned about the properties of the clay primarily through the physical actions involved while manipulating it. Vygotsky agrees that physical activity contributes to cognitive growth, but explains that language and social context influence learning, too:.

[C]an children change their schema for modeling clay to include the notion that it is stretchy without their hearing or using the word "stretchy"? Can they pretend that modeling clay is bread dough without hearing someone else say, or being able themselves to say, that both are "stretchy"? Another way to put these questions is to ask: How important is it for the child to have the word *stretchy* available as a label for what is experienced in such a situation? Piaget and Vygotsky would answer this question differently. Vygotsky placed more importance on the child's having language along with action in order to learn. He stressed the importance of having someone with the child who could supply that language. According to Vygotsky, a mother who says to her child, "Look at the stretchy clay!" plays a vital role in her child's learning about clay. Vygotsky placed a strong emphasis on the social component of cognitive . . . development. (p. 7)

For Piaget, concepts develop primarily from direct action on physical objects; adults play only a minor role—organizing the environment and creating problems. For Vygotsky, concepts are socially mediated; they grow from interactions with others.

Intellectual "Tools"

Central to Vygotsky's thinking is the idea that humans are fundamentally different from animals because they make and use tools. They do so to enhance their natural abilities and to solve problems—to do things impossible to accomplish without them. Tools can be classified as *physical tools* (implements such as wheels or axes that are invented to help master the environment) or *mental tools* (complex cognitive processes used to solve all kinds of problems). Because physical and mental tools are invented by humans, they must be transmitted from generation to generation—taught to others. And since the significance of specific tools varies among groups of people (fishing nets are more valued by people living in New England than in Iowa), cultures influence how people should think. Cultures determine the kinds of things their members should learn and what they should believe.

Cultures have invented language, which is considered a cultural tool. That is because concepts take form in a culture, and the culture's language is used to represent and communicate ideas; for example, children in Mexico learn about the *peso* when studying their country's monetary system, while Russian students learn about the *ruble.* These concepts are best communicated in social experiences because they would be virtually impossible to construct without the input of an adult or a more knowledgeable peer.

Shared Experiences

Good social studies programs are based on an understanding that social interactions are essential for real learning to take place. For Vygotsky, the social context influences learning more than any other factor; it has firm control over how we act and think. When Vygotskians talk about the social context, they refer to everything in the child's environment that involves interactions with people, including family and school. In the social studies classroom, this means that children learn or acquire knowledge through a process of interacting with others—normally their teachers and peers. Only after this social interaction can the student internalize and use the concepts independently. Through these shared interactions, children are encouraged to discover, make choices, move at will, discuss, and grapple with personal challenges.

Shared Activities With Teachers (Scaffolding)

In order to implement socially based techniques, teachers must develop sophisticated interaction skills. Vygotsky suggests that these interactions serve as guides during learning activities, providing information and support for the child to grow intellectually. The adult observes the child and provides just the right help to assist him with a problem he is on the verge of solving by himself, but would fail if left to his own resources. This could be accomplished by asking questions or offering information, clues, reminders, demonstrations, and encouragement at just the right time and in the proper amount (a process referred to as conducting *educational dialogues*). The following example illustrates how an adult might conduct an educational dialogue with a child having difficulty finding an original answer for the question, "How would life have been different for the Navajo if they had lived in the Pacific Northwest instead of the Southwest?"

Teacher:	Teddy, what solution did you come up with?
Teddy:	I can't think of one idea.
Teacher:	What are some things the Navajo would find in the Pacific Northwest that are not found in the desert of the Southwest?
Teddy:	Lots of fish, big trees, and, uh, water. I guess.
Teacher:	Well, how would these things make the Navajo's lives different?
Teddy:	They could eat fish and maybe build wooden houses?
Teacher:	There you have it! Now try coming up with one or two more ideas."

Bodrova and Leong (1996) inform us that an educational dialogue is similar to a Socratic dialogue where there is give and take among all participants. It is a teacher-guided journey; the teacher gently leads the students to discover meaning, helping them correct misconceptions and avoid dead-end lines of thinking. This kind of adult assistance is called *scaffolding,* a term not originally used by Vygotsky but introduced by scholars (Wood, Bruner, & Ross, 1976) attempting to explain his instructional recommendations. Scaffolding helps support children's thinking until they reach a point where they can solve problems by themselves. As children demonstrate increasing awareness of a problem situation, the adult gradually relinquishes her leadership role and eventually turns over the management of the learning experience to the child.

As the teacher relinquishes full control, her questions should become internalized by the child and the child will achieve self-regulation, or personal control over the learning situation. Notice, however, that throughout the entire progression of the preceding dialogue, the teacher did not furnish Teddy any answers, but rather led the child to solve his own problem. While this event-specific sequence of verbal interaction cannot be used for every learning experience in the social studies classroom, it does illustrate how the process of questioning and prompting assists the child during varied learning experiences.

According to Vygotsky, many classroom happenings confront children with problems that they come close to solving but cannot completely work out without the prompts and questions of an adult or a more advanced peer. The area where the

Children learn from the teacher; she must be able to pass on accurate information.

child cannot solve a problem alone but is able to succeed with the collaboration of another is known as the *zone of proximal development (ZPD).* This is the zone where instruction can succeed, a "construction zone" where an adult supports children in their attempts to understand. The major implication of Vygotsky's ZPD is that teachers are responsible for doing more than arranging the child's environment. They must guide by asking timely questions, offering appropriate prompts, and providing stimulating demonstrations. Because children learn from each other, plentiful opportunities for cooperation and collaboration also must be offered.

Regardless of whether the children's learning is a spontaneous event or contrived by an adult, teachers must become familiar with the types of questions and prompts that are most likely to create a positive impact on the learning situation. One of the most important considerations in formulating questions and prompts is, "Will my comments encourage further exploration, or do they guarantee immediate closure?" When working with preservice teachers during early field experiences, I often find that they habitually ask questions resulting in closed-ended responses—for example, "Did you have fun trying the musical instruments from Japan?" or "How many stars did you count on Old Glory?" In the scaffolding process, however, teachers should try to ask questions that require more than simple, pat answers. Figuring out what the child is thinking is one of the most intricate challenges of experiential teaching, for that affects the kinds of prompts we offer the child during any activity. Sigel, McGillicuddy-Delisi, and Johnson (1980) suggest three levels of adult assistance for the scaffolding process:

1.   *Low-level distancing.* The teacher's questions or statements label or describe the immediately observable characteristics of materials in the classroom. For example, "What material is the mask made from?" or "This mask shows the face of a feared monster in Norse myths."

2. *Medium-level distancing.* Teachers elaborate on the readily observable characteristics of materials in the classroom by calling the child's attention to relationships. For example, "How was the journey of the Pilgrims on the *Mayflower* like the journey of the first astronauts?" or "Kansas grows much more wheat than Ohio. Why do you suppose this is true?"

3. *High-level distancing.* Teachers encourage children to go beyond that which is readily observable in the immediate environment by elaborating on an idea or formulating hypotheses. For example, "Imagine that it is 1840 and you are preparing to move west with your family, traveling in a wagon that is about 16 feet long and 5 feet wide. Knowing that you must pack food and only a few necessary items, what will you choose to take ?"

Some prompts are designed to help children observe an object or event more carefully; others are designed to encourage thought processes like prediction and finding relationships. Through such questions and comments, the teacher helps the children better understand or more effectively accomplish a task or problem.

Shared Activities With Peers

Shared activities in the social studies classroom are not limited to teacher-student interactions; in the Vygotskian framework, the social context for learning goes far beyond teacher-student dialogue. Equally important are the interactions that go on among peers. Bodrova and Leong (1996) caution, however, that interacting only with one's peers is not sufficient to promote learning. Although casual interaction can help some children learn, this learning can often be haphazard, and the children can be misled by one anothers' misunderstandings. Teachers must understand that the social situation involves many complex interactions; to be a worthwhile experience, the situation must be deliberately structured and the types of interactions must be carefully spelled out. This means that during the early stages of a learning episode, when the child has not developed a skill or strategy sufficiently or when the concept is yet quite vague, it may be more productive for the teacher to facilitate the sharing interactions. Giving students responsibility for sharing at these times could confuse learners. As children refine a skill or solidify a concept, peer interaction can become very beneficial.
Bodrova and Leong (1996) suggest the following patterns of peer interaction:

1. *Cooperating to successfully complete a task.* Activities in which students must work together to complete a task or solve a problem motivate students and lead to productive learning. For example, the students must independently locate information and coordinate that information, like the pieces of a puzzle, to solve a problem or create a whole. This is called *cooperative learning* and is more comprehensively described in Chapter 7.

2. *Assuming assigned roles.* Another way to promote peer interaction is to assign projects that involve nonoverlapping roles. For example, in peer editing (see Chapter 12), children write and then check each other's work. In building a model

During the elementary grades, children work hard to discover new learnings with the help of their classmates.

colonial village, one child draws the plan for a blacksmith shop, another builds it, and the first checks to see if the final model matches the plan. This type of activity is based on the idea that other-regulation precedes self-regulation.

3. *Acting as a sounding board for a peer.* Often, children can be paired together to explain things back and forth or to think through a problem. An example is the Think-Pair-Share structure for cooperative learning (see Chapter 7). In this structure, the students individually *think* about an answer to a question posed by the teacher. Then they *pair* with a partner to discuss their ideas. After acting as a sounding board for each other's ideas, the students *share* their thinking or ideas with the whole class. This social context for learning makes learning meaningful for all grade levels.

4. *Acting for an imaginary person.* Sometimes, creating something for an imaginary character or someone who cannot be present in the classroom creates a shared learning opportunity. For example, one teacher wrote the students a "letter" as a pioneer crossing the Appalachians to settle in Kentucky in the late 1700s. The letter described the not-so-good points about moving (Cherokee attacks, severe storms, wagons that broke down, deep streams to cross, and steep banks to climb). In small groups, the students were asked to write a dialogue for and role-play one of the hardships faced by the pioneers. This type of activity forces students to prepare explicit or detailed explanations of concepts under study.

EDUCATIONAL IMPLICATIONS OF PIAGET AND VYGOTSKY

From this discussion of Piaget and Vygotsky emerge three major elements necessary for leading students through the process of gaining meaning from information shared during any learning experience involving social studies content:

1. *Children's previous experiences must be associated with the new source of knowledge.* Children construct meaning by activating their prior knowledge and connecting it to the demands of the new learning task.

2. *Children must be active learners.* New or deepened understandings are most effectively constructed through a combination of actions on objects (physical action) and mental activity (organizing sensory input). Learners must be physically and mentally active.

3. *Social knowledge, a form of arbitrary knowledge, is constructed by the learner through scaffolded support from the teacher and peers.* Children construct meaning by participating in many types of shared activity, gradually becoming responsible for their own learning.

For social studies teachers, the basic implications are clear. Because a major objective of social studies education is to enhance children's acquisition of knowledge, educational methods must be consistent with the process of constructivism. How do classroom teachers go about helping students advance through this process? Although there are many variations, in the most general sense two major instructional models are most commonly employed in social studies classrooms: (1) the concept reception model and (2) the concept production model.

1.   *Concept reception.* This plan of instruction can best be described as the act of carefully regulating the presentation of information and concepts for learners. To carry out this strategy, teachers must clearly designate a targeted concept, select the specific information to which the learners will be exposed, and design and conduct systematically planned experiences that will help students compare, contrast, and classify essential information. The overall aim is to directly help students classify information into concept categories.

2.   *Concept production.* This is the application of discovery and inquiry strategies that help children become self-directed learners. Concepts are not transmitted directly by the teacher, but are formed by the students as they ask questions, seek information, and conduct independent investigations. There is no predetermined body of knowledge that all students must learn; the learners themselves are responsible for initiating the ideas and questions to be explored.

THE CONCEPT RECEPTION MODEL

We will consider the first approach, the *concept reception model,* in this chapter. It is arguably the most widely employed system of social studies instruction in the United States. The concept recepton model is particularly attractive to beginning teachers because it allows them to assume more direct control of all the children (whole-class instruction is usually employed), requires all the children to use the same learning materials (the method is usually textbook- or literature-based), provides specific objectives and clear direction for teaching/learning behaviors, and minimizes classroom management concerns.

Teachers help children form new concepts by carefully arranging a deliberate sequence of learning events so that new models grow from the old; they help students put new pieces of information together in ways that are wholly meaningful to them. In concept reception instruction, teachers exercise primary control over the process of attaining new concepts. Although learners are led to construct meaning for themselves, the teacher facilitates the process by helping students connect to already existing concepts or experiences. To choose this model, teachers must be convinced that common understandings of specific concepts are necessary prerequisites to undergird a complete grasp of the nature of particular cultures, places, or objects.

In its most basic form, concept reception strategies consist of four interrelated instructional components: (1) connecting to prior knowledge, (2) selecting instructional resources, (3) summarizing and interpreting the information, and (4) providing follow-up experiences.

Connecting to Prior Knowledge

In the concept reception approach, the teacher's primary responsibility is to facilitate the children's ability to access and activate relevant knowledge before encountering any learning experience. Students must be directed to think about what they already know about the topic to be explored; as they participate in the learning task, they will add new information to their existing schemata. There are several primary techniques for accomplishing this responsibility. Among the most widely used are *discussion techniques, external mediators,* and *real experiences.*

Discussion Techniques

It is important to plan a presentation or discussion session prior to the new learning experience to help bring out students' existing background knowledge. Sometimes, brief comments or questions related to the topic of the lesson can bridge the gap between what the children already know and the new content to be introduced. For example, one teacher wanted her children to understand how goods were transported during colonial days. To achieve this goal, she chose to read aloud the book *Ox-Cart Man*, written by Donald Hall and illustrated by Barbara Cooney. Before the book was read, she said to the class, "Today I am going to read to you the book *Ox-Cart Man*. Before I read it, look at the title and illustration on the cover; what do you think this book is going to be about?" The teacher asked this question not to elicit "right" answers from the students, but to get them to think of possibilities. As the students offered their predictions, the teacher recorded them on the chalkboard. The predictions would be confirmed or revised as the children listened to the story. The teacher then asked, "What is an ox-cart?" and paused as the students offered responses. The teacher displayed a large study print of an ox and discussed why it was such an ideal beast of burden. Finally, she thought aloud, "In thinking about all we have already learned about colonial America, I wonder what kinds of things the man might be carrying in his ox-cart," and, once again, paused for responses. After she constantly nudged the children's thinking with scaffolding prods such as, "What makes you think that?" she invited the students: "Let's listen to find out."

The teacher in this example pursued this line of discussion because she realized it was important for students to understand the concepts *ox* and *ox-cart* before she read the book. Compare her approach with a second teacher who began his class discussion with the statement, "Today we're going to listen to a book titled *Ox-Cart Man*." Then he asked, "Have you ever seen an ox-cart? Where did you see it? What was it used for?"

Notice that the second teacher's questions are quite general and deal only with contemporary times. The background development is vaguely related to the main concept of the book. In contrast, the discussion plan of the first teacher required students to use whatever background information, or schemata, they had developed about the specific story topic to make their predictions. Key concept attachment was made to the context of the historical period rather than to the present. Additionally, she guided the students to listen by asking them to listen for a purpose that was directly linked to the discussion.

This type of discussion strategy is beneficial because it creates disequilibration, brings the students' existing knowledge to the forefront, offers the teacher some insight into the students' current level of cognitive functioning, and furnishes a base from which to reconstruct existing schemata.

External Mediators (Anticipation Guides)

In addition to arousing conceptual attachment to the new information through deliberate discussion strategies, teachers often find it helpful to facilitate their students' thinking with attention-grabbing external mediators such as diagrams, charts, drawings, and other visual displays. Yopp and Yopp (1992) call these external mediators *anticipation guides,* or graphic displays of categorized information that help students consciously focus their attention on the targeted concepts under study.

Information Retrieval Charts.   One form of anticipation guide is the *information retrieval chart.* The major purpose of an information retrieval chart is to help students place information into conceptual grids. Retrieval charts typically consist of two interrelated elements: concept labels and the information to be classified. Most of us have seen information retrieval charts put together by children with the help of the teacher *after* sharing a purposeful learning experience when teachers want to encourage reflection on important facts or details, such as how much water was used in a town during a six-month period from May through October. In addition to serving as important summary devices, however, information retrieval charts can also stimulate children to attach previous knowledge to the new learning experience if introduced *prior* to the learning experience. Let us suppose that a class is studying dinosaurs and that a videotape full of interesting information is the planned learning experience for the day. The teacher might construct an information retrieval chart as illustrated in Figure 5–2, gluing Velcro strips onto each section that will eventually hold Velcro-backed information cards. An information card is given to pairs of students who predict into which portion of the grid it might go. Some pairs will surely be able to pick the correct segment while others will not be sure; all students, however should feel psychologically safe to risk placing their cards somewhere on the retrieval chart. Now the students will read for the purpose of determining how accurate their predictions were and then change cards around on the basis of newly uncovered data.

FIGURE 5–2
Information Retrieval Chart

Name of Dinosaur	Length	Diet	Habitat
Triceratops	▬	▬	▬
Tyrannosaurus Rex	▬	other dinosaurs	land
Brachiosaurus	▭	▭	▭
Allosaurus	▭	▭	▭
Pterodactyl	4 feet	▭	air

K–W–L Charts.   Another highly useful anticipation guide that can guide children's thinking before, during, and after the learning experience is the *K–W–L chart*. Each letter represents a different activity that guides learners not only prior to, but also during and after the learning experience. *K* represents what the students already *know* about the topic. Before the learning experience actually takes place, students discuss and brainstorm all the ideas they can associate with the topic and record their ideas on a chart, as shown in Figure 5–3 for the example *oceans*. The teacher might elicit suggestions with a question such as, "Before we read this article on oceans, think for a few moments about what kinds of information might be included." You may need to model one or two suggestions so that students begin to see what you mean. *W* represents what the students *want* to know. As the students reflect on what they already know about the topic, they form questions related to gaps in their understanding. Again, the teacher might need to model a personal question and write it down on the chart to give the children an idea of what they are expected to do. *L* represents what students *learn* about the topic. After reading the article, students record what they have learned. They should check their questions to see if each has been answered; if not, you may want to suggest other sources of information.

The K–W–L strategy is a favored social studies activity because it helps students actively associate their previous knowledge and experiences while establishing personalized purposes for becoming involved in a new learning experience. This procedure effectively bridges teacher-directed learning and more independent learning in social studies.

Opinionnaires.   One more exemplary anticipation guide is the *opinionnaire*. Opinionnaires contain a series of statements related to concepts or issues with which students are asked to indicate a strength of feeling. Keep in mind that the purpose of the opinionnaire is to elicit students' honest attitudes, not "correct" answers. Therefore,

FIGURE 5–3
K–W–L Chart

K = What We Know	W = What We Want to Find Out	L = What We Learned

waves
salt water
large bodies of
   water
sandy beaches
vacation spots
sea shells
Atlantic Ocean
Pacific Ocean
	Where does sand
	   come from?
	Why do some beaches
	   have rocks
	   instead of sand?
	What animals live
	   in the ocean?
	What are the names
	   of the oceans?
	How many are there?
	Which ones border
	   the United
	   States?	

teachers must be nonjudgmental, accepting students' feelings even if they are contrary to their own. Typically, three to five statements are used in an opinionnaire, each of which is intended to stimulate discussion prior to the learning experience. Yopp and Yopp (1992) suggest the following steps for using opinionnaires:

1. Identify major themes or ideas in the [learning experience].
2. Write three to five statements related to selected themes or events that are likely to arouse discussion.
3. Present the statements to the students on an overhead projector, the chalkboard, or as a handout.
4. Allow a few minutes for students to respond privately to each statement by indicating their agreement or disagreement on paper.
5. Engage the students in a discussion about the statements by asking for their reactions. This discussion should include reasons for responses. (p. 18)

A sample opinionnaire is shown in Figure 5–4.

Bodrova and Leong (1996) note that using external mediators to assist students' thinking is not a new idea; adults use them all the time. We often write a list before going shopping or lay out our daily schedule with a pocket calendar. These external mediators regulate our thinking and keep us on task. In the Vygotskian framework, these "tools of the mind" are not acquired naturally, but must be taught to children so that they can eventually develop the ability to organize and monitor their own thinking. External mediators, then, build the scaffolds that help children make the transition from being regulated by adults to becoming self-regulated learners.

FIGURE 5–4
Opinionnaire

> Put a mark next to the things a long-ago farmer might take to town.
>
> _____ potatoes   _____ pizza
>
> _____ candles   _____ apples
>
> _____ frozen peas   _____ potato chips
>
> _____ mittens   _____ goose feathers

Real Experiences

If the children's backgrounds on a specific topic are quite limited, you will find it helpful to provide real experiences to establish a concrete framework for understanding new ideas. For example, think how much more meaning students who have no knowledge of traditional Mexican clothing would attach to a discussion of this topic if an actual _serape_ were displayed in the classroom. My college students often scoff at this suggestion and ask me how they would be able to obtain such items for their own classrooms. My response is simply, "Send a note home prior to studying a topic to explain to the parents that you need certain items related to that topic—and get ready." In my own elementary school teaching experiences, I've always ended up with more than I could handle by using that technique.

You know that children are full of questions as they continually attempt to discover the hows, whats, and whys of life. They are extremely curious and enjoy getting their hands on everything. You could introduce a new learning experience on tools by motivating children this way: Arrange on a worktable a number of tools used by early American farmers. Ask questions about them: "What are these tools? Are these hand tools or machines? Who do you suppose used these tools? How do you think they were used?" Use their predictions to establish a meaningful purpose for a forthcoming learning experience.

Jackdaws, collections related to special topics or themes of instruction, can motivate children to learn and help develop their conceptual readiness for a particular learning task. Jackdaw collections may be pulled together by teachers, but are available from commercial sources, too. For example, the Institute of Texan Cultures in San Antonio rents to teachers several kits, one of which, "Cowboys and Cattle Drives," contains a branding iron, lariat, and spurs, as well as photographs and documents. Jackdaw items can be effectively used to relate background information to new learning experiences.

As ideal as they are for establishing backgounds for building or enriching concepts, real hands-on items cannot be brought to the classroom for every new lesson. Suppose your class is going to learn about how prairie schooners were used by pioneers for cross-country travel. Obviously, it would be impossible to display a real schooner prior to the day's learning experience. What would be the next best choice: a model, photo, study print, transparency, slide, or other depiction? Certainly, something must be shared; true learning will not occur without a common perception of the major idea to be examined.

Even though vicarious experiences are not as deeply meaningful as the real thing, these attempts to fill in or bring out past experiences are much more effective than words alone.

Learning Experience Responsibilities

The types of learning experiences you offer to follow these introductory experiences depend on your students; you will need to provide a wide range from which to produce accurate concepts. Children eagerly seek new ideas through alternative sources, and a good social studies classroom focuses on *balance:* the children see, hear, taste, touch, *and* listen and read.

Most school districts encourage teachers to employ a variety of materials in their social studies program because not all pupils learn in the same way, and different media appeal to different learning styles. Each medium has particular strengths and limitations in the way it conveys messages; the impact of a message is likely to be stronger if more than one sensory system is involved in receiving it. Different sources can provide different insights on the same subject, while some discrepancies or inaccuracies may go undetected if a single source is used.

Bruner and his associates (1966) identify three ways of knowing, as shown in Figure 5–5. These levels—*enactive, iconic,* and *symbolic*—describe the modes through which individuals receive and store concepts, starting with the more concrete sources and moving to the more abstract. Children may need one type of experience as opposed to another for any given topic, or may need to use two or more of them together.

FIGURE 5–5
Three Modes of Knowing

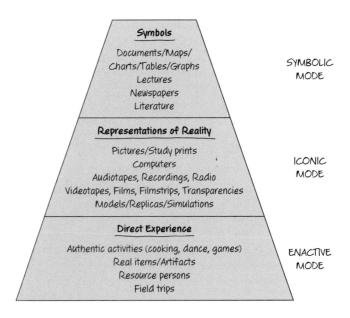

Enactive Mode

This broad category includes objects, people, places, trips, visitors, and real-life classroom activities. Most of all, children are active participants while exploring, manipulating, choosing, and using real materials. Children need these real, direct learning opportunities to observe reactions and discover relationships. For example, if you want to help the children conceptualize the nature of Mexican and south-western American homes made of adobe brick, you may choose to bring in a real adobe brick, take a trip to a home made from adobe, or actually have the children make adobe bricks from clay, straw, and water.

Children learn by doing; they "mess about" and naturally get into or try out every-thing. They do whatever it takes to discover things; they strive to see, hear, touch, smell, and taste all the special things around them. They want to know all about the mysterious people, places, and things that confront them each day. They may come to elementary school knowing a little bit about a lot of things, but one characteristic they all share is a thirst for experiences that will help them find out more. When these enthusiastic, energetic youngsters come to school they expect to learn about all that interests them in much the same way, through activity and involvement. They are not greatly interested in memorizing information or in confining activities such as completing ditto sheets or workbook pages. They want to try things out.

The concept of *whale*, for example, can be most truly constructed from, and elab-orated on, the children's direct "acting on" whales. Pictures of whales, stories of whales, or a videotape of whales cannot replace the sounds, smells, sights, and tac-tile sensations of the real thing. Wadsworth (1978) explains how direct action in-volving a beached whale helped him and other members of a combined 5–8 class, none of whom had ever before seen a real whale, know exactly what a whale was: "We looked at it, we listened to it, we went up to touch it (it could not move much), we ran away from it when it opened its massive mouth, we threw water on it, we made faces at it—we did all sorts of things. From that day on we all knew exactly what a whale was" (pp. 54–55).

Certainly, direct experiences constitute one critical category of classroom activity, but the act of constructing concepts in the social studies does not happen automati-cally after children experience something firsthand. Piaget (1964) writes, "Experi-ence is . . . necessary for intellectual development . . . but I fear that we may fall into the illusion that being submitted to an experience . . . is sufficient. . . . But more than this is required. . ." (p. 4). In emphasizing the need for a child's *construction* of knowledge, Piaget stresses the crucial role of the teacher; teachers must not only be effective *organizers* who are able to select rich materials and intriguing situations· that arouse learners' interest in learning, but they must also be thought-provoking *guides* who know how to stimulate and direct learners' thinking to effectively orga-nize the information taken in during the experience.

Iconic Mode

This activity mode involves "imagery," or using representations of real objects when the objects themselves cannot be directly experienced. For example, you realize that the children's concepts of an adobe house will not be accurately developed unless they can actually see a house constructed from adobe brick. Unable to travel to an adobe house, you might bring in a scale model, display a photograph of an adobe home, or even show a videotape of one being constructed. Representations help children form concepts when real things are not available.

Symbolic Mode

This mode involves using arbitrary symbols in written or oral form to communicate and store concepts. For example, you might choose to reinforce the concept of an adobe home by asking the children to read a selection from their textbook or a trade book that describes living in an adobe home.

Understanding these three ways of knowing is important for planning and organizing learning activities for your social studies program. They help you recognize the need for *balance* among the activities you choose, so that there is not too much symbolism (workbooks, practice sheets, reading) and too little enactment, or vice versa, in your programs.

As a rule of thumb, you should remember that all students thrive on a variety of solid learning experiences, but that younger students need direct contact and real experiences (a visit to an orchard) and visual representations (a videotape of apple-growing procedures). Older students still require concrete experiences but are increasingly able to gain knowledge from written symbols (a folktale from China) and verbal symbols (listening to a well-planned lecture).

Post-Learning Experience Responsibilities

Whether you engage the children in reading a magazine article, interviewing someone, viewing a videotape, or examining a historical document, they must ultimately face the task of processing and interpreting the information to which they were exposed. Over the years, the most frequently used technique to accomplish this has been leading discussions with follow-up questions.

Follow-Up Discussions

Class discussion, a valuable teaching procedure in any subject, is essential to successful learning in social studies. Discussion is used to develop cognitive skills by getting the most possible benefit from the content to which the learners were exposed. There are many discussion models, but one that has withstood the test of time is the *Taba strategy* (named after Hilda Taba). The Taba discussion strategy is a controlled strategy in which the teacher asks a carefully planned sequence of questions, similar to the Vygotskian process of scaffolding. The questions are designed to help students process data by using such cognitive strategies as:

1. *Developing and attaining concepts.* Students list, group, and regroup a number of items and then label the groups.
2. *Inferring and generalizing.* Students make inferences and generalize about the relationships they observe among various kinds of data.

3. *Applying generalizations.* Students are asked to apply previously learned generalizations and facts to predict what might logically occur in a new situation.

Developing Concepts.   The Taba strategy consists of sequentially ordered questions designed to elicit a specific set of responses from the students. To illustrate, let
us suppose that the students in Mr. Holcroft's sixth-grade class are gathered in front
of a large chart posted on the wall. They are in the final week of a unit, "Mountain
Regions Around the World." Today, Mr. Holcroft has divided the class into cooperative learning groups to review what they learned after reading the text, viewing
videos, and being exposed to quality literature. He begins by asking the groups to
brainstorm any specific information about mountains. A scribe from each group lists
the group's data on notebook paper. When the groups exhaust their thinking, Mr.
Holcroft asks the scribes from each group, in turn, to list its first five items on the
chalkboard so that the class can create a cumulative list. As each group lists its data,
scribes from the other groups crossoff the duplicate items from their group charts so
no data are repeated on the cumulative class chart. Once students complete the cumulative chart, Mr. Holcroft helps them search for relationships among the data. He
underlines the words *Andes* and *Himalayas* in red marker and asks, "What makes
these two words alike?" The students respond, "They are both names of mountain
ranges." Mr. Holcroft continues by asking, "What other words are names of mountain ranges?" At that point, students come to the board and underline in red words
such as *Rockies, Alps,* and so on. Next, Mr. Holcroft directs a similar discussion sequence by asking each cooperative learning group to gather the remaining data into
categories, underline each category with a different color marker, and give each category a name. The students suggest various categories such as *animal life, plant life,*
and *human conditions.*

When the students finish categorizing the data, Mr. Holcroft helps them construct
a written informational paragraph. He begins by saying, "There appear to be many
facts on our list. What do you suppose they are telling us?" Silence drops over the
class, for this is a tough question. Mr. Holcroft allows some wait time. Shortly,
Sheena volunteers, "Mountains are found all over the world." "Yeah," agrees Brody.
"Some are really high and others aren't."

"That's a nice start," replies Mr. Holcroft. "Let's write your ideas here on our
chart." He continues writing sentences until he records all the children's ideas. He
then reviews those ideas. He asks the students to examine the first two sentences to
see if they can be combined or explained to form one sentence. Each group toys
with the words; the whole group eventually settles on "Large and small mountains
are found all over the world." Progressively, the students edit and rewrite the other
sentences in the same way until they complete a jointly composed, descriptive paragraph of mountain regions around the world.

Why did Mr. Holcroft organize his lesson this way? For the most part, he is convinced that social studies and language are so closely interrelated that it is impossible
to teach one without the other. He operates with a deep conviction that most children,
as they become exposed to new information, delight in opportunities to share what
they have learned with others. Therefore, Mr. Holcroft avidly grasps any opportunity to

Teachers must be able to help children understand how broad concepts grow from a body of facts.

functionally utilize the skills of language in his social studies program. He views learning as an active process where learners construct ideas as they use language.

The Taba strategy, as used by Mr. Holcroft, begins with a series of "opener questions" requiring students to do the following:

1. *List items.* "What did you learn (see, find, notice) here?"
2. *Group similar items.* "Do any of these items seem to belong together?"
3. *Identify common characteristics of items in a group.* "Why would you group these together?"
4. *Label the groups.* "What would you call these groups?"
5. *Regroup and relabel items.* "Could some of these belong in more than one group?"
6. *Summarize information.* "What could you say in one sentence about each of these groups?"

Each step in the Taba strategy is a prerequisite for the next, but the necessity for uniformly sequencing the steps should not be interpreted as imposing a rigid procedure. The lesson pace and style of questions should vary according to such factors as the background students have with the content and the experience they have had with the procedure.

Generalizing.   As you have read throughout this chapter, concepts are most often represented by a word or phrase, such as *neighborhood, radiocarbon dating, agriculture, continent,* or *inflation. Generalizations,* on the other hand, state the relationship among two or more concepts, usually in complete-sentence form. "Modern transportation and communication systems help to make easier lives possible for people in metropolitan areas" is a generalization that contains two or more concepts and establishes a relationship among them. Can you name the concepts included in the generalization?

Teachers can help students form thoughtful generalizations by asking them to make a statement about the ideas selected for any particular category. Returning to Mr. Holcroft's mountain example, the students might be asked: "What is an important idea we got from this information?" or "Offer a statement that includes much of the data in this category." or "What is the big idea that this data communicates? What are the facts telling us?" Such narrowly focused questions lead students to make appropriate generalizations. (A more inexplicit question such as, "Can you give me a generalization about mountains?" may produce few responses.)

Taba's belief is very compatible with Vygotsky's: She is convinced that if children repeatedly go through the process of answering questions from a logical model, they will learn to internalize the procedure and begin to create thinking patterns on their own. Consequently, the nature and the organization of the Taba strategy encourage learners to do their own thinking, develop their own ways of categorizing information, and evaluate their own ideas. Additional questioning strategies are presented in Chapter 11.

Graphic Representations

Graphic representations serve as external mediators that help students organize ideas and participate in meaningful discussions about the learning act. Although oral discussion strategies can be effective instructional methods by themselves, graphic organizers make them even more effective by helping children focus on major ideas and perceive relationships among details.

Any conceptual relationship can be presented with external mediators—charts, graphs, and drawings, for example, are commonly used to summarize large amounts of information. We discuss some of the most popularly used forms of graphic representation in the sections that follow.

Webbing.   A key external mediator designed to help students organize complex ideas is the *web.* Webs help children discern a central idea as well as its distinguishing attributes. Webs have three basic elements: core concept, web strands, and strand supports.

The *core concept* serves as the focus of the web. All the details, facts, and information generated in a discussion should relate to the core concept. An example of a core concept is "Daily Life in New England Colonies." Place the core concept in the center of a growing matrix (see Figure 5–6) and begin a group discussion with a thought such as, "Think about the kinds of activities that made up daily life in the homes of New England colonists."

As the students suggest categories such as jobs, school, food, furniture, entertainment, religion, and sports place their suggestions at various points around the core to represent different categories of information related to the concept. These points are referred to as *web strands*.

The specific facts or details the students use to support each web strand are called the *strand supports*. The strand supports extend from each web strand, summarizing important information and relationships. Here the students should select such particulars as *apprentices, hornbook, doll, New England Primer, ladder-back chairs, Puritans,* and *stool ball.*

Venn Diagrams.   Venn diagrams are graphic representations that students can use to compare and contrast two distinct cognitive elements. Introduce Venn diagrams by drawing two overlapping circles on the chalkboard. Suppose you have just read a

FIGURE 5–6
Web: Daily Life in Colonial America

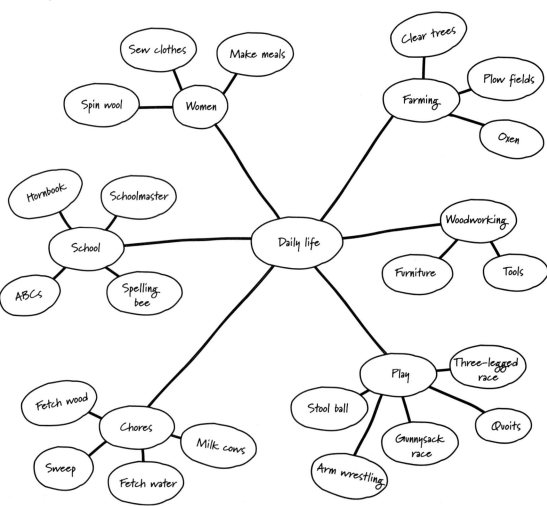

FIGURE 5–7
Venn Diagram

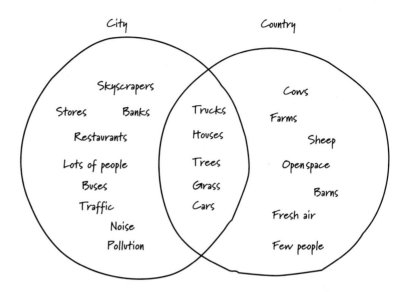

selection contrasting life in the city and in the country. One circle represents the city and the other represents the country. The attributes unique to each environment are listed inside the separate circles, and the attributes common to both are listed in the area where the two circles intersect (see Figure 5–7). When students know how to use the Venn diagram, you can use it to guide comparisons of a variety of topics; for example, two (or more) people, forms of government, communities, nations, religions, and so on.

Comparison Charts. Often, you will want students to create a chart that compares the attributes of two or more contrasting elements (people, places, events, ideas, etc.). For example, if your students are examining the concept of *settlements*, studying the reasons why early settlers were motivated to seek out new territories in different parts of the United States, a chart can be designed to focus on these questions: "What things are being compared?" "How are they similar?" "How are they different?" (see Figure 5–8).

Similarly, students might, as a group activity, make charts out of heavy posterboard listing the voyages of significant Spanish, Portuguese, French, Dutch, and English explorers; the dates of their expeditions; what each explorer wanted to accomplish; and the results of each expedition. Such a chart can be an ongoing activity, where students contribute information as they progress through a thematic unit.

Bubble Trees. This type of graphic organizer visually represents relationships among people or events. Bubble tress work best with information that can be categorized beneath a *core* (or *main*) *understanding*. The top of the structure contains the core understanding; in Figure 5–9 this is "The fall of Rome." Information related to the core understanding should fall neatly into major *idea categories*: "barbarians" and "other causes." The tree begins, therefore, as a top bubble containing the core understanding and branches labeled as major idea categories. Finally, students must

FIGURE 5–8
Comparison Chart

Characteristic	Mexico	Japan
Food		
Recreation		
Music		
Art		
Pets		
Hobbies		
Religion		

FIGURE 5–9
Bubble Tree

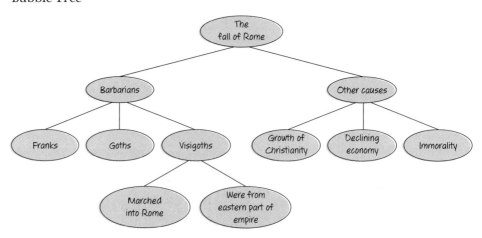

organize the *facts* associated with each of the major idea categories, eventually constructing a structure of branching information.

Bubble trees can be used in a variety of ways in the social studies classroom: (1)
completed by the teacher before a lesson, they can present an overview, or advance
organizer, for the students; (2) presented only as blank bubbles, they can tap students' prior knowledge before the lesson—as the lesson progresses, students add to,
modify, and refine their suggestions; and (3) after a lesson, they can be used by students to review and organize content.

Event Chains.   At times, a social studies learning experience may deal with a sequence of important happenings (major events of the Revolutionary War) or the significant milestones in the life of a historical figure (the rise and fall of Alexander the
Great). An event chain is useful in describing the sequence of events, and how one
event led to the other, by presenting a series of frames that separate the key parts of
the whole. Figure 5–10 illustrates a sample event chain.

FIGURE 5–10
Event Chain

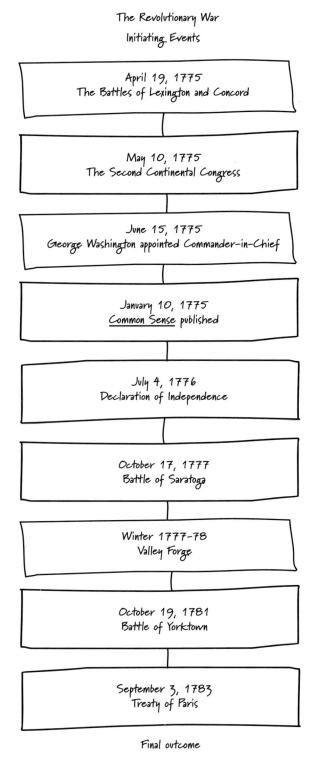

The Revolutionary War

Initiating Events

April 19, 1775
The Battles of Lexington and Concord

May 10, 1775
The Second Continental Congress

June 15, 1775
George Washington appointed Commander-in-Chief

January 10, 1775
Common Sense published

July 4, 1776
Declaration of Independence

October 17, 1777
Battle of Saratoga

Winter 1777–78
Valley Forge

October 19, 1781
Battle of Yorktown

September 3, 1783
Treaty of Paris

Final outcome

Timelines.   Elementary school students often have difficulty placing information in a historical framework. Event chains help them conceptualize chronology; constructing timelines on topics of study is another useful way to promote the organization of meaningful information. Timelines are graphic representations of events arranged into chronological order. They differ from event chains in that the lines are divided into proportioned units, each unit representing a specific number of years. To create a timeline, it is important to involve the students in helping decide on a unit to represent the sequence of events. Suppose that you are considering "snack food favorites," the first of which was introduced in 1853. Emphasize that the students will be dealing with over 150 years of time, so they will need a unit that can reasonably fit into an allotted space. Once the students solve this problem, have them discuss the information they uncovered about favorite snack foods. Emphasize the dates, such as the following:

chewing gum—1860

root beer—1877

hot dog—1890

Oreos—1912

pizza—1945

"Big Mac"—1968

Next, begin organizing these events on the line. Start with 1850 and add colorful construction paper circles at 20-year intervals until reaching the year 2010. Select students to write the date below each paper circle. Have small groups of students randomly select one of the snack foods, make a drawing of it, and position it on the timeline at a point corresponding to its popularization in the United States. Then ask the students to summarize in a short oral report how each snack was originated. Prod them to think more deeply about the information by asking discussion questions such as, "Was the hot dog introduced closer in time to the 'Big Mac' or to the potato chip?" When you come to the year 2010, ask the small groups to brainstorm what they think might be the next favorite snack food (see Figure 5–11).

Process Chains.   Process chains are graphic representations of the stages of something (life cycle or water cycle, for example). Suppose that your fifth-grade class has just read a short passage on how communities treat water to make it safe to drink. You might follow the exposure-to-information phase of the lesson with these questions: "We just read about the process of water treatment. If you were to tell someone about this process, how would you go about doing it?" "What clues in this passage let us know that the information is given in a certain sequence?"

As you lead the students through a discussion of the text, you constantly model how to extract meaningful information. The final stage involves the construction of a graphic organizer to help bring order to the students' learning. You assign the students to cooperative teams, each of which is to illustrate a step in the water treatment process. You then tape the illustrations to the wall in sequential order and tell students to write a short descriptive narrative about each (see Figure 5–12).

FIGURE 5–11
Timeline

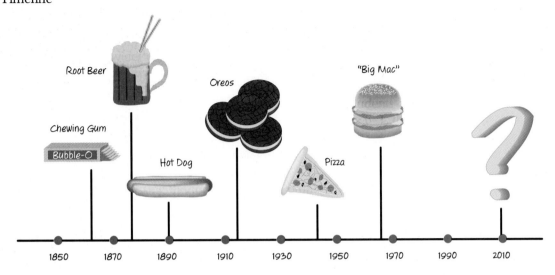

FIGURE 5–12
Process Chain

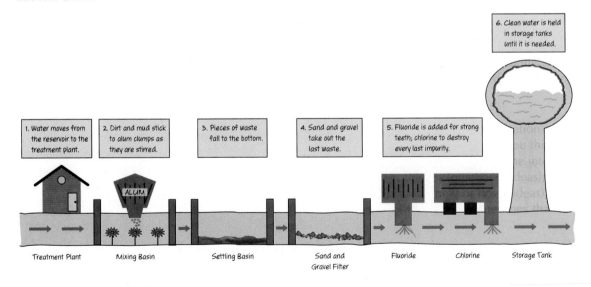

Main Idea Hamburger. A good way to help students remember the details of what they have learned is to help them make a graphic summary of it. Various techniques can aid in this process, but one I have found to be especially enjoyable for elementary school youngsters is the Main Idea Hamburger. Ask the students to identify the main idea of something they just read and place it in the top of the bun (see Figure

FIGURE 5–13
Main Idea Hamburger

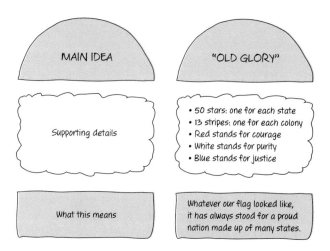

5–13). Then ask them to recall or search for the details that support the main idea. List these in the burger part of the illustration. The bottom of the bun contains a personal statement of what this information means to the learner.

Cycles.   This variety of graphic organizer helps students visualize a series of connected events that occur in sequence and produce a repeated result. The months and seasons of a year, for example, exemplify a cyclical process, as do the water cycle and the metamorphosis of a caterpillar. One cyclical phenomenon treated in most social studies programs is recycling. Help your students understand this process by first writing the word *recycling* on the chalkboard. Discuss why so many communities in the United States recycle their waste and why our country has developed a wasteful attitude throughout its history. Then have the students complete a cycle graphic organizer as they read about the process of recycling. See Figure 5–14 for a sample.

   Graphic organizers are fundamental to concept formation in the social studies. They provide the stimulus for cognitive development in ways that questioning and discussion strategies alone cannot do. Clearly, you should offer opportunities to develop and use graphic representations whenever you ask children to seek relationships among ideas. Jones, Pierce, and Hunter (1989) suggest these steps for introducing the use of graphic organizers in a positive way:

1. *Present at least one good example of a completed graphic outline.* The graphic outline should match the type of organizer you will teach.
2. *Model how to construct the graphic organizer.* Describe the decisions you had to make while completing your organizer.
3. *Provide procedural knowledge.* Discuss when and why your students should use this type of organizer.
4. *Coach the students.* Have students work as a whole class or in groups to plan their first organizers. Ask them to share and compare their graphics and to explain how and why they made their decisions. Provide them with ample feedback. Help them

FIGURE 5–14
Cycle Organizer

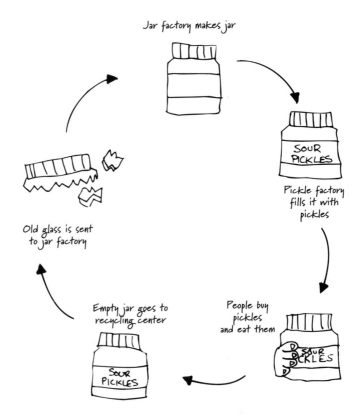

understand that planning and revision are important parts of constructing any graphic organizer.

5. *Give the students opportunities to practice with individual organizers.* Offer plenty of constructive feedback.

Follow-Up and Extension Activities

Follow-up and extension activities provide additional practice on certain skills through special projects or independent activities that encourage children to apply or extend concepts to a variety of situations, as in the following sample activities.

- Dramatize the firing of the "shot heard around the world."
- Cook and eat Harry S. Truman's favorite food, brownies.
- Give first-person accounts of famous historical events as if the students were the actual characters.
- Select a location students would like to "cheer" about. Then design paper pennants with colors and illustrations that have some meaning to the location.
- Choose a favorite scene from a historical era to recreate in a three-dimensional model, or diorama.

- Write a historical period news magazine. Students write their articles in the style of popular news magazines using headlines, drawings, eyewitness statements, and so on.

By reading professional journals and organizing an idea file, you will begin to accumulate ideas for follow-up and extension experiences that will bring more meaning to the learning experience. Remember, though, that these activities must be an integral part of the total learning experience, not "extra busy work" or "icing on the cake" that gets done only because you have a few minutes to kill. Activity 5-1 presents a sample follow-up activity.

Activity 5-1

 ## Case Study

A Sample Follow-Up Activity

Ms. Hudson's fifth-grade students had been learning about America's struggle for independence from Great Britain. As part of their study, they had learned about many important people, places, and events of the Revolutionary War. As a follow-up activity, Ms. Hudson divided her class into seven groups, assigned a specific Revolutionary War figure to each, and asked the groups to compose a short skit highlighting the major experiences of their figures. She asked each group to apply the content of what they had learned about the Revolutionary War to develop the setting and dialogue for a scene involving General Thomas Gage, Deborah Sampson, George Washington, King George III, Thomas Jefferson, Jonas Parker, and Paul Revere.

While the children worked together to create scenes depicting the major events in the lives of their assigned figures, Ms. Hudson acted as a resource person, ready to help in any capacity required. When each scene was complete, Ms. Hudson asked the groups to meet together to discuss the order of presentation. The group determined the order and decided it would be helpful to have a narrator explain how the scenes were interrelated.

After the presentation, Ms. Hudson related the content of the skits to the material covered beforehand, emphasizing cause and effect as well as chronological order.

Because follow-up experiences often tend to focus on creativity and choice, they may include such things as painting, group murals, writing, construction projects, drama, puppetry, and music. In all of these activities, children use what they have learned to construct deeper meaning. The key to success in this phase of thematic planning is the same as was stressed for success in all of social studies teaching—variety. Vary your activities to keep interest and motivation high. Because social studies topics differ in their complexity, some strategies will be more useful than others for enriching, reinforcing, or extending the concepts under study. Ms. Hudson realized this consideration and selected an activity that not only involved her students in a worthwhile expressive experience but also enriched and reinforced the major understandings introduced in the unit.

AFTERWORD

Throughout this chapter we have examined various components of teaching that lead children toward the acquisition and refinement of social studies concepts. Let us now consider what a lesson might look like when a teacher plans a learning experience with the chapter's suggestions in mind. A sample plan for an upper elementary grade lesson follows in Activity 5–2. You will also find it useful at this point to attempt one of your own. Such an experience will help you understand the connections between what you are learning and the classroom world that will soon surround you.

Activity 5–2

Lesson Plan

Theme: Regional likenesses and differences
Grade: Four
Teacher: Regina DeMarco

General Objective
The students will understand how two geographic areas in the United States can be quite different.

Specific Objective
The students will compare and contrast the geographic likenesses and differences between Maine and the prairie.

Materials
1. Handmade quilt.
2. Duplicated 9-square quilt block.
3. Crayons, markers, construction paper, and glue.
4. Large chart with the headings *Things About the Prairie* and *Things About the Sea.*

Procedure

1. On a map of the United States, locate Maine and the prairie states. Show large study prints depicting the regional characteristics of each. Invite the students to talk about the differences in life on land and near water. Tell the students that they will be reading *Sarah, Plain and Tall* (Harper & Row). Explain that at the time this story took place, a move from Maine to the prairie was a major event; there were no airplanes, automobiles, buses, or railroads to take people there. So, if a person decided to move, it would be a permanent decision.

2. After reading the book, brainstorm a list of features that could be placed under the chart headings, *Things About the Prairie* and *Things About the Sea.*

3. Bring in a special "gift" to stir students' interest and enthusiasm: "I brought something with me to show you. Yesterday a friend brought it to me after school. What do you think it might be?" Slowly uncover the quilt.

4. Explain that this is a special kind of blanket or bedspread. It's called a *quilt.* Describe how quilts are made from pieced patterns and demonstrate how the patterns fit together precisely as a finished quilt. Show several patterns and explain their meaning. Finish up by discussing the history of quilts—the Chinese thought of the process first—and their evolution into an American art form, especially during Colonial days.

5. Each child is given a nine-patch quilt block. The students design a quilt for Sarah. They first sketch a likeness of Sarah in the middle block. In four squares, they draw or piece together construction paper to show some things that she loved about Maine's countryside. In the other four, they illustrate what she loved about the prairie.

6. Each child's "Sarah quilt block" is then mounted on a large sheet of paper and fastened to the wall for display.

Assessment

1. Have the students complete these sentences: "The things Sarah misses from her old home in Maine are...." and "The things Sarah learned to like about the prairie are...."

Helping elementary school students classify and categorize information into meaningful concepts is one of the foremost challenges to social studies teachers. A major part of this challenge is to help learners attach their backgrounds to the learning experience and to organize new information into appropriate schemata. As Piaget and Vygotsky emphasize, meaningful learning takes place only when learners are able to bridge the gap between the unknown and the known. To that end, this chapter has described a system of instruction through which the teachers are able to effectively direct their students through the process of concept reception.

Developing a teaching plan is a complex professional responsibility involving a great deal of knowledge, hard work, and skill. As a new teacher, you may wonder whether the results are worth the effort. In effect, you may say, "Why bother? After all, the textbook and teacher's manual were written by experts in the field who really know the social studies." To an extent, you are correct. Manuals can be very helpful, especially for student or beginning teachers. As guides, though, they must be viewed as suggestions, not as prescriptions. You will probably want to start your career by using the teacher's guide closely, but as you gain experience, you will adapt it to the changing needs of the different groups of children you will teach each year. The constructivist approach described in this chapter allows you the flexibility to constantly change your teaching approach within a framework of sound planning.

TECHNOLOGY SAMPLER

Some useful sources for related social studies topics include these Internet sites:

4Kids Detectives (answers to almost every question your children might have)
http://www.4Kids.org/detectives/

The CIA World Factbook (source of maps and data on population, geography, economics, and governments of countries A through Z)
http://www.odci.gov/cia/publications/nsolo/

Publishers Hunt Questions (practice seeking out information by probing the Internet to answer "hunt questions")
ftp://ftp.cic.net/pub/hunt/questions

Some useful sources for related social studies topics include these Software titles:

Imagination Express—Destination: Rainforest
Edmark
Using the rainforest as the setting, this tool blends creativity and education as children make their own books.

Logical Journey of the Zoombinis
Broderbund
An adventure format presents deductive reasoning and logic games that are entertaining and educational.

The Magic School Bus Explores the Rainforest
Microsoft
Ms. Frizzle is on the go again with her students; this time, they ride to the rainforest on the Magic School Bus. The excursion is filled with interesting information and enjoyable games.

What's the Secret?
3M Learning Software
Full of activities and information on a variety of topics.

WHAT I *NOW* KNOW

Complete these self-check items once more. Determine for yourself whether it would be useful to take a more in-depth look at any area. Use the same key as you did for the preassessment form ("+", "?", "-").

I can *now*

_____ define the term *concept.*

_____ explain the relationship between facts and concepts.

_____ summarize the theories of Piaget and Vygotsky as they relate to concept development.

_____ describe what is meant by *constructivist* teaching practices.

_____ plan developmentally appropriate concept-oriented lessons.

_____ explain the importance of graphic organizers.

_____ plan a lesson centering on concept development.

REFERENCES

Ausubel, D. P. (1961). In defense of verbal learning. *Educational Theory, 2,* 16.

Bodrova, E., & Leong, D. J. (1996). *Tools of the mind: A Vygotskian approach to early childhood education.* Englewood Cliffs, NJ: Prentice Hall.

Brooks, J. G., & Brooks, M. G. (1993). *In search of understanding: The case for constructivist classrooms.* Alexandria, VA: Association for Supervision and Curriculum Development.

Bruner, J., et al. (1966). *Studies in cognitive growth.* New York: John Wiley.

Jones, B. F., Pierce, J., & Hunter, B. (1989). Teaching students to construct graphic representations. *Educational Leadership, 46,* 20–25.

McGee, L. M., & Richgels, D. J. (1996). *Literacy's beginnings: Supporting young readers and writers.* Boston: Allyn and Bacon.

Piaget, J. (1952). *The origins of intelligence in children.* New York: International Universities Press.

Piaget, J. (1964). Three lectures. In Ripple, R. E., & Rockcastle, U. N. (1964). *Piaget rediscovered.* Ithaca, NY: Cornell University Press.

Remy, R. C. (1990). The need for science/technology/society in the social studies. *Social Education, 54,* 204.

Sigel, I. E., McGillicuddy-Delisi, A. V., & Johnson, J. (1980). *Parental distancing, beliefs, and children's representational competence within the family context.* Princeton, NJ: Educational Testing Service.

Smith, F. (1975). *Comprehension and learning: A conceptual framework for teachers.* New York: Holt, Rinehart and Winston.

Smith, F. (1982). Understanding reading: A psycholinguistic analysis of reading and learning to read: New York: Holt, Rinehart and Winston.

Van Doren, M. (1982). Quoted in E. L. Boyer, Seeing the connectedness of things. *Educational Leadership, 39,* 384.

Vygotsky, L. S. (1978). *Mind in society.* Cambridge, MA: Harvard University Press.

Wadsworth, B. J. (1978). *Piaget for the classroom teacher.* New York: Longman.

Wood, D. J., Bruner, J., & Ross, G. (1976). The role of tutoring in problem solving. *Journal of Child Psychology and Psychiatry, 17,* 89–100.

Yopp, R. H., & Yopp, H. K. (1992). *Literature-based reading activities.* Boston: Allyn and Bacon.

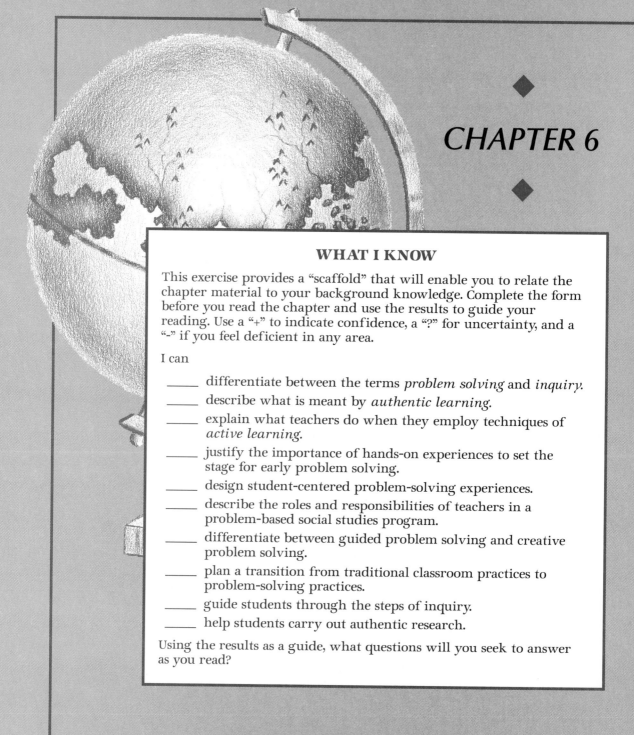

CHAPTER 6

WHAT I KNOW

This exercise provides a "scaffold" that will enable you to relate the chapter material to your background knowledge. Complete the form before you read the chapter and use the results to guide your reading. Use a "+" to indicate confidence, a "?" for uncertainty, and a "-" if you feel deficient in any area.

I can

_____ differentiate between the terms *problem solving* and *inquiry*.

_____ describe what is meant by *authentic learning*.

_____ explain what teachers do when they employ techniques of *active learning*.

_____ justify the importance of hands-on experiences to set the stage for early problem solving.

_____ design student-centered problem-solving experiences.

_____ describe the roles and responsibilities of teachers in a problem-based social studies program.

_____ differentiate between guided problem solving and creative problem solving.

_____ plan a transition from traditional classroom practices to problem-solving practices.

_____ guide students through the steps of inquiry.

_____ help students carry out authentic research.

Using the results as a guide, what questions will you seek to answer as you read?

Investigating the
Social World

◆ CLASSROOM SKETCH

"Econ the Spider" is a friendly spider toy who dangles from
an elasticized string helping children learn all about their
world by integrating language arts, mathematics, art, music, and
economics. "Econ" rules the "Land of Economics" and invites the
children to journey to his kingdom. The kingdom consists of 26
towns, each with an economic alphabet letter name. In each
town live producers whose occupations begin with the town
letter. A-Town is the home of artists, actors, and
advertising executives; B-Town houses bar-
bers, bankers, and butchers; in C-Town live
chefs, carpenters, and coal miners. Several
days are spent in each town, where children
learn about occupations starting with that
letter. Mrs. Yohe invites parents to class to
talk about their occupations—for example, Isaiah's mother, a landscaper,
visited during L-Town week. Parents
become members of the VIP (Very Important Parent) Club, and all are encouraged to visit during the weekly
studies. Mrs. Yohe must stretch the limits of her creativity while trying to ensure that each occupation has
only one VIP visitor (if there are two truck drivers eager to
come to the classroom, for example, one would be the

227

"truck driver" and the other a "delivery person"). VIPs are classified as either producers of goods or providers of services. Appropriate storybooks, videos, field trips, and other sources of information help fill in the content while students visit a specific town; creative dramatics, art projects, writing activities, and reinforcement games supplement instruction and provide for information processing and enrichment. One activity, "Econ's Web of Interdependence," is a special favorite of Mrs. Yohe's children. Here is how it works: The children sit in a circle on the floor. One player holds a large ball of yarn, names a producer, gives the corresponding economic alphabet letter, and tells what the producer's job involves. Holding the yarn in one hand, the player then rolls the ball to a classmate. The children hold the yarn tautly enough to keep it six to eight inches off the floor. The player receiving the ball names another producer, gives the correct economic alphabet letter, describes what the producer's job entails, and also tells, if possible, how that occupation relates to or depends on the previous producer. The student then rolls the ball of yarn along the floor to the next player. Thus, the web is spun.

For example, Angelica begins, "I am a dancer in the ballet. My economic alphabet letter is 'D'. I entertain people by dancing." The ball goes to Danny. He says, "I am a teacher. My alphabet letter is 'T'. I help children learn things in school. I took my family to see Angelica in the ballet." The ball goes to Maurice. Maurice says, "I am a typist. My economic alphabet letter is also 'T'. I type letters. I typed a letter for Danny, the teacher, to send home to his students' parents." Econ's web grows and grows, clearly demonstrating our world of interdependence. When the web is completed, the students place Econ in the center to dance on the strings.

Topics for "Econ's Web of Interdependence" may vary in difficulty according to class needs. Mrs. Yohe suggests the following:

- Children name occupations of their fathers and/or mothers.
- Children name producers living in selected towns (only producers living in B-Town, D-Town, etc.).
- Children name only producers whose occupations involve construction in some way (carpenter, electrician, mason, roofer, architect, and so on).

As the journey through the economic alphabet comes to an end (usually during the busy holiday weeks in December), Econ welcomes the children to a beautiful shopping mall, unfortunately not completely constructed because of an untimely strike. Econ leads the children in a discussion of some of the causes and effects of strikes. Even though the strike has now been settled, it will take more workers to complete the mall in time for the holiday shoppers. Econ asks the children to work for him.

Children work and plan the shopping center with Econ's help. He hires them to staff the shops, paying them in play money for their "labor" in completing the mall. Finally, they become eager consumers at the luxurious new shopping center. Each day, half of the class is assigned to work in the shops, while the other students are consumers. The groups reverse roles daily. The shopping center includes a bank in which students may deposit and withdraw the play money they earn in class. They thus experience opportunity cost daily, choosing to purchase some items at the expense of not being able to purchase others.

Suggested stores include a restaurant, a card and a gift shop, a travel agency, a bank, a flower shop, a fast food service, a shopping market, a jewelry store, an electronics boutique, a shoe store, a clothing shop, and so forth. For example, Mrs. Yohe's "Brown Bag Market" provides the following learning opportunities after the children visit an actual supermarket:

- The children bring in empty food containers from home. Working in groups, students label, price, and classify food items as vegetable, meat, dairy products, and so on.
- Students print signs to indicate store sections.
- The children glue pictures of meats and cakes to plastic plates, and then cover them with clear plastic wrap. Plastic toy shopping carts add excitement to the activity.
- The following workers are hired each day: Two cashiers, two checkout baggers, two stock workers, sales personnel, and a store manager.
- Mrs. Yohe assigns various language arts tasks to the shoppers. She may ask children to go shopping with a shopping list where they must buy three balanced meals, five foods beginning with the same sound, such as *me*, or three items grown on a farm. She also asks children to select items independently and write a list of what they have purchased.
- Mrs. Yohe includes mathematics challenges such as counting, classifying, and comparisons throughout the shopping activity.

You can take similar field trips to other kinds of stores and set up related learning activities in your own "classroom shopping mall."

◆ CLASSROOM CONNECTION

Mrs. Yohe demonstrated how social studies teachers can inspire and nurture their students' learning through engaging, meaningful classroom experiences. These teachers want their students to understand that there's an interesting world out there and that they have access to that world through their curiosity, interest, and sense of wonder. Teachers often build their social studies instruction on their children's natural interest in the world, often getting a good idea of what to do by listening to and watching them—looking for clues about what students find interesting and puzzling.

It is easy to see that children look at life around them with interest and wonder. They take nothing for granted; hardly anything ever passes them by. They enjoy being taught about their world by wise, helpful teachers who use accepted constructivist approaches such as concept reception models, but they also have a strong urge to be independent—to learn by themselves through trial, error, and experimentation. Finding out about things by themselves is a matter of profound importance; unmitigated pride flows from learners who master important skills or uncover meaningful knowledge by themselves. Perhaps this natural spirit to learn was demonstrated best by one fifth grader who was asked what it would be like to know everything. "Awful," the child replied. "Why?" the teacher asked. "Because then there would be nothing to *wonder about!*"

Children are quite exceptional wonderers. They radiate natural curiosity about the world around them and look at life as a mystery to be searched and solved. Nothing is too small for their eager minds; nothing is so insignificant that it passes without generating curiosity. They are utterly infatuated with the mind-stirring phenomena that excite their senses. Observations of children in "their world" would lead almost everyone to conclude that they are doers, thinkers, and natural scholars. Jean Piaget was so impressed by these natural childhood tendencies that he used them to support his idea of *active education*, noting that "active methods . . . give broad scope to the spontaneous research of the child . . . and require that every new truth to be learned be rediscovered or at least reconstructed by the student and not simply imparted to him" (p. 21).

A good social studies classroom encourages its students to look at the world as a neverending mystery. No matter how compelled teachers feel to "follow the textbook" or any other strategy inflexibly, they should foster a sense of wonder by giving fullest support to the questioning mind: "Why?" "What is it?" "How could it be done differently?" "What is it for?" "What does it mean to me?" When we work to build a sense of wonder, we move toward a system of teaching that supports children's own fresh, creative ways of responding to their world. This responsive planning results in what Piaget (1969/1970) refers to as "authentic work" taking place within *active schools.* He notes that, "When the active school requires that the student's effort should come from the student himself instead of being imposed, and that his intelligence should undertake authentic work instead of accepting pre-digested knowledge from outside, it is therefore simply asking that the laws of all intelligence should be respected" (p. 159).

ACTIVE SCHOOLS

Teachers in "active schools" do not place a high priority on any single method or source of information as the exclusive "right way to teach." They realize that the heart of instruction is balance and proportion. Sometimes, as concept reception teachers, they will "bring the action to the children," using *deductive approaches* to help their students organize a body of knowledge into concept categories (concept reception). But, at other times, they will allow the children to "bring the action to them" through an *inductive approach*—supporting students emotionally and intellectually as they independently discover information and construct new concepts by themselves. Good teachers realize that the key to effective social studies instruction is *flexibility*—looking at options, weighing the advantages and disadvantages of each, determining the relative value of the choice, and selecting the most appropriate approach.

There is no special way to plan for active learning; teachers basically turn the children loose and follow their lead. Holt (1967) suggests:

> We do not need to "motivate" children into learning by wheedling, bribing, or bullying. We do need to keep picking away at their minds to make sure they are learning. What we need to do, and all we need to do, is bring as much of the world as we can into the school and the classroom; give children as much help and guidance as they need and ask for; listen respectfully when they feel like talking; and then get out of the way. We can trust them to do the rest. (p. 185)

Rogers advises that the role of the teacher changes drastically in active social studies programs. Instead of the "technician" who employs carefully prescribed patterns of instruction, the teacher becomes a "facilitator" who provides something meaty for the children to sink their teeth into and then sits back to wait for their response. There is no prescribed place to start or end. Facilitators do not check the teacher's manual; they begin where the action is liveliest. Only one thing matters: a teacher who stays close to the significant interests of students. Rogers (1974) distinguishes between "teachers" and "facilitators" with his "mug and jug" theory.

> The teacher asks himself: "How can I make the mug hold still while I fill it from the jug with these facts which the curriculum planners and I regard as valuable?" The attitude of the facilitator has almost entirely to do with climate: "How can I create a psychological climate in which the child will feel free to be curious, will feel free to learn from his environment, from fellow students, from me, from experience? How can I help him recapture the excitement of learning which was his in infancy?" (p. 102)

Holt and Rogers argue that the adult logic behind planned sequences of instruction looks fine on paper, but in practice it conflicts with the energy and enthusiasm most children have for becoming actively involved in their own learning. Social studies teachers cannot limit their roles to that of content experts for, as highly knowledgeable people, they can be tempted to limit instruction to telling others what they need to know. However, education must progress beyond transmitting information toward using information in more advanced ways. The following items summarize the nature of such active, authentic social studies instruction:

1. *Students construct meaning and produce knowledge through their own activity.* Social studies is not only a body of information to be learned, but also a way of acting. Students should be seen as "social science apprentices" who learn about

the world not only through teacher-centered practices, but also by trying out problem-solving and inquiry strategies used by real social scientists—observing, questioning, and searching for answers.

2.   *Students aim their work toward products and performances that have value and meaning beyond success in school.* Learners and their teachers work on problems or issues that they see as connected to their personal lives or to contemporary public situations. Students are involved in efforts to influence an audience beyond their classroom.

3.   *The teacher's role shifts from that of managing director to guiding facilitator.* The teacher becomes a guide who helps students identify problems and find things out for themselves.

4.   *Social engagement is a stimulus for learning.* Collaboration between teacher and students, among students, and between the class and people outside it are crucial to authentic learning.

5.   *Teachers are active inquirers.* They should model ways of approaching problem situations, and offer assistance for mastering investigative techniques, while sharing their own curiosity and interest in the world around them, prompting children to take more responsibility for independent learning as their skills increase.

For the purpose of this chapter, the concept of "authentic" or "active" learning will be referred to by the more popular social studies terms, *problem solving* and *inquiry*.

PROBLEM SOLVING

The term *problem solving* has been used to cover a variety of things we do in social studies, from putting puzzles together to suggesting solutions for pressing social issues. However, no description of the problem-solving process has had more impact on elementary school social studies instruction than the one advocated by Dewey (1916) during the early part of this century. Dewey proposed an entire elementary school curriculum based on problems—situations that he described as *anything that creates doubt and uncertainty in learners.*

Problem solving has continued to be an important part of the social studies program since Dewey's time. Today, the process is especially applicable to authentic learning because the problems that Dewey promoted had to meet two precise criteria: (1) the problems to be studied had to be important to the culture and (2) the problems had to be important and relevant to the student (Orlich et al., 1990, p. 305).

Dewey believed that a curriculum based on problem-solving skills was important because it provided individuals with the thinking tools they would use throughout life—a basic aim of all of education. Gagne (1977) supports this contention: "Educational programs have the important ultimate purpose of teaching students to solve problems . . ." (p. 177).

Problem-Solving Skills

There seems to be no doubt that problem-solving skills are rooted in the rich sensory adventures of very young children as they explore and act on their environment. Mitchell (1971) maintains that, as inexperienced learners, children

> seldom reach further than the range of their own first hand explorations. The things that [they] are told about, but which do not start specific associations of muscles, eye or ear or of some sensory apparatus, are not genuinely intelligible to [a young child]. I elaborate this point because so often I find teachers that are satisfied if they get a correct verbal response from small children. (p. 16)

Despite its natural affinity to childhood, if you choose student-centered problem solving for your social studies program, you must first be sure that the processes involved do not run against the grain of the way students have been taught in school. If your students have had little or no previous experience with student-centered learning, there must be a transition period during which they participate in exercises carefully designed to move from teacher direction to more independence. Student-centered learning cannot emerge spontaneously in elementary school classrooms; it is a product of helping students work together in new ways. It may take several weeks or months to reach the point where you and your students work together to investigate problems productively. Wasserman (1989) describes the rationale for this supportive guidance:

> We must not . . . make the mistake of expecting that . . . thinking for oneself will occur in the absence of classroom instruction and practice aimed at these specific goals.
>   It may be a lot easier to teach children to read and spell than it is to teach them to . . . function on their own cognitive power. I have heard teachers give it up after a single attempt, saying, . . . "Children cannot think for themselves," and proceed thereafter to do children's thinking for them. But these very same teachers would *never* say, "These children cannot read by themselves," and thereafter remove any opportunity for them to learn to read. Nor would they deplore children's inability to add or multiply, or spell or write stories as the reason NOT to teach them to acquire these skills. (p. 204)

Before you make this mistake and end up crying, "Bring back the textbook! Give me back my workbook sheets—this business of promoting autonomous learning just doesn't work," you must know that, even though new stimuli may be needed in your social studies program, children must move slowly. You must give them many opportunities to grow and learn; the skills needed for problem solving will not be achieved after a single experience. Time, patience, and your belief in the importance of autonomous learning are the key ingredients of a successful transition from teacher-directed instruction to student-centered learning.

According to Piaget, the foundation of all higher order thinking lies in problem-solving activities that involve direct manipulation and observation. Children require rich opportunities to interact with real things before they can begin to conceptualize more abstract ideas. They discover the physical properties of objects (color and feel, for example), as well as how objects respond to actions (bouncing or rolling, for example), through actions on objects. Smith (1987) advises, "As physical knowledge develops, children become better able to establish relationships (comparing, classifying, ordering) between and among the objects they act upon. Such relationships are essential for the emergence of logical, flexible thought processes" (p. 35).

Teachers help students learn independently by offering early problem-solving experiences that consist of the following elements: (1) designing captivating classroom displays, (2) discussing the displays, and (3) recording observations.

Classroom Displays (Mini-Museums)

Classroom displays, or "mini-museums," stimulate children to explore, comment, and ask questions. You may refer to these areas of your classroom as *interest areas, curiosity centers, theme tables,* or any other name. Whatever you call them, you should arrange exhibit areas in your classroom to provoke the children's curiosity. Today's exhibit might be a ship's bell, origami, a Chilean rainstick, foreign coins, a butter churn, a cotton boll, shark's teeth, Colonial tools, a tape recording of city sounds, or a sombrero. You can obtain display items from the school resource center or from parents, but all items in the mini-museum should be treated like exhibits in the best public, child-oriented museums—not with a "hands-off" policy, but with a policy that invites touching, exploration, and investigation.

Most elementary school students have visited museums during a school trip or with their families (if they haven't, you should take them), so they will have many ideas on how to create a museum in their classroom. Even upper-grade and middle school students enjoy designing exhibits and sharing their cultural collections. You must remember, though, that these collections should not be haphazardly displayed, nor should they be briefly explained and then put on a shelf and forgotten. Such practices run contrary to the early problem-solving process.

In essence, the practices involved in setting up a regular museum display should be employed when setting up mini-museums. Monhardt and Monhardt (1997) suggest that the best place to start is to have the children share their past museum experiences. The authors suggest a discussion guided by questions such as these:

- "What are some different museums you've visited?"
- "What museums were most interesting?"
- "What made them so?"
- "What is involved in setting up a museum display?"
- "How can we find out more about museums?"

Introduce the idea of a social studies mini-museum to your class. One teacher modeled the process by arranging a table display of a cultural artifact—a stiff brush used by dog groomers. Behind the table was a display board on which a cartoon-type anthropologist was carefully examining an artifact. Carefully printed above the anthropologist were the words *Social Studies Mini-Museum.* Almost instantly the children began looking at the brush, touching it, and talking about what it might be. The teacher watched and listened, occasionally asking open-ended questions and making comments to stimulate the children to think more deeply about the artifact. One child tried to use the brush on her own hair. She was surprised to see just how stiff the bristles were. Naturally, the other children had to try, too.

A good social studies classroom does not operate on the assumption that children must sit down and listen in order to learn.

Rosa eventually identified the object. Her mother was a veterinarian and Rosa often helped around the office. She was obviously thrilled to share her knowledge with the class; their interest became much deeper as they listened to the expert description by their friend. To capitalize on this growing fascination with the brush and what veterinarians do, the teacher invited Rosa's mother to visit the class to talk about her job.

You can see from this example that it is a good idea to plan what you display at the curiosity center rather than selecting items hit-or-miss. You want something to happen at the center—interests to grow and concepts to deepen as the activity extends in the direction of the children's interests. Some teachers prefer to introduce the items in a mini-museum during a meeting time that can involve a small group or the entire class. If you prefer this approach, inform the students about how a social scientist works, as well as about how the mini-museum will operate. The following dialogue illustrates one teacher's initial meeting at an interest area. That teacher, Mr. Kurlak, opens the meeting by calling the children's attention to a large study print of an archaeologist examining some artifacts.

Mr. Kurlak:	Today we're going to try something new—work with our social studies mini-museum. But first, look carefully at this photo. The person you see is called an *archaeologist*. Have you ever heard that word? (Mr. Kurlak holds up a word card for *archaeologist*.) This is how the word looks. What is it that archaeologists do?

Adam:	She's looking at something.
Mr. Kurlak:	Yes, she's looking at, or examining, something. What kinds of things do you suppose archaeologists examine?
Denise:	Fossils?
Tamara:	Yeah. To see what the earth was like a long time ago.
Mr. Kurlak:	They examine old objects and use that information to describe what people were like very long ago. That's a good start. Does anyone else have an idea?
Patrick:	They dig for old tools and things. Even bones.
Mr. Kurlak:	They might study fossils, bones, tools, paintings, clothes, furniture, and other objects. These things are called *artifacts*. Studying artifacts can help us understand the lives of people. Have you ever seen an archaeologist examine artifacts?
Nelson:	I saw a picture of an archaeologist in a museum. It was in an exhibit about China.
Lucinda:	On a TV show once, I saw some archaeologists looking in old pyramids for mummies.
Mr. Kurlak:	Yes, archaeologists study many things to learn about the lives of people. Artifacts can tell about the games they play, the tools they use, and even the way they eat their meals. From now on, this table will be called the mini-museum. It is a place where you will come to discover things about the lives of people by doing some of the important jobs archaeologists do—examining things and keeping a record of observations. (Mr. Kurlak brings out a corn husk doll.) I've brought something for you to examine today. Look at it carefully and try to make a discovery. Wangto, what are some of the things you notice? What is the item made of? What parts does it have?
Wangto:	It looks like a toy—a doll, maybe?
Mr. Kurlak:	What makes you think it's a doll?
Wangto:	It looks like it has arms and legs. The top is like a head.
Mr. Kurlak:	It is shaped like a doll. What do you notice, Raphael?
Raphael:	It looks like it might be made out of corn. It feels like the dried corn plants we put out at Halloween.
Mr. Kurlak:	That part of a corn plant is called a *husk*. Here, look at this. It is a corn husk before it was made into a doll. (Shows corn husk.)
Moira:	How do people ever make dolls out of corn husks?
Mr. Kurlak:	Here, I'll show you. It's quite simple. (Takes a few minutes and demonstrates how to construct a corn husk doll as the

children follow his lead to make their own. Mr. Kurlak is demonstrating that people can be a very important source of information. He emphasizes the importance of checking other sources, too, calling the children's attention to a set of five books, each of which contains information about corn husk dolls.) What does the doll tell you about the people who used it? (The craft activity continues for several more minutes.) You've been examining our artifact very carefully today. You made some interesting discoveries. Archaeologists don't stop with discoveries, though. They must keep careful records of everything they do so their findings can be shared with other people. We will use a special way of recording our discoveries—*observation sheets.* (Mr. Kurlak passes out the observation sheets.) There's a place for your name and the date, and then the paper says, "What I Know About . . ." followed by a long blank. What words should I put in the blank?

Martha:	Corn husk dolls!
Mr. Kurlak:	That's right. There is also a big box for you to draw an illustration of what you examined. Please make a careful drawing there. Finally, at the bottom you will find some space to write. What are some things archaeologists might write about this corn husk doll?
Denise:	The doll is made from dried corn husks.
Amanda:	It was made in a place where people grew lots of corn.
Martin:	It could have been a gift for a boy or a girl.
Louise:	There weren't many stores around selling toys then. People had to make their toys from things around them. (The suggestions flow forth for several minutes. The children then complete their observation sheets. Figure 6–1 shows a sample completed sheet.)

Mr. Kurlak explained to the class that he planned to display something in the mini-museum every few days and that it would be directly related to the thematic unit under study.

Discussing the Classroom Displays

As important as they are, observational experiences alone do not guarantee acquisition of problem-solving skills. Teachers must use carefully worded questions or comments to help children gain meaning from the mysteries that confront them. Because they often have relatively limited backgrounds of experience, children could misinterpret new experiences if an adult's guidance is not offered. Seefeldt (1974) advises:

FIGURE 6-1
"Archaeology Attic"
Observation Sheet

"ARCHAEOLOGY ATTIC"
OBSERVATION SHEET

NAME _Jesse_   DATE _4|6|94_

WHAT I KNOW ABOUT _Corn husk dolls_

The doll was made from corn husks.
It is a toy for a young child. It
probably came from a place where corn
is plentyful, like Nebraska.

Observing young children, talking to them, asking them questions about how they think engines work or why they think clouds move reveals to the adult the level of their . . . thinking. Often the children have misconceptions that need clarification and revision. They may believe, for example, that the wind moves because it is happy or the shadows move to get out of their way. . . . Engines, air, the clouds, according to the young child, move because they want to. Often the young child's egocentricity influences his concepts: He may believe that the sun sets because he goes to bed or that the rain is falling because it does not want him to go outside. (pp. 176–177)

Skillful guidance must be provided to help children make accurate observations. You can guide their investigation with questions like the following:

- "What do you see here?"
- "How do you suppose it is used?"
- "I wonder what would happen if . . . ?"

- "If we try it again, do you think the same thing will happen?"
- "Is this like anything you've ever (used, seen, tried out) before?"
- "How can we find out more about . . . ?"
- "Can we find out if we watch it carefully?"
- "What makes you think so?"
- "Who do you think might use this?"
- "Where do they live? What makes you think so?"
- "What can you tell about the people who use this?"
- "What do you think of the people who use this?"

Some of these questions and comments help children look for specific things; others are more open ended, to encourage higher thought processes such as predicting and discovering relationships. Through such experiences, children develop the rudimentary scientific observation skills required for more sophisticated data collection activities.

The goal of direct observation is to lead the children toward careful investigations that result in clear, accurate descriptions. Your questions and comments lead to deeper observations, and the children discover and record evidence. The situation is described, and the question is partly answered but open to further research.

Observing and talking about interesting things under the teacher's direction are important components of early problem-solving experiences; another component is encouraging children to ask their own questions about the experience. Children often have a lot of questions of their own to ask. For example, Thomas Edison's last day in school came when he asked, "How can water run uphill?" after he noticed that a river in Ohio did just that. Young Tom was then expelled for expressing himself in ways that were unacceptable at the time. Children come to us with a strong need to ask questions. Respect that fact and guide them in exercising this childhood gift. Here are a few questions and comments I remember while working with children: "I heard something pretty disgusting. I read in my book about a guy who *chewded* wood. And about a guy they found alive in a whale's stomach!" "Are babies born with brains?" "Where does the water go when I flush the toilet?" "Look! That man has a hole in his hair (he was balding)." When children blurt out such comments, ask yourself, "Am I listening as carefully and sensitively as I am able?" When you do listen, you communicate to the child that she or he is a worthwhile individual whose honest thoughts are valued. This is something the children need to know, for question asking is an indispensable part of the problem-solving process.

We do not "teach" children about their world; we join them and investigate it together. Asking good questions and being a good listener are important parts of that responsibility, but to be truly helpful, teachers must be tuned in to learning, too. You need not understand everything about each phenomenon that captures a child's interest, but you should have enough knowledge to support children whenever they need your help. You should constantly read and search for new knowledge related to the social studies themes you teach. It is amazing how enthusiastic teachers are to pass on the new knowledge that they steadily accumulate. As Rachel Carson (1965) writes, "If a child is to keep alive his inborn sense of wonder, he needs the companionship of at least one adult who can share it, rediscovering with him the joy, excitement and mystery of the world we live in" (p. 45).

Recording Children's Ideas

As children investigate their world, they will be acting much as social scientists do. To deepen their scientific pursuits, we must help them realize that scientists not only observe interesting phenomena in an effort to find out as much as they can, but that they also compile careful records of their discoveries. Suppose you had arranged a collection of seashells as a curiosity experience, for example. You might invite the children to orally describe what they have observed by asking an open-ended question such as, "What can you tell me about these seashells?" You might encourage the children to examine the shells closely to compare colors, shapes, textures, sizes, or other physical characteristics and invite them to make separate collections based on the criteria jointly suggested. It is important to keep a written record of these experiences. For the very young child (kindergarten or first grade), an experience story or illustration might do. For older children, a journal entry or graph would be appropriate.

Using Problem-Solving Skills

"That's it! That's how I'll prove to Mrs. Shofner that this mystery coin is actually from ancient Rome!" The excitement in Jenny's voice was as clear as the pleasure reflected in her teacher's face. Her sixth-grade class had been working at the sand table digging up and brushing off replicas of artifacts their teacher had hidden beneath the sand. Acting as "apprentice archaeologists," the students were to examine the uncovered clues to identify the culture from which they came. Jenny was not hasty in drawing her conclusion; she had learned that all valid conclusions are based on factual evidence and that the accepted procedure for determining validity involves three basic steps:

1. *Study the evidence.* Jenny looked carefully for any information that might unlock the mystery. She observed what she thought was a likeness of a Roman emperor wearing a laurel crown. The word *AUGUSTUS* was printed above the likeness.

2. *Interpret the clues.* Jenny used her observations from step one to formulate a reasonable explanation. She searched through a series of reference books arranged beforehand by her teacher and learned about the history of Roman coins. Coins were decorated with the likeness of the emperor in power at the time. She discovered that laurel crowns were used to adorn emperors and also that the title "Augustus" was given to the popular Roman leader Octavian when he succeeded Julius Caesar following his death at the hands of Brutus. There was no date on the coin, but Jenny compared her information about Roman coins and emperors and formed a tentative conclusion that this coin was made in Rome between 31 B.C. and A.D. 14.

3. *Reevaluate the evidence.* Jenny reconsidered whether or not the evidence supported her initial interpretation. Working with an open mind, she stood ready to

alter her initial interpretation should further evidence demand it. She compared the replica she uncovered with an artifact found by a classmate, Russell. He had dug up a miniature banner with the letters *SPQR*. His research indicated that these were the initials for Latin words translated as, "The senate and the people of Rome." Together, Jenny and Russell believed that they had enough corroborating evidence to substantiate their contention that these replicas were from ancient Rome.

In conducting this simulated archaeological dig, Jenny and her classmates demonstrated many of the qualities of authentic problem solving—basing testable, valid conclusions on the collection and examination of factual evidence.

General problem solving turns notions of traditional teaching topsy-turvy. Students confront a challenging problem before they receive any instruction and, instead of covering the predetermined content of an established curriculum, probe deeply into a variety of resources to locate the information needed to solve it. In problem-based social studies instruction, students assume the roles of probing social scientists who have strong personal stakes in the problem.

Good Social Studies Problems

What are good social studies problems? The best are those that capture the interest of the students. Herein lies the real challenge of problem-solving–based instruction: "How can I know what will interest my learners?" First and foremost, children will be interested if they are able to attach themselves to the problem; they must be convinced that the problems they encounter are worth thinking about. The problems must be clear, understandable, and meaningful, and involve a high degree of mystery. Additionally, the problems must lie within the learners' sphere of competence. Problem situations that generate the most interest are those that offer the proper balance of "disequilibrium" or those that offer just the proper level of mystery to challenge previously established ideas. If the problem is foreign to previously established ideas, students will not be motivated to solve it; they have no personal stake in it. In contrast, if the problem is easily unraveled by the children's current level of knowledge, it will be considered too routine, and the students will quickly lose interest. A sample episode growing from a developmentally appropriate problem is described in Activity 6–1.

Activity 6–1

Case Study

Problem Solving

The adventure started when Mr. Shudlick showed his fifth graders a print of the painting *Last of the Buffalo*, created in 1888 by the artist-adventurer Albert Bierstadt. The print depicted the cruel slaughter of buffalo at a time when these majestic animals nearly became extinct. The children's interest and enthusiasm heightened as they propelled themselves into a serious discussion of the sacredness of buffalo to the Native Americans on the Great Plains of North America. Mr. Shudlick asked a series of questions designed to challenge his students to think:

- "What is happening?"
- "Where is it taking place?"
- "How did it happen?"
- "Why did it happen?"
- "When do you think this event took place?"
- "What took place before this happened?"
- "How does this compare with other events you know about?"

As the students reacted to the picture, Mr. Shudlick recorded their comments and questions on a large sheet of newsprint. Mr. Shudlick fashioned a social studies environment where new learning challenges emanated from the interests and aspirations of the students themselves. He ultimately brought closure to the discussion with the query, "Let us take time to answer your questions about how this buffalo became an important part of the lives of the Native Americans living on the Great Plains?"

The study began as Mr. Shudlick helped the students compare and contrast their comments and questions as recorded on the chart, finding many that could be grouped together—buffalo myths and legends, landscape where buffalo gathered, cultural beliefs, the hunt, and uses of the buffalo. Mr. Shudlick then listed each category on separate sheets of chart paper and provided a different-colored marking pen for each chart. He then formed student committees to research related information and listed the children's names on the appropriate charts.

The next day, Mr. Shudlick gathered about twenty-five books (of different reading levels) and a variety of other resources to help the children research their topic. Each committee understood that it was responsible for choosing a chairperson, deciding how to go about answering its questions, and making plans to present what they found out to their classmates.

After two or three days of gathering, analyzing, and selecting pertinent information, the committees were ready to share their findings. One group's chart was filled with fascinating information about the uses of the buffalo, as shown in the following list. As each of the other charts became filled, the committees designed strategies of sharing: One group planned a program of Sioux myths and legends; another group made a scrapbook of pictures depicting scenes from a hunt; a third group developed a mock television exposé about the factors leading to the demise of buffalo herds; and a fourth created replicas of pre-hunt headdresses and demonstrated the pawing, milling, and stampeding movements of buffalo that were part of the ceremonial dances held before every hunt.

Uses of the Buffalo

Committee Members: Harold, Karen, Eugene, Louella

- Women and older girls butchered the buffalo with sharp flint knives.
- As women worked, hunters devoured thin slices of raw liver dipped in the salty juices of gallbladders.
- Mouthfuls of raw brains were eaten.
- Remainders of hides and meat were loaded on packhorses.
- Buffalo hearts were scattered on the plains; magical power of the hearts was thought to renew the herds.
- Choice bits of meat were sliced off, held up to the spirits to see, and buried as an offering.
- Nearly every part of the buffalo was eaten—one buffalo had enough meat to feed over 100 people.
- Some of the meat was preserved:
  - Strips of meat were hung over high poles to dry. The sun-dried meat was called *jerky.*
  - Some of the dried meat was pounded into pulp, mixed with fat, and flavored with crushed nuts, berries, and fruit. This was called *pemmican.* Pemmican could last for years without spoiling.
- Hides were used as robes, cloaks, bedding, caps, earmuffs, leggings, or mittens. Some hides were smoked over fires to make them waterproof. They could then be used as walls for tepees, or to make moccasins, pouches, purses, or saddlebags.
- Sinew from the neck and back was used to make bowstrings and thread.
- Every part of the buffalo was used—the hair could be twisted into ropes or stuffed into balls, the stomach became a water jug, and even the tail was used as a flyswatter. Buffalo horns were used for cups or spoons, hooves produced glue, and the fat was used as a base for soap. The bones were shaped into tools of many kinds. The backbone, with ribs attached, made a toboggan for the children in winter. The dried buffalo droppings were used as fuel.

Teachers' Responsibilities

When students become engrossed in problem-solving ventures, they acquire knowledge and construct concepts through self-directed learning. Interest in a problem becomes "fuel" for constructive learning. Students probe deeply into what interests them, searching for data to return their minds to a state of equilibrium. In general, problem-solving strategies involve the following basic responsibilities for the teacher:

1.   *Create genuine interest in a challenging problem.* It is fascinating to observe students construct meaning when they really want know about a topic. Try putting your students into situations like the following:

- For a homework assignment, ask the students to find out which of their relatives immigrated from other countries to the United States. In class, discuss their results and find the relevant countries on a map, attaching push pins with the family's name. Ask the students, "Why do you suppose your relatives left their homelands?" Develop a joint plan to find out answers.

- In October, most elementary school children eagerly anticipate the celebration of Halloween. Capitalize on their interest by discussing the costumes the children plan on wearing. Such a discussion often prompts the question, "Why do people wear costumes for Halloween?" Ask the class to suggest how they could find an answer to their question.

- Have the children select one object from a box containing common everyday items such as a pencil, a toothbrush, a drinking cup, and a hat. Invite the children to explain the different ways their objects are used. Then ask, "How would our lives be different if your item did not exist?"

- While studying a historical period such as the Westward Movement, raise questions about the problems people faced: "If you were part of a family moving from Boston to San Francisco in the mid-1800s, what items would you bring with you?"

2.   *Build a varied collection of research materials.* Do not limit your students' problem-solving resources to the textbook. Certainly, textbooks can be effectively used as one source of data, but be sure to use other informational books, magazines, travel brochures, audiotapes and videotapes, real objects, resource people, field trips, and other tools.

3.   *Investigate together.* When children have a real stake in a problem, motivation soars; they realize they own the problem and are able to use data in their own personal way to arrive at a solution. Teachers have a crucial role in enhancing this spirit. They act as models, thinking aloud with the students and practicing every behavior they want their students to use. They ask questions: "What's going on here? What do we need to know more about?" They coax and prompt students to ask similar questions as they assume responsibility for their own learning. They are open to

Social studies teachers encourage puzzling and wondering when they give fullest support to the questioning mind.

new experiences. Children relish teachers who reach out for the different and un-usual; teachers who look at life with a sense of wonder. The world is full of mirac-ulous phenomena, a neverending mystery. Teachers stop, look, and listen; they feel, taste, and smell. They ask, "What is it? Where does it come from? What is it for?" They perform their own careful examinations and, through their enthusiasm for new discoveries, offer the greatest form of encouragement to their children. We must do our best in the social studies program to nurture curiosity for life; one of the best ways to do this is to be a teacher who responds to the world with a probing, wondering mind and regularly proposes, "Let's find out!" Discovery is usually accompanied by a strong feeling of elation. This is what drives people to explore: *It feels good.*

4.   *Provide adequate time.* If students are going to conduct authentic research, they will become deeply and personally involved in seeking solutions. They must have opportunities to work for extended periods of time. You should allot a min-imum of one hour for each problem-solving session during which students conduct research to explore problems that interest them.

5.   *Facilitate social interaction among your students.* Students learn to solve prob-lems by interacting with one another as well as with the teacher. Thus, you will often divide your class into cooperative learning groups (see Chapter 7) where students share the responsibility for problem solving. This social context offers students oppor-tunities to experience the desires and ideas in other minds and motivates them to seek agreement if conflict in perspective is encountered. Part of the problem-solving effort, then, is to establish an environment where students develop both a growing con-sciousness of others' ideas and a need to cooperate and share with them.

Lifelong problem solvers and researchers get their start in elementary social studies classrooms as teachers arouse curiosity in stimulating problems and propel their students into research to obtain answers or solutions. This problem-solving process, oriented and constantly monitored by the teacher, leads to the intellectual independence we so often find in lifelong learners. This is but one view of the problem-solving process. Another problem-solving model challenges students to ex-plore problems of personal interest and to generate novel, creative solutions. We will refer to this model as *creative problem solving.*

CREATIVE PROBLEM SOLVING

During problem-solving episodes, we challenge learners to explore and discover new learnings on their own, much as detectives search for clues to solve a baffling crime. Some students do this well: They sort out the clues, pull them together, look for patterns, and very deliberately arrive at valid conclusions. Others, however, ad-dress problems in quite different ways. Sternberg (1989) uses the following story to describe differences in approach:

> A [insert the name of your college or university] student and one from [insert the name of your chief rival] were hiking in the woods when they came across a grizzly bear.
> One student quickly calculated the mathematical differential between his speed and the bear's.
> The other student simply traded his hiking boots for his jogging shoes and took off.
> "Boy, you ARE stupid," the first guy hollered to the second. "You can't outrun a grizzly bear!"
> "I don't have to," the runner yelled back. "I only have to outrun you!"

Cognitive Styles

Sternberg's story demonstrates two types of *cognitive styles* that people call upon when they are confronted with a problem. The two styles are generally referred to as *systematic* (the first student) and *intuitive* (the second student). Regardless of whether you are solving the problem of how to study for an exam when a big football game is scheduled for the weekend before, or where to get money for next year's tuition hike, you are likely to rely on one of these cognitive styles.

Where do these differences in style originate? Research into the human brain (Ornstein, 1972) has revealed that there are two sides, or hemispheres, each capable of processing information in a unique way—in effect, giving us two minds in our heads. The *left brain* controls the logical, rational thought processes (as well as the right side of the body); the *right brain* controls intuitive, abstract thought (and the left side of the body). In most people, then, *logic* resides in the left hemisphere, *intuition* in the right. During childhood, as with left- or right-handedness, one hemisphere becomes dominant. When confronted with a problem, most of us solve it in our preferred style. Before these breakthroughs into brain functioning, little was known about the right hemisphere. Since speech and language were known to be functions of the left hemisphere, and most schoolwork called upon systematic rather than intuitive thinking, schools (and society in general) tended to overemphasize left-hemisphere skills at the expense of right-hemisphere skills, giving our children an apparently "lopsided" education.

Bruner (1965) examined the research into brain hemisphere characteristics and informed educators of its importance in *On Knowing: Essays for the Left Hand.* In the book, Bruner criticized the nearly exclusive emphasis on teaching toward systematic, rational (left-hemisphere) thinking in our schools and advocated teaching strategies that also encouraged exploration of innovative, experimental thinking (right-hemisphere). De Bono (1969) looked at this "left-handed" (or right-hemisphere–controlled) thinking and found it to be quite distinct from logical thinking, and more useful in generating new ideas. He used the term *lateral thinking* to describe intuitive thinking, and *vertical thinking* to denote logical thought. De Bono explained that lateral thinking is easiest to appreciate when seen in action, as in the situation illustrated in Figure 6-2. Although this problem looks simple, it is actually quite difficult. As a matter of fact, only about one person in a hundred is able to solve it the first time around. There are four volumes of Shakespeare's collected works on the shelf. Each volume is exactly 2" thick (pages only); the covers are each 1/6" thick. A bookworm starts eating at

FIGURE 6–2
Bookworm Problem

page 1 of volume I and eats through to the last page of volume IV. What is the distance the bookworm covers? Try to work the problem before you look at the answer at the beginning of the next paragraph.

Remember that the bookworm started at page 1 of volume I. Put your finger on that point; do not count the back cover and all the pages in between. Are you catching on? Similarly, the bookworm ate only to the last page of the last volume, so do not count the front cover and all the pages of the last volume. The answer is five inches.

Sources of Creativity

What causes so many of us to generate incorrect answers by looking only at "obvious" solutions to problems? Torrance (1963) believes that a great deal of blame should be placed on the schools:

> Creative imagination during early childhood seems to reach a peak between four and four-and-a-half years, and is followed by a drop at about age five when the child enters school for the first time. This drop has generally been regarded as the inevitable phenomenon in nature. There are now indications, however, that this drop in five-year-olds is a man-made rather than a natural phenomenon. (p. 79)

New, creative solutions to problems come from the ability to shift directions in thought: to move beyond the obvious to the subtle. The vertical thinker attacks a problem by first establishing a direction of thought and then digging deeper and deeper until finding an answer or solution. The lateral thinker also attacks a problem by establishing a direction of thought, but when digging in that direction appears to be leading nowhere, he or she stops and begins digging at a new spot. A lateral thinker keeps digging at new spots until arriving at a novel idea or new possibilities.

Just as a person can become, with practice, more proficient with the nondominant hand, so can children become more novel problem solvers by looking at situations in more ways than just the most probable—by practicing with the right hemisphere of the brain in classroom activities. I do not mean to persuade you that all vertical thinking experiences are "bad," or that all lateral thinking experiences are "good." My intention is to create an awareness that a child's mind is capable of different thought processes, and that children may demonstrate greater skills in some processes than in others. Just as children's physical development may result in greater mastery of running than throwing skills, so their intellectual development may be characterized by greater skills in lateral thinking than in vertical thinking. Teachers must be aware of this variability and plan classroom experiences that foster an assortment of thought processes.

This perspective is especially important when we consider that the organization of the brain is quite plastic in young children. Galin (1976) reports that lateralization is in flux up to about the age of ten. Knowing this, we must develop classroom practices that encourage interaction between both sides of the brain.

Classroom Applications

Samples (1977) has designed educational strategies that bring both brain hemispheres into equal partnership. He has found three characteristics in the resulting learning process: (1) higher feelings of self-confidence, self-esteem, and compassion; (2) wider exploration of traditional content subjects and skills; and (3) higher levels of creative invention in content and skills. We must encourage in the social studies classroom not only systematic problem solving, but also the inventive, intuitive thinking associated with creative discovery. Students able to solve problems creativly reflect the characteristics outlined in Table 6–1; these are the thinking abilities that help originate unique, creative solutions.

Strategies for Creative Problem Solving

In discussing the topic of creative problem solving, we here define *creativity* in its broadest context. Our basic assumptions are that creative thinking varies among individual students, is something that is not copied, and is original to each student. The purpose of creative problem solving is not to develop creative geniuses, but to free all children to express and discover themselves.

To encourage creative problem solving, you must emphasize divergent thinking—rewarding original thought and respecting differences of opinion. Basic to developing or encouraging creative thought is to place students into situations where they can generate a variety and quantity of ideas. Rather than converge on a single "correct" answer, inspire students to free their imaginations to explore many possibilities. In the social studies classroom, you can achieve this in two important ways: (1) by asking stimulating questions that motivate students to think in different ways about the information and concepts they are learning about and (2) by presenting situations that force students to associate two or more normally unrelated problems or ideas.

Brainstorming.   You can ask questions that inspire and provoke the ideation associated with creative thought. A question such as, "How many uses can you think of for an automobile tire other than for moving a car?" encourages each of the intellectual characteristics associated with creative thinking: *fluency* (number of ideas); *flexibility* (different kinds, or categories, of ideas); *originality* (new or novel ideas); and *elaboration* (adding on to ideas). Further samples of the types of questions that release children's creativity and invite it to flourish and grow follow:

- "How can one person make a difference in the world?"
- "Suppose the Statue of Liberty could talk. What would she say about the citizens who make up our country?"
- "Why is it important to remember special people from the past?"
- "Suppose your family just moved to Thailand. How might your life change?"
- "If one more national holiday could be added to those we already celebrate, what might it be? How would it be celebrated?"

TABLE 6–1
Intellectual and Emotional Characteristics of Creative Individuals

Intellectual Characteristics	Emotional Characteristics
1. *Fluent thinking abilities:* Generates large quantities of ideas as possible solutions to problems. The child who responds to the question "What things are red?" with "apple, book, car, beet, crayon, and shoes" is a more flexible thinker than one who says, "fire engine and candy."	1. *Risk Taking:* Has the courage to take wild guesses and expose self to criticism or failure. The creative thinker is strong-willed and eager to defend his or her own ideas.
2. *Flexible thinking abilities:* Offers a variety of different categories of responses to problems. The child who indicates that a pencil may be used for such diverse purposes as writing, holding up a window, tapping on a drum, or leading a song is more flexible than one who suggests a pencil might be used to draw, write numbers, write words, or compose secret messages.	2. *Complexity:* Enjoys looking at the way things are and thinking about the way they should be. Delves into intricate problems and seeks alternatives so that order can be brought from chaos.
3. *Original thinking abilities:* Offers highly unusual or clever responses to a problem. The child who finishes the incomplete sentence "He opened the bag and found . . ." with "a giant spotted butterfly" is more original than the child who suggests "an orange."	3. *Curiosity:* Is inquisitive and full of wonder. The creative thinker is open to puzzling problems and toys with many ideas while pondering the mysteries of things in the surrounding environment.
4. *Elaborate thinking abilities:* Adds on to or expands simple ideas or responses to make them more "elegant." The child who responds to a teacher's invitation to add more information to the sentence "The cat sat on the porch" with "The lazy black and white alley cat sat on the top of the rotten old porch" demonstrates greater elaborative ability than the child who says, "The black cat sat on the old porch."	4. *Imagination:* Dreams about things. The creative thinker often is a "dreamer" who visualizes and builds mental images and reaches beyond the boundaries of reality.

- "What is one event that our current President will remember for a long time?"
- "How would you have felt in 1620 if you were a Pilgrim watching the *Mayflower* sail away from Plymouth Colony?"
- "What might we do to get more computers for our school?"

- "What design would be best for our room's class flag?"
- "Suppose the United States had been colonized by China. How might our country be different today?"

A stimulating question or problem and an accepting classroom atmosphere are keys for implementing the creative problem-solving process, but the question remains, "What do I do from there?" The step recommended by most proponents of creative problem solving is to engage the students in active brainstorming sessions. You can begin brainstorming immediately after sharing a problem. The process is described in Activity 6–2.

Activity 6–2

Classroom Exercise

Brainstorming

Generate Possible Solutions

Group members think of as many new (and wild) ideas for possible solutions as fast as they can. One group member records all ideas; no evaluation or judgment of ideas is allowed at this time. Every suggestion is added to the list, no matter how ridiculous it may sound. The main objective of this phase is to generate the greatest number of ideas possible without regard to quality; quantity is the objective for each group. This part of the brainstorming process often lasts between 5 and 15 minutes.

Critically Evaluate Ideas

This phase begins as groups restate the problem and narrow down lists of suggestions by addressing such concerns as, "Will this idea actually solve the problem? Will it create new ones? Will it work? Is it practical? Will we be able to use it in the near future? What are the strengths and weaknesses? Can any of the ideas be combined into one useful solution?" After narrowing their lists, each group should work toward a common decision. The ultimate choice might contain one idea or a combination of ideas.

One special strategy useful in helping students examine their potential solutions is *attribute listing*. In this process, students list all the attributes of the problem in one column, generate ideas for improvement in the next, list positive features in the next, and list negative features in the last column. In this way, they are able to consider the positive and negative features of each alternative suggestion.

PROBLEM ATTRIBUTES	SUGGESTED SOLUTIONS	POSITIVE FEATURES	NEGATIVE FEATURES
Playground swings are too high for the young children.	1. Lower them.	1. Children can reach them.	1. If too low, they can get hurt.
	2. Have someone lift up the children.	2. Children will be able to swing.	2. Will someone always be around to help?

Put Ideas Into Use

The final stage of brainstorming is to consider all possible ways that the tentative solution might be elaborated on or improved. Your contribution to this phase of creative problem solving is to guide the students' thinking with thought-provoking questions, such as those that follow:

- New Ideas
  Can it be used in new ways as it is?
  Can it be put to other uses if it is changed in some way?
- Adaptation
  What else is like this?
  What other idea does this make us think of?
  What new twist could we add to the idea?
  Could we change the color, shape, sound, odor?
- Enlargement
  What can we add?
  Should we make it longer, wider, heavier, faster, more numerous, thicker?
- Condensation
  What can we take away?
  Should we make it smaller, shorter, narrower, lighter, slower, thinner?
- Substitution
  What else can we use to do the same thing?
  What other materials or ingredients might we use?

Forced Associations.   You may also stimulate creativity by encouraging your students to discover relationships—to sense how one thing is like another and apply these connectors to solve a problem. While exploring the relationship of ideas, you might simply ask a question such as, "How can we improve a mailbox by making it like a garbage can?" First, students must list the attributes of a garbage can, such as carries large loads, has two handles, moves. Then, they must use one or a combination of these attributes to improve the mailbox: "Attach two handles and make it portable so that on bad weather days it can be brought inside where the mail can be unloaded."

Another forced association strategy is described in Activity 6–3. It is a mind-stretching exercise that helps students think in different ways about the content with which they are dealing.

Activity 6–3

Classroom Exercise

Making Forced Associations

1. Put a word related to a social studies theme, such as *mesa*, in a box at the top of a growing display. Then ask, "What two words does *mesa* make you think of?"

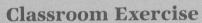

2. Place those two words in the boxes as shown.

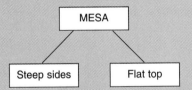

3. Ask the students what other word comes to mind as they examine these two words. For example, "What word do you think of when you see the words *steep sides* and *flat top?*"

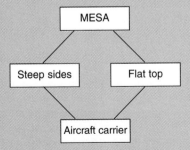

4. Ask the students to establish a relationship between the top and bottom boxes: "How is a mesa like an aircraft carrier?"

Synectics. Gordon's (1961) synectics approach is an interesting creative problem-solving strategy. Instead of a specific, clearly defined problem, the strategy begins with a general account. For example, our actual problem might be to devise a plan to find adequate parking for automobiles in a large city. Instead of specifying this problem, the students would be told that the problem is one of storing things: "How many ways can you think of to store things?" In a general way, students might come up with ideas such as: "Put them in boxes," "Pile them up," "Can them," "Put them on shelves," "Hang them on hangers," or "Put them in bags."

As the students continue brainstorming, the teacher gradually narrows the problem. At first, she tells the students that the items to be stored are large and then asks them to eliminate suggested possibilities. Next, she informs the students that the items to be stored cannot be cut up or folded. Finally, the actual, specific problem is given to the class. By now, the students should pull together ideas from their list to come up with solutions that they might never have considered had they been given only the clear problem. For example, one group created an interesting parking garage that resulted from the idea of "putting things on hangers."

Creative problems differ from closed-ended problems in that they call for divergent solutions to problems. They offer built-in motivation for children with right-hemisphere strengths, and essential practice for children with left-hemisphere talents. Both types of problems, however, are crucial to today's social studies classrooms in that they encourage children to dig into things, turn over ideas in their minds, try out alternative solutions, search for new relationships, and struggle for new knowledge.

INQUIRY

As you studied the previous section on problem solving, you learned that there are no set patterns of instruction in carrying out the process. The inquiry model, however, can be viewed as a more systematic way to investigate a question or problem, as it is designed to bring students directly into the scientific process. Like problem solving, inquiry originated in a belief that independent learning should be a major goal of social studies instruction. And, like problem solving, it views children as curious and natural explorers. Because of these similarities, problem solving and inquiry are often discussed synonymously. Sound confusing? Don't feel alone, for, as Thomas and Brubaker (1971) contend:

> From time to time, a term intended to signify a new teaching procedure rapidly gains popularity among educators. In recent years, the expression *inquiry method* has achieved this distinction, particularly in the fields of science and social studies. However, as use of the term has spread, so has confusion about what it really means. Some people consider inquiry an approach to instruction that is indeed new. Others say it is at least as old as ancient Greece but has previously traveled under such names as the Socratic method, problem solving, critical thinking, scholarly investigation, scientific analysis, and the development of thinking processes. (p. 239)

Despite this apparent dilemma, the characteristic that sets inquiry apart from problem solving is the sequence of specific phases students must use to solve a problem. So, for the purposes of this text, inquiry will be considered as a *systematic process for solving problems.* Descriptions of its system of investigation vary from source to source, but the most common pattern in elementary school social studies classrooms seems to be the time-honored pattern recommended by John Dewey (1916):

1. The students confront a problem they would like to solve.
2. The students generate hypotheses, or unproven suppositions, that are tentatively accepted to explain the problem.
3. The students collect data for the purpose of testing the hypotheses.
4. The students analyze the data and form generalizations that can be applied to this problem and to similar ones encountered in their lives.
5. The students share their results with an audience.

When teachers use the inquiry process in their social studies classrooms, they guide children through these five inquiry steps. They assume that students have first developed problem-solving skills and are now ready to perform the systematic steps of the inquiry model.

Confronting a Problem

In order for inquiry to work, students must first have an interesting, motivating problem to solve. The problem must hold a degree of mystery for the students to capture their interest. The major concern here is appeal—children will not want to investigate anything they do not care about. I vividly recall one insightful youngster reacting to a teacher's suggested problem: "Research is boring when you don't care about the topic." There are three basic types of problems that interest students: (1) problems generated by the students, (2) problems generated by asking a stimulating question or presenting a perplexing dilemma, and (3) problems produced by arranging the classroom environment and encouraging exploration of various items on display.

Problems Generated by the Students

To illustrate this type of problem, let's examine a social studies teacher's use of the model. Ms. Hasson's fourth-grade students returned from lunch upset about seeing their peers unload huge amounts of food from their trays into the trash containers. The developing discussion inspired a searching "why" from one of the students. Antonio suggested that most children didn't like meat loaf, the meal served that day. There were competing views; however, most thought that the quality of food needed to be improved. Ms. Hasson realized student interest in this situation was deep and sensed that their concerns centered about two questions: "What is the least favorite food served for lunch?" and "What is the favorite food served for lunch?" Rather than have the children engage in a "heated exchange of ignorance," Ms. Hasson decided to help the students substantiate their opinions about what lunches the children "really liked" by turning their problem into an inquiry episode.

Problems Generated by a Stimulating Question or Perplexing Dilemma

Mr. Reid's third-grade class had been involved in a series of lessons focusing on the concept of *historical change* as it related to the passage of time. Today, Mr. Reid chose to stimulate deeper interest in the topic by bringing to class several items typically used by kindergarten children: simple puzzles, primary writing paper, picture books, blocks, and an easel brush. He asked the children to identify the items and to talk about the time of their life when these items were commonly used. Mr. Reid recorded their comments related to kindergarten memories on a chart labeled *Kindergarten Memories (Past).*

Mr. Reid then shifted their attention to a second chart, labeled *Third Grade (Present).* He asked the students to talk about things they could do in third grade that they were unable to do in kindergarten. As they offered ideas such as, "Tie our shoes," "Do multiplication problems," and "Read harder books," Mr. Reid wrote them on the "present" chart. Then Mr. Reid asked the children, "How do you think your school life will be different in the future—in fifth grade?"

Problems Generated by Examining Objects or Written Sources

Tony Light, a fifth-grade teacher, learned about the inquiry process during his graduate-level social studies course and was won over to the approach. However, he had not yet had a chance to put his knowledge and interest to use. Tony had learned not to jump headlong into a new mode of instruction without first making sure his students were ready for the change. He remembered his professor's advice to introduce children slowly to any new pattern of instruction. A particular quote stuck out in Tony's mind: ". . . the presence of any new element in a classroom is potentially distracting. . . . Introducing [new expectancies] all at once produces a situation in which the children's cognitive systems collapse under an 'overload of input,'. . ." (Fisk & Lindgren, 1974, p. 58).

Tony's chance to put his ideas to work turned up quicker than he had planned. A small group of students had arrived at school that day eager to discuss a magazine article describing fads of youth today—their clothing styles, favorite television shows, most popular entertainers, and so on. An extended verbal interchange about whether the poll accurately reflected the interests of students in their community dominated the lively discussion. As the students critiqued the article's accuracy, one questioning student looked at Tony and decisively shifted the direction of the conversation: "Mr. Light," he asked, "what fads were popular when you were our age?"

Realizing that the spark for inquiry often comes from meaningful personal questions, Tony shared a few of his recollections from life about fifteen years ago and found that the rest of the class had begun to share the questioning student's interest. Without deliberately planning an inquiry experience, Tony Light found himself in the midst of one. Building on the knowledge gained from his graduate course, Tony seized upon the spontaneous interest generated by the magazine article and launched an inquiry episode. He started by writing the question on the board in an *IWW* format: "I WONDER WHAT fads were popular among fifth graders in 1985."

The problem, often stated as a question, is the initial spark for further discussion. For the problem to be effective, you must be aware that the problem must match what the children already know. If children are confronted with a problem with which they have little or no previous experience, they often reject it because of its unfamiliarity. On the other hand, the problem should not simply be an opportunity for children to "rehash" information they already know. Instead, the problem situation should be balanced between what students already know and what is new to them. That balance seems to stimulate elementary school children's greatest need to explore and search for answers.

This first step of the inquiry process is crucial; if children cannot accurately define a problem based on previous experiences or if they are not interested enough to pursue it, the subsequent steps of the process are futile.

Developing the Hypotheses

Once students understand the problem and develop a sincere interest in it, they are ready for action; it is now time to work systematically toward a solution. You might begin by asking: "What do you already know about this situation? What have you already learned that we might be able to use now? How could this information help us come up with an answer to our problem? What answers can you suggest based on what we've just discussed?" The purpose of these questions is to help children associate information they already know and to encourage them to offer assumptions, or *hypotheses*, about the problem. Formulating hypotheses involves a certain amount of risk to the child, so you must be especially careful to value individual contributions. Remember that these assumptions are, in most cases, nothing more than predictions. Definitive solutions and opportunities to reject hypotheses arise when children become involved in carrying out their investigations and selecting the appropriate data that support or refute the hypotheses.

Ms. Hasson's fourth-grade students offered responses such as, "Spaghetti is one of the favorites. The other kids hardly throw any away," "Tacos are a favorite because everybody likes tacos," "No one likes meatloaf. It ends up in the trash container every time it's served," and "Chicken fingers are awful. They don't even look like chicken!"

Mr. Reid's class, on the other hand, suggested such thoughts as, "We'll learn Spanish. My sister's in fifth grade and she says it's cool to learn how to count in Spanish" and "Learn about the early colonies in our country. I think you have to know the states and capitals, too."

In Tony Light's class, the students came up with ideas such as, "They listened to songs by Bruce Springsteen. My older cousin always talks about how great he is" and "I think everybody was wearing striped or checkered sneakers then. My sister has about six pairs in the back of her closet."

Gathering the Data

Having generated their hypotheses, students are now ready to gather data to test them. The collection process can take several forms, depending on the nature of the investigation. In most elementary school classrooms, data are collected in one of three ways: *survey, descriptive,* or *historical.* The format selected depends on the problem and its hypotheses.

Surveys

The first step in conducting a survey is to make sure the questions asked of the individuals to be polled are so precise that they will yield the specific data required to test the hypotheses. For example, in the case of Ms. Hasson's problem, the class wants to find out exactly what the students prefer for lunch as it is prepared by the cafeteria staff. So their survey question could be, "Of the following, what is your favorite lunch served in the lunchroom?" or "Of the following, what is your least favorite lunch served in the lunchroom?" On the other hand, a question such as "What do you think of the food served at school?" is too general and would not yield the necessary data.

Once the clear-cut polling question has been determined, the actual survey instrument must be constructed. Should the students poll their peers orally and keep a running record of the results, or should they distribute questionnaires similar to the one illustrated in Figure 6–3? Regardless, after they determine how they will conduct the survey, the students must decide on the sample population for their investigation.

Do they need to question every child who eats lunch in the cafeteria? Should only a small portion of the student body be surveyed? Since it is unnecessary to gather data from every child eating lunch in the cafeteria, the students would be wise to

FIGURE 6–3
Sample Survey Questionnaire

Lunchroom Survey

Put an "x" in front of your favorite lunch served in the lunchroom.

_____ pizzas   _____ hot dogs

_____ tacos   _____ chicken fingers

_____ spaghetti   _____ meat loaf

_____ hamburgers   _____ sloppy joes

As avid social scientists, children dig into many resources to get the facts.

choose some type of *sampling* strategy. Perhaps they will interview every third child who gets through the lunch line. If they want an equal boy/girl distribution, they might poll every third boy, every third girl, and so on. If possible, they could randomly select fifty students by drawing names out of a hat. Whatever the choice, the students must do all they can to ensure that their survey data is gathered from a representative sample of the larger population.

Descriptive Research

Descriptive research is probably the most frequently used of all data-gathering techniques in the elementary school social studies classroom. It involves two major strategies: direct observation and indirect observation. *Direct observation* includes all the real-life experiences that involve children in touching, handling, trying out, and viewing objects or events. A trip to the commuter train station to observe the "crunch" of rush hour, a trip to a dairy farm to see how a cow is milked, and a visit by the town's mayor to question her about the need for a traffic light near the school are all examples of direct observational experiences offering data for problem solving.

Indirect observation involves the use of information sources other than direct experiences. These sources often include library resources such as encyclopedias, informational books, magazines, newspapers, pamphlets, almanacs, catalogs, dictionaries, travel brochures, atlases, guides and timetables, posters, films, videos, photographs, and even the phone book.

Mr. Reid's students were involved in a study with considerable possibility for using direct observation, so he followed the listing of hypotheses with the following directions: "We will now divide our class into four groups. Each group will visit a fifth-grade classroom. I have arranged your visit with the fifth-grade teachers, so they know you are coming. You will spend one-half hour watching what the fifth graders do. You must sit quietly and record anything that fifth graders do that you do not now do in third grade."

Historical Research

When children delve into conditions of "long ago," they must gather and evaluate relevant traces of the past. These may include physical remains (artifacts, relics, and other "accidental survivors") and oral or written records (stories and documents).

Tony Light's students decided to examine the fads of 1985 by gathering an oral record of the past—interviewing family members and neighbors who were upper elementary grade students that year. Students designed a written list of questions each would ask their interviewees.

Analyzing the Data

In contrast to traditional research conducted in elementary school social studies programs that use written sources such as encyclopedias and other informational books as their data source, *authentic research* is more likely to involve data-gathering techniques of primary research: surveys, observation, interviews, and document analysis. Once students have gathered the data, it must be analyzed and interpreted.

When Ms. Hasson's surveys were completed, for example, the children tallied the responses and organized the data into categories. Figures 6–4 and 6–5 show the tally sheet and summary graph used by the class.

After they recorded the information, the children examined and analyzed the data to draw accurate conclusions. Naturally, you don't impose a complicated treatment that you learned in a college statistics course on the children, but you do want them to interpret the data accurately. The findings of the lunchroom survey included the following interpretations, or *generalizations*:

FIGURE 6–4
Tally Sheet

Our Favorite Lunch							
Pizza	Tacos	Spaghetti	Hamburgers	Hot Dogs	Chicken Fingers	Meat Loaf	Sloppy Joes
~~1111~~ ~~1111~~ ~~1111~~ 11	~~1111~~ ~~1111~~ ~~1111~~ ~~1111~~ 11	~~1111~~ ~~1111~~ ~~1111~~ 1	~~1111~~ 11	111	~~1111~~ ~~1111~~ ~~1111~~ ~~1111~~ 1		11

FIGURE 6–5
Graph of Survey Results

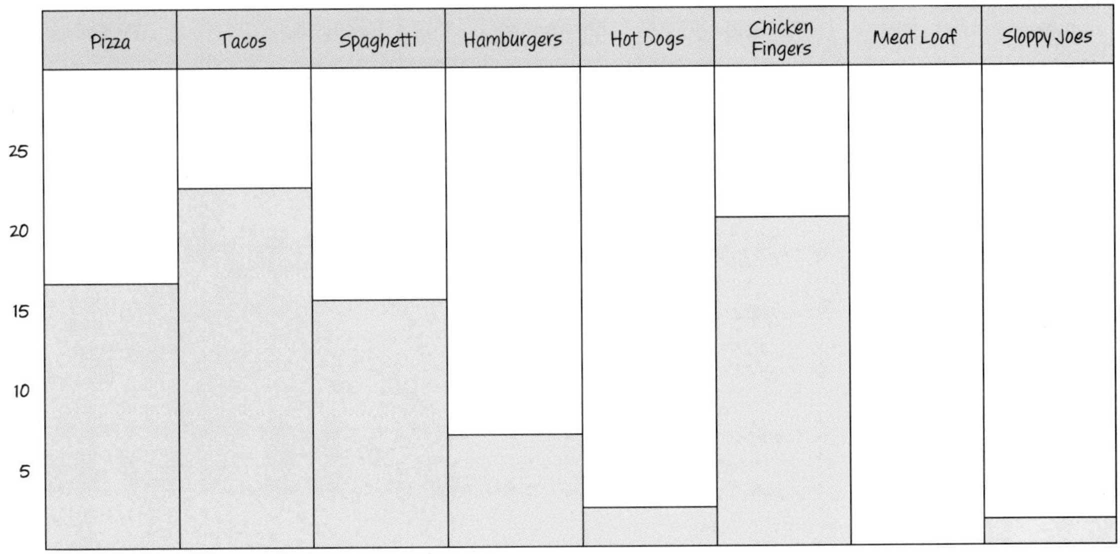

Pizza	Tacos	Spaghetti	Hamburgers	Hot Dogs	Chicken Fingers	Meat Loaf	Sloppy Joes

1. Most of the children like tacos for lunch.
2. Chicken fingers are almost as popular as tacos.
3. Meat loaf, sloppy joes, and hot dogs are the favorite of the fewest people.

Because of the nature of his students' research, Mr. Reid found that a comparative analysis of their observations was more appropriate than a tally sheet or graph. When the children returned from their observational visits to the fifth-grade classrooms, Mr. Reid asked each group to come up with a list of observed activities. After each group tabulated its list, Mr. Reid asked group one to share its first two observations. If either was duplicated on another group's list, that group's recorder was to remove it from the list. Mr. Reid then invited group two to share two additional observations as he listed them on the chart. Continuing, Mr. Reid listed all unduplicated observations on the "Fifth Grade (Future)" chart. Using a Taba concept reception strategy, Mr. Reid encouraged his students to group and regroup the data and culminated the experience with these generalizing questions: "What changes have happened between your kindergarten year and third grade? How do you think fifth grade will be different from third grade? Why will these changes occur? What other things change over time?"

Tony Light's students summarized and rank ordered the responses to each query on a large chart. The results are shown in Figure 6–6. Tony helped his students make descriptive statements of the data by asking such questions as, "What did you discover about fads of 1985? How does this list compare to present fads? Why do you think this has happened? How might this list change in the future? What makes you think so?"

FIGURE 6–6
Summary of Interviews

Sayings	Toys	Clothing	Entertainers	Sports Stars	TV Shows
Awesome	Cabbage	Camouflage	Bill Cosby	Mary Lou Retton	Cosby Show
Rad	Patch	clothes	Michael J. Fox	Walter Payton	He-Man: Masters
Cool	Kids	Fingerless	Ralph Macchio	Greg Louganis	of the Universe
	He-Man	gloves	Madonna	Larry Bird	Punky Brewster
	Transformers	Legwarmers	Wham!	Evelyn Ashford	The A-Team
	My Little	Jams	Cyndi Lauper	Pete Rose	Webster
	Pony	Parachute	Emmanuel Lewis	Kareem Abdul-Jabbar	Who's the Boss?
	G.I. Joe	pants	Ricky Schroder	Carl Lewis	Silver Spoons
	Stickers	Cutoff	Gary Coleman		Knight Rider
		shirts	Mr. T		Family Ties
		Collars	Michael Jackson		
		turned up	Sylvester Stallone		
		Checkered			
		shoes			
		Jeans			
		Belts below			
		the waist			

Sharing Results

The final step of conducting an inquiry is sharing the results with an *authentic audience* using appropriate vehicles of communication. In the adult world, much of the reward gained from researching comes from having an impact on desired audiences; professors of education take great pride in discovering ways to improve academic performance, and medical researchers want to uncover treatments for difficult-to-control diseases. The resulting recognition and excitement are often missing for students whose primary audience is usually limited to the teacher and fellow classmates.

When sharing the results of the lunchroom survey with an authentic audience, who will benefit from the results (cafeteria manager, principal, school newspaper)? Ms. Hasson's students may choose to show the principal their findings after summarizing the lunchroom survey on large charts with precise data. The students would then need to orally communicate this data with accurate, effective statements. What might constitute an authentic audience for Mr. Reid's and Tony Light's students? As you ponder that question, keep in mind that authentic research goes beyond the traditional formal written report by engaging children in varieties of communication possibilities—oral presentations, graphics, photographs, audio- or videotapes, debates, dramatic skits, and other means.

Once students have experienced some authentic research, they will want to address, independently or as a group, other absorbing questions, problems, or situations, such as the following:

- How to get the money needed to finance a trip to the state capital.
- How to curb vandalism on the school playground.
- How to make the school building or classroom more attractive.
- How to care for the homeless on the city's streets.
- How to celebrate Dr. Martin Luther King, Jr.'s birthday.

THE SUCHMAN INQUIRY MODEL

One of the problems of using inquiry in the elementary school classroom is that it takes more time and effort than can be realistically extracted from an already crowded day. Suchman (1966) has designed a data-gathering procedure that attempts to alleviate that problem by encouraging students to seek information through less time-consuming questioning strategies. Eggen and Kauchak (1988) offer this middle-school classroom scenario to illustrate the Suchman inquiry model. First, the teacher, in this case Mr. Smith, presented a problem:

> In the mountains of the Southwest a number of years ago deer were quite numerous, although the population would fluctuate slightly. There were also wolves in the mountains. Some people from a small town witnessed a wolf pack pull down two of the smaller deer in the herd and were horrified. As a result, the people launched a campaign to eliminate the wolves. To the dismay of the people, the years following the elimination of the wolves showed a marked decrease in the population of the deer. Why, when the wolf is the deer's natural predator, should this occur? (p. 223)

Yes–No Responses

After Mr. Smith shared the problem and was sure the students understood it, he encouraged them to ask questions, but they had to follow two rules: (1) the questions must be answered "yes" or "no" and (2) the answers to the questions must be observable. Part of the questioning sequence went as follows:

> "I have an idea, I think," Steve said tentatively. He went on, "After the wolves were eliminated, other predators such as bobcats, coyotes, and large birds, such as eagles, were able to prey more successfully on the deer, so their population went down."
> Steve then appeared to be finished for a moment, so Mr. Smith returned to Pam.
> "Jim and I have another idea," Pam suggested.
> "Excellent," Mr. Smith praised. "Go ahead."

"After the deer's predator was eliminated, the population expanded so their habitat couldn't support them, and they became susceptible to starvation, and the population went down," Pam said.

"OK," Mr. Smith said. "Can we gather some information to support your idea?"

"Were more bobcats seen in the deer's habitat after the wolves were eliminated?" Ronnie queried.

"No," Mr. Smith said.

"How about coyotes?" Ronnie continued.

"No again," replied Mr. Smith.

"Were numerous barkless dead trees found in the region after the wolves were eliminated?" Sally continued.

"Yes," Mr. Smith said. (Eggen & Kauchak, 1988, p. 223)

As you can see, Mr. Smith's strategy began with a problem: "Why should a population of animals decline rather than expand when their primary predator was eliminated?" The students were then involved in seeking out data while testing their hypotheses.

Arriving at Conclusions

The discussion pattern continued until the students uncovered sufficient data to test their hypotheses. One student made a final comment:

"That does it then," Jackie asserted. "That supports Bill's idea about wolves taking the weaker members of the population."

The class was satisfied that their hypothesis was supported by the data, and Mr. Smith continued the lesson by discussing the hypotheses that had been formed and linking them to generalizations about prey–predator relationships. (Eggen & Kauchak, 1988, p. 223)

The Suchman inquiry model is summarized in the following sequence:

1. The teacher presents a problem, which typically asks the students to explain why a particular phenomenon has taken place.
2. Students hypothesize a solution to the problem.
3. Students gather data as they ask the teacher factual questions that can be answered yes or no.
4. The students revise their hypotheses as more data is accumulated, until they develop a solution.

AFTERWORD

To conclude our discussion of inquiry in the social studies, it will be instructive to examine an inquiry-based lesson plan that details the classroom procedures. Activity 6–4 presents this sample plan. After studying and discussing this plan, try to construct one of your own. What major instructional processes must be central to your plan?

Activity 6–4

Lesson Plan: Life on the *Mayflower*

Theme: Settling Plymouth Colony
Grade: Five
Teacher: Terri Snyder

General Objective

The students will participate as authentic, self-regulated learners in exploring solutions to a problem.

Specific Objectives

1. The students will compare and contrast their lives with the lives of children aboard the *Mayflower* in 1620.
2. The students will use independent study skills to locate and record information.

Materials

1. Set of books on early life in the colonies.
2. Drawing paper.
3. Crayons and markers.

Procedure

1. Help the students recall from previous lessons that the Pilgrims came to Plymouth Colony in 1620 on a ship called the *Mayflower*. Explain that the *Mayflower* was a small ship sailing on a large ocean for over two months. Ask the students to imagine that they were children on the *Mayflower* and to predict what the routine for a typical day on the ocean might be. Chart their responses on the chalkboard.

2. Call the children's attention to a collection of books you have arranged on a study table; for example, *Eating the Plates* by Lucille Recht Penner (Macmillan). Each of these books describes daily routines such as playing games, eating meals, and sleeping.

3. Help students use the books to uncover information dealing with daily routines and to compile notes on the nature of each routine. A simple study sheet helps guide the research. It contains such questions as, "What routine are you describing? At what time of the day is the routine carried out? How is the routine carried out?"

4. Ask the students to summarize their findings by creating a whole-class timeline identifying and characterizing the routines experienced

during a typical day on the *Mayflower.* Then have students share what they consider to be the most interesting feature of each routine. They should compare the results of their research with the predictions.

5. Tell the students that many people on the *Mayflower* kept diaries to help them remember what happened on the voyage. Have each student compose a daily diary entry describing any of the routines outlined previously.

Assessment

1. Examine the *Mayflower* timeline to determine whether the sequence of daily routines is accurate. Check to see if relevant information was used to solve the problem.

2. Listen to the descriptions of the daily routines to assess whether the context for and conditions of each routine were clearly and accurately described.

3. Read the diary pages to determine whether students were able to write an understandable description of a daily routine on the *Mayflower.*

It often happens that when the word *research* is mentioned to college students, groans and steely glares accompany the predictable questions, "How long does the paper have to be? How many references do we need? What's the topic?" Schack (1993) comments that exposing students exclusively to this form of research often builds negative attitudes toward the processes of problem solving and inquiry: "Written reports on teacher-determined topics using secondary sources not only generate negative attitudes from students but also present an unrealistic view of research in the real world. While this kind of research has a place, to present it as the only form of research does students a disservice" (p. 29). We cannot limit elementary school research to such practices; remember that most elementary school youngsters are natural problem finders. They revel in the mysteries of their world. On their own, they deftly uncover problems of interest—the important first step of research: "Why do farmers cut off the corn and leave the lower part of the plants behind? During what month of the year do most of my classmates celebrate their birthday?" What they need at school is to learn the methods by which these queries can be investigated. Schack (1993) explains that while all the particular problems children bring to school may not be particularly significant, the processes they go through and the feelings they gain about themselves as capable researchers *are*. So, authentic research associated with problem-solving and inquiry processes teaches students that they have the skill and ability to pursue knowledge in a meaningful way and that their efforts have real value now and in the future.

TECHNOLOGY SAMPLER

Useful sources for related social studies topics include this Internet site:

4Kids Detective (answers children's questions on almost any topic)
http://www.4Kids.org/detectives/

Some useful sources for related social studies topics include these software titles:

Compton's Interactive Encyclopedia
Compton's New Media

Encarta
Microsoft Corporation

Grolier
Grolier Interactive

World Book Multimedia Encyclopedia
World Book Multimedia

WHAT I *NOW* KNOW

Complete these self-check items once more. Determine for yourself whether it would be useful to take a more in-depth look at any area. Use the same key as you did for the preassessment form ("+", "?", "–").

I can *now*

_____ differentiate between the terms *problem solving* and *inquiry.*

_____ describe what is meant by *authentic learning.*

_____ explain what teachers do when they employ techniques of *active learning.*

_____ justify the importance of hands-on experiences to set the stage for early problem solving.

_____ design student-centered problem-solving experiences.

_____ describe the roles and responsibilities of teachers in a problem-based social studies program.

_____ differentiate between guided problem solving and creative problem solving.

_____ plan a transition from traditional classroom practices to problem-solving practices.

_____ guide students through the steps of inquiry.

_____ help students carry out authentic research.

REFERENCES

Bruner, J. (1965). *On knowing: Essays for the left hand.* New York: Atheneum.

Carson, R. (1965). *The sense of wonder.* New York: Harper & Row.

de Bono, E. (1969). The searching mind: Lateral thinking. *Today's Education, 58,* 20–24.

Dewey, J. (1916). *Democracy and education.* New York: Free Press.

Eggen, P. D., & Kauchak, D. P. (1988). *Strategies for teachers.* Englewood Cliffs, NJ: Prentice-Hall.

Fisk, L., & Lindgren, H. C. (1974). *Learning centers.* Glen Ridge, NJ: Exceptional Press.

Gagne, R. M. (1977). *The conditions of learning.* New York: Holt, Rinehart & Winston.

Galin, D. (1976). Educating both halves of the brain. *Childhood Education, 53,* 20.

Gordon, W. J. J. (1961). *Synectics: The development of creative capacity.* New York: Harper & Row.

Holt, J. (1967). *How children learn.* New York: Pitman.

Mitchell, L. S. (1971). *Young geographers.* New York: Bank Street College of Education.

Monhardt, R. M., & Monhardt, L. (1997). Kids as curators. *Science & Children, 35,* 29–32; 80.

Orlich, D. C., Harder, R. J., Callahan, R. C., Kauchak, D. P., Pendergrass, R. A., Keogh, A. J., & Gibson, H. (1990). *Teaching strategies: A guide to better instruction.* Lexington, MA: D. C. Heath.

Ornstein, R. E. (1972). *The psychology of consciousness.* New York: Viking.

Piaget, J. (1969/1970). Science of education and the psychology of the child. New York: Viking Compass.

Piaget, J. (1973). *To understand is to invent.* New York: Grossman.

Rogers, C. R. (1974). Forget you are a teacher. In M. D. Gail & B. A. Ward (Eds.), *Educational psychology.* Boston: Little, Brown.

Samples, R. (1977). Mind cycles and learning. *Phi Delta Kappan, 58,* 689–690.

Schack, G. D. (1993). Involving students in authentic research. *Educational Leadership, 50,* 29.

Seefeldt, C. (1974). *A curriculum for child care centers.* Columbus, OH: Merrill.

Smith, R. F. (1987). Theoretical framework for preschool science experiences. *Young Children, 42,* 35.

Sternberg, R. (1989). Comments made at a meeting of parents and teachers at the Episcopal Academy in Philadelphia, PA, March 14, 1989.

Suchman, R. (1966). *Inquiry development program: Developing inquiry.* Chicago: Science Research Associates.

Thomas, R. M., & Brubaker, D. L. (1971). *Decisions in teaching elementary social studies.* Belmont, CA: Wadsworth.

Torrance, E. P. (1963). Adventuring in creativity. *Childhood Education, 40,* 79.

Wasserman, S. (1989). Children working in groups? It doesn't work! *Childhood Education, 65,* 204.

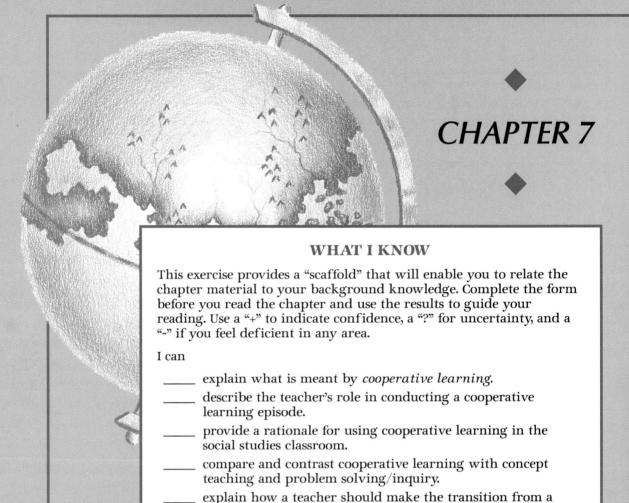

CHAPTER 7

WHAT I KNOW

This exercise provides a "scaffold" that will enable you to relate the chapter material to your background knowledge. Complete the form before you read the chapter and use the results to guide your reading. Use a "+" to indicate confidence, a "?" for uncertainty, and a "-" if you feel deficient in any area.

I can

_____ explain what is meant by *cooperative learning*.

_____ describe the teacher's role in conducting a cooperative learning episode.

_____ provide a rationale for using cooperative learning in the social studies classroom.

_____ compare and contrast cooperative learning with concept teaching and problem solving/inquiry.

_____ explain how a teacher should make the transition from a traditional classroom to cooperative learning.

_____ design a cooperative learning experience for a social studies topic or theme.

_____ identify basic principles of managing a cooperative classroom.

_____ suggest methods of rewarding positive cooperative efforts and for resolving group conflict.

Using the results as a guide, what questions will you seek to answer as you read?

Using Cooperative Learning as "Social Study"

◆ CLASSROOM SKETCH

Ms. Nguyen divided her class into groups of four, assigned heterogeneously by ability level. These groups were called *home groups.* To start the lesson, each home group member drew a slip of paper out of a box. Written on the slips was either of the four elements of the natural landscape of the United States—*forests, prairies, mountains,* and *deserts.* Each *home group* member who drew a slip of paper with *forests* on it left her or his *home group* and joined with the others who drew the same landscape feature to form an *expert group* to study forests. At the same time, the students who drew the other natural landscape features regrouped themselves into expert groups to study either prairies, mountains, or deserts. Therefore, expert groups of four or five students were established to investigate each of the four landscape features.

After studying their textbook and other reference materials with the other members of their expert groups, the

271

students discussed their assigned landscape feature, designed a graphic overview of the information uncovered, and pondered the possibilities of representing this information on a diorama that they would construct upon return to their home groups.

When they went back to their home groups, students began constructing their dioramas. Each "expert" constructed her or his own diorama; then, using the graphic overview and diorama, each "expert" in the home group taught the others in their group about her or his landscape feature. To complete the project, the home group students connected each of the dioramas into a sequence that they believed would tell a story about the natural landscapes of the United States. Using their displays and the graphic overviews, each home group presented its story of the natural landscapes of the United States.

◆   CLASSROOM CONNECTION

Elementary school students learn in a variety of ways. Some prefer to read and write while others like to explore and manipulate. Some enjoy listening to a stirring lecture while others opt to be wired in to a computer terminal. Picture *your* ideal classroom setting. Is it one where the teacher presents a lesson to the whole class, or does it engage learners in problem solving and inquiry? Regardless of which style you've chosen, you should realize that we all become most highly motivated to learn when instructional styles match our learning preferences.

Up to this point in our consideration of flexible teaching in social studies, we have considered two major models of instruction—concept teaching (Chapter 5) and problem solving/inquiry (Chapter 6). Ms. Nguyen used a third—the cooperative learning model. Although cooperative learning has become a hot topic in education these past few years, Ms. Nguyen understands that it is not really a *new* instructional approach. As we have found with many other teaching practices, the roots of cooperative learning go back to 1916 when John Dewey wrote a book called *Democracy and Education*. In this time-honored piece, Dewey described an educational system that mirrored society—a laboratory for real-life learning. Central to Dewey's philosophy of learning was a democratic social system that emphasized small-group investigations into important social and interpersonal problems.

Years later, Lev Vygotsky ([1930–1935] 1978) supported the importance of a social context in the classroom with his contention that learning occurs most effectively under adult guidance or in collaboration with more capable peers. In Vygotskian classrooms, however, merely interacting with peers is not in itself sufficient to promote learning; casual interaction, although at times productive, often becomes haphazard, and the children can become confused by one another's misunderstandings. By structuring the social situation, the teacher uses peer interaction to satisfy learning goals.

In more recent years, scholars of cooperative learning have conceived highly applicable models for "structuring the social situation." The best known of this group include Robert Slavin, Roger and David Johnson, Elliot Aronson, Schlomo Sharan, and Spencer Kagan. So, an old idea resurfaced in the 1980s and has been vigorously promoted as a "new" strategy for teachers through the 1990s.

DEFINING COOPERATIVE LEARNING

In today's social studies classrooms, students interact with one another in two fundamental ways; they either (1) *compete* to see who is best or (2) *work cooperatively* with a vested interest in one another's learning as well as their own. Of these two, competition is perhaps the most familiar. In competitive classrooms, students spend much of their day striving to be "first" or "best," trying to achieve the highest grades, best jobs, most lavish praise, or a star on the weekly achievement chart. In such competitive situations, few succeed while the majority become known as "losers." Johnson and Johnson (1988) explain:

> The research indicates that a vast majority of students in the United States view school as a competitive enterprise where you try to do better than the other students. This competitive expectation is already fairly widespread when students enter school and grows stronger as they progress through school. . . . Cooperation among students where they celebrate each other's successes, encourage each other to do homework, and learn to work together regardless of ethnic backgrounds, male or female, bright or struggling, handicapped or not, is rare. (p. 34)

Ellis and Whalen (1990) warn that not only do excessively competitive classrooms often cause "losers" to drop out of the education game, but they often hurt the "winners," too: "They fear failure and the loss of approval they fear it will bring. And while they're winning, they're often ostracized by the other students—labeled a brain or a nerd or a brownie. By the time they get to middle school, many students would rather be caught dead than have one of these labels" (p. 13). As for the average children, competition rarely offers them opportunities to shine.

COOPERATIVE LEARNING AS "SOCIAL STUDY"

Many educators spurn highly competitive programs and favor more noncompetitive approaches that encourage children to work together. That philosophy is reflected in today's popular proposition that *learning is primarily a social activity*. In other words, effective social studies teaching involves cooperative "social study." Stahl and Van Sickle (1992) explain:

> *Social* . . . refers to the need to engage in worthwhile, goal-oriented tasks within supportive interpersonal environments. . . . Within such environments individuals must

become active, contributing, and integral parts of the social community that benefits from their participation. To be effective within this social environment, students must learn and practice the knowledge, abilities, and attitudes necessary to function effectively within the social group.

. . . By *study* we mean the systematic and focused pursuit of knowledge and the ability to apply that knowledge when needed. (pp. 2–3)

Social study, then, refers to a process through which teachers enable students to acquire new knowledge and abilities within viable groups, or social communities. Social studies teachers carefully define student roles and deliberately structure classroom activities so that youngsters are able to participate together as members of a social community focused on the common task of achieving shared learning goals. Cooperative learning strategies can help make *social study* a useful, meaningful part of the elementary school social studies classroom.

Slavin (1992) offers two points of justification for using cooperative learning in social studies: "First, these methods enhance and deepen students' learning of the formal curriculum. Second, they help to accomplish goals. These include traditional

Our society gains a great deal when we help children learn from each other.

affective goals of social studies such as commitment to civic values and empathy for other peoples in other cultures and eras" (p. 21). Cooperative learning can accomplish these things, but simply putting students into groups to work together is not enough. There is a major difference between putting students into groups to learn and structuring true cooperative learning opportunities. Johnson and Johnson (1991) clarify this thought by explaining that cooperation is *not* having students sit side-by-side at the same table to talk with one another as they do their individual assignments. Cooperation is *not* assigning a report to a group of students where one student does all the work and the others simply put their names on the product. Instead, the authors make clear that cooperative groups are much more than collections of students who sit together completing individual tasks that are then pulled together for a "group project."

Positive Interdependence

Johnson and Johnson (1991) define *cooperative learning* as a process through which students work together to maximize their own and one another's learning. Cooperative learning is characterized as the true exemplification of the saying, "All for one and one for all." The authors call this concept *positive interdependence* and use it to detail the major difference between traditional group work and cooperative learning groups. Think of "positive interdependence" much as the type of teamwork taking place on a basketball court when one player passes the ball to another who, in turn, slams the ball through the hoop. The actions of both players were positively independent (they both did different things to contribute to the joint goal of scoring two points); neither player could have succeeded without the other. Both needed to perform competently for success to result. Slavin (1984) upholds this "sink or swim" concept of cooperative learning: "the critical feature of [cooperative learning] is that two or more individuals are interdependent for a reward they will share if they are successful as a group. . . . [Cooperative learning happens in] situations in which two or more individuals are allowed, encouraged, or required to work together on some task, coordinating their efforts to complete the task" (p. 55).

PLANNING A COOPERATIVE EXPERIENCE

Teachers use cooperative learning groups in social studies to accomplish the goals and objectives that drive the selection of any other instructional approach: learning from the textbook; solving a baffling problem; interpreting maps, charts, or graphs; examining personal values or attitudes; or reading literature, documents, pictures, or news articles. The basic cooperative learning format conforms to the following general script:

1. Determine group size.
2. Assign students to groups.
3. Establish the classroom's physical arrangement.

4. Select a pattern or structure.

5. Enable students to employ positive interdependence.

6. Evaluate the successes of each group.

7. Reward students' efforts appropriately.

Determining Group Size

There is no magic recipe to help all teachers arrive at the ideal number of students for a cooperative learning group; you will need to experiment to see what works best for you. From my own experience, I have found that the larger the group, the more skilled the members must be for the group to function well. So the best advice is to think small. First cooperative learning groups (for primary-grade children or older children with little prior group-work experience) should be formed of pairs, or *dyads*. Primary-grade students work best in pairs because young children more easily reach agreement with only one other person. By grade three or four, as the children become more skilled at working together, you might assign them heterogeneously to three-member teams. Students through middle school can function as quartets, but they need much success working in dyads and trios before they can work in groups of four. The problem in working with groups larger than two is that trios often tend to separate into a tight pair and a castaway, and quartets tend to separate into pairs. Therefore, you need to offer many successful opportunities to work as dyads before you separate students into trios or quartets. Unless your project demands it, four members stretches the upper limits of cooperative group membership. Freiberg and Driscoll (1992) have examined the common group sizes found in elementary school social studies classrooms and detail some of the benefits of each:

Elementary school children function beautifully as cooperative learners, especially if they can work in small groups.

Two-person group. This size promotes a relationship and generally ensures participation. This is a good way to begin with inexperienced "groupies" (students who have not been grouped before). In a pair, students gain experience and skill before working in a complex group arrangement.

Three-person group. This arrangement allows for a changing two-person majority. Participation is very likely because no one wants to be the odd person out. Roles in this size group can be those of speaker, listener, and observer, and learners can experience all three roles in a brief period of time. This size group is appropriate for creating descriptions, organizing data, drawing conclusions, and summarizing ideas.

Four-person group. In a four-person group, there will likely be different perspectives. This size is small enough that each member will have a chance to express himself and can be comfortable doing so. Often this size groups [*sic*] emerges as two pairs when opinions are expressed. A group of four people requires basic communication and cooperation skills, but offers ideal practice for learning group process. (p. 277)

Selecting group size will mean carefully examining your students and the maturity they have developed through informal and formal group experiences. A common mistake many teachers make is to have students work in larger groups before they have the skills to do so.

Assigning Students to Groups

The actual "coming together" of cooperative learning groups begins with careful assignment of students to teams. The first question teachers often ask is, "Should these groups be homogeneous or heterogeneous?" For most tasks, you should use heterogeneous grouping—place "high," "middle," and "low" achievers within the same learning group. If the groups are dyads, the fastest way to form a group is to have the students count off by two. You might also have fun experimenting with random strategies such as having students blindly draw a riddle and an answer from a box and then match the riddle with the answer. Trios should consist of "high," "middle," and "low" learners. A useful technique is to arrange your students according to ability level and assign numbers according to how many teams you want. Figure 7–1 illustrates one teacher's heterogeneous breakdown of students into four-member teams. Darcee is the top-ranked student while Donald is ranked lowest. This teacher will then group all the ones, twos, and so on, and will have teams balanced according to ability (see Figure 7–2).

Notice that even though the teacher carefully divided the teams on the basis of ability, other minor adjustments needed to be made as he deliberated about each group's mixture. Think about the many characteristics you will need to consider as you adjust heterogeneous teams: "Are all the talkative (or quiet) children in one group? Have I put together children who act up? Did I balance gender, race, or ethnic factors? In order to complete the group's goal, must I add someone with a special skill (e.g., to draw an illustration)?"

Cooperative learning groups should be carefully put together and should reflect a range of differences that make cooperative learning effective; a major purpose of cooperative teams is *social study*—to help students learn to work with everyone. For

FIGURE 7–1
Establishing Heterogeneous
Groups

STUDENT	GROUP		STUDENT	GROUP
1. Darcee	1		11. Jeffwan	1
2. Warren	2		12. Inez	2
3. Holly	3		13. Patty	3
4. Ahmad	4		14. Gina	4
5. Johnny	5		15. Linda	5
6. Penny	5		16. Mack	5
7. Mike	4		17. Bobby	4
8. Luis	3		18. Laura	3
9. Nate	2		19. Robin	2
10. Carla	1		20. Donald	1

FIGURE 7–2
Teams Balanced in Ability

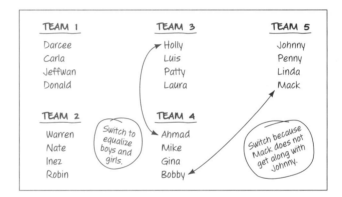

this reason, having students select their own groups is often unsuccessful. Self-selected groups often become homogeneous: high achievers working with other high achievers, boys working with boys, girls choosing girls, and so on. According to Johnson and Johnson (1991), "More elaborative thinking, more frequent giving and receiving of explanations, and greater perspective taking in discussing material seem to occur in heterogeneous groups, all of which increase the depth of understanding, the quality of reasoning, and the accuracy of long-term retention" (p. 65).

How long should the groups stay together? Some teachers prefer to keep them together until they complete a special project. Others form new groups every day (especially dyads). Some teachers keep cooperative groups together for an entire year or semester. The most frequently recommended approach is to allow groups to remain together for three to four weeks; students should have an opportunity to work along with every other classmate, if possible.

Arranging the Classroom

Students working together must be near one another and separated from other groups as much as possible so they will not interfere with one another's learning.

FIGURE 7–3
Physical Arrangements

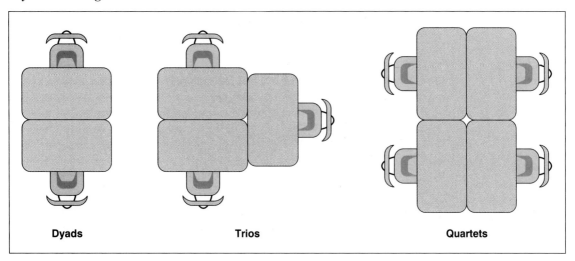

Dyads   Trios   Quartets

The best way to accomplish this is to have group members push their desks together so they can see one another and talk at a level without disturbing other cooperative teams (see Figure 7–3).

Selecting a Pattern or Structure

Several people have developed patterns, or "recipes," for cooperative learning that can be used for a variety of purposes in social studies classrooms. The following are examples of specific, tried-and-true strategies that you might find useful.

Turn-to-Your-Partner Discussions

This is the simplest structured cooperative learning pattern, most appropriately used during teacher-directed lessons (see Chapter 5). You may stop at natural 'break' points within a lesson and say something like, "Turn to your partner and . . ." (think about what makes the San Joaquin Valley a good place for farming; predict where the river begins; tell why the Cheyenne held Medicine Dances; and so on), and then give the children a minute or two to share their ideas. You may ask a few groups to share their ideas with the class, but you should not normally require all groups to share each time. In the case of predictions, for example, you may follow the sharing minute not with a whole-class discussion but simply with a comment such as "Let's go on and see what happens," and continue with the lesson.

The idea of sharing aside, Turn-to-Your-Partner discussions have four components: students should (1) *compose* an individual response to the question or problem, (2) *reveal* their idea to their partner, (3) *listen* thoughtfully to their partner's view, and (4) together *develop* a new response that is better than either member's original idea. Turn-to-Your-Partner discussions are intended to actively engage students in the content you are teaching by getting them to think about the material being presented.

Think-Pair-Share

Think-Pair-Share is much like Turn-to-Your-Partner, except that the process must culminate with each pair sharing its ideas with the entire class. Developed by McTighe and Lyman, Jr. (1988), Think-Pair-Share is a discussion cycle during which students are (1) presented with a question, (2) given time to think individually about the problem, (3) asked to talk about the question with a partner, and (4) invited to share responses with the class. Each phase is special, with distinct responsibilities required of the students. Signal children to switch from observing some type of presentation to the *think, pair,* and *share* modes by using cues. McTighe and Lyman, Jr. (1988) suggest hand signals similar to those illustrated in Figure 7–4. You may also use printed cards labeled with the four cues or illustrated cartoon figures to signal student responsibilities.

Cuing enables you to manage the efforts of the group more effectively by focusing the children's attention on a response process, rather than by encouraging the impulsivity that normally surfaces when children respond to questions in traditional recitation models of instruction. A basic script for Think-Pair-Share follows:

1. Present the children with a learning experience (read the text, observe a process, etc.).
2. Pose a question while giving the listening cue.
3. Signal the children to think silently by using the thinking cue.
4. Give the children 3–10 seconds of silent thinking time after the question has been posed.
5. Offer the pairing cue and encourage the partners to share their thoughts with one another.

FIGURE 7–4
Hand Cues for Think-Pair-Share Experiences

Listen

Think

Pair

Share

6. Give the children a sharing cue and have them raise their hands on that signal to give a response.

7. Allow a "wait time" (3-second pause) after each response to encourage deeper listening and thinking.

8. Encourage students to express their thoughts in a number of ways, such as through illustrations, dramatic skits, written products, oral reports, and the like.

Because of the sharing emphasis, Think-Pair-Share takes longer than Turn-to-Your-Partner, but it can also encourage higher-level conversations, especially those involving generalizing or critical thinking. The cuing system also helps you manage classroom learning more effectively.

Numbered Heads Together

Spencer Kagan (1989) created Numbered Heads Together, another approach to cooperative learning. It involves a simple, four-step structure:

1. The teacher has students count off within groups, so that each student has a number: 1, 2, 3, or 4.

2. The teacher asks a question, such as, "What were the roles of men and women inside a castle?"

3. The teacher tells the students to "put their heads together" to make sure that everyone in each group knows the answer.

4. The teacher calls a number (1, 2, 3, or 4). The students with that number may raise their hands to respond.

Kagan (1989) reports that positive interaction and individual accountability are both included in this approach since "the high achievers share answers because they know their number might not be called, and they want their team to do well. The lower achievers listen carefully because they know their number might be called" (p. 13). Therefore, students work together and help one another find answers, and all students learn what is being studied.

Jigsaw

Jigsaw is a cooperative learning technique developed by Elliot Aronson and his colleagues (1978) that is a combination of cooperative and individual learning. The process starts as the teacher assigns students heterogeneously to groups of four each, called their home group. Each home group works on content material that the teacher has broken down into sections. Each team member is responsible for one of the sections. Next, members of the different home groups who are responsible for the same sections meet in expert groups to study and discuss their assigned sections. Then these students return to their original home groups and take turns sharing with their teammates about their respective sections.

Mr. Emerson and his fifth graders, for example, use Jigsaw frequently during social studies class. To introduce the activity, Mr. Emerson tells his students that they will be assigned to a home group of four members each. Each home group is to meet and select a team name. The teams followed this procedure for a lesson on Helen Keller:

1. The class started out with five home groups, each team consisting of four members.

2. Mr. Emerson gave each member of a home group a different-colored adhesive dot (red, yellow, blue, green). These signified membership in an Expert Group.

3. Students left their home groups and went to a section of the room designated by colored sheets of construction paper that matched their dots, becoming members of expert groups. Mr. Emerson had four expert groups, each focused on an aspect of the life of Helen Keller: Helen's childhood, Helen's first accomplishments, Helen's adult life, and Helen's influence on history.

4. While in expert groups, the students focused on reading and discussing tasks designed to help them understand their sections. Finally, they summarized the information in a form that could be used to teach the members of their home groups about their sections. Then they returned to their home groups. Now there was an expert on every section in each home group.

5. Every expert shared information on his or her section with other members of the home group. Because students were able to learn about other sections only by listening carefully to their teammates, they were motivated to attend to one another's work.

6. Each home group planned a special presentation to share its collective learnings about Helen Keller.

Jigsaw II

Slavin (1986) offers slight modifications to Aronson's Jigsaw model, calling it Jigsaw II. Students work in four-member teams as in Jigsaw but, instead of each student being assigned a unique section, all students take part in a *common learning experience* (read a biography, for example). Like Jigsaw, the students then receive a subtopic on which to become experts, meet in expert groups to examine the subtopics, and return to their home groups to teach their teammates. Finally, students take individual quizzes, which result in team scores. Teams that meet minimum standards may earn certificates or other rewards.

Pick Your Spot

Pick Your Spot is a useful cooperative group strategy that helps students identify and declare their beliefs and opinions and then explore them with like-minded classmates. Developed by Ellis and Whalen (1990), the structure has the following four steps:

1. Ask the students a question from which they are to select an answer from among alternatives: "What is the one national symbol that best reminds us that we are a nation of free people?"

2. Identify "spots" in the room designating a variety of alternatives. Word cards can identify options, such as "The Flag," "The Bald Eagle," "The Liberty Bell," "The Statue of Liberty," or "The Washington Monument." Ask students to quickly pick a spot and quietly congregate there.

3. Tell students at each spot to discuss their choice to see how many good reasons they can generate for their position. Have a large sheet of chart paper available so the students can record their reasons.

4. After allowing sufficient time to build a strong case, call on one student from each group to share the group's reasoning with the rest of the class. After each group has reported, ask if any students would like to convert and pick a new spot. If they do, ask which argument persuaded them. (This step can be expanded by including questions or challenges from other groups.)

These are among the most popular of all patterns of cooperative learning. As you try one or more, you will discover variations and create new approaches. Concentrate and enlarge upon what works well for you. Gaining knowledge of and confidence in the approach, you will be naturally motivated to learn more.

Creating Positive Interdependence

The essence of cooperative learning is that it has two interrelated components: an *academic* element and a *social* element. Students must know that you value their success in attaining social skills as much as you value academic outcomes. A large part of cooperative learning, then, has to do with children understanding that they are linked with the others in their group and that the group's responsibilities can be most effectively carried out when its members coordinate their efforts. How do teachers promote positive interdependence in cooperative learning situations? Major techniques include (1) distributing materials, (2) assigning group roles, (3) teaching social skills, and (4) fostering group pride.

Distributing Materials

An effective way to entice all members to participate in group projects is to provide only one set of materials ("materials interdependence"). By passing out only one book, one list of questions, or one object, you communicate the idea that the assignment is collaborative and that the students are in a "sink or swim together" learning situation. Sometimes you may give individual group members different books or resource materials that *all* group members must then synthesize into one arrangement ("information interdependence"). This process requires that all members contribute so that the group can be successful.

Assigning Group Roles

You may also encourage positive interdependence by assigning interrelated roles to the group members. Each member must enact her or his role successfully for the group to function effectively. Different tasks call for different roles; you will need to reassign roles as the demands of unique group pursuits change from situation to situation. Some popular cooperative group roles include the following:

Group Captain	Reads the task aloud to group. Checks to make sure everyone is listening. Makes the task as clear as possible. Coordinates the group's efforts; provides leadership.
Materials Manager	Gathers, distributes, and collects all research books and other supplies.
Recorder	Fills out forms and writes down and edits the group's report. Shares the group's result with the class.
Illustrator	Draws any pictures, graphs, charts, or figures that help communicate the group's findings.
Monitor	Keeps the group focused on the task. Makes sure each member of the group can explain the answer or information and tell why it was selected.
Coach	Sees that everyone has an equal chance to participate. Offers praise and encouragement to members as they work.

Teaching Social Skills

Elementary school students require help while learning to work cooperatively with others. Students exposed only to traditional instructional practices and primary-grade children are limited in their groupwork experiences, so as you must teach them to read or write, you must also teach them group skills. Ellis and Whalen (1990) offer valuable examples of the kinds of skills students need to work effectively in cooperative learning groups: basic group skills, functioning skills, and higher-order thinking skills (see Figure 7–5).

Ellis and Whalen (1990) advise teachers not to become overwhelmed by the length of their skills list. *All* of the skills cannot possibly be taught in a week, month, or even the school year. Primary-grade teachers may work on three or four skills in need of special attention each year, while intermediate-grade and middle school teachers may focus on more; however, you should work on no more than two or three at a time and should never move so fast that students can't experience success.

Wasserman (1989) recalls her frustrations with moving sixth-grade children from highly directed, teacher-controlled classroom experiences into responsible cooperative groups, focusing on the social behavior of her children: "The first weeks of so-called 'cooperative' group work was anything but. All manner of uncooperative behavior emerged. . . . They couldn't focus on the tasks; they didn't care about each other; they didn't understand 'what they were supposed to do.' In the absence of clear and specific teacher direction (i.e., 'Do this now and do it THIS way!'), they fell apart" (p. 204).

Wasserman describes her biggest disappointment in watching her students become unruly: "My biggest disappointment was *not* that the children were unable to

FIGURE 7–5
Categories of Social Skills

Basic Group Skills are those bottom-line skills without which a group can't get anything done:

- getting into your group quietly and quickly
- bringing necessary materials with you
- staying with your group until the task is done
- talking in quiet voices
- listening to your partner(s)
- calling your partner(s) by name
- knowing your task(s)

Functioning Skills enable group members to work together effectively so that the group can accomplish its task and each member can learn the material. Most functioning skills can be learned to some degree by all elementary and middle school students:

- taking turns
- contributing your ideas
- supporting your point with evidence*
- asking for help when you need it
- encouraging others to contribute
- complimenting others' contributions
- checking for understanding
- keeping the group focused on the task

Higher-Order Thinking Skills deepen group members' understanding of the material being learned and the points of view of other students. While young children can learn some of these skills, others are appropriate only for students in grades 4 through 8 who have developed good Functioning Skills:

- asking for clarification
- providing clarification
- building on another's ideas
- paraphrasing another's idea to show you understand it
- analyzing your group's process
- coming to consensus
- synthesizing several ideas
- evaluating the group's work
- criticizing an idea, not the person who presented it

*This is a difficult skill for elementary students, but it is essential for them to learn it.

Source: Susan S. Ellis and Susan F. Whalen, *Cooperative Learning: Getting Started* (Jefferson City, MO: Scholastic, 1990), pp. 40–41. Reprinted with permission.

function in . . . sophisticated, mature and self-disciplined ways. . . . The killing blow was that the children wanted, asked, *begged* for a return to 'the way we did it in Grade 5' (p. 203).

It was at that point that Wasserman realized that she needed to help the children learn the skills required to function as thoughtful, responsible, cooperative learners. She needed to provide experiences for students to gain practice in those skills. This was not an easy task either, for as she (1989) admits: "It may be a lot easier to teach children to read and spell than it is to teach them to behave cooperatively . . . with each other" (p. 204).

To involve students in cooperative learning, you must help them gain control of themselves as group members. You do this by making interpersonal functioning an important learning goal. This is good news—cooperative skills can be taught and learned just like any other skill. And, like any other skill, you must exercise great patience and offer meaningful opportunities to help children learn. It may be February before you are able to recognize any major shift in students' group work, but you must follow the children's lead, never moving so fast that students are overwhelmed by your efforts.

When you want to teach a special skill, it may be most productive to begin with game-type tasks, especially those where team members must cooperate to reach a

The essence of cooperative learning is "social study"; excessive competition cannot teach elementary school children to live together.

common goal. A game I have found to be particularly useful is Puzzle Squares (see Activity 7–1). Fortunately, many books and professional magazines contain suggestions for similar cooperative games.

Activity 7-1

Classroom Exercise

Puzzle Squares

Materials

1. Cut out five heavy tagboard squares, each about five inches square.
2. Cut each square into three segments using the following patterns.

3. Scramble the fifteen pieces and put them into a large manila envelope.
4. Repeat the procedure for each set of five children in your classroom.

Goal

Each child in a group must use the puzzle pieces to complete a five-inch square consisting of only three pieces.

Procedure

1. Place children into groups of five and have them select a group leader.
2. Give each group leader one of the envelopes containing fifteen puzzle pieces.
3. On signal, the group leader opens the envelope and randomly passes three puzzle pieces to each group member.
4. Direct the students to examine their puzzle pieces and try to make a square from them. Signal the students to begin. Most groups will complete this task within twenty minutes, so allow the proper amount of working time. If the students discover their segments will not form a perfect square, they may exchange pieces with other members of their group, but only under these rules:

a. No talking. The game must be played in complete silence.

b. No eye signals, hand signals, or gestures. Communication of any kind is discouraged.

c. No taking another puzzle piece from another player, unless he or she first offers it to you.

When the time is up and several puzzles have been completed, discuss questions such as, "How did you feel when you first started working with the group? Did you find it difficult to cooperate with others as you kept working? What were some of the problems that your group experienced? How could they be resolved? What feelings did you have toward the other members of your group? What made you feel that way?"

As you help students acquire important group work skills through pleasurable cooperative games and eventually challenging social studies-related tasks (see Activity 7–2), you will need to keep a number of important processes in mind.

Activity 7–2

Classroom Exercise

Cooperative Writing on a Theme or Topic

1. *Bring in a number of objects related to a topic or theme of instruction.* For example, after reading about the traditions of Hanukkah during a thematic unit on Winter Holidays, Mr. Livingston brought in six objects: a menorah, a dreidel, latkes, an oil lamp, a replica Torah scroll, and a model Jewish temple. One object was displayed on each of six tables spread out around the room. Taped to the wall near each table were two large sheets of chart paper.

2. *Divide the class into cooperative learning groups of four students each.* Mr. Livingston explained that the objects were to be used for a writing activity that would take place in stages, each lasting for about five minutes. One group would start out at each of the tables, brainstorming words associated with the object on the table and writing them down on one of the sheets of chart paper.

3. *Rotate each group to the next table;* each group will now have an object different than the one it had brainstormed. The menorah group, for example, moved to the oil lamp table, the oil lamp table moved to the Torah table, and so on. The groups must write a short story about their new object on the second sheet of chart paper, using the brainstormed words of the previous group.

4. *Rotate again to the next table.* This time, each group revises the story written by the previous group—adding to, deleting, or revising ideas.

5. *Rotate once again.* Now each group edits the work of the previous groups, checking for such mechanics as spelling, punctuation, and grammar.

6. *On this fourth rotation, students examine the edited piece and compose a final copy* on a clean sheet of chart paper (leaving room for an illustration).

7. *Rotate still one more time,* assigning each group the responsibility to create an illustration for the final written piece.

8. *On the last rotation,* each group should be back at its original position, examining the story written for its object and sharing its reactions. The separate pages could be read aloud, and then bound together as a chapter in a class-generated book on Winter Holidays.

1. *Define the skill clearly and specifically.* Be sure the students understand their responsibilities (your procedures) as distinctly as possible. For example, "When I say, 'talk in quiet voices,' I mean that you will need to use your 'yard voices.'" You can then show your students a yardstick to demonstrate how far a "yard voice" should carry.

2. *Ask students to characterize the skill.* Brainstorming with your students is essential for determining cooperative group expectations. Place your students into dyads. Have each dyad write a list of behaviors that it thinks best characterizes a particular social skill, such as being able to form groups efficiently. Johnson and Johnson (1989/1990) recommend using what they term a "T-chart" to effectively accomplish this characterization (see Figure 7–6). To construct a T-chart, draw a horizontal bar and write the skill in question above it. Draw a vertical line down from the middle of the bar. On one side, list student responses to the question, "What would this skill look like?"; on the other side, list their responses to the question, "What would this skill sound like?" You then model the skill until all students have a clear idea of what its correct performance looks and sounds like.

3. *Practice and reinforce the skill.* You cannot teach students to work cooperatively with a single lesson or experience. Growth occurs over time with meaningful

FIGURE 7–6
T-chart Characterization of a
Social Skill

Skill: Getting into your group quickly and quietly

Looks Like

- wait for a signal to go
- gather all materials
- stand up and push chair
  in smoothly
- walk slowly and softly
  to your group area
- wait for all members to
  arrive before you start
  your work

Sounds Like

- silence
- quiet
- peacefulness
- stillness

- noiseless movements

- hushed voices

practice and effective reinforcement. Johnson and Johnson (1991) describe a first-grade teacher's efforts to practice the skill of "encouraging others to contribute":

> One day . . . she formed groups and handed out five poker chips to each group member, with a different color for each group member. The students were instructed to place a chip in the box every time they spoke while they worked on the worksheet. When a student had "spent" all his or her chips, he or she could not speak. When all the chips were in the box, they could get their five colored chips back and start again. There were several surprised students when their five chips were the only chips in the box! Teachers only have to use this device once or twice to get the message across (although first-grade students can get addicted to chips, so watch out). This technique was later used in a monthly principal's meeting. As the principals came in, each was handed several colored strips of paper. When they spoke . . . (p. 75)

You must constantly clarify instructions, review important procedures, and teach task skills as necessary. To master social skills, students must practice again and again. So, after you have defined and demonstrated the skill, you should ask the students to role-play it several times. At the end of cooperative group experiences, tell how many times a skill was observed. New skills must be practiced constantly and reinforced for some time.

Fostering Group Pride

If you plan on keeping the groups together for more than a day, help each group develop a sense of group identity. Have each decide on a group name, and perhaps also select a motto, color, symbol, and so on. Give each group a large piece of posterboard that can be decorated with the group name, the members' names, and illustrations or symbols. When completed, the groups may hang the charts above or near their meeting areas.

In all effectively structured cooperative learning experiences, students perceive that they are linked with their teammates in such a way that no one can succeed unless everyone works toward the completion of a task. Positive interdependence is an avenue to maximize the learning of all team members.

Assessing Individual and Groups Efforts

Has cooperative learning been successful in your classroom? Teachers obtain answers to this important question in two basic ways—by checking to see if students have accomplished their academic tasks effectively and by observing to see if students are collaborating and using the social skills being taught. Both involve highly complex skills and systems of recordkeeping. Chapters 3 and 4 discussed assessment procedures appropriate for various types of instruction in the social studies, including cooperative learning.

Rewarding Students

Slavin (1984) purports that teachers must provide clear incentive for children to work together—*rewards* (stickers, bonus points, snacks) or *recognition* ("super team," "great team," or "good team"). Under these conditions, Slavin believes, children are driven toward productivity by reinforcing one another's behavior. He notes that students' accomplishments should be recognized whenever cooperative learning groups succeed at a task—academic or social. All group members must receive a reward for the accomplishment; everyone is rewarded or no one is rewarded. For example, every group member gets ten minutes extra recess time when all group members correctly associate at least 45 capital cities with their states. The rewards should be both enticing and inexpensive. Ways of rewarding groups include the following:

- Bonus points added to all members' scores when a team achieves an academic task.
- Nonacademic rewards such as free homework passes, stickers, erasers or pencils, or extra recess time.
- Social rewards such as smiles or verbal praise. Noticing special accomplishments becomes sufficient reward in most cases ("You improved your previous best test score by 5 points!").

Teachers are discouraged from giving lots of stickers or other material rewards for success in acquiring social skills. Children must become motivated to behave for reasons other than to receive extrinsic (outside) rewards. Students should listen, for example, because they want to listen; they regard listening as an important social skill. They learn this not because someone gives them a cookie when they demonstrate a skill, but because they are convinced that caring interaction is a key to accomplishing group goals. You can help children develop an internal, rather than an extrinsic, locus of motivation through various means:

- *Be responsive to children.* Respond to their actions in attentive, affectionate ways.
- *Make sure children accept consequences for their actions.* If they run to their work area, they must go back and practice getting there quietly.
- *Give students developmentally appropriate responsibilities.* "Synthesizing ayn-thesizing several ideas" is a skill more appropriate for middle schoolers than for primary-grade children.

- *Provide feedback.* Let students know when they have performed well ("Super! you remembered to use encouraging words today") or how they can improve ("When someone can't understand you, it helps to say your idea another way").
- *Allow students to make appropriate decisions.* "How could you get the information you need?"

Ellis and Whalen (1990) advise that rewards can be gratifying and fun, provided that a few rules are followed:

- Students must compete only with others who are on the same ability level.
- The number of winners must be maximized.
- The situation must not be life or death, like a test or final exam.
- Competition should be used for fun, for review, or for a change of pace.

Critics (Damon & Phelps, 1989) reject the notion of offering external rewards for peer collaboration, emphasizing that it holds the potential for harm. They argue that collaboration should result in such heightened learning that it serves as its own reward. In other words, cooperative learning should be pursued not for external rewards but because it is an intrinsically satisfying experience.

After examining the arguments on both sides of the issue, you might have serious questions about the "right" way to approach the use of external rewards in your classroom. What should *you* do? My contention is that the abuses of rewards are not as much associated with the reward itself as in how the teacher uses it. Anyone who has ever stepped foot in an elementary school classroom would probably agree that not all learning tasks can be intrinsically rewarding for the children every day. Sometimes children need an "extra push." For example, if a teacher thinks that her students need some type of reinforcement for producing a high-quality mural, a reward such as a pencil topper can be enjoyable. However, to use grades as external rewards for group efforts can cause group members to focus too narrowly on the end product rather than on the collaborative procedures necessary to complete the task.

Children gradually develop a sense of inner (intrinsic) motivation when they discern a sense of control over their environment and perceive that teachers are responsive to their needs. For example, Ms. Rawlings often encourages her sixth-grade students to make their own decisions on the basis of one of the following three methods:

1. *Consensus.* Perhaps the most appropriate technique for social studies groups, all members offer suggestions so that the group as a whole can agree on a common plan of action.
2. *Compromise.* This technique is a form of "give and take" where group members with sharply conflicting ideas each modify their positions so that agreement can be reached.
3. *Voting.* Perhaps the most popular decision-making process among children, this technique simply decides the direction of a group based on the wishes of the majority.

Children's relationships with each other are of primary importance: "My classmates are a joy; they make learning a pleasure!"

To illustrate how each of these techniques could be used to solve an impasse, consider the following episode from Ms. Rawlings's classroom:

> While building a model of a Navajo village, a cooperative learning group argued over the shape of the Navajo houses, called *hogans*. Some said the shape of the hogan under construction was right; others argued that something was wrong. The group decided to clear up the controversy by taking a vote. The vote ended up three to two in favor of the shape currently under construction, resulting in some very unhappy losers.
>
> Ms. Rawlings joined the discussion at this point and asked whether a satisfactory solution was arrived at through voting. "No," "Yes," "No" . . . the children volleyed in response, and further discussion ensued. The three children voting for the current shape showed their teacher a picture of a crude brush and mud hut they had been using as their model. "But we saw other pictures of hogans showing much larger houses," argued the contenders. Ms. Rawlings encouraged a library visit to find the pictures, and the group agreed to wait and see if both parties might be able to compromise. Soon the contenders returned, book in hand, ready to defend their point. Indeed, they found that the hogan under construction was like those from the primitive Navajo civilization, while the hogans researched by two children—large, permanent structures of earth-covered logs—were from a more advanced Navajo civilization.
>
> After a short discussion, the group agreed that their model village should show both types of hogans, one labeled "primitive" and the other "advanced." So in a very short time, the children moved from *voting* to *compromise* to *consensus*.

You should encourage children to handle their own problems in cooperative groups, but be near to furnish appropriate guidance. In this way, children not only learn about social studies content in their group work, but also get firsthand experience in the operation of a democratic system of decision making.

RESEARCH ON COOPERATIVE LEARNING

Is it worth the time and hard work to transform your class into a cooperative learning environment? Is cooperative learning a fad that will come and go like so many others in recent years?

Slavin (1987), a leading advocate of cooperative learning, reports that in 35 out of 40 studies, results favored cooperative learning strategies over more conventional methods of instruction. In short, the research reveals that cooperative learning, done well, improves children in nearly all the areas of concern to elementary teachers, especially when compared to other alternatives. Johnson and Johnson (1992) assert that cooperative learning is here to stay because we know the approach does what people say it will do. Teachers can use it with confidence in a variety of ways because it is based on substantial research that validates its effectiveness. Speaking with conviction, Johnson and Johnson (1992) explain that "because of its effects and likely widespread use in the future, social studies educators need to understand the various approaches to implementing cooperative learning" (p. 45). Tom Bernagozzi (1988), a teacher who has used cooperative learning strategies extensively in his classroom, agrees with the Johnsons and adds that, despite its pitfalls, the benefits of the approach are considerable:

> Of course, cooperative learning can intensify personality conflicts. At first, some children hold on to their prejudices and don't want to work with their teammates. Loners can find it hard to share answers. Aggressive children try to take over. Some bright students tend to act superior. But those problems are typical of any classroom and needn't be barriers to cooperative learning. . . .
>
> Then there are the benefits. Watching students adjust to cooperative learning must be something like watching survivors on a life raft. Students quickly realize that they'll either sink or swim together. They learn to be patient, less critical, and more compassionate. If they see a teammate in need, they go to his aid. . . . Many times I'd stand back, watch the teams, and think: *This is what good teaching and learning should look like.* (p. 39)

There are no shortcuts to becoming a highly skilled cooperative learning social studies teacher; gaining expertise requires years of effort and long-term commitment to self-improvement. Seek help from colleagues, attend professional workshops, exchange ideas, and read widely.

AFTERWORD

Of all the options available, teachers seem to prefer whole-group instruction more than any other mode in our nation's social studies classrooms. Among the reasons for this state of affairs is that (1) teachers are more familiar and more comfortable with whole-group instruction because this is how they themselves were taught in elementary school and high school; (2) most classrooms are crowded, so teachers find whole-class instruction more efficient than other forms of instruction; and (3) with so many subjects to teach each day, elementary school teachers have little time to plan specialized social studies instruction for small groups and individuals.

For today's classrooms and those of the future, however, teachers must subscribe to the notion that children learn best when exposed to a *variety* of instructional strategies. Teachers must offer their students a wealth of organized activity: Children may compare and contrast ideas with Venn diagrams, complete project work in small groups, pursue independent activities at learning centers, grapple with real-life problems on the computer, or collaborate in groups with their peers. Sometimes you may choose to teach the whole class, but not always. You must realize that because elementary school students learn in many different ways, they must be offered a range of learning opportunities. Be careful not to fall into a "sit-and-listen" routine; you must guide and support students in different ways. In the social studies, this includes whole-class instruction, cooperative group work, and opportunities for problem solving and inquiry. In effect, you must be an experimenter, trying a wide range of techniques to reach each child, sensitive to the diversity present in every classroom.

WHAT I *NOW* KNOW

Complete these self-check items once more. Determine for yourself whether it would be useful to take a more in-depth look at any area. Use the same key as you did for the preassessment form ("+", "?", "-").

I can *now*

_____ explain what is meant by *cooperative learning.*

_____ describe the teacher's role in conducting a cooperative learning episode.

_____ provide a rationale for using cooperative learning in the social studies classroom.

_____ compare and contrast cooperative learning with concept teaching and problem solving/inquiry.

_____ explain how a teacher should make the transition from a traditional classroom to cooperative learning.

_____ design a cooperative learning experience for a social studies topic or theme.

_____ identify basic principles of managing a cooperative classroom.

_____ suggest methods of rewarding positive cooperative efforts and for resolving group conflict.

REFERENCES

Aronson, E., Blaney, N. T., Stephan, C., Sikes, J., & Snapp, M. (1978). *The jigsaw classroom.* Beverly Hills, CA: Sage.

Ayers, W. (1989). Children at risk. *Educational Leadership, 46,* 72.

Bernagozzi, T. (1988). The new cooperative learning. *Learning, 88,* 39.

Boyer, E. L. (1989). What teachers say about children in America. *Educational Leadership, 46,* 74.

Damon, W., & Phelps, E. (1989). Critical distinctions among three approaches to peer education. *International Journal of Educational Research, 5,* 331–343.

Dewey, J. (1916). *Democracy and education.* New York: Macmillan.

Ellis, S. S., & Whalen, S. F. (1990). *Cooperative learning: Getting started.* New York: Scholastic.

Freiberg, H. J., & Driscoll, A. (1992). *Universal teaching strategies.* Boston: Allyn & Bacon.

Goodlad, J. I. (1984). *A place called school.* New York: McGraw-Hill.

Johnson, R. T., & Johnson, D. W. (1988). Cooperative learning. *In Context,* 34.

Johnson, D. W., & Johnson, R. T. (1989/1990). Social skills for successful group work. *Educational Leadership, 47,* 29–33.

Johnson, D. W., & Johnson, R. T. (1991). *Learning together and alone: Cooperative, competitive, and individualistic learning.* Boston: Allyn and Bacon.

Johnson, D. W., & Johnson, R. T. (1992). Approaches to implementing cooperative learning in the social studies classroom. In R. J. Stahl and R. L. Van Sickle (Eds.), *Cooperative learning in the social studies classroom* (pp. 42–45), Bulletin no. 87. Washington, DC: National Council for the Social Studies.

Kagan, S. (1989). The structural approach to cooperative learning. Educational Leadership, 47, 12–15.

McTighe, J., & Lyman, F. T., Jr. (1988). Cuing thinking in the classroom: The promise of theory-embedded tools. *Educational Leadership, 45,* 18–24.

National Commission on Excellence in Education (1983). *A nation at risk: The imperative for educational reform.* Washington, DC: Author.

Slavin, R. (1984). Students motivating students to excel: Incentives, cooperative tasks and student achievement. *The Elementary School Journal, 85,* 53–62.

Slavin, R. E. (1986). *Using student team learning.* Baltimore: Center for Social Organization of Schools, John Hopkins University.

Slavin, R. E. (1987). Cooperative learning and the cooperative school. *Educational Leadership, 45,* 7–13.

Slavin, R. E. (1992). Cooperative learning in social studies: Balancing the *social* and *studies.* In R. J. Stahl and R. L. Van Sickle (Eds.), *Cooperative learning in the social studies classroom,* (pp. 20–23) Bulletin no. 87. Washington, DC: National Council for the Social Studies.

Stahl, R. J., & Van Sickle, R. L. (1992). Cooperative learning as effective social study within the social studies classroom: Introduction and an invitation. In R. J. Stahl and R. L. Van Sickle (Eds.),*Cooperative Learning in the Social Studies Classroom,* (pp. 2–3) Bulletin no. 87. Washington, DC: National Council for the Social Studies.

Vygotsky, L. S. ([1930–1935] 1978). *Mind in society: The development of higher mental processes,* Eds. & Trans. M. Cole, V. John-Steiner, S. Scribner, & E. Souberman. Cambridge, MA: Harvard University Press.

Wasserman, S. (1989). Children working in groups? It doesn't work! *Childhood Education, 5,* 204.

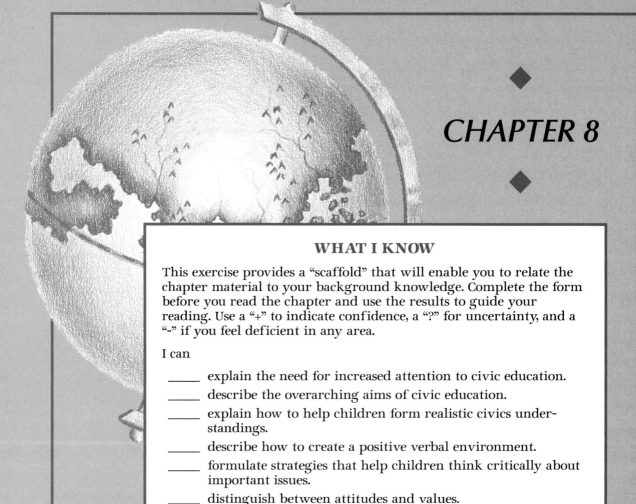

CHAPTER 8

WHAT I KNOW

This exercise provides a "scaffold" that will enable you to relate the chapter material to your background knowledge. Complete the form before you read the chapter and use the results to guide your reading. Use a "+" to indicate confidence, a "?" for uncertainty, and a "-" if you feel deficient in any area.

I can

_____ explain the need for increased attention to civic education.

_____ describe the overarching aims of civic education.

_____ explain how to help children form realistic civics understandings.

_____ describe how to create a positive verbal environment.

_____ formulate strategies that help children think critically about important issues.

_____ distinguish between attitudes and values.

_____ identify the fundamental values of American constitutional democracy.

_____ give examples of how good citizens participate in responsible actions.

_____ give a sound rationale for including civics education in the elementary school social studies curriculum.

Using the results as a guide, what questions will you seek to answer as you read?

Promoting Civic Education

◆ **CLASSROOM SKETCH**

Mrs. Holzwarth's fourth graders were about to wind up their study of Pennsylvania's state symbols when Naisha brought in a newspaper story about Maryland having just adopted the monarch butterfly as its state insect. "Does Pennsylvania have a state insect, too?" the children asked with sincere interest. That was all it took to launch Mrs. Holzwarth's class into one of the most rewarding learning events it had ever tackled.

After the children asked their genuine question, Mrs. Holzwarth stood back a bit and responded, "How do you think we can find out?" After looking up information in various books and pamphlets, the students found a state flower, a state song, a state tree, a state nickname, and various other official state symbols, but no official "state bug." They reasoned that they should write to the president of the United States to see if they could have one, but Mrs. Holzwarth explained that since this was a state matter they should direct their inquiry to their district legislators in Harrisburg (the state capital).

Before they did so, however, the children decided to conduct a regular democratic election to determine what the state insect should be. Several insects were nominated; each nominee became the subject of intensive scrutiny. The students explored the pros and cons of such bugs as the dragonfly, ladybug, and grasshopper. After weighing the advantages and disadvantages of each, a class vote settled the matter: the firefly was their choice. Why? One reason was that the scientific name, *Photuris pennsylvanica*, closely resembled the name of their state, Pennsylvania. Students also liked the fact that summer evenings often reflected the soft glow of hundreds of these insects; many a summer night was spent by these youngsters catching "lightning bugs." (The children had been taught that to catch a firefly and let it walk all over their hands for awhile is "okay" but to hurt the insect in any way is very wrong.)

Now that the children had designated their choice for state insect, the next step was to write to their two district legislators. Both lawmakers were impressed with the children's enthusiasm toward their special project and visited Mrs. Holzwarth's classroom. They discussed the process of initiating a law in the state legislature and advised the students how to go on from where they were. The children learned that their next step would be to gather the support of other legislators for their cause. They wrote to every state legislator requesting his or her support. These 26 children wrote over 250 letters—203 to the House, 50 to the Senate, and 2 to the governor and his wife. The children also learned that they needed support from voters in their area, so they circulated a petition and obtained more than 2,100 signatures.

So, Harrisburg was saturated with support from "firefly fans," but the children's backing was too regional. They needed help from throughout the entire state, not only from their county. At this point, the students felt like throwing in the towel in frustration and abandoning the whole project, but Mrs. Holzwarth came to the rescue, encouraging them to pick up the pieces and move on. She contacted the people she knew best—representatives of the state teachers' organization—telling them about the firefly bill. They responded enthusiastically. Each representative canvassed his or her district, and Harrisburg was deluged with more than 5,000 letters from firefly fans throughout the state. The children were on their way!

The class continued their work, printing 600 luminous bumper stickers proclaiming "Firefly for State Insect." They also kept up their letter-writing campaign, asking legislators to vote YES when the bill came onto the floor.

Eventually, the Senate passed the firefly bill by an overwhelming vote of 37 to 11. The children were invited to Harrisburg two days later for the House Government Committee hearings on their bill. They went to Harrisburg armed with banners on the side of the bus and singing an original song they wrote especially for this occasion:

Oh firefly! Oh firefly!
Please be our state bug.
Photuris pennsylvanica,
You'll fly forever above.
Oh firefly! Oh firefly!
You light up so bright.
It's fun to see such a pretty sight.
Oh firefly! Oh firefly!

Imagine the thoughts of the children as they arrived in Harrisburg and were met by television cameras and reporters from the major newspaper wire services. The hearing itself was held according to established decorum, the children testifying with all their knowledge about fireflies for a period of about two hours. The committee reported its unanimously favorable feeling toward the bill to the House of Representatives, and eventually the bill passed the House by a vote of 156 to 22. When the governor finally signed the bill (Act 59), the children were again in Harrisburg to watch the creation of a new state law. How many people, whether they be 9, 19, or 90, have given birth to a state law?

Photuris pennsylvanica has taken its place alongside the whitetail deer, ruffed grouse, and Great Dane as official state animals. However, for Mrs. Holzwarth's class, this experience was much more than an exercise in choosing a state insect. It was a civic participation episode in which they actively learned about political action and legislative processes in ways that most of us have not experienced. The students learned about petitioning and writing letters to their representatives, and they saw firsthand how government works. As one child noted, "Now we have something to tell our grandchildren." Another, when asked if she would like to get another law passed, blurted, "Darn right! I'd like a law against homework. Homework gives you pimples!"

◆ CLASSROOM CONNECTION

After this priceless experience, Mrs. Holzwarth's students tackled other civics-related topics with great vigor. They adopted a local park and pledged to keep it clean, raised $200 for a classmate's family whose house was destroyed in a tragic fire, collected food at Thanksgiving and brought it to the Salvation Army for distribution to needy families, and took handmade gifts to the senior center during the holiday season in December.

Through their considerable involvement in political institutions and processes, Mrs. Holzwarth's students ventured forward into the realm of civic education. Civics as a curricular area (sometimes called *political science* or *government* in high school or college) involves the study of political institutions and governmental processes. Civic education includes an understanding of how people attempt to maintain order, with emphasis on the structures and functions of government—how people get power, what their duties are, how they carry out their duties, and the relationship of authority and power.

Many of the most important decisions affecting our lives are political decisions; yet, to most students and adults, the study of the institutions and processes involved in these matters is all too confusing and uninteresting. Brody (1989) is convinced that resulting apathy toward civic life (the public life of a citizen) is the result of "a failure of civic education. Americans fail to see connections between politics and their lives because they have not been taught that the connections exist and are personally relevant" (p. 60). Historically, civic education has studied the structure and functions of governments with little regard to how they affect one's life. In effect, civics *education* was equated with civic *knowledge*. Barber (1989) argues, however, that, "if democracy is to sustain itself a richer conception of citizenship is required" (p. 355). Barber (1989) calls this richer concept *strong democracy* and describes it thus:

> If the point were just to get students to mature into voters who watch television news diligently and pull a voting machine lever once every few years, traditional civics . . . would suffice. But if students are to become actively engaged in public forms of thinking and participate thoughtfully in the whole spectrum of civic activities, then civic education and social studies programs require a strong element of practical civic experience—real participation and empowerment. (p. 355)

The task of citizens in a strong democracy includes real, active participation in civic processes (such as by helping with a local effort to provide shelter for the homeless) and institutions (such as by volunteering to lead a group of Girl Scouts). Individuals must not only know about these things, but must also be willing to engage in associated civic experiences. As witnessed in Mrs. Holzwarth's classroom, elementary school students can practice the skills of citizenship through relevant study and active participation.

The ultimate goal of contemporary civic education is "informed responsible participation in political life by competent citizens committed to the fundamental values and principles of American constitutional democracy. Their effective and responsible participation requires the acquisition of a body of knowledge and of intellectual and participatory skills" (Center for Civic Education, 1994, p. 1). *CIVITAS* (Center for Civic Education, 1991), a widely respected framework for civics education, adds that "[t]he first and primary reason for civic education in a constitutional democracy is . . . the widest possible civic participation of its citizens. . . ." Although the unquestionable goal of civic education is active participation, we are not speaking of just any kind of participation by any kind of citizen; it is the participation of informed and responsible citizens. How can elementary school teachers facilitate the acquisition of this goal? Essentially, schools should build upon a steady foundation that takes form during the earliest years of schooling. In addition to the traditional and central role of imparting civic knowledge and skills, this foundation must include helping students perceive the relevance of their "civic mission."

THE COGNITIVE REALM OF CIVICS INSTRUCTION

The civic mission of our schools requires formal and informal instruction in the knowledge and skills required of strong citizens in a constitutional democracy. The Center for Civic Education in its influential National Standards for Civics and Government (1994) maintains that such knowledge is communicated to students through formal instruction by providing students with "a basic understanding of civic life, politics, and government. It should help them understand the workings of their own and other political systems as well as the relationship of American politics and government to world affairs. Formal instruction provides a basis for understanding the rights and responsibilities as citizens in American constitutional democracy and a framework for competent and responsible participation" (p. 1). In addition to the formal curriculum, The Center for Civic Education recommends that adults help students through an informal curriculum centered on the governance of the school community and relationships among those within it: "Classrooms and schools should be managed by adults who govern in accordance with constitutional values and principles and who display traits of character worth emulating. Students should be held accountable for behaving in accordance with fair and reasonable standards and for respecting the rights and dignity of others, including their peers" (pp. 1–2).

Good citizens must be rational thinkers. They make up their minds on the basis of fact.

Formal Instruction to Help Develop Concepts

Effective civic education, then, must have a content base, but not superficial coverage of facts—for example, "The federal system of government divides power among the executive, legislative, and judiciary branches"—without regard for what they mean. Students often find such instruction trivial because their teachers fail to establish the relevance of civic knowledge to their lives.

Civic knowledge is most effectively imparted by involving elementary school children directly as participants playing a role of "citizen" in a democratic classroom. Rather than limiting instruction to the memorization of First Amendment rights, for example, you might challenge the students to assemble a "First Amendment Diary" (Mertz, 1991) after they learn about the rights guaranteed under the First Amendment. One student's diary of protected activities experienced over one weekend is illustrated in Figure 8–1. When comparing the diaries of each student, it would be productive to discuss the following points:

- How frequently did you rely on First Amendment protections?
- What might your weekend (week) have been like without the First Amendment rights?
- Which rights were exercised most? Least? (You might chart and analyze the entries.)

This activity does not imply that substantive knowledge is unnecessary; its purpose is to go beyond knowledge by demonstrating the relevance of civic understanding to students' lives. Further examples of activities that help involve students as active participants in civic instruction follow.

FIGURE 8–1
First Amendment Diary

Activity	Establishment Clause	Free Exercise	Speech	Press	Assembly	Petition
Read newspaper				X		
Went to church		X				
Went to a basketball game					X	
Phoned my friend to get homework assignment			X .			
Wrote letter to principal to request better playground equipment						X
Went to a movie with my parents					X	

Rules and Laws

Passe (1988) considers civic education as something more than studying flow charts of "How a Bill Becomes a Law" or reading a textbook chapter on the "Separation of Powers." Students from their earliest days of schooling learn about civics from the ways the classroom is governed—from the ways teachers respond to behavioral issues:

> Too often, when students violate standards of behavior, it is because they do not recognize the need for the rule. This is especially common in the early grades. Some of our youngest students have never been taught about the need for such rules as being quiet in the hallways or not calling out. The effects of those misbehaviors had never occurred to them. The cure is simple: We must teach them about behavior. We must teach them how the world works. That is basic citizenship education. It is the primary emphasis of social studies education. (pp. 19–20)

Simulations and Games.   One approach to teaching about rules is through simulations or games. For example, the following game sequence often works very well:

- *Phase 1.* Divide your class into equal-size groups. Give each group member a wooden block and tell them to play a game. Watch the children as they try to figure out what to do. When you notice the groups reaching a point of frustration, stop them and lead a discussion, asking these questions: "What took place when you started to design the game? Did you have any problems? Why? How did you decide to make the rules? Who made up the rules?"

- *Phase 2.* Ask each group to pass its blocks to one member. Declare that person the winner. Then discuss these questions: "Did this rule bother anyone? Is it important for you to share in making the rule? Why? How can we all share in decisions?"

- *Phase 3.* Follow the suggestions the children offer in their response to phase 2 and create rules for a game using the blocks distributed to each group. After writing down the rules, have them play the game. Many will have designed a good sequence to follow, but some groups may have created rules that contradict each other or are too difficult to follow. Frustration will certainly result. At this point, the children will eagerly discuss their feelings about the problems that arise from unclear rules or too many rules.

After this game sequence, focus on these concepts:

1. What is a rule? (a guide that helps us know how to act)
2. Where are rules? (everywhere—home, school, community, etc.)
3. Why do we need rules? (they protect us and help us to live together in groups)
4. Who makes rules? (everyone can help make rules in our country)
5. Why should we follow rules? (people will find it hard to get along; it may be dangerous or unsafe; someone might be punished)

Literature Sources.   A second approach to teaching about rules is to tap the rich storehouse of children's literature. Marie Winn's book *Shiver, Gobble, and Snore* (Simon and Schuster) is a particularly suitable story. It focuses on a funny king who made silly rules. In his kingdom lived three unhappy subjects: Shiver, who was always cold; Gobble, who was always hungry; and Snore (guess what he liked to do). Many of the king's rules severely limited the cravings of these characters, so they decided to move away to a place where there would be no rules. Alas, the three friends discovered that disputes could not be resolved in their new land—because they had no rules. They finally decided that to live peacefully, they must make rules. After reading them the story, you can lead children through a discussion: "What are rules? Who made the rules in the kingdom? Did the rules make sense or were they foolish? Did all the people want to obey the rules? Why or why not? What did they decide to do? What else could they have done? What have you learned about rules?"

Another excellent literature resource is one of the episodes from *The Tale of Peter Rabbit* by Beatrix Potter, in which Peter is instructed not to go into Mr. McGregor's garden. After reading the story, you may discuss the following: "What rule did Peter's mother give him? Why do you suppose she made it? Did Peter obey? What happened to Peter because he did not follow the rule? Who makes rules in your family? Why are those rules made? What happens when those rules are not obeyed?"

The purpose of these questions is to encourage children to realize that rules are necessary to protect people's rights and to keep them safe from others' unacceptable behavior.

Children Help Create Rules.   A third approach, challenging students to think about and construct the rules guiding their own classroom, also is a constructive way to engage them in authentic learning experiences dealing with democratic processes. Rather than imposing your list of rules at the beginning of the school year with little or no input from your students, define and implement rules democratically with their help, as outlined in Activity 8–1. The activity calls upon students to reflect upon rules as contributing members of classroom governance. Students who have had this opportunity are more likely to remember the rules and sense their importance. They also appear more interested in studying established forms of government.

ACTIVITY 8-1

Instructional Outline

The following sequence of activities is designed to help students think about how rules help govern the classroom community.

1. Following the reading of a book such as *Shiver, Gobble, and Snore,* divide your class into small discussion groups. Have each

group list the rules they believe would be suited for their class-room and for the times they must leave the classroom (use the restroom, go outside for recess, or attend a special class, such as physical education). Allow the groups to brainstorm for one-half hour or more.

2. Ask the question, "What rules do you wish to recommend?" To guide discussion, randomly select one group to list its first two choices on the chalkboard as the other groups cross off similar items from their lists (so they won't be repeated). As each rule is recorded, discuss specific examples of behavior that caused the group to suggest it. This allows students to see that rules are cre-ated for particular reasons. Select another group to do the same, continuing in this manner until you have a whole-group list on the board. This list, and the related discussion, will most certainly be long, as groups will want to bring up specific incidents to go along with each. Be sure to allow each group its fair chance. You may end up with a list of 30 or more rules, most of which will be stated neg-atively: "Don't fight," "Don't talk out loud unless you raise your hand," "Don't take things without permission." Groups will want to make a specific rule for every single behavioral situation they can imagine.

3. Ask the question, "Can any of these rules go together?" Lead stu-dents to combine those that are related: "Don't talk out of turn," for example, might be combined with "Raise your hand when you want to talk." Use colored chalk to underline those you can group together. Discuss the question, "Why did you group these rules together?" to help students verbalize common characteris-tics. The question helps students see how one general rule can sup-plant several specific ones. To further develop this idea, ask, "Can someone create one rule to take the place of all the rules in each group?"

4. Erase all the specific rules until only the three or four general rules remain; the general rules are usually along the lines of, "Don't do anything to damage the classroom" or "Don't do anything to hurt someone else." Encourage students to rephrase negatively stated rules as positive ones. Sometimes, students suggest one overarching rule, such as "Everyone and everything must be treated with re-spect." This procedure helps students acquire ownership of rules and they will participate more constructively as class members when they feel this psychological attachment.

5. Construct a permanent chart listing the classroom rules and display it prominently in your classroom.

Classroom Constitution.   As children experience the dynamics of a democratic classroom, they should become involved in activities that help them apply their understanding to society in general. In a democratic society everyone is bound by the rules and laws fairly established by its members. To help make this connection, one teacher extended a discussion of the U.S. Constitution by encouraging the students to create their own classroom constitution. See Figure 8–2.

Formal Instruction to Help Facilitate Critical Thinking

Intellectual skills grow from personal involvement in challenging subject matter content; students develop basic understandings of subject matter that they apply to higher level cognitive processes such as critical thinking. The Center for Civic Education explains, "To be able to think critically about a political issue . . . one must have an understanding of the issue. . . ." (p. 3). The ultimate purpose of critical thinking is to facilitate the development of strategies and tactics that help students evaluate, take, and defend positions about a particular topic or issue. Boyer (1990) emphasizes that "citizenship training, if it means anything at all, it means teaching students to think critically. . . ." (p. 5). The National Council for the Social Studies Task Force on Early Childhood/Elementary Social Studies (1989) takes a strong position on the role of critical thinking in social studies: "For children to develop citizenship skills appropriate to a democracy, they must be capable of thinking critically about complex societal problems and global problems. . . . Continually accelerating technology has created and will continue to create rapid changes in society. Children need to be equipped with the skills to cope with change" (p. 16).

Defining Critical Thinking

What is critical thinking? Critical thinking is a complex mental process; although there are many definitions of what it is, Ennis (1985) offers an explanation that is particularly appropriate for social studies instruction. He defines it as "reasonable reflective thinking that is focused on deciding what to believe or do" (p. 54). Ennis contends that thinking is *reasonable* and *reflective* when students make earnest efforts to analyze arguments carefully, search for valid evidence, and reach sound conclusions on a variety of civic issues. Beyer (1985) does not characterize critical thinking as any singular thinking skill, but rather as a collection of ten skills, or operations, that function in various combinations, depending on the situation:

- Distinguishing between verifiable facts and value claims.
- Determining the reliability of a source.
- Determining the factual accuracy of a statement.
- Distinguishing relevant from irrelevant information, claims, or reasons.
- Detecting bias.
- Identifying unstated assumptions.

FIGURE 8–2
Classroom Constitution

Grade Six Constitution

We the students of Grade 6, Room 14, in order to form a more perfect class, do establish this *Constitution of the Sixth Grade.*

Article I. Officials

1. There will be two branches of our government: the executive branch and the legislative branch.
2. The executive branch is made up of the President, Vice President, Secretary, and Treasurer.
3. The legislative branch is made up of all the rest of the members of the class.
4. Two candidates each for the offices of President, Vice President, Secretary, and Treasurer shall be nominated the Friday before the third Monday of each month.
5. Election of officers shall take place the third Monday of every month by secret ballot.
6. A student may hold a term of office only once.

Article II. Qualifications of Officers

1. Everyone automatically becomes a member of the legislative branch when entering Room 14 as a student.
2. Students must have these qualifications to be an officer:
   a. must be a member of Room 14 for at least two weeks.
   b. must be honest and trustworthy.

Article III. Duties of Executive Branch

1. *President*
   a. The President shall run all class meetings.
   b. The President shall take charge of the class in the teacher's absence.
   c. The President shall help the substitute (show him or her where things are).
   d. The President shall appoint class helpers.
2. *Vice President*
   a. The Vice President shall help the President when necessary.
   b. In the absence of the President, the Vice President shall take over.
3. *Secretary*
   a. The Secretary shall take notes at all class meetings.
   b. The Secretary shall take care of all class mail (letters, thank you notes, etc.).
4. *Treasurer*
   a. The Treasurer shall take care of all class funds.

Article IV. Duties of Legislative Branch

1. To approve, by majority vote, class helper assignments.
2. To approve, by majority vote, any decision for which the class is responsible.
3. To volunteer for class helper assignments:
   a. clean chalkboard
   b. feed fish
   c. water plants
   d. pass out papers
   e. take lunch count
   f. serve as class librarian
   g. greet room visitors
   h. keep art materials orderly
   i. check attendance
   j. run errands
4. To approve, by two-thirds vote, any amendment to this constitution.

Article V. Presidential Vacancy

The Vice President shall take over if the President's office is vacant, followed by the Secretary, and then the Treasurer.

Article VI. Class Meetings

Meetings shall be held each Friday from 2:30–3:00 P.M.

Article VII. Amendments

1. An amendment may be proposed by any member of the class.
2. An amendment must be approved by two-thirds vote of the legislative branch.

Amendments

Amendment 1.
An elected official shall temporarily give up any classroom helper jobs held during his or her term of office. (Approved: February 10)

- Identifying ambiguous or equivocal claims or arguments.
- Recognizing logical inconsistencies or fallacies in a line of reasoning.
- Distinguishing between warranted or unwarranted claims.
- Determining the strength of an argument.

Therefore, as a *mental operation*, critical thinking can be characterized by Beyer's (1985) ten skills, or operations. But, we must also consider a second dimension of critical thinking if we are to use the process effectively in the elementary school classroom. Fraser and West (1961) labeled this crucial second dimension *frame of mind*. In describing a proper frame of mind, Fraser and West explained that critical thinkers have (1) an *alertness* to the need to evaluate information or ideas, (2) a *willingness* to test opinions, and (3) a *desire* to consider all viewpoints. Paul (1987) adds that to be effective critical thinkers, we must learn to control our natural human tendency to consider our own views superior to those of others: "A . . . critical thinker is not routinely blinded by his own point of view. . . . He realizes the necessity of putting his own assumptions and ideas to the test of the strongest objections that can be leveled against them" (pp. 3–4). Critical thinking, then, involves not only a process for judging the worthiness of something, but also a proper frame of mind that enables one to do so.

Instructional Strategies

How do elementary social studies teachers help build critical thinking skills in social studies? Walsh (1988) suggests that teachers must nurture the attitudes or dispositions essential to critical thinking in the social studies:

1. *Intellectual curiosity*—seeking answers to various kinds of questions and problems; investigating the causes and explanations of events; asking why, how, who, when, where.
2. *Objectivity*—using objective factors in the process of making decisions; relying on evidence and valid arguments and not being influenced by emotive and subjective factors in reaching conclusions (in deciding what to do or believe).
3. *Open-mindedness*—willingness to consider a wide variety of beliefs as possibly being true, making judgments without bias or prejudice.
4. *Flexibility*—willingness to change one's beliefs or methods of inquiry; avoiding steadfastness of belief, dogmatic attitude, and rigidity; realizing that we do not know all the answers.
5. *Intellectual skepticism*—postponing acceptance of a hypothesis as true until adequate evidence is available.
6. *Intellectual honesty*—accepting a statement as true when there is sufficient evidence, even though it conflicts with cherished beliefs; avoiding slanting facts to support a particular position.
7. *Being systematic*—following a line of reasoning consistently to a particular conclusion; avoiding irrelevancies that stray from the issue being argued.

8. *Persistence*—supporting points of view without giving up the task of finding evidence and arguments.

9. *Decisiveness*—reaching certain conclusions when the evidence warrants.

10. *Respect for other viewpoints*—listening carefully to other points of view and responding relevantly to what was said; willingness to admit that one may be wrong and that other ideas one does not accept may be correct. (p. 280)

Beyer (1988) advises that if we want our students to be critical thinkers, then critical thinking should be encouraged while attacking "real issues." You can accept this charge even though it means hard work. Students must be freed up to deal with significant civic issues by challenging ideas, offering divergent viewpoints, supporting controversial thoughts, or expressing beliefs that deviate from the majority point of view. When students know that their own ideas are important, they are more likely to be tolerant of others' ideas.

Teachers help students think critically by exposing them to arousing content that stirs intense feelings. Substance is crucial if thinking is to progress higher into the cognitive domain. Children must examine the content, seek key relationships, and, with thinking at its peak, arrive at personal judgments and opinions. Critical thinking, then, cannot happen in a vacuum. Before students can think critically, they must understand the underlying facts, concepts, and generalizations and use them as standards for stating and defending opinions and judgments. Therefore, you first teach for understanding. If students don't understand, they have nothing on which to base higher-order thoughts.

The following are areas of social studies activity commonly exploited as avenues to involve students in acquiring and refining critical-thinking skills:

- Examining how language is used.
- Distinguishing facts from opinions.
- Understanding the purpose for communication.
- Judging sources.
- Inferring character traits.
- Analyzing statistics.
- Investigating pictures and study prints.
- Detecting bias.

Examining How Language Is Used.   Children get most of their social studies content from a variety of sources, but words-in-print seem to predominate: textbooks, children's literature, newspaper items, or information books such as encyclopedias. These resources often contain problems, issues, or ideas that become the lifeblood of meaningful classroom discussions. Whether these discussions involve controversial current issues or historical events, lead students to ponder reasons for acts and try to view issues from all sides. Consider the two excerpts in Figure 8–3. Examine them to judge which most closely represented conditions of African American slaves. What

FIGURE 8–3
Controversial Issue

Statement A

Rules on the Estate of P. C. Weston

"The Proprietor wishes the Overseer to understand that his first object is to be, the care and well being of the negroes. The Proprietor never can or will excuse any cruelty, or want of care towards the negroes [but] it is absolutely necessary to maintain obedience, order, and discipline; to see that the tasks are punctually, and carefully performed." (Metcalf, 1992, p. 6)

Statement B

Recollections of His Experiences in Bondage: Frederick Douglass

Mr. Severe was rightly named: he was a cruel man. I have seen him whip a woman, causing the blood to run half an hour at the time; and this, too, in the midst of her crying children, pleading for their mother's release. He seemed to take pleasure in [showing] his [cruelty.] From the rising till the going down of the sun, he was cursing, raving, cutting, and slashing among the slaves of the field in the most frightful manner. (Douglass, 1845, p. 9)

---

skills or clues did you use to decide which excerpt was most accurate? Gunning (1992) suggests that a good starting point for most people is to examine how language is used.

According to Gunning (1992), words are used in four ways: *to describe, to evaluate, to point out,* and *to interject*. The words *proprietor, overseer,* and *whip* describe things and actions; the words *cruelty, punctually,* and *frightful* go beyond description to judgment, or evaluation. Yet other words both describe *and* evaluate; *take pleasure, raving,* and *slashing* describe, and also attempt to sway one's opinion. Pointing out (*and, on,* or *a,* for example) and interjecting (*Oh! Wow!)* words do not involve critical thinking, so they will not be discussed here. A key strategy in critical thinking is to note which terms simply describe, which evaluate, and which do both. You enable your students to appraise the uses of language by encouraging them to determine the purpose and effect of the words chosen: Why did the writer choose these words? What reaction is the writer trying to draw out from the reader? Is the writer's purpose to inform or to persuade?

Distinguishing Fact From Opinion. Critical thinkers must be aware of the existence of both fact and opinion in social studies materials. *Facts* can be defined as statements that are demonstrable or provable, such as, "In January of 1863, President Lincoln signed the Emancipation Proclamation." *Opinions* are views, judgments, or conclusions one makes about certain matters; an individual may believe them to be true but cannot verify their validity. For example, the statement, "Harriet

Tubman was the most remarkable woman in the history of our country," is, as stated, an opinion. You must help your students to distinguish fact from opinion as they weigh statements for objectivity. Turner (1983) suggests that students apply the following criteria to judge whether or not a statement is factual:

1. The statement comes from a believable authority.
2. The statement is substantiated by other evidence or other authorities.
3. The statement is reconcilable with what we know from personal experience.
4. The statement seems logical and reasonable.
5. It is stated in terms that are value-free or that do not require value judgement.
6. The statement is generally accepted to be true or accepted by those we trust.
7. The statement is open to few or no exceptions.
8. The statement has been repeated often with little or no contradiction to this point.
9. The statement is made with authority.
10. The statement *can be* checked. (p. 179)

Help students locate facts and opinions in social studies materials. They should realize that evaluative words often signal statements of opinion: *Good, bad, modest, brave, excellent, immoral, tightwad,* and *admirable* are all evaluative words. Ask students to locate such signal words while searching through a variety of social studies material.

Understanding the Purpose for Communication.   People communicate with one another for four major reasons: *to inform, to entertain, to express an opinion or philosophy,* and *to persuade.* When students recognize which of these purposes can best be associated with a particular source of communication, they are able to interpret the speaker's or author's intent. This is an important foundational skill of critical thinking—one that can be broadened by bringing in various print resources, such as a front-page newspaper story, editorial, editorial cartoon, news magazine article, or trade book excerpt, and having students determine the author's intent.

Advertising.   One subject that you can use effectively to help children examine how language is used is *advertising*—a special form of mass communication that openly tries to influence the thinking of individuals. You might begin a study of advertising by having your students examine ads in newspapers and magazines and categorize them into the following types of persuasive appeal:

• *Bandwagon.* Everybody's buying it. You are encouraged to follow the crowd or be left out.

- *Authority.* A well-known person endorses the product or service.
- *Snob appeal.* The product or service brings special status. For example, "Charmies are sold only in the finest stores."
- *Glittering generality.* Making information appear factual, even though it isn't. For example, "Most people agree that . . ."
- *Plain folks.* People just like you are buying the product or service.
- *Transfer.* The attributes of someone else will be transferred to the buyer. For example, using a photograph of a sweaty, dirt-stained football player transfers a feeling of toughness to the product or service being advertised.

For a research-oriented project, you might have your students count the number of commercials shown on television from ten to twelve o'clock during typical children-oriented Saturday morning programming. Compare this data with a two-hour slot of family broadcasting from seven to nine o'clock, or from eight to ten, if possible. Is the count similar for both time slots? Is the advertising appeal the same? If the number of commercials in the time slots varies, try to come up with an explanation.

To help students apply critical thinking skills to the study of advertising, ask them to search through magazine advertisements to find one product manufactured by at least two different companies. Have them respond to the following queries in a journal writing assignment: "What products are advertised? Which ad would you notice first? Why? Which ad is more appealing? Using the ads as a guide, which brand would you buy?"

The goal of these experiences is not narrowly limited to informing students of the ploys used by advertisers so they can be wary consumers, but to engage them in the process of making decisions and choices so they may more fully understand the role of consumers in today's world. It is important to emphasize that you must fairly present the concept of advertising. To have students come away from such educational experiences with a negative attitude toward advertising is grossly unfair to both the advertisers and your students. By offering a nonbiased view of advertising, students may decide for themselves what is fair.

Political Cartoons and Editorials.   Like advertisements, political cartoons also use special persuasive techniques to sway one's opinion about a particular issue. Sometimes the message of a cartoon is just plain fun—an illustrated joke. Other times, however, cartoons carry serious messages intended to influence a reader's opinion about an important issue, even though they use humor or sarcasm to make their point.

Most political cartoons deal with one central idea and are fairly uncomplicated. Cartoonists use few words to express ideas because the illustrations communicate most of the message. In addition, cartoonists will exaggerate certain physical characteristics of people to make them instantly recognizable. George Washington's hair or Abe Lincoln's beard are examples of the kind of distinguishing traits cartoonists select to highlight the central cartoon figure. Cartoonists also use standard, quickly recognized symbols—Uncle Sam, the Russian bear, dollar signs, the Republican elephant and the Democratic donkey, and the hawk and the dove quickly communicate an idea or feeling.

While selecting political cartoons for your classroom, choose those that convey the simplest of ideas in as uncomplicated a fashion as possible. Help the children identify the standard symbols and central characters, recognize the activity in which the characters are engaged, analyze the cartoonist's point of view, determine the cartoonist's purpose, and decide whether they agree or disagree with the cartoonist.

Figure 8–4 is a political cartoon. You could ask children the following questions about this particular cartoon to help them understand the purposes of political cartoons in general:

1. This cartoon contains illustrations of people you may know. Are these real people? Can you recognize any of the people in the cartoon?

2. Who are the people in the dark clothing? Who are the others?

3. What is happening? Why are they looking at each other that way? How do they appear to feel about what is going on?

4. Have you ever had anything like this happen to you?

5. What issue do you think the cartoonist is trying to highlight? What point is he making about the issue?

6. How would you react to this situation if you were a tourist? If you were a member of the Amish family?

FIGURE 8–4
Political Cartoon

Source: Daily Local News, West Chester, PA (14 March 1993).
Reprinted with permission of Rick Cole.

The purpose of newspaper editorials is similar to that of political cartoons, but editorials use words rather than cartoon figures to express a specific feeling or attitude. Like political cartoons, editorials should be discussed carefully, keeping the following thoughts central to the exchange of ideas:

- Interpreting the main issue.
- Recognizing the variety of possible reactions to the issue.
- Relating personal experiences to the issue.
- Exploring reasons for various emotional reactions to the issue.
- Comparing students' own reactions with those of others.

As students begin to understand the nature of editorials and cartoons as persuasive media, they develop strong interests in creating their own. John Kerrigan, for example, became deeply concerned about his principal's decision to remove the hallway door to the boy's restroom as a move to curb vandalism. To express his dislike for the principal's ploy, John wrote a cutting editorial. After he read it aloud to the class, his friend Chris drew an accompanying political cartoon. Figure 8–5 displays their joint effort.

Judging Sources.   Elementary school students have a tendency to believe everything they read, so you should help them deliberately examine materials for the purpose of judging the source: "What is being written or spoken? Who is writing or saying those things? When was this written or spoken? Where? Why was this written or spoken?" Students should constantly question any source they examine.

I can clearly recall David, for example, as he walked up to me one day, his darting eyes and furrowed brow expressing deep concern. "Mr. Maxim," he announced, "we're having some trouble in our group and we don't know what to do about it. [The group was researching life in the Andes Mountains of Peru.] This book says that the highest peak in the Andes is 500 feet higher than the other book says. We don't know which one is right." Inconsistencies often exist when "facts" are cited in various resources, so I was challenged with the responsibility of helping David come up with a plausible resolution to his problem. We began by checking the dates of both sources, examining who published them, their language (did it say "exactly" or "approximately"?), and whether one type of document itself might be more reliable then the other (for example, a travel brochure versus an atlas). David's look of concern was transformed into a beam of satisfaction as he proudly weighed all the evidence and bounded back to his group to eagerly announce a resolution to their conflict. David illustrates how critical thinking can emerge spontaneously from children's needs, but there are planned ways to do this, too. One method is to use phony documents in a classroom exercise.

Phony Documents.   Vanderhoof and his associates (1992) have developed a technique for encouraging critical thinking by using phony documents. For example, a teacher opens a lesson with the following statement: "I have an opportunity to purchase an original letter purportedly written by Harriet Tubman when she was a leader of the Underground Railroad. I have concerns, however, about the authen-

FIGURE 8–5
Persuasion Using Both an
Editorial and a Cartoon

"Are bathrooms private anymore

Mr. Towson has a great scence of hummer, his last joke was the funnyest of of all. You better sit down for this Ready? Okay - He took... you sure your ready for this... Well, he took the bathroom door off. See! I told you should sit down. Now you propally think all the resoribillaty has gone to his head. Well for once I think he's absolutely almost right. Heres his side. Somoone took three rolls of tolite paper in the toilet and flush it. It flooded the bathroom and the boys locker room. But taking the bathroom door off is to much. I mean you ever try and go in the bathroom with about 50 girls standing in front. But, there is a good part, the vandalism has gone down.
Now Mr. Towson has something to worry about that is weather the school board impeaches him and if the health board calls the school a health hazrd.

Har! A littel town with a littel school has there own Watergate. I can see the head of linds now "First Princepal to be Impeached." I thought Mr. Towson is a nice guy (sometimes). But the health hazard is yet a nother thing. But don't worry Mr. Towson will figure out some and we hop bathrooms are still private

                                    Chris

OH The Bathroom, first open Door
on the right

ticity of this letter. Perhaps it was not written by Harriet Tubman. I need your help to determine whether I should invest my hard-earned money in this letter." The teacher then reads the letter, which contains several factual errors, to the class. Part of this letter is excerpted in Figure 8–6.

FIGURE 8–6
Phony Document

March 31, 1913

When I crossed the Mason-Dixon Line from Virginia into the state of Pennsylvania I finally reached freedom. Free black families, white Quaker families, and friendly German farmers risked their own safety to give me food and shelter on my journey. The journey was hard; I slept soundly under the stars each night to restore my spent energy.

　　I looked at my hands to see if I was the same person now that I was free. I felt like I was in heaven! Crowds of enthusiastic supporters greeted me when I reached Philadelphia and welcomed me to the land of freedom. In the throng of humanity was the one face I had longed to see at the end of my journey—my dear husband, Clarence Tubman . . . .

The teacher then asks, "Do you think I should purchase this letter?" Of course, the letter is not authentic, but it motivates the students to read the textbook and other sources of information for detailed information that might corroborate or refute details of the document. The students support a recommendation to purchase (or refuse) the letter based on information contained in the sources they consult. Phony documents like Harriet Tubman's letter can motivate students to read critically and to judge sources for the accuracy of their content.

Inferring Character Traits. In social studies, content that stimulates critical thinking often emerges from people as they are encountered in stories, articles, written statements, or documents. By examining the personal characteristics of people, students become engaged in processes associated with critical thought. How do you plan for such experiences? The procedure can best be described as evolving through this sequence: (1) share a source of content suitable to the interests and abilities of your students; (2) help the students describe the setting, characters, and problem or conflict; (3) show them how to examine the issue from all sides; (4) encourage them to formulate their own opinions and to support their choices with sound reasons; and (5) provide appropriate forums for the opinions to be expressed. Activity 8–2 presents a sample lesson plan in which a teacher asks students to explain whether they think the person making statement A in Figure 8–3 was honest or deceitful, based on what they had previously studied about the conditions of slavery.

ACTIVITY 8–2

Lesson Plan

Theme: Inferring Character Traits
Grade: Five
Teacher: Harry Gilbert

General Objective

The students will identify key character traits, using them to formulate opinions about a controversial issue.

Specific Objectives

1. The students will summarize and clarify the character traits of a person described in a short reading selection.
2. The students will write a short passage telling whether or not they feel the person is honest or deceitful.

Materials

1. Portrait of Abraham Lincoln
2. Two conflicting written statements

Procedure

1. Display a portrait or caricature of Abraham Lincoln. Ask the students to call upon what they already know about Lincoln to suggest words or short phrases to describe his character. List the responses on the chalkboard.
2. Ask the students to explain how character perceptions are formed from the information we already know about a person.
3. Pass out statement A (see Figure 8–5) and ask the students to study it carefully for the purpose of telling what kind of person they think this historical figure was, "honest" or "deceitful."
4. Encourage the students to think critically be asking the following questions about the selection: "Who is the character? Do you think he is honest? Deceitful? What did he do or say to make you feel that way?"
5. To motivate students to think more deeply about these questions, pair them off into conversation dyads. Each dyad will complete the following discussion grid to prepare for sharing its ideas with the class.

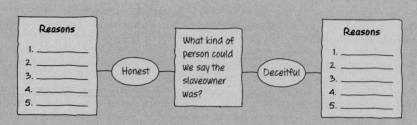

6. Have the dyads summarize their conclusions and share them with their classmates. Throughout, ask students to consider the ways some findings were similar and different and to compare the criteria used for judgment.

7. Students will reflect on all the positions shared by the dyads and compose individual one- or two-paragraph summary statements explaining their own stance on the issue.

Assessment

1. Examine the discussion grids to determine the degree to which the students supported their conclusions with sound reasoning.

2. Read each statement to determine whether each student was able to express a personal opinion and back it up with pertinent information.

Notice that the lesson permitted the students to make different interpretations of the same action; this is vital to programs stressing critical thinking. One student, for example, believed that the owner was an honest person, while another disagreed (see Figure 8–7). The rest of the class was equally flexible in their interpretations.

It is important to note that students will find it difficult to construct logical character portrayals unless they are initially helped to identify specific examples. More abstract thinking, where students must consider complex interrelationships, occurs most effectively in situations where teachers sequence review discussions with questioning patterns that evolve from less to more highly abstract thinking demands.

Analyzing Statistics.   To analyze statistics, students must be able to use collections of data to support their conclusions, and most data in elementary school social studies programs are summarized in the form of tables and graphs. Tables and graphs represent lengthy data in summary form, allowing students to gather information, visualize relationships, and make comparisons much more easily than with narrative materials. All forms of graphics appear in social studies materials, but to use them well, children must be able to comprehend on three levels: literal, inferential, and critical.

FIGURE 8-7
Critical Thinking Interpreting a Writer's Honesty (see Figure 8-3)

I think the owner was honest. I Think he was honest because he seemed to really care about the way slaves were treated. Not all slave owners were mean, or were they?

By,
Chris Smith

I think the slave owner was mean. When he said that it was absolutely necessary to maintain obedience, he probably use a lot of cruel techniques to keep the slaves in line.

By,
Becky
Reilly

At the level of *literal* comprehension, children locate specific factual data with questions such as "How many . . . ?" or "What are . . . ?" Literal comprehension is the basic level of understanding and is essential to the thinking required on the next two levels.

At the *inferential* level, children compare and contrast factual data to form generalizations and draw conclusions. Guided interpretations of the graphic material through thoughtful questions is the best way to develop inferential comprehension: "In what ways is _____ similar to (or different from) _____ ?" "Explain what is meant by . . ." or "Why did _____ happen?" These questions require the student to project beyond the immediate factual data in more abstract ways than when answering literal questions.

Developing *critical* comprehension of graphic materials helps children examine and recognize biased or inaccurate information. Questions that guide critical thinking occur in many forms, including the following: "For what reasons would you favor . . . ? Which of these _____ would you consider to be of greatest value? Do you agree with these conclusions? Is this information useful or valuable?" In all cases, the student must indicate the basic criteria and supply the appropriate data that caused her to make a decision.

Just as we apply developmental learning principles to all phases of children's skills acquisition, we must also introduce graphic materials by using something children have previously experienced. Young children grasp the relationships shown in graphic representations only if they first go through the process of representing things graphically themselves.

Detecting Bias.   As teachers of elementary school children, we have a deep obligation to make our students aware of harmful "isms" that create fear, hatred, and biases in our country: *racism, sexism, ageism, handicapism,* and *classism,* for example. We need to closely examine our social studies materials for any biased, judgmental, unfair, or stereotypical content. Children and teachers should ask themselves the questions listed in Table 8–1.

Informal Instruction to Help Facilitate Critical Thinking

An important ingredient of informal civic education is to experience the free exchange of ideas in a way that is basic to citizens in a constitutional democracy—to explain, negotiate, and communicate with others within a respectful classroom environment. Like rules and laws, good classroom discussions do not burst forth without help; they are the products of careful teaching and learning.

Children love to talk with one another about issues that matter to them if you establish the conditions for them to do so. They will talk about their experiences—who they prefer in the presidential election, how to resolve a playground dispute, what the cat did to a bird's nest in a back bush—as they enter the room, sit next to a classmate, or win the ear of the teacher. Children of all ages should be given every opportunity to talk about things that matter to them.

Table 8–1
Question Guide for Selecting Appropriate Learning Experiences

1. How well do pictures, posters, games, and other materials represent *real people*?
   a. Are people respectfully depicted as positive, active, considerate, and cooperative?
   b. Are the numbers of males and females balanced?
   c. Are people with a variety of physical and mental abilities depicted?
   d. Are people from various ethnic/cultural groups pictured in traditional and contemporary settings, dress, and hairstyles? Are facial features, skin tones, and other characteristics accurate? Are artifacts and information authentic?
   e. Are people of many ages represented?
   f. Are work activities, dwellings, natural resources, and families depicted with diversity?
   g. Do displays feature children's own original artwork?
   h. Are materials placed where children can see and touch them?

2. How well do the messages in children's books and recordings—both individual titles and the collection as a whole—reflect reality?
   a. Are the characters and illustrations diverse (see *a–f* above)?
   b. Do characters speak and act like real people?
   c. Are text and illustrations accurate in their information?
   d. Are both historical and contemporary settings depicted?
   e. Are situations resolved in ways we expect children to emulate?
   f. Are children urged to think critically about what they read, hear, and see?

3. How are children encouraged to succeed?
   a. Do people, learning materials, toys, and activities reflect children's cultures and the world's peoples? Do children and families feel respected? Are people within the community seen as primary resources? Are differences resolved through discussion with families?
   b. Do adults have realistic, individualized expectations for children based on their ages, abilities, learning styles, family values, and life experiences?
   c. Are children taught—and expected to use—skills such as decision making, democratic conflict resolution, and acting to solve problems? Are children interested and absorbed in worthwhile activities?
   d. Do adults support children's curiosity, self-motivation, and desire to control themselves?
   e. Are various types of play offered (small-/large-motor, quiet/noisy, mostly child-directed/some adult-directed, individual/small group, cooperative/individual)? Are children encouraged to engage in a variety of activities?
   f. Are children urged to evaluate their own efforts and progress?

Source: From Janet Brown McCracken, *Valuing Diversity: The Primary Years* (Washington, DC: National Association for the Education of Young Children, 1993), p. 30. Reprinted with permission.

Kostelnik, Stein, and Whiren (1988) advise that we cannot simply "will" the children to conduct productive discussions, however; discussions in democratic classrooms must take place in a "psychologically safe" environment in which discussion sessions have the following attributes:

1. *Teachers use words to show affection for children and sincere interest in their lives.* They greet children as they arrive at school. They make remarks showing children they care about them and are aware of what they are doing: "I notice your bike's fender is dented. How did that happen?" When a teacher laughs with children and responds to their humor, the children know their teacher enjoys being with them.

Part of our job as teachers is to convince students that concentrated study leads to improved critical thinking skills.

2. *Teachers send congruent verbal and nonverbal messages.* As they are showing interest verbally, they stand, squat, or sit near the child at a similar height from the floor, look directly at the child, and thoroughly pay attention. Other actions, such as smiling or offering sincere praise and encouragement, open up the doors of communication.

3. *Teachers extend invitations to children to interact with them.* They may say, "Let's take a minute to talk. I want to find out more about that." When children seek them out, teachers accept the invitation enthusiastically: "That sounds like a very interesting state of affairs." "Oh good, now I'll have a chance to talk with you."

4. *Teachers listen attentively to what children have to say.* They show their interest through eye contact, smiling, and nodding. They encourage children to elaborate on what they are saying by using such statements as "Tell me more about that" or "Then what happened?" In addition, teachers pause long enough after making a comment or asking a question for children to reply, giving them time to gather their thoughts before responding. Such thoughtful considerations make children feel valued and interesting.

5. *Teachers speak courteously to children.* They resist the temptation to interrupt children, allowing them to finish what they have started to say even if they get "stuck" on a thought. The tone of voice used by adults is patient and friendly, and social amenities such as "Please," "Thank you," and "Excuse me" are part of the verbal package.

6. *Teachers use children's interests as a basis for conversations.* They speak with them about the things elementary school youngsters want to talk about. This is manifested in two ways. First, they follow the child's lead in conversations. Second, they bring up subjects known to be of interest to a particular child based on past experience.

7. *Teachers plan or take advantage of spontaneous opportunities to talk with each child.* During the course of a day, children have many chances to talk with adults about matters that interest or concern them; waiting for the bus, playing outdoors at recess, or eating lunch in the cafeteria provide superb settings for informal teacher–child conversation. Teachers do not need to wait for special, planned times to talk with their students. Some of the best opportunities spring up when you least expect them.

8. *Teachers avoid making judgmental comments about children either to them or within their hearing.* Children are treated as sensitive, sensible human beings whose feelings must be respected. Discussions about children's problems or family situations are held in strictest confidence.

9. *Teachers refrain from speaking when talk would destroy the mood of the interaction.* When they see children deeply absorbed in activity or engrossed in conversation with one another, teachers do not break into the course of action. They treat silence as a sign of absorption and respect child–child discussions. Teachers who are good communicators refrain from too much talk at the wrong time.

10. *Teachers focus their attention on children when they professionally engage with them.* In a positive verbal environment, adults are available, alert, and prepared to respond to children. They put aside personal socializing or less important routine tasks when students have something interesting to talk about.

Positive verbal interactions communicate to children a message that they are important, thereby enhancing their perceptions of self-worth. As a result, children are likely to express their feelings and opinions more openly and interact more spontaneously with other children and adults. A positive verbal environment is characterized by a teacher who exhibits sincere warmth, acceptance, respect, and compassion.

Spontaneous conversations can occur at different times and in varied contexts in the social studies classroom. As children develop conversational maturity, you will be able to gather a group of youngsters together to talk about a focused topic.

Small-group or whole-class discussions are appropriate if you desire to increase shared conversations centering on meaningful topics. Group discussions are best carried out in a place where children are encouraged to share freely and realize that what each has to contribute is worthwhile. A comfortable seating arrangement in a circle, semicircle, or oval provides the greatest attention and maximum participation, as children are able to see one another as they talk. A democratic group leader, the teacher first serving as a capable model, helps the children to grasp the difficult procedure of discussion:

- Sit in an unassertive position so that the leader is not perceived as the most important person with all the "right answers."
- Clearly present the topic of discussion. Make sure everyone understands the subject.
- State the rules of good discussion—raise your hand when you want to speak, listen thoughtfully to the ideas of others, and be respectful of the ideas of others.
- Use *active* listening strategies (e.g., paraphrase a student's comments or ask clarifying questions).
- Summarize the ideas shared. All of the ideas should be concisely repeated: "Let's go back and recall what each person said."

Many occasions arise when students are energized to discuss issues that involve civic issues. Therefore, students need a climate of openness, honesty, and trust. From such a constructive environment, students come to know their thoughts are important and that it is psychologically safe to test out new ideas. In Activity 8–3, Olsen (1970) describes a small-group discussion experience with primary grade children that encouraged them to freely share feelings—things that make them happy or sad.

ACTIVITY 8–3

Case Study

Group Discussion: What Words Make Us Feel Bad?

Teacher:	Some people use words to make us feel bad or make us feel happy. Different words make different people feel bad. I don't feel happy when someone calls me stupid. Did someone ever use words that made you feel bad or unhappy?
Billy:	My sister calls me "stinky."
Teacher:	How does that make you feel? (No response.) Do you like to be called "stinky"?
Billy:	No. It makes me feel bad.
Teacher:	Would someone else like to share a word?
Susan:	It makes me feel bad when someone says, "Shut up."
Teacher:	I know what you mean, it makes me feel angry when someone says "shut up" to me.

John:	Big boys say, "Get out of here."
Teacher:	How does that make you feel?
John:	I don't like it.
Susan:	My sister calls me "stupid."
Chris:	"You can't play." I don't like it when they say that.
Teacher:	I can tell by your voice that you feel hurt when someone won't let you play. Alice, you look like you have something to say.
Alice:	My brother calls me "puny." I don't like it.
Teacher:	It isn't a nice feeling inside when a brother calls you "puny." Did anyone ever say some words that made you feel happy? (Two children start to smile but don't respond verbally to the questions.) I can tell that you're thinking of something that makes you happy because you're smiling.
Chris:	You get to ride a trike.
Teacher:	How would that make you feel?
Chris:	I'd say, "Goodie," and I'd tell everyone.
Susan:	(Blurts out) I like you!
Teacher:	How does that make you feel when someone says, "I like you"?
Susan:	It makes me feel good.
Teacher:	It makes me feel happy when my son says to me, "Mom, that pie was delicious." John, what did someone say to make you feel good?
John:	Someone said, "You're nice."
Teacher:	How did that make you feel?
John:	I liked it.
Susan:	I like it when it's my birthday.
Teacher:	What do you like about your birthday?
Susan:	The presents make me happy.
Teacher:	(Smiles and nods) I like presents, too. Words can make people feel happy or sad. Different words can make people feel happy or sad. I'm going to say something that might make you happy. I think you did a very nice job of sharing how you feel.

The best way to introduce productive discussions to elementary school children, then, is to serve as a discussion guide. Until children become familiar with the discussion process, which often is not until the third or fourth grade, they need careful, caring direction and guidance from their teacher.

Today's civics education takes on a much different role today than it did in the past. The ultimate goal of civic education has shifted from imparting knowledge to producing citizens who are not only knowledgeable, but also committed to the principle of voluntary participation. A commitment to civic responsibility—voting, letter-writing to public officials, volunteering one's service in various public capacities, and a wide range of other activities—begins in the elementary school classroom and manifests itself in the dispositions of adult citizens who participate fully in our democratic society.

THE AFFECTIVE REALM OF CIVICS INSTRUCTION

Up to this point, we have limited our discussion of civics education to helping students develop rich understandings of governmental practices and public policy as well as aiding them to make connections between what they learn in school and their lives as citizens in a democracy. But the vision of contemporary civics education transcends even these two noble goals; an essential part of civics education includes thinking in the affective domain. In its *Curriculum Standards for Social Studies,* the National Council for the Social Studies (1994) described the affective realm as going beyond the content of civics to the formation of dispositions required of effective citizenship–Standard X (Civic Ideals & Practices) states: "Social studies programs should include experiences that provide for the study of the ideals, principles, and practices of citizenship in a democratic republic" (p. 30). In defending the importance of this cognitive-affective connection, NCSS emphasized that it is critical to full participation in society and is "the central purpose of the social studies" (p. 30). The ultimate goal of *CIVITAS* (Center for Civic Education, 1991) is to enable students equipped with civic knowledge "to make their own commitment to the civic values necessary for the nurture and strengthening of the ideals of American democracy" (p. 11).

Ryan (1993) comments that this cognitive-affective connection of civic education has emerged as a popular trend "because people are banging on the schoolhouse door. The invitation is coming from the outside. Parents and policymakers are disturbed by a total inability of our culture to pass on its values" (p. 1). Lickona (1993) sees the motivating force as a "growing national sense of moral crisis and what people speak of as a steady moral decline" (p. 1). Society is now turning back to the schools to renew the core values underlying American society and help students appreciate how these values ensure the freedoms associated with a democratic society. Shaver (1985) highlights the role of social studies in this movement: "It is crucial that instruction in social studies be based upon an adequate conception of the role of values in our democratic society. Anthropologists have commonly noted that shared commitments are critical to the survival of any society" (p. 194).

Table 8–2 shows how the National Council for the Social Studies apportioned various essential democratic values and behaviors many deem necessary for the nurture

TABLE 8–2

Illustrative Examples of Applications of Democratic Beliefs and Values

	Central Focus	Democratic Rights, Freedoms, Responsibilities, of Beliefs Addressed	Illustrations of Opportunities
KINDERGARTEN	Awareness of self in a social setting	1. Right to security 2. Right to equal opportunity] 3. Respect of others' rights 4. Honesty	1. Explore how rules make a room safe for everyone. 2. Schedule every child to be a leader for a day. 3. Emphasize that when someone speaks we should all listen. 4. As teacher, reinforce honesty as exhibited by children.
GRADE 1	The individual in primary social groups	1. Impartiality 2. Freedom of worship 3. Consideration of others	1. When an altercation is reported, the teacher tries to find out exactly what happened before taking action. 2. Stress that each family decides whether or not or how to worship. 3. Make clear that everyone has a right to his/her turn.
GRADE 2	Meeting basic needs in nearby social groups	1. Respect for property 2. Respect for laws 3. Values personal integrity	1. Discuss vandalism in neighborhoods. 2. Demonstrate how laws protect the safety of people. 3. Explore the importance of keeping promises.
GRADE 3	Sharing earthspace with others	1. Pursuing individual and group goals 2. Government works for the common good	1. Explain how goods are exchanged with other places in order to meet the needs of people. 2. Discuss how government is concerned about the unemployed and works to reduce unemployment.
GRADE 4	Human life in varied environments	1. Respect for the rights of others 2. Respect for different ways of life	1. Stress the importance of respecting the right of individuals from other cultures to have different values. 2. Help appreciate that lifestyles of people in other places are different from ours.
GRADE 5	People of the Americas	1. Freedom to worship 2. Right of privacy	1. Point out that people came to the Americas because of religious persecution. 2. Explain that a home cannot be searched without a warrant except under most unusual circumstances.

Source: Task Force on Scope and Sequence, "In Search of a Scope and Sequence for Social Studies," *Social Education 48* (April 1984): 258.

and strengthening of the ideals of our democracy. They are listed according to grade level and suggested classroom procedures for teaching and reinforcing them. (The NCSS cautions that these are examples only and should not be construed as a recommended curriculum.)

In the elementary grades, students are introduced to civic ideals and practices throughout the day as they experience life in democratic classrooms. The dispositions and values of our nation are exemplified by the sense of community created in a democratic classroom—everyone operates for the common good of all. How do teachers address the responsibility of treating civic virtues (values) in ways other than establishing a democratic classroom environment? To begin our search for the answer to this question, let us examine Mr. Young's classroom as he facilitates the discussion of a very sensitive topic.

The first step transpired as Mr. Young's fifth graders returned to their classroom after recess. The soft, plaintive strains of "Negro spirituals" filled the room. Slaves had created these songs not only to express their deep longing for freedom, but also as coded messages that passed on secret information for escape, such as where to find escape routes and hideaways: "Steal Away to Jesus," "Go Down, Moses," "The Drinking Gourd," and "Swing Low, Sweet Chariot."

Mr. Young assembled the class and read the book, *The Story of Harriet Tubman: Conductor of the Underground Railroad* by Kate McMullan, a fascinating story of one of America's most famous abolitionists and a valiant conductor on the Underground Railroad. At the story's end, Mr. Young asked, "What kind of a person was Harriet Tubman? What evidence from the story supports your feelings?" The students contributed many ideas, most of which revolved around the ideas of "toughness," "intelligence," and "courage"—Harriet Tubman worked hard in the fields, was whipped by owners, learned to read without her owner's knowledge, was injured while helping a slave escape, went on many Underground Railroad journeys, learned to use special ways to escape (such as navigating by the north star), and helped slaves whose owners refused to let them go after the Civil War. During this captivating discussion, one student served as the scribe, recording the specifics on a large data-retrieval chart strategically placed near the story reading area.

After spending a good deal of time discussing the story, Mr. Young shifted gears slightly. "So far," he said, "we have been talking about the many accomplishments that made Harriet Tubman stand out as a famous American. Now I would like you to do some *really* deep thinking. Certainly, you have indicated that each of Harriet Tubman's accomplishments were important, but now I want you to think about which you consider to be her *most important* contribution of all." After much debate, small groups of students agreed that it was her efforts to hide and carry slaves to freedom with the Underground Railroad.

Mr. Young then shared a few ideas about the dangers of running away from slavery and of aiding fugitives. Then he shared this dilemma faced by Sie, a real slave from Maryland in 1825, when his extremely troubled master came to his cabin with an unusual request:

One night in the month of January . . . he came into my cabin and waked me up. . . . For awhile he said nothing and sat . . . warming himself at the fire. "Sick, massa?" said I. "Can't I help you in any way, massa?" I spoke tenderly for my heart was full of compassion at his wretched appearance. At last . . . he cried, "Oh, Sie! I'm ruined, ruined, ruined. . . . They've got a judgment against me, and in less than two weeks every [slave] I've got will be . . . sold." I sat silent. . . . "And now, Sie," he continued, "there's only one way I can save anything. You can do it; won't you, won't you?" In his distress he rose and actually threw his arms around me . . . "I want you to run away, Sie, to . . . Kentucky, and take all the servants along with you." . . . My master proposed to follow me in a few months and establish himself in Kentucky. (Henson, 1935, pp. 162–167)

After discussing the situation to make sure the students understood what it was all about, Mr. Young said, "Isn't it interesting that after being Sie's master for over thirty years, the plantation owner is so dependent on him? Should Sie help out the owner?" Mr. Young divided the children into discussion groups and asked them to decide what Sie should do.

Throughout this lesson, Mr. Young employed sophisticated instructional strategies designed to move his students beyond the realm of conceptual thinking and into the affective domain. He did this by sharing rich material that incorporated thought-provoking content. Thought-provoking content sets in motion affective adventures, for it provides the essential substance of productive discussions dealing with feelings, attitudes, values, and civic ideals. Note that the first part of Mr. Young's lesson involved a "concept reception" strategy (see Chapter 5) that centered on making sense from the content—understanding the major contributions of Harriet Tubman. He operated with a conviction that, if his students were going to be required to share their feelings and attitudes about an issue, they must first have an extensive storehouse of information on which to base their ideas.

Mr. Young realized that limiting instruction to the *content* of values such as "individual rights," "justice," or "equality" could help his students understand what the lives of slaves might have been like, but could not offer them a deep appreciation for their great courage and intelligence, or a deep compassion for the intensity of their aspirations for freedom; nor could it foster a genuine pride in the cultural background of African American children, or serve as an excellent example of social protest fueled by the cooperation of both blacks and committed whites. Mr. Young was convinced that social studies instruction has much more to offer than information, so he incorporated elements of affective thinking.

Mr. Young realized that the lives of his young learners are deeply involved in questions concerning what is good or bad, right or wrong—issues that do not simply have one "right answer." Paul (1987) believes that how children learn to respond to these questions in the elementary school has a profound influence on how they will later define and deal with personal issues as adult citizens. He offers the following examples of such questions:

Who am I? What am I like? What are the other people around me like? What are people of different backgrounds, religions, and nations like? How much am I like others? How much am I unlike them? What kind of a world do I live in? When should I trust? When should I distrust? What should I accept? What should I question? How should I understand my past, the past of my parents, my ethnic group, my religion, my nation? Who are my friends? Who are my enemies? What is a friend? How am I like and unlike my enemy? What is most important to me? How should I live my life? What responsibilities do I have to others? What responsibilities do they have to me? What responsibilities do I have to my friends? Do I have any responsibilities to people I don't like? To people who don't like me? To my enemies? Do my parents love me? Do I love them? What is love? What is hate? What is indifference? Does it matter if others do not approve of me? When does it matter? When should I ignore what others think? What rights do I have? What rights should I give to others? What should I do if others do not respect my rights? Should I get what I want? Should I question what I want? Should I take what I want if I am strong enough or smart enough to get away with it? Who comes out ahead in this world, the strong or the good person? Is it worthwhile to be good? Are authorities good or just strong? (p. 129)

Questions such as these form the backbone of values-oriented or affective-based, civic education.

Defining Affective-Based Education

What is the affective domain and how can it strengthen civics education? Jacobsen, Eggen, and Kauchak (1993) explain that the affective domain is the area of thinking that deals with feelings and emotions, likes and dislikes. It is the domain that embraces the dispositions we commonly refer to as *attitudes* and *values*. Attitudes are personal expressions of like and dislike directed toward objects, ideas, or people around us. We can have positive or negative attitudes about things like broccoli and spinach; we can also have positive or negative attitudes about certain college professors and the way elementary school social studies should be taught.

Like other aspects of human behavior, attitudes are greatly shaped by one's life experiences. Over the years, for example, you may have developed strong feelings toward cats. If your past experiences with cats were pleasurable, then you might enjoy holding one in your arms and petting it. On the other hand, if you were badly scratched by a cat as a youngster or if you suffered a series of bad experiences with cats, then your reaction might be to get it out of your sight. Jacobsen, Eggen, and Kauchak (1993) add that "[t]he fact that attitudes are formed through experiences is good in the sense that it allows teachers to influence positively the attitudes of their students, but it also places a burden of responsibility on teachers not to contribute to the development of negative attitudes toward various aspects of schooling" (p. 83). Because they are described as emotions accumulated through past experiences, attitudes are considered cognitive in nature.

Individual boys and girls, because of diverse external factors, may exhibit varied attitudes and values in the classroom.

Like attitudes, *values* are cognitive in nature, too. Shaver (1985) explains: "[V]alues have both affective and cognitive elements. That is, values evoke feelings in us (due process of law is 'good,' something we feel positive about) and so are affective. But values also have a cognitive component. They are concepts. We can define what we mean by due process, and argue about the appropriateness of each other's meanings and about the validity of proposed applications of 'due process' in policy decisions" (p. 195). Despite these similarities, values are considered to be much more abstract in nature. Attitudes prompt us to order a pepperoni pizza over a veggie pizza or to root for the New York Yankees rather than the Baltimore Orioles. Values are more deeply held; when we speak of values we refer to such virtues as honesty, truthfulness, cleanliness, and civic-mindedness.

Turner (1983) defines *values* as strong, prevailing, qualitative attitudes; they are deeply felt points of view about how people ought to act or lead their lives rather than qualitative feelings about specific things:

1. *Goodness* (moral values, social values, religious values)
2. *Power* (political values, physical values)
3. *Beauty* (aesthetic values)
4. *Satisfaction* (personal values, psychological values)
5. *Truth* (philosophical values, scientific values)
6. *Order* (organizational values)
7. *Worth* (human values, economic values, historical values) (p. 184)

Parker (1988) explains that values permeate our daily lives; there is no escape from them: "There is no human activity and therefore no citizenship education . . . independent of values. Those who argue that schools should not teach values are missing the point. Like it or not, schools do teach values and cannot do otherwise" (p. 3).

Although affective citizenship education has generated widespread interest among social studies educators, implementing the approach can be quite controversial. This is because two traditions have regularly vied for a central place of instruction in our nation's schools: (1) the classical tradition and (2) the liberal tradition.

The Classical Tradition

Early in our nation's history, educational leaders used the terms *public dispositions* and *civic virtues* to describe affective education—the willingness of citizens to subjugate their personal wishes on behalf of the common good was its primary goal. So, students were engaged in rigorous intellectual exercises demanding strong conformity to thoughts viewed as important for the common good. Early learning materials were primarily of a religious flavor, as we see in this selection from *The Boston Primer* of 1808 (Hersh, 1980):

> Let Children who would fear the LORD,
> Hear what their Teachers says,
> With rev'rence meet their Parents' word,
> And with Delight obey. (p. 16)

Direct moral teachings also occurred during teachers' day-to-day interactions with the children, as in this sample recitation from *A Manual of the System of Discipline and Instruction* (1980):

T: You must obey your parents.

S: I must obey my parents. (The pupils, at each repetition, place the right hand, opened, upon the breast.)

T: You must obey your teachers.

S: I must obey my teachers. (p. 16)

At those rare times that children questioned their superiors about a behavior, the dialogue might have gone like this:

Master: You must not do so.

Child: And why must I not do so?

Master: Because it is naughty.

Child:	Naughty! Why is that being naughty?
Master:	Doing what you are forbidden.
Child:	And what harm is there in doing what one is forbidden?
Master:	The harm is, you will be whipped for disobedience.
Child:	Then I will do it so that nobody will know anything of the matter.
Master:	O, but you will be watched.
Child:	Ah! But then I will hide myself.
Master:	But you must not tell fibs.
Child:	Why must not I?
Master:	Because it is naughty. (Rousseau, 1971, p. 397)

Educators of the time justified the direct approach with arguments like this: "Thus, we go round the circle: and yet, if we go out of it, the child understands us no longer. . . . I could be very curious to know what could be substituted in the place of this fine dialogue. . . . To distinguish between good and evil, to perceive the reasons on which our moral obligations are founded, is not business, as it is not within the capacity, of a child" (Rousseau, 1971, p. 397).

Children were considered incapable of making their own decisions because it was believed that they had not yet acquired the ability to think rationally. Therefore, their thinking had to be done for them.

As our nation grew and new educational needs arose, systematic instruction moved from the use of religious materials to the recitation of patriotic slogans, oaths, flag salutes, creeds, and pledges designed to instill the values of citizenship. Moralistic stories of great leaders eventually replaced religious stories. "The Power of Kindness" (The American Educational Readers, 1873) is a sample of this kind of story:

The Power of Kindness

William Penn, the founder of Philadelphia, always treated the Indians with justice and kindness. The founders of other colonies have too often trampled on the rights of the natives, and seized their lands by force; but this was not the method of Penn. He bought their lands, and paid for them. He made a treaty with the Indians, and faithfully kept it. He always treated them as *men.*

After his first purchase was made, Penn became desirous of obtaining another portion of their lands, and offered to buy it. They returned to answer that they had no wish to sell the spot where their fathers were buried; but to please their father Onas, as they named Penn, they said they would sell him a part of it.

A bargain was accordingly concluded, that, in return for a certain amount of English goods, Penn should have as much land as a young man could travel round in one day. (pp. 56–57)

Elementary school children need the freedom to talk about important issues. They are the ones who do most of the talking in good social studies classrooms.

The Liberal Tradition

Through the years, then, teachers used lectures, children's stories, and textbook readings in which specific values such as "honesty" and "respect" defined the character of good citizenship. But the 1960s and 1970s ushered in values programs that emphasized individual rights and freedoms rather than personal obligation to the public good. Now, instead of having their behavior shaped by a teacher who demanded devotion to predetermined sets of values, students were asked to identify and clarify their own beliefs and values. The two most widely recognized of these approaches were values clarification and moral reasoning.

Values Clarification.   Values clarification is an approach to helping students bring to light their beliefs and points of view in an environment where they can learn from others, even from their objections and differing ways of thinking. The approach is based on a supposition that individuals recognize and refine their values only as they progress through these major valuing processes:

- *Choosing freely.* A value must be a result of free choice, not coercion.

- *Choosing from among alternatives.* Only when a choice is possible, when there is more than one alternative from which to choose, can a value result.

- *Choosing after thoughtful consideration of the consequences of each alternative.* Impulsive or thoughtless choices do not lead to values. Only when one clearly understands the consequences of each alternative can one make intelligent choices.

- *Prizing and cherishing.* In this definition, values flow from choices that one prizes, cherishes, and holds dear.

- *Affirming.* One must affirm choices publicly and be willing to speak publicly about them in appropriate forums.

- *Acting upon choices.* A value shows up in all aspects of our living. Nothing can be a value that does not, in fact, give direction to our lives.

- *Repeating.* When something reaches the stage of a value, it is likely to reappear in a number of contexts in one's life. Values tend to have a consistency, to make a pattern in life.

As applied to content in the social studies, a teacher might involve her students in a simulated seventeenth-century voyage from England to the Massachusetts Colony. Students are asked to imagine that it is the year 1625 and that they are members of a Pilgrim family joining a group of hired workers to sail from England to Massachusetts. The ship is large and each family is given the luxury of packing all of these supplies: books, clothing, tools, guns, fishing equipment, medical supplies, pots and pans, furniture, fresh water, food, seeds, and livestock.

As the day of departure grows near, the ship's captain confronts the voyagers with an announcement that the original ship has been severely damaged by a storm at sea and will not be ready for the journey. In consequence, they must sail on a ship half as big, one unable to hold large stores of cargo. All families must meet in their groups to rank-order the items from their original list and specify the top six as the items they will take. Then, all families gather together as a group to debate with one another, determining a whole-class ranking of the supplies deemed most important for their journey.

In this context, the students knew that there were no department stores or super-markets in Massachusetts to buy supplies, so settlers had to make hard decisions about what they needed to take with them. When they made their hypothetical lists, students clarified their personal, family, and whole-group values by selecting supplies and defending their choices with sound reasons.

Values clarification experienced widespread popularity throughout the 1960s and 1970s; handbooks of activities could be found on every teacher's bookshelf. However, well-publicized problems associated with some of the activities generated considerable controversy. In a school district in southeastern Pennsylvania, for example, a third-grade teacher decided to use a values clarification activity that appeared in a popular teaching magazine. As the activity directed, the teacher held a mirror in her hand and asked the children why people use such an implement. After a short discussion, she informed the class that the mirror in her hand was a magic mirror—one that allowed people to see not only what they looked like on the outside, but also what was deep inside their thoughts. To help make this point, the teacher read a poem about this "magic mirror"; it gave examples of the kinds of deep thoughts people might have. Following this poetry reading, the teacher asked the children to write a short piece about what deep thoughts the mirror might see if they were looking into it.

Since this activity took place late on a Friday afternoon, the teacher put the students' papers in her briefcase and took them home to read over the weekend. Late Sunday afternoon, she took out the papers and was shocked by one little boy's piece. In it, he wrote about strong inner feelings about suicide. Not wasting a moment, the teacher grabbed the phone and called the boy's family. Naturally, they were extremely upset with the news and ran to their son immediately: "Oh, I didn't mean anything by it," he said innocently, "I just thought suicide was something that the teacher might want to read about!"

The parents subsequently discussed the situation with other families and soon a ground swell of protest grew. There was unanimous agreement that the children should never again be placed in such a position. The child's family went so far as to initiate legal action against the school district and the teacher, claiming negligence on her part for not heading off a potential catastrophe by reading the papers sooner.

Not all values clarification activities were quite so powerful (many less intense suggestions contributed greatly to social studies instruction), but such instances caused school systems to carefully reassess the role of values clarification in their elementary school classrooms. The resulting controversy became so great that the approach eventually was banned or restricted in many school districts.

Moral Reasoning.   The moral reasoning approach was developed by Lawrence Kohlberg and his associates (1973) to explain how children learn to reason about moral issues (what is "good," "bad," "right," or "wrong"). Kohlberg became interested in Jean Piaget's ideas of moral development and sought to validate them by carrying out intensive studies throughout the world. Kohlberg found that all individuals, despite differences in cultural, social, economic, and religious backgrounds, move through the stages of moral development described in Figure 8–8.

Kohlberg's approach to affective education was based on the assumption that growth through the stages can be stimulated by involving children in "moral dilemmas"—stories in which individuals face situations that involve issues of trust, fairness, or taking advantage. Children are encouraged to examine situations and make judgments about the various actions the characters might take.

An example of a moral dilemma suitable for upper-grade elementary school children is the case of Rosa Parks, a courageous African American woman from Montgomery, Alabama, who refused to give up her seat on a bus in defiance of the prevailing segregation customs in 1955. Activity 8–4 is a teaching plan to encourage children to think about the difficult decision Rosa Parks faced.

FIGURE 8–8
Kohlberg's Stages of
Moral Development

Preconventional Level: Egocentric in Nature

Stage 1: To be "well-behaved" means unquestioned obedience to an adult authority figure. The child considers being either good or bad solely because of the physical consequences involved (punishment, reward) or because of the desires of authority figures (teacher, parent, etc.).

Stage 2: The child is basically egocentric (self-centered) at this stage and regards goodness or badness on the basis of whether it satisfies personal needs. Children at this stage begin to consider the feelings of others, but elements of fairness and equal sharing are interpreted in a manner of "what's in it for me?" Children are out to make the best "deal" for themselves. Being "right" is viewed in a context of fairness: "You scratch my back and I'll scratch yours."

Conventional Level: Orientation to Conformity

Stage 3: Good behavior is that which pleases or helps others. Children conform to what they imagine to be a "good" or "nice" person and begin to see things from another's viewpoint for the first time (put themselves into the shoes of another person). Behavior begins to be judged on the basis of intent—a conscience is beginning to form. Children are strongly oriented to being labeled "good boy/nice girl."

Stage 4: The individual is oriented to obeying authority and following fixed rules for reasons of law and order. A good person does one's duty, shows respect for authority, and maintains the given social order for its own sake. One earns respect for performing dutifully, living up to one's socially defined role, and maintaining existing social order for the good of all.

Postconventional Level: Individual Moral Principles

Stage 5: Since laws have been critically examined and agreed upon by the whole society, they continue to guide decisions regarding goodness or badness. However, right and wrong begin to be characterized by personal feelings; the result is an emphasis upon the "legal point of view," but with an emphasis upon the possibility of changing laws, rather than obeying them as in Stage 4. One makes an internal commitment to principles of "conscience"; individuals are guided by a respect for the rights, life, and dignity of all persons.

Source: Adapted from Lawrence Kohlberg, The claim to moral adequacy of a highest state of moral judgment. *The Journal of Philosophy,* 70, no. 18 (October 25, 1973): 631–632.

ACTIVITY 8–4

Classroom Exercise

Rosa Parks's Choice

Warmup Questions

Ask these questions to orient children to the situation: "How many of you have ever ridden on a bus? Were you able to sit anywhere you liked when you got on the bus? Did you ever hear of people being told that they couldn't sit on any section of the bus because of the color of their skin? their height? their sex? their religious persuasion?"

Presentation

Explain to the students that they are to read a short story about a woman who is told she cannot sit on a particular seat on a bus because of the color of her skin. She must decide whether to sit in that seat. Her name is Rosa Parks and the city in which the decision took place is Montgomery, Alabama. Tell the children to decide what they would do if they were faced with Rosa Parks's decision. Supply them with an account of the incident.

Rosa Parks's feet hurt, for good cause. Her job as a seamstress in the Montgomery Fair kept her on the run. All that day of December 1, 1955, she had pinned up hems, raised waistlines, and carried dresses back and forth. When the closing time buzzer sounded, she hurried out of the store. Then she boarded a Cleveland Avenue bus, dropped her dime in the box—and hesitated. Where should she sit?

By law and custom, the front rows of seats were reserved for white people. [Black people] sat in the back. Halfway up the aisle there was a no man's land where [black people] might sit until the space was needed for white passengers. There were no signs announcing these rules. In Montgomery, the capital city of Alabama, everybody knew them.

But this bus was half empty, and Mrs. Parks sank into the first seat behind the "white" section. Her feet began to feel as if they were almost ready to stop hurting. It was a feeling that made it impossible for her to think about anything else. She scarcely noticed that the bus was getting fuller from one stop to the next. Soon all the seats were taken. A few minutes later people were standing in the aisle. White people.

The bus driver, with one eye on his rearview mirror, called, "All right, you niggers [sic], move back!"

The woman next to Mrs. Parks and two men across the aisle rose and silently made their way to the back of the bus. Mrs. Parks sat still. A white man stood beside her, waiting, but she didn't budge.

The bus driver left his wheel and strode up the aisle. "Get up!" he ordered.

Rosa Parks took a deep breath.

From Should Rosa Parks Go to the Back of the Bus? (Sterling, 1968, pp. 1–2)

Follow-Up Decision

The first questions should help clarify the story. "Where was Rosa Parks before she got on the bus? How did she feel? Why was she asked to leave her seat? When did the story take place?"

Group Dialogue

Split the children into groups and ask them to decide what Rosa Parks should do. Move from group to group and offer questions to guide the children's thinking. "Why do you think some cities had rules establishing separate facilities for blacks and whites? Did Rosa Parks have a right to break those rules? Were the rules fair? What could happen if she did not give up her seat to the white person?"

Follow-Up Activity

In this case, encourage each group to role-play the scene on the bus, stopping at the point of Rosa's decision. Then have them portray what Rosa should have done and what the consequences would have been. What other follow-up activities might be appropriate?

Enrichment

The children will naturally be curious about the real outcome of this dilemma, and their questions will flow spontaneously: "What did Rosa Parks do? What happened to her?" The questions will indicate a perfect starting point for an inquiry session. You may wish to offer the information yourself, or encourage the children to search for the answers in material you have collected for them. (For your information, Rosa Parks refused to give up her seat and was arrested. Her arrest touched off a bus boycott in Montgomery and was one of the major events in launching the campaign for black civil rights.) In 1980, Mrs. Parks received the Martin Luther King, Jr,. Peace Award for the inspiration she provided to resolve racial differences through nonviolent means.

When the children share their responses to story situations, they provide teachers with insight into the different stages of moral reasoning at which they are operating. The stages of moral reasoning are not defined by the nature of the decision itself, but on the basis of the reasons the students give for each decision. For example:

Stage 1:   "Rosa Parks should get up from her seat because she would be in real trouble if she didn't. The bus driver would probably throw her off the bus." (People cannot disobey authorities or they will be punished.)

Stage 2:   "Rosa Parks should not go to the back of the bus because she is awfully tired and there wouldn't be anywhere else for her to sit." (Everyone has a right to do what she wants to fulfill legitimate needs.)

Stage 3:   "Rosa Parks should start to move to the back of the bus because if the white man sees how tired she is, he will be sure to understand and let her stay in her seat." (Children have a sense of fair play at this stage— what would a *good* person do?)

Stage 4:   "Rosa Parks should move to the back of the bus because she would be breaking the law if she didn't. People are expected to follow the law." (Conforming to law and order emerges as a central value.)

In the moral reasoning approach, the presentation of each moral dilemma followed a careful script that emphasized the importance of backing up decisions with sound reasoning. However, several suggested dilemmas presented such intricate issues (some having to do with deciding who should live or die) that children simply could not handle the complex thinking demands. As with values clarification, then, moral reasoning became the target of sharp criticism. One of the areas of greatest concern was that children were asked to reveal their deepest feelings about morality, which often placed the teacher in the role of "amateur psychologist." Too many situations arose that teachers simply were unprepared to handle. An equally strong criticism was leveled at Kohlberg's contention that higher-stage reasoning is better than lower-stage reasoning. Because Kohlberg stressed that the defining standard for a moral stage is not the *content* of one's decision but the *reasoning* that goes into making it, Jesus Christ, Buddha, Mother Theresa, and Ghandi would be at the same level of moral reasoning as Hitler and Charles Manson—an obviously ludicrous suggestion. Therefore, if "higher" is not "better," school districts decided there was no justification for using classroom activities selected for the sole purpose of moving children through Kohlberg's stages.

Balancing the Traditions

The current emphasis in values instruction is to find a balance between the classical and liberal approaches. The Center for Civic Education (1991) describes effective citizenship as reflecting both sets of values—those of the public good and those of freedom, diversity, and individual rights: "We believe that civic virtue embraces thinking and acting in such a way that individual rights are viewed in light of the public good and that the public good includes the basic protection of individual rights. Whether one prefers to stress balance . . . between these traditions, or views them as a blend . . . we believe that the effort to identify and understand their ingredients is the first major step toward the practice of civic virtue [commitment to civic values]. . ." (p. 12).

In addressing the question of what fundamental values are important for the preservation and improvement of American democracy, the Center for Civic Education (1994) recommended several civics content standards dealing with the most important values and principles of American democracy. Two of these standards are explained here:

Fundamental values and principles. *Students should be able to explain the importance of the fundamental values and principles of American democracy.*
To achieve this standard, students should be able to

- explain the importance for themselves, their school, their community, and their nation each of the following fundamental **values** of American democracy:
- individual rights to life, liberty, property, and the pursuit of happiness
- the public or common good
- justice
- equality of opportunity
- diversity
- truth
- patriotism (p. 22)

American identity. *Students should be able to explain the importance of Americans sharing and supporting certain values, principles, and beliefs.*
To achieve this standard, students should be able to

- explain that Americans are united by the values, principles, and beliefs they share rather than by ethnicity, race, religion, class, language, gender, or national origin.
- explain the importance of shared values, principles, and beliefs to the continuation and improvement of American democracy
- identify basic documents that set forth shared values, principles, and beliefs, e.g., Declaration of Independence, United States Constitution and Bill of Rights, Pledge of Allegience
- identify symbols used to depict Americans' shared values, principles, and beliefs and explain their meaning, e.g., the flag, Statue of Liberty, Statue of Justice, Uncle Sam, Great Seal, national anthem, oaths of office, and mottoes such as *E Pluribus Unum*
- describe holidays Americans celebrate and explain how they reflect their shared values, principles, and beliefs, e.g., the Fourth of July, Labor Day, Memorial Day, Presidents' Day, Columbus Day, Thanksgiving, Veterans Day, Martin Luther King, Jr.'s Birthday (p. 25)

Many instructional opportunities can be offered to deal with these standards; teachers use situations such as these:

- Students may write letters to Benjamin Franklin stating why they agree with or oppose his suggestion to make the turkey our national symbol. Students may suggest various other animals—bear, buffalo, wildcat, deer—as a national symbol.
- As you study national symbols, students may select a classroom animal, motto, flag design, song, flower, and so on. These can be displayed throughout the school year as indications of pride and cohesiveness of the classroom group.

- As you study national holidays and their celebrations, students may choose a month during which national holidays are scarce, suggest a national holiday for that month, describe who or what should be honored, and explain how that holiday could be celebrated.
- Debate this question: "Should citizens and noncitizens of the United States have equal rights and responsibilities?"
- To help your students understand the concept of voting for our country's leaders, put them in situations where they can make a choice and vote. Imagine they can choose your school's mascot. Invite them to submit proposals along with support for each one, hold a primary election to determine the two most popular choices, and have students develop a campaign for each (banners, posters, slogans, speeches, etc.). Hold a general election to determine the community animal.
- Students may write editorials or draw political cartoons expressing opposing views on a controversial issue.
- Have students make posters urging citizens of the 1800s to work toward the abolition of slavery.
- Assign students in groups to represent the states at the Constitutional Convention of 1787. Each state should discuss the New Jersey and Virginia plans and decide which it should support.

In addition to these general activities, students will enjoy participating in values-laden discussions and debates. Perhaps the currently most accepted strategy for guiding careful, deliberate discussions of values issues is *values analysis*. The idea behind values analysis is, as its name implies, to take an issue, carefully analyze it, take a position, and then justify it.

Values Analysis

The values analysis approach is designed to help students use logical thinking abilities and scientific inquiry skills to make decisions about values-laden issues. The format of instruction usually contains structured, rational discussions that demand evidence to support personal feelings. In essence, the values analysis strategy follows this general pattern of instruction:

1. Identify and clarify the issue.
2. Gather and organize evidence related to the issue.
3. Assess the accuracy and relevance of the evidence.
4. Select alternate solutions.
5. Consider potential consequences of each alternative.
6. Select the most personally suitable alternative.

Values Analysis Discussions.   In helping children analyze values, teachers often use a carefully planned sequence of questions. The purpose of such question-generated discussion is to help students realize that attitudes and values are most firmly based on a rich foundation of understandings. For example, suppose you have read the following selection about Harriet Tubman to a group of children.

> Harriet Tubman fell in love with John Tubman, a free black man. Since slaves were permitted to marry free blacks, Harriet and John married in 1844. Harriet remained a slave because slaves were still owned by their masters even after they were married to free blacks. Harriet and John Tubman lived in a small cabin by themselves, but Harriet never stopped dreaming about being free. She would talk to John day and night about how she would escape to freedom in the north, but her husband only snickered at her plans. "I'm pleased with what I have here," John remarked. "I have no desire to go with you."
>
> In 1849, Harriet endangered her own safety and escaped to freedom in Pennsylvania. Shortly thereafter she risked her life by going back to the plantation to get John. "I will not go back," announced John uneasily. Harriet was saddened that he had already had a new wife.

Upon completing the story, you would lead the children through a discussion by asking the following questions:

- "What happened in the story?"
- "What do you think were John's reasons for doing that?"
- "What do these reasons tell you about what was important to him?"
- "What things might Harriet do?"
- "What might happen to her if she does these things?"
- "How do you think Harriet or John would feel in each case?"
- "If you were faced with this situation (as Harriet or John), what would you have done?"
- "What does this tell you about the things *you* think are important?"

After completing a stirring discussion, children commonly ask questions like, "What did Harriet Tubman *really* do?" When the children ask their own questions, they will have eagerly thrust themselves into a scholarly posture. A values discussion, then, can often immerse children so deeply in a topic that they are internally motivated to learn more about it. It would then be appropriate for you to provide information sources that explain how Harriet Tubman helped a small group of slaves escape in place of her ex-husband and how this process was repeated for six years as Harriet helped more than 300 slaves escape to the north with the aid of the Underground Railroad.

When children deal with controversy, the eventual goal is to have them initiate their own questions. Controversial issues often motivate students to want to learn more. The major assumption of the values analysis approach is that through empathizing with the feelings of others faced with intense, conflicting choices, students will acquire a deeper understanding of their own behaviors and values.

Values Analysis Graphic Organizers.   In conjunction with good questioning strategies, teachers often choose to help their students organize their thinking with the use of graphic organizers. As an example, let us suppose that you have been charged with the responsibility to teach any or all of the four basic economics concepts—production, distribution, exchange, and consumption—within a context of studying early civilizations. You begin with the premise that one of the major characteristics of a settled civilization is a stable food supply, and you decide to stress the evolution of nomadic gatherer-hunters into sedentary civilizations. As early gatherer-hunters domesticated wild animals and learned to sow seeds instead of moving about in constant search of edible wild plants, they gradually settled down and became farmers and herders. As farming methods improved, people often found themselves with food surpluses; such economic largesse led to trade. A village with an overabundance of grain, for example, exchanged it for tools, pottery, cloth, or other goods from nearby villages. An overabundance of anything is called a *surplus*, and early civilizations had to learn how to face important decisions regarding surpluses—it wasn't always the best move to trade them for other goods. To help your students understand this, set up a situation such as the one shown in Activity 8–5.

Activity 8–5

Classroom Exercise

Feast and Famine

Students pretend they are citizens of an ancient village on the land between the Tigris and Euphrates rivers. Their village is fortunate; unlike others whose farmland has been scorched by the sun, theirs has an irrigation system that helped produce an abundance of grain. While other villages face a devastating famine, theirs is thriving. Hold a discussion focusing on the following questions: "How do you feel about having surplus food while your neighbors are starving? Is it fair that one village should have so much while the others face famine? Do wealthy civilizations have a responsibility to help those that have less?"

To delve more deeply into these issues, initiate a cooperative learning opportunity in which you consider the problem of what your village should do with its suplus grain. Divide your students into base groups of three, and assign the students in each a number from one to three. Ask all the ones, twos, and threes to move from their base groups into study groups, each study group assigned to focus on a single alternative: (1) store the grain, (2) sell the grain, (3) give it away. Have each group use the following figure to help them consider the positive and negative consequences of their alternative.

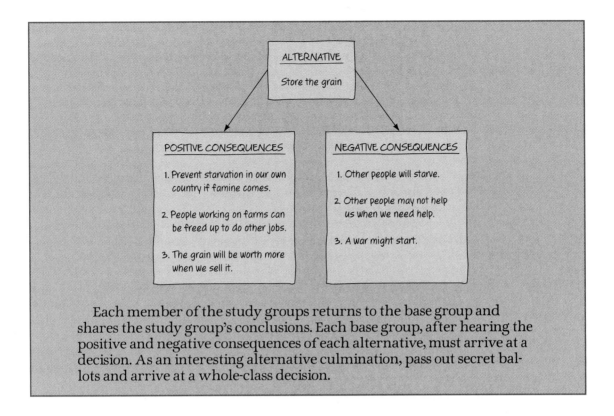

ALTERNATIVE

Store the grain

POSITIVE CONSEQUENCES

1. Prevent starvation in our own country if famine comes.

2. People working on farms can be freed up to do other jobs.

3. The grain will be worth more when we sell it.

NEGATIVE CONSEQUENCES

1. Other people will starve.

2. Other people may not help us when we need help.

3. A war might start.

Each member of the study groups returns to the base group and shares the study group's conclusions. Each base group, after hearing the positive and negative consequences of each alternative, must arrive at a decision. As an interesting alternative culmination, pass out secret ballots and arrive at a whole-class decision.

Climbing a Decision Tree.   An interesting values analysis program has been developed by Richard Remy and his associates (no date) at the Mershon Center of The Ohio State University. *Skills in Making Political Decisions* was planned as a supplement to a teacher's regular social studies program. Several creative techniques were developed to help youngsters make political decisions, but one of the most imaginative and long-lasting strategies is "climbing a decision tree."

To begin climbing the decision tree, ask how many students notice that they make decisions as they climb a tree or wall. Do they plan their attack by examining the obstacle or seek alternative routes should their first choice fail? Do they foresee the consequences of a weak branch or a sharp point? Inform them that they are going to use their ability to see alternatives and consequences that grow out of an occasion for decision—they are going to help Sir Lottalance make a decision about fighting Dingbat the Dragon.

Tell the children to put themselves in the place of the knight, Sir Lottalance, as they listen to the following story:

One day very long ago, the country's bravest knight, Sir Lottalance, was riding along on his faithful steed minding his own business when he came across some very sad townspeople. They were sad because the vile, nasty, gruzzled old dragon, Dingbat the Dimwitted, had lumbered out of his deep, dark cave and carried off the beautiful princess from the king's castle. The grief-stricken king had offered a huge reward for anyone who could destroy the dragon and save his daughter's life. But the first knight to try was overpowered by Dingbat and barbecued by his fiery breath. The second knight to try ran away in panic at the sight of the hulking creature, tripped over his own sword, and become the dragon's shish kabob. Sir Lottalance could hear the princess beating her fists fiercely against the dragon and calling him the nastiest names you ever heard. He could hear Dingbat's tummy rumbling as the dragon eyed Lottalance and eagerly waited for another tasty meal of fried knight. Sir Lottalance was the fastest, strongest, and bravest knight in the kingdom. What could he do?

Now point to a bulletin board display showing Dingbat, Lottalance, and a large construction-paper decision tree bedecked with the sign "Occasion for Decision" (as in Figure 8–9). The "Alternative" and "Consequences" areas on the tree are initially blank. For the children to climb the tree, they will have to think of Sir Lottalance's alternatives. Ask them for alternatives. When they have described fighting or fleeing, write the responses on the alternative branches of the tree and congratulate the children for starting their climb up the decision tree.

Help the students climb higher into the branches of the tree by looking at the consequences of Sir Lottalance's decision. Ask, "What would be a good (or positive) consequence of getting out of there fast? What would be a bad (or negative) consequence of getting out of there fast?"

When the students have suggested ideas corresponding to "stay alive" "enjoy dragonburgers for life," or "be called Lottalance the Sissy," add them to the blank areas above the "getting out of here fast" alternative. Again, reinforce your students for doing a good job of climbing and remind them they still have an alternative branch to explore. Ask, "What would be a bad (or negative) consequence of fighting Dingbat the Dragon? What would be some good (or positive) consequences of fighting Dingbat the Dragon?"

Again, list each contribution as it is offered. Examine the whole tree and look for the students' sense of accomplishment. Then, weighing the consequences, ask the class to vote, deciding whether they should run away or fight. Finally, place their decision high in the top of the decision tree.

To reiterate, the decision-tree strategy involves the following steps:

1. Decide what question to examine and label it at the base of the tree.
2. Abbreviate the decision in the "Occasion for Decision" sign.
3. Encourage children to think up alternatives and write them in the boxes on the branches of the decision tree.
4. Discuss positive and negative consequences of each alternative, one at a time.
5. Write in the consequences, ask the children to weigh each, and write in their goal.
6. Congratulate the children as successful decision makers.

Initial experiences with the decision tree should center on relatively uncomplicated problems, such as where to go on a field trip or what to do with friends on a free afternoon. As the children become more competent, deeper issues could be considered, such as the use of tobacco products, voting for political candidates, or drug prevention.

FIGURE 8-9
The Decision Tree

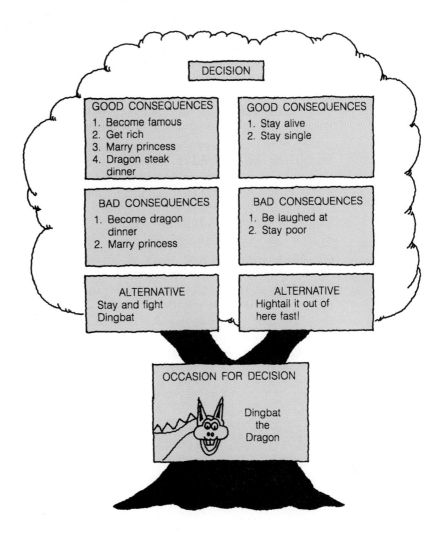

PARTICIPATORY SKILLS

Good citizenship requires a clear understanding of public issues, an awareness of the mechanisms used to rectify difference of opinion, and a willingness to partake in responsible action directed toward the welfare of one's community. Criticizing the failure of U.S. citizens to become effectively and personally involved in preserving their nation's well-being, Parker (1989) describes the American spirit as being stuck in a state of "individualism." Parker cites de Tocqueville's (1969) 150-year-old description of individualism to clarify: "Individualism is a calm and considered feeling which disposes each citizen to isolate himself from the mass of his fellows and withdraw into the circle of family and friends; with this little society formed to his taste, he gladly leaves the greater society to look after itself" (p. 506).

Parker believes that the demise of effective citizenship today is directly linked to individualism. Where can such an attitude lead? According to Parker (1989), "No one knows to what it may lead. Political chaos, economic collapse, urban warfare, a quiet lapse into tyranny, or something less dramatic—anything is possible (p. 353). Newmann (1989) agrees with this outlook and warns that "[It] threatens the very survival of the human species and the planet" (p. 357).

The mission of participatory citizenship, then, is to offer direct experiences in civic life that can evolve into deepened understandings of democratic principles. At the beginning of this chapter, you read about how Mrs. Holzwarth and her 26 fourth-graders from Upper Darby, Pennsylvania, undertook a legislative project that ideally exemplifies the participatory citizenship mission. Good community service programs also consistute an important element of citizenship education when they are made an integral part of the regular curriculum and not treated as frills or add-ons.

The concern for encouraging public service and involvement is mushrooming today and, with growing public support, many schools have been quick to adopt an explicit civic participation program. In a sense, they concur with the sentiments of one astute 11-year-old who observed, "We have freedom in this country but it stinks. Drugs . . . alcohol . . . crime . . . war. There's no good news anymore. We need someone to come in and clean out America!" Education for democratic citizenship means we must practice what we preach in our social studies classrooms. Telling students about the worth of civic participation is one thing; involving them in community service is better. When students roll up their sleeves and get involved, they understand what we really mean by citizenship responsibilities.

AFTERWORD

Some experts have considered the way adults assist children through their youth so important that their methods have been singled out from all other pressing issues of our day—drug abuse, war, environmental concerns, crime—as the major factor influencing social change. DeMause (1975), an authority on the history of childhood, asserts: "The major dynamic in historical change is ultimately neither technology nor economics. More important are the changes in personality that grow from differences between generations in quality of the relationships between [adult] and child" (p. 85). What a powerful thought! And what a mighty challenge for you—to affirm your devotion to children by striving faithfully to help them develop the values and habits of responsible citizenship. A classroom for young citizens should have a distinctly democratic flavor. Children should know what our country is now, and envision the best our country can be. As a teacher of young children, you will be an important nurterer of maximum civic growth. You will help make society. You must have a vision of good citizenship—much the same kind of vision as Michelangelo had when he peered intently at a monumental slab of Carrara marble and saw within it the Pieta, waiting to be liberated. Will you work with the fervor of Michelangelo to release a responsible democratic citizen? Should society expect anything less?

TECHNOLOGY SAMPLER

Useful sources for related social studies topics include these Internet sites:

Character Education: Teaching Kids to Care (strategies for citizenship education; Strategies for Empowering Students is a comprehensive collection of activities)
http://www.aces.uiuc,edu/~uplink/Schools Online/charactered.html

Fourth and Fifth Rs: Respect and Responsibility (a detailed 12-step approach to character education)
http://www.cortland.edu/www/c4n5rs/index.html

Kids Voting USA
http://www.pbs.org/democracy/

United Nations
http://www.un.org/

U.S. House of Representatives
http://www.house.gov/

U.S. Senate
http://www.senate.gov/

White House
http://www.whitehouse.gov/

Wiseskills: Character Education for Grades K–8 (sample lessons for character education)
http://www.cric.com/~Wskills

WHAT I *NOW* KNOW

Complete these self-check items once more. Determine for yourself whether it would be useful to take a more in-depth look at any area. Use the same key as you did for the preassessment form ("+", "?", "–").

I can *now*

_____ explain the need for increased attention to civic education.

_____ describe the overarching aims of civic education.

_____ explain how to help children form realistic civics understandings.

_____ describe how to create a positive verbal environment.

_____ formulate strategies that help children think critically about important issues.

_____ distinguish between attitudes and values.

_____ identify the fundamental values of American constitutional democracy.

_____ give examples of how good citizens participate in responsible actions.

_____ give a sound rationale for including civics education in the elementary school social studies curriculum.

REFERENCES

Barber, B. R. (1989). Public talk and civic action: Education for participation in a strong democracy. *Social Education, 53,* 355.

Beyer, B. K. (1985). Critical thinking: What is it? *Social Education, 49,* 270–276.

Beyer, B. K. (1988). *Developing a thinking skills program.* Boston: Allyn and Bacon.

The Boston Primer (1808), cited in *Models of moral education,* R. H. Hersh (Ed.), (1980). New York: Longman.

Brody, R. A. (1989). Why study politics? In *Charting a course: Social studies for the 21st century.* Washington, DC: National Commission on Social Studies in the Schools.

Center for Civic Education (1991). *CIVITAS: A framework for civic education.* Calabasas, CA: Author.

Center for Civic Education (1994). *National standards for civics and government.* Calabasas, CA: Author.

DeMause, L. (1975). Our forebears made childhood a nightmare. *Psychology Today, 8,* 85.

de Tocqueville, A. (1969). *Democracy in America.* G. Lawrence (trans.), J. P. Mayer (ed.). New York: Doubleday. (Original work published 1835–1839).

Douglass, F. (1845). *Narrative of the life of Frederick Douglass, an American slave, written by himself.* Boston: Anti-Slavery Office, 9–15.

Ennis, R. H. (1985). Goals for a critical thinking curriculum. In A. Costa (Ed.), *Developing minds: A resource book for teaching thinking.* Alexandria, VA: Association for Supervision and Curriculum Development.

Fraser, D. M., & West, E. (1961). *Social studies in secondary schools.* New York: Ronald Press.

Gunning, T. G. (1992). *Creating reading instruction for all children.* Boston: Allyn and Bacon.

Henson, J. (1935). A slave's dilemma. In B. Brawley (Ed.), *Early negro American writers,* (pp. 162–167). Chapel Hill, NC: University of North Carolina Press.

Jacobsen, D., Eggen, P., & Kauchak, D. (1993). *Methods for teaching: A skills approach.* Upper Saddle River, NJ: Prentice Hall.

Kohlberg, L. (1973). The claim to moral adequacy of a highest state of moral judgment. *The Journal of Philosophy, 70,* 631–632.

Kostelnik, M. J., Stein, L. C., & Whiren, A. P. (1988). Children's self-esteem: The verbal environment. *Childhood Education, 65,* 29–30.

Lickona, T. (1993). In M. Massey (1993). Interest in character education seen growing. *Update, 35,* 1.

A manual of the system of discipline and instruction (1980). New York: Longman.

Mertz, G. (1991). Strategies for teaching about the First Amendment in grades 4 to 6. *Social Studies and the Young Learner, 4,* 10–13.

Metcalf, F. (1992). When rice was king. *Social Education, 56.* In special section following p. 408.

National Council for the Social Studies Task Force on Early Childhood/Elementary Social Studies (1989). Social studies for early childhood and elementary school children preparing for the 21st century. *Social Education, 53,* 16.

National Council for the Social Studies (1994). *Curriculum standards for social studies: Expectations of excellence.* (Bulletin 89). Washington, DC: National Council for the Social Studies.

Newmann, F. M. (1989). Reflective civic participation. *Social Education, 53,* 255–258

Olsen, M. (1970). It makes me feel bad when you call me "Stinky." *Young Children, 26,* 120–121.

Parker, W. C. (1988). Why ethics in citizenship education? *Social Studies and the Young Learner, 1,* 3–5.

Parker, W. C. (1989). Participatory citizenship: Civics in the strong sense. *Social Education, 53,* 353.

Passe, J. (1988). Citizenship education: Its role in improving classroom behavior. *Social Studies and the Young Learner, 1,* 19–20.

Paul, R. W. (1987). Critical thinking and the critical person. In *Thinking: Report on research.* Hillsdale, NJ: Erlbaum.

The power of kindness (1873).*The American educational readers,* Fourth Reader. New York: Ivison, Blakeman, Taylor, & Co.

Remy, R. C. (no date). *Skills in making political decisions.* Columbus, OH: Mershon Center, The Ohio State University.

Rousseau, J. (1971). Selections from Emilius. In R. Ulich (Ed.), *Three thousand years of educational wisdom.* Cambridge, MA: Harvard University Press.

Ryan, K. (1993). In M. Massey (1993). Interest in character education seen growing. *Update, 35,* 1.

Ryan, K. (1994). Lecture to the Center for Advancement of Ethics and Character, Boston University, Boston, MA.

Shaver, J. P. (1985). Commitment to values and the study of social problems in citizenship education. *Social Education, 49,* 195.

Sterling, D. (1968). *Tear down the walls!* New York: Doubleday.

Turner, T. N. (1983). Higher levels of comprehension: Inference, critical reading, and creative reading. In J. Estil Alexander (Ed.), *Teaching reading.* Boston: Little, Brown.

Vanderhoof, B., Miller, E., Clegg, L. B., & Patterson, H. J. (1992). Real or fake?: The phony document as a teaching strategy. *Social Education, 56,* 169–171.

Walsh, D. (1988). Critical thinking to reduce prejudice. *Social Education, 52,* 280–282.

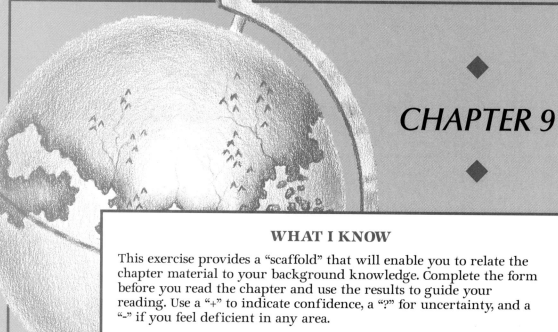

CHAPTER 9

WHAT I KNOW

This exercise provides a "scaffold" that will enable you to relate the chapter material to your background knowledge. Complete the form before you read the chapter and use the results to guide your reading. Use a "+" to indicate confidence, a "?" for uncertainty, and a "-" if you feel deficient in any area.

I can

_____ explain what is meant by *geographic literacy*.

_____ define *geography* and explain its role in the social studies program.

_____ identify and describe the National Geographic Standards.

_____ select activities most appropriate for enhancing skills associated with the standards.

_____ identify and describe the four cognitive skills that link geography and the other social sciences.

_____ explain how premapping readiness experiences lead to successful map-reading skills.

_____ describe the six skills required for successful map reading.

_____ suggest developmentally appropriate map instruction experiences for younger learners.

_____ explain how map skills instruction changes in emphasis during the middle and upper grades.

_____ select appropriate maps and globes for an elementary school classroom.

_____ defend a central role for geography in the social studies curriculum.

Using the results as a guide, what questions will you seek to answer as you read?

Understanding
Geography

◆ CLASSROOM SKETCH

Diane McCarty (1993) and Judy Dollard, classroom teachers trained as geography consultants by the National Geographic Society, have tried many geography projects with their classes, but rate their "Travelmates" project as the best:

The project began in the fall with their fourth graders preparing to send their Travelmates into the wide, wide world. . . .

Each fourth grader chose a doll or stuffed animal from home to be his or her Travelmate. A dog tag with a class picture was placed around the Travelmate's neck. On one side of the dog tag were the school's name, address and phone number; on the other side was a brief statement of what the project was all about. Included in the statement was a request that the Travelmate be returned to our school by April 15.

Once the preliminary details were taken care of, the students were ready to start sewing backpacks. . . . The backpack was where the diary was kept, and the diary was where the details of the Travelmate's journeys were recorded.

We took a lot of trouble with the diary. On the cover were the words "Passport to the World," along with these instructions: "Dear Friend: Please sign my diary. Include places I've been and sights I've seen. A souvenir, or best yet, a photo of you and me together would be wonderful! My only form of transportation is from person to person, so please pass me on. Sincerely, (Travelmate's name). P.S. Please assist me in sending home an occasional postcard!". . . . [A] send-off party, which included music and food, was a huge success. Each student shared a moment alone with his or her Travelmate by reading the card created for the party. I saw one child pretending to feed her Travelmate as she said good-bye. The confetti thrown on the Travelmates before the students took them out of the classroom door was the last hurrah.

Monty's Adventure

Most of the Travelmates began their adventures sometime between Thanksgiving and the end of Christmas break. The adventures began with a trip home to the student's family. The family's job was to find someone traveling during this time period—be it near or far, be it Dad, Grandma or a neighbor.

Example: Monty, Laura's Travelmate, went along with Laura's father on a business trip to San Diego. There, the father handed Monty to a flight attendant, and Monty was off and winging. He visited Germany, Australia, and Hawaii. We know he was there because people sent us postcards.

After Monty had been gone for about two months, the class received a phone call from another flight attendant who was in Paris. She reported that Monty was fine and had traveled around the world with four major airlines. What's more, she said that Monty's picture would be on the cover of Southwest Airlines' next travel brochure for being a world class traveler. . . .

Aukland, New Zealand; Surfers' Paradise, Australia; Sitka, Alaska; Guanjxi, Peoples' Republic of China; Kingston, Jamaica; Tokyo, Japan. . . . Postcards, letters, pictures, books and gifts from wonderful places such as these were some of the items the fourth graders received in the mail while the Travelmates were seeing the world. . . .

Incorporating Literature

. . . .The use of reference materials became an important skill as we located the wonderful places our Travelmates were visiting. Example: Locating Aruba, a small island north of Venezuela, was a thrill for Adrienne. We had received a postcard from someone in Aruba, and she was eager to show the entire class just where Cherish had been. . . .

We learned new names and new places. We discovered how humans interact with their environment in different cultural and geographical regions. People often included information about time zones, population count and size of a particular area. We compared this information with what we knew about ourselves and then began to apply, interpret and speculate on global connections.

Welcome Home!

By April 15, most of the Travelmates had returned from their journeys. The diaries were full of fabulous information about their worldly adventures. The backpacks were often overflowing with treasures. Foreign currency was a favorite with the children. . . .

One Travelmate, Sylvester, held a piece of history in its paws as his owner told about Sylvester's trip to the Berlin Wall. We honored the Travelmates who had not returned yet with a Missing in Action poster, complete with pictures of the absent Travelmates and their owners.

On the Map

Our social studies period during the last week of school was spent with the children working in teams of two or three. The teams read through the journals and recorded all locations in sequence to show each Travelmate's itinerary. A sticker was placed on a large, laminated map to mark each location that had been visited.

Addresses of new friends were also recorded by the teams. It was time to send thank-you letters—as well as updated news about the Travelmates—to the many people who had assisted us in the project. . .

We never dreamed that this one small idea could teach us so much about ourselves and about the world around us. (pp. 32–35)

◆ CLASSROOM CONNECTION

Teachers constantly strive to provide the best possible experiences for their students. The integrated geography unit of McCarty and Dollard met this aspiration commendably. It gave these creative teachers the opportunity to communicate important geographical concepts effectively and efficiently and to embrace other befitting disciplines as they related to the specific instructional theme. In today's world and that of the future, individuals must possess the ability to communicate and make decisions that will reach far beyond one's local community. To help prepare elementary school students for these new roles as communicators and decision makers, teachers must constantly design creative activities from geography with the goal of motivating students to explore the world.

WHAT IS GEOGRAPHY?

Effective, efficient communicators and decision makers must know about the world around them. Understanding geography helps develop perspectives on our changing world and provides a better understanding of world cultures. Gritzner (1981) describes people's incapacity to make sense of the world when lacking crucial geographic understandings:

To individuals lacking a global "mental map" the world must be little more than a confusing hodgepodge; places without location, quality, or context, faceless people and cultures void of detail, character, or meaning; vague physical features and environments for which terminology, mental images, causative agents and processes, and human patterns are lacking; temporal events that occur in a spatial vacuum; and a host of critical global problems for which they have no criteria on which to base analyses, judgments, or attempts at resolution. Such individuals are prisoners of their own ignorance or provincialism. (p. 264)

Although citizens living in a democracy need to be familiar with both local and world environments ("geographic literacy"), alarming statistics have indicated that students in the United States are woefully illiterate in geography (Denko, 1992):

- Forty-five percent of Baltimore's junior and senior high school students could not locate the United States on a map of the world.
- Twenty-five percent of high school students in Dallas could not name the country directly south of Texas.
- Forty percent of high school seniors in Kansas City, Missouri, could not name three of South America's dozen countries.
- Sixty-five percent of 2,200 college students in North Carolina could not name a single African country south of the Sahara.
- In a geography quiz administered to students in many countries, those from the United States ranked at the bottom.

At no time on record has the level of geographic literacy been so low. Do you make the grade in geography? How well do you know your way around? Activity 9–1 contains questions that were put to high school and college students in various surveys. Try them. Do not look at the answers until you have attempted them all. If you and your classmates have trouble, it may help make the point that efforts to improve geographic literacy in the schools are crucial as we enter a new millennium.

Activity 9–1

Classroom Exercise

Geography Quiz

1. What mountain range stretches from Alabama to Quebec?
2. Define what is meant by a *landlocked country*. There are two landlocked countries in South America. Name one.
3. What is the largest country in the world in terms of area?
4. In what country is the city of Manila located?
5. Name the largest city in Africa.

6. From what Southeast Asian country did U.S. forces withdraw in 1975?
7. What are the seven continents?
8. What are the six New England states?
9. Name the smallest state in the United States in terms of area.
10. Name the two largest states in the United States in terms of area.

Answers

1. The Appalachians
2. One that does not border a major body of water and has no ports or access to international waters. Bolivia and Paraguay are landlocked countries.
3. Russia
4. The Philippines
5. Cairo
6. Vietnam
7. North America, South America, Europe, Asia, Australia, Antarctica, Africa
8. Massachusetts, Connecticut, Rhode Island, Vermont, New Hampshire, and Maine
9. Rhode Island
10. Texas and Alaska

Although these questions require place names for answers, geographic educators do not simply encourage memorization of facts. Although they recognize that developing geographic literacy is an important goal of a geography program, they assert that geography should not simply teach students to recall national and state capitals or learn where diamonds are mined and bananas are grown. Some of these facts are certainly necessary, but today's geography places a greater emphasis on critical thinking, problem analysis, and understanding the fundamental relationships between human beings and the earth. Factual data must be used more as a prelude to discovery than as a conglomerate of information appropriate for game show-type challenges. New geography is about ocean dumping, droughts, voting patterns, the demise of the Soviet Union, the revitalization of cities, and not only knowing *that* Washington, DC is our nation's capital, but *why*. New geographers are curious: "Why is there so much forest in northeastern Pennsylvania? Why is the Pennsylvania Turnpike located where it is? Why did Pittsburgh develop into a large city?" Risinger (1992) describes how a fifth-grade class used new techniques of geography to study the historical evolution of their small midwestern river town:

The students learned that during the mid-1800s the town's commercial life centered on the riverfront. That is where the banks, major businesses, and wealthy homes were located. By the late 1800s and early 1900s, the focus had moved away from the river to the railroad line that came through town. The big buildings near the river were turned into warehouses and the fancy homes became apartment buildings. New businesses and modern homes were built near the railroad station. By 1980 the new interstate highway had been built about two miles east of town. The new mall near the interchange and the subdivisions of new homes caused a dramatic decline in the business and housing areas near the now-closed railroad station. Windows in businesses and homes were boarded up. Through this kind of analysis students learn how some people became wealthy while others lost jobs—all because of how humans moved themselves and goods over the land. Students in this fifth-grade class have learned geography in the truest sense of the term. (pp. 2–3)

This approach to teaching helps students view geography as more than a collection of facts—rather, geography is defined as "an integrative discipline that brings together the physical and human dimensions of the world in the study of people, places, and environments. Its subject matter is the Earth's surface and the processes that shape it, the relationships between people and environments, and the connections between people and places" (Geography Education Standards Project, 1994, p. 18). Natoli and Gritzner (1988) agree that treating geography solely as a body of facts is not really what the discipline is all about but, "On the other hand, knowledge of geography should stimulate students' curiosities about the wonders as well as the problems of the world in which they live. It might also help to cultivate in them a sense of stewardship for the fragility of many of the earth's environments. Such knowledge about and appreciation of the world can lead students to satisfying lives and improve their participation as citizens in this democratic society and as partners in the world community" (p. 9). In our schools, then, students must be taught to answer the same questions used by geographers as they look at Earth: Where is something? Why is it there? How did it get there? How does it interact with other things?

THE COMPONENTS OF GEOGRAPHY EDUCATION

One of the most intensive efforts to stress geography education was completed by the Geography Education Standards Project (1994). The project addressed the issue of geographic literacy and issued its National Geography Standards as a vital contribution to the achievement of the goal to demonstrate competency in geography. The National Geography Standards offer a blueprint of the scope of geographic study organized around six essential elements: *The World in Spatial Terms, Places and Regions, Physical Systems, Human Systems, Environment and Society,* and *The Uses of Geography.* Grouped within each essential element is a set of standards summarizing what a student should be able to understand or do. A total of eighteen standards are distributed among the six essential elements. Table 9–1 presents the framework of the National Geography Standards.

The National Geography Standards serve as a guide for current efforts to improve geography instruction in our elementary schools. The standards are applicable to all

It is important that children have a basic understanding of their world, both locally and globally.

school districts in the United States, but districts are encouraged to tailor each to their local contexts. Teachers who want to create programs that use such activities to enhance the geographic literacy of their students create an atmosphere in which children become eager, enthusiastic learners. Generally, they do so by offering two major types of learning experiences: (1) developing the cognitive skills that allow students to better understand the world around them and (2) learning to use maps and globes.

Cognitive Skills

A set of four specific cognitive skills that link geography to the other social sciences is critical to effective instruction in the social studies. These skills are (1) observation, (2) deliberation, (3) data gathering and analysis, and (4) evaluation. This set of skills allows students at any level of schooling to examine geographical phenomena for the purpose of gaining greater insight into the world around them.

Observation

The process of geographic inquiry begins with observing an actual physical location (such as a pond, building, or road) or representation of a physical location (video or

TABLE 9–1
The Eighteen Standards

The World in Spatial Terms

Geography studies the relationships between people, places, and environments by mapping information about them into a spatial context.

The geographically informed person knows and understands:

1. How to use maps and other geographical representations, tools, and technologies to acquire, process, and report information from a spatial perspective
2. How to use mental maps to organize information about people, places, and environments in a spatial context
3. How to analyze the spatial organization of people, places, and environments on Earth's surface

Places and Regions

The identities and lives of individuals and peoples are rooted in particular places and in those human constructs called regions.

The geographically informed person knows and understands:

4. The physical and human characteristics of places
5. That people create regions to interpret Earth's complexity
6. How culture and experience influence people's perceptions of places and regions

Physical Systems

Physical processes shape Earth's surface and interact with plant and animal life to create, sustain, and modify ecosystems.

The geographically informed person knows and understands:

7. The physical processes that shape the patterns of Earth's surface
8. The characteristics and spatial distribution of ecosystems on Earth's surface

Human Systems

People are central to geography in that human activities help shape Earth's surface, human settlements and structures are part of Earth's surface, and humans compete for control of Earth's surface.

The geographically informed person knows and understands:

9. The characteristics, distribution, and migration of human populations on Earth's surface
10. The characteristics, distribution, and complexity of Earth's cultural mosaics
11. The patterns and networks of economic interdependence on Earth's surface
12. The processes, patterns, and functions of human settlement
13. How the forces of cooperation and conflict among people influence the division and control of Earth's surface

Environment and Society

The physical environment is modified by human activities, largely as a consequence of the ways in which human societies value and use Earth's natural resources, and human activities are also influenced by Earth's physical features and processes.

The geographically informed person knows and understands:

14. How human actions modify the physical environment
15. How physical systems affect human systems
16. The changes that occur in the meaning, use, distribution, and importance of resources

The Uses of Geography

Knowledge of geography enables people to develop an understanding of the relationships between people, places, and environments over time—that is, of Earth as it was, is, and might be.

17. How to apply geography to interpret the past
18. How to apply geography to interpret the present and plan for the future

Source: The Geography Education Standards Project (1994). *Geography for life: National geography standards 1994.* Washington, DC: National Geographic Research & Exploration, pp. 34–35.

film, photograph, slide, etc.) and seeking answers to the question, "What do you see here?" The process of understanding begins with what the students can observe. You will find it especially useful to engage students in observation activities at the beginning of new topics of study.

Ms. Fessier, for example, initiated a thematic study of "Homes Around the World" by inviting her fourth graders to draw models and tell stories about their own homes and families. She thought it a good idea because the focus of her topic was "different kinds of homes," and she wanted to heighten students' awareness of the concept by starting with their own backgrounds of direct experience. Then she showed large study prints of general scenes from around the world and guided the observation and discussion with these questions: "What kinds of homes do you see here? In what ways are these homes similar to our homes? In what ways are they different?"

The ability to note, describe, compose, and contrast what one sees is the most basic skill of geography; it begins the process of understanding.

Deliberation

The process of understanding evolves from observation to wondering why something looks the way it does: "What do you think has caused the landscape to look this way? What forces (historical, economic, social) have led this scene to have these elements?" Students must not stop the process of examining a geographic location simply by looking at and describing it; they must be led to speculate on why such a condition exists.

Ms. Fessier, continuing the discussion of "Homes Around the World," asked her students to look for clues in the pictures about how climate, natural resources, and other physical features of locations around the world might influence the choice of building materials as well as the design of a home. She asked, "How have the people in these pictures adapted their homes to the environment?" This process should not be pure guesswork, but rather a systematic form of deductive thinking, asking students to bring elements from other experiences to the observation.

Data Gathering and Analysis

In this third phase of geographic inquiry, students gather information as they strive to examine or test their speculations. In the earlier elementary grades, this might be done by using literature, showing videos, inviting resource persons to the classroom, or any other suitable source of direct information. In the middle and upper elementary grades, students can engage in investigative activities such as library research or interviews. Regardless of the grade level, all pertinent information should be recorded on a chart or study sheet, followed by a probing discussion: "What has happened? How did this happen? Why did this happen? What took place before this happened? How does this compare (to something we experienced)?"

While examining adobe homes, for example, Ms. Fessier asked, "What kind of homes are these? Where are they found? What are they made of? How were they made? Why are they made this way? How do these homes compare with ours? Why are adobe homes so popular in different parts of the world? Do you think that homes in these areas will always be built this way?"

After discussing similar questions about each different type of house, Ms. Fessier built toward a general statement regarding all the pictures being studied. When such a statement is made *by the class*, successful geographic inquiry is demonstrated; in this case, "People from different places on the earth build their homes from materials readily found nearby."

You may extend and reinforce your lesson by using small-group writing activities, constructing models, or examining all kinds of literature. Having had such a stimulating data-gathering experience, children will have much to share. See Activity 9–2 for a sample extension and reinforcement activity.

Activity 9-2

Case Study

Travel Agency

Mr. Jordan designated sections of his classroom as "travel agencies," posted a United States map at each, and included the names of selected regions of the United States at each designated section: Middle Atlantic region, Great Lakes region, and so on. Groups of students were assigned to each agency and given the charge to design an advertising campaign for its respective region. They were required to produce a guidebook, travel poster, travel brochure, magazine advertisement, and a radio/television campaign.

Before they began the poster, Mr. Jordan asked the students in each group to think about what its region was noted for: sandy beaches, scenic mountain trails, historic sites, industry or agriculture, and so on. He directed the children to illustrate that feature with a large drawing and use a few well-chosen words to characterize the region (for example, "Water Helps Industry: The Great Lakes").

The brochures were eye catching. Patterned after commercial brochures, the covers were adorned with scenes associated with the locale, such as "The Central Plains: Our Nation's Breadbasket." The children chose six important features of the region to highlight on the inside, each feature accompanied by text and illustration. The back of each brochure included a small map of the region, directions on how to get there, and sources of further information.

The purpose of the magazine ads and radio/television campaigns was similar—to draw visitors by describing the essential features of the region.

The guidebooks were much more comprehensive. Mr. Jordan showed commercial guidebooks as models, which students used to create their own, with these features:

- A *preface* that briefly promoted the attributes of the region
- An *introduction* that served as a slightly more comprehensive guide to the region's attractions, climate, geographical features, chief products, and so on.
- A *history* section that included significant dates and events as well as the important people who have lived in the region.
- A *calendar of events* that highlighted fairs, celebrations, and seasonal attractions
- A *places to see* section that included descriptions of major cities, museums, parks, zoos, recreational activities, historical sites, businesses, and the like.
- A *food and shelter* section that provided information about hotels, restaurants, and campsites, as well as their costs.

To culminate the activity, Mr. Jordan requested that each travel agency share its advertising campaign with the class. All children learned a great deal about the various regions through participating in this enjoyable, productive activity.

Evaluation

The final phase of geographic inquiry is making personal judgments of the situation: "Have the people been wise in using the environment in such a way? Is this the most productive use of the land or its resources?" All personal expressions of opinion must be supported with sound reasons: "If not, why not? If so, why?" Since so many conditions of our world are intimately associated with the wise use of our physical environment, skills in this realm are of primary importance to children—the adult citizens of the future.

It is this physical environment–people linkage that makes geography such a valued component of today's elementary school social studies curriculum. Geographic terms and place locations are important; students need to know and use correctly the appropriate geographic terms and concepts. However, to become truly geographically literate, students must extend basic skills and concepts to understanding relationships among people, places, and other phenomena. For example, generalizations about the influence of weather on homes or elevation of a region on agriculture are fundamental geographic relationships necessary for increasing geographic literacy.

By engaging children in geographic discussions and activities such as these, you open up avenues of interest in many lands and cultures. Some generic suggestions for classroom activities follow.

- *Pen pals.* Encourage students to write to children from other countries. Published lists are available from the U.S. Postal Service.
- *Weather trackers.* Have the students track weather patterns around the globe.
- *Geographic gourmets.* Hold a food fair where students put together a collection of tasty treats from around the world.
- *Global newscasters.* Have students bring in news articles about events in other countries. Rather than being open ended, these efforts are usually more successful if they are focused: "Students in Other Countries," "Sports in Other Countries," "Food in Other Countries," "Entertainment in Other Countries," and so on.
- *Real estate agents.* Have students prepare a sales brochure for a building (the White House) or place (Great Salt Lake).
- *Global congress.* Have groups of students discuss global issues such as world hunger, pollution of the environment, world trade, international terrorism, or poverty.

USING MAPS, THE TOOLS OF GEOGRAPHERS

Of all materials essential for geographic education, maps are the most important. Natoli (1988) stresses that "[i]n the sequence of geographic learning, maps are indispensable for collecting data by earth locations, analyzing area and regional information, and formulating generalizations about spatial relationship. One cannot teach or learn geography without using a map or even several maps simultaneously. . . . Thus, desk and wall maps, globes, and atlases create distinctive requirements for classroom use" (p. 98). The Geography Education Standards Project (1994) supported this outlook with its comments about the first essential element—the world in spatial terms: "The first element . . . captures the essence of the geographic eye: the structuring of geographic education, the ordering of knowledge into mental maps, and the spatial analysis of that information [using maps]" (p. 33). One of your major tasks in developing a solid geography component in your social studies program is to help children acquire the basic skills necessary to construct and interpret maps.

Premapping Considerations

Learning to read maps, like learning to read the printed word, depends on a student's ability to associate arbitrary symbols with something real in the environment for the purpose of communicating ideas to others. Jean Piaget offers us a vivid idea of how children acquire the ability to attach meaning to arbitrary labels. Central to Piaget's explanation is the term *signifier*, which may be used to refer to any of three systems of representing something within the environment: *index, symbol,* and *sign.*

1.   *Index.* This is the actual physical contact with an object. When the child first comes into contact with a pencil, for example, she performs many physical operations on it to perceive what it is: Her eyes fix on it and perceive its color and shape,

she reaches out to touch it and find out how it feels, and she experiments with it to discover its function. The experience gained from such direct physical contact with the object opens the door to extracting meaning from the environment.

2.   *Symbol.* This is where the child deals not with the objects themselves, but with representations of the objects. The child may call upon previous direct experiences to bring meaning to a representation of a pencil—a photograph or drawing, for example.

3.   *Sign.* This is the most abstract representation of something in the environment; this level relies on systems of words and other symbols to communicate ideas. Index and symbol systems are considered *personal signifiers* because they involve an individual's own internalization of direct experiences with the environment, while the sign system is a *social signifier* because it utilizes abstractions (words and other symbols) that must be mutually agreed upon to communicate meaning. Sign signifiers require abstract thought from students because, for example, the word *pencil* bears no physical resemblance to a real pencil, or even to a drawing of one.

Maps, then, are a sign system of arbitrary representations (social signifiers). To have true meaning, you must patiently develop these social signifiers through a series of activities that starts with direct experiences, evolves to representations of those direct experiences, and culminates with the use of more abstract symbols. This process is not unlike learning to read the printed word; instead of reading a printed page, however, students go through the complicated process of attaching meaning to maps. That process begins with a basic knowledge of the physical world.

Knowledge of the Physical World

Inherent in the acquisition of map-reading skills is the formation of basic concepts of the physical world to which map symbols can later be associated. Preschool and kindergarten children acquire these concepts as they explore and manipulate objects in their immediate environment. As they participate in firsthand experiences, they are continually gathering, sorting, and storing the kind of information that subsequent map-reading processes demand. Three important premapping learning areas must be emphasized as children gather and assimilate knowledge about their physical world: physical features, the earth, and representation.

Physical Features.   Children continually "read their environment" for clues as to what the still-undefined people, places, and objects in their young lives are all about. You can help children begin to make sense of their surroundings by directing them toward certain data or significant discoveries. This guidance does not stifle a child's interest in the experience, but provides the necessary direction to make the most of it. You may help children inspect and identify physical features in their environment in a variety of ways:

• If your playground has several different surfaces (sand, dirt, grass, asphalt, concrete, etc.), have the children observe each carefully and decide which is best for riding a trike or running in bare feet. Discuss why the hardest surface is easiest for some tasks and the softest is easiest for others. Ask children to find the area that would be best for digging, for tumbling, for resting, or for other uses.

• You can use sand and water play to help children build model rivers, lakes, roads, mountains, farms, cities, and the like. Toy vehicles add additional fantasy to free play and help develop awareness of the different types of geographical features on the earth's surface and how people use those features in their daily lives.

• Take a walk outside the school and locate various physical features. Identify churches, houses, apartment buildings, trailers, row homes, stores, parking lots, and parks. Help the children understand the ways people use these parts of the physical environment.

• Take a trip to an area different than the one in which your school is located—to a rural area if your school is in the city, for example. Encourage the children to look for different land formations and buildings, such as rivers, ponds, mountains, valleys, fields, farmhouses, or barns. Lead a discussion of the ways this environment differs from their own, especially regarding clothing, work, play, and living arrangements. You should lead discussions to help the children compare and contrast the ways people use these neighborhood features.

The Earth.   Complete understanding of the earth and its features is certainly impossible for young children—consider, for example, the youngster who busily burrows with his shovel because he wants to "dig all the way to the bottom of the world." Despite maturational limitations, children need to participate in experiences that focus on apparent features of the earth's surface:

• When standing in the sun, ask the children to find their shadows. Explain that the sun's strong light makes the shadow. Move to the shade and talk about the differences.

• Digging in the dirt and playing with water introduce children to the two basic features of the earth. Take the children to a lake or pond to help them more fully understand large bodies of water. Have the children classify objects or pictures of things that belong primarily on land or in the water.

• Have the children look at the many varieties of cloud formations to learn that large, puffy, white clouds mean fair weather, and large, dark, thick clouds warn of rain or snow.

• During a windy day, point out the nature of the wind by asking the children to run into the wind and then turn away from the wind and run. Discuss the differences experienced during each effort.

• Use the globe to point out locations of stories whenever you read to your children of faraway places.

This kindergartner will spend his entire recess period exploring the fascinating properties of sand, thereby testing out one of the earth's many physical wonders.

Representation.   The actual symbolic representations on maps are too abstract for kindergarten and early primary-grade children to use. This does not mean, however, that young children are incapable of using symbols of any kind; their oral language skills show that they are able to use verbal symbols. For that reason, a variety of informal representational activities will help children discover relationships between some physical aspect of their environment and its symbol. These activities help promote initial instruction in representation:

• Allow children ample time to play with blocks and other building materials. Youngsters often construct model environments that simulate real locations. If toy vehicles, traffic signs, and people figures are also available, children will dramatize their knowledge of the real world in their play.

• Take a class trip around the neighborhood and photograph the buildings as you go. Mount the pictures on blocks of wood and encourage the children to use them as they would use regular blocks in their play.

• Use photographs of the children to illustrate that familiar things can be represented by scale models. Point out to them, "The picture shows you, but the picture is very small and you are really much bigger." Take photographs or draw pictures of a variety of classroom features and ask the children to point to or pick up the real object. This leads children to understand that symbols represent real things or real places, but in much smaller ways.

- Provide picture puzzles and map puzzles to help children develop accurate conceptualizations of real objects.

Some children use these experiences as springboards to successful map and globe consciousness, while others derive little benefit. What accounts for the variability? Perhaps the most reasonable explanation is that many children have not yet developed the perceptual skills required for reading and understanding maps.

Perceptual Skills

Egocentrism and Conservation.   Perceptual skills involve a child's ability to receive sensory input, interpret it, and respond to it. Two perceptual factors—Piaget's "egocentrism" and "conservation"—are particularly important to successful map reading. *Egocentrism* refers to childrens' ability to see the world only from their point of view and their belief that everyone else sees it the same way. Children have difficulty imagining that a view of any physical feature changes if it is examined from a position other than their own. To test this characteristic, Piaget devised a square board with three distinctly different model mountains, arranged as shown in Figure 9-1. Interviewers ask children to sit at a table so that they see the view shown. Then the interviewers show the children drawings of the mountains as viewed from several different perspectives and ask the children to select the view they presently see. Next, the interviewers introduce a doll who "strolls" around the table along the edges of the model, stopping at each side of the square. The children remain seated and select pictures showing how the doll sees the mountains at each stop. Results showed that some children were able to make firm choices before the age of 8 or 10, but not until that age could most children answer with confidence.

In addition to egocentrism, Piaget found that children younger than about 7 or 8 have difficulty counterbalancing how things look now as opposed to how they looked a short while ago (*conservation*). Manifestations of the concept of conservation are illustrated in Figure 9–2.

Informal Play with Blocks.   Because children younger than age 8 are egocentric in their view of the environment and have difficulty conserving, teachers of young children should learn to work *with* and not against these natural tendencies. Teachers of children 5 to 7 years old provide the foundation for helping the child conceptualize space by arranging blocks, boxes, and other construction materials in

FIGURE 9–1
Piaget's Arrangement of
Mountains on a Square Board

FIGURE 9–2
Piagetian Tests to Estimate Children's Ability to Conceptualize Space

	Have the children agree that there are:	Then make this change:	And ask the children:
CONSERVATION OF LIQUIDS	two equal glasses of liquid. 	Pour one into a taller, thinner glass. 	Do the glasses contain more, less, or the same amount? Why do you think so?
CONSERVATION OF NUMBER	two equal lines of coins. 	Lengthen the spaces between the coins on one line. 	Do both lines have the same number of checkers or does one line have more? Why do you think so?
CONSERVATION OF MATTER	two equal balls of clay. 	Squeeze one ball into a long thin shape. 	Which piece has more clay—the ball or the snake? Why do you think so?
CONSERVATION OF LENGTH	two pencils of equal length. 	Move one pencil. 	Would two ants starting a hike at this end of the pencils and walking at the same speed both travel the same distance? Why do you think so?
CONSERVATION OF AREA	two identical pieces of green construction paper representing a field of grass on which are placed the same number of red blocks representing barns. Add a toy cow to each field. Establish that both cows have same amount of grass to eat. 	Rearrange the barns. 	Do the cows still have the same amount of grass to eat? Which has more? Why do you think so?

a variety of informal play situations. Children can build structures, large enough to play in, that represent neighborhood, school, shopping area, or airport. Although the emphasis is on creative play and not on constructing accurate representations, the children are making a symbolic representation of some real part of their environment; in essence, that is what a map is.

Blocks are exciting materials for youngsters to work with. With blocks, children can make "real" things to touch, move, reach through, go around, and even to crash into on occasion. Children build, play, destroy, and build again as they gain mastery not only of their physical capabilities but also of their ability to represent some real place. Watch a group of kindergartners or first graders strive to build a neighborhood with their blocks: cars, buses, and trucks maneuver up and down the streets, reacting to pedestrians and traffic signals or coming into a service station for a fill-up. The active involvement, role playing, and mental exercise help make this a valuable initial learning experience.

Your role during this kind of activity is to *observe* and *encourage*. You may offer help and advice, but do not build or participate in the actual block construction. Maintain a lookout for safety reasons and interfere only if there is continued disarray or confusion, or physical danger. The atmosphere is one of independence and responsibility, encouraging the children to work hard toward their own purposes.

In addition to informal learning with block play, what specific map and globe skills can you encourage in a more planned way? We can best answer this question if we think of a small group of children building with blocks who become aware they have made some structures and what appear to be streets. They have included toy people, animals, cars, and other "props" that were near the block area. Skillful teachers will interact with the children, asking questions that lead to the development of specific

During the earliest years, children pile up concrete experiences that give them a truer sense of what map symbols stand for.

perceptual skills necessary for successful map reading. The following are appropriate questions and comments:

- "Which automobile will fit through the garage door?"
- "How can you make this road longer?"
- "Does your road have curves or is it straight?"
- "Where would that car go if this road were closed?"
- "What made your building fall down?"
- "Let's see if that building is as tall as this tower."
- "Jimmy's foot is two blocks long. How many blocks long is my foot?"
- "How can you build a bridge so that the truck can get to the other side of the river?"
- "Are these blocks the same size?"
- "I wonder what would happen if you put a round block here."

By interacting in this way, you can encourage expansion of perceptual concepts such as size, shape, weight, measurement, classification, symbols, and categorization. Mastery of these concepts, according to Piaget, is essential before formal map instruction begins.

You can learn much about children by listening and watching. As the children investigate and discuss, you may wish to introduce new materials unobtrusively or pull together random ideas. Do this carefully, because children's free experimentation and creativity can be stifled by teachers who fail to maintain the delicate balance between informal guidance and formal direction. Your creativity, added in proper proportion to the children's, will bring interesting new aspects to the play. Your role during this initial map-reading experience includes the following aspects:

- *Arranging the environment.* Provide blocks, boxes, boards, barrels, cardboard, spools from telephone cable, ramps, rugs, trucks, cars, fire engines, trains, boats, wagons, tractors, airplanes, rope, gas pumps, traffic signs, barns, animals, family dolls, community worker dolls, and a variety of other equipment.

- *Informal guidance.* Allow children to experience the materials and to discover their dramatic possibilities. Creative play provides the necessary foundation for developing more sophisticated understandings.

- *Evaluation.* Observe the children at dramatic play to pick up clues as to what areas need strengthening or which children are becoming ready for more formalized map instruction.

Beginning Map Instruction

During children's experiences with premapping activities, skills and understandings will evolve at different rates. If you are in the process of building a truly developmental map-reading program in the primary grades, children who do not have adequate experiential and perceptual characteristics should be given more opportunities for readiness activities. Children who are able to move ahead should be encouraged to do so with directed learning experiences that promote confidence and motivation to succeed and that develop these map-reading skills:

1. Locating places.
2. Recognizing and expressing relative location.
3. Interpreting map symbols.
4. Developing a basic idea of relative size and scale.
5. Reading directions.
6. Understanding that the globe is the most accurate representation of the earth's surface.

Planned instruction in map and globe skills is easy to begin with children identified as ready because of *direct involvement* and *concrete experiences,* two essential components of a program. Children learn best when they experiment with challenging materials that stimulate mental processes to organize and integrate new information into already present mental perceptions. This means that children can learn only if they have previously developed the perceptions necessary to make a logical progression to a new task.

Three-Dimensional Classroom Maps

Because of the importance of providing a continuous, developmental approach to instruction, the experiences in the initial phases of planned instruction should remain concrete and not vary greatly from those of the premapping period. However, the emphasis changes from informal play to planning and developing accurate representations of some real observed environment.

Siegel and Schadler (1981) advise that the first environment to be mapped should be thoroughly familiar to the children. To support this point, the researchers conducted an experiment to determine whether familiarity with the environment enhances young children's ability to produce spatial representations (map constructions). They found that increased experience in the environment to be mapped (a classroom, in this instance) significantly facilitated the accuracy of the representations. Perhaps the most desirable environment in which to begin, then, is the classroom. In this way, children are able to constantly observe the environment they are to represent, enabling them more readily to make direct comparisons and contrasts.

Begin this initial mapmaking project (it usually works best with second graders) by asking the children to bring their empty half-pint milk containers back from lunch. Clean carefully and cut off the tops of the containers at a point below where they meet so that you have a square, open-top box. Turn the box over and cut away parts of the sides with scissors so that the cartons appear to have legs and begin to represent the forms of the children's desks (see Figure 9–3).

FIGURE 9–3
Stages of Constructing Milk
Carton Desks

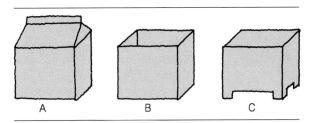

Discuss the representation with the children, pointing out that these model desks are to look like their real desks. Encourage the children to paint the desks with tempera paint, to glue construction paper books or pencils on top, and to put their name cards on the fronts of the desks.

When the desks are completed, ask one child to put her desk on a large sheet of cardboard or paper that you have placed on a worktable or on the floor. Show the child that the large cardboard represents the classroom on a smaller scale. Let her observe the room and then the cardboard to see where to place the desk. Once she is satisfied with the placement, you may ask for the child who sits next to the first to place his desk. Actually, you are introducing three basic map-reading skills as you continue to have the children place their desks on the cardboard:

1. Recognizing that their milk carton desks *stand for* their real desks (interpreting map symbols).
2. Finding where their desks should be placed (locating places).
3. Determining the placement of individual desks in relationship to the other desks (recognizing and expressing relative location).

To continue the activity, ask the children to bring to school the next day empty boxes they might have around the house, from small jewelry boxes to boxes about the size of a toaster. Divide the members of the class who are able to work together into committees, each of which is responsible for constructing a classroom feature such as the piano, teacher's desk, learning center, and so on. Keep a careful eye on the children as they select the boxes most appropriate for their particular models. Often, the group responsible for the teacher's desk will select the largest box, even though that box is much larger than the relative size of the desk, because children view the teacher as an extremely important person in their lives and thus deserving the largest available box. But encourage the children to observe their own real desks in comparison to yours so they can eventually select a box that represents the true relationship. Sometimes children create amusingly novel approaches to depicting relative size associations. For example, one teacher found that all students had completed their assigned tasks and were ready to place their features on the growing three-dimensional map, but Alice was still busy at the back of the room finishing her model wastebasket. When the teacher went back to watch he found that Alice's progress had been impeded by a sincere desire to represent the relative size as accurately as possible. Since the classroom wastebasket was full of paper scraps, Alice was folding and cutting dozens of tiny pieces of paper for her wastebasket in order to reproduce the real object with precision.

When you have chosen all classroom features, decorate and paint them so they are ready for placement on the floor or table map. This phase of map-reading instruction is crucial for its contribution to what Preston and Herman (1974) describe as the "bird's-eye-view" concept. They found that a major reason for children's failure to read maps in the upper grades is the lack of ability to mentally view the environment as it would look from above, the way a map is constructed. You can help develop this key ability by encouraging the children to place their classroom features on the map and view them from above. That way, they will see only the tops of the desks, tables, file cabinets, and so on, and begin to understand that this is how a real map is constructed.

Notice that during this phase of construction, the three previous map-reading skills are extended and reinforced, and a new skill is introduced: developing an idea of relative size and scale.

Once the classroom has been properly arranged, you can further extend and reinforce map skills with questions and tasks such as the following:

Locating Places

- "Place your desk on the spot where it is located in our classroom."
- "Where would you place the piano? The file cabinet?"

Teachers in good social studies programs know geographic content and sound ways of teaching it to elementary school children.

- "Point to the box that shows the puppet stage . . . the worktable . . . the teacher's desk."
- "James, can you find Michelle's desk? Put your finger on it."
- "Put your finger on the aquarium. Now trace the path you would take to answer the door."

Recognizing and Expressing Relative Location

- "Whose desk is closest to the coat rack?"
- "Trace the shortest path from the reading corner to the door."
- "Which is closer to the door, the science learning center or the teacher's desk?"

Interpreting Map Symbols

- "Pick up the box that stands for the learning center table."
- "What does the red box stand for?"
- "How can we show the coat rack on our map?"

Developing an Idea of Relative Size and Scale

- "Which is larger, the spelling center or the piano?"
- "Which box should be smaller, the teacher's desk or the worktable?"
- "Point to the smallest (or largest) piece of classroom furniture."

Class discussion of their three-dimensional representation affords children opportunities to understand that objects can be used to symbolize other objects. This skill is vitally important in a developmental plan of instruction, since Piaget tells us that children most effectively acquire understandings according to the three levels of representation explained earlier in this chapter.

Beginning map activity moves through these levels by giving students opportunities to construct symbols that represent real objects (index and symbol levels of representation) and to put their experiences into words (sign)—whereby you have provided an accurate language base for still newer ideas.

Flat Maps

Begin a transition from this three-dimensional classroom experience to one that is slightly more abstract. To move to the construction of a simple flat map, have the children look at their 3-D map from directly above and discuss their perceptions. Then ask them to put a piece of construction paper beneath each feature and trace around the outside of each with a crayon. As the 3-D features are removed and the outlines cut out with scissors, the children should label the remaining outlines, such as "file cabinet" or "Bart's desk," and glue the outlines in their appropriate places. The 3-D map gradually becomes a flat map as outlines replace the models. For the children to perceive accurately how the flat map is similar to the 3-D map, you should ask questions like those suggested for the 3-D map. Effective discussion is as important for this flat map phase as for the 3-D phase.

Children's Literature

Early primary-grade children are not too young to begin developing a basic foundation of concepts and skills, provided they are actively involved in the process. Children's stories can extend the children's learnings by providing opportunities for creative skill-building activity.

Good children's books offer superb opportunities for exposure to informal mapping activities. Some books are perfect; *chain stories* that the children (or teacher) can illustrate easily are excellent selections. For example, in Eric Hill's popular "lift-the-flap" story *Spot's First Walk* (Putnam), a curious puppy meets all kinds of new animal friends as he wanders behind fences, by a chicken coop, and near a pond on his first venture away from home. As you read the story, invite the children to predict who they might meet under each flap. When the story is finished, ask the children to draw pictures of the snail, fish, bees, hen, and other friends Spot met along the way. Their simple illustrations can be arranged as a floor display, creating a sequence map of Spot's travels. Other stories that are appropriate for informal representational purposes include *Katie and the Big Snow* by Virginia Lee Burton (Houghton Mifflin), *Rosie's Walk* by Pat Hutchins (Macmillan), and *Harry the Dirty Dog* by Gene Zion (Harper).

Telling Stories

Norton (1994) has created "The Mystery of the Kidnapped Chemist" as an innovative approach to reinforcing map skills for young children. The activity involves a map (see Figure 9–4) and a story, which you may either read aloud or tape-record and play in class:

> You are going to have an opportunity to solve the case of the kidnapped chemist. The heroine in this story is a girl who invented a formula for making people invisible. Two companies want the formula; one company is honest and the other one is not. When our heroine refuses to sell the formula to the dishonest company, they kidnap her, blindfold her, and put her in the back seat of a car. The kidnappers tell her she will be taken to a secret laboratory where she will be forced to make the formula. She cannot see where the car will be taking her. She wonders how she will be able to tell the police how to find the secret laboratory; she knows she will try to escape, and she needs to know the location of that laboratory. The kidnappers have covered her eyes, but they have not covered her ears. She decides that if she listens carefully, she may be able to get enough clues to identify the route the car is traveling in. She is afraid, however, that she will not be able to listen carefully enough to recognize all the sounds and to remember the order she hears them in. The order is very important, since the sounds will form a sound road map and provide the clues for locating the secret laboratory. When you finish listening to the clues, you will make her trip on a sound road map. Ready? The car is starting!
> The first sound she hears is a [church bell]. The sound is loud, so the car must be beside the sound. The car stops at the corner by the sound and turns toward the right. She can hear a new sound off in the distance. The car is coming closer to [zoo animal

sounds]. As she rides past these sounds, she knows it is 8:00 because she can hear the [clock striking]. Many sounds are now heard in the sky. She can hear an [airplane] overhead. The road is getting bumpy, and she can hear [road construction noises]. Something big just passed the car. A pleasant sound is heard as the car travels on. She can hear [children laughing and talking] in the distance. She must be driving in the country because she can hear the sound of [frogs]. She hears a [railroad crossing bell], and thinks the car is stopping at a railroad crossing. The car moves ahead, slows, and stops. Her kidnappers tell her to get out because she has reached the secret laboratory. She strains her hearing and thinks she hears the sound of [turkeys gobbling]. Can you help her remember her trip? Where did the car travel? Where is the secret laboratory? To show that you remember the car's movements, draw the direction the car took on the Sound Road Map in the listening center. After you have finished, listen to the tape a second time and check to see if you are correct. If you are not correct, draw in the right directions with a red pencil. (pp. 82-83)

FIGURE 9-4
Sound Road Map for "The Mystery of the Kidnapped Chemist"

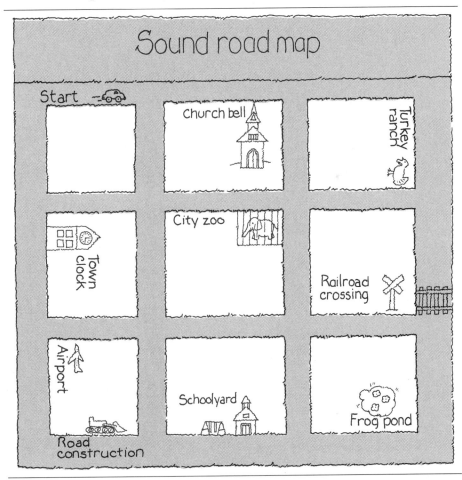

Refining Map Skills

Because an initial construction or story experience cannot guarantee complete competency, you will need to offer various other opportunities to build specific map and globe skills. With appropriate experiences spread out over an extended period of time, most new skills can be developed and strengthened in a rewarding and satisfying manner.

Map Symbols

To reinforce the concept of map symbols through activities that go beyond classroom maps, present the children with a few easily recongized symbols they might see every day, such as those in Figure 9–5. Ask the children what each symbol or sign means to them. What do they stand for? Emphasize that symbols represent real people, places, things, or ideas. Following the discussion, ask the children to pair up and each draw a secret symbol without allowing the partner to see. Then have each pair try to guess each other's picture. If they have difficulty getting started, offer suggestions such as road signs, punctuation marks, math symbols, and the like. Prepare a bulletin board display of their efforts after they have shared the symbols with each other.

FIGURE 9–5
Recognizable Symbols

Explain that a *symbol* is a sign that stands for something. Illustrate this idea by sharing a familiar object, such as a toy airplane. Ask the children to draw an airplane, say the word, and write the word on the chalkboard. Help children understand that some sounds are symbols, pictures are symbols, and printed words are symbols. The children should now be ready to understand that the special set of symbols a group of people commonly use to communicate ideas is called a *language*. In the United States, most citizens use the English language to communicate orally and in print. In school, we learn English as our main language, but we also learn other languages, such as the language of maps.

To move from this introductory lesson on symbols, write the word *tree* on the chalkboard and ask the children what a tree looks like. After discussing their many interpretations, emphasize that the written *tree* stands for a real thing the same way a map symbol does. Ask the children to suggest what the symbol for *tree* would be in the special language of maps. Follow this procedure while helping the children make up their own symbols for houses, factories, stores, libraries, lakes, roads, mountains, and so on. Don't be overly concerned if their symbols are not the same as standard map symbols; at this point you are most concerned not with accuracy of representation, but with the overall concept of symbolization.

The children can practice their ability to make symbols and place them on "maps" with the following activity. Clear a large area of your classroom or take the children outdoors or to a multipurpose room. Outline the area as a diamond shape with a long piece of yarn, tape, or string. Have the children stand above the yarn and observe it from eye level. Show them a rough outline of this yarn shape that you have previously drawn on a large sheet of paper. Discuss how the drawn outline shows a real area as it would look from the ceiling. Then ask the children to draw their own copies with crayon on sheets of drawing paper—a large, simple diamond is fine. Place a box on the floor near one corner of the large quadrangle and invite the children to stand over it and look at it carefully. Then ask them to draw a picture of what they saw as they observed it from above and put a work label on it. Add several more objects to this activity, each time following the same procedure. Use objects such as books, chairs, blocks, toys, and so on. Compare the relative size and distance of each item so children will see how position and proportion affect the accuracy of maps. Now split the class into groups of three or four. Have each group draw a special "map" showing how they would arrange the objects. The groups then challenge one another by exchanging and determining where the real objects should be placed on the floor within the large diamond. Now invite the groups to further challenge one another by having one group rearrange the objects on the floor and asking the others to make the map of the resulting configuration.

You may now gradually introduce standard map symbols now that the children are more familiar with the concept of *symbol*. Remind the children that maps are symbols on paper—that they stand for real things. Show them photographs or slides of a railroad, a bridge, and a building. Then show the children the three corresponding map symbols. Ask them to match the symbols to their corresponding pictures and add the word labels. Follow this progression (photo or picture—symbol—word label) whenever new map symbols are introduced in your classroom (see

FIGURE 9–6
Introducing Map Symbols

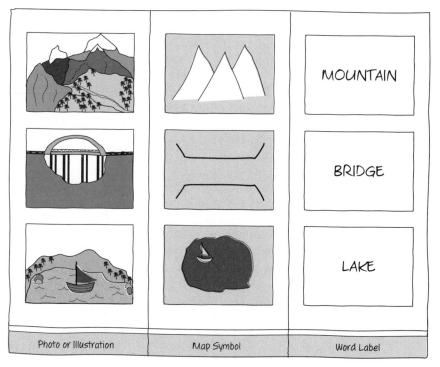

| Photo or Illustration | Map Symbol | Word Label |

Figure 9–6). After completing the entire map transfer and symbol recognition procedure, the children will be ready for an introduction to a new map skill—reading directions.

Direction

The best method of introducing children to the skill of finding directions on a map is to design a participatory learning experience. Primary-grade children enjoy going outdoors with simple compasses to find the cardinal directions (north, south, east, and west). After they locate north on the compass, the children will soon learn that south is behind them, east to the right, and west to the left. If the children are outside at noon on a sunny day, they will find a new clue for determining direction—that, in our northern hemisphere, at noon their shadows will point in a northerly direction. Once they determine north this way, the other directions will be easy to find. To help them remember the other directions, ask the children to search for outstanding physical landmarks. Have one child face north and select the first obvious feature, such as a large building. Give him a card labeled *North* and ask him to stand facing north with the card in his hands. Then select a second child to stand back-to-back to the northerly child. Ask the children what direction this child is facing. If no one says "south," tell them. Ask this child to find an outstanding physical feature to the south (such as a large tree) and give her a labeled card to hold. Repeat this procedure when explaining the east and west directions. Encourage the children to plot the position of the sun in the sky from morning through afternoon. By associating landmarks with directions, the children begin to understand that directions help us locate places in our environment. You may ask, for example, "In what direction must I walk if I want to go to that large hill?" To help reinforce these directional skills, provide a number of follow-up activities; for example, "Simon Says" can be adapted to a directional format—"Simon says, 'Take three steps west.' Simon says, 'Turn to the south.'"

After the children have had this fundamental introduction to direction, extend the learnings to their classroom maps. Ask the children to place their direction labels on the appropriate walls in the classroom after completing the outdoor experience. Do not label the front of the room *north* and the back of the room *south* if these are not the true directions. After checking the classroom directions by using the compass or checking with the previously established reference points, teach the children always to orient their maps in the proper direction whenever they use them. This may involve turning chairs or sitting on the floor, but by always turning themselves and their maps in the direction of true north, children avoid the common misconception that "north" is the direction toward the front of the room.

The skill of reading cardinal directions can then be extended with the use of the children's classroom map and these questions or requests: "Point to the south wall. Put your finger on the worktable. Someone dropped a pencil near the chalkboard on the west wall. Show the path you would take to pick it up. Put your finger on the puppet stage. In which direction should you walk to get to the teacher's desk? In what direction would you go to get from your desk to the drinking fountain? True or false—Richard's desk is north of Marie's desk." You may also use the children's textbook maps to reinforce directions. Use "Who Am I?" riddles such as, "I am north of California and south of Washington. Who Am I?"

Scale

The idea of scale should be introduced in a relative way rather than in a mathematical sense in the primary grades. Children should be led to realize that maps need to be small enough to be easily carried and readily used. Give the children sheets of drawing paper in shapes that approximate their classroom and tell them to construct their own maps using the 3-D map as a model. Some children will immediately reduce the size of the classroom features proportionately. Others will have greater difficulty trying to reproduce the large classroom features on their smaller papers.

Children move toward an understanding of maps as they master the skills of locating places, recognizing and expressing relative locations, interpreting map symbols, reading directions, and developing the ideas of relative size and scale. These skills are best developed in a program that stresses activity and concrete experience.

The Globe

Since the early primary-grade child's view of the earth may be fairly restricted, planned instruction in globe-reading skills is usually not recommended. But you should not totally omit globe-related activities from the primary classroom. With simplified 12-inch globes, children can understand that the globe is a visualization of the earth much as their map was a model of their classroom. The globe should include a minimum amount of detail and preferably should show the land masses in no more than three colors and the bodies of water in a consistent shade of blue. Only the names of the continents, countries, largest cities, and largest bodies of water should appear. Globes that show more detail can confuse the very young child.

You should use the globe as a valuable, informal teaching tool. When reading stories, children may wish to find where their favorite characters live; you can show them the geographical location. For example, if your second-grade class is in Philadelphia and you are reading the children a story about Los Posados in the city of Los Angeles, you may want to show them where Los Angeles is in relation to Philadelphia. However, even this would be a meaningless activity unless you relate it to the children's own experiences. You may ask, for example, "How many of you have ever taken a trip for a whole day in a car? Were you tired? If you wanted to go to Los Angeles by car, you would need to spend about eight days in a row riding in a car. That's how far Los Angeles is." Children who hear about the North Pole at Christmastime may want to know where this cold place is located. Television stories or newspaper articles may suggest places the children wish to find. The teacher can use instances like these to familiarize young children with characteristics of the globe and with the fact that they can use the globe to find special places. The basic globe concepts for development in the primary grades are (1) to understand the basic roundness of the earth, (2) to understand the differences between land and water areas, and

Once children begin to acquire some basic understandings of maps and globes, the world of the far away is opened up to them.

(3) to begin to locate the poles, major cities, and the United States. Teaching suggestions follow:

- Use the names of large bodies of water and land masses, such as Atlantic Ocean, Pacific Ocean, North America, or Africa. Show the children where their home state is located.
- Have the children distinguish large land areas from bodies of water.
- Talk about how it would feel to be an astronaut and to be able to look at the earth from a satellite. Have the children describe how the land masses and bodies of water would look. Show a satellite photo and map of the earth.
- Show the children that the earth is composed of much more water than land and that most of the land is located north of the equator.
- When studying about families around the world, tape small pictures of people in typical dress to their corresponding countries on a large papier-mâché globe constructed by the children. Discussion of the need for different types of clothing can lead to an awareness of warm and cold regions of the earth.

Subsequent Map Skills Instruction

The basic map and globe skills introduced and reinforced during the early grades are used in the later grades in more highly sophisticated contexts and for different purposes. Children in the early grades are developing concepts of what a map is and how to read one. They primarily use maps in their textbooks and practice exercises that (1) are simple in nature, usually depicting familiar places such as a zoo, park, or neighborhood or imaginary places such as Playland, Fantasyland, or Spaceland, (2) contain mostly pictorial or semipictorial symbols, (3) often represent a real environment shared by all the children, and (4) begin to introduce children to the locations of people or places under study in other contexts, such as in literature. In later grades, children refine the skills to include using maps to gather information and to solve problems. Children are expected to extend their basic skills to using detailed maps of areas well beyond their immediate location and direct observation. In short, the direction changes from *learning to read maps* to *reading maps to learn*.

Place Location and Direction

As children progress through the elementary grades, they are still required to use directions and examine a map to find places. The major difference, however, is the level of sophistication of the map itself. Comparing this process to reading a book, you might say that children are taught to recognize stories in first grade but only at a level appropriate for their stage of development. Later, as the children's skills mature, they are introduced to newer, more difficult stories. Likewise, the maps that early primary-grade children read gradually evolve into more specialized maps, many of which require skill in using grids, a skill requiring students to combine place, location, and direction. Middle- and upper-elementary-grade children move toward functionally employing maps, such as road maps, to acquire information for a specific purpose. As with the primary grades, provide older children with a variety of activities that go beyond workbook maps designed to reinforce specific map-reading skills. See Activity 9–3 for suggestions.

Activity 9-3

Classroom Exercise

Place Location

Tic-Tac-Toe
Divide your class into groups of three. For each of the following phases, designate two players and an umpire. During Phase 1, the umpire draws a regular tic-tac-toe grid and places Xs or Os into the squares for each player. The players indicate the squares they want by pointing to the spaces only. Discourage any other form of communication. Play three games during Phase 1, alternating responsibilities so that each child has an opportunity to be an umpire and a player. For Phase 2, the umpire draws a regular tic-tac-toe grid but adds a new feature. On each row, she places the numerals 1, 2, and 3. Again playing three games, the players now indicate the Xs and Os to the umpire by calling the numeral and then pointing to the appropriate square. The umpire writes in the proper mark. Finally, in Phase 3, the traditional tic-tac-toe grid is drawn with numerals for each row, and an added feature—letters for each column. Allow the children to play at least three games again, this time indicating their moves to the umpire by stating the row and column.

Tap-Tap
Arrange desks or chairs into rows. Tape a sheet of construction paper labeled with a different letter of the alphabet for each row to the first desk of each row so that it can be easily seen by someone standing in the front of the room. For each column, label a sheet of construction paper with a different numeral. Draw the names of five children from a hat and ask them to go to the front of the room and stand with their backs turned and eyes closed. Select five more children to sneak to the front, tap each child lightly, and return to their seats. Opening their eyes and facing the class, the original group of five must try to guess who tapped each of them by calling out the appropriate grid placement; for example, "The one who tapped me is seated at C-4." Alternate places so that everyone has a chance to participate.

Odd Town

Creative story writing and map-skills instruction can be combined as an extension of the preceding activities. For example, encourage each child to look at a road map index and determine the oddest name of a town or city in the state. In Pennsylvania, for example, children have many from which to choose—Snowshoe, Bird-in-Hand, Potato City, and Conshohocken, to name a few. Using the coordinates specified in the index, mark the location of the city with an *X* on the map so it cannot be used again by someone else. Encourage children to then write an original story telling how the town they selected got its name.

Map Display

Display a large map on the bulletin board. Encourage the children to collect postmarks, business cards, matchbook covers, newspaper mastheads, clothing labels, and so on. Pin them on the board and attach a piece of string to the location.

Follow Directions Game

The teacher gives each child a sheet of paper that has a marked grid, as shown below. The children start at the dot placed on the graph paper by the teacher. They make their own dots at each location given, such as, "Place a dot at the point 10° west." As they place the dot locations, the children connect them. An outline of an object, state, country, or continent results.

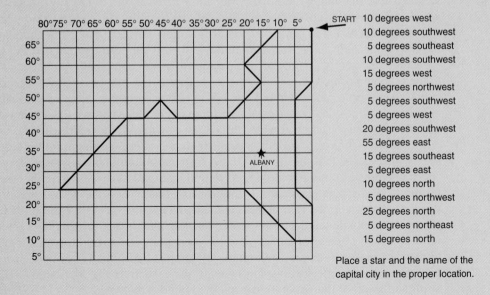

START 10 degrees west
10 degrees southwest
5 degrees southeast
10 degrees southwest
15 degrees west
5 degrees northwest
5 degrees southwest
5 degrees west
20 degrees southwest
55 degrees east
15 degrees southeast
5 degrees east
10 degrees north
5 degrees northwest
25 degrees north
5 degrees northeast
15 degrees north

Place a star and the name of the capital city in the proper location.

FIGURE 9–7
The Earth's Grid System

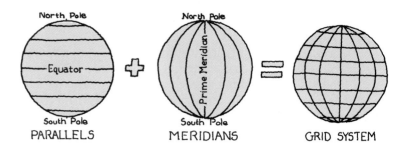

Latitude and Longitude.   In the upper elementary grades, children extend their knowledge of grids as place location devices to the system of latitude and longitude. This system consists of east-west lines called *parallels of latitude* and north-south lines called *meridians of longitude* (see Figure 9–7).

The parallels of latitude, imaginary lines encircling the earth, measure distances in degrees north and south of the equator (designated as zero degrees latitude). The parallels grow smaller in circumference as they approach both poles. The meridians of longitude, also imaginary lines encircling the earth, converge at the poles and measure distances in degrees east and west of the prime meridian (designated as zero degrees longitude).

The importance of grids as means of locating places can be illustrated with a large, unmarked ball. Lead a discussion comparing the similarities of the large ball and the earth as represented by the classroom globe. Glue a small plastic ship to the ball and ask the children to describe its exact location, imagining themselves ship-wrecked and needing to radio their location to be rescued (the ship marks their wreck). They will discover that this is nearly impossible, since there is no point of reference from which to describe an exact location. For example, if the children say the ship is located on the front side of the ball, you can turn the ball and the statement will be incorrect. If they say the ship is on the top of the ball, turn it back again to the original position. Gradually, the students will experience the frustration of locating places on a globe without agreed-on reference points. After some deliberation, they will most likely suggest the addition of parallel east-west lines and instruct the rescue squad to search an area "three lines down from the middle line."

On closer examination of this arrangement, and after prodding from the teacher, they will discover that the rescuers need to travel all around the world along the "third line down from the middle line" to find them unless given even more precise locations by devising *meridians*, or north-south lines. Then the rescue squad only needs to find where the two points meet. Eventually, the children can be led to locate many well-known places in the world using latitude and longitude. Exact locations by actual *degrees* of latitude and longitude may be beyond the mental development of most fourth- and fifth-grade children. Guide them, however, in using latitude and longitude for locating general areas, such as the low latitudes (23½° north and south of the equator), the middle latitudes (between 23½ and 66½° north and south of the equator), and the high latitudes (between 66½° north and the North Pole and 66½° south and the South Pole). Children can generalize about the climatic similarities within these areas. In which latitudes are most cities located? Where is the weather warm (or cold) throughout most of the year? Show them how to find places east or west or north or south of their location by using meridians. After careful scrutiny, they may find many surprising facts—for example Rome, Italy, is nearer the North Pole than New York; Detroit is actually north of Windsor, Ontario; Reno, Nevada, is actually farther west than Los Angeles; the Gulf of California does not touch California at any point; and the Pacific Ocean is actually east of the Atlantic Ocean at Panama. All early grid instruction should be general and avoid as much as possible the use of degrees in place location.

In the sixth grade, after grid concepts have been firmly developed, children can begin to make increasingly precise locations. They can locate places they are studying, such as, "If you were at 20° south latitude and 20° east longitude, you would be in _____."

In addition to these activities, you may wish to reinforce the understanding of grid systems with other activities.

Relative Location

Place location, a significant map-reading skill, must be expanded so that children perceive greater meaning from maps. Children must understand the influence of location on people's lives and how one physical feature may influence another. Recognizing and expressing relative location is a more sophisticated map skill because it involves not only finding places but also interpreting the interrelationships among geographical features, such as location, topography, and climate. For example, upon examining a rainfall map of an area such as Africa, shown in Figure 9–8, children should be able to determine the type of vegetation that might grow there and how its inhabitants use the land.

In the early primary grades, children can develop concepts of relative location by relating different places in the classroom ("Why do you think the science center is next to the sink?"). The concept is expanded in the intermediate grades as children

FIGURE 9–8
Yearly Rainfall and Vegetation Maps of Africa

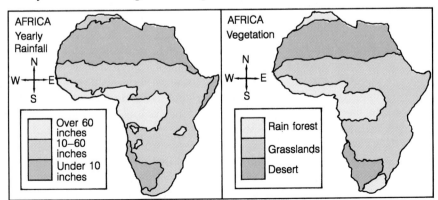

develop the ability to interpret the significance of physical factors, such as mountains, deserts, valleys, and oceans, on human life. The effects of these geographic features should be discussed, along with humans' attempts to change conditions for their own benefit.

One way of doing this is to ask the children to participate in a simulation activity. Distribute a map of a community's downtown business section through which a new highway must be constructed. Assign each student a building in the section through which the highway must pass (bakery, florist shop, hospital, church, historic house, apartment building, department store, pizza parlor, movie theater, YMCA, auto dealership, supermarket, and so on). Construct a large master map and ask the children to write their names next to their respective businesses. Tell them that the highway must be completed with minimal delay, so the entire business community must meet to decide where to put the final route. How complex you get at this point is your decision, but insist that the children arrive at one solution. Tunnels or bridges are acceptable alternatives, but don't encourage children to choose them before they contribute those ideas by themselves. In similar ways, children can learn about other environmental interactions between humans and nature, such as the effect of a large shopping mall on an undeveloped rural area or the effect of a housing project on what had been farmland.

The following experiences further develop concepts of recognizing and expressing relative location:

- Discuss the relationships among latitude and climate, temperature, land use, and living conditions.
- Discuss people's attempts to modify the physical characteristics of their environment. Locate dams, highways, cities, communications networks, and so on.
- Have children locate areas of high population density in our country and cite possible reasons for growth.
- Note relationships among topography and natural resources, population, vegetation, climate, and transportation.

Map Symbols

Maps and globes use symbols to represent a region's characteristics. In the primary grades, pictorial or semipictorial symbols are recommended; as a rule, the younger the child, the less abstract the symbols should be. As children move into the upper grades, you may use conventional map symbols, as illustrated in Figure 9-9. Be careful to provide children with clear interpretation and visualization of newer map symbols. Present a picture of pictorial symbols (or the real thing). After discussing a new symbol, review it without its label so children will learn the symbol and not rely on the label. Emphasize the importance of looking at the legend before using a map.

Many maps and globes use color or shading as a symbol, most commonly to show elevation of land from sea level. Color should be taught as a special kind of symbol. Children should understand that elevation is measured from sea level and that colors show the height above sea level. Discuss profiles of mountains and explain that color used in this way helps us determine elevation.

FIGURE 9–9
Common Map Symbols for Legends

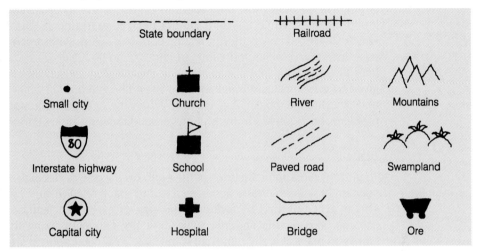

The following additional activities help children grow in their ability to understand and use map symbols :

- Provide a blank "profile drawing" of the United States. Have children plan a trip from Maine to the Pacific Coast. As they proceed west, the children use crayons to color mountains, valleys, and plains to represent proper elevations.
- Encourage children to look through magazines you provide for them, select pictures of outstanding physical features, and paste them next to the labels and map symbols you have organized on a chart.
- Examine aerial photographs to illustrate the relationship between an area's actual conditions and the symbols used to represent them.
- When studying world regions, supply children with outline maps and encourage them to provide symbols to represent features such as main products, vegetation, population trends, elevation, and rainfall.

Direction

In the early grades, children learn the cardinal directions and participate in related map-reading experiences. As they become more mature and learn to grasp the concept of cardinal direction, they can begin more complex map work such as intermediate directions (northeast, southwest, etc.). The ability to use directional skills is often combined with latitude and longitude skills for locating places on maps. Note that the reinforcement activities for place location also include directional knowledge that can be used to strengthen latitude and longitude concepts.

An even more sophisticated skill than *interpreting* maps is the ability to *communicate* directions. An illustrative activity is to divide your classroom into teams of three. One student thinks of an easily accessible place somewhere in the school or around the school grounds but cannot reveal that place to the other members of the group. The student must then hide an object at the location and tell the second group member (while the third cannot hear) how to find it. The "teller" describes which directions to go (north, south, northeast, etc.), what features the other will pass (lavatory, drinking fountain), and how far to go. Child 2, the "translator," translates the directions into a map showing the location chosen by Child 1. The map is given to the third team member, who must find the hidden object. Each team that finds the hidden object is a winner. When the activity is completed, discuss the problems encountered in translating verbal directions into accurate maps.

Scale

To portray geographic features of the earth on a globe or flat map, you must use the concept of scale to ensure accurate size and space relationships among the features. This is accomplished by reducing the size of every real feature in an equal percentage. Very young children have difficulty conceptualizing that sizes and distances on maps actually represent some large, real geographical area. Therefore, you should not introduce the formal use of scales until a child is past third grade, when gradual instruction can begin. Introduce children to the concept of scale by comparing a class picture to the actual size of class members. Lead them to realize that the picture represents a real group of children, but in a much smaller way.

You must be careful to move forward gradually. Have the children measure the distances between prominent landmarks on walking trips around the school. They can make maps of their experiences and discuss the actual distances between the landmarks and the amount of space on their maps. Although their scale will probably not be accurate, have the children discover that although the walking trip covered a distance of 2,000 feet, it is represented by only 20 inches on their map.

Perhaps the most appropriate formal map scale to use at the elementary school level is the graphic scale. Place a scale of miles at the bottom of the child's map. Children can place a cardboard marker between any two points (Los Angeles and San Francisco) on their maps, place a dot for each city, and then lay the edge of the marker along the scale. The segments of the scale on Figure 9–10 are of equal length and represent miles on the map. Comparing the marks on their cardboard marker to the scale, children will see that the distance between Los Angeles and San Francisco is approximately 350 miles.

The following additional activities will help children grow in their ability to understand scale:

- Show an aerial photograph of their city or neighborhood and have the children pick out recognizable landmarks. This will help them visualize that a small map can represent a large area on the ground.
- Using a camera, take a close-up picture of an object and then take another at a greater distance. Compare the amount of detail shown in each picture to develop the concept of scale.
- Have children compare two maps of the same area drawn to different scales. Discuss the likenesses and differences.

FIGURE 9-10
A Graphic Map Scale

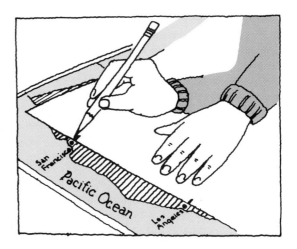

Reading a Globe

Recall the basic globe-reading skills we discussed for the primary grades: informal instruction aimed mainly to help the children realize that the globe is a model that represents the earth. Their major formal map-reading experiences up to this time dealt with flat maps on which they located cities and other places of interest. They learned how to tell direction and how to compute the distance between one place and another. Now they must learn that a globe is the only accurate map of the earth, and is an even better tool for studying locations, directions, or distances than a flat map. To emphasize this, you may want to show a satellite photograph of the earth and compare it to a classroom globe. It is fairly easy to find satellite photographs; one option is to request them through the United States Weather Service.

After you compare satellite photographs to a classroom globe, illustrate just why the globe is more accurate than flat maps. Using a large, thin rubber ball or a globe made from papier-mâché, cut the ball in half and draw an outline of North America (or any random shape) on the ball. Have the children apply hand pressure to flatten the ball and discuss the resulting distortions. Then use scissors to cut through the ball along lines that represent longitude lines. Have the children try to flatten the ball again. Although the ball flattens more easily, the drawn outline still becomes distorted. Help the children discover that this is a major problem faced by mapmakers (*cartographers*) when they attempt to make flat maps of places on the earth (see Figure 9–11).

Globes help to show shapes of areas exactly as they would appear on the earth's surface. Unfortunately, maps are not able to do this. Representing a curved surface precisely on a flat map has confounded cartographers for years. The resulting distortion has been responsible for such honest comments as, "I didn't know Greenland was such a large country!" In fact, it isn't. Although it appears huge on some map projections, Greenland is actually one-third the size of Australia. A classroom globe shows shapes and areas more accurately than maps. Therefore globes and maps should be used reciprocally while developing the skills outlined in this chapter.

FIGURE 9–11
Globe as a Flattened Ball

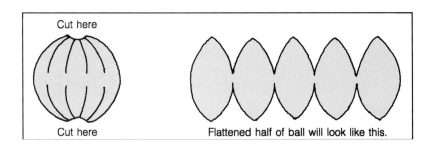

Cut here

Cut here

Flattened half of ball will look like this.

As a third step in establishing the true characteristics of globes, lead the children to realize that the earth, a planet, is a large, spherical, solid body that moves through space around the sun, from which it receives heat and light. Accompanying the earth as components of our solar system are eight other planets, the largest of which is Jupiter and the smallest, Pluto. Earth, the third planet from the sun, is a relatively small planet, the only one in our solar system that sustains life. Establish that the earth *revolves* around the sun, making one complete revolution each 365¼ days. As it revolves, the earth also turns around or *rotates* in a west-to-east direction once every 24 hours. Point out that the earth turns on an *axis* that always leans a little (23½°) from a true vertical line. The axis is an imaginary line that runs through the earth from the North Pole to the South Pole. Show how the earth rotates on its axis by spinning a gyroscope and having the children observe how it tilts to one side as it moves.

After familiarizing the children with these basic globe concepts, explain that the earth can be divided into *hemispheres* (*hemi* is a prefix meaning "half of"; thus, "half of a sphere"). If we live in the United States, we live in the northern half of the globe, or the Northern Hemisphere. At the same time, we live in the western half of the globe, or the Western Hemisphere. The *equator* and the *prime meridian* split the earth in half in each direction to form the hemispheres. Other significant lines that encircle the earth and run parallel to the equator are the parallels of latitude, discussed previously. Two important latitudes are the tropic of Cancer and the tropic of Capricorn. The region between these two lines, including the equator, is called the *tropics*. The tropic of Cancer is north of the equator; the tropic of Capricorn is south of the equator. Lead the children to discover that a combination of all these factors accounts for seasons. They have learned that the earth is tilted 23½° on its axis and that the axis always tilts in the same direction. Note the angle shown on the four positions of the earth illustrated in Figure 9–12. As the earth moves around the sun, there are certain times when the Northern Hemisphere leans toward the sun and receives direct rays, and other times when it leans away from the sun and receives less direct rays. This gives us our summer season (when the direct rays are between the equator and the tropic of Cancer) and our winter season (when the direct rays are between the equator and the tropic of Capricorn). On what major parallel of latitude do the direct rays shine on March 21 and September 21? What seasons do we have in the Northern Hemisphere at those times? Why? It should be apparent to you at this

FIGURE 9-12
Position of the Earth During the Four Seasons

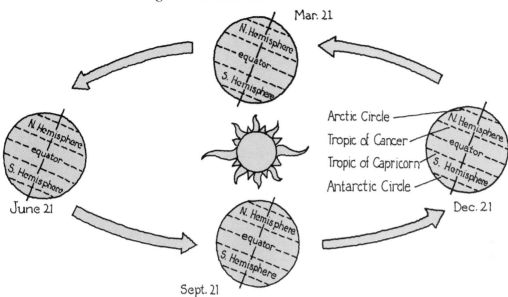

time why the tropic of Cancer and the tropic of Capricorn are located 23½° north and south of the equator. How could you explain this fact to your children? Regardless of the season, though, it is always hot in the tropics. The two zones that lie outside of the tropics receive less direct sunlight and have more moderate climate. It is in these regions that the seasons change. These are the northern mid-latitude region and the southern mid-latitude region. Seasons in the two regions are opposite because of the tilt of the earth's axis. As we move toward the North and South Poles, we encounter the polar regions, which receive little direct sun and are cold all year around.

Map Selection for the Classroom

Teachers need to select maps and globes that are appropriate for their children's developmental levels. Every school should be equipped with a large variety of maps, including wall maps, special-purpose maps, outline maps, atlases, and globes. A variety of information can be shown on these maps, as in Figure 9–13. A *relief map* gives information about land elevation, a *vegetation map* shows what grows naturally, an *export map* shows what products are sold to other countries, and a *rainfall map* shows how much rain falls yearly in a region. These materials should be available in schools: physical–political maps of the home state, United States, each continent, and the world; plastic-coated washable maps of the United States and the world; plastic raised relief maps of the United States and each continent; outline

FIGURE 9–13
Special Subject Maps

maps of the home state, United States, each continent, and the world; physical–political globes; large markable globes; world atlases; pictorial charts of geographic terms; special purpose maps; and satellite photographs.

Besides using commercial maps in the classroom, children should also make their own maps. To be of value, however, these maps should directly relate to a specific topic or unit of study and suit the children's developmental level. As mentioned, initial mapmaking experiences should relate to the child's immediate environment and should be realistic and concrete. As children mature, these activities can be extended to include areas beyond their immediate environment.

Outline Maps

Having children produce freehand map drawings of specific locations can be an unnecessary, time-consuming activity. When the need arises for an outline map, you should provide one as quickly and efficiently as possible. The opaque projector is one good source to use in constructing outline maps. You can project enlargements from textbooks, magazines, newspapers, atlases, or similar reference materials, and trace their outlines on the chalkboard or large poster paper. You can use an overhead

FIGURE 9–14
The Proportional Squares
Technique

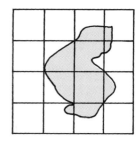

projector if the necessary transparencies are available. If transparencies are not available, you can make tracings on clear plastic or glass. In the proportional squares technique, cover the map to be enlarged with small squares. Draw the same number of squares on a much larger piece of paper, resulting in much larger squares. Match the outline shown in each small square with the corresponding large square, as shown in Figure 9–14.

You can make chalkboard outline maps by punching large pinholes approximately one inch apart on an outline map. Hold the map up against the chalkboard and dust an eraser full of chalk over the holes. An outline of the map will appear on the chalkboard, which you can trace over with chalk.

You may make small outline maps for individual student use by tracing original maps on a master for reproduction on a duplication machine or photocopier. Commercial publishers also produce inexpensive printed outline maps.

Maps are everywhere in today's world; learning how to read them makes children more powerful and more independent learners.

Relief Maps

Maps that incorporate raised features are useful aids for visualizing topographic features and for determining the effects of those features on distance, travel, weather, terrain, and other conditions. One of the problems in constructing relief maps is the distorted vertical–horizontal relationship. Children must understand that the relationship of height to distance is highly exaggerated to show the topographic features more clearly. If true height–distance relationships were shown while scaling the earth down to the size of a large beach ball, the beach ball model would be smooth, and no actual topographical features could be shown. If you use relief maps, students must understand that they show vertical distortion of topographical features.

Construct relief maps on a firm base, such as plywood. Posterboard or similar materials are not strong enough to support wet modeling materials and can buckle and curl as the materials dry. Carefully prepare an accurate outline for the relief map, and keep a second map nearby to serve as a working guide while placing the modeling material over the outline. Sketch in rivers, lakes, mountains, valleys, and other features where needed. After identifying elevation and other land features, use nails, pins, brads, and other materials as supports for mountains, peaks, ranges, and hills. Add color to represent changes in elevation, to identify lakes and rivers, and to highlight other natural phenomena.

You may use several different recipes to produce modeling materials. The following are among the most popular:

- *Papier-mâché.* Cut newspaper or paper towels into strips about ½ to ¾ inch wide and soak them overnight. Squeeze the paper and drain off excess water. Add wheat paste until the mixture assumes the consistency of dough. You can build surface features by applying this mixture to the modeling surface. After drying for three to six days, the surface becomes extremely hard and is ready for painting.

- *Paste and paper strips.* Cut paper towels into ½-inch strips and dip them into wheat paste. Place them over crumpled paper used to build up the surface features. Cover the entire surface with two layers of material. After this has been done, apply a coat of wheat paste over the surface. After the material is dry, paint it as you wish.

- *Salt and flour.* Mix equal parts of salt and flour with enough water to ensure a plastic consistency. Add the mixture to a map outline and mold the terrain according to specifications.

- *Modeling dough.* Mix together three cups of flour and one cup of salt. Stir and knead these materials together, gradually adding water until the mixture attains the consistency of dough. Add dry tempera paint to produce a bright-colored product.

Puzzle Maps

You can make puzzle maps from cardboard, posterboard, or plywood. Trace the major features as you would on an outline map. Color in rivers, lakes, mountains, and other significant topographical features. Cut the map into a variety of shapes and encourage the children to reconstruct it.

Topographic Maps

Nearly everyone at one time or another has used a topographic map. In fact, the U.S. Geological Survey distributes more than seven million topographic maps annually. Chances are the children you teach will eventually have contact with a topographic map—as adults in jobs as diverse as fishing or engineering. Older children may use the maps for a variety of purposes in the classroom, including simulations involving highway and airport planning, selecting industrial sites and pipeline and powerline routes, making property surveys, managing natural resources, conducting agricultural research, and planning recreation areas.

Topographic maps provide detailed records of land areas, showing geographic positions and elevations of both natural and fabricated features. They show the shape of the land (mountains, valleys, and plains) with brown contour lines; water features are shown in blue; woodland features are shown in green; roads, buildings, railroads, and power lines are designated by black markings; and urbanized areas are shown in a red tint. Other special features are shown by appropriate symbols.

The physical and cultural characteristics of the terrain are determined by precise engineering surveys and field inspections by U.S. Geological Survey personnel, who then record the data on a map. Topographic maps are published for each state and are free upon request from Branch of Distribution, U.S. Geological Survey, 1200 South Eads Street, Arlington, VA 22202.

AFTERWORD

If elementary school youngsters are going to develop geographic competency, they must receive a sound, basic education in geography; they must acquire the necessary tools and techniques to think geographically. Geographic information is compiled, organized, and stored in many ways but, to think geographically, maps are central to understanding and analysis. The following list summarizes the teacher's role in developing map and globe skills in the early primary grades.

• *Prepare the environment.* Encourage the children to observe carefully the environment and compare the physical features of objects in the classroom for use in their map.

• *Plan a developmental sequence.* Reproduce the environment with an accurate three-dimensional model. Gradually transform this model to a flat map, substituting outlines for each feature. Finally, construct individual maps from the larger models. Make large "yarn maps" for the purpose of understanding map symbols. Use compasses and the position of the sun to teach directions.

• *Stimulate thinking.* Develop a sound questioning strategy that encourages children to think concretely and creatively throughout the entire map instruction sequence.

- *Evaluate progress.* Observe the children at all times to see who is frustrated and who is bored. If either symptom is evident, you need to find the cause and adjust your instruction accordingly. Frustration occurs if you move too quickly with some children or present them with tasks for which they are not ready. If you fail to challenge gifted students or move too slowly for them, chances are they will become bored or apathetic. Remember that map instruction, like any other learning in the primary grades, must be developmental in nature and geared to individual needs.

The following summarizes the teacher's role in developing and reinforcing map skills in the upper elementary grades.

- *Prepare the environment.* Provide a variety of maps and globes, both commercially produced and child-constructed.

- *Plan an instructional sequence.* Continue with the developmental sequence begun during the primary grades. Reinforce and extend those skills with increasingly sophisticated maps such as relief maps or special-purpose maps. Use concrete experiences to teach new concepts such as grids or those related to the globe. Remember, your emphasis has changed from learning to read maps to reading maps to learn.

- *Stimulate thinking.* Encourage youngsters to think logically and creatively while constructing and interpreting maps. Help them see how maps summarize and explain geographical phenomena and their influence on humankind.

- *Evaluate progress.* Remember that map instruction, like any other teaching task in the elementary grades, must be geared to each individual. Failure to challenge the gifted or meet the special needs of the slow learner will result in a classroom of uninterested, dissatisfied youngsters. Be constantly aware of the children's progress and adjust your teaching strategies accordingly.

Planned instruction in these skills should offer *direct involvement* and *concrete experiences,* for when children experiment with challenging materials that stimulate mental processes, they are best able to organize and integrate new information into existing mental structures.

TECHNOLOGY SAMPLER

Useful sources for related social studies topics include these Internet sites:

Hoops Nation (travel across the country in a van looking for the best pickup basketball games)
http://www.hoopsnation.com/

Maps and References (maps, atlases, and other geographic references)
http://www.cgrer.uiowa.edu/servers/servers_references.html

MapQuest (for a variety of maps)
http://www.mapquest.com

National Geographic (outstanding educational site that visits places all over the world)
http://www.nationalgeographic.com

Street Map (a detailed street map appears as you type in a street address and ZIP code)
http://www.proximus.com/yahoo<

Tiger Map Server (create detailed, full-color maps, and much more, by typing in a ZIP code)
http://tiger.census.gov/cgi-bin/mapbrowse-tbl

Window on the World (see the world from the computer screen)
http://www. globalearn.org/

Useful sources for related social studies topics include these software titles:

Encarta Virtual Globe
Microsoft
World Atlas offers short videos and photos from a variety of foreign cultures; join a Sarajevo family at dinner or relax in a South African living room.

Madeline: European Adventure
Creative Wonders
Madeline, a storybook favorite, embarks on a trans-European train trip that opens up a host of new dilemmas and adventures.

SimAnt

SimCity

SimEarth

SimPark

Maxis

Students describe, create, and control systems from ant colonies to park ecosystems.

Where in the World Is Carmen Sandiego?

Where in the USA Is Carmen Sandiego?

Where in Europe Is Carmen Sandiego?

Where in Time Is Carmen Sandiego?

Where In the World Is Carmen Sandiego? Junior Detective Edition (for beginning readers)

Broderbund
Children become detectives, using visula and auditory clues to track down Carmen Sandiego—an ex-secret agent turned thief.

WHAT I *NOW* KNOW

Complete these self-check items once more. Determine for yourself whether it would be useful to take a more in-depth look at any area. Use the same key as you did for the preassessment form ("+", "?", "–").

I can *now*

_____ explain what is meant by *geographic literacy*.

_____ define *geography* and explain its role in the social studies program.

_____ identify and describe the National Geographic Standards.

_____ select activities most appropriate for enhancing skills associated with the standards.

_____ identify and describe the four cognitive skills that link geography and the other social sciences.

_____ explain how premapping readiness experiences lead to successful map-reading skills.

_____ describe the six skills required for successful map reading.

_____ suggest developmentally appropriate map instruction experiences for younger learners.

_____ explain how map skills instruction changes in emphasis during the middle and upper grades.

_____ select appropriate maps and globes for an elementary school classroom.

_____ defend a central role for geography in the social studies curriculum.

REFERENCES

Denko, G. J. (1992). Where is that place and why is it there? *American Educator, 16,* 20.

Geography Education Standards Project (1994). *Geography for life: National geography standards 1994.* Washington, DC: National Geographic Research & Exploration.

Gritzner, C. F. (1981). Geographic education: Where have we failed? *Journal of Geography, 80,* 264.

McCarty, D. (1993). Travelmates: Geography for kids (and stuffed pets). *Teaching K–8, 23,* 32–35. Reprinted with permission.

Natoli, S. J. (1988). Implementing a geography program. In S. J. Natoli (Ed.), *Strengthening geography in the social studies, NCSS Bulletin 81.* Washington, DC: National Council for the Social Studies.

Natoli, S. J., & Gritzner, C. F. (1988). Modern geography. In S. J. Natoli (Ed.), *Strengthening geography in the social studies, NCSS Bulletin 81.* Washington, DC: National Council for the Social Studies.

Norton, D. E. (1994). *Language arts activities for children.* New York: Merrill/Macmillan. Reprinted by permission.

Preston, R. C., & Herman, W. L., Jr. (1974). *Teaching social studies in the elementary school.* New York: Holt, Rinehart and Winston.

Risinger, C. F. (1992). *Current directions in the social studies.* Boston: Houghton Mifflin.

Siegel, A. W., & Schadler, M. (1981). The development of young children's spatial representations of their classrooms. In E. M. Hetherington & R. D. Parke (Eds.), *Contemporary readings in child psychology.* New York: McGraw-Hill.

CHAPTER 10

WHAT I KNOW

This exercise provides a "scaffold" that will enable you to relate the chapter material to your background knowledge. Complete the form before you read the chapter and use the results to guide your reading. Use a "+" to indicate confidence, a "?" for uncertainty, and a "-" if you feel deficient in any area.

I can

_____ define the term *history*.

_____ compare and contrast *old history* with *new history*.

_____ explain the role of content in a modern history curriculum.

_____ describe the National Standards for History.

_____ plan history lessons using quality literature and storytelling sources.

_____ describe how community resources contribute to historical study.

_____ justify the role of family history in the social studies program.

_____ understand how documents, witnesses, and physical remains offer clues to historical mysteries.

_____ justify a central role for history in the social studies curriculum.

Using the results as a guide, what questions will you seek to answer as you read?

Exploring History

Ms. Guyton used a group activity to introduce the idea of historical study to her fifth graders. She divided the class into groups of three and supplied each with a Lincoln penny. The groups were given a list of questions to guide their investigation of the historical artifact:

- How old is the coin?
- What is the coin made from?
- What languages are found on the coin?
- What figures are depicted on the coin?
- In what country was the coin made?
- How much is the coin worth?
- What is the coin used for?
- Might religion be important to the people who made this coin?

After the groups had completed their investigations, Ms. Guyton helped them verify their hypotheses by providing this information:

- Answers will vary according to the date on the penny.
- Metal (mostly copper).
- English and Latin (*E Pluribus Unum* means "one out of many").
- Abraham Lincoln on the "heads" side; the Lincoln Memorial on the "tails" side.
- The United States.
- One cent.
- To pay for things.
- Yes, as indicated by the phrase *In God We Trust* above Lincoln's head.

After the penny exercise, Ms. Guyton handed each group a reproduction of an incident pulled from Mason Locke Weems's (Parson Weems) fifth edition of *The Life and Memorable Actions of George Washington* (published in 1806). Weems wrote that when Washington was six years old, he cut down an English cherry tree with a hatchet he received as a gift. Questioned by his father, George confessed with the words, "I can't tell a lie, Pa; you know I can't tell a lie." After examining Weems's story, Ms. Guyton explained to the class that when they study the past, historians must rely on two major kinds of evidence: *primary sources* and *secondary sources*. Primary sources are produced at the time of the historical event, whereas secondary sources are produced after the event. She then gave each group a list of questions that historians use to determine whether a source of evidence is considered primary or secondary:

- When was the source produced?
- Where was the source produced?
- What kind of source is it (artifact, written piece)
- Why was the source produced?

Ms. Guyton led a discussion of how these questions related to the two sources of evidence—the penny and the quote. To culminate the experience, Ms. Guyton helped her students apply the four questions for assessing historical evidence to artifact boxes that were passed out to each group. For example, one artifact-filled box contained a photograph of players playing a baseball game, baseball trading cards, a baseball, and a copy of Alfred Slote's *The Trading Game* (HarperCollins), a story about collecting baseball cards. Articles were varied among the boxes. The students were to identify each object in their group's artifact box and describe each item, classifying it as a primary or secondary source. Then the groups were asked to tell the story suggested by the artifacts.

◆ CLASSROOM CONNECTION

Ms. Guyton bases her overall approach to teaching history on a conviction that history is not something found exclusively in textbooks. It can be found in museums or newspapers. It can be found in a box of old receipts; in games children play; in stories people tell; in paintings, clothes, tools, furniture, books, newspapers, letters, and diaries. Almost everywhere we look, we can find clues to a culture's past. Ms. Guyton wants her students to know that the past is not just names and dates, but a story that emerges as new evidence is encountered by historians working much like detectives, sifting through a maze of sources to explain what life was like in other times.

Unfortunately, not all children experience history like Ms. Guyton's students. When asked to share their feelings about history, many children echo Henry Ford's reaction that history is "bunk"; they don't like history because it is "boring." The main reason children feel this way is that they perceive history as merey a collection of facts in a textbook—who discovered what lands and when, what famous people did, who won and lost what wars, who won and lost what elections, and when certain treaties were signed. Ms. Guyton, however, avoided this traditional complaint and accomplished the goals of historical study in a much more creative way. Her students learn history, but the parts that they like best are the emphases on the personal "story" in history—making history seem real in their lives. Ms. Guyton believes that a study of history should begin by looking into how a historian reconstructs the past—determining what happened at the Boston Massacre or describing the toys little children played with in 1890.

WHY STUDY HISTORY?

Ms. Guyton's history is today's history; students do much more than recall facts. Students learn that by inquiring into the past, history offers an insightful perspective of how events from days gone by have influenced our lives today. I enjoy using the following story to make that point:

When Bismarck was Prussian ambassador to the court of Alexander II in the early 1860s he looked out a window and saw a sentry on duty in the middle of the vast lawn.

He inquired of the Czar as to why the man was there. The Czar asked his aide-de-camp. The aide didn't know. The general in charge of the troops was summoned.

In answer to the question, the general replied, "I beg to inform his majesty that it is in accordance with ancient custom."

"What was the origin of that custom?" interrupted Bismarck.

"I don't recall at present," answered the general.

"Investigate and report the result," ordered Alexander.

The investigation took three days. They found that the sentry was posted there by an order put on the book eighty years before.

It all started one morning in the spring of 1780. Catherine the Great looked out on the lawn and saw the first flower thrusting above the frozen soil. She ordered the sentry posted to prevent anyone's picking the flower, and in 1860 there was still a sentry on the lawn.

A memorial to custom, habit, or just everyone saying, "BUT WE'VE ALWAYS DONE IT THAT WAY."

And so today . . . far too few ask "WHY?" Far too few, when told that something can't be changed, fail to ask "WHY NOT?" "Why can't we find a new or better way?" "How can it be done more easily or effectively?" "What is a good solution to our problem?"

As reported in the *National Standards for History* (National Center for History in the Schools, 1996), history—along with literature and the arts—provides young children one of the most interesting studies in which they can be engaged: "History connects each child with his or her roots and develops a sense of personal belonging in the great sweep of human experience" (p. 2).

Ravitch (1985) furnishes these additional justifications for history:

Properly taught, history teaches the pursuit of truth and understanding; properly taught, it establishes a context of human life in a particular time and place, relating art, literature, philosophy, law, architecture, language, government, economics, and social life; properly taught, it portrays the great achievements and the terrible disasters of the human race; properly taught, it awakens youngsters to the universality of the human experience as well as to the magnificence and the brutality of which humans are capable; properly taught, history encourages the development of intelligence, civility, and a sense of perspective. It endows its students with a broad knowledge of other times, other cultures, other places. It leaves its students with cultural resources on which they may draw for the rest of their lives. These are values and virtues that are gained through the study of history. Beyond these, history needs no further justification. (p. 17)

HISTORY PROPERLY TAUGHT

History as a component of social studies instruction, then, has many reasons for existing, with one precautionary note—it must be "properly taught," a two-dimensional concept that will be examined in terms of *instructional content* as well as *instructional methodology.*

Instructional Content

Recognizing the values of history in the lives of citizens of our country, authorities and professional groups have become engaged in heated debates about what content, or core of knowledge, should form the backbone of the history curriculum in our nation's schools. Gagnon (1987) clarifies: "The fate of the entire educational reform movement, from kindergarten through college, depends upon the willingness of educators to take up the intellectual challenge of deciding upon a common core of what is most worth learning in late 20th-century American society, as well as where it most critically affects education for intelligent citizenship" (p. 19).

E. D. Hirsch, Jr. (1987) has proposed a lengthy common core of knowledge in his controversial book, *Cultural Literacy: What Every American Needs to Know.* Hirsch suggests over 5,000 facts that he contends should be known by our students. The popularity of this appeal has become so widespread that Hirsch has organized a nonprofit foundation, Core Knowledge, to put his ideas to work. The foundation has created a core knowledge curriculum that is used in well over 50 schools across the United States. In addition, Hirsch has established a second organization (Core Publications), which has been producing a series of children's books. In 1992, Doubleday published Hirsch's *What Your First Grader Needs to Know* and *What Your Second Grader Needs to Know*, books that begin with the working list of core knowledge contents and provide the background a teacher or parent would need to introduce a specific concept or tell a Greek myth. Books for the third through sixth grades have followed this initial flood of interest.

This growing trend to select and teach a body of core content has caused some to warn of the dangers of reverting back to the days of requiring students to memorize historical information. Skeptics of core knowledge lists contend that "students often fail to demonstrate knowledge of essential material despite having been exposed to it because they did not engage in thoughtful interaction with the material. Coverage

Memorizing names and dates is not what history is all about. Elementary school children need a fuller diet—they must carry out investigations just like real historians.

does not necessarily equate with student learning" (Schneider, 1989, p. 151). Other concerns of a core curriculum approach are that (1) a common core is too elitist—it is oppressive and insulting to segments of our culture and (2) knowledge expands at such a fantastic rate that core content considered crucial today may be rendered obsolete by the time our elementary school students reach adulthood.

How, then, with this deep controversy, can elementary school teachers help students connect with history? Downey and Levstik (1988) conducted a review of research on the teaching and learning of history and arrived at the following conclusions:

• A shallow cultural literacy approach should be avoided. Instead, schools should focus on subject matter that is both culturally significant and pedagogically engaging. Rather than choose information for the curriculum primarily because it makes students "culturally literate," emphasis should be placed on "big ideas" that help students make sense out of mindless collections of information.

• Content and process form a sophisticated partnership in teaching and learning history. Command of content is not sufficient as a teaching skill or learning outcome. Teachers must engage students in stories, projects, and other devices that make the people, events, and conditions of the past seem memorable and as real-to-life as possible. As we help students discover and enjoy history with engaging learning experiences from whatever source, we must do more than ask them to recite facts. They need to be taught to reflect and compare—to form important concepts and build meaningful general understandings.

Cheney (1987) recognizes the critical need to balance a "*how* to teach" and a "*what* to teach" approach to teaching history. On one hand, Cheney writes that the decline of students' achievement in history can be traced to a lack of emphasis on meaningful content: "we can teach our children *how* to think without troubling them to learn anything worth thinking about, the belief that we can teach them *how* to understand the world in which they live without conveying to them the events and ideas that have brought it into existence" (p. 5). On the other hand, Cheney asks for more "activities that involve imaginative thought and introduce children to great figures of the past" (p. 28). If we hope to arouse an interest for historical study in our students, we must have a firm grasp of not only *what* to teach, but *how* to teach.

National History Standards

Perhaps the currently most influential source of recommendations for determining the content of elementary school history is the *National Standards for History* (National Center for History in the Schools, 1996). The standards have made explicit the goals that all students should have the opportunity to acquire through the K–4 social studies curriculum. The Standards Committee recommends that, to bring history alive, historical studies should be centered on four topics under which eight standards are distributed (see Figure 10–1).

FIGURE 10–1
Standards in History for Grades K–4

Overview

Topic 1:   **Living and Working Together in Families and Communities Now and Long Ago**

Standard 1:   Family Life Now and in the Recent Past; Family Life in Various Places Long Ago

Standard 2:   History of Students' Local Community and How Communities in North America Varied Long Ago

Topic 2:   **The History of the Students' Own State or Region**

Standard 3:   The People, Events, Problems, and Ideas That Created the History of Their State

Topic 3:   **The History of the United States: Democratic Principles and Values and the Peoples From Many Cultures Who Contributed to Its Cultural, Economic, and Political Heritage**

Standard 4:   How Democratic Values Came to Be, and How They Have Been Exemplified by People, Events, and Symbols

Standard 5:   The Causes and Nature of Various Movements of Large Groups of People Into and Within the United States, Now and Long Ago

Standard 6   Regional Folklore and Cultural Contributions That Helped to Form Our National Heritage

Topic 4:   **The History of Peoples of Many Cultures Around the World**

Standard 7:   Selected Attributes and Historical Developments of Various Societies in Africa, the Americas, Asia, and Europe

Standard 8:   Major Discoveries in Science and Technology, Their Social and Economic Effects, and the Scientists and Inventors Responsible for Them

---

Source: National Center for History in the Schools (1996). *National standards for history.*
Los Angeles, CA: Author.

Instructional Methodology

Although the *National Standards for History* pinpoint the content for a K–4 social studies program, the National Center for History in the Schools (1996) does not ignore the important matter of instructional methodology. The *National Standards for History* stresses that teachers should bring history alive by using "stories, myths, legends, and biographies that capture children's imaginations and immerse them in times and cultures of the recent and long-ago past" (p. 3). The Standards further recommend that

In addition to stories, children should be introduced to a wide variety of historical artifacts, illustrations, and records that open to them first-hand glimpses into the lives of people in the past: family photos; letters, diaries, and other accounts of the past obtained from family records, local newspapers, libraries, and museums; field trips to historical sites in their neighborhood and community; and visits to "living museums" where actors reenact life long ago. (p. 3)

The modern history curriculum engages students in a mixture of learning experiences. Teachers go beyond the textbook and use a variety of media such as literature, field trips, and artifacts. They also draw upon the family and community and use the ideas and experiences of the students themselves as important inputs for learning. Content in history classrooms is not taught in the form of isolated facts, but as ideas linked to one another and to students' previous experiences. Good teachers value active learning and use ideas to solve problems. A sample lesson plan (see Activity 10–1) illustrates how one teacher engaged her children's historical thinking, even when the source of content was a social studies textbook.

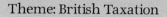

Activity 10–1
Sample History Lesson Plan

Theme: British Taxation
Grade: Five
Teacher: Charles Kunkle

General Objective
The students will understand the major factors that transformed many of the colonists from loyal British subjects to dissidents on the verge of revolutionary war.

Specific Objectives
1. The students will identify the taxes levied by the British to help recover expenses imposed by the Seven Years' War.
2. The students will compare and contrast the reactions of the colonists and the British to these taxes.

Materials
1. Large sheets of chart paper.
2. Marker pens.

Procedure

1. Ask the class to imagine that the school district budget has just bottomed out and very little money is available to purchase the supplies necessary to finish out the school year. A committee of teachers has met to study the problem and decided that a good source of revenue would be to have students pay a small charge each time they put something into the wastebasket. Ask the students if they think this is a fair solution to the money problem, especially since they had never before been required to pay such a "tax." Also, raise the issue of whether teachers have the right to levy such a tax on the students. Promote a discussion of the options available to the students—avoid paying the fee, protesting the plan, complaining to others, and so on.

2. Have the students recall that the Seven Years' War drained the treasury of Great Britain, so the government was in desperate need to raise money. Britain began to do something it had never done before—it decided to tax the colonies. (This was the topic of a previous lesson.) Have the students predict how the colonies might react to these taxes.

3. Ask the students to read the next section in their textbooks to find out (1) what some of those taxes were, (2) the colonial reaction to each, and (3) the British reply to the colonies.

4. Ask the students to summarize the three taxes described in the reading selection: (1) the Stamp Act, (2) the Townshend Duties, and (3) the Tea Act. Have the students chart each on a graphic organizer. (Note how the organizer directly relates to the stated purposes for reading.)

The Tea Act	Colonial Reaction	British Reply
Parliament taxed the tea sold to the colonies by the British East India Company.	Dumped tea from three ships waiting to unload tea chests in Boston Harbor. The event was known as the Boston Tea Party.	Passed the "Intolerable Acts," which closed Boston Harbor and limited the power of the colonists.

Assessment

1. Examine the graphic organizers to determine whether each event was described accurately.

2. Study the posters to determine whether the exaggeration of conditions or portrayal of characters conveys the feelings experienced by the citizens of Boston.

Historical Fiction

One of the most satisfying ways to study past events is to put the story, with a historical setting, back into history. Fiction, biographies, picture books, and informational books all make the people, conditions, and events of the past seem well defined and real. Crabtree (1989) writes of the power of storybooks to bring history alive for elementary school learners:

> Parents, children's librarians, and teachers of the young have long known the power of superbly written biographies, myths, legends, folktales, and historical narratives to capture children's imagination and to hold their interest. Incorporating enduring themes of conflict and personal choice; of sacrifice and responsibility; of power and oppression; of struggle, failure, and achievement . . . these stories connect in powerful ways with these same impulses and conflicts in children's own lives. They engage children vicariously in the experiences and perspectives of others, expand their ability to see the world through others' eyes, and enlarge their vision of lives well lived and of their own human potential. (p. 36)

To gain genuine historical understandings, students must discover the "story" of history from all available sources. Hickman (1990) explains how this happens by recalling the way books affected her life as a young learner:

> First in my heart were the books of Laura Ingalls Wilder. My teacher in third and fourth grade read aloud the early titles: *Little House in the Big Woods, Little House on the Prairie, On the Banks of Plum Creek.* My favorite was *Plum Creek.* I marveled at the family's dugout, at the plague of grasshoppers they endured, and at the way Pa kept himself alive in a blizzard snowbank by eating Laura and Mary's Christmas candy. . . . I didn't know that Laura Ingalls Wilder was introducing me to the influence of geography and climate on history—but she was! (p. 22)

Hickman's description illustrates how she was intrigued by the experience of real people. Likewise, a picture book like Donald Hall's *Ox-Cart Man* (Viking) gives primary-grade children a personal glimpse of life in early nineteenth-century New England as it describes how a farmer packs everything his family made into a two-wheeled cart and travels to town where he sells the goods, the cart, and the ox. In return, he purchases a few items and walks home. Eve Bunting's *The Wall* (Clarion) tells the moving story of a little boy and his father visiting the Vietnam Memorial in Washington, DC, to find the boy's grandfather's name. Historical stories dramatize and humanize the sterile facts of history. They transport children to the past and enable them to more clearly understand that today's way of life is a continuation of what people did in the past; that the present will influence the way people live in the future. To guarantee these benefits, however, historical stories must not only be written and illustrated well, they must also relate the past authentically and accurately—the information must be precise. Native Americans, for example, have strongly objected to the portrayal of tribal life in one book, Bill Martin's *Knots on a Counting Rope* (Henry Holt) that tells a tale about a young boy and his grandfather sitting around a campfire telling stories. The boy's favorite is one about himself that he had heard many times before. Native Americans point out several flaws. One deals with the way the young boy persists in interrupting his grandfather to tell the parts he knows. Native Americans maintain that elders are always respected and would never be interrupted by a child. Other flaws are that the clothing and hairstyles depicted are not authentic to any particular nation, and the naming ceremony described is not correct. Historical stories are capable of shedding light on the past, but they can do so only when there is no distortion of the facts.

Advanced readers might tackle powerful historical novels and biographies to gain information about and perspectives of the past. Katherine Paterson's *Lyddie* (Dutton) helps learners visualize the courage and strength of a young lady employed in a nineteenth-century textile mill. The inspiring story of Sarah, an eight-year-old who accompanies her father into the wilderness to cook for him as he builds a cabin for their family, is the subject of Alice Dalgliesh's popular book, *The Courage of Sarah Noble* (Scribner's). In *Brady* (Penguin), Jean Fritz tells the engaging story of a curious young boy who discovers that his father is an agent for the underground railroad

Children love to read and listen to stories about noteworthy people and events from the past. To share what they have read about, these students will simulate a television interview during which their classmates will appear as famous historical figures.

during the pre-Civil War era. And, of course, we cannot forget the trials and tribulations of the Ingalls family during frontier days in the nine "Little House" books by Laura Ingalls Wilder.

Countless books have memorable impact and may serve as the substance around which you could plan multiple learning opportunities in the social studies. When students become engaged in books that are especially meaningful to them, they are intrinsically motivated to pursue those opportunities to extend, enrich, and clarify what they have read. Linda S. Levstik conducted an extensive review of the research on teaching history to elementary school students, and used a fifth grader's comment to illustrate the benefit of good historical literature: "The social studies book doesn't give you a lot of detail. *You don't imagine yourself there*" (Levstik, 1989, p. 4). Levstik continues:

> "One way to gain the kind of imaginative entry into the past that the fifth grader missed is through historical literature. Stories remain a familiar form to children well into adolescence, and beyond. . . . History embedded in literary narrative [elicits] strong interest among students, and could be channeled into study using more traditional sources. When given a historical fiction format, for instance, children [engage] in interpretation and analysis more readily than previous studies would suggest.

To be sure these important benefits actually emerge from the use of historical literature, you must carefully research the associated content so that an accurate context for the story is developed. I recall observing a university field experience student read Elizabeth George Speare's *The Sign of the Beaver* to a group of fourth graders. During the introductory phase, she told the children that the story took place long ago in the Maine wilderness, where Matt is left by his father to tend a new cabin while he returned to Massachusetts for the rest of the family. To establish the story context, the field experience student introduced a large study print depicting Native Americans of the past because their interactions with Matt are central to the story. The story is wonderful, but it is an Eastern Woodlands story. The study print, however, depicted a Plains Indians buffalo hunting camp with its cone-shaped tepees and campfire. The student complicated her error by discussing the shelters she thought were "wigwams" portrayed in the study print. As the regular classroom teacher stepped in to help correct the error-filled presentation, I couldn't help wonder about how pre-service teachers might be convinced of the need to confirm the accuracy of what they are teaching.

You must grasp that the many benefits of historical literature can be realized only if you place the story content in an accurate context. Historical literature is based on a strong background of fact and should be used as a vehicle to enlighten, not confuse.

Norton and Norton (1994) selected the story *Caddie Woodlawn* (Scholastic Book Services) to show how good literature can launch a study of life during the early 1800s. Their excellent example begins with the teacher sharing information about the author, Carol Ryrie Brink:

> Carol Ryrie Brink had a very special reason for writing *Caddie Woodlawn*. The heroine of the book was Mrs. Brink's grandmother. When Mrs. Brink was eight years

old, she went to live with her grandmother. Her grandmother, Caddie, told her many stories about growing up in Wisconsin in the 1800s. During Mrs. Brink's childhood, she amused herself by drawing, writing, reading, and telling herself long stories.

When Mrs. Brink was an adult, she remembered the stories of Caddie's childhood and thought other children would also like to read them. She wrote *Caddie Woodlawn* while her grandmother was still alive. She wrote letters to her grandmother to ask questions about details she could not remember.

Carol Ryrie Brink says the facts in *Caddie Woodlawn* are mostly true. Some of the facts are changed slightly to fit the story. *Caddie Woodlawn* won the Newbery Medal for the best children's book in 1936. (pp. 297–300)

After sharing information about the author, Norton suggests these highly appropriate activities, among others:

1. Oral Language, Interviewing, Writing—Carol Ryrie Brink wrote *Caddie Woodlawn* because she enjoyed her grandmother's stories. Ask the children to interview older relatives or other older people in the community. In their interviews, they should ask people to retell experiences they remember from childhood, or stories they heard from their grandparents. During the interviews, the students can also gather information about what these people did for entertainment, how they traveled, where they got their food, how they dressed, and what toys they played with. Have the children share their information orally with the rest of the class or ask them to write stories using the information. Develop a bulletin board to display the stories.

2. Creative Writing—Have the students choose a favorite chapter from *Caddie Woodlawn*. Ask them to pretend they are Caddie, and write a diary entry for that chapter.

3. Reading for Details—After reading *Caddie Woodlawn*, have students complete the following chart with drawings that show details for each category.

Life in Wisconsin in 1864

Clothing   Entertainment   Transportation   Education   Home Furnishings   Food

4. Evaluative Reading—Place in the learning center several reference and history books that give factual descriptions of the 1860s. Ask students to compare their readings about the historical period with the picture of daily life presented in the book. Are the historical facts accurate in *Caddie Woodlawn?* Make a list of accurate facts and a list of any inaccurate information.

5. Reference and Art—Caddie has a special friend named Indian Joe. Caddie even visits the Indian camp. Provide several reference books describing the Native Americans who lived in that part of Wisconsin. Students can read reference material about these peoples, then design and build a model of an authentic Native American camp.

6. Map Skills—Nero, the Woodlawn's dog, goes on a long trip with Uncle Edmund. They travel in a steamship all the way from Downsville to St. Louis. Nero runs away after he reaches St. Louis and finally reaches his home in Wisconsin.

- Look at a map of the United States. Draw in the route Nero and Uncle Edmund followed to reach St. Louis.
- On page 53 of the Scholastic Book Services edition, there is a river named that is not near Downsville. What is the current name of the river on which Nero and Uncle Edmund started their journey?
- Now look at the map again. Imagine the route that Nero traveled on his lonely trip back to Wisconsin. What states did he go through? What was the country like? Draw in the route you think he followed.

7. Several types of transportation characteristic of the 1860s are mentioned in *Caddie Woodlawn:* canoes, horses, steamships, horsedrawn wagons, and rafts. Provide reference pictures and books describing these forms of transportation. Ask children to construct a mobile illustrating these early means of travel. (pp. 297–300)

Informational Books

Historical fiction helps children to feel history—the jolt of a buckboard as Pa hurries home from town, the agony of a thousand-mile trek through the wilderness to reach a missionary station, the joy of receiving a corn husk doll as a thank-you gesture from a runaway slave. There is room in every child's mind to soak up and consider the plights of those who hold a prominent place in the sweep of human history.

Like historical novels, informational books help bring a historical perspective to the lives of our young learners. New wonders await students in informational books—the secrets of the first voyage of Columbus, the tombs of mummies, and the construction of castles. Such books hold a wealth of historical information.

Children exhibit a natural curiosity about the past. They develop a heartfelt attachment to books that answer their many questions about what has gone on in this world before they were born. Whether in the form of lavishly illustrated picture books for younger learners, such as the "Magic School Bus" stories by Joanna Cole and Bruce Degen (Scholastic), or the high-quality illustrated essays for older students, informational books function as a major content resource for the history program. Elementary school social studies texts, the traditional source of content, are frequently oversimplified in an attempt to keep them readable. However, a rich collection of informational books can provide the depth not possible in a textbook treatment of the same topic.

Although some elementary school children are capable of searching for and selecting good informational books, most cannot. For this reason, you should display informational books in the classroom and make them available for browsing or in-depth reference study. This requires a significant time investment on your part; however, you can simplify the process by requesting the assistance of librarians who can readily direct you to specialized resources.

Storytelling

Fine literature is the lifeblood of a quality social studies program, carrying the content for many legitimate learning experiences. There are so many books for young learners, however, that we often allow little time for telling stories. Yet, children love to hear stories; the mode of storytelling creates an intimate bond between teller and audience.

From earliest history, storytelling has been considered an art. Many teachers are afraid to try it. However, teachers who truly delight in working with children, enjoy stories, and are thoroughly familiar with the theme or plot, will find that effective storytelling techniques come quite naturally. No amount of study of actual storytelling techniques will substitute for the desire, confidence, and practice that emerges from a sincere drive to breathe life into social studies instruction.

Teacher Stories.   A good storyteller is not an actor, but the avenue of communication through which a story is told. The teacher as storyteller projects mental images to the listeners through spoken words and gestures, reacting and responding to audience needs. Through captivating stories based on real events, teachers help children reach beyond the boundaries of immediate time and into the world of the past. Believing that elementary school teachers are natural storytellers, Schreifels (1983) brought life to history by telling stories within the context of mini-simulations. She describes her approach thus:

The day I discovered my fifth grade class had no idea who Vasco da Gama was—and cared less to find out—was the day I vowed to come up with some way to provoke interest in historical personalities. If da Gama and the rest of the early explorers were to become more than hard words to be stumbled over in a textbook, I realized, something drastic—and dramatic—had to be done.

The next morning during social studies class, I slipped into the hall, plunked an old beehive hat on my head, swept a wraparound skirt over my shoulders and reappeared as an unreasonable facsimile of Vasco da Gama, fifteenth century sea captain. I introduced myself with my best Portuguese accent and invited questions.

At first there were merely giggles, until I threatened to make every student walk the plank unless I got some proper, respectful questions. The first was about how I got there (via a time machine that just happened to look like a filing cabinet). Eventually someone wanted to know just who I was.

"I'm Vasco da Gama, and I'm very famous."

"For what?" they all demanded.

I then proceeded to regale them with stories of my sailing prowess. Ever since that time, I've found I need only lean on the filing cabinet to get everyone's undivided attention. "Is the time machine going to bring us another mysterious person?" students plead. Quite often the answer is yes. And although these time machine visitors may have fuzzy historical memories, they serve to stimulate real interest in people of the past. (p. 84)

As Schreifels advises, you need not "go overboard" to involve students personally and motivate them to learn. Some of the most effective techniques require very little extra teacher preparation time to organize.

Oral History. Bringing in someone to tell stories of personal experiences related to particular places or times is an idea with exciting possibilities for any classroom. Known as *oral history*, these stories need not be major projects; all that is needed is an individual to spin tales of times gone by. Take the time Mrs. Frazer, 97 years old, visited my classroom and fascinated my children with firsthand accounts of turn-of-the-century life. "When we got automobiles around here, you couldn't use them in the winter," Mrs. Frazer said. "My father had one of the first cars in town. It was one of those open cars with leather seats and brass lamps. I'll never forget one Sunday; we had eleven flat tires!"

Mrs. Frazer had the children's undivided attention when she told what a dollar would buy in 1939: one dozen eggs, a loaf of bread, a pound of butter, and a half-pound of bacon. She also told the children about a whistle-stop campaign during which Teddy Roosevelt visited town in 1912 ("I can see him to this day") and the transfer of the Liberty Bell on a flatbed car from Philadelphia to San Francisco for safekeeping during World War I. You should use such valuable sources of historical information both for the children's enjoyment and as a source for researching and recording details from the past. These experiences give students a clearer understanding of and appreciation for people and events of the past.

Community Resources

The local environment offers special opportunities for participation in historical study. Every community, regardless of size or population profile, has something to offer your history program. Whether a child brings to school a brooch worn by her grandmother, a parent visits to model a Civil War uniform, or the class visits a local mansion to inspect examples of turn-of-the-century architecture, you are making use of community resources.

Regardless of which of virtually hundreds of possibilities you choose, community resources can be classified into two major types: *resource persons,* who bring history to the classroom, and *field trips,* which take the students to the community for the purpose of historical study.

Resource Persons.   Resource persons are individuals within or outside the school who bring certain expertise, experience, skill, or knowledge to the classroom. Generally, children enjoy contact with outside visitors and the interesting materials they have to share. Regardless of whether you choose a parent or the school custodian as a resource person, the key to success lies in the way you use the individual; merely having someone come into school to talk with your students will not guarantee a successful experience. Activity 10–2 provides two examples of resource person utilization to illustrate the benefits of careful planning.

Activity 10–2

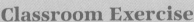

Classroom Exercise

Creatively Using Resource Persons

Mr. Perry understood that his third graders' perceptions of chronology were inexact and that historical concepts develop slowly. To help his class refine these skills and see themselves and their present place in time as a part of a larger picture, Mr. Perry read Bonnie Pryor's book, *The House on Maple Street* (Morrow). In the story, the past is linked to the present as lost objects from early times are unearthed in a contemporary child's yard.

A spirited discussion of dramatic changes in the American family through the course of history followed. Students talked about several eras, but became particularly focused on how hard it must have been for people to grow up without television to watch. "What was their primary source of family entertainment back then?" asked these youth living in the cable television–VCR era. Seizing the moment, Mr. Perry suggested inviting his grandfather to school to talk about what it was like for him. Mr. Perry's grandfather was an antique radio buff with an extensive collection of radio tapes from the 1930s and 1940s (the "Golden Age" of radio). Jointly, Mr. Perry and the students developed a set of questions to ask about radio programs and the reasons they were popular.

Mr. Perry's grandfather not only visited class, but he staged an Old-Fashioned Radio Night. Using a replica of an old console-style radio, he recreated an atmosphere of family and friends gathered around the radio. He played excerpts from sports and news events, the "Hit Parade," and even a popular comedy show of the era, "The Jack Benny Program." He dressed in the style of the 1930s and 1940s, and enlivened his stories with small "Baby Ruth" candies, a popular snack of the time.

The children watched, listened, commented, and asked questions as they became immersed in radio's days of glory. After his grandfather left the room, Mr. Perry gathered the children together and invited them to share their thoughts. Sensing their interest was still high, Mr. Perry asked the students to bring in family photos from the 1930s and 1940s, looking especially for pictures showing the family radio. The photos were examined for clothing and hair styles, furniture, and other characteristics.

In contrast, Mrs. Orlando, fifth-grade teacher, assumed quite a different posture in having a resource person visit her classroom. To deepen her students' study of colonial America, Mrs. Orlando invited a local history buff who was particularly skilled at weaving at a loom.

When the weaver arrived, Mrs. Orlando called for the children's attention.

"Quickly and quietly, children, put away your math work and clear your desks. Show Mr. Quinlan what good boys and girls you are."

Promptly and efficiently, the children put away their materials, folded their hands on the tops of their desks, and directed their attention to the front of the room.

"Weren't they just terrific?" commented Mrs. Orlando, as if attempting to convince her friend of her superlative classroom control. The children, who had not been prepared beforehand, listened to a lengthy introduction of the visitor without completely understanding why he was there. When the resource person eventually got a chance to speak, he explained his craft in such minute detail that even the most mature child's attention wandered. Nervous glances from Mrs. Orlando informed fidgety children of her displeasure over their actions. At the end of the long presentation, Mrs. Orlando eagerly thanked the speaker for visiting and warned the children of the danger of going too close to his weaving loom for fear of damaging it.

"Stay in your seats, children," she admonished. "Work on your math papers until our speaker packs up his materials. First, we'll all show how much we enjoyed his visit. Everyone clap now." Dutifully, the children followed Mrs. Orlando's instructions.

Compare Mr. Perry's and Mrs. Orlando's techniques. What were the strengths in Mr. Perry's approach? What were the flaws in Mrs. Orlando's technique?

Field Trips.   The world outside the classroom is rich in potential learning experiences, too. By organizing trips into the community, students experience firsthand learning impossible to provide in the classroom. As with resource persons, however, the quality of the field trip is directly related to the quality of your planning. A poorly planned field trip is worse than no field trip at all. (See Chapter 14 for more information about planning field trips.)

The list of places to visit can range from A to Z—from antique shops to the zoo. Regardless, the challenge is to effectively use wherever you choose to go. One enterprising teacher, for example, took a trip to a local cemetery as a place for historical study. The teacher, Edward Stranix (1978), writes that the project, described in Activity 10–3, developed when a group of middle school students took a walk through their community with the intent of noticing and listing as many interesting places as they could.

The world outside the classroom is a stimulating place for active learning. Explore your community for these "hidden" resources and you, too, may discover fascinating outdoor classrooms.

Activity 10–3

Case Study

Making Local History Intriguing

Mr. Stranix's students found a local cemetery to be particularly historically fascinating, and decided to study what went on within its boundaries. Mr. Stranix listened to the children's questions and comments as they examined the gravestones: "What is an epitaph? How are headstones decorated? What is the average age of death for men and women? Why did so many young children die? Look at the names; they're sure different!" In this context, the students became involved in the first step of historical investigation: *identifying interesting problems.* When the class returned to school, Mr. Stranix encouraged further discussion and recorded the children's interests on the chalkboard as each contributed.

The next stage of historical investigation (data collection) began with hundreds of gravestone rubbings the children made by placing large sheets of newsprint against the gravestones and rubbing crayons over the paper. Everything on the gravestone (names, dates, epitaphs) transferred to the paper and provided excellent research material for the classroom. Mr. Stranix grouped the children according to their interests and used the rubbings, along with a selection of library materials, for a variety of activities, giving students the following instructions:

- Record the ages at death for any twenty men and twenty women. Determine the average for each group. Which group lived longer? Look through the material on this table (books and magazine articles) and find as many reasons as you can.

- Record the average age at death for any ten men who died during each of the following periods: 1800–1849, 1850–1899, 1900–1949, 1950–present. During which period did they live longest? Think of some reasons why this happened. Check the resources at this table to see if you were right.

- Look at the gravestones for epitaphs. Record the longest, shortest, funniest, most interesting, most religious, and so on.

- Examine the form of writing on the gravestones. Do any of the words or letters seem peculiar to you? List the ones that do.

- Suppose you were appointed to design a gravestone for the president of the United States (or other popular figure). Draw a picture of the gravestone and display it on the large bulletin board.

- How are the gravestones of the past like ours? How are they different? What changes can you predict for gravestones in the future? Use the large boxes to design a possible gravemarker of the future.

- Make a list of the most popular names on the gravestones. Are they popular today? What nationalities seemed most prevalent at the time? Why?

The groups then gathered and analyzed their data, formed conclusions, and shared their findings.

Family History

Studying family histories in school has become a popular trend in historical research. This can be a beneficial strategy, but its value depends on well-developed skills of historical research. Thavenet (1981) offers a comprehensive list of suggestions designed to transform family research into stimulating historical study.

Begin by showing the students a sample portfolio containing the kind of historical evidence found in most homes—photographs, certificates, yearbooks, diaries, report cards, letters, military records, newspaper clippings, and scrapbooks—and asking them to reconstruct as much of a family biography as they can from these materials. Have students identify the kinds of materials they used for this project, suggest others that may have been helpful, and develop a list of possible sources they might find in their own homes.

Going on a field trip to examine grave markers is an excellent way to engage children in gathering firsthand historical data.

Second, encourage students to visit, write, or telephone family members who may provide additional information. Students need instruction on interview techniques, and it would be useful to brainstorm a list of questions that can be asked during the interview. Thavenet (1981) recommends the sample questions shown in Figure 10–2 as a helpful guide.

Genealogical data are easiest to handle in chart form. You may choose from many different types of charts; one currently preferred is the "family tree" chart. The chart represents one's family heritage, and you can note on it important dates and places (see Figure 10-3).

The family tree is one effective method of helping students collect and organize family historical data. Haas and Wylie (1986) have designed another, a "Family History Coat of Arms." To start, distribute a blank coat of arms to the students (see Figure 10-4). Have the students take the form home along with this set of questions to be asked of parents and grandparents:

FIGURE 10–2
Interview Guide

Personal Data

When and where you born?
Were you ever told about any special circumstances of your birth?
What have been the most memorable events of your life?
Where did you fit in your family? Were you the oldest? Did it make a difference?

Growing Up

Where did you grow up? Have you moved often? For what reasons?
Did you have any brothers and sisters?
Can you describe your home and home life as a child?
What jobs did each member of your family perform?
How could you tell when you were considered grown up?

Education

Where did you go to school?
What did you study?
How important was education in your family?
What were your teachers like?

Parents

How did your parents meet?
Had they grown up together?
What education and occupations did they have?
Have they told you how their lives differed from your own?
What particular jobs did your father do in the family? Your mother?

Achievements

Did your family have any particular goals? An "American Dream"?
Did you share their goals?
How did you try to achieve your goals?
Which of your goals are you still working on?

Family Members and Kin

Do you remember any family members who died before the children were born?
What do you remember about any of your family history prior to the family's coming to the United States?
Are there any family traits or heirlooms that have been in your family for a long time?

Source: D. J. Thavenet (1981). Family history: Coming face-to-face with the past. *How to do it series,* no. 15. Washington, DC: National Council for the Social Studies, 2. Reprinted by permission.

FIGURE 10-3
Ethinic Family Tree

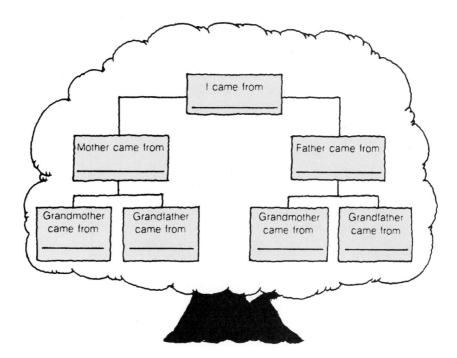

1. What is the name and age of the person in your family who lived the longest?
2. What occupation was practiced by at least three members of your family?
3. What physical trait is common among members of your family?
4. What is the national origin of your family?
5. In what wars have members of your family fought?
6. What is either the oldest or most important of your family's possessions?
7. What is the meaning of your family's name? If your family changed its name, what was the name before the change? What is a common first name among your family members?
8. Who is someone that everyone in your family (or almost everyone) admires and respects?
9. What tragedy or crisis did your family face?
10. What are some words of advice or sayings passed on from generation to generation in your family?

Encourage students to draw symbols and use words to fill in the coat of arms, making it interesting and attractive. After they finish, hold a brief discussion session with the whole class so they can share their reactions to the activity. Then divide the class into groups of four to six students and ask each group to answer the following questions:

FIGURE 10–4
Coat of Arms

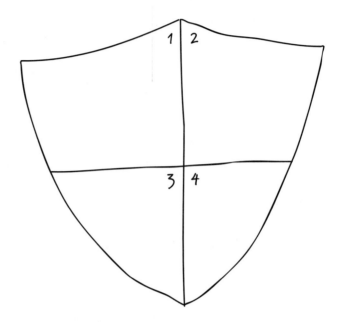

- What two questions received the largest number of similar answers?
- What two questions received the greatest variety of answers?
- Why do you think those questions received so many similar or so many different answers?
- What was the most surprising answer found by your group?

   In a follow-up discussion with the whole class, list the answers on the chalkboard and compare the group lists by citing similarities and differences. Then ask whether the answers might be similar for other students in the school, in other schools throughout the district, or in other regions of the nation. Their ideas could be checked by comparing classes, reading biographies, or examining the text.

   I must add here an important caveat. Although nine out of ten children will approach the study of family history enthusiastically, some will not want to research the past because of special family circumstances they do not wish to address or reveal. If students raise questions about how much they should reveal from their research, reassure them that they need not share anything they do not want others to know.

   Family trees and coats of arms are a start to historical data collection, but students have not yet completed their historical study without interpreting the data, elaborating on the facts to turn them into a story. Students will need to *explain* events, *analyze* causes and effects, and *generalize* about patterns they uncover. Without the *story*, all history is a sterile collection of facts.

As the students become involved in their own historical research, they begin to realize the difficulties faced by professional historians who attempt to put together the story of humanity's past. When this happens, students may become motivated to study areas of history other than family history by examining direct sources of evidence.

Documents, Witnesses, and Physical Remains

Students must learn that historians are much like detectives, searching for and interpreting pieces of evidence that offer clues to perplexing mysteries. But, since neither detectives nor historians were present at the original event, they must rely on a combination of material evidence (heirlooms, recipes, wills, cemetery records, etc.) and witnesses to piece together a riddle.

Documents.   Examining original evidence from the past helps students form a personal attachment to history. How can you use such evidence in your classroom? What questions would a historian ask about the evidence? Using a scientific approach, encourage students to analyze, ask questions, and interpret information based on individual frames of reference. Consider this example of an advertisement for a runaway apprentice from the early 1800s:

RUN AWAY

on the 1ft of March inftant,
an INDENTURED SERVANT
boy to the
Boot and Shoemaking Bufiness,

named MARBLE LAPLANT:

he is between 16 and 17 years of age,
dark complexion
has a fcar on his right cheek,
and is a REMARKABLY UGLY LOOKING FELLOW.

Among the advertisements in old newspapers, you will often find in such reward notices interesting clues to nineteenth century life. Young boys were commonly hired out to artisans to learn a craft. They were housed and fed at the craftperson's expense in return for training, working for free during their apprenticeship. Such advertisements usually include such clues as the clothing the runaway wore and comments on his appearance and temperament. With their "striped row trousers," "gingham roundabouts," "brown flannel jackets," "old straw hats," or "dark fustian pantaloons," these "remarkably ugly fellows" may have "lost two of their fore teeth" or "had three fingers cut off at the first joint on the right hand." These descriptions provide remarkable portraits of working-class people of 150 years ago; when children read original accounts of their escapades, they emerge as real individuals rather than as statistics or textbook portrayals. In this case, help your students analyze the evidence by asking questions:

- Why did the apprentices run away?
- What hardships did they face?
- Why did boys want to be apprentices?
- Why were apprentices mostly boys?
- How valuable was an apprentice to his master?

A sample front page from a newspaper such as Benjamin Franklin's *Pennsylvania Gazette* would give students insight into life in our country over 200 years ago. Published in Philadelphia, our country's biggest city in 1787, an average front page would contain items similar to the following:

FOR SALE

A large and general affortment of
SCYTHES and SICKLES.

Made by the fufcriber at his
SCYTHE AND SICKLE MANUFACTORY

in Market ftreet,
between Fourth and Fifth ftreet,
next door to the fign of the Black Horfe.

THOMAS GOUCHER.

Students could understand several different concepts as a result of examining this evidence:

- The front pages at that time were mostly ads.
- The letters "f" and "s" looked alike.

- Advertisers referred to themselves as "subscribers."

- There were no building numbers. People were guided by signs that had pictures, not words. Many people could not read.

As a follow-up to examining the sample newspaper, you could have students research other occupations that might be advertised in the *Pennsylvania Gazette* during Franklin's time—blacksmiths, milliners, tinsmiths, gunsmiths, wig makers, sail makers, shipbuilders, bootmakers, weavers, and so on. Then the students could publish their own front page, trying to duplicate the language and other conventions consistent with the early history of our country.

Witnesses.   Encourage your students to critically examine the testimony of witnesses in addition to investigating direct evidence. These can be either *primary* witnesses (those who were part of an event) or *secondary* witnesses (people who got information secondhand). A spacecraft launch illustrates these sources of historical data. Thousands, perhaps millions, of people watch the launch on television and become secondary witnesses to the event, while newspapers carry accounts of the event and give us accurate written records for future reference. Who might be the event's primary witnesses?

Children should understand that when examining secondary accounts, historians must carefully check the information. But even after they check their information for accuracy, problems remain, such as witnesses who offer conflicting testimony of a crime in court. Even the most well-meaning primary witnesses *interpret* what they see differently. This is part of the problem with history; people who examine the facts cannot interpret them in a vacuum. The life situation of the historian influences what the facts mean to her. For that reason, you must teach students to read historical accounts critically. Consider the following accounts of the Russian Revolution, one written for young children by a Russian author and the other by an American (King, 1970, p. 262):

The Soviet Story

During 1917, a revolution took place in Russia. The working people overthrew the *czar* (zär), a Russian king. The czar and his family were killed. Everyone longed for freedom. They had never had it under the czar.

Under the slogan, "All power to the Soviets," a new government was formed. It was a dictatorship of the people. At last the people had their own government. All land was owned by the government. Since the government was the people, the people owned all the land.

The government also took over the banks, factories, mines, and stores. The people then owned everything.

The Communist (käm-y -nəst) party was the wise leader of the working people. It led the people along the right path. It led them to liberty and a classless life. The Revolution was a people's revolution. It threw out those who would make slaves of the workers. It established the dictatorship of the people.

The Revolution brought a new life to all mankind. It brought them the victory of communism.

The American Story

In 1917 the Russians revolted against their czar. The Communists cruelly killed the czar and his family. The Russians hoped to win freedom.

Most of them hoped that the Russian Revolution would make their lives better. The Russian peasants hoped to divide the land among themselves. The workers wanted better wages. They wanted their living conditions improved.

After the bloody Revolution, a new government was set up. It was a government controlled by Communists. It took over all the property owned by the people. The property became the property of the government. It took over factories, banks, and stores.

The people did not get what they wanted. They did not control the government. The government was controlled by the Communist party. No one could disagree with the party. Those who tried to disagree were put in jail or killed.

The Revolution made the Soviet people slaves of their government. It took away their religion. It took away their property. It took away their freedom.

Do you notice the similarities and differences in these accounts? For one, they report the same facts: (1) the Russian Revolution took place in 1917; (2) the czar and his family were killed; (3) the government owned everything after the Revolution; (4) the government was led by the Communist party. But the Russian historian and the American historian disagree about what the facts mean. Who was right? Both writers are convinced they are right, and it is here, when writers try to explain what facts mean, that the historian has trouble.

When children begin to understand the concept that a historian *interprets* facts, it is fun to place them into creative writing situations. Here is what one student wrote when the teacher said: "Just suppose that a Native American wrote the accepted account of the sale of Manhattan. What would it say?"

Indians Give Us Maxi-Ha-Ha

A bunch of natives from Brooklyn paddled over to Manhattan in 1626 to eyeball the strange white guys who had landed and camped there. The Brooklyn Bridge wasn't built yet, but the natives of the land knew they had a bunch of yokels on the hook as soon as the settlers brought up the subject of buying an island no one was living on anyway.

Besides Manhatte's (that's what it was called back then) lousy reputation as a hunting land, the natives didn't have the white man's concept of land ownership— they figured the land was given by God to anyone who wanted to use it. So, when Peter Minuit kept heaping trinkets before them, the Canarsee Indians (the natives of Brooklyn) just stood straight-faced until they got enough loot to fill their canoes— about sixty guilders' (twenty-four dollars) worth of beads, needles, fabric, buttons, and fishhooks.

Then America's first fly-by-night real estate brokers paddled away hurriedly—probably to tell their friends about the easy "marks" the new neighbors were. It was later that Minuit realized he was swindled. Manhattan actually belonged to the Weckquaesgeeks who finally were paid for Manhattan, too. But, as businesspersons, the Canarsees had a way to go to catch the Raritan Indians. They sold Staten Island six times!

Notice that the creative experience was more than a "fanciful" activity. The student drew on creative talent to produce something original, but still based the product on actual knowledge gained in the classroom. Through the use of historical research, teachers establish a basis of involvement that makes all inquiry an exciting learning process.

Physical Remains. Physical remains include artifacts, relics, and other accidental survivors of the past. By examining these sources, the historian is able to partially reconstruct the story of human life. I use the term *accidental survivors* because few historical artifacts or relics were planned to be preserved to describe a way of life to people in the future. Take a coin, for example. What do you think historians can learn from a coin? Suppose a recently unearthed coin has a figure of a person on one side and a series of fish on the other, along with some words that can not be read. What can we tell about the people who used the coin? Think about that question for a moment, and then compare your ideas to the following:

1. The people were advanced enough to use a monetary system.

2. They were advanced enough to use metal.

3. Their clothing and hairstyles can tell us something about their lifestyle.

4. The fish indicate something about the economy.

5. A stamped date puts the people in a specific time frame.

Artifacts, or handcrafted/manufactured items, are one of the two kinds of physical remains historians use to study the past. They also study written and oral sources—letters, diaries, songs, speeches, myths, and legends. By inspecting letters from the past, for example, we have learned that one of the most famous opponents of the bald eagle as our national symbol was Benjamin Franklin, who believed that the turkey would have been far more representative of the newly formed United States. Franklin was in France when Congress chose the national symbol in 1782. He wrote a letter complaining of the decision. Of the eagle, Franklin wrote, "He is a bird of bad moral character; he does not get his living honestly; you may have seen him perched on some dead tree near the river, where, too lazy to fish for himself, he watches the labour of the fishing-hawk; and when that diligent bird has at length taken a fish and is bearing it to his nest for the support of his mate and young ones, the bald eagle pursues him and takes it from him. Besides, he is a rank coward; the little kingbird, not bigger than a sparrow, attacks him boldly and drives him out of the district."

Franklin continued, "The turkey is in comparison a much more respectable bird, and withal a true original native of America. . . . He is . . . a bird of courage, and would not hesitate to attack a grenadier of the British Guards who would presume to invade his farmyard with a red coat on."

All of us have heard stories of Franklin's displeasure at recognizing the bald eagle as our national symbol, but few have ever read his words of expression. Think about how much actual written accounts, or replicas, would enliven the pursuit of knowledge in the social studies.

Part of studying history is functioning as a historian. Students must examine oral and written records as well as artifacts or relics for evidence to explain the past. Regardless of the source, however, they must establish the information's validity and authenticity. Much as detectives prepare a criminal case for court, historians must carefully gather information from more than one source and decide what is truthful. The historian's final responsibility is to write about the information without showing personal bias. This is perhaps the ultimate challenge, because historians see various meanings in the facts they uncover. In summary, the historian's role is to search carefully for facts, use a variety of sources for evidence, judge the evidence for accuracy, and write about the facts without showing personal bias.

You will want to teach history in a way that allows children to investigate as historians. Provide situations where they can examine historical materials firsthand. Bring artifacts to the classroom, invite guest speakers to demonstrate items from the past, visit museums and historical sites to examine original written materials, and compare written accounts of historical events to detect personal biases. Encourage children to make their own hypotheses about what they observe and give them opportunities to test their guesses. They should use the historian's methods of investigation to study a variety of local, regional, state, national, or international topics.

Timelines.   You may use a variety of activities to help children disclose and interpret the historical concepts developed through any topic of study. We have discussed many of them throughout this book—murals, illustrations, displays, dioramas, classroom museums, story retelling strategies, crafts and construction, journals, diaries, story construction, cooking experiences, and so on. These experiences, when carefully planned, are generally successful in the elementary school classroom and are universal in application. You can use all of these activities to deal with a topic in geography as easily as in history. In addition, some activities involve tools specific to the subject. As maps offer a specialized tool for geography, timelines offer the historian a distinctive tool to organize history. They help children develop a concept of chronology, or sense of historical time.

FIGURE 10–5
Sequence Skills

Timelines are graphic representations of a succession of historical events, constructed by dividing a unit of time into proportional segments. As children study the past, timelines help them put events into perspective by seeing a picture of when important things happened. Very often, young children experience difficulty understanding time beyond yesterday, today, and tomorrow. We often compound this difficulty by talking about Christopher Columbus on Columbus Day, George Washington and Abraham Lincoln in February, and Dr. Martin Luther King, Jr., in January. As far as young children are concerned, all of these people could have been alive at the same time or recently deceased. We need to help children gain a proper historical perspective. Placing events in a historical framework can help accomplish this goal.

For the very youngest children, construct timelines on topics of immediate experience. Illustrate routines of the daily schedule. Extend sequencing of major events over a period of time by cutting out a symbol for each major holiday. The children can use clothespins to clip the symbols in sequence (see Figure 10–5). The children must decide which symbol comes first, second, and so on as they place the cards in proper sequence.

Gradually apply the same strategy to specific topics under study. For example, to introduce the general topic of U.S. history, put up a large section of butcher paper (one yard by four yards) and mark off sections to represent centuries. Tell children that you will be creating a timeline of U.S. history (see Figure 10–6). For most elementary school purposes, the history of the United States begins at 1492, so you can have one segment for each century beginning in the 1400s. As you read about people such as Columbus, Washington, Lincoln, or King, place symbols on the appropriate centuries to help the children see when these people lived.

Use timelines the same way you use other semiabstract or abstract learning aids—initial experiences should be as concrete as possible. A wise way to begin the study of chronology is to start with the children's own lines. You can prepare large cards (and add appropriate photos, if possible) with the labels "Birth," "Learn to Walk," "Go to School," "Enter Grade _____," and "Graduate from

FIGURE 10–6
Beginning Timeline

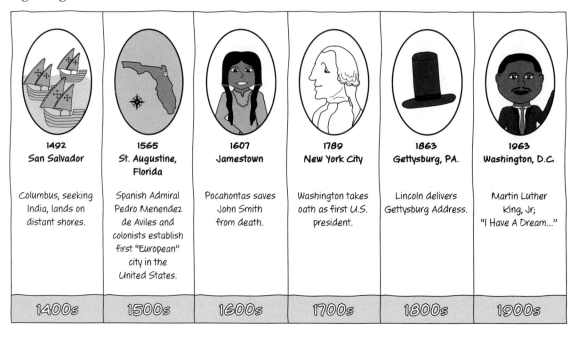

1492 San Salvador	1565 St. Augustine, Florida	1607 Jamestown	1789 New York City	1863 Gettysburg, PA.	1963 Washington, D.C.
Columbus, seeking India, lands on distant shores.	Spanish Admiral Pedro Menendez de Aviles and colonists establish first "European" city in the United States.	Pocahontas saves John Smith from death.	Washington takes oath as first U.S. president.	Lincoln delivers Gettysburg Address.	Martin Luther King, Jr; "I Have A Dream..."
1400s	1500s	1600s	1700s	1800s	1900s

High School." Take the children to the playground and assign one card to each child. The child holding the "Birth" card is the starting point for the timeline. The children can next suggest the age at which they began to walk. Have the child holding the "Learn to Walk" card pace from the "Birth" point the number of steps as years from birth to walking. Use the same process for each of the other cards. Discuss the relationships between the distances. In the same way, you may wish to develop time concepts related to other key events, such as important inventions, famous explorers, changes in transportation, notable events in the community, and the like.

This procedure can also be used to show the sequential development of historical events. The children can first be presented with a random number of cards listing events of history. They can go to the playground, organize the cards in sequence, and walk off one step for each year between events. This practice is especially appropriate in the upper grades, since history facts are difficult for most primary children to understand. You would use a similar procedure when transferring this practice into the classroom, but the children will soon realize that if they take one step for each year between events, they will soon run out of room and not be able to complete their task. You can then direct them toward discovering that a smaller unit of measure will be needed, perhaps one inch to represent a year.

FIGURE 10–7
Group Work on Timeline

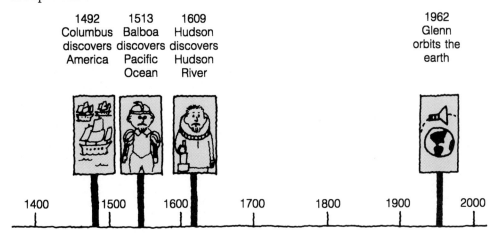

1492	1513	1609		1962
Columbus	Balboa	Hudson		Glenn
discovers	discovers	discovers		orbits the
America	Pacific	Hudson		earth
	Ocean	River		

1400   1500   1600   1700   1800   1900   2000

When working on smaller scale timelines in the classroom, emphasize exactness and consistency. An inexact or inconsistent scale distorts time relationships and hinders true conceptualizations of chronology.

For timelines such as the one in Figure 10–7, give groups of children a set of cards identifying events from a current topic of study. Ask the children to look up information about their assigned event and draw an illustration about it. From there you can direct the children to find the date for each event and place their illustrations in chronological order on the timeline. Following this, have each group share pertinent information about the different events with the rest of the class. By completing this project, your class will have constructed a master guide of the major events under study and will have begun to develop a historical perspective of particular events.

AFTERWORD

History has long been a valued part of schooling in America; it continues to exert a strong influence on social studies programming and practices. Many have praised its value over the years, but none more eloquently than Winston Churchill, who once said, "The further backward you look, the further forward you are likely to see." Such statements underscore the importance of furthering historical consciousness in our schools. In a society steeped in triumphs and tragedies, knowledge of our past helps us to develop pride in our successes and discontent with our errors. We cannot, however, expect children to become interested in the study of history when all we ask them to do is memorize facts from a textbook. Surely, facts about people and events are an important part of history, but we must also be aware of the processes of history. Children must be given regular opportunities to *explore* history rather than simply be *exposed* to it. We must lead students to perceive the nature of history itself by helping them understand the concept of historical time, investigate their personal and family histories, and examine other sources of historical data. Such techniques of personal involvement will help students acquire a more balanced sense of history—it is not only something one *knows* but also something one *does.*

TECHNOLOGY SAMPLER

Useful sources for related social studies topics include these Internet sites:

First Thanksgiving/Plymouth Plantation
http://media3.com/plymouth/thanksgiving.html

Historic Documents
http://www.ukans.edu/carrie/docs/docs_us.html

The HistoryNet
http://www.TheHistoryNet.com/

Teaching With Historic Places
http://www.cr.nps.gov/nr/twhp

U.S. Historical Documents
http://www.law.uoknor.edu.ushist.html

Virtual Tour of Historic Philadelphia
http://www.libertynet.org/iha/index.html

Useful sources for related social studies topics include these software titles:

American Girls Premiere
The Learning Company

Based on a collection of dolls and histroical-fiction books of the same name (from Colonial times to post-World War II America). Children write, produce, and direct plays starring any of the collection's five characters.

American Heritage: The History of the United States for Young People
Byron Preiss Multimedia

A resource for older children (9–12 years). Full of engaging stories and substantial information, presented with winsome multimedia support.

Eyewitness History of the World
DK Multimedia

Children 8 years old and up board a virtual time machine in 500 B.C. and travel to the present, stopping along the way to experience important events in world history.

Go West
Edunetics, Ltd.

An imaginative simulation that takes students to 1880s Kansas as homesteaders. They make decisions related to everyday struggles.

The New Oregon Trail
Minnesota Educational Computer Consortium

Children face decisions that confronted pioneers in 1847 as they set out in wagon trains to find new homes in the Oregon Territory.

Putt-Putt Travels Through Time
Humongous Entertainment

Putt-Putt and his dog Pep take younger children (3–8 years) on an exciting blast to the past.

Skytrip America
Discovery Channel

Children board a flying time machine to meet numerous historical personalities, from Lief Ericsson to Bill Clinton. Real-life sports and entertainment figures are added for a "curtural perspective."

WHAT I *NOW* KNOW

Complete these self-check items once more. Determine for yourself whether it would be useful to take a more in-depth look at any area. Use the same key as you did for the preassessment form ("+", "?", "–").

I can *now*

_____ define the term *history*.

_____ compare and contrast *old history* with *new history*.

_____ explain the role of content in a modern history curriculum.

_____ describe the National Standards for History.

_____ plan history lessons using quality literature and storytelling sources.

_____ describe how community resources contribute to historical study.

_____ justify the role of family history in the social studies program.

_____ understand how documents, witnesses, and physical remains offer clues to historical mysteries.

_____ justify a central role for history in the social studies curriculum.

REFERENCES

Cheney, L. V. (1987). *American memory: A report on the humanities in the nation's public schools.* Washington, DC: National Endowment for the Humanities.

Crabtree, C. (1989). History is for children. *American Educator, 13*, 36.

Downey, M. T., & and Levstik, L. S. (1988). Teaching and learning history: The research base. *Social Education, 52*, 336–344.

Gagnon, P. A. (1987). *Democracy's untold story: What world history textbooks neglect.* Washington, DC: American Federation of Teachers.

Haas, M. E., & Wylie, W. (1986). The family history coat of arms. *Social Education, 50*, 25–28.

Hickman, J. (1990). Put the story into history. *Instructor, 100*, 22.

Hirsch, E. D., Jr. (1987). *Cultural literacy: What every American needs to know.* Boston: Houghton Mifflin.

King, F. M. (1970). *Using the social studies 1970.* (By permission of Laidlaw Brothers, a Division of Doubleday & Company, Inc.)

Levstik, L. S. (1989). Once upon a time past—History in the elementary classroom. *Social Studies and the Young Learner, 2*, 3–5.

National Center for History in the Schools. (1996). *National standards for history.* Los Angeles, CA: Author.

Norton, D. E., & Norton, S. (1994). *Language arts activities for children.* New York: Merrill/Macmillan. 1994. Reprinted by permission.

Ravitch, D. (1985). The precarious state of history. *American Educator, 9*, 11–17.

Schneider, D. O. (1989). History, social sciences, and the social studies. *Social Education, 53*, 148–154.

Schreifels, B. (1983). Breathe life into a dead subject. *Learning*, 84.

Stranix, E. (1978). The cemetery: An outdoor classroom. *Teacher, 93*, 66–67.

Thavenet, D. J. (1981). Family history: Coming face-to-face with the past. *How To Do It Series*, no. 15. Washington, DC: National Council for the Social Studies.

CHAPTER 11

WHAT I KNOW

This exercise provides a "scaffold" that will enable you to relate the chapter material to your background knowledge. Complete the form before you read the chapter and use the results to guide your reading. Use a "+" to indicate confidence, a "?" for uncertainty, and a "-" if you feel deficient in any area.

I can

_____ define the concept of *literacy across the curriculum.*

_____ describe the pattern of instruction characterized by the Directed Reading–Thinking Activity (DR–TA).

_____ explain the processes involved with the Mediated Reading Thinking Activity (MRTA).

_____ delineate the benefits and problems associated with textbook use in the social studies program.

_____ support the use of trade books in the social studies curriculum.

_____ identify the major trade book genres adaptable to the social studies curriculum.

_____ defend the use of traditional and contemporary techniques to help children read to learn from various print resources.

Using the results as a guide, what questions will you seek to answer as you read?

Reading as a Meaning-Making Activity

◆ **CLASSROOM SKETCH**

Mr. Dawkins has been reading folk tales to his first graders with the overall goal of helping them understand that a culture's folklore echos its beliefs and customs. Today, he selected the book, *The Mitten: A Ukrainian Folktale* by Jan Brett (Putnam). The story is about a little boy who lost a fancy mitten while in the woods looking for some firewood for his grandmother. The animals found his lost mitten and crawled inside to keep warm. The parade to the inside of the mitten started with a field mouse, who was joined by a frog, owl, rabbit, fox, wolf, wild boar, and bear. To the children's surprise, all were able to get inside the mitten until a tiny cricket joined them. Then the mitten exploded!

To start the reading experience, Mr. Dawkins reached into his story bag (a colorfully decorated cloth bag that holds a surprise associated with each book he reads). He pulled out a beautiful shirt from a Ukrainian folk costume that he had borrowed from a friend. The children were fascinated by the intricate embroidery and ornate stitchery. He showed the children a photograph of a Ukrainian family dressed in traditional attire. Mr. Dawkins explained that this folk costume was from

Ukraine, a large country in Eastern Europe, and together they located Ukraine on a globe.

Mr. Dawkins reached into the bag once more and took out a pair of fancy mittens. He encouraged the children to talk about why people wear mittens and how the mittens feel on a cold winter day. Mr. Dawkins called the children's attention to the illustration on the front cover and asked the children to think about what might go through an animal's mind if it saw a mitten like the one on the cover lying on the ground in the forest. He encouraged several predictions and then read the book.

After the reading, the discussion began. The children did not raise their hands in response to the teacher's questions, but joined in a natural conversation about the book. As they talked, Mr. Dawkins listened and helped make connections. But the children controlled the discussion.

Following the discussion, Mr. Dawkins involved the children in a readers' theater skit. To begin, the children recalled the animals who squeezed into the mitten. Then they suggested the movements each animal would probably use while approaching the mitten—springing like a frog, hopping like a rabbit, flapping one's arms like an owl, and lumbering like a bear. Mr. Dawkins selected volunteers to play each of the animals as the story was reread. He placed an elegant construction paper glove covered with sequins and beads in the middle of the group meeting rug. The players dramatized the story as volunteer readers read each part. The readers used their voices to bring life to the animals they were reading about, while the players entered and left the area around the glove according to the script. The emphasis was not on the quality of the production, but on the interpretive qualities of the children's voices and bodily movements.

◆ CLASSROOM CONNECTION

Mr. Dawkins embraces a philosophy of teaching social studies that is popularly referred to as *literacy across the curriculum*. To understand what this means, we must first understand what is meant by the term *literacy*. According to Tompkins (1997), the term *literacy* was used in the past to refer exclusively to reading, but now has been broadened to encompass the skills and processes associated with both reading and writing. Thaiss (1986) uses that definition of literacy as a base from which to explain the broader concept of literacy across the curriculum:

> "[Literacy] across the curriculum" means basically two things. First, it means that gaining power in all the modes of language . . . must take place in every school course and at every school level, if this growth is to be deep and substantial. This meaning rejects the notion that the diverse uses of language are best learned in specific "skills" courses in, for example, [spelling, grammar, reading, or writing]. Second, "[literacy] across the curriculum" stresses the interrelationship of the modes: One learns to write

as one learns to . . . read. Each ability, therefore, improves to the extent that all are exercised. This second meaning rejects the teaching of, for example, writing or reading in relative isolation from the other. Ultimately, these two meanings of [literacy] across the curriculum come together in a third: the inseparableness of language, thinking, and learning. If we do not apply the full range of our language resources to our learning of any subject, then we stifle thought, conscious and unconscious, and so deprive ourselves of more than the most superficial understanding. (p. 2)

Think back to this chapter's opening sketch. In how many ways did Mr. Dawkins encourage his students to use language? How was the literacy across the curriculum philosophy maintained throughout the lesson? Mr. Dawkins adopted the literacy across the curriculum philosophy after his first few years of classroom teaching. Each year, while constantly reconsidering the curriculum requirements of his first-grade program, he began to raise some captivating "Why" questions: *"Why* is it that when my students read a story about Sojourner Truth at nine-thirty in the morning and I follow that up with a creative writing project, it is called *literacy*? *Why* is it that when we read about Sojourner Truth at two-thirty in the afternoon and I follow that up with a dramatic skit, it is called *social studies*? *Why* do my teaching strategies need to change in each setting?" Mr. Dawkins found answers to these questions when he read what literacy experts had to say about learning in the content areas. In essence, their message was, "Language is a powerful learning tool, and reading and writing are valuable ways to learn in all content areas. Effective teachers encourage students to use reading and writing in meaningful ways in theme studies so that they learn information better and refine their literacy competencies" (Tompkins, 1997, p. 32). Today, Mr. Dawkins operates with a firm belief that literacy should be the heart of a good elementary school social studies program. His beliefs are supported by these three significant beliefs (Thaiss, 1986):

1. Students understand the content better when they use reading and writing strategies to learn.
2. Students' literacy learning is strengthened when they use related skills and strategies in authentic daily experiences (meaningful activities).
3. Students learn most effectively through active involvement, collaborative projects, and interaction with their classmates, the teacher, and their environment.

Although reading and writing are viewed as parallel processes of meaning construction, they will be described separately in this text for ease of discussion. The reading process will be presented in this chapter; the writing process will be explained in Chapter 12.

SOURCES OF READING IN THE SOCIAL STUDIES

Students in elementary school social studies classrooms typically read two major types of books to learn social studies concepts and skills—*textbooks* and *trade books.* Traditional textbook content has been written in a structured, expository manner, but many current editions include interesting stories and poetry. Trade books (books that are not textbooks), on the other hand, have special story structure elements, including character and plot. Recently, there has been a great deal of controversy about whether textbooks or trade books should serve as the base for teaching social studies in the elementary school. Goodman (1988), for example, argues that textbooks are written too unimaginatively for young children; their shortened sentences and controlled vocabulary result in dull, uninteresting reading. Conversely, Lapp, Flood, and Farnan (1992) suggest that textbooks and trade books are compatible and that there is a place for both in a quality social studies program. Tompkins (1997) believes that the use of textbooks is especially important for beginning teachers who "often rely on [textbooks] and move toward incorporating trade books in their [social studies] programs as they gain confidence in their teaching abilities . . . " (p. 203). So, what should teachers of elementary school social studies do—use trade books only, textbooks only, or a combination of both? The point of view of this book is that students need a wide variety of reading materials in their social studies program, including textbooks and selections from quality trade books.

Accompanying the controversy surrounding the issue of whether to center social studies instruction on textbooks or trade books is the issue of how to teach from these resources. The traditional pattern of instruction can be characterized by the *Directed Reading–Thinking Activity* (Stauffer, 1969), a somewhat structured form of guidance offered to students during group readings of textbooks or trade books. The more contemporary view of instruction is exemplified by the *Mediated Reading Thinking Activity,* a strategy that treats reading as a constructive process during which teachers support children as they become active participants in the meaning-making process.

The position taken in this book is that effective social studies instruction calls for a combination of, or balance between, these two approaches. Although many schools are implementing the more contemporary MRTA approach, others remain attached to the traditional DR-TA pattern of instruction. The question is therefore not whether either of these approaches is more beneficial than the other, but whether teachers are best able to improve instruction by utilizing contemporary knowledge to strengthen ongoing, time-honored practices. Toward that goal, the DR–TA will be explained in connection with textbook-based instruction, while the MRTA will be treated in the section on trade books. Do not, however, think of these two instructional strategies as attached to either source of reading; balancing and using ideas from each can be used with either textbooks or trade books. Both employ, in unique ways, the basic essentials of the reading process.

USING SOCIAL STUDIES TEXTBOOKS

Social studies textbooks are graded sets of reading materials traditionally used by teachers as a source of planning and instruction. Normally published as a sequential series from kindergarten through grades six or eight, textbooks are developed by large publishing companies under the direction of a senior author who is usually a

There is a wide array of reading materials appropriate for social studies classrooms, containing informative and thrilling accounts of the human experience.

respected name in social studies education. Most social studies textbook series contain an array of instructional materials, most typically the following:

- *Student's book.* Students normally receive individual copies of their own texts designed to teach social studies concepts, strategies, and skills.
- *Teacher's manual.* The teacher's edition duplicates the student text, augmented with easy-to-use instructional support: key terms, background information, discussion questions, precise lesson format, and ideas for extension and reinforcement.
- *Study guides.* Students may receive their own workbooks that provide reinforcement for each lesson, including practice in key concepts and skills. An accompanying teacher's guide contains exact copies of the student pages along with directions and correct answers.

- *Study prints.* Enlarged color visuals illustrating key instructional concepts (e.g., "A Williamsburg Household") are often available. They usually come with suggested discussion questions or ideas for related projects.

- *Tests.* Mastery tests for every chapter help assess each student's command of major skills or level of comprehension. Test items usually appear in a variety of formats, including short-answer and essay questions.

Benefits of Textbooks

Because most social studies textbook programs offer a convenient instructional package and a carefully researched, systematized body of content, teachers often become strongly attached to them. Such a bond to a textbook-based social studies curriculum is not hard to understand. When elementary school teachers are required to plan developmentally appropriate learning activities in all school subjects, including math, reading, spelling, and science, the thought of having specially "packaged" help in social studies greatly reduces the pressure and anxiety of daily planning. In addition, textbooks offer a common core of knowledge organized sequentially from one grade level to the next. Each teacher from kindergarten through grade eight knows what was done in earlier grades and what will be expected in later grades, thereby minimizing gaps or repetition. Finally, school districts and teachers appreciate the carefully researched, comprehensive nature of the teacher's manuals, which come complete with goals, objectives, lesson plans, suggestions for activities, and tests. The utility of textbook programs is acknowledged by teachers at all levels of experience, but beginning teachers find them especially attractive. Jarolimek and Parker (1993) explain:

> Beginning teachers are usually most comfortable starting with [textbooks]. The teaching environment can be controlled sufficiently well to reduce management concerns to a minimum, the objectives can be made specific, the children's study materials can be preselected by the teacher, and the process can be entirely teacher directed. . . . This initial [textbook experience relies heavily] on the suggestions presented in the teacher's manual that accompanies the book. (pp. 30–31)

Although textbooks take teachers "by the hand" and guide them through the instructional process, teachers must plan and execute specialized instructional strategies that help students complete their reading tasks effectively. Vacca and Vacca (1986) describe the teacher's specialized role as a *process helper*: "When textbooks are the vehicle for learning, the teacher has a significant role to perform. In effect, the teacher is a 'process helper,' bridging the gap that often exists between students and the [textbook material]. . . " (p. 11). As process helpers, teachers provide appropriate experiences that help students develop special reading-to-learn strategies that involve much more than covering the material. The following sections describe the elements of a reading-to-learn process designed to help your students experience success in a textbook-based social studies program: the *Directed Reading–Thinking Activity.*

Directed Reading–Thinking Activity (DR–TA)

In essence, the DR–TA (Stauffer, 1969) is activated by applying specific *pre-reading, reading, postreading,* and *extension activities* to the pertinent reading material.

Prereading

The prereading phase is the first step of the DR–TA; it is subdivided into the following four elements: (1) *vocabulary development*, (2) *concept attachment*, (3) *prediction*, and (4) *purpose.*

Vocabulary Development.   Understanding a textbook reading selection depends a great deal upon whether or not the students are familiar with the words. Students often encounter words in their social studies textbooks that they will rarely, if ever, find in other subject-area books. Examples of specialized social studies vocabulary are *junta, shaman, boycott, cassava, legislature, longitude, archaeologist,* and *tundra*. To understand what they are reading, students must know these words; teachers must carefully direct their attention to particular vocabulary, phrases, and sentences before they read. Comprehending a text heavily laden with specialized vocabulary presents a clear challenge to social studies teachers. Harp and Brewer (1996) elaborate:

> It is impossible to write about content subjects without using specialized vocabularies. Despite authors' attempts to write in simple language, the expository selection must inevitably present the reader with vocabulary challenges. It would be ridiculous, for example, to write a piece about the Constitution and avoid the multisyllabic word Constitution by referring to it as "the big paper" (p. 369).

The paragraph below is an excerpt from a fourth-grade social studies text (Armento, Nash, Salter, & Wixson, 1991). The authors probably could not have made this selection any easier to read, yet the term *imports* is a specialized word students must relate to their own experiences if the passage is to have meaning.

> National borders begin to fade even more when we try to figure out where our belongings come from. Consider your family's car, for example. Even if your car was made in the United States, many of its parts are imports from all over the world. (p. 339)

Textbook writers anticipate such challenges and often provide the reader with *contextual help*—cues that help the reader derive a word's meaning from the way it is used in a sentence. In this case, the sentence immediately following the paragraph above offers a direct explanation: "An **import** is a product that a country brings in from another country to buy" (Armento, Nash, Salter, & Wixson, 1991, p. 339). Sometimes a brief explanation might be given in parentheses; for example, "The *vaquero* (Mexican cowboy) worked on a large ranch." Or, a synonym, clause, or phrase that explains the meaning of a word may be inserted in the sentence: "The vaquero practiced for many hours with his *reata,* or rawhide rope." If such contextual help is unavailable, the teacher's guide will identify key terms and suggest that teachers plan special instruction to clarify the vocabulary so the reading can be understood. Photographs, demonstrations, diagrams, drawings, and other aids help fill in the gaps.

Combs (1996) recommends these options for preteaching vocabulary:

* Preteach only those words that are critical to the understanding of the material.

* Preteach critical words that cannot be understood in the context of the material.

* Preteach words that the children will not be able to independently decode.

Concept Attachment.   The ability to comprehend a social studies textbook passage depends not only on a student's ability to recognize the words, but also on a reader's capacity to associate previous experiences with the ideas presented in the text. That is, students must be able to connect their past experiences to the author's ideas. In social studies, the most appropriate experiences for accomplishing this goal are direct experiences; the most abstract are words and symbols.

Provide Direct Experiences.   Direct experiences not only enhance students' cognitive backgrounds, they also motivate students to read the assignment. Think how much more interested students would be to read about coal mining if a few lumps of coal, a bandanna, and miner's helmet were on exhibit. Dolch (1951) emphasizes the value of providing such direct experiences:

> The average adult tries again and again to tell children with words what things are . . . .
> The child asks, "What is a snake?" The adult says, "An animal that crawls along the ground." The child imagines such an animal and asks, "But his legs will be in the way." The adult says, "Oh, he hasn't any legs." So the child takes off the legs and sees a legless body lying there. "But how does he crawl around without legs?" "He wiggles," says the adult. The child tries to make the legless body wiggle. "How does that get him to go forward?" The adult loses his temper. The peculiar way in which part of the snake pushes the other part cannot be described. It has to be seen. "Let us go to the zoo." (p. 309)

Look back to Figure 5–5. It is a helpful design for thinking about the kinds of experiences we offer students in the social studies program. A general rule of thumb is that the closer a teacher stays near the base of the figure, the more concrete and meaningful the experiences will be.

Jackdaws, collections of objects related to special topics or themes, are often created by social studies teachers to motivate children to read. The term *jackdaw* comes from the British name for a blackbird that deviously picks up brightly colored objects and carries them off to its nest. In speaking about jackdaws related to material to be read, Dowd (1990) advises the following:

Creating a jackdaw for a particular historical period authenticates the experience for children and helps them visualize and synthesize knowledge. . . . Jackdaws can help young children learn abstract historical concepts contained in the increasing numbers of historical and biographical . . . books being published. . . . Preservice teachers who need jackdaws in their classroom . . . report that these artifacts increased students' interest, enhanced their understanding . . . , and made classroom discussions more meaningful and interesting. (p. 228)

One teacher compiled a jackdaw kit for a unit on Egypt. It contained a timeline, model mummy coffin, necklace with a dangling ankh, panel from a false door of a tomb, a tablet with heiroglyphs, as well as photographs and documents. These jackdaw items not only motivated the students to read about Egypt in their texts, but also helped them relate background information to new learning experiences throughout the unit of study.

Offer Vicarious Experiences.   As ideal as they are for building or enriching concepts, hands-on items will be impossible for teachers to locate for every new reading experience. Suppose your students were going to read about the importance of prairie schooners for cross-country travel during pioneer days. Obviously, it would be impossible to display a real prairie schooner prior to the day's reading experience. Examine Figure 13–1 and use it as a guide to decide whether the next best choice might be a model, photo, study print, transparency, slide, or other depiction of the real thing.

One teacher used a vicarious experience to motivate her students to read about the topic of building railroads during the mid-1800s. She played a recording of the song, "I've Been Working on the Railroad." The students discussed how the people singing the song felt about railroads, and then read the textbook selection to verify their thoughts.

The surest way to bring children and books together is to plan a captivating introduction.

Although vicarious experiences are not always as motivating as the real thing, these attempts to fill in or bring out past experiences are much more effective than motivating through words alone.

Comments and Questions.   Sometimes a brief comment or question can bridge the gap between a previous learning experience and the new reading. Holmes and Roser (1987) have identified five techniques for connecting one's background knowledge with comments and questions. I have applied their suggestions to the new reading material, *A Wampanoag Child's Day:*

1. *Free recall.* "Tell me what you know about the Wampanoag Indians."

2. *Word association.* "When you hear the names Massasoit and Hobbamock, what do you think of?"

3. *Recognition.* Display key terms and ask the students to identify which might be directly related to the selection they are about to read—*wigwams, longhouses, deer stew, breeches, loincloths, petticoats.*

4. *Structured questions.* In preparation for the reading, ask prepared questions that will help connect the children's prior knowledge—"Who were the Wampanoags? What was life like in a Wampanoag village before the Pilgrims came to New England in 1620? How did the Wampanoags help the Pilgrims survive in New England?"

5. *Unstructured discussion.* "We are going to read about the Wampanoag Indians. What do you know about them?"

Charting.   A charting technique popularly used to help children associate what they already know about a topic to new content is the *K–W–L chart.* Each letter represents a different activity that guides learners before, during, and after the reading experience. *K* represents what the students *know* about the topic. Before reading, students brainstorm all the ideas they can associate with the topic, recording their ideas on a class chart, as shown in Figure 11–1. *W* represents what the students *want* to know about the topic. Students share questions that establish their own purpose for reading and motivation for learning. *L* represents what students actually *learn* from the reading experience.

After the students fill in the *L* column, they note what information addresses the purposes they established beforehand in the *W* column. Should some questions not be answered, students can reexamine the book or research the answers elsewhere.

The K–W–L technique is a favored social studies strategy because it helps students actively associate their previous experiences before becoming involved in a new reading activity. This procedure effectively bridges directed learning and more independent learning in content areas.

A contextual perspective, therefore, is most effectively achieved as children are presented activities designed to associate their backgrounds of experience to the new textbook reading requirements.

FIGURE 11-1
K-W-L Chart

What We Know About Buddhism	What We Want To Know About Buddhism	What We Learned About Buddhism
Started in India	How did Buddhism get started?	
Popular world religion	What is reincarnation?	
Follows spiritual callings of Buddha	Who is Buddha?	
Followers beleive in reincarnation	What are the laws and teachings of Buddhism?	
Karma (good or bad deeds during your life) travel with you to the next life	What are some Buddhist rituals and ceremonies?	
People should live in moderation	How many people practice Buddhism today? Where do they live today?	

Prediction.   A third prereading process is to encourage students to forecast what new ideas the reading will hold for them. For example, a textbook reading assignment the students will soon read describes how life in times past was different from life today. Before reading, the teacher writes on the board the names of two locations familiar to the students—a popular fast food restaurant and a local shopping mall. She asks the students to list all of the possible ways they might get from their homes to those locations. The responses are listed on the board. Next, the teacher asks the students to list all the ways they might get to another city. Then, calling their attention to a colonial-era scene depicted in the opening photograph of their reading assignment, the teacher continues, "What different kinds of transportation moved people during colonial days?" After the students' predictions are listed on the board, the teacher uses them as a source for the reading purpose: "What made you think that? Let's read the next page to find out." After they finish reading, the students will decide whether the evidence has confirmed their predictions or whether their ideas need to be changed.

When reading social studies textbooks, students often begin the prediction cycle by examining the title. Then they look at the pictures and illustrations to get an overall idea of what the selection will be about. They examine the section headings and look for key words in the passage. Connecting these clues and their prior knowledge, the students predict what the textbook reading assignment will be about. After completing this preview, students read to verify their predictions. This prediction-making portion of the reading preview should be adjusted for the developmental qualities of the children you teach.

Hennings (1990) suggests these uncomplicated predictive strategies for teachers of *young learners* as part of a prereading routine:

1. Read the title, study the cover, look at the pictures, and then predict: What is this going to be about? What do you already know about this topic?
2. Look at the way the words are put on the paper and how the lines are organized. Predict: Is it a story? Is it a poem? Is it about facts?
3. Set your purpose: What do you want to get out of this? fun? facts? feeling?
4. Decide: How should you read this? fast? carefully? (p. 455)

Hennings (1990) suggests these advanced predictive strategies for *upper elementary learners*:

1. Read the title. Study the cover, the pictures, charts, graphs, and tables. Scan the passage and read the words in italics and boldface. Read headings and subheadings, if any. Scan the first paragraph and the last. Predict: What is this going to be about? What do you already know about this topic and about this form of writing? Do you need to get more information from another source before you begin?
2. Decide: What kind of piece is this? story? poem? factual article? very detailed informational piece? humorous piece?
3. Decide: How is the selection organized? Is there an introductory part? a summary section at the end? study questions at the beginning or end? What kind of material is up front? at the end? How are the headings and subheadings laid out on the paper? Will the graphics be useful to you? How?
4. Decide: What do you want to get out of this? fun? fantasy? feelings? facts?
5. Decide: How shall you read this? just skim for big ideas? read fast? read for details? take notes? (pp. 455–456)

Sometimes teachers can help children acquire these special textbook-reading skills by serving as good models while demonstrating how to use them. Mr. Rosado, for example, introduced a new reading topic by asking his fifth-grade students to turn to a specific page in their social studies text. He pointed to and read aloud the main heading, "Saving Our Land." He explained to the class that when he sees a new heading, he always thinks for a moment about what it might mean. He then asked the class to tell him what the heading meant to them. Mr. Rosado wrote their thoughts on the chalkboard.

After activating what the children already knew about the topic, Mr. Rosado asked the students to look at the text photos and the first minor heading, "The Need to Protect Land." He said to the class, "I always look at the pictures and headings before reading because they give me an idea of what all the subsections will be about.

By doing that, I always come up with questions. What are some questions I might have asked myself?" Mr. Rosado went through the next section, "Conservation Efforts," the same way and continued with the succeeding sections, writing each set of questions on the chalkboard.

Modeling is a process of motivating through example; if the students see you are excited about performing certain reading skills, they will pick up your enthusiasm and become stimulated to follow your lead.

Purpose. "Why is my teacher assigning this social studies reading assignment?" is a question many students have asked over the years in classrooms around the country. Bush and Huebner (1970) address the same question and speculate that the way it is answered separates the scholar from the indifferent learner and nonreader:

> Try this question aloud with the varying inflections of the enthusiastic scholar, the indifferent learner, and the older nonreader. The first knows why he reads—to find out something he is vitally interested in knowing, to follow certain directions, to get a central idea, even to stimulate some personal thinking on a subject of deep interest. The second may read when prodded to answer the teacher's questions, to do his homework, or occasionally to find an answer when there is no one to tell him what he needs to know. The third has not learned to read, therefore he considers reading as impossible or unnecessary or completely frustrating; he cannot, so he does not read for any purposes. (p. 32)

Establishing a purpose for reading is a deeply personal process; doing so can be the most important step students take to read for meaning. It is unreasonable to involve students in any reading activity without letting them know why. Primary-grade children read "to find out why bells ring every half-hour on a ship." Upper-grade students read to prepare informative arguments for a class debate or to follow the directions to construct a table model of a tepee. Learners set their own purpose when they preview the reading material and ask the question, "I wonder why banana farmers cut the stalks while the fruit is still green?" Then they read to find out. Readers also set their own purpose when they check the heading of a new chapter, "Religions of the Roman Empire," and turn it into a question, "What religions were practiced in the Roman Empire?"

The prereading phase of a DR–TA usually culminates in a purpose-setting statement, a "launching pad" from which children propel themselves into the reading selection. It stimulates awareness of the material and informs the students why a particular textbook reading assignment is about to be shared with them. A teacher who thoughtlessly directs the students with the statement, "Your assignment is to read pages 68–71 and write answers to the questions on the board when you finish," fails to stimulate meaningful learning. The students will most likely read aimlessly; many "stumble read" their way through the assignment, wondering what is important for them to remember. Nothing is more deadly. Such a teaching mistake stifles any interest the children may have had in the topic and often turns off children to the reading process altogether.

Purposes for reading are usually framed as predictions, but are sometimes worded as direct statements. If the material does not seem to be the type conducive to making predictions, or if the children cannot yet formulate their own purposes, teachers will directly inform their students of the purpose for reading with something like an "I wonder" statement: "I wonder how the Incas used pieces of string to keep important records." With such guidance, the related information should unfold before the students. You will need to examine the material to determine whether a purpose-setting statement or a prediction would be most helpful for your students. If the beginning of the reading selection offers little help for making natural predictions, introduce the reading by using "I wonder . . . ." statements.

The purpose-setting activity closes the prereading phase of the DR–TA. Examine the classroom scenario described in Activity 11–1 and try to detect how one teacher, Mr. Scarcelli, blended several of the prereading techniques that you have just read about.

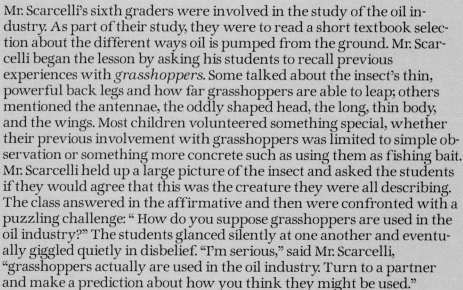

Activity 11–1

Structured Prereading Narrative

Mr. Scarcelli's sixth graders were involved in the study of the oil industry. As part of their study, they were to read a short textbook selection about the different ways oil is pumped from the ground. Mr. Scarcelli began the lesson by asking his students to recall previous experiences with *grasshoppers.* Some talked about the insect's thin, powerful back legs and how far grasshoppers are able to leap; others mentioned the antennae, the oddly shaped head, the long, thin body, and the wings. Most children volunteered something special, whether their previous involvement with grasshoppers was limited to simple observation or something more concrete such as using them as fishing bait. Mr. Scarcelli held up a large picture of the insect and asked the students if they would agree that this was the creature they were all describing. The class answered in the affirmative and then were confronted with a puzzling challenge: " How do you suppose grasshoppers are used in the oil industry?" The students glanced silently at one another and eventually giggled quietly in disbelief. "I'm serious," said Mr. Scarcelli, "grasshoppers actually are used in the oil industry. Turn to a partner and make a prediction about how you think they might be used."

After a few minutes, Mr. Scarcelli wrote down the predictions as each of the partner pairs came up with one: "They have special senses that cause them to jump around real fast if oil is underground. They help find new oil wells." "The brown 'tobacco' that they spit on your hand when you hold them can be collected and used to lubricate the machinery until the well begins to produce oil." After each pair contributed its prediction, Mr. Scarcelli made a connection to their reading: "These answers are very interesting. I would like you to read pages

78–81 in your textbooks to find out if any of your predictions explain how grasshoppers are actually used in the oil industry." After the children finished reading the selection, they discovered that oil industry "grasshoppers" were large pumps shaped somewhat like grasshoppers that pump oil from low pressure wells. Although these oil "grasshoppers" weren't of the insect variety, signs of learning were obvious as the students, in a friendly way, chastised Mr. Scarcelli for "tricking" them.

Reading

The second step of the DR–TA is the actual act of reading for the stated purpose. In general, teachers might use any of these five types of reading (Tompkins & Hoskisson, 1995) while facilitating the reading process with social studies texts:

1. *Reading aloud.* Students listen as someone else reads the text aloud. They do not have a copy of the material they are listening to, but try to gain insight into the topic by focusing on the information they hear, not on the experience of reading itself.

2. *Shared reading.* Students follow along in their own copies of a text while the teacher reads it aloud or as the class reads it together.

3. *Buddy reading.* Two students read the text together. They may take turns reading aloud or they may both read silently. This process is especially recommended for students who are not fluent readers.

4. *Guided reading.* Students read the text silently to address the stated purpose for reading or to confirm or reject predictions. Guided reading is usually done with the whole class, especially when the students need special help in order to interpret the social studies text.

5. *Independent reading.* Students read independently. They might all use the same text, or their teacher might distribute multiple texts on the same topic. Regardless, the students are responsible for achieving the reading goals with little formal direction from the teacher.

One of the most widely used reading-to-learn strategies in the social studies that can be used to help students read independently was developed by Robinson (1970). Called the *SQ3R* approach, this technique consists of the following elements:

1. *Survey.* Students skim through the material quickly, paying close attention to the major headings, subheadings, illustrations, charts and graphs, questions posed by the author, and the first and last paragraphs.

2. *Question.* This step involves turning the information examined during the survey phase into questions the reader wants to answer. In this way, readers set their own purpose for reading, an important component of reading in the social

studies. For example, the heading "California's Farm Belt" would become, "What is a farm belt?"

3. *Read.* The student reads, using his or her individually established purposes to guide the reading (to see if the purposes can be met).

4. *Recite.* The students attempt to recite from memory the material that helps satisfy the purposes established for reading.

5. *Review.* Students refer back to the textbook for the purpose of reviewing the content and verifying whether they answered their questions accurately.

Cheek, Flippo, and Lindsey (1997) comment that the SQ3R method may take students extra time to read through social studies text material, but the sacrifice is worth the rewards:

> If you have never been taught or used . . . SQ3R. . ., you are probably thinking you could not use [it] because [it] would take too much time! We want you to know that your thinking is quite true . . . and that your students will come to the same conclusion when you introduce these strategies to them. Nevertheless, we believe that you and your students will read, comprehend, and recall more pertinent information when using [the] strategy than reading without using a systematic procedure. Using such strategies will indeed require additional time, but if they are used often and internalized as a habit, they promote content-reading success. (p. 258)

Postreading

During the third stage of the DR-TA, teachers plan and conduct activities that focus on comprehension skills, including literal information and higher level thinking skills. Three ways that teachers help students construct understandings of the material presented in the text are by *asking questions, retelling,* and *using charts and diagrams.*

Asking Questions.   Over the years, social studies teachers have believed that the most efficient and effective way to teach a child to comprehend the text is by leading discussions with well-designed questions. Teachers' guides have reinforced this thinking by offering lists of questions to ask the children immediately after they finish reading. So the most frequently utilized technique to aid children in comprehending a reading selection has been participating in follow-up discussions where students respond to questions asked by their teachers. However, research studies have shown that the way these questions have been asked has resulted in little or no benefit to the learner. Durkin (1978–1979) observed instruction in a number of fourth-grade classrooms and reports that rather than using a pattern of questions to foster learning, most teachers used questions as tools of "interrogation." Little was done to help students seek and master information, organize it, and apply what they learned about the world around them. Out of a total of 4,469 minutes of observation, only 28 minutes were spent on actual information processing. The remaining 4,441 minutes were devoted to a quiz show-type format—testing the student's retention abilities with a series of rapid-fire, factual questions. Taba and her associates (1971) point out the difficulties of such narrow instructional methodology:

> A closed question such as, "When did Columbus sail?" permits only one child to respond. If the first student knows the answer that's the end of it. The teacher must then ask a second question to elicit another fact. A series of closed questions inevitably develops a teacher–student sequence. It also prevents the child who has a particular piece of information to offer from entering the discussion if the teacher does not ask "the right question." . . . A teacher whose opening question lacks focus may himself be unsure of the focus or the purpose of the discussion and his students will suffer accordingly. (p. 105)

Unfortunately, closed questions permeate most classroom discussions as teachers start out discussions with statements like, "Let's answer a few questions to see if everyone understands what we've just read." To which Manning (1985) says, "If the student knows the answer to the question . . . why ask? And . . . if the students do not know the answer to the question . . . why ask?" (p. 136). Manning (1985) advises replacing such questioning sequences with more appropriate instruction.

Realistically, teachers can ask many different kinds of questions, and good social studies teachers *must* use a variety of the right kinds of questions. The kinds of questions you choose, however, are primarily determined by the established *purpose* of the reading activity. A teacher, concerned about the readers' ability to *conceptualize the information,* might ask, "How is desert life during the day different from desert life during the night?" On the other hand, a teacher interested in a student's ability to *apply information* to the solution of unique problems might ask, after the students finished reading a selection on the various elements of U.S. coins, "What kinds of monuments from our area might be appropriate for placement on a coin?" A crucial discussion-leading skill is to tie in the stated instructional purpose to the initial question. During the prereading phase, a teacher might have stated the purpose for reading this way: "Please read pages 71–72 to find out how the Kwakuitl used wood in their everyday life." After the reading, the teacher's first question should be something like, "What did you find out about the ways the Kwakuitl use wood in their everyday life?" Can you imagine the difficulty students would have in making connections if the teacher instead asked, "How did living near water affect Kwakuitl life?"

The logic of the connection between *purpose* and *initial question* is apparent, but we sometimes neglect to make it. Be sure to keep in mind the importance of this connection and ask yourself, as you develop your discussion sequence, "What was the purpose of this reading assignment?" Begin the process of framing your questions at that point.

Questioning Strategies.   A common approach to asking comprehension questions involves the use of three levels of questions: *literal, inferential,* and *critical.* Read the following paragraph (Chase, 1971); we will then examine how to ask each type of question.

A Japanese word, *mokusatsu*, may have changed all our lives. It has two meanings: (1) to ignore, (2) to refrain from comment. The release of a press statement using the second meaning in July 1945 might have ended the war then. The Emperor was ready to end it, and had the power to do so. The cabinet was preparing to accede to the Potsdam ultimatum of the Allies—surrender or be crushed—but wanted a little more time to discuss the terms. A press release was prepared announcing a policy of *mokusatsu*, with the no comment implication. But it got on the foreign wires with the ignore implication through a mix-up in translation: "The cabinet ignores the demand to surrender." To recall the release would have entailed an unthinkable loss of face. Had the intended meaning been publicized, the cabinet might have backed up the Emperor's decision to surrender. In which event, there might have been no atomic bombs over Hiroshima and Nagasaki, no Russian armies in Manchuria, no Korean War to follow. The lives of tens of thousands of Japanese and American boys might have been saved. One word, misinterpreted. (p. 32)

Literal questions ask for information directly from the material. Learners need to contribute little complex thinking.

- "In what year did this incident take place?"
- "What are the two meanings of the Japanese word *mokusatsu*?"
- "Which meaning did the cabinet wish to communicate in its message to the Allies?"
- "Which meaning was actually communicated?"
- "What caused the mix-up?"

Inferential questions ask for information not explicitly stated in the material, which must be supplied by learners through the process of reading between the lines. Students must combine their own background knowledge with literal meaning to respond appropriately.

- "During which war did this incident take place?"
- "Which side had the upper hand in 1945?"
- "How did the Allies plan to carry through their threat, 'Surrender or be crushed'?"

Critical questions ask learners to make personal judgments about the material to which they were exposed.

- "What could have been done to prevent the mix-up in translation?"
- "What could you have done as a member of the Japanese cabinet when you realized there was a mix-up in translation?"
- "What might nations do to prevent similar incidents from happening in the future?"

Morgan and Schreiber (1969) contend that one should not burden beginning teachers with even these three questioning categories. They believe that it is much more important to have an intuitive feel for types of questions that stimulate either closed-ended or open-ended responses:

> Any discrete categorization of questions is inherently artificial. It seems more reasonable to conceive of classroom questions as being on a continuum. One extreme of the continuum may be characterized by lower levels of mental activity such as pure recall . . . and questions which are likely to have one "correct" answer. The social studies classroom in which questions of this type predominate will tend to be teacher dominated, with minimal student involvement. . . . Conversely, questions at the other extreme of the continuum involve more complex, higher mental activity. . . . Student participation in class discussions would consume a greater proportion of class time. (p. 2)

Closed questions are those that expect predictable or correct responses from the point of view of the questioner. *Open questions* are likely to bring forth unpredictable responses. They usually ask for opinions or feelings; there is no single correct answer. Check your ability to discern open from closed questions by categorizing each of the following questions:

1. When early pioneers built their homes, other people came to help. What can we do today for people who have no homes?
2. How much grain does Kansas produce annually?
3. What are the major differences between oceans, lakes, and seas?
4. How would our lives be different today if plastics did not exist?
5. What are the names of the five Great Lakes?

Did you select questions 1 and 4 as *open questions?* They are open because each student has his or her own "correct" answer. These are the most generally successful discussion starters because they make all ideas important to the group instead of confirming a single answer: "How do you feel about it?" "What do you think?" Questions 2, 3, and 5 are *closed* because they deal either with the recall or organization of specific information. There usually is only one correct answer held in common by all students and, once the answer is given, discussion usually comes to a halt.

Questioning Patterns.   Knowing the levels of questions is only one step in leading group discussions in the social studies. Teachers must also be skilled at ordering or "patterning" the questions so their students can be systematically guided toward intended learning outcomes. How to pattern questions is a personal decision, for two teachers may view the same material in completely different ways. Let us look at two questioning sequences planned by different teachers who wanted their classes to identify some of the characteristics of Sitting Bull. One teacher initiated the sequence by asking, "From all you have learned about Sitting Bull, what kind of a person do you think he was?" In other words, the teacher used an *open question* to set his discussion in motion. The students offered several characteristics, and the teacher continuously asked them to support their suggestions with accurate data: "What evidence from the reading supports your feeling that he was brave? What evidence supports your feeling that he was clever?"

The second teacher, by contrast, set the discussion in motion with this question: "As you think about the section we just read, what were some of the important things you learned about Sitting Bull?" The teacher added each suggestion to a growing list of important things about Sitting Bull, and then asked, "Let's look at the idea that he urged his Dakota Sioux warriors to fight to keep their Dakota hunting grounds. What kind of a person do you think would do that?" She then said, "Let's think of Sitting Bull chanting these words as he was arrested: 'A warrior I have been; now it is over; a hard time I have.' What kind of person would say these words?" She pursued a number of Sitting Bull's actions and then asked, "Let us think of a statement that would tell what kind of a person Sitting Bull was."

The first teacher used an *open question* to start the discussion and asked his students to support their personal ideas with relevant information. The second teacher did just the opposite; she asked the students to recall specific information and then draw their personal conclusions from the data. Which approach is best for elementary school social studies instruction? Both are acceptable; instead, the major considerations of question schemes should be thought of in terms of Dewey's (1933) popular "art of questioning" guide, as proposed over sixty years ago:

1. Questions should not elicit fact upon fact, but should be asked in such a way as to delve deeply into the subject; that is, to develop an overall concept of the selection.

2. Questions should emphasize personal interpretations rather than literal and direct responses.

3. Questions should not be asked randomly so that each is an end in itself, but should be planned so that one leads into the next throughout a continuous discussion.

4. Teachers should periodically review important points so that old, previously discussed material can be placed into perspective with that which is presently being studied.

5. The end of the question-asking sequence should leave the children with a sense of accomplishment and build a desire for that which is yet to come.

Many questioning sequences are possible following a social studies reading assignment, but the main consideration should be to consider carefully what you want to achieve with any plan. Random questioning with no end in mind gives the illusion of teaching, but wise teachers know that questions with the most positive impact on the learning situation are planned so that one leads to the other throughout a logical sequence, deliberately provoking deeper thought or creating new learnings.

Sustaining Discussions.   Once you set a questioning sequence in motion, you must use the right words to the right person at the right time in a way that not only encourages constructive learning but also shows that you are listening and that you care. To achieve this goal, you will sometimes need to ask questions or offer comments other than those that are directly related to the content. *Probing* is a popular technique for sustaining classroom discussions. This process, mastered centuries ago by Socrates (and referred to as the *Socratic method),* remains a valuable teaching tool today. By probing, Socrates was able to prod students (offer them hints) if they were unclear in an answer or unable to answer a question at all. To understand the technique, you must realize that it consists of two subprocesses: prompting and clarifying.

Prompting utilizes short hints or clues whenever children give an unsatisfactory response to a question, usually a lower level question. Several prompts or leading questions help children organize their thinking patterns relative to the original question.

Teacher:	Why was the bald eagle chosen as our national symbol?
Student 1:	One reason is that it has great strength. There was another reason, uh-h-h . . .
Teacher:	Think about where the eagles lived during the days of the early settlers.
Student 1:	They flew high and free above the land. Eagles lived only in North America.
Teacher:	That's right. Now can you tell a second reason why the eagle was chosen as our national symbol?
Student 1:	Because it lived only in North America.

Children are not told that their initial response is wrong; instead, they are led, reinforced, and encouraged. Because the teacher does not imply that a student's initial response is incorrect, prompting also helps to enhance the student's self-confidence.

Clarifying calls for enlargement or restatement of a student's original answer. The teacher uses clarification when an answer is correct but insufficiently accurate and complete, or when children are asked to defend a position when there may be differences of opinion. Thus, clarification can usually be applied to questions at the higher levels of thinking.

Teacher:	Was there widespread agreement 200 years ago that the eagle should be our national symbol?
Student 2:	No—Benjamin Franklin favored the wild turkey.
Teacher:	Why did Franklin favor the wild turkey?
Student 2:	Because he thought it was a wise and clever bird.
Teacher:	Which bird do you think makes the best symbol for our country?

To carry out a good discussion, teachers must say the right words to the right children at the right time.

Student 2:	The eagle.
Teacher:	What are your reasons for feeling this way?
Student 2:	The eagle stands for freedom and power—just like the United States.

The probing technique helps children express ideas individually and intuitively. It enables learners to operate on all levels of thinking while they develop solutions to problems. The success of your questioning technique, however, depends on your ability to adapt questions to the individual without expecting the same quality of response from all students.

Framing Questions.   Your chances of eliciting thoughtful responses to appropriate questions are greatly enhanced by effective methods of framing questions. The basic approach for framing questions is: (1) ask the question, (2) pause for 3 to 5 seconds (wait time I), (3) call on someone to respond, and (4) pause for 3 to 5 seconds again while the students think about the response (wait time II). The process is grounded on the principle that students attend better to questions if a short pause follows. Orlich and his associates (1990) offer several justifications for pausing. First, wait time gives students a chance to think about their responses. Second, the nonverbal message (pause) indicates that any student may be selected for a response. Thus the attention level remains high. Third, a pause provides the teacher with a little time to "read" nonverbal clues from the class. With experience, teachers can readily observe such signals as pleasure, fright, or boredom. Fourth, teachers who pause after asking questions become more patient while awaiting student responses. The message, then, is not to expect rapid-fire exchanges during discussions. Make the decision to pause after you ask a question. You may discover that children make longer responses, offer more complex answers, interact more with one another, and gain more confidence in their ability to make worthwhile contributions.

Although there may be more effective ways to help children comprehend what they read in their social studies textbooks, the fact remains that teacher's guides urge teachers to ask questions, and many teachers seem to have been conditioned to think that asking questions is a most effective way to learn from print. Harp and Brewer (1996) maintain that this creates problems because "[w]hen students have difficulty answering comprehension questions, teachers often assume they have not read the text carefully. We suspect that this failure may often be attributable to the fact that children have not been taught how to analyze a question in order to find the correct answers" (p. 297). In place of the teacher-directed questioning format, Harp and Brewer (1996) recommend that teachers facilitate comprehensive discussions (retellings) during which students share with one another what they have read.

Retelling.   Retelling is a way to actively engage children in sharing their own understandings of an author's message. Combs (1996) suggests that guided retelling experiences are an excellent means of activating students' learnings from textbook reading; they are effective tools that help students think back and recall the information. Combs describes several different forms of retelling; the content of the reading assignment would determine which to employ in your classroom. Those with particular applicability to social studies textbooks are:

1. *Dramatic retelling.* It is easier for some children to retell what they have read by pretending to be a character they have read about and to playact important parts of the character's life.

2. *Illustration retelling.* After reading the text, students return to the beginning and retell important events by explaining the significance of the photographs and illustrations.

3. *Story map retelling.* Students illustrate a visual arrangement of the events in the reading material. A story map may be written or drawn, but it should show the main parts of the selection.

4. *Artistic retelling.* Combs (1996) advises that "[d]rawing is a good activity for young children because it slows down their thinking and allows them time to re-call details and organize ideas . . . " (p. 266). As the children draw an illustration that highlights a major idea from the reading selection, the teacher (or the students themselves) could write a retelling statement.

5. *Written retelling.* Individuals or small groups of students record their retellings in journals or learning logs.

6. *Taped retelling.* A tape-recorded retelling can supplement other retellings such as drawings or writings. One benefit to this strategy is that children can replay the retelling to see how complete it is. Group retellings can be accomplished by having the children take turns retelling parts of the selection in order from be-ginning to end.

Retelling helps children notice details in the reading assignment; it is a very helpful meaning-making strategy.

Graphic Representations.   Graphic representations are visual depictions of knowl-edge gained from the reading experience. Although the previous strategies can be ef-fective instructional methods, graphic organizers are perhaps the most accepted method today for helping children focus on major ideas and perceive relationships among details.

We discussed many types of graphic representations in Chapter 6—charts, graphs, tables, and other commonly used methods of summarizing large amounts of information. Such representations help students make sense of the information they encounter in their reading. In deciding what kind of a graphic organizer to use while helping students read expository material, teachers must be aware of the way the text is structured. Tompkins (1997) describes five patterns and presents sample pas-sages that illustrate the use of each pattern. Tompkins also illustrates a general graphic organizer appropriate for each pattern. See Figure 11–2.

Reader's Response to the Text (Enrichment Activities)

Reader's response activities serve as the culmination of the entire DR–TA. Up to this point, students have been involved in what Rosenblatt (1982) has described as taking an *efferent stance* with the text. They are reading to take something from the text—primarily information. However, Rosenblatt adds that teachers must help chil-dren approach the text with a second stance, too, an *aesthetic stance.* Here, the readers attach personal feelings or perceptions to the text. Harp and Brewer (1996) explain that "[t]eachers often invite children to respond to texts through what are called *enrichment activities,* which build bridges between reading and other curric-ular areas—and offer students opportunities to enrich and extend their comprehen-sion of [the] content" (p. 286). These enrichment activities are usually special projects that help children personalize the reading content and apply or extend concepts to a variety of situations, as in the following sample activities.

FIGURE 11–2
The Five Expository Text Structures

Pattern	Description	Cue Words	Graphic Organizer	Sample Passage
Description	The author describes a topic by listing characteristics, features, and examples.	*for example* *characteristics are*		The Olympic symbol consists of five interlocking rings. The rings represent the five continents—Africa, Asia, Europe, North America, and South America—from which athletes come to compete in the games. The rings are colored black, blue, green, red, and yellow. At least one of these colors is found in the flag of every country sending athletes to compete in the Olympic games.
Sequence	The author lists items or events in numerical or chronological order.	*First, second, third* *next* *then* *finally*	1. _____ 2. _____ 3. _____ 4. _____ 5. _____	The Olympic games began as athletic festivals to honor the Greek gods. The most important festival was held in the valley of Olympia to honor Zeus, the king of the gods. It was this festival that became the Olympic games in 776 B.C. These games were ended in A.D. 394 by the Roman Emperor who ruled Greece. No Olympic games were held for more than 1,500 years. Then the modern Olympics began in 1896. Almost 300 male athletes competed in the first modern Olympics. In the games held in 1900, female athletes were allowed to compete. The games have continued every four years since 1896 except during World War II, and they will most likely continue for many years to come.
Comparison	The author explains how two or more things are alike and/or how they are different.	*Different* *in contrast* *alike* *same as* *on the other hand*	[diagram: box pointing to "Alike" and "Different"]	The modern Olympics is very unlike the ancient Olympic games. Individual events are different. While there were no swimming races in the ancient games, for example, there were chariot races. There were no female contestants and all athletes competed in the nude. Of course, the ancient and modern Olympics are also alike in many ways. Some events, such as the javelin and discus throws, are the same. Some people say that cheating, professionalism, and nationalism in the modern games are a disgrace to the Olympic tradition. But according to the ancient Greek writers, there were many cases of cheating, nationalism, and professionalism in their Olympics, too.

Source: Tompkins, G. E. (1997). *Literacy for the 21st century: A balanced approach.* Englewood Cliffs, NJ: Merrill/Prentice Hall, 219–220.

FIGURE 11–2
The Five Expository Text Structures (continued)

Pattern	Description	Cue Words	Graphic Organizer	Sample Passage
Cause and Effect	The author lists one or more causes and the resulting effect or effects.	*reasons why* *if…then* *as a result* *therefore* *because*		There are several reasons why so many people attend the Olympic games or watch them on television. One reason is tradition. The name *Olympics* and the torch and flame remind people of the ancient games. People can escape the ordinariness of daily life by attending or watching the Olympics. They like to identify with someone else's individual sacrifice and accomplishment. National pride is another reason, and an athlete's or a team's hard-earned victory becomes a nation's victory. There are national medal counts and people keep track of how many medals their country's athletes have won.
Problem and Solution	The author states a problem and lists one or more solutions for this problem. A variation of this pattern is the question-and-answer format in which the author poses a question and then answers it.	*problem is* *dilemma is* *puzzle is* *solved* *question . . .* *answer*		One problem with the modern Olympics is that it has become very big and expensive to operate. The city or country that hosts the games often loses a lot of money. A stadium, pools, and playing fields must be built for the athletic events, and housing is needed for the athletes who come from around the world. And all of these facilities are used for only two weeks! In 1984, Los Angeles solved these problems by charging a fee for companies who wanted to be official sponsors of the games. Companies like McDonald's paid a lot of money to be part of the Olympics. Many buildings that were already built in the Los Angeles area were also used. The Coliseum where the 1932 games were held was used again, and many colleges and universities in the area became playing and living sites.

Writing

- Write a historical period news magazine for the Pilgrims of Plymouth. Students compose their articles in the style of popular news magazines, but reporting on such areas of interest as the birthday of Peregine White (the first child born in Plymouth Colony), the "lawful recreations" (games) that children were allowed to play, Pilgrim manners, Pilgrim meals, boy and girl chores, Pilgrim clothing styles, and a description of village life.
- Students imagine they are passengers on the *Mayflower* and keep a weekly diary of their 66-day journey to the New World.

For additional information about Plymouth Colony and the Pilgrims, students may write a business letter to request a free kit on the history of the Pilgrims to:

Plymouth Area Chamber of Commerce, 225 Water Street, Suite 500, Plymouth, MA 02360

Cooking

- Students cook and eat Harry S. Truman's favorite food—brownies.
- Students prepare and eat cornmeal mush, a staple food of the pioneers on their journeys westward.
- When studying about Pilgrims, show the students how the colonists had to preserve food for storage over the winter months. Drying apples is a great harvest time activity.

Art

- Students select a location they would like to "cheer" about. Then they design paper pennants with colors and illustrations that have some meaning to the location.
- Students make their own natural dyes from beets, onion skins, grapes, berries, and other foods. They make designs on cotton cloth with the dyes.
- Students draw a scene from Mexico on one side of an index card to make a postcard. On the other side, students write a brief message about their impressions of Mexico.

Music

- Play a recording of the humorous folk song, "Old Dan Tucker." Invite the students to clap time to the rhythm and sing along. Ask them to write an additional verse to the song.
- Students can learn songs from a variety of countries—including China, Japan, and West Africa—from the audiotape, *Multicultural Rhythm Stick Fun* (Kimbo). Simple directions help them respond to the music with rhythm sticks.
- Make ankle bells by attaching small metal "jingle bells" to elastic or ribbon. Students can "dance" to Native American music following authentic steps.

Drama

- Students pantomime the firing of the "shot heard around the world."
- Students prepare a puppet presentation retelling their text reading about animal life on the prairie.
- Students work in groups to prepare a readers' theater skit in which they role-play various aspects of life long ago in an Inuit community.

By searching a variety of teacher activity books and organizing an idea file, you will soon begin to accumulate a rich collection of ideas for extension experiences and bring more personal meaning to the DR–TA. Remember, though, that these activities must be part of the total learning experience, not "extra busy work" or "icing on the cake" that gets done only because you have a few minutes to kill. Some teachers (especially those planning these reader's response experiences for the first time) tend to select the "cutest" activities, thinking that the more alluring an activity is, the more benefit it will bring to the students. Certainly, charm is an important criterion for selection, but even more critical is how suitable the activity is for enriching or extending the concepts the children just finished reading about.

Developing a DR–TA is a demanding responsibility involving a great deal of hard work and expertise. As a new teacher, you may wonder whether the results are worth the effort. In effect, you may say, "Why bother? After all, the textbook and teacher's manual were written by experts in the field who really know the social studies, so they must be good." To an extent, you are correct. Social studies textbook series can be very good, and the accompanying manuals can be extremely helpful, especially for student teachers or beginning teachers. As part of the social studies curriculum, though, textbooks must be viewed as a single resource, not as the complete curriculum. Do the experts in the field know your fifth graders as well as you do? You will probably want to start your career by using the teacher's guide closely, but as you gain experience, you will adapt it to the changing needs of the different groups of children you will teach each year. The DR–TA allows you to constantly change your teaching ideas within a framework of sound planning.

Cooper (1997) suggests that structured patterns of content-area reading instruction, such as the DR–TA, are most useful on these occasions:

- When the text is particularly difficult.
- When students are second-language learners.
- When students are having difficulty constructing meaning.
- When you know students have limited prior knowledge about the topic or about the type of text (p. 135).

Although DR–TAs are most commonly associated with expository materials such as social studies textbooks, teachers can guide students through the reading of trade books with the technique, too. Whether reading from a textbook or from a trade book, you should present the basic DR–TA outline whenever you believe your students need a framework to guide their thinking and organize the information.

Criticisms of Textbooks

Despite publishers' attempts to provide social studies classrooms with substantial, captivating materials, textbooks are not without their critics. Some, for example, complain that textbooks are often used as the curriculum—the only instructional resource to which the children are exposed. In surveying the reactions of a dozen teachers to the question, "What do you associate with social studies teaching that is clearly not creative in the elementary school?" Solomon (1989) discovered that the exclusive use of textbooks was a prevalent response:

> In these classrooms, wrote one of the teachers surveyed, the "teaching [is] only from the textbook. . . . Students answer questions from the textbook or [do] nothing but worksheets, worksheets, worksheets." Another responded, the teacher is "following each page and paragraph within a textbook—giving the same emphasis to every paragraph and calling for learning." All twelve respondents had the same message: Teachers in these classrooms allow one textbook to determine what they teach, with students simply expected to learn the material in it. (p. 3)

Sewall (1988a) inquired into the quality of social studies textbooks, with a particular accent on content: what information textbooks include and omit, how that information is presented, and the impact these factors have on young learners. Four of Sewall's general conclusions are summarized as follows:

1. *The physical size and weight of textbooks discourage enthusiasm for their contents.* Reviewers stressed that young children would not be drawn to "curl up and read" the social studies texts merely because of their sheer size.

2. *The prose style of most textbooks is bland and voiceless.* Even though quality varied from publisher to publisher, reviewers thought that the overall literary style of the texts fell well short of the mark: "Reviewers found textbooks generally to be more catalogues of factual material . . . , not sagas peopled with heroic and remarkable individuals engaged in exciting and momentous events" (p. 35).

Much of this difficulty in writing style can be attributed to a publisher's concern that the content match the reading skills normally associated with children at each grade level. Because the word recognition and comprehension skills of younger learners are considered somewhat limited, publishers often resort to a practice popularly referred to as "dumbing down" the material. Leu and Kinzer (1987) offer this example of dumbing down:

> It is night. A man is very sick. The man comes here in a fast car (p. 341).

In the passage, the publisher chose to use the word *here* for *hospital* and the words *a fast car* for *ambulance*. As Leu and Kinzer (1987) inform us, "These decisions were undoubtedly made because children had not yet been taught to recognize the words *hospital* and *ambulance,* but had been taught the words *here* and *a fast car.* As a result, children must infer the real meanings of these seemingly easier words; a task that can make the comprehension of this passage more difficult." The problems created by a fixed-sequence textbook series, then, may involve serious instructional disadvantages.

3.   Excessive coverage makes textbooks boring. Many textbooks are most effective as almanacs, encyclopedias, or reference guides; names and dates seem to dart past like telephone poles seen from the window of a swiftly moving train.

4.   Textbook formats and graphics diminish the style and coherence of the running text. To be competitive with television and other mass media, textbooks have lost the narrative content that made up 90 percent of their pages just a generation ago, and now substitute "endless photographs, diagrams, charts, boxes, subunits, [and] study exercises . . . especially in lower-grade-level textbooks" (Sewall, 1988a, p. 35). The result is a limited reading sample.

To be fair, it must be emphasized that most of these criticisms cannot be as closely attached to the textbooks themselves as to the ways teachers use them. Textbook publishers encourage teachers to supplement and enrich their materials with auxiliary literature sources, information books, videos, field trips, realia, computer programs, and other instructional resources. Texts are not meant to furnish the total social studies experience, but to serve as a single resource among an array of several possibilities.

TRADE BOOKS IN THE SOCIAL STUDIES PROGRAM

Disenchanted by the dry and tedious practices that have often been associated with unimaginative approaches to textbook-based social studies instruction, more teachers than ever before are turning to literature-based support in their social studies classrooms. Their learning-through-literature programs help students broaden their knowledge and understandings by reading trade books about other people, places, and ideas.

Most of us shared our childhood with a menagerie of storybook companions. Some we recall with sweet memories and special fondness. Their adventures and misadventures were sources of great delight, and the thoughts of missing out on the likes of Peter Rabbit, Winnie-the-Pooh, the Cat in the Hat, the Little Red Hen, or the Three Billy Goats Gruff is unthinkable. Zinsser notes that "[n]o kind of writing lodges itself so deeply in our memory, echoing there for the rest of our lives, as the books that we met in our childhood" (p. 3). First and foremost, then, literature brings delight and enjoyment to children. But literature can educate at the same time it entertains. Huck, Hepler, and Hickman (1993) explain:

> The experiences children have with literature give them new perspective on the world. Good writing can transport the reader to other places and other times and expand his life space. The reader feels connected to the lives of others as he enters an imagined situation with his emotions tuned to those of the story. . . .

How better can we feel and experience history than through a well-told story of the lives of its people and times? . . . A history textbook tells; a quality piece of imaginative writing has the power to make the reader feel, to transport him to the deck of a slave ship and force him into the hold until he chokes on the very horror of it. (p. 11)

Textbooks, with their expository style, can tell children that racism is wrong, but one need not be told while reading a book such as *Marching to Freedom: The Story of Martin Luther King, Jr.* by Joyce Milton (Dell). Readers are made to feel the atrocities of racism as they are carried on the wings of Milton's words to the seats of a bus where they enter a new dimension of imagination to discover racism's horrors. Milton describes an event in 1943, when Martin Luther King, Jr. (then known as M. L.) was only fourteen and had an encounter with "Jim Crow" laws that he would never forget. M. L. and his teacher (Mrs. Bradley) had boarded a bus that was pulling off the road to make a local stop:

Suddenly, the bus driver started yelling at them. Some new passengers were boarding the bus—white passengers. "Get up, you two," the driver shouted. "The white folks want to sit down." Mrs. Bradley started to gather her belongings. But she didn't move fast enough to suit the driver. He began to curse. "You black _____ _____. You git up. Now!" M. L. sat frozen in his seat. No one had ever talked to him that way before. Ever so slowly M. L. stood up. . . .
  "That night will never leave my memory," he said years later. "It was the angriest I have ever been in my life." (pp. 4–5)

Texts are primarily concerned with facts; literature is primarily concerned with feelings—compassion, humanness, misfortune, happiness, awe, and grief. This intrinsic value of literature, by itself, should make it a valued part of the social studies program. However, the public assigns very low priority to school experiences that bring enjoyment only; what is enjoyable can't be very good for children. Ravitch (1978) echoes this sentiment as she criticizes the displacement of quality literature with textbooks based on the expanding environment approach:

Until expanding environments managed to push historical material out of the social studies curriculum children in the early grades in most public schools learned about . . . myths, biographies, poems . . . fairy tales, and legends. The story of Robinson Crusoe and the study of Indian life were particular favorites. Stories about explorers, pioneer life, American heroes . . . , and famous events in American history were the staples of the first three grades. The line between historical literature and general literature was virtually nonexistent. Teacher guides emphasized the importance of telling stories. (p. 38)

Ravitch (1978) goes on to describe the status of literature in today's classrooms:

Today, children in most American public schools do not read fairy tales, myths, folklore, legends, sagas, historical adventure stories, or biographies of great men and women unless the teacher introduces them during reading period. And we know from recent studies of reading instruction that current reading methods depend almost entirely on basal readers, a species of textbook containing simple stories of ordinary children, families, and neighborhoods. (pp. 38–39)

Trade books (both fiction and nonfiction) contribute much to the social studies program; they present information about people, places, events, and times in inspiring, memorable, and relevant ways. But implementing a literature-based social studies program means that teachers must be familiar with the books that can teach students something. Children learn facts and concepts from both expository and narrative forms of literature, but three types (genres) of books seem particularly adaptable to the social studies program: *historical fiction, biographies,* and *folk literature.*

Historical Fiction

Historical fiction is a term describing realistic stories that are set in the past; the facts are accurate but the characters are fictional (although they sometimes interact with actual historical figures). Historical fiction offers children opportunities to vicariously experience the past by entering into a convincingly true-to-life world of people who have lived before them. By being transported to the past through the vehicle of literature, students enter into the lives of the characters and, through mental imagery, become inspired to think as well as to feel about their condition.

The theme of many historical fiction stories is social conflict and its resulting confusion and animosity. In *Early Thunder* by Jean Fritz (Coward McCann), 14-year-old Daniel West faces a struggle to sort out his loyalties during events leading to the American Revolution. Set in Salem in 1774, when people were either Tories (loyal to the king) or Whigs, Daniel is a staunch Tory who hates the acts of the rowdy Liberty Boys. But as the story unfolds, Daniel becomes equally disenchanted by British attitudes. Eventually, Daniel must come to terms with himself and sort out his allegiance.

Mildred D. Taylor is an African American author who has written with great sensitivity and understanding about racial injustice in rural Mississippi during the 1930s. *Mississippi Bridge* (Bantam Skylark) is a tale based on a true story told to Taylor by her father. It centers on the Logan family and their determination to fight racial injustice. The story opens with Jeremy Simms, a 10-year-old white child, watching from the porch of the general store as the weekly bus from Jackson splashes through a heavy rainstorm to stop at the store. His neighbors, Stacey Logan and his sister Cassie, are there to see their grandmother off on a trip. Jeremy's friend, Josias Williams, is taking the bus to a new job. But Josias and the Logans are black; black people can't ride the bus if that means there won't be enough room for white people to ride. When several white passengers arrive at the last minute, Taylor describes the injustice that unfolded as the driver sends Josias and Stacey's grandmother off the bus. The author's words make it impossible not to attach deep emotions to the event:

Josias stood. He picked up his bundle of clothes and he give up his seat. He took himself some slow steps to the front of the bus. I moved over to the door waiting to say my spell to him, but he still ain't got off. He stopped hisself right front of that driver and he gone to pleading. "Please, boss . . . I got to get to the Trace t'day. Please, boss. I done got my ticket. I done made all my plans. Folks spectin' me. I got t' go on this bus!"

"Nigger, I said you gettin' off."

"Boss, please . . ."

That bus driver, he ain't give Josias chance to say no more. He jerked Josias forward to the door, put his foot flat to Josias's backside, and give him a push like Josias wasn't no more 'n a piece of baggage, and Josias, he gone sprawling down them steps into the mud. The bus driver, he throw'd Josias's bundle after him, his ticket money too. (p. 31)

Shortly after this episode, the bus skids off the bridge and all are drowned. The nightmare changes the lives of the townspeople forever.

The varied settings and conflicts of colonial America have inspired a large number of books about young children. *The Sign of the Beaver,* by Elizabeth George Speare (Houghton Mifflin), is a widely used book in many literature-based social studies programs around the country. It is the story of 12-year-old Matt, who is left by his father to survive on his own in their cabin in the Maine wilderness while his father returns to Massachusetts to bring back the rest of the family. Matt is a brave boy, but he is not prepared for an attack by swarming bees. He is rescued by Saknis, the chief of the Beaver clan, and his grandson, Attean. The boys get to know each other well; Matt teaches Attean to speak English, and Attean teaches Matt crucial survival skills. The story describes their friendship that grows through the months until Matt's family returns.

If written well, historical fiction offers children fuller understandings of human problems and human conditions. To be considered for social studies programs, well-written historical fiction should reflect the following guidelines:

1. It must tell an interesting story—the book should "set the reader on fire."
2. It should be accurate and authentic—the historical period should be so precisely described that the people within the book "walk right into the room."
3. It should reflect the spirit and values of the times—the stories cannot be made to conform to today's ethical values (such as contemporary points of view concerning women and minorities).
4. It should contain authentic language—the spoken words should give the flavor of how people actually talked.
5. It should provide insight into today's problems—such as putting the conditions of women and minorities into historical context.

Biographies

Biographies are much like historical fiction in that they are based on historical facts that can be documented. Rather than focusing on fictional characters, however, biographies are carefully researched accounts of the lives of real people. The work of Esther Forbes offers an excellent comparison of a biographical story and historical fiction. In 1942, Forbes won the Pulitzer Prize for her adult biography, *Paul Revere and the World He Lived In.* While she was researching the book, she uncovered many fascinating stories about the duties of Boston's apprentices. As a result, she created a book for children, *Johnny Tremain* (Houghton Mifflin), that won the New-bery Medal in 1944. The book is about a fictional silversmith's apprentice to Paul Revere who lived in Boston in the days leading to the American Revolution. A skilled craftsperson, Johnny becomes one of the best at his trade. But a practical joke back-fires, and Johnny's hand becomes maimed for life. Johnny then becomes involved in pre-Revolutionary War activities. The book remains one of the most popular works of historical fiction to this day.

Children are introduced to Deborah Sampson, Hammurabi, General Santa Ana, Neil Armstrong, Sojourner Truth, Abraham Lincoln, Molly Brown, Lewis and Clark, Mary McLeod Bethune, Hiawatha, or Frederick Douglass in their social studies texts, but these figures seem to spring into life as the biographer chooses and presents de-tails in ways that engage the minds of the readers. Consider this account of a portion of the ritual, led by his tribe's shaman (spiritual leader), that transformed Sitting Bull from a boy into manhood:

> Following Moon Dreamer's [the shaman's] instructions, Sitting Bull entered the [sweat lodge] and sat by the [hot] stones for what seemed like an eternity. Soon his skin was hot and throbbing, and sweat poured down his back and sides. Finally, when the boy felt as if his body were on fire, the shaman ordered him back outside. There he told Sitting Bull to jump into a freezing creek.

An attractive display of trade books is a great way to launch children into meaningful and productive inquiry.

Without questioning the shaman's command, Sitting Bull raced across the ground and leaped into icy water, gasping at the shock. As he climbed up out of the creek, he saw that Moon Dreamer was getting ready to say farewell and leave. Naked and without food or water, Sitting Bull remained alone on the hill [for several days]. (Eisenberg, 1991, pp. 30–31)

Well-written children's biographies personalize social studies subject matter with a degree of vividness unattainable with the straight reporting style of most textbooks. Biographies impress children with a sense of historical reality. Even early primary-grade children become interested in biographies if you give them picture biographies, such as those by Ingri and Edgar Parin d'Aulaire (Abraham Lincoln, Benjamin Franklin, Pocahontas, and others). Gradually, you can move on to many excellent biographies suitable for children at each age level: Fernando Monjo's *The One Bad Thing About Father* gives a son's view of Teddy Roosevelt; James T. DeKay's *Meeting Martin Luther King, Jr.* is a picture essay describing King's early childhood and growth into adulthood; Dan D'Amelio's *Taller Than Bandia Mountain: The Story of Hideyo Noguchi* tells of a Japanese doctor's efforts to combat serious obstacles while achieving success in bacteriological research; and Evelyn Lampman's *Wheels West: The Story of Tabitha Brown* describes a 66-year-old woman's wagon train trip to Oregon, where she became a famed educational pioneer.

The same guidelines for selecting historical fiction apply to biographies. Be sure the story is a well-researched, carefully documented account of the person's life with fast-moving narrative and a clear, readable writing style.

Folk Literature

Fables, myths, legends, and folktales belong to the great component of literature we refer to as *folklore*. In essence, these are the stories that began with illiterate people and were handed down by word of mouth for generations. Originating wherever people gathered—in marketplaces, during tasks such as weaving or sewing, in taverns, or around the hearth—the stories were told not only for the entertainment of the listener but often as an expression of philosophies and living conditions. The rich oral tradition of these stories was kept alive by generations of storytellers; the tales eventually found their place within printed literature.

Because folktales have been retold from generation to generation within every culture, they reflect those cultures' beliefs, values, lifestyles, and histories. An authentic tale from Chinese culture, for example, will include references to the land on which the people lived, their food, their homes, their customs, and their beliefs. Take, for instance, this passage from *Lon Po Po* by Ed Young (1989), a Red Riding Hood story from China:

"Po Po, Po Po [wolf]," she said, for she was not only the eldest, she was the most clever, "you must be hungry. Have you eaten gingho nuts?"

"What is gingho?" the wolf asked. (p. 13 of an unnumbered text)

Much like the wolf, disguised as the children's grandmother (Po Po), elementary school children learn about the nuts of a gingho tree as they read this fascinating tale.

Since folktales reflect a culture so plainly, it is nearly impossible to confuse a folk-tale from a village in China with a folktale from central Africa. This is a major reason folktales belong in social studies classrooms; they help children understand a culture's inherent values, beliefs, and customs.

Huck, Hepler, and Hickman (1993) inform us that despite these distinct cultural nuances, the following characteristics are common to all folk literature: *repetition* ("Fee, fi, fo, fum"); *conflict* (Anansi needs a wife but is afraid he won't find one because of his bad name), *characterization* (wolf, stepmother, or witch is a symbol of evil; innocent children are symbols of goodness), *theme* (reflects goals of people—long life, good spouse, beautiful home, plenty of food, freedom from fear, power, courage); and *motifs* (magical powers, such as the ability to spin straw into gold; transformations, such as Cinderella going from rags to riches; magic objects, such as a lamp containing a genie who grants a number of wishes; trickery, such as when children entice Lon Po Po, the Chinese wolf, into a basket to taste a gingho nut).

The study of folktales enlightens students about distinct cultures and contributes greatly to their understanding of people around the world. A cross-cultural study of folk literature also adds an extra dimension to helping children discover the universal qualities of all humankind. For instance, the theme of reward for a good, generous person and punishment for a greedy, disobedient one seems to be universal. In our culture, Cinderella illustrates this characteristic. She also receives her rewards in different ways in cultures throughout the world:

Mrs. Gilland, a third-grade teacher, used such a cross-cultural study to enrich her unit on China. To begin, Mrs. Gilland read two books to her students: the Charles Perrault version of *Cinderella* (retold by Amy Ehrlich and illustrated by Susan Jeffers [Dial]) and the Chinese version, *Yeh-Shen* (retold by Ai-ling Louie and illustrated by Ed Young [Philomel]). She then constructed a large chart with the titles of the books across the top and the areas for comparison along the side (see Table 11–1).

TABLE 11–1
Chart Comparing Cinderella Variants

Title	Country	Outcome
Cinderella (Bradbury, 1973)	France/USA	marries the prince
Yeh-Shen (Philomel, 1982)	China	marries the king
Mufaro's Beautiful Daughters (Lothrop, 1987)	Africa	marries the king
The Egyptian Cinderella (Crowell, 1989)	Egypt	marries the Pharaoh
Princess Furball (Greenwillow, 1989)	Germany	wins a prince
Vasilissa the Beautiful (HarperCollins, 1991)	Russia	saved from wrath of Baba Yaga
The Rough-Face Girl (Putnam, 1992)	Village by the shores of Lake Ontario	marries the "Invisible Being"

To help the children fill in the information, Mrs. Gilland asked timely and appropriate questions: "Who were the main characters in the stories? How were they alike? Different? Where do the stories take place? When? How are the settings alike? Different? What problems did Cinderella face? Yeh-Shen?"

Mrs. Gilland's overall goal was to help the children understand that, despite many differences in cultures around the world, similar problems often motivate people to generate similar ideas. Mrs. Gilland brought this phase of her China unit to closure by having her students dramatize the events of both stories.

Folk literature has deep roots in all distinct cultures. Through this genre, students broaden their understandings of those cultures, as well as sense the common bonds that have linked together cultures for centuries.

Teaching With Trade Books

Trade books do not typically come with teacher's manuals, so teachers must establish for themselves the course instruction will take. DR–TAs are used by many teachers to guide their children through trade books as well as their social studies textbooks. However, in contemporary circles, whether reading aloud to the children or asking them to read silently, a widely advocated technique (Combs, 1996) designed to focus students' thinking as they read or listen to trade book stories is the *Mediated Reading Thinking Activity (MRTA)*. The MRTA is referred to as a "mediated experience" because the teacher leads the children through their reading experience in a more open-ended manner than with the DR–TA. In comparing the DR–TA to the MRTA, Combs (1996) explains that, although the DR-TA has been shown to improve children's comprehension of text, current views of meaning making discourage viewing the teacher as one who directs and the reader as one who is directed. Instead, the teacher must be seen as a *mediator* who gradually reduces support as children become self-regulated readers.

This perspective is based on a "constructivist" view of learning. Constructivists believe that comprehension occurs as readers relate ideas from books to their acquired or prior knowledge. Because comprehension is based on prior experiences, students' ability to comprehend may be limited or impossible if they do not already possess schemata (concepts formed from past experiences) related to the topic. The paragraph below may help illustrate this point (Freedman, 1987).

> Five doctors worked over the president that night. Now and then he groaned, but it was obvious that he would not regain consciousness. The room filled with members of the cabinet, with congressmen and high government officials. Mary waited in the front parlor. "Bring Tad—he will speak to Tad—he loves him so," she cried. Tad had been attending another play that evening. Sobbing, "They killed my pa, they killed my pa," he was taken back to the White House to wait. (pp. 125–126)

To comprehend this paragraph, the reader must have already built a schema about presidents of the United States. Associating that schema with information in the paragraph, the reader is able to tell that it is about a president. However, if the reader's schema does not include something about assassinated presidents, the paragraph will have very little or no meaning. But, let us say that the reader's schema does include background knowledge of assassinated presidents. He or she will then search through the paragraph looking for clues to determine the president's identity. To do so, the reader must pull from several of his or her schemata to narrow down the possibilities to the four former presidents, who were assassinated, even though none were specifically mentioned in the passage. Relying even more heavily on one's schemata and the clues in the paragraph, the reader recognizes names and events that eventually help pinpoint this passage as describing the horrific assassination of Lincoln. In other words, the reader *constructed* meaning as he or she associated personal schemata with the clues contained in the paragraph. Therefore, constructivist views of reading comprehension hold that effective comprehenders use an interactive process to bring meaning to the text; they rely heavily on the interplay of their schemata and clues from the story. Cooper (1997) offers a succinct definition of reading comprehension that underlies the constructivist practices associated with the MRTA: *"Comprehension is a strategic process by which readers construct or assign meaning to a text by using the clues in the text and their own prior knowledge. . . . The meaning the reader constructs . . . does not come from the printed page; it comes from the reader's own experiences that are triggered or activated by the ideas the author presents "* (pp. 11–12).

The Mediated Reading Thinking Activity (MRTA)

Essentially, teachers plan the MRTA in three segments, similar to the DR–TA, mediating meaning-making efforts: (1) before the reading, (2) during the reading, and (3) after the reading. The process is summarized in Figure 11–3.

At first glance, the two processes appear to be quite similar; only the terms labeling each segment seem to differ. However, the major difference between the two processes is that the MRTA is more open-ended. As students listen to the teacher read or read a book by themselves, they are involved in a four-step cycle that is repeated several times from start to finish: *predict–listen–explain–connect.* Combs (1996) explains that "[t]he cycles occur because you pose open-ended questions and statements that continue to nudge children's [listening] and thinking. In response to your questions and comments, children [listen to or read] the text, explain and provide support for their thinking, make connections to what they already know, and think ahead about where the text seems to be going" (p. 256). The teacher activates the children's thinking with a series of open-ended questions throughout the reading. At the *beginning* of the story, for example, the students might be asked to examine the cover of the book and its title, connect their observations to their own backgrounds of experience, and, on the basis of these attachments, predict what they think might happen in the story. Then they listen to verify their predictions. For example, let's suppose that the students are about to read the book *Death of the Iron Horse* by Paul Goble (Bradbury). It is a story about a group of young Cheyenne braves who derail and raid a freight train encroaching on their territory in 1867. To construct meaning from the book, the teacher asks the students to look at the front cover and examine the illustration (a freight train and Cheyenne brave drawn in the traditional style of Cheyenne art). Then, reading the title of the book and pointing out the illustration, the teacher would ask the students, "What do you think this book might be about?" Teachers should not expect "right" answers at this point; they only want students to think of possibilities based on their background experiences and the

FIGURE 11–3
Mediated Reading Thinking Activity

Before Reading

Teacher should:

- Establish clear purpose(s) for reading a particular text.
- Identify strategies for meeting that purpose.
- Consider how to adjust support during the reading to help children move toward independent thinking.
- Encourage children to anticipate reading, using text and background knowledge.
- Focus reading for identified purpose(s) (e.g., discuss how stories have beginnings, middles, and ends, and how these are used to make meaning).

Children should:

- Predict what might come in the reading using available information.
- Connect the prediction to current background knowledge.
- Be prepared for meeting the purpose(s) of the reading.

During Reading

Teacher should:

- Read aloud in a fluid and lively manner.
- Stop the reading at appropriate places to assist children in making meaning and meeting reading purposes.
- Encourage children's use of identified strategies.
- Encourage children's responses, listening thoughtfully.
- Adjust support according to need reflected in children's responses.

Children should:

- Use listening-thinking strategies to meet reading purpose(s).
- Give feedback to teacher about thinking during the reading.
- Meet purpose(s) of reading.
- Use background knowledge and text to understand essential vocabulary.

After Reading

Teacher should:

- Encourage response through open-ended questions, such as "Well, what did you think of that story?"
- Elicit retelling, first unaided through open-ended questions, and then aided by probing for specific points.
- Based on response, determine what essential words may warrant further discussion.
- Reaffirm strategies used to meet reading purposes.
- Depending on purposes and children's responses, determine whether repeated readings are warranted or desirable.

Children should:

- Share responses to the reading (creative/personal meanings).
- Retell most important points (explicit meaning).
- Discuss understanding of essential vocabulary.

Source: Combs, M. (1996). *Developing competent readers and writers in the primary grades.* Englewood Cliffs, NJ: Prentice Hall, 150.

clues on the cover. Responses should be treated as predictions that will be verified as the story is read or listened to.

Then the teacher says, "The title of our book is *Death of the Iron Horse.* What is an iron horse?" Wondering aloud, the teacher then asks, "I wonder what might cause the death of a steam locomotive." Students are asked to support their predictions: "What makes you think that?" This topic is discussed as long as there is interest. Finally, the teacher says, "Let's read to find out."

During the reading, the teacher asks other open-ended questions and encourages the students to uphold their thoughts with supporting evidence, which may include citing information from the text or rereading specific portions of the text. For example, the teacher might say, "I wonder how the Cheyenne will defend their lands. What leads you to think that?" Or, "What will the Cheyenne do with the goods from the train?" At the end of the reading, the teacher once again encourages response through open-ended questions: "Do you think the Cheyenne's deed will be enough to stop expansion of the white men? What makes you say that?"

After the reading, there are many ways that children can respond to literature, but the four procedures that appear to be most popularly used while employing the MRTA in social studies classrooms include (1) *discussions,* (2) *response charts,* (3) *journals,* and (4) *readers' theater.*

Discussions and Response Charts.

Teachers who value children's ideas ask questions other than those that always require students to come up with the "right answer" or supply a thought they agree with. If students sense that you are open to a variety of responses about what has just been read, they should eventually imitate your behaviors and, in turn, become more tolerant of other people and of ideas that differ from their own. Most literature-based social studies programs value open-ended thinking in response to stories, but they operate with a conviction that the students need some support in understanding the content of the story, too. Therefore, teachers in social studies classrooms often begin a story discussion with a series of "comprehension checks" that determine whether or not the children understand the main direction of the story, followed by a number of more open-ended questions that invite a variety of responses. Sloan (1984) has developed a helpful list of sample questions that invite "comprehension check" responses to a story:

> "Where and when does the story take place? How do you know? If the story took place somewhere else or in a different time, how would it be changed?"
>
> "What incident, problem, conflict, or situation does the author use to get the story started?"
>
> "Trace the main events of the story. Could you change their order or leave any of them out? Why or why not?"
>
> "Who is the main character of the story? What kind of a person is that character? How did you know?"
>
> "Did you have any feelings as you read the story? What did the author do to make you feel strongly?" (pp. 104–106)

Oftentimes, teachers will help facilitate student responses to these "comprehension check" questions with concrete teaching aids that help them organize and represent graphically ideas and relationships. These concrete teaching aids help students rehearse what they want to talk about. For example, Mr. Jacobs read to his third-graders the book *Nannabah's Friend* by Mary Perrine (Houghton Mifflin), a sensitive story of how a young Navajo girl bridges the gap between the security of home and the world outside. He thought this was an excellent book to use for character analysis, especially since the children would immediately identify with Nannabah and her plight. To help analyze Nannabah's character, Mr. Jacobs and his students made a web of her traits. See their character web in Figure 11–4.

FIGURE 11–4
Character Web

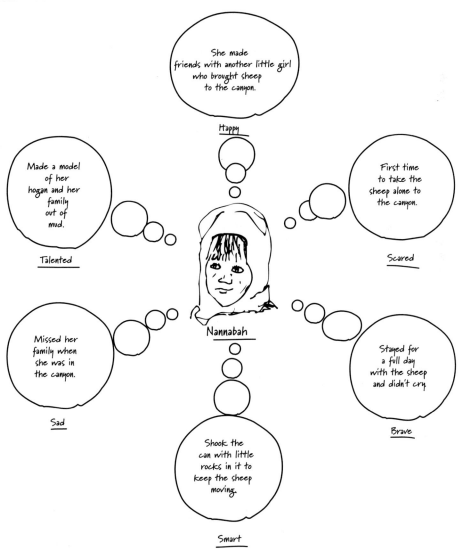

She made friends with another little girl who brought sheep to the canyon.

Happy

Made a model of her hogan and her family out of mud.

Talented

First time to take the sheep alone to the canyon.

Scared

Missed her family when she was in the canyon.

Sad

Nannabah

Stayed for a full day with the sheep and didn't cry

Brave

Shook the can with little rocks in it to keep the sheep moving.

Smart

When teachers want to prompt individual responses to a story, their questions prompt students to think more openly. Vandergrift (1980) offers examples of such questions:

- "What idea or ideas does this story make you think about? How does the author get you to think about this?"
- "Is there one character that you know more about than any of the others? Who is this character and what kind of a person is he/she?"
- "Are there other characters important to the story? Who are they? Why are they important?"
- "Did you notice any particular patterns in the form of this book?"
- "Were there clues that the author built into the story that helped you anticipate the outcome? What were they?"
- "What questions would you ask if the author were here? Which would be the most important question? How might the author answer it?"

Open-ended questions are often used to initiate literature-based discussions called *grand conversations* (Tompkins, 1997). In place of the traditional "inquisitions" during which students recited answers to factual questions teachers asked about books they had read, grand conversations shift the focus to making connections between the text and the students' own lives. Tompkins elaborates:

> Teachers often participate in grand conversations, but they act as interested participants, not leaders. The talk is primarily among the students, but teachers ask questions regarding things they are genuinely interested in learning more about and share information in response to questions that students ask. . . .
> Grand conversations can be held with the whole class or in small groups. Young children usually meet together as a class, while older students often prefer to talk with classmates in small groups. (p. 259)

Literature Response Journals.   Literature response journals are booklets or notebooks in which students record personal reactions to what they read or listen to. Tompkins and Hoskisson (1995) advise that literature response journals should not be used to simply summarize stories, but to relate students' reading to their own lives or to other literature they have read. In addition, "Students may also list interesting or unfamiliar words, jot down quotable quotes, and take notes about characters, plot, or other story elements; but the primary purpose of these journals is for students to think about the book, connect literature to their lives, and develop their own interpretations" (p. 172).

Literature response journals are being used with children as young as kindergarten age. Most typically, kindergarten children listen to their teacher read a story and draw their response. When children start writing words to accompany their drawings, their entries usually summarize the plot. In time, the drawings become less significant and the written entries take on a more interpretive or personal nature (see Figure 11–5a and 11–5b, parts 1 and 2).

FIGURE 11–5a
Upper-Grade Literature Response Log

THE GIVER
by Lois Lowry

A book that made a difference for me is one called <u>The Giver</u>. It is about a twelve year old boy who lives in the future world where there is no fighting, poverty, or injustice. In this book no one can see color. All they can see is gray. When they are twelve, all children get assigned the job they have to do for their adult years (like Caretaker of the Old). The main character, Jonas, is selected by the Giver for a special job called The Receiver of Memory. This job requires one to remember the past when everyone could see color and had a choice of what they could do. But it also helped Jonas discover some very important secrets about his world.

The book made me realize that the future may not be as good as everyone thinks it will be. So I think that our time is good enough. The reason I liked this book was because it was not in our place of time. It was a future book but not with space ships and robots. It made the future look boring and very lonesome instead of fun and really high tech. Also, it showed me how one person could make a difference. Jonas left the village so that all the memories of the past would flood the minds of the people in the town in order for everyone to see color and have feelings as in the past. <u>The Giver</u> is a great book to get so check it out.

by Gayle Westover
Grade 7- Ms. Summers

Journals can be powerful reading-response tools, and teachers are now using them widely in literature-based social studies programs. Cooper (1997), however, cautions teachers against their improper use:

- *Beware of overuse of journals.* Sometimes teachers get so excited about journals that they use them in every subject. Students become bored, and the journals lose their effectiveness.
- *Don't require all students to write in their journals every day.* To get everyone to write, teachers often require a daily entry. This turns students off to journals.

> Amy L.
> The BAd Gise
> SaiD You CAn't
> PrAy To god. You
> hAve To PrAy To us
> not god. And The
> BAd reckT Their HouES.
> But thAt WAS not
> nice. And A
> Little Kid fouNd
> Some oeL. And
> The LigHt StAd
> for eigHt DAYS.

Therefore, allow students to use journals as a choice. Some teachers require a minimum number of entries each week, especially in middle school.

- *Make sure you know your reason for having students use journals.* Be confident about why you are using journals before you begin. Avoid using journals just for the sake of using them.

- *Remember that journals are instructional tools.* Journals should replace other, less meaningful types of activities that students might do. They should not become just more "busy work" that is added on to what students already need to complete. (p. 319)

Readers' Theater.   The term *readers' theater* is used to describe the process in which children are encouraged to act out characters and experiences from the sto-

FIGURE 11–5b (part 2)
Lower-Grade Literature Response Log

ries they have listened to or read independently. Performances are not formal; there is no need to memorize lines or create elaborate sets and costumes. Select a story with a good deal of dialogue and an engaging plot (an easy introduction to readers' theater is a repetitive story such as Verna Aardema's *Why Mosquitos Buzz in People's Ears*).

The following course of action is useful in planning for readers' theater in the social studies classroom:

- Discuss the plot and variety of story characters. Identify the characters needed to dramatize the story and how the characters might have gone about their tasks or how they might have spoken important lines. For example, "How do you suppose python might have moved as he said, 'wasawusu, wasawusu, wasawusu'?" Also, decide on one or two narrators who will read aloud the parts between the dialogue. For kindergarten or first-grade children, the teacher may need to read aloud while the children share the dialogue, but older children can read or retell the story.

• Guide the children to improvise the actions of each character and to practice their parts several times. Dramatization techniques will differ depending on the book involved and the students. If students are to do the read-aloud portion, they should enliven the performance by using variations in pitch, intonation, and reading rate.

• Remember that informality is the key to successful readers' theater experiences. Although the readers' theater is scripted, we expect neither a superb performance nor extensively memorized lines. Rather, the emphasis is on enjoyment.

Saltz and Saltz (1986) describe how *The Three Little Pigs* was used as a readers' theater episode:

> After reading the fairy tale to the children, the teacher led a brief discussion of the story theme and motivations of the characters ("Why did the little pig run to the brick house?" "How did the little pig feel when the wolf said, 'I'll huff and I'll puff!'?"). Roles were then chosen or assigned, and the children reenacted the story. Props and costumes were minimal and often chosen or constructed by the children themselves. Children were strongly encouraged to follow the original story line. Reproduction of the original dialogue was not, however, considered important, and rephrasing was accepted. . . . Initially, the teacher's role was very directive, perhaps serving as narrator, or frequently prompting, as the children engaged in the actions indicated. If necessary, the teacher might even physically lead a child through an action. . . . As the children became more experienced, the teacher's active direction was decreased and sometimes even eliminated; the children themselves would often direct each other in the reenactments, as in, "Wolf, [you're not supposed] to run away now, [you're supposed] to get stuck in the chimney!" (pp. 157–158)

Folktales from around the world are excellent sources for readers' theater productions, especially when used with young children. Books heavily laden with dialogue work especially well with older students: for example, *Sarah, Plain and Tall* by Patricia MacLachlan or *The Lorax* by Dr. Seuss. Even though the children re-telling these stories will be older, the readers' theater need not become a big production. Children simply take turns being the readers, actors, and audience.

AFTERWORD

Although it might be controversial to recommend both the DR–TA and the MRTA as integral components of elementary school social studies programs, I believe it is possible to use each technique as a source of helpful support when reading from the textbook or a trade book. For students or teachers comfortable with receiving or offering a higher degree of deliberate guidance, the DR–TA can be productive. For students or teachers who thrive in open-ended environments, the MRTA might provide the most productive system of support. Only by knowing yourself and your students can you make the best decision. A sample read-aloud episode using the DR–TA is shown in Activity 11–2; a sample read-aloud episode based on the MLTA approach is shown in Activity 11–3.

Good literature and the social studies are inseparable. Through various genres, students are able to recognize concerns common to people of all ages, places, and times. Your social studies program will be enriched by using these materials that engage the minds and hearts of your students.

Activity 11-2
DR-TA for *Mufaro's Beautiful Daughters*
Backgrouund

Mafaro's Beautiful Daughters (Lothrop) is John Steptoe's version of an African folktale of two equally beautiful daughters with two completely different personalities. The daughters are called before the king, who must choose a wife from among the most beautiful and worthy women in the land. The daughters' virtues earn their just rewards. This story will be read to the children as part of a thematic unit on African folklore.

Prereading

A clever pirate puppet with a secret treasure chest is all you'll need to capture interest in this read-aloud book. Tell your students that "Pete the Pirate" is a special friend of yours who travels the world over in search of exciting adventures. He has just returned from a trip on his pirate ship and, in his treasure chest, has brought a number of interesting souvenirs along with a storybook. Have Pete show students on the globe where his last adventure took him—Africa. Pinpoint Zimbabwe (in southern Africa) and compare its location to your city. Have Pete reach into the teacher-constructed treasure chest and take out a study print showing the land and people of Zimbabwe (Pete's "souvenir photo"). Discuss the scene. Then reach back into the treasure chest and, one at a time, take out a bit of millet, a handful of sunflower seeds, a gnarled yam, and a wiggly rubber snake. Ask the children to suggest what each item is. If they can't, have Pete furnish the background information. Pete should explain that the snake is a major character from *Mufaro's Beautiful Daughters* and the items play especially significant roles in the story. Emphasize that although snakes are helpful creatures that contribute to productive natural cycles, they are often feared and scorned undeservedly by people around the world. In this story, the snake is a very helpful and special character. Ask students to listen carefully as you read the story to learn how the snake becomes a treasured creature, as well as to discover the significance of each of the other tems in Pete's treasure chest.

Examine the cover of the book. Have the children look at the title and the illustration for clues as to what the story might be about. What does the young lady on the cover appear to be doing? What kind of a person does she seem to be? Introduce her as Manyara (mahn-YAR-ah), one of Mufaro's (moo-FAR-oh) two beautiful daughters. Write both names on the board. Add two other character names—Nyasha (nee-AH-sha) and Nyoka (nee-YO-kah). Tell the students that John Steptoe selected these four names for the characters in the story because each name is descriptive of the character. Show them that you have written the meanings on separate cards. Ask the students to listen to the story to see if they can tell which name card can best be associated with each meaning card (Mufaro = *Happy Man,* Manyara = *Ashamed,* Nyasha = *Mercy,* Nyoka = *Snake*). Ask the students to predict what they can about the story elements from their preview. Then inform them that they are to listen to the story for three purposes: (1) to uncover the significance of each item in the treasure chest, (2) to associate names with character traits, and (3) to verify their predictions.

The Reading Experience

Read the tale aloud to the class as they listen for the established purposes.

Postreading

1. Lead a discussion about the significance of each item that was removed from the treasure chest during the prereading phase of this story.

2. Ask students to match the name cards to each of the character cards and defend their reasons for doing so.

3. Prepare an information-summary chart. Give each studnet a card containing a specific piece of information from the story. Each student must help finish the chart puzzle by attaching their data card to the appropriate slots until the missing details fit together to tell a story.

WHO?	WHAT?	WHERE?	WHEN?	WHY?
MUFARO	proclaimed he was the happiest father	in all the land	at the wedding feast	he had two beautiful and worthy daughters
NYASHA	tended her crops	in her garden	day after day	it was part of her chores
MANYARA	sneaked away	to the city	in the middle of the night	to be first to see the king
NYOKA	hid in the garden	under the leaves and vines	while Nyasha worked	to keep the garden pests away

Enrichment Activity

Have the students brainstorm words to describe additional personality characteristics of Mufaro (e.g., proud, trusting), Nyasha (e.g., compassionate, generous), and Manyara (e.g., selfish, greedy). Ask them to support their words with evidence from the story ("What makes you say this?"). Then as a follow-up, have the students write their names on circles cut from white construction paper. Each student then glues construction paper petals of various colors and shapes around the circle to form a flower. Have students complete the flowers by writing their personality traits on the petals. Display the flowers on a bulletin board display entitled "(Teacher's Name)'s Beautiful Students."

Activity 11-3

MRTA for *The Wave*

Background

The Wave by Margaret Hodges (Houghton Mifflin) is a captivating story of the people of a small village in Japan who are threatened by a powerful tidal wave. While the unsuspecting villagers are having fun near the edge of the ocean, Ojisan, an old man who lives at the top of the hill, is the only one who senses the potential danger. To warn them, Ojisan uses a technique guaranteed to catch their attention—burning his precious rice fields.

Prereading

Examine the illustration on the front cover of the book. Look at the title and ask, "From looking at the cover of the book, what ideas do you have about the story? What makes you think that?" The emphasis should not be on who comes closest to the "right" answer, but only on the possibilities presented by the information contained on the book's cover. Think aloud, "I wonder why the people of the village are so terrified of an ocean's wave." Pause for responses and then suggest, "Let's listen to the story to find out."

Reading

Begin by reading only the part that describes the people enjoying themselves in their village at the base of the hillside. Ask, "What did we find out? Do we have enough information yet to tell why the villagers are terrified of the wave?" Connect to the next section by asking, "Did you find any clues that might inform us that something destructive might soon happen?" Pause for the children's responses.

In the next section, Ojisan sets fire to his precious rice fields. Ask, "What caused the old man to do something like this? Why would he do such a thing?" Connect to the next section by asking, "What do you think the people will do when they see the fire? Why do you think that?"

In the next section, the people rush up the hillside to help save Ojisan's rice fields. Ask, "Were you right? How did your ideas compare to what the author wrote?" Connect to the next section by asking, "Do we have enough information yet to tell why Ojisan set fire to the rice fields? Let's listen to find out more."

Next, the huge *tsunami* crashes into the beach and wipes out the entire village. The villagers were saved because they had rushed up the hillside to help put out the fire in Ojisan's rice fields. Ask, "What did you find out about Ojisan? What makes you think that?" Connect to the next section by asking, "What do you think will happen in the next scene? How will the story end?"

In the last section, the villagers look down at their devastated village; only an empty beach can be seen where their village once stood. Ask, "How do you think the people now feel about Ojisan? What makes you say that? How do you think they will thank him for sacrificing his rice to save their lives?"

Connect to the next section of the MRTA by saying, "Let's take a few minutes to think back on what we heard."

Postreading

Because most second and third graders enjoy this suspenseful story, it is beneficial to start out with a discussion about their personal feelings. Ask, "What do you think of Ojisan? What makes you feel that way?" As they respond, look for a way to lead the children through a retelling of the story. Use the suspenseful changes in scenes to help students realize that the story is organized in a Beginning–Middle–End structure. Say, "Let's think back to what we listened to."

Help the students recall the story and the feelings associated with the major events. Say, "I like the way the author described how the characters felt during each part of the story." Then display a chart divided into Beginning–Middle–End segments. Reread the story, pausing at the end of each significant event. Have the students summarize the events during each pause in reading. For example, the beginning might be summarized: "The ocean was calm and everyone was having fun in the village." Divide the class into three groups. During each pause in events, students in Group 1 would write a single word on a slip of self-sticking paper to describe Ojuisan's feelings; students in Group 2 would each write a single word describing Tada's (Ojisan's grandson) feelings; and students in Group 3 would do the same for the villagers. After each section break, students would stick their words onto the chart in the appropriate place.

After the entire story is reread, each contribution should be discussed and supported with appropriate evidence from the story.

Finally, as an extension activity, the students would creatively dramatize the story events by participating in a readers' theater production.

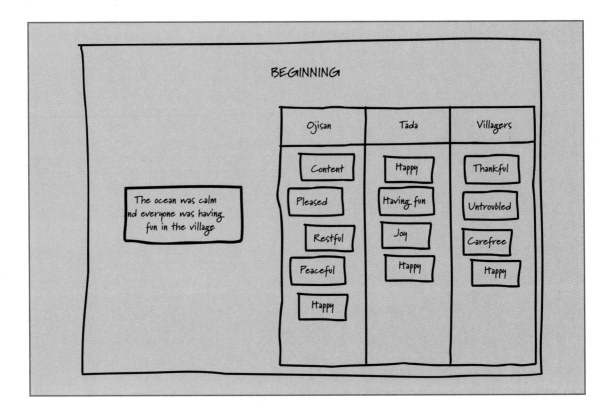

TECHNOLOGY SAMPLER

Useful sources for related social studies topics include these Internet sites:

Literature Links (K–12 literature links)
http://www.npac.syr.edu/textbook/kidsweb/

Schoolwide Study Skills (lessons for teaching study skills)
http://www.studyskills.com

Textbook Resources (ideas, lessons, and interactive games)
http://kcs.kana.k12.wv.us/edcomer/textbook.html

Useful sources for related social studies topics include these software titles:

Writing for Readers

Pierian Spring
Challenges children to apply higher-order thinking skills to their reading and to read for a variety of purposes.

WHAT I *NOW* KNOW

Complete these self-check items once more. Determine for yourself whether it would be useful to take a more in-depth look at any area. Use the same key as you did for the preassessment form ("+", "?", "–").

I can *now*

_____ define the concept of *literacy across the curriculum.*

_____ describe the pattern of instruction characterized by the Directed Reading-Thinking Activity (DR–TA)

_____ explain the processes involved with the Mediated Reading Thinking Activity (MRTA).

_____ delineate the benefits and problems associated with textbook use in the social studies program.

_____ support the use of trade books in the social studies curriculum.

_____ identify the major trade book genres adaptable to the social studies curriculum.

_____ defend the use of traditional and contemporary techniques to help children read to learn from various print resources.

REFERENCES

Armento, B. J., Nash, G. B., Salter, C. L., & Wixson, K. K. (1991). *Houghton Mifflin social studies: This is my country.* Boston: Houghton Mifflin.

Bush, C. L., & Huebner, M. H. (1970). *Strategies for reading in the elementary school.* New York: Macmillan.

Chase, S. (1971). Mokusatsu. In Littell, J. F., *The language of man, Book 5* (p. 32). Evanston, IL: McDougal, Littell.

Cheek, E. H., Jr., Flippo, R. F., & Lindsey, J. D. (1997). *Reading for success in elementary schools.* Madison, WI: Brown & Benchmark.

Combs, M. (1996). *Developing competent readers and writers in the primary grades.* Englewood Cliffs, NJ: Merrill/Prentice Hall.

Cooper, J. D. (1997). *Literacy: Helping children construct meaning.* Boston: Houghton Mifflin.

Dale, E. (1969). *Audiovisual methods in teaching.* New York: Holt, Rinehart and Winston.

Dewey, J. (1933). *How we think.* Boston: D.C. Heath.

Dolch, E. W. (1951). *Psychology and teaching of reading.* Champaign, IL: Garrard.

Dowd, F. S. (1990). What's a jackdaw doing in our classroom? *Childhood Education, 66,* 228–231.

Durkin, D. (1978–1979). What classroom observations reveal about reading comprehension instruction. *Reading Research Quarterly, 24,* 481–533.

Eisenberg, L. (1991). *The story of Sitting Bull, great Sioux chief.* New York: Dell.

Freedman, R. (1987). *Lincoln: A photobiography.* New York: Clarion.

Goodman, K. S. (1988). Look what they've done to Judy Blume!: The "basalization" of children's literature. *The New Advocate, 1,* 29–41.

Harp, B., & Brewer, J. A. (1996). *Reading and writing: Teaching for the connections.* Fort Worth: Harcourt Brace College Publishers.

Hennings, D. G. (1990). *Communication in action.* Boston: Houghton Mifflin.

Holmes, B. C., & Roser, N. L. (1987). Five ways to assess readers' prior knowledge. *Reading Teacher, 40,* 646–649.

Huck, C. S., Hepler, S., & Hickman, J. (1993). *Children's literature in the elementary school.* Fort Worth, TX: Harcourt Brace Jovanovich.

Jarolimek, J., & Parker, W. C. (1993). Social studies in elementary education. New York: Macmillan.

Lapp, D., Flood, J., & Farnan, N. (1992). Basal readers and literature: A tight fit or a mismatch? In K. D. Wood & A. Moss (Eds.), *Exploring literature in the classroom: Contents and methods* (pp. 35–57). Norwood, MA: Christopher Gordon.

Leu, D. L., Jr., & Kinzer, C. K. (1987). *Effective reading instruction in the elementary grades.* New York: Merrill/Macmillan.

Manning, J. C., (1985). What's needed now in reading instruction: The teacher as scholar and romanticist. *The Reading Teacher, 39,* 136.

Morgan, J. C., & Schreiber, J. E. (1969). How to ask questions. *How to do it series,* no. 24. Washington, DC: National Council for the Social Studies.

Orlich, D. C., et al. (1990). *Teaching strategies: A guide to better instruction.* Lexington, MA: D.C. Heath.

Ravitch, D. (1978). Tot sociology. *American Educator, 6,* 38.

Robinson, H. A. (1970). *Effective study.* New York: Harper & Row.

Rodgers, F. A. (1975). *Curriculum and instruction in the elementary school.* New York: Macmillan.

Rosenblatt, L. M. (1982). The literary transaction: Evocation and response. *Theory into Practice, 21,* 268–277.

Saltz, R., & Saltz, E. (1986). Pretend play training and its outcomes. In G. Fein & M. Rivkin (Eds.), *The young child at play* (pp. 155–173). Washington, DC: National Association for the Education of Young Children.

Sewall, G. (1988a). Literary lackluster. *American Educator, 12,* 35.

Sewall, G. (1988b). Framework will force textbook changes. *ASCD Update, 30,* 2.

Sloan, G. D. (1984). *The child as critic: Teaching literature in elementary and middle schools.* New York: Teachers College Press.

Solomon, W. (1989). Teaching social studies creatively. *Social Studies and the Young Learner, 2,* 3–5.

Stauffer, R. G. (1969). *Directing reading maturity as a cognitive process.* New York: Harper & Row.

Taba, H., Durkin, M. C., Fraenkel, J. R., & McNaughton, A. (1971). *A teacher's handbook to elementary social studies.* Reading, MA: Addison-Wesley.

Taylor, M. D. (1992). *Mississippi bridge.* New York: Bantam Skylark.

Thaiss, C. (1986). *Language across the curriculum in the elementary grades.* Urbana, IL: National Council of Teachers of English.

Tompkins, G. E. (1997). *Literacy for the 21st century: A balanced approach.* Englewood Cliffs, NJ: Merrill/ Prentice Hall.

Tompkins, G. E., & Hoskisson, K. (1995). *Language arts: Content and teaching strategies.* Englewood Cliffs, NJ: Merrill/Prentice Hall.

Vacca, R. T., & Vacca, J. L. (1986). *Content area reading.* Boston: Little Brown.

Vandergrift, K. (1980). *Child and story.* New York: Neal-Schuman Publishers.

Young, E. (1989). *Lon Po Po.* New York: Scholastic.

Zinsser, W. (Ed.) (1990). *Worlds of childhood: The art and craft of writing for children.* Boston: Houghton Mifflin.

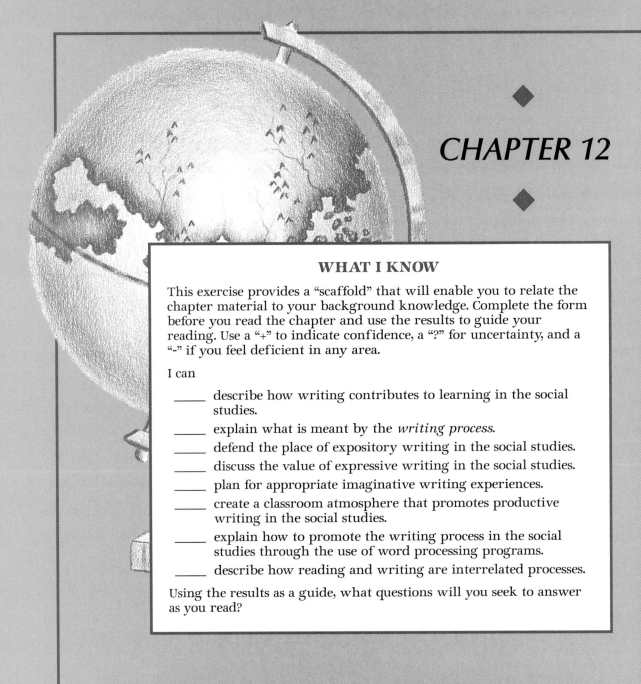

CHAPTER 12

WHAT I KNOW

This exercise provides a "scaffold" that will enable you to relate the chapter material to your background knowledge. Complete the form before you read the chapter and use the results to guide your reading. Use a "+" to indicate confidence, a "?" for uncertainty, and a "-" if you feel deficient in any area.

I can

_____ describe how writing contributes to learning in the social studies.

_____ explain what is meant by the *writing process.*

_____ defend the place of expository writing in the social studies.

_____ discuss the value of expressive writing in the social studies.

_____ plan for appropriate imaginative writing experiences.

_____ create a classroom atmosphere that promotes productive writing in the social studies.

_____ explain how to promote the writing process in the social studies through the use of word processing programs.

_____ describe how reading and writing are interrelated processes.

Using the results as a guide, what questions will you seek to answer as you read?

Writing to Learn

◆ CLASSROOM SKETCH

Students in Mr. Bonelli's fifth-grade classroom gathered around a yellow rug they called their "Rap Ring." The "Rap Ring" was a meeting place where the class would come together whenever there were special ideas to be shared. Mr. Bonelli set up this unique sharing center because he believes that classroom communication can be most effectively facilitated when the children are able to see one another in a functional setting.

On this day, the students were getting ready to share group reports they had written while researching the topic, "Flags in Early American History." Before beginning the presentations, Mr. Bonelli wanted to make sure the students could link their background information to the shared information, so he displayed a large, present-day flag of the United States and asked the students if they could explain the meaning of the colors, stars, and stripes. Mr. Bonelli then explained that clues to test their predictions would be offered by groups of students as they shared reports about how the flag has evolved into its present form. Mr. Bonelli then drew a diagram on the chalkboard to help students classify the information related to what they would be listening to (see Figure 12–1). After each presentation, students would add pertinent details to the chart. To aid them in the listening process, Mr. Bonelli asked the students to duplicate his diagram on a sheet of paper and take notes as they listened to each report.

FIGURE 12–1
Organizing the Details

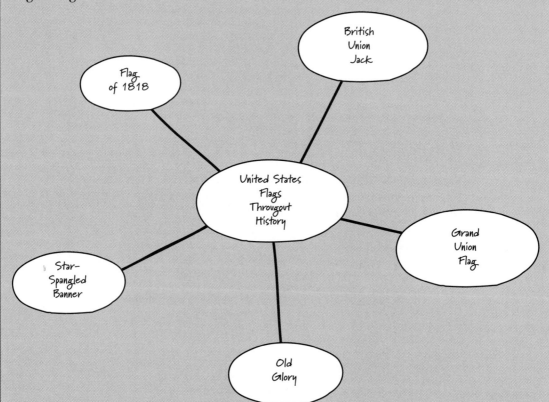

As part of its presentation, each group displayed a drawing of its selected flag and shared a short report describing the flag's historical significance. Figure 12–2 is an example of the report that was read aloud by the first group as it described our Colonists' earliest flag, the "Grand Union Flag."

After each flag group read its written piece aloud, classmates asked questions and contributed ideas in an attempt to pull together the separate flag descriptions. Details were then added to Mr. Bonelli's chalkboard diagram from the notes the children had taken. Finally, students synthesized the information gathered from the reports to explain the symbolism of our present-day flag.

Because Mr. Bonelli subscribes to the idea that the *informative function of language* is dominant both in school and out, a major component of his social studies program involves writing as a part of learning.

FIGURE 12-2
Student Report

The Grand Union Flag

The Grand Union Flag served as America's first national flag. It had a British Jack in the top left corner out of loyalty to the crown. It had 13 stripes to show the unity of the 13 colonies. It was raised the first day of January 1776 over George Washington's headquarters. It lasted untill 1777.

Luke Darigan

◆   CLASSROOM CONNECTION

Why should elementary school children write in social studies? Much of what we say in response to that question is based on the work of contemporary researchers and educators such as Nancie Atwell, Donald Graves, and Donald Murray. According to Templeton (1997), these scholars are clear on one important point: "Children do not learn to write by working exclusively on exercises in grammar texts; they primarily learn to write by writing" (p. 230). If this is true, then classroom teachers must create diverse contexts, or environments, where writing can be experienced as a functional and educative process. These classroom contexts are rich and varied, but must include social studies, a curriculum area "that is as appropriate for writing as the gym is for basketball" (Murray, in Atwell, 1987, p. 54). The social studies curriculum offers contexts in which students are able to write frequently and for different purposes—an environment in which writing in different forms can be perceived as necessary and useful.

In this chapter, we will explore the writing process as it is applied to the social studies program and examine the many ways we can enhance learning in the social studies through writing.

─────────

THE WRITING PROCESS

If students are going to write for meaning in social studies, they must understand the specific aspects of the writing process as it is applied to the content areas. Research indicates that everyone—from the professional adult writer to the kindergarten-age author—follows a similar course before, during, and after they write (Murray, 1980). This shared course of action consists of five major elements that, when combined, define the writing process: *experiencing, prewriting, composing, rewriting,* and *publishing.*

Experiencing

Throughout this text, you have read about the how a rich background of experiences serves as the fundamental wellspring from which children develop knowledge, establish concepts, and come to understand the actions and consequences of people and things around them. Children derive meaning from direct, firsthand experiences; they must touch, feel, taste, see, hear, and manipulate in order to comprehend their environment. Teachers facilitate this process by taking their students on a field trip to a television studio, offering a prickly pear cactus plant to examine, or inviting the local mayor to visit the classroom. These direct experiences stimulate writing by providing opportunities for input of information, discussion, exploration of ideas, and expression of feelings.

As important as direct experiences are for furnishing the raw material for writing, however, teachers will find it inconvenient or impossible to provide firsthand experiences for every social studies topic. For example, suppose that a teacher wishes to discuss the invention of the cotton gin. She would like to show her students an example of the machine, but the nearest one is in a museum hundreds of miles away! In such a case, a videotape, photograph, diagram, or illustration must substitute for the real thing. While studying the construction of the transcontinental railroad, limitations related to time and distance would certainly prevent most teachers from taking their students to Promontory Point, Utah, to see where the final spike was driven. Reading a picture-book story or showing a videotape to the class might be an acceptable vicarious experience. Readiness for writing depends on understandings that emerge from experiences, both direct and vicarious.

Writing in social studies is based on the premise that meaning comes from within the writer. Nowhere can this discovery be illustrated more clearly than this episode from the life of Helen Keller (1920), who lost her sight and hearing after a fever at the age of 19 months. The following high point in Keller's life occurs when her teacher, Anne Sullivan, places the hand of her then seven-year-old pupil under the spout of a pump:

> We walked down the path to the well-house, attracted by the fragrance of the honeysuckle with which it was covered. Someone was drawing water and my teacher placed my hand under the spout. As the cool stream gushed over one hand she spelled into the other the word *water,* first slowly, then rapidly. I stood still, my whole attention fixed upon the motions of her fingers. Suddenly I felt a misty consciousness as of something forgotten—a thrill of returning thought; and somehow the mystery of language was revealed to me. I knew then that "W-A-T-E-R" meant the wonderful cool something that was flowing over my hand. That living word awakened my soul, gave it light, hope, joy, set it free! (pp. 23–24)

Writing in social studies is comparable to the adventure of Helen Keller; it is awakened and set free by mind-stirring experiences, both real and vicarious.

Prewriting

Prewriting involves the process of guiding children to reflect on their direct or vicarious experiences for the purpose of bringing meaning to the written work. For kindergarteners or first graders, for example, artwork (drawing) is a preferred prewriting activity. As these youngsters draw pictures of stimulating experiences, they think about what information they want to disclose and then represent their ideas as a drawing. After a trip to a farm, for example, children's drawings would most probably reflect a variety of interests: Naisha draws a barn and silo in great detail, Brandon paints a large orange pumpkin, and Maria's white cow reflects her great interest in animals. Creative one- or two-sentence "stories" grow naturally from such experiences; they are usually dictated to the teacher, who writes them on the children's artwork. The children might also be encouraged to use "invented spelling" in order to compose their own stories. "This is a Guernsey cow," offered Maria as she explained her drawing. "It gives yellowish milk."

Writing about their experiences will deepen children's impressions of the people they have met and the places they have seen.

Children in the upper elementary school grades may organize their thoughts about an experience through such information-processing strategies as webbing, charting, brainstorming, and other techniques such as those presented in Chapters 5 and 11. The overall purpose of the prewriting stage is to reflect on background learning experiences in order to build ideas for writing. The prewriting stage thus becomes a vehicle for thought; it helps students get ideas "out of their heads" in a purposeful, systematic manner. Murray (1980) recommends that at least 70 percent of writing time should be spent in the experiencing and prewriting phases, where students gather information, brainstorm, process information, and prepare for writing.

Composing

The foremost task of the composing stage is to create words, phrases, and sentences that best express the ideas generated and organized during the prewriting stage.

Composing should be a time when children are encouraged to pour forth words onto the page, easily and freely. Certainly, it is a time of making decisions, too: what to put in, what to leave out, in what order ideas should be presented, and which words to choose. The objective of the composing phase is not to produce a polished piece of writing; good handwriting, punctuation, spelling, grammar, and other such conventions take a back seat to the expression of ideas. Important content decisions must be made at this early point of the writing process, and an unreasonable concern for writing conventions can impinge on what the author is trying to say. If children become more concerned about mechanics than the expression of ideas, their writing often become dull and lifeless. Graves (1983) explains:

> When a writer struggles to find meaning in an early draft, conventions are less important. I want the writer to focus on discovering the one thing the piece is about. Teachers who insist on full accuracy in early drafts are wasting both the students' time and their own. On the other hand, when the focus of the piece is clear, the use of conventions can be a delightful, interesting experience. (p. 39)

What has been said about writing conventions should not be construed as a laissez-faire approach to writing in the social studies. On the contrary, a major part of the writing process is to guide children in the correct use of conventions. But composing is a time when we encourage fluent thinking; noticing and using conventions calls for a greater degree of deliberation and formality. The ABCs of writing conventions can be addressed in the rewriting phase (although all writing in the social studies need not result in an edited composition).

Rewriting

This phase of the writing process is commonly referred to as *editing* or *revising*; whatever we choose to call it, this is the time when the composition is reread and polished in terms of both content and writing conventions. The role of the student now changes from free thinker to deliberate reader with the goal of making several decisions about the content. Farris (1993) explains: "The writer must consider possible adjustments in the organization of the material, the clarification of meanings, and the expansion of general ideas. . . . At this juncture, the writer must also analyze and correct punctuation, spelling, and usage errors" (p. 184). Although this can be an individual task, students usually exchange papers with one another or discuss their drafts in small groups. These groups usually form spontaneously whenever four or five students finish their rough drafts. Sitting around a table or assembled on the rug in a corner of the room, the children take turns reading their rough drafts to one another. After they finish, group members first offer polite compliments (what they liked about the piece) before suggesting content revision. Tompkins and Hoskisson (1995) offer these suggestions for helping children offer polite compliments:

- "I like the part where you. . . ."
- "I'd like to know more about. . . ."

- "I like the way you described. . . ."
- "Your writing made me feel. . . ."
- "I like the order you used in your writing because. . . ."
- "Your characters seemed realistic because. . . ."

So that suggestions for improvement are made in a helpful rather than a hurtful way, Tompkins and Hoskisson (1995) add these prompts:

- "I got confused in the part about. . . ."
- "Do you need a closing?"
- "Could you add more about. . . ?"
- "I wonder if your paragraphs are in the right order. . . ."
- "Could you combine some sentences?"

Shifting from the content of the students' writing, the second part of the revision process involves examining the composition to determine whether there are problems with conventions: capitalization, punctuation, spelling, sentence structure, and usage. This is most commonly accomplished by proofreading one's own work. Students are encouraged to read slowly, in word-by-word fashion, searching carefully and deliberately for errors. When they are found, errors are usually corrected with special proofreader marks, like those illustrated in Figure 12–3.

Tompkins and Hoskisson (1995) suggest that editing checklists often help students focus on particular errors. The authors explain:

> Teachers can develop checklists with two to six items appropriate for the grade level. A first-grade checklist, for example, might include only two items—perhaps one about capital letters at the beginning of sentences and the second about periods at the end of sentences. In contrast, a middle-grade checklist might include items such as using commas in a series, indenting paragraphs, capitalizing proper nouns and adjectives, and spelling homonyms correctly. Teachers can revise the checklist during the school year to focus attention on skills that have recently been taught. (p. 220)

An editing checklist appropriate for fourth graders is shown in Figure 12–4.

Students can work with a partner to edit each other's compositions. First, each author proofreads her or his own work, looking for errors as designated on the checklist and checking off each item in need of attention. The compositions are then exchanged and edited by the partner, who also uses the checklist as a guide. The goal is to correct as many errors as possible before meeting with the teacher for a final editing.

Publishing

This is the final phase of the writing process—a time when children have an opportunity to share the final versions of their compositions with an audience, most typically their teacher and classmates. Teachers often designate a special section of the

FIGURE 12–3
Editors' Proofreading Marks

Mark	Meaning	How to Use
✗	Delete; take out	Iroquois Indians
,...•	Put back what was deleted	Fort Orange ~~later~~ became Albany.
∧	Add a letter, word, or words	Fur trade killed nearly all the beaver.
#	Make a space	Trading post
⌒	Close up a space	North east Indians
∼	Transpose; reverse letters or words	settlements
∧̦	Put in a comma	Susquehanna, Delaware, and Iroquois tribes
⊙	Put in a period	Europeans wanted beaver pelts⊙
⌄/	Put in an apostrophe	the beavers' dam
« »	Put in quotation marks	The Iroquois said, "Two axes for one beaver pelt."
≡	Capitalize the letter	The fort stood along the Hudson river.
/	Make the letter lowercase	Settlers canoed up the Rivers.
¶	Start a new paragraph	Traders loaded boats with pelts they got from the Iroquois.

classroom for sharing compositions; writers sit in and read their selections from a distinctive "Author's Chair." Listeners are encouraged to react to the reading with comments and questions for clarification, but initial comments must be positive and reassuring.

In addition to reading from the Author's Chair, a variety of publishing forms appropriate for the social studies curriculum exist, such as making a class book, displaying writings on a bulletin board, recording the composition on an audiotape, producing a videotape, reading works to children in other classrooms, publishing a class newspaper, reading for parents, presenting compositions at assembly programs, contributing selections to the local newspaper, or sending copies to a "partner school" in another city. Such opportunities communicate to the children the message that their work is valued and entitled to special recognition.

FIGURE 12–4
Fourth-Grade Editing
Checklist

Editing Checklist

I remembered to check that . . .

_____   all proper nouns begin with a capital letter.

_____   all sentences begin with a capital letter.

_____   all sentences end with the proper punctuation mark.

_____   all sentences are complete sentences.

_____   all sentences make sense.

_____   sentences are in order.

_____   each paragraph is indented.

_____   commas are used to separate items in a series.

_____   all words are spelled correctly.

_____   my handwriting is neat and readable.

_____   the story has a good beginning, middle, and end.

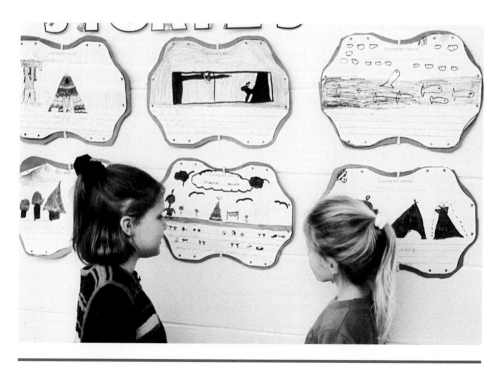

Teachers who seek mind-stretching experiences in social studies are alert to the many possibilities for publishing their children's written pieces.

Children become fulfilled as writers only when they publish their work. Writers write to be read, so be sure to share your students' work with an audience.

In summary, the writing process is a way of enriching social studies instruction by providing the skills and strategies that help students take in and express ideas and feelings related to important social studies content. By bringing literacy and subject-area content together in the elementary school classroom, students not only learn more effectively, they also master important writing skills.

The writing process addresses only one major aspect of writing. To maximize the contributions of writing to the social studies program, we must also have clear ideas about what forms the writing might take. Called *voice* or *form*, this aspect of writing describes the different types of writing used by elementary school children. Although there are many types of writing, many individuals insist that writing in the social studies should take only one form: "Children should write in social studies class to record or report information about a particular topic under study. Writing is functional—it enables students to organize or express what they have learned." Certainly, the process of clearly and cogently organizing and expressing information is a valued goal of elementary school social studies instruction; indeed, practicing social scientists often write in a functional way, recording and communicating important observations and discoveries. Because social studies instruction attempts to help children search for ideas and information the way social scientists do, writing about what they learn is a very important part of the curriculum. However, communicating the content of their learning experiences is only one way children write in the elementary school classroom. Called *expository writing,* this form joins *expressive writing* and *imaginative writing* as the three approaches most applicable for specific instructional purposes in the social studies.

EXPOSITORY (TRANSACTIONAL) WRITING

When students write to inform, explain, or persuade, they are practicing *expository writing* (sometimes called *transactional writing*). Frye, Baker, and Perkins (1985) define expository writing as "explanatory writing, the presentation of facts, ideas, or opinions, as in short forms like the [informational report, book report, or biography]" (p. 184). Britton et al. (1975) and Applebee (1984) report that teachers have considered expository writing such an important part of the social studies program that it is the most common type of writing found in elementary school social studies classrooms today. Teachers use expository writing strategies because they are convinced that the essence of the scientific method is precise observation, accurate data collection, orderly analysis of the data, and clear communication of applicable information. Expository writing strategies become functional tools that help students operate as competent social scientists.

Expository Writing in the Primary Grades

Perhaps the most widely used approach to expository writing with younger children is the *language experience approach,* which is based on the oral language generated by children following experiences that can be either direct or vicarious. In this approach, children dictate words and sentences about their experiences to their teacher, who writes them for everyone to see. As the children observe their speech being written, they begin to sense that the purpose of writing is communicating ideas; since the language comes from the children's own experiences, the approach helps children learn about their world and language simultaneously.

The Language Experience Approach (LEA)

The first step in carrying out an LEA is to make sure that the children have had a common experience interesting enough to stimulate lively discussion. Topics may be initiated by the teacher or by the children themselves. A trip to the post office, the hatching of a chick, a classroom visitor, tasting ethnic foods, a videotape of the breadmaking process, a new class pet, an interesting book, or last night's trick-or-treat adventures are examples of topics that are sure to generate a great deal of talk.

After the shared experience, discuss the things the children noticed. The purpose of doing this is to review the experience so that the children can clarify and organize ideas that will be used in their writing. Good ideas usually flow from these discussions as one child's thinking stimulates another's. Some teachers choose to work with groups as large as fifteen to twenty children, but I prefer to limit the size of kindergarten or first-grade groups to ten or fewer. Lower numbers get more children involved.

When you think the children have expressed an adequate sense of the experience, you can begin to record individual ideas. Start with a comment like, "We've been talking about the firefighters who came to visit our school. Now we're going to write about them. Who can tell me something to write on our chart?" As they write, most teachers prefer to use lined chart paper and a black marking pen or crayon. (Others would rather use the chalkboard, the overhead projector, or even the computer. The medium is not as important as the opportunity children get to see their ideas written down.) Teachers print the children's contributions clearly, being sure to model correct handwriting elements: *letter formation* (form should correspond to the handwriting method being taught), *spacing* (must be consistent), *slant* (all letters should be slanted consistently to the left, right, or straight up), *alignment* (comparable letters should be the same height), and *size* (should be consistent and easily read). You must master these mechanics of writing because you will want to move quickly and efficiently as the chart is composed; drawn-out, tiring efforts from a teacher with unpolished mechanical skills will certainly cause the children to lose interest.

In response to the teacher's opening question about the firefighters, James suggests, "Dial 911 if you have a fire."

"Yes, James," responds the teacher. "I'll write that down. As usual, I'll start at the top left and begin with a capital letter. Everyone watch and listen as I do that."

The teacher begins printing, starting near the top left margin. She first writes, "James said," and then writes exactly what he said. She starts with each child's name because most young children have learned to recognize their own names and will use them later to locate their dictated sentences. The teacher pronounces the words as she writes them and then reads the entire sentence back to the children, moving her hand under each word: "James said, `Dial 911 if you have a fire.' "

"Good start," comments the teacher. "What else can we say about the firefighters? Shantelle."

Shantelle offers, "They wear hard helmets to keep their heads safe."

The teacher repeats the writing scheme she used for James' sentence and then asks, "What else can we write?"

When recording children's ideas, teachers must be very careful not to correct or edit their contributions. If the child uses a colloquialism like "y'all," "youze," or "younze," the teacher should write it. The LEA should be a total language experience in which the children get to see their ideas written down, so the expression of ideas is much more important during early writing than using correct grammar or speech patterns. Sometimes, however, children will offer words that test our ability to comprehend what they are saying; then teachers must become skilled active listeners. For example, I remember a child who offered this statement after returning to the classroom from a trip to a farm: "We saw a big halo." "A halo," he repeated pensively as I listened. "It had lotsa corn; like the picture in our book." Realizing what a wonderfully creative act had begun, I invited him to talk more about the "halo" and printed his sentence on the chart. By listening carefully to what the child had to say and asking him to enlarge upon his idea, I became convinced that he had ingeniously interwoven the words *hay* and *silo* into a fascinating new word. Imagine what could have happened to the child's future interest in sharing ideas if I had responded with a tactless comment like, "I'm not sure what you're saying here. Farms don't have halos, angels do. We'd better move on."

Do not break the link between speech and writing. If we constantly correct children for their "errors," they may eventually become reluctant to share ideas. Spelling should be proper, however. If a child says "lotsa'" for "lots of," spell the word correctly and let the child pronounce the word the way she likes as she reads it back. The only other modification a teacher should make is to ask a child to rephrase the rare comment like, "I didn't like the damned siren." Words you would not normally accept in your school should not be written down on the chart.

The teacher in our example continues accepting ideas about firefighters in a like manner until everyone who wants to talk has an opportunity. This is another reason to limit the number of children in an LEA group to less than ten—you do not want to make the story go on and on. After the teacher prints the whole chart, she reads it back for the children and asks them to suggest a title that would sum up their story. The completed firefighter chart is shown in Figure 12–5.

Now the chart is read several times both by the teacher and the children, each time in a slightly different way:

1. The teacher leads the children as they choral-read with her.
2. The teacher may ask the children to read what they individually contributed on the chart as she points to each word. Some may read only one word, while others may be able to read the entire sentence.

FIGURE 12–5
A Language Experience Story

The Fire Fighter

James said, "Dial 911 if you have a fire."
Shantelle said, "They wear hard helmets on their head."
Nina said, "A light on the helmet shines in a dark room."
Norene said, "The suit keeps the fire fighter safe from the hot flames."
Pablo said, "Girls can be fire fighters, too."
Do Yong said, "The oxygen tank helps them breathe when there's smoke."
Jimmy said, "I learned how to stop, drop, and roll."

---

3. The teacher may use follow-up activities:
   a. "Find the sentence that Pablo told us about."
   b. Hold up a card containing a key word in the story and see if anyone can recognize it on the chart.
   c. Ask questions to check comprehension: for example, "Why does a firefighter need special clothing?"

The children often demonstrate a strong interest in illustrating the story when it is complete. Provide crayons, markers, or paint and let them highlight individual contributions with creative illustrations placed directly on the chart.

Drawing and Invented Spelling

In addition to language experience stories, teachers of kindergarten and first-grade children augment their children's social studies writing repertoires by supporting their efforts to get ideas down on paper in a variety of ways—usually drawing or invented spelling. When their teacher offers a piece of drawing paper or primary-grade writing paper, most kindergartners and first graders will draw a picture of something that happened in their own lives and then talk about it. Graves (1983) refers to drawing pictures and talking about them prior to writing as a "rehearsal" process inasmuch as children use their drawings as a way to reflect on what they have experienced. For example, as one group of first graders came back to school at the close of winter vacation, they were excited to share the interesting things that happened to them while they were away. Hands flew into the air during sharing time in eager anticipation of who would be the first to talk. Teri's words exploded as she told about helping her father shovel the driveway after a heavy winter snowstorm. Robert's eyes sparkled with pride as he described the new furniture that arrived at his house a week ago ("A beautiful yellow sofa, just beautiful!"). Wendy sadly recounted her family's heavyhearted task of saying good-bye to their 10-year-old beagle, who was struck down by a speeding car. Enrique happily described the party his family organized in celebration of his seventh birthday, and Kyle told of his family's trip to the city aquarium. After they shared orally, the teacher could have chosen to compose a group-dictated experience story, but instead passed out drawing paper and asked each child to draw a picture of his or her special contribution to the discussion. After the children finished their drawings, the teacher could either print their "stories" in the space below as each child dictated it, or encourage the children to employ their own writing system—most kindergartners and first graders scribble and use invented spelling as they write. In this case, the teacher decided to have the children use their own writing systems. Figure 12–6 is a sample of Kyle's story about his family's trip to the aquarium. Kyle's attraction to the dolphins was particularly strong; when asked about his written piece, Kyle explained that the dolphin was saying, "Ouch!" Then he read back what he had written above the drawing: "Animals should definitely not wear clothing because a dolphin might have trouble with its fin."

FIGURE 12–6
Young Child's Early Writing Effort

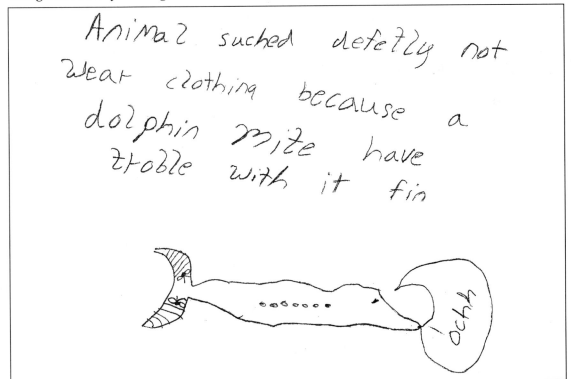

From her own classroom experience, Mary Ellen Giacobbe (1981), a first-grade teacher, explains how children use the written word to tell about their experiences: "As the blank pages . . . came alive with drawings and words telling of their experiences, I could see these children had entered school ready to engage in the active process of writing. . . . They were showing me what they knew as well as what they needed to know (pp. 100–101).

We teach elementary school social studies by surrounding young children with a richly literate environment where they are involved in a variety of writing activities. Group-generated experience stories hold a significant place in a social studies program for young children, as do the children's individual pages of drawings, scribbles, and invented spellings. But this is only the beginning; we must now find a way to take what the children already know about writing and use it as a base to bring about more diverse expository-type compositions in the social studies.

First Written Reports

Ultimately, writing informationally in the social studies will involve much more than pulling from a single major experience and putting a crayon or pencil to paper to tell about it; to stretch the children's writing repertoires, we will want to consider a developmental extension of what was has already been accomplished in the children's writing. We must learn how to create other stimulating contexts that will involve children in more advanced processes—gathering, organizing, and synthesizing information about a topic and presenting it as a written piece (a process most commonly referred to in social studies circles as the *written report*).

To accomplish this charge effectively, we must abandon the stereotype of the social studies report as being nothing more than copying or paraphrasing from an encyclopedia or other informational book. As Atwell (1990) emphasizes:

> Report writing per se, isn't the problem. . . . the problem with school reports lies in our methods of assigning them. We need to put the emphasis where it belongs—on meaning—and show students how to investigate questions and communicate their findings, how to go beyond plagiarism to genuine expertise and a "coming to know." (p. xiv)

Like the experience story, individual drawings, scribbling, and invented spellings, prerequisites to writing first reports with primary-grade children are stimulating firsthand and/or vicarious experiences. Mr. Greenberg realized this was important because children's first social studies reports are usually of the "Let Me Tell You About . . ." variety. That is, children most commonly create booklets that provide information or tell a story about something familiar to them. Therefore, when Mr. Greenberg began his unit on "bread," he showed his children an assortment of real bread, as well as pictures and plastic models: bagels, pita, baguettes, paska, challah, tortillas, rye bread, croissants, fry bread, injera, and the like. Mr. Greenberg did this not only to provide his students with a direct experience, but also to generate enthusiasm and interest, to prime the pump for a flurry of activity that naturally follows.

Mr. Greenberg invited the children to taste the different breads and, as a class activity, marked the country of origin of each on a large map. Mr. Greenberg added another hands-on experience by giving the children small balls of prepared bread dough (available in supermarkets) and asking them to place the balls on sheets of aluminum foil labeled with their names. Before they put their dough into the oven, the children were encouraged to shape the balls any way they wished. The bread was baked according to directions, and the children discussed their sensory experiences as well as the physical changes they observed from start to finish. Everyone responded to this activity with enthusiasm and interest; a profusion of questions and comments followed.

To begin the actual writing phase, Mr. Greenberg formed committees around common topics of interest which, after much discussion, were narrowed down to four: bread bakers and bakeries, bread from around the world, what bread is eaten with (condiments), and homemade bread. The children wrote on a piece of paper the two topics they would most like to pursue. Mr. Greenberg formed interest committees that would meet the next day.

The next day, Mr. Greenberg assigned to each committee the task of writing its own information booklet on its chosen topic. He specified the form the writing would take, but the children would eventually determine the content. To set the scene and familiarize the children with the form that their booklets were to take, Mr. Greenberg brought to class an example of informational writing: *Bread, Bread, Bread* by Ann Morris (Lothrop, Lee, & Shepard). The book contains exceptional photographs of various breads being made around the world. As the class surveyed the book, it paid particular attention to the photographs and text on each page. On the easel, Mr. Greenberg specified what each of the children's information pages should include: a drawing and a sentence with some information about the drawing.

The children worked on their bread books for about three days during social studies class. The committees decided that each of their books should be about five pages long (one page for each child), but a few committees wrote more. To help the committees find information about bread, Mr. Greenberg located suitable trade books and inserted bookmarks at the proper places. At the end of the first day, Mr. Greenberg and the children sat in a circle with their papers and the books they had used. They shared what they had done and how things had gone for them. Most had gotten as far as locating something they wanted to write about and starting their drawing. The next day, the children completed their drawings and wrote the text in their own words.

On the third day, Mr. Greenberg talked to the children about book titles and discussed how the covers of several of the books the children had been reading contained illustrations that represented the main idea of the text. The children illustrated the covers of their own books, added titles, listed their names as authors, put the pages in order, and stapled them together. The committees shared their books with one another, and the final copies were ceremoniously added to the classroom library. The "Bread From Around the World" committee compiled this book, which they entitled *The Bread Book:*

Page 1:   Navajos eat fry bread almost every day. It is fried, not baked.

Page 2:   People from France eat baguettes. They are long loaves of bread.

Page 3:	Ukrainians eat paska bread at Easter. Paska is very special.
Page 4:	Mexican people like to eat tortillas. Tortillas are cornmeal bread.
Page 5:	Jewish people bake challah to eat at their Friday meal. It is a white bread with braids.

The fact that most of the children could not yet read independently nor write conventionally did not deter them. The main thing about writing in the social studies during the primary-grade years is that children are motivated to write; you must help fuel that motivation by providing "grabbers"—objects or books that just can't be ignored. These launch the children into personal writing projects that help them both describe what they know and begin to ask questions on their own.

Expository Writing in the Middle and Upper Grades

Initial report writing for middle- and upper-grade children should also be collaborative. However, "[f]rom the third grade on, children are asked to do increasingly more writing in the [social studies], so they must learn to deal with new writing formats and new sentence and paragraph structures" (Harp and Brewer, 1991, p. 408). Cullinan and Galda (1994) suggest that quality sources of children's literature offer models for young authors to imitate; good models produce good results:

> Literature provides a rich resource to use in any writing program. It can be used as a model for writing, as examples of interesting language used well, and as an illustration of topics to write about. There are books that illustrate unique formats: journals, letters, postcards, diaries, and autobiographies. . . . No matter what point you want to illustrate about writing, there are books to help you make it clear. (p. 399)

As they read increasingly more complex literature over the years, children are able to model its structure for their own writing projects. Therefore, their writing in social studies becomes more complex, too. By grades three and four it includes the use of specialized skills such as notetaking, outlining, and constructing charts and graphs. These skills do not emerge naturally, but must be taught and used in meaningful situations requiring authentic communication. Children do not learn notetaking, for example, by completing contrived workbook exercises, but by engaging in the preparation of purposeful writing pieces in content areas such as social studies. To write effectively, then, children must sense the value and applicability of the skills they are being taught—social studies offers a superior setting for this to happen.

Templeton (1997) suggests that we can effectively use writing in the social studies by involving third-grade children and older in writing projects that involve progressively more "abstract" steps—from the self, to others, to print resources.

The Student as "Expert" (Self)

Graves (1983) recommends that when students begin to write expository pieces, they should start from within their own domain of experiences. The use of books and other resources will come later. Start by asking each child to describe something he or she is very good at, inviting a resource person to share his or her area of expertise with the class, or reading a poem or story based on the "expert" theme. Jack Prelutsky's (1984) humorous poem, "Clara Cleech" ("the poorest juggler ever seen") is an excellent source from which to launch a discussion of the children's special talents. Follow up this introductory experience by modeling the process described by Templeton (1997):

- Pass out several index cards to each student.
- Ask the students to think of one area where they are "experts" and write it on a card.
- Ask the students to think of other things or ideas that relate to their areas of "expertise" (students can use this word, especially if you explain how it is related to "expert"). They write each on a separate card. Each card will be a "heading" or "main idea" for the area of expertise.
- Ask the students to write information that will elaborate on their headings on the cards—one piece of information per sheet of paper.
- The students arrange the cards sequentially until they are satisfied with their explanation.
- Using the cards as "organizational handles," the students then write about their areas of expertise. The reports need not be long; one or two pages will do nicely.

Figure 12–7 shows one "expert's" card exhibit and written report on the topic of "dancing the hula."

Using Other Resources: Interviews

Conducting interviews is a superb way to introduce children to the process of collecting information for their expository writing without having to draw from print resources. Most children are familiar with the process; they see people interviewed on television nearly every day. Help beginning classroom interviewers understand the process by videotaping a television interview on a topic of interest and then discussing what an interviewer does. Emphasize the types of questions an interviewer asks; some seek facts while others are designed to find out about personal feelings and opinions. Since children seem to ask many questions that elicit *yes* or *no* answers, point out that interviewers ask few, if any, of those questions because they do not help obtain much information. *Why, how,* and *what* questions produce much more. Offer the children an opportunity to be interviewers by bringing to school an interesting object and encouraging the children to ask questions in an attempt to get at the story behind the object. Play the "interviewee" as the children assume the roles of "interviewers." For example, one day Ms. Lee walked into her classroom with a Native American dream catcher dangling from her left hand. "I have something interesting here," she announced. "Ask some questions to find out as much information about it as you can. I will give only the information you ask for." Twenty excited pairs of eyes took in every feature of the dream catcher: "What is it? What is it used for? Why does it have feathers on the side? Who made it? Why is it important for Native Americans?"

FIGURE 12–7
Using Cards to Organize Expository Writing

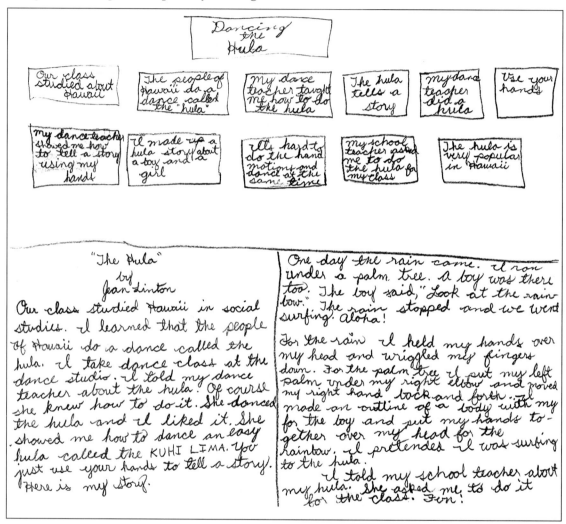

A special interview had begun! Notice that the youngsters started asking "What" questions and eventually moved to other types that gave them a more complete collection of information. Children soon learn how different questions can give them different types of information, but most of all they learn that people possess information, and that they can extract interesting knowledge with a series of strategic queries.

When children have acquired some proficiency in asking questions, have them plan an interview with a person who might contribute new insights into a topic under study. During a unit titled "Our Changing Times," for example, Ms. Lee asked her students to brainstorm a series of questions they might ask their grandparents to unlock what life was like when they were growing up. Each suggestion was written on a notecard. The students examined the collection of notecards, discarding those requiring simple *yes* or *no* answers and keeping those which stood the best chance of eliciting the information they were looking for. Then the cards were placed in a logical order for conducting the interview.

Once they established their questioning sequence, the students conducted their interviews. Students were free either to use a tape recorder or to jot down notes to help them remember what was said during the interview, but most found that the tape recorder worked best. The children listened carefully to the interviewee's responses to determine whether the desired information was being gathered. If not, they asked probing follow-up questions to clarify points or elicit additional information.

Once the children carefully listened to their tapes and examined their information, they wrote individual accounts of their interviews. Each was read in class, and one set of copies was bound into a class book. Another set was taken home. Haley-James and Hobson (1980) describe one teacher's feelings about her interviewing program: "Children can learn from this sort of experience more easily than they can from a text. Having the interviews, writing them up, reading them, listening, all these skills that we use (in doing so) come naturally during an interviewing program" (p. 500). A sample interview conducted by a fifth-grade student is shown in Figure 12–8.

FIGURE 12–8
A Student's Interview With His Grandfather

FIGURE 12–8 (continued)

> Question: What kind of hobbies did you have when you were 12?
>
> Answer: He liked to go fishing and hunting. He couldn't get a hunting license untill he was 12. Most of his time he worked on the slackpile. His job was helping the family. Once and a while he went swimming. He paid $.10 for a movie. His brother would take them in his Model-T-Ford. He still fishes but does not hunt.
>
> Question: What was your first car? How much did it cost?
>
> Answer: Grampy's first car was a 1929 Essex. It cost him $500 to get it. He was 23 years old when he got it.

Using Other Resources: Print Materials

The final part of Templeton's three-step expository writing program is to use books and other print material as the source of content for students' writing in the social studies. Their ability to take notes and to organize content from various print sources are foundational skills for promoting these purposeful writing activities. The types of expository writing experiences using print materials should appeal to the students and depend largely on their developing interests and skills. Many creative possibilities meet this responsibility, but the key to enjoyable, productive efforts lies in whether the writing is enjoyable and promotes understanding. Two types of expository writing seem to be most popularly employed in social studies classrooms to explain or inform—*written reports* and *biographies*. Two others are employed to influence the actions or opinions of others—*political cartoons* and *editorials*. And one, the *newspaper*, is an interesting way to publish the results of interviews, biographies, reports, political cartoons, editorials, and other purposeful writing endeavors.

Written Reports

As a format for writing in the social studies, the written report has had wide acceptance at all grade levels. However, you cannot expect students to compose good

The teacher becomes a resource as the children search for just the right place to begin and the right steps to take in completing their social studies reports.

written reports simply by announcing, "Write a report on Sitting Bull for next Tuesday." Giving such an assignment only frustrates many students and encourages them to copy every bit of information from a written resource. Instead, they must be helped to evolve as writers of expository text by learning how to apply the principles of the writing process to composing written reports. To that end, students need help in (1) selecting a topic, (2) formulating questions for study, (3) organizing the content, (4) drafting the report, (5) composing the report, and (6) publishing the report.

Selecting a Topic   Meaningful, successful topics for written reports are usually selected by the students themselves. The topics should come from the students' own interests—most commonly something related to what they are studying or what they want to learn more about. Going back to our opening Classroom Sketch, while covering the American Revolution, Mr. Bonelli discovered that his students were fascinated by the many different emblems used by the colonists before they decided on a flag of their own. Impressed with the enthusiasm of his fifth graders as they asked their questions, Mr. Bonelli judged that the time was right to initiate an expository writing project, "Flags In Early American History." This general topic was too broad for a single report, so Mr. Bonelli chose to break it down into manageable segments. This was an important step, because Mr. Bonelli also understood that successful first reports for middle- and upper-grade elementary school students should be limited and conducted as collaborative ventures in which groups of three or four students are assigned manageable segments of a broad topic. By splitting the overall topic into manageable sections, Mr. Bonelli was able to concentrate the content each group needed to complete its report. Separate group reports, therefore, focused on the topics "British Union Jack," "Grand Union Flag," "Old Glory," "Star-Spangled Banner," and "Flag of 1818." These topics would eventually be shared orally and compiled into separate chapters in a class book, "Flags in Early American History." At the conclusion of the writing, Mr. Bonelli planned to help his students connect the separate group reports into a unified piece.

It is during this planning stage that students must consider the purpose of the piece they are about to write. In social studies, two purposes for expository writing appear to be the most popular—*writing to inform or explain* and *writing to persuade.* Since the purpose of this writing exercise was to inform or explain, Mr. Bonelli thought his students needed to witness a model of expository writing, since children tend to write original pieces after patterns they find in books. No matter what point you want to illustrate about writing, there is a book to make it clear. As an illustrative model, Mr. Bonelli brought to class the book *Flag Day* by Dorothy Les Tina and illustrated by Ed Emberley (Crowell). He read the first six pages of the book; they provided a short history of flags. Mr. Bonelli helped his students understand the organizational pattern of the section by leading a discussion of how the author developed her ideas. To help crystallize their thinking, Mr. Bonelli and his students diagrammed the organizational pattern for one flag, as shown in Figure 12–9.

Modeling is a very important, but frequently overlooked, part of the expository writing process. It must be included in the prewriting phase of all expository writing experiences, for it not only helps the students understand the pattern appropriate for their piece but also directly influences the quality of their work. As students gain more experience examining the organizational patterns used in expository writing, they will independently learn to choose those they believe are most appropriate for their specific writing purposes.

Formulating Questions for Study.   The second stage of the report-writing process involves developing a list of questions that the students ask about their topic. As the students brainstorm these questions, each should be recorded on an organizational chart and used for planning.

Mr. Bonelli's class decided that each small group should answer the same questions as modeled in the book they had just listened to: What colors were used? What symbols were used? When was it adopted? The questions provided a starting point for the information search and served as a focus for the students' writing. The students used the questions as a guide to write their sections of the report.

Organizing the Content.   During this phase of report writing, the students search through resource materials for the purpose of locating information to satisfy their questions. Children must learn to choose relevant information and avoid word-for-word copying from a book or encyclopedia. Nothing can be more deadly than to

FIGURE 12-9
Organizational Pattern for Writing

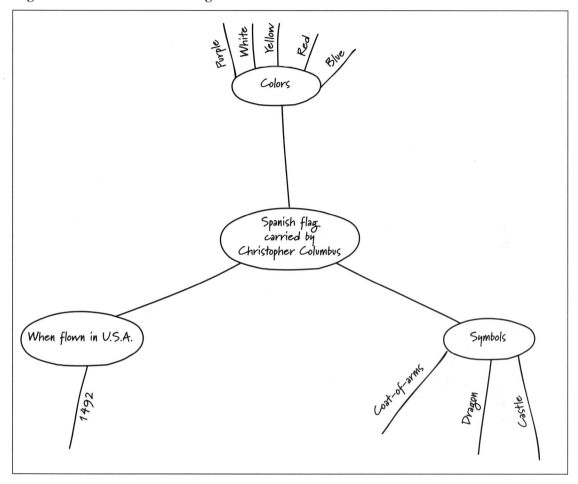

allow a child to stand in front of a classroom and read a report that was copied verbatim. Frequent pauses will occur as the child reads in monotone and struggles to pronounce unfamiliar words.

Since his students had little previous experience gathering and organizing information from print sources, Mr. Bonelli used several different approaches to guide them through this new experience—*note cards, data webs,* and *data charts.*

Note Cards.   Mr. Bonelli gave the students a number of index cards. He explained that these would be referred to as *information cards* for two different reasons: each was to be (1) decorated with a large lowercase "i" (the first letter in the word *information*) and (2) used to summarize important information. Duplicating his model, the students divided a note card into two major sections: a large circle at the top of

FIGURE 12-10
An "I" Notecard

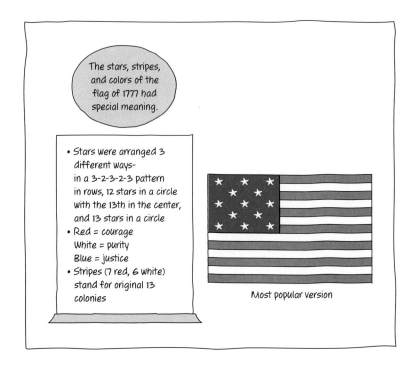

the card represented the dot of the letter "i," and the bottom rectangular section represented the stem. The students then printed the main idea (usually the first sentence of a paragraph) on the top section (the dot of the "i"); in the bottom section they listed all the supporting details (see Figure 12–10). This visual aid helped the children summarize the information effectively.

Data Webs.   Teachers who have used webs to help their students organize social studies content (see Chapter 5) may find this strategy useful in helping their students record and catalog data for written reports. Mr. Bonelli drew a circle on the chalkboard and labeled it with the class topic. This served as the center of a web. He wrote the names of the individual flags on lines connected to the central topic. Then Mr. Bonelli and the students referred to the charts holding the questions they asked about each flag: "What were the colors of each flag? What symbols were used? When was the flag adopted?" As each group collected its information, it was recorded on lines connected to the flag names. The groups used the outlined data as the skeletal framework for their written reports. Figure 12–11 shows a sample data web for one flag.

Data Charts.   Mr. Bonelli knew from past experience that one of the most difficult tasks for student writers is to take notes on a topic, especially when more than one reference is being used. Mr. Bonelli considered various options to help his students with this skill, but eventually selected a data chart like the the one

FIGURE 12–11
Data Web for "Old Glory"

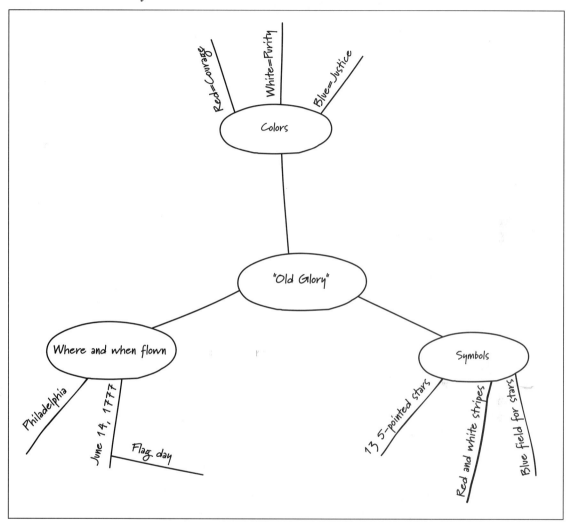

illustrated in Figure 12–12. He listed key questions about each individual topic as column heads and placed reference designations in each row. The students completed the chart as they searched for and gathered the information to complete each block.

Drafting the Report.   In this phrase, students use all of their notes as well as the information from their data webs and charts to write the rough draft, implementing the

FIGURE 12–12

Data Chart for "Old Glory"

Source of Information	What Colors Were Used?	What Symbols Were Used?	When Was It Used?
Encyclopedia	Red, white, and blue	12 stars in a circle, with the 13th star in the center.	1777–1795
Information book	Red, white, and blue	13 stars in alternating rows of 3-2-3-2-3. 13 stars in a circle rarely used.	1777–1795
Textbook	Red, white, and blue	13 white stars in a circle on a field of blue.... No historical basis for assigning a star to each state.	Not sure when it became official. Changed in 1795 when 2 new states were added.

Write 3 paragraphs.

Paragraph 1: What colors were used? What was the meaning of each?

Paragraph 2: Describe the symbols. Why were they chosen?

Paragraph 3: Explain the time period it was used. Why was it replaced?

components of the writing process as described earlier. These initial drafts are best sketched out by writing on every other line so there is room for additions or corrections; children are encouraged to cross out unwanted or irrelevant words and sentences and to write in the margins with arrows to indicate where new words or sentences might go. In effect, the draft is not thought of as a finished copy, but more of what Mr. Bonelli referred to as a "sloppy copy," where children focused on communicating clear content and meaning rather than mechanical accuracy. To aid in the editing process, Mr. Bonelli thought it would be helpful for his groups to share their drafts with peer groups using general feedback and editing checklists to help locate areas of strength and weakness.

Written reports are most effective when the author captures the attention of the readers with an engaging statement, question, or other "interest grabber" at the beginning of the piece. A strong beginning makes the written piece more interesting to its readers, so as the report is reworked and polished, the children should search for a "lead in" sentence or two to make it stronger. Likewise, a brief conclusion should summarize the "big idea" the students learned from their report.

Bromley (1992) has designed an interesting web to help readers conceptualize the activities that occur during the drafting phase (see Figure 12–13).

FIGURE 12–13
Activities That May Occur During Drafting

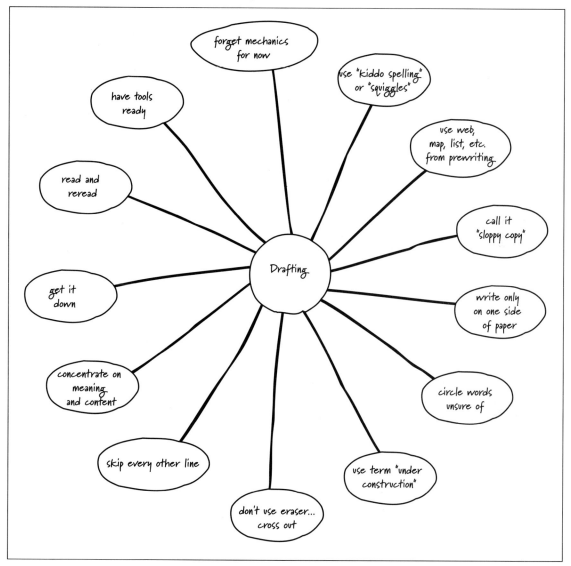

Source: Bromley, K. D. (1992). *Language arts: Exploring connections.* Boston: Allyn and Bacon, 342.

Composing the Report.   During this phase, the students revise their reports on the basis of the feedback they receive from their classmates and teacher. In Mr. Bonelli's class, students copied each report in their best handwriting (a word processing program could also be used). The finished piece was read aloud so students could see if it flowed smoothly and with clear meaning. Drawings were added to illustrate what each flag looked like.

Mr. Bonelli helped his students compile the separate group reports as chapters of a book. A cover was designed for the book and a list of authors for each section was presented. Everything was joined together in the proper sequence.

Publishing the Report.   The last step of writing a report is to publish it. Many formats can be used for this phase—dramatizing, oral reading, and videotaping are only a few. In our example, Mr. Bonelli added to the book publishing strategy by using a tactic devised by Hennings (1997) called the "Idea Fair."

In the Idea fair a reporter from each interest group set up an area of the classroom where he or she shared the group's written piece with four or five classmates (or children from other classrooms). Several reporters functioned simultaneously and repeated their presentations as their classmates revolved through the Idea Fair. The reporters donned simple costumes or used simple props to help those attending the fair get a feel for the historical era presented. For example, the reporter giving the "Grand Union Flag" presentation wore a pair of glasses pulled down over his nose like Benjamin Franklin, and the reporter who told of "Old Glory" placed a feather alongside her copy of the Declaration of Independence. Hennings (1997) contends that this pattern is ideal because (1) students refine their presentations as they repeat their reports, (2) listeners in small groups are more willing to offer feedback, (3) speakers are more at ease when reporting to small groups, and (4) each group will hear a slightly different presentation as they rotate, resulting in more exuberant total-class discussion following the Idea Fair.

Although the written report is the most frequently used form of expository writing, it is not the only technique appropriate for informing and explaining in the social studies classroom.

Biographies

Biographies join the written report as an especially relevant form of writing in social studies because they allow students to conduct research into and write about a person's life, thereby helping them gain a clearer vision of what life was like in the past or a more complete understanding of a particular theme. As with other forms of writing in social studies, students should use the writing process and employ sources from children's literature as models. Teachers must share these models with students so their own biographies can become more accurate and realistic. Farris (1993) comments:

> Beginning any composition is a challenge for all writers; however, initiating a biographical sketch can be especially difficult for children. Because children have problems establishing a frame of reference for a setting (both time and place), their biographies often fail to describe a distinct period and locale. As a result, it is not unusual for a child's biography about a historical figure . . . to begin with "Once upon a time, there was a boy [girl] named. . . ." (p. 227)

Farris (1993, p. 226) cites several authors of biographies who would serve as exemplary models for students' attempts, but has especially strong recommendations

for the works of Jean Fritz, "a master biographer" who has written about several periods in American history, particularly the Revolutionary War. In *Why Don't You Get
a Horse, Sam Adams?* (Putnam), for example, Fritz describes the colorful hero this
way: "His clothes were shabby and plain, he refused to get on a horse, and he hated
the King of England." Her series on the Revolutionary War contains several stories
that show historical characters as real people, helping children enrich their understandings of history in an enjoyable way.

Another "master biographer" whose works serve as emulative models for elementary school students is Russell Freedman. Freedman has reacted strongly against the
"I cannot tell a lie" make-believe stories that were previously popular and presents a
more objective treatment of historical figures in his biographies. In *Lincoln: A Photobiography* (Clarion), for example, Freedman contrasts the physical differences between Lincoln and Douglas as they prepared for one of their famous debates:

> The striking contrast between Douglas and Lincoln—The Little Giant and Long Abe, as
> reporters called them—added color and excitement to the contests. Douglas was Lin-
> coln's opposite in every way. Barely five feet four inches tall, he had a huge round head
> planted on massive shoulders, a booming voice, and an aggressive, self-confident
> manner. He appeared on the speakers' platform dressed "plantation style"—a navy coat
> and light trousers, a ruffled shirt, a wide-brimmed felt hat. Lincoln, tall and gangly,
> seemed plain in his rumpled suit, carrying his notes and speeches in an old carpetbag,
> sitting on the platform with his bony knees jutting into the air. (pp. 58–59)

In writing their biographies, students must focus on (1) a realistic description of
the time when and place where the person lived (biographies can be written about
living people or historical figures), (2) an accurate characterization of the subject, (3)
a careful accounting of the significant events in the person's life, and (4) the values
and interests influencing the person to act as he or she did. Cullinan and Galda
(1994) suggest that social studies teachers look at biographies in two major ways.
The first and most popular is the biography in terms of a historical period such as the
Civil War or the Great Depression. The second contains stories of people who relate
to a particular theme such as "the struggle for human rights," "great explorers," or
"immigration." Whatever the choice, biographies hold an important place in the social studies writing program. Conducting research for their biographies and putting
thoughts together to form a written portrait of a historically significant person help
students more clearly understand the people who have made history and elucidate
the strengths and weaknesses influencing the great decisions of their lives. A section
from a sample biographical sketch of Sacagawea is shown in Figure 12–14.

Newspapers

Classroom newspapers provide a stimulating expository writing medium especially
appropriate for the social studies because they offer a realistic forum where students
can express factual accounts of what they are learning or attempt to influence others
with cartoons or editorials. While discussing other forms of expository writing, we
learned that children must be exposed to models of the style their piece is expected

FIGURE 12–14
Biographical Sketch of Sacagawea

> Mike   Mar. 7, 1991
>
>   Sacagawea
>
> She was a Shoshoni Indian Woman
> who guided Lewis and Clark, She
> was helpful because her presence was a
> Sign of peace to different tribes,
> they encountered. She could find many
> plants and herbs to eat. She wanted
> to see the Pacific Ocean and
> the whales, Clark took her all
> the way to the Great Stinking Pond,
> The trip took two years and 6 months.
> Sacagawea was a brave woman,

to take; the same is true for newspapers. A trip to a newspaper publisher and careful examination of a local newspaper can help the children understand how newspapers are planned and produced. Although newspaper publishers differ in their organization, all generally include the following positions, which can be simulated in the classroom:

- *Publisher.* Owner or person who represents the owner; responsible for the overall operation of the newspaper. (The teacher usually assumes this position.)
- *Editors.* Responsible for several facets of newspaper production, such as deciding what goes into the newspaper, assigning reporters to cover events, determining where to position the stories, or writing their opinions of significant events (editorials).
- *Reporters.* Cover the stories. Columns to which reporters can be assigned include class news; school news; local, state, national, and world news; sports; or special events. Reporters can interview others as primary sources for gathering their news or use secondary sources such as radio, television, newspapers, or magazines.
- *Feature writers.* Produce special columns such as jokes and riddles, lost and found, a version of "Dear Abby," recipes, and so on.
- *Copy editors.* Read stories for mistakes and adjust length to meet space requirements.

After assigning several students to the news gathering and processing activities, you will want to get the rest of the class involved in these "behind the scenes" departments:

- *Production department.* Put pictures and stories together and get them ready for printing. (Children who know how to use the word processor, or have a desire to learn, make special contributions here.)
- *Art department.* Create ads (with pictures) that highlight coming events, special sales, parent meetings, special assemblies, or other important school functions.
- *Mechanical department.* Run the printer or copier, collate the newspaper pages, staple them, and get them ready for distribution.
- *Circulation department.* Deliver the newspaper to the principal, other teachers, and classmates.

Newspapers may be written in either a contemporary or a historical setting. Consider Mr. Rivera's fifth-grade classroom, for instance. The students were involved in a unit on the Revolutionary War. They created a period newspaper for 1776 with front-page stories blaring these headlines: "British Evacuate Boston," "Grand Union Flag Unfurled Over Boston," "Redcoats Invade New York," "Congress Approves Declaration of Independence," and "Washington Stuns Hessian Fighters." Feature articles detailed such items of interest as quilting, candle-making, and the steps of drying food for winter. An advertising section offered articles for sale (spinning wheels, bed warmers, teams of oxen, pewter tableware, flintlock rifles, wigs, and the like). An employment section offered such jobs as post rider, saddler, tanner, wigmaker, tavern keeper, chandler, mason, cooper, hatter, and printer. An editorial page displayed a political cartoon showing a crowd of Continental soldiers pulling down an equestrian statue of King George III as they celebrated the signing of the Declaration of Independence in Philadelphia, and an editorial soliciting funds for the relief of widows and children of the patriots "murdered" at Lexington. There was a book review of Thomas Paine's *Common Sense,* and a sports section detailing the results of such popular events as stool ball, quoits, arm wrestling, and gunny sack races. When finished, the various sections were stapled together and distributed to the other fifth-grade classrooms.

By simulating a real newspaper, children bring more interest and excitement to their learning. Be careful, though, to make sure that all children have an opportunity to assume as many different newspaper responsibilities as possible. Let them try the various jobs so they develop a complete understanding of the many duties performed on a real newspaper.

Teachers of elementary school social studies should use a variety of expository writing formats in purposeful ways to avoid the dullness associated with such drab routines as copying a report from the encyclopedia. Teachers employing useful formats must share good examples from textbooks and trade books; with exposure to these models, children will learn to write quality expository pieces. The list below suggests expository writing formats that will supplement the major suggestions in this text.

- ABC books where each letter of the alphabet tells something about a topic (for example, *The ABCs of Native American Culture).*
- Calendars where each page incorporates an illustration and information (for example, a glimpse of monthly life in colonial America).
- Picture books where each page contains a combination of drawings and brief text about a concept (for example, a book about trains).
- Information books or pamphlets where groups of students write separate pages or chapters (for example, a description of life in the Southwestern United States).
- Radio, television, or movie scripts that can be performed by the students.
- Historical fiction where students write about events of the past through the stories of people who seem real to us (for example, a day in the life of a child who accompanied Lewis and Clark in their journey west).
- How-to books where students write instructions for something related to a unit of study (for example, *How to Make a Tepee).*
- Travel brochures that describe a particular location under study.
- Recipe books that describe foods eaten by particular groups of people (for example, favorite foods of our nation's presidents).

EXPRESSIVE WRITING

A second popular category of writing found in elementary school social studies classrooms is more relaxed and personal than expository writing. Called *expressive writing,* this genre encourages children to write in much the same way as they speak. Norton (1997) defines expressive writing as "very close to speech and, consequently, very close to the writer. It is relaxed and intimate. It reveals the writer and verbalizes his or her consciousness. . . . Expressive writing is frequently characterized as thinking aloud on paper" (pp. 499–500). Since most young children learn to write at home as an outgrowth of natural oral language experiences, they come to school with an idea that the major function of writing is to compose personal narratives. With this understanding, Britton et al. (1975) suggest that children's earliest writing should be in the expressive genre; from this starting point, they can move on to exposition.

Many forms of expressive writing are employed in typical social studies programs, but the most frequently used are *journals and diaries, stories (narratives),* and *letters* written to real or imaginary people. Regardless of the form selected, expressive writing strategies are important in social studies classrooms because they encourage students to tell about their personal experiences, express what they already know about a topic of investigation, or communicate their personal feelings about a theme or learning experience.

Journals and Diaries

Starting with young children who draw simple pictures and scribble invented spelling words to tell about interesting people and objects and progressing through adult learners who write about their ideas, beliefs, and concerns, journals are a favored way to record personal thoughts. As such, they become students' dialogues with themselves that express ideas in highly personal ways. Journals can be a handmade booklet or a purchased notebook. Journals may take several forms, but the two most applicable to the social studies program are the *personal journal* and the *dialogue journal.*

Personal Journals

Personal journals are informal and unstructured. They serve mostly as diaries in which students record events in their lives and their reactions to them. Teachers might ask the students to write a brief daily entry (a drawing for younger learners) summarizing an important idea immediately after they finish social studies class. The content should be open-ended, but teachers often find that upper-grade children are suspicious of open-ended assignments (Farris, 1993) and need support in learning how to record meaningful events. You might want to read Beverly Cleary's *Dear Mr. Henshaw* (Morrow) or its sequel, *Strider* (Morrow), as models of a journal-writing approach. Or you might need to supply clear direction for the journal entry. Some teachers request specific entries, such as writing about the most significant learning gained from a particular experience. For example, a child might write in her journal about one memorable characteristic of Nat Turner, a literate slave and radical preacher. Others might ask their students to brainstorm a list of possible topics for the journal entry. Some teachers give their students a form to follow. In one case, a teacher asks the students to *state* the main ideas covered during the daily social studies experience, *clarify* the ideas by adding supportive data, and *analyze* the content in terms of what it means to them. Regardless of the form the personal journal takes, students should record no more than two or three entries per week, limiting their writing time to no more than five minutes. When the structure of a daily entry is so specified, the written piece is often called a *learning log.*

Dialogue Journals

Dialogue journals are the second popular type of journal writing in the social studies. They are designed specifically to promote interaction between a student and the teacher. Using this format, each student writes what she or he learned or felt about a learning experience, and the teacher writes a brief response directly on the journal page (see the sample in Figure 12–15).

Diaries

Diaries are "private records of personal observations . . . , or a daily record of thoughts and feelings" (Cooper, 1997, p. 307). Like journals, diaries are unplanned, spontaneous means whereby children record events and their reactions to those events. However, diaries are not made public as are journals.

Sometimes, imaginative situations (such as Columbus's journey to America) can serve as a stimulus to write daily diary entries. For example, these imaginative diary

FIGURE 12–15
Page from a Dialogue Journal

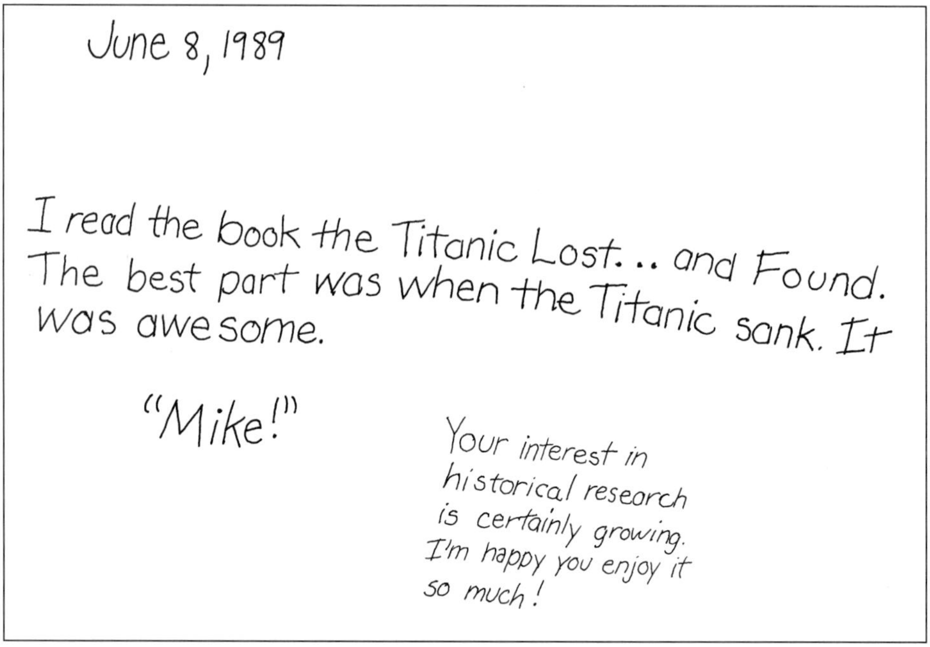

June 8, 1989

I read the book the Titanic Lost... and Found.
The best part was when the Titanic sank. It
was awesome.

"Mike!"

Your interest in
historical research
is certainly growing.
I'm happy you enjoy it
so much!

entries were written by a student pretending to be a sailor on one of Magellan's ships that was unable to complete the circumnavigation of the globe in 1522 :

> *Day 10.* The storm lasted two days and two nights. I never saw waves so high or the wind blow so hard. Our ship was thrown against huge rocks and was smashed to bits. We held onto our lifeboats for longer than I could remember—every sailor was scared stiff. We finally spotted some land. . . .
>
> *Day 11.* Fresh water is disappearing. Our captain divided us into four groups. Each group was to go in a different direction to search for fresh water. In midafternoon the fourth group found a freshwater spring on the west side of the island. . . .

Writing is easy for children if they write about what they know, something they have read about or lived. Regardless of the source of motivation, children have much to share in the social studies classroom. Throughout the social studies program, the children use writing as a tool to understand their world and communicate their knowledge of it.

Stories

As children are exposed to a wide variety of literature throughout the curriculum, including the social studies, they will become interested in using the styles of their favorite authors as a model to write their own stories. Tompkins and Hoskisson (1995) point out: "As students read and talk about literature, they learn how writers craft stories. They also draw from stories they have read as they create their own stories, intertwining several story ideas and adapting story elements to meet their own needs" (p. 347). Templeton (1997) adds that this penchant for imitation is important: "Imitation plays a seminal role in students' learning to write. All writers, either by accident or design, begin by imitating the style and structure of other writers" (p. 259). Templeton urges teachers to take advantage of this imitative nature and encourage it. So when students are studying the folklore of Africa, for example, they might want to compose their own "pourquoi tale" patterned after Verna Aardema's *Why Mosquitos Buzz in People's Ears* (Dial) or a "trickster tale" after Eric A. Kimmel's *Anansi and the Talking Melon* (Holiday).

Templeton (1997) recommends that the groundwork for story writing begins in the primary grades as children begin to understand at least four important story elements: *plot* (what happened?), *setting* (where did it happen?), *conflict* (what problem did the characters face?), and *characterization* (what were the characters like?). A deeper explanation of these story features is shown in Figure 12–16.

The key to getting good stories from the students is to help them understand how story plots are developed. Start during the primary grades by having the children retell a story you have read to them. Illustrate the story structure on a chart or the chalkboard. These plot structure illustrations are called *story maps*. Combs (1996) advises that:

> A story map will be an excellent planning tool for narrative writing. A *story map* is a word or picture diagram that shows the main events in a story and the relationship of those events. Making a map of a story can help children identify the detail and sequence they want to use in their plot. (p. 201)

When using a story related to the social studies theme, develop a story map to help children examine how authors constructed the plot. After the class has mapped a particular book, they will be ready to write an original group story using an identical pattern. For primary-grade children, the story map might summarize events from the beginning, middle, and end of the story. A story map for *Why Mosquitos Buzz in People's Ears* by Verna Aardema (Dial) is ahown in Figure 12–17.

Middle- and upper-grade students could use various forms such as charts, webs, and Venn diagrams to construct their story maps. These class-generated maps are used for group writing projects; after group writing, the children will be ready to plot personal stories, following the writing process guidelines explained earlier in this chapter.

Hennings (1990) suggests that to use any narrative form, a teacher must take the following steps:

1. Read a sample of the form to the students to serve as a model.

2. Discuss and map the key story elements.

3. Engage students in composing a group story using the map.

4. Invite the students to compose individual stories.

FIGURE 12–16
Four Story Elements

Plot

Plot is the sequence of events in a story. It has four parts:

1. A Problem: The problem introduces conflict at the beginning of the story.
2. Roadblocks: Characters face roadblocks as they try to solve the problem in the middle of the story.
3. The High Point: The high point in the action occurs when the problem is about to be solved. It separates the middle and the end.
4. The Solution: The problem is solved and the roadblocks are overcome at the end of the story.

Setting

The setting is where and when the story takes place.

1. Location: Stories can take place anywhere.
2. Weather: Stories take place in different kinds of weather.
3. Time of Day: Stories take place during the day or at night.
4. Time Period: Stories take place in the past, at the current time, or in the future.

Conflict

Conflict is the problem that characters face in the story. There are four kinds of conflict:

1. Conflict between a character and nature
2. Conflict between a character and society
3. Conflict between characters
4. Conflict within a character

Characters

Writers develop characters in four ways:

1. Appearance: How characters look
2. Action: What characters do
3. Dialogue: What characters say
4. Monologue: What characters think

Source: Templeton, S. (1997). *Teaching the integrated language arts.* Boston: Houghton Mifflin, p. 260.

Letters

Letters offer another major type of expressive writing for social studies classrooms. Children typically write two types of letters: friendly letters and business letters. As Tompkins and Hoskisson (1995) explain, "Friendly letters might be informal, chatty

FIGURE 12–17
Story Map for Why
Mosquitos Buzz in People's
Ears

Beginning

Mosquito tells iguana a big lie
Iguana puts sticks in his ears.
Snake crawls into rabbit hole.
Rabbit runs away.
Crow spread the alarm.
Monkey breaks limb.
Limb kills an owlet.
Mother Owl does not hoot to wake up the sun.

Middle

King Lion calls a meeting of all the animals.

End

Mosquito is found guilty.
Mother Owl was satisfied.
Mother Owl hoots to wake the sun.
Mosquito has guilty conscience.
Mosquito buzzes in people's ears.
KPAO!

letters to pen pals or thank-you notes to a television newscaster who has visited the classroom. . . . When students write to General Mills requesting information about the nutritional content of breakfast cereals or letters to the President expressing an opinion about current events, they use the more formal business style" (p. 383). Because friendly letters and business letters are written in conventional styles, some teachers find it helpful to provide models (charts, samples, etc.) for the children to follow as they write. This is important, for as we explained with the other types of writing, form and content are interchangeably essential for effective communication.

Numerous experiences encourage both types of letter writing in the social studies. There are stories from children's literature, for example, in which characters write letters in a historical context. Patricia MacLachlan's *Sarah, Plain and Tall* (Harper-Collins) contains a series of letters written by Sarah, who lives in New England, to a frontier family to whom she will eventually become wife and mother. Using the writing process, students enjoy writing letters back to Sarah. After reading Chapter 1 of the book, which ends with an introductory letter sent from Sarah to Anna, Caleb, and Papa, the children begin charting their background knowledge as they are asked, "What words would you use to describe Anna? What evidence from the story supports your choice of these words?" Chart their responses and repeat the process for Caleb and Papa. Then ask, "If you were Anna, what are some things you would write in a return letter to Sarah? What would you tell Sarah? What would you ask

her?" Record these responses and repeat the process for Caleb and Papa. Then, referring to a friendly letter format chart, the students write their letters, imagining that
they were from Anna, Caleb, or Papa. The letters could be displayed on a bulletin
board or read aloud in the classroom.

Mrs. Whitehead, a sixth-grade teacher from Flagstaff, Arizona, constructed a different type of letter-writing experience within the context of an "exchange package."
She asked her students to collect objects in a package that could clearly describe life
in Flagstaff to students in a colleague's classroom in San Francisco. The students selected items such as a small chunk of volcanic cinder, a branch of ponderosa pine, a
plastic fish, a cowboy hat, a pair of mittens, and a small piece of silver jewelry with
turquoise stones. The students then wrote a letter that explained each of the items.
Figure 12–18 shows one paragraph of the letter; it describes the significance of including the pair of mittens. The students in San Francisco reciprocated by preparing
a package and explanatory letter describing their city.

Ms. Hernandez, a fifth-grade teacher discussing disagreements that led to the
Civil War, asked half of her class to imagine that they lived in the North and had relatives living in the South. Each "Northern" student was to write a letter to the
"Southern" relative, encouraging him or her to remain loyal to the Union. The letters
were randomly delivered to classmates, who were then responsible for composing
a response. Ms. Hernandez employed writing process strategies to complete this
project, making sure her students understood the issues before they presented their
arguments in the letters.

Mr. Littlejohn, a second-grade teacher, took his children on a trip to the post office
as part of their study of community helpers. After the class returned, he read them
the book *The Jolly Postman* by Janet and Allan Ahlberg (Little, Brown). The children
delighted in the imaginative tale about a mail carrier who delivers letters to such fantasy characters as Cinderella and The Three Bears. Mr. Littlejohn used the story as a
springboard for his children to write letters to their favorite authors.

Mr. Pronchik asked his students to examine the yellow pages of the telephone direc-
tory to locate the names of travel agencies. They wrote letters to the agencies requesting

FIGURE 12–18
Paragraph From a Student's Letter

In Flagstaff it snows a lot during wintertime.
Sometimes it snows as much as 2 feet.
There are many winter sports in Flagstaff.
People especially like to go to the mountains
to snow ski. I like to go snowboarding.
Jeffwan

information about important historical sites around Philadelphia, including Convention Hall, the Betsy Ross House, and the Liberty Bell. Writing business letters to request information and free materials is important to social studies instruction.

Writing letters is an excellent way to encourage expository writing in social studies, for experiences in social studies provide varied contexts that motivate students to write in that form.

The goal of expository and expressive writing is to present ideas accurately as teachers carefully arrange an environment where students can acquire and refine communication skills. Salinger (1988) describes the possibilities for selecting expository and expressive writing activities in the primary grades during a unit on Thanksgiving:

> A unit on Thanksgiving, for example, could lead to a factual report on the Pilgrims or Indians, a letter from Plymouth colony, a description of the first Thanksgiving dinner (with drawings), a thank-you note to Squanto, a script to reenact the first Thanksgiving dinner, a report on Thanksgiving celebrations in other nations, or a recipe for cooking turkeys. A few children may find some of the assignments "silly"; others may have trouble handling a full "research report"; but because there are varied opportunities for writing, the whole class—avid story writers to meticulous fact seekers—can accomplish something. Through assignments like these, children gain valuable practice writing in different modes, for different purposes, and to different audiences. (p. 258)

IMAGINATIVE (CREATIVE) WRITING

Expository and expressive writing are primarily concerned with communicating facts and ideas, or personal thoughts, opinions, and feelings. When educators talk about writing in content areas such as social studies, these two genres seem to dominate their recommendations. However, we must be aware that young writers enjoy writing in original ways, too. Called *creative writing* or *imaginative writing*, this genre is intended not only to communicate information, but also to express original ideas that are the personal product of the child's experience and imagination. Murray (1979) states that creative writing "not only communicates information, it makes the reader care about the information, it makes him feel, it makes him experience, it gets under his skin" (p. 253). Because the purpose of imaginative writing is often thought to be to delight or entertain, the process is primarily encouraged during "language arts" or "literacy" classes where the mechanics of skillful writing are emphasized. As important as these skills are, however, imaginative writing is best cultivated not in the exercise of grammatical rules but through the experience of life and the discovery of meaning. Therefore, the discoveries unearthed while engaged in social studies themes and topics provide a strong background of content for creative writing. Caprio (1986) has found that when social studies topics are used as stimulation for creative writing, kindergarten and first-grade children write both longer and higher quality products. O'Day (1994) notes that his students were more deliberate in thinking out concepts or questions after being involved in creative writing processes. Consequently, students need many opportunities in the social studies to write and to gain pleasure from sharing their creative products. Proett and Gill (1986) emphasize that this process consists of two major considerations:

> Seen in one way, [the writing process] is the flowing of words onto the page, easily, naturally, rapidly. But it is also a time of making decisions, of choosing what to tell and what to leave out, . . . of determining what order, what structure, what word works best. In some ways these functions even seem contradictory; the first needs to be fluid and fast while the other calls for deliberation and reason. The teaching task is to help the writer coordinate these two functions. (p. 11)

Poetry

One of the most powerful ways to encourage imaginative writing in social studies is to involve children in poetry, a form of writing that allows individuals to concoct word pictures as they express ideas in highly original ways. Through poetry, children organize their thinking about social studies content in order to convey clear images of what they have learned.

Free-Form Poetry

A most effective ways to introduce poetry to children is to focus on the content of a learning experience. For example, one teacher began a lesson on popcorn by holding up a cup of popcorn and asking how many of her second graders liked popcorn and what they knew about it. To help the students access their background knowledge, the teacher recorded their comments on a knowledge chart. They listed everything they knew about popcorn in a column labeled, "What We Know About Popcorn." Then she read aloud *The Popcorn Book* by Tomie de Paola (Holiday), a delightfully illustrated picture book that tells about varieties of corn and where and when popcorn was discovered. The book includes interesting information about popcorn such as how much is eaten each year and the "popcorn blizzard" in the Midwest. After the book was read, the teacher helped the students record in the second column ("What We Learned About Popcorn") what they learned about popcorn after hearing the story and corrected any information in the first column that was inaccurate. Because de Paola also devotes much of the book to the popping process, the teacher followed up this information-processing activity by inviting the children to help her pop some corn. Throughout the entire popping experience, the teacher stressed both awareness of what the children were discovering as well as the impressions they received from their senses. They talked about the color, size, weight, and shape of the popcorn. Children offered words to describe the aroma of the popcorn as it popped. They commented on the exploding noises, as well as the puffy new shape the kernels were taking. More words described its feel and taste as the popcorn was eaten. As the children contributed their ideas, the teacher recorded them on a data chart.

After the children talked about things they experienced with popcorn, the teacher led them through the process of writing a free-form poem, each line beginning with "Popcorn." Here is the result:

Popcorn was discovered by Native American Indians long ago.
Popcorn was worn as trinkets by some Native American Indians.
Popcorn jumps up and down when you cook it.
Popcorn looks like a puffy cloud when it is done.
Popcorn tastes delicious with salt and butter.
Popcorn tastes good.

This type of poetry is called *free-form poetry* because the children choose words freely to express their thoughts without concern for rhyme or a particular structure. In social studies, it is important to create free-form poems only after the children have experienced a meaningful learning episode and brainstormed lists of words to describe what they learned.

Although free-form poetry need not rhyme, some children create unintentional rhymes as they play with words, combining them in novel ways. Denman (1988) calls this "wordsmithing," or an awareness of the functions of language. In the example shown in Figure 12–19, a child demonstrates that a particular sound can be repeated within a unique combination of words. In addition to experimenting with words, teachers should encourage children to experiment with different formats and patterns.

Patterned Poetry

In recent years, teachers have found structured poems such as haiku, tanka, senryu, diamante, or cinquain to be especially useful in helping students convey ideas about social studies topics. As we discovered with free-form poetry, teachers who want children to compose structured poems must organize instructional efforts so that the children both acquire sufficient knowledge on which to build their creations and understand the literary form that the final product is expected to take. One teacher understood these basic principles of writing in the social studies program, so the initial phase of his fourth-grade thematic unit involved the process of *exploring the topic*, a period of content investigation during which children were encouraged to think deeply about something new to them. Therefore, as the "Southwestern United States" interdisciplinary theme unfolded, the teacher carefully prepared a variety of fact-finding experiences. The emphasis of the unit was on the land and the people, so one particular section dealt with early Spanish settlers and life on their large cattle ranches *(ranchos)*. The focus of learning was on *vaqueras* (female cattle workers) and *vaqueros* (male cattle workers), expert riders who spent most of their day on horses rounding up cattle. To help children learn about these rancho workers, the teacher selected a quality resource from children's literature: *Carlota* by Scott O'Dell (Houghton Mifflin). The students collected and organized information from the book on an information processing web titled "Life of a Vaquera." The process of collecting, thinking about, organizing, and talking about the content was an important initial step for the teacher's young writers.

The second step in creating a written product in social studies is to guide children through the process of *brainstorming what they already know* about the topic and

FIGURE 12–19
Experimental Poem

organizing the data into categories of shared relationships, the categories reflecting the form of written expression identified as the final goal of the process. In this case, for example, the teacher selected a *cinquain* as the form of written expression, so his brainstorming and data organization activities needed to correspond to the basic pattern of the cinquain. Teachers have adapted cinquain patterns over the years; this teacher selected one that consisted of a *first line* with one word (or short phrase) naming the theme, the *second line* having two words describing the theme, the *third line* consisting of three words describing some action related to the theme, the *fourth line* naming something associated with the theme, and a *fifth line* designating another word (or short phrase) for the theme. Because the children needed to generate ideas for each line, the teacher began by dividing his class into three groups to brainstorm information related to vaqueras. He asked one group to brainstorm all the words they could think of to *describe* vaqueras, another group to generate *action* (doing) words associated with vaqueras, and a third group to list *things* associated with these cattle workers. After about ten minutes of enthusiastic deliberation, each group selected an individual to place its word inventory on a large sheet of chart paper. Words such as *expert rider, skillful, lonely, tired, hard working, Spanish,* and *woman cowboy* were written on the "Describing Words" chart; the "Doing Words" collection contained *roping, herding, riding, camping out, tending cattle, branding,* and *rounding up;* the "Vaquera Things" chart included *reata (rope), silla (saddle), chaparreras (chaps), blanket, horse, cattle, rancho, spurs, cattle drive, stampede, hat,* and *bandanna.* By creating a comprehensive list for each grouping, the teacher not only helped the students organize an extensive word bank from which to select words for their cinquains, but also reviewed and organized into meaningful categories the content under study.

After the charts were completed and displayed, the teacher directed the "Describing Words" group to carefully examine the "Doing Words" list and select three words they felt best characterized what vaqueras do. The "Doing Words" group was to choose from the items on the "Vaquera Things" chart the four things they thought were most closely associated with the rancho workers. The "Vaquera Things" group examined the "Describing Words" chart to select the two words that best described vaqueras. Lively discussion continued for some time as the children in each group argued strongly for their personal choices. Key information from previous learning experiences bubbled forth as the children sought to convince their group partners of the value of their word choices.

When each group made the appropriate number of selections from its assigned chart, the teacher directed the class toward the third phase of the writing continuum—*composing a group model.* He posted a large sheet of chart paper that exhibited a writing guide, as shown in Figure 12–20.

On the top line, the teacher wrote the word identifying the idea under study—*Vaquera.* He then asked the "Vaquera Things" group to reveal the two describing words it had selected. Then he wrote the words in the blanks on the next line—*hard working* and *expert rider.*

In the same way, the "Describing Words" group offered its three action words for the third line (*roping, herding,* and *rounding up*) and the "Doing Words" group

FIGURE 12–20.
Cinquain Pattern

shared its choice of four vaquera things for the next line (*rancho, mustang, reata,* and *stampede*). "Try to think of another word for *vaquera* so we can put it in the last blank," was the teacher's last challenge. After considering all suggestions, the class decided upon *rancho worker* because the term defined these women. The group composition is shown in Figure 12–21.

During the fourth stage of the writing process—*editing and rewriting*—the teacher encouraged the students to read the cinquain with him, and they revised the text appropriately. Commas were added to separate items in a list and the first word of each line was capitalized. After the corrections were made, the class chorused the selection once again.

To begin the next stage of the writing process—*individual writing*—the teacher helped his students analyze the pattern of the group cinquain they had just completed: "How many blank spaces do you see on each line? What kinds of words were used on each line? How have the words helped paint a mental picture of what we have been studying about life in the Southwest?"

The teacher had previously decorated a large bulletin board with illustrations depicting a vaquera twirling a rawhide reata above her head and a herd of cartoon-like cattle of the size to hold a 4" x 5" piece of paper (the display was titled "Poetry Roundup"). He asked the students to read their cinquains and staple them to the sides of the cattle. This final phase of the writing process—*publishing*—encouraged the students to share their products with an audience. In this case, publishing took the form of oral reading and displaying the individual cinquains on the bulletin board.

Other forms of structured poetry are especially useful in the social studies. A discussion of some popular options follows.

FIGURE 12–21
Completed Group
Cinquain

Vaquera
hard working   expert rider
roping   herding   rounding up
rancho   mustang   reata   stampede
rancho worker

The Haiku.   This form of Japanese poetry consists of three lines with a total of seventeen syllables; the first and third lines have five syllables each, and the second line has seven. These poems usually describe the spirit of nature, and appeal to children of all ages.

The rain is falling. *(five syllables)*
Soon the flowers will burst forth. *(seven syllables)*
Spring is beautiful. *(five syllables)*

The Senryu.   This form of Japanese poetry is structurally similar to the haiku, but expresses ideas about human beings rather than nature.

The strong ox-cart man *(five syllables)*
Trudges down the lonely trail. *(seven syllables)*
His cart is his life. *(five syllables)*

The Tanka.   Tanka are extensions of haiku; they add two lines of seven syllables to the haiku and contain a total of thirty-one syllables.

Big puffy white clouds *(five syllables)*
Floating across a blue sea. *(seven syllables)*
A white castle there? *(five syllables)*
Maybe a giant white ship? *(seven syllables)*
What do you want them to be? *(seven syllables)*

The Cinquain.   The cinquain is not a form of Japanese poetry, but is often thought to be because its form is based on a specific number of words for each line. Actually, the word *cinquain* is based on the French word for five, *cinq*. Cinquains consist of five lines following this pattern:

Noun (The title)
Two describing words, or adjectives (Describe the title)
Three action words, or verbs (describing some action related to the theme)
Four words naming something associated with the theme
Another word (or short phrase) for the theme

The Simile.   Similes are comparisons made between two things or ideas that people normally tend not to associate. The words *like* or *as* often signal the associations, as in "as quiet as a mouse." Here is an example of a fourth grader's simile, written in response to the teacher's suggested title, "How Brave Can You Be?"

I can be as brave as a tree in a thunderstorm.
I can be as brave as a seed sprouting under the dirt.
I can be as brave as writing this poem!

Persona.   Ms. Blumenreich extended the study of tribal societies by guiding her fifth graders through the use of *persona* as a writing technique. To begin, the students had just learned that in many tribal societies a person has a "bush soul" as well as his or her own soul. The bush soul can take the form of an animal, tree, rock, or some other existence in nature that might give one strength and courage. This characterization aspect can be applied to writing poetry—putting oneself in the place of someone or something else (real or imaginary) to say what might not normally be revealed.

Ms. Blumenreich started her class by displaying a large poster print of a young African woman adorned in ceremonial attire, gazing wistfully into a brilliant sunset. Ms. Blumenreich asked her class to extend their imaginations and try to actually "become" that young woman.

At this point, the students were asked questions about the scene: Who are you? What are doing in the picture? Where do you live? How do you feel? What is it like to be you? What changes have you been through in your life?"

Ms. Blumenreich wrote the children's responses in a few short lines of interesting poetry:

> There was a young woman
> Adorned with jewels
> And painted with earthen ashes.
> It seemed like only yesterday
> When she frolicked freely in the fields.
> Now she prepares for a wedding ritual.
> What lies ahead is invisible.

Ms. Blumenreich began her writing sequence with a direct experience and used oral activities to create a written product. The model product was then kept in full view as the students each received their own photos depicting tribal life cut from old *National Geographic* magazines. They were to write their own "persona poetry" using the writing process techniques described earlier in this section. Once completed, the poems and photos were mounted on colored construction paper to be displayed for all to enjoy.

Although most elementary school social studies classrooms primarily use expository and expressive writing, considerable opportunity exists to integrate creative writing strategies as well. By encouraging children to explore and experiment with written words in contexts associated with social studies themes, we help them realize that language is used both to communicate information clearly and to express that knowledge through creative texts. Creative writing should be accepted as a natural element of social studies instruction—a treasured tool for pleasurable learning.

The instructional sequence for creative writing in social studies is summarized below:

1. *Experience.* Offer a series of meaningful direct or vicarious learning experiences through which the students gather meaningful information upon which to base their writing.

2. *Brainstorm and organize the data.* Help students process what they learned by charting relationships among the data.

3. *Compose a group text.* Help students cooperatively compose a model written sample.

4. *Edit the sample and rewrite, if necessary.* Reread the written piece to determine whether ideas are expressed clearly and accurately, and whether there are any errors in spelling, grammar, or other writing mechanics.

5. *Create individual pieces.* Offer an opportunity for each student to write a unique product based on the model generated by the group.

6. *Publish the written products.* Share what the classroom authors have created by asking them to read aloud to their classmates, contribute a page to a class-made book, post their work on a bulletin board, and so on.

WORD PROCESSING AND DESKTOP PUBLISHING

Word processing programs (computer programs for writing) have become extremely valuable tools for writing in the social studies classroom. We learned earlier in this chapter that writing is viewed as a continuous process during which an author generates ideas, creates drafts, edits, revises, and publishes a finished piece. That process is common to everyone—from kindergarteners as they compose stories with drawings and invented spellings to teachers who compose letters to parents. This writing process is as suited to the computer as it is to the paper and pencil. Like the paper and pencil, computers can be used to compose any kind of written work.

Word Processing

Although many word processing programs are available for classroom use, all share certain common characteristics; they facilitate the efficient entry, editing, storing, and printing of text (Simonson and Thompson, 1997; Newby, Stepich, Lehman, & Russell, 1996).

Text Entry

With most programs, text is entered into the computer much as it is typed on a typewriter—using a keyboard. Unlike most typewriters, however, word processing programs allow students to format text and lay out pages easily and efficiently. Common formatting and page layout features include:

- *Fonts.* The appearance of the text itself can be altered through the selection of various fonts, or typefaces, that come in various sizes. Common fonts include Times, Helvetica, Calligrapher, and Courier.

- *Type styles.* Word processors allow various type styles to be applied to any of the fonts included in the word processing program. Type styles include **boldface**, *italics,* underline, outline, and others.

- *Graphics.* Most new word processing programs allow students to embed a wide variety of graphics into the document.

In addition, word processors set margins and tabs easily, automatically page the document, and allow line spacing to be changed quickly. Word processors also have what is called a *wrap-around* feature. This means that the student does not need to use the return key to move to the next line; the program determines the end of each line of print and automatically moves the next whole word down. Mistakes are also much easier to fix on the computer than on the typewriter. All the student must do is move the cursor immediately to the right of the character that needs to be changed and press the backspace or delete key. The correct entry can then be substituted.

Editing

Clearly, there is much more to word processing than entering text and making corrections. In addition to these features, word processors allow the student to revise and edit once the written piece has been completed. In the days before word processors, if writers wanted to move parargraphs from one part of a composition to another, they used scissors to carefully cut them out and then taped them to the new spot. With word processing systems, however, students learn to perform "block operations." That is, they can manipulate blocks of text in several ways: delete an entire block, move it to a new location in the piece, or copy it to be added somewhere else.

Word processing systems also allow students to experiment with language by inserting or deleting material with ease. To insert, all one needs to do is position the cursor where the material is to go and then simply begin to type. After the insertion, the text is automatically reorganized. To delete, the cursor is placed at the end of the material to be stricken, and then the backspace or delete key is pressed to eliminate unwanted text. Again, the material is automatically reorganized.

Word processors simplify the writing process with special technical features. A *thesaurus* offers a wealth of synomyms for the writer; a *grammar checker* identifies such errors as improper capitalization, lack of subject–verb agreement, split infinitives, and the like; and a *spell checker* searches through the document to find misspelled words and then suggests possible corrections. Simonson and Thompson (1997) inform us that teachers have expressed mixed reactions to spell checkers:

> Some teachers do not allow their use, saying these programs inhibit the learning of good spelling habits. Many of these teachers seem to believe the spelling checker spells for the student, which of course is not true.
>
> The majority of teachers who have worked with spelling checkers are enthusiastic about their possibilities. Spelling checkers seem to encourage students to edit their writing. . . . Using a spelling checker usually means that students will do more spelling work when writing a paper than they would without it. (p. 178)

As with the spell checker, teachers are split on the use of grammar and usage aids. On one hand, teachers appreciate the fact that these aids make the oftentimes tedious editing process faster, easier, and more enjoyable; on the other hand, teachers fear that students could become lazy and not focus critical attention on needed areas of improvement.

Storing

A third key benefit of word processors is their ability to save and retrieve documents from a disk or the operating system's hard drive. An incomplete or unpolished version of a written piece can be placed into storage and retrieved later to be altered or completed. Disks can store a multitude of files; compositions from everyone in a typical classroom could be easily stored on a single disk.

Printing

Of course, the final word processing activity is the paper copy of a written piece. All of the features described to this point would be useless if they could be printed on paper. So, after the text is laid out as desired, the writing process culminates in the printing of a "clean" copy. The word-processed text can then be stored on a disk for repeated retrieval, updating, or reuse.

In support of word processing activities in the elementary school classroom, Bangert-Drowns (1993) concludes that the use of word processors results in both longer written texts and better-quality writing. Galda, Cullinan, and Strickland (1993) point out the effectiveness of word processing in classroom writing activities:

> [Teachers] have found that when the computer replaces paper and pencil many children write more, revise more willingly and more extensively, and thus work longer on single pieces. The result is not only longer, more detailed, and generally "better" pieces, but a realization by the children that they can manipulate text, changing it at will and as often as they like to produce the effect they want. (p. 197)

Galda, Cullinan, and Strickland (1993) caution that, if teachers are not careful, the positive effects of computer-aided writing could be blunted if they place too much emphasis on the technical aspects of writing and not enough on the creative aspects:

> For some writers, revision becomes easier, faster, less tedious, and thus both more frequent and more complete. However, this revision may be limited to editing concerns such as spelling, mechanics, and syntax rather than encompassing whole-text concerns. . . . Perhaps the computer allows young writers to process their texts so quickly that they do not spend time thinking about what they are writing. They may see surface errors clearly on the screen and focus on those rather than on larger concerns. (p. 197)

In addition, Hennings (1997) forewarns teachers that:

> The use of word processing programs in writing . . . does not teach children what revising and editing are all about. Often upper-graders who are taught how to type stories

One important way to encourage children to engage in wide and purposeful writing is to make the computer readily available.

into a computer and use the editing commands to produce another draft simply make cosmetic changes; they do not expand thoughts, clarify ideas, or reorganize even though the computer program lets them make these changes. (p. 352)

Templeton (1997) has determined that while the research in this area is quite new and mixed, three fundamental observations seem to emerge:

1. The [classroom environment] in which computer use occurs may significantly affect children's awareness of their writing and how it communicates with an audience.
2. In the early stages of computer use, students' motivation to write can be enhanced.
3. Revising and editing can become easier and perhaps more effective on the computer than on paper. (pp. 256–257)

Advancements in technology now offer word processing programs to facilitate the writing process. Positive results can be expected if students have the opportunity to experiment and create rather than become bogged down with technical demands. Motivated writers are not only able to prepare attractive, well-edited reports, but also to apply creative thinking to the production of a wide variety of written products

FIGURE 12–22
Student Report Written with
a Word Processing Program

JADE SNOW
WONG

Jade Snow Wong was born to a Chinese family in America. She and her family lived in San Francisco's Chinatown. Her family owned a garment shop there. The shop was attached to their house. As she got a little older she played close to home. Her family told her that they only had enough money to send their sons through college. She worked at poor-paying jobs to earn money.

Jade Snow Wong started her own pottery business in San Francisco. She was very good in art so she got a scholarship to college. Despite all her hardships growing up, she was sucessful in her life. Jade did not let obstacles stand in her way.

such as poetry, folktales, travel brochures, newspapers, and the like (see Figure 12–22 for an example of a written report with an illustration).

Computers cannot be embraced as a panacea for problems with composition, but they can be accepted as highly regarded word processing tools to aid in composing diverse written texts. The Technology Sampler lists useful word processing software appropriate for elementary and middle school classrooms.

AFTERWORD

Many kinds of writing give balance to elementary school social studies programs. Through informal and formal writing experiences, the elementary school child learns to use language for a variety of purposes. Of all these purposes, perhaps the most powerful initial desire of young children is to communicate the message, "I've got something to tell you." The idea that writing can be used to communicate information is very important to social studies and depends on a complex set of language competencies that grow from varied classroom experiences. Of all curriculum areas, students and teachers use literacy strategies more often than any other to fulfill the demands of learning in social studies. (In this text, *literacy* has been defined as an integrated language arts approach where writing is nestled among reading, listening, and speaking experiences, resulting in a more cohesive command of all language tools than possible when they were taught in isolation—traditional *language arts*.)

It is during infancy when we take our first wobbly steps on the journey toward literacy, an enterprise that continues throughout our lives. Vygotsky explains that it is this language process that separates humans from all other animals. Specifically, Vygotsky proposes that humans differ from animals because they are able to make and use tools in an effort to adapt to their environment and solve problems. Tools can be classified as *physical tools* (things such as saws or a hammers) or *mental tools* (complex thought and language processes). In speaking of mental tools, Vygotsky emphasizes that symbols have been created by human beings to communicate what goes on in one's mind and how these thoughts might transform the physical environment. These symbolic tools might be expressed through such forms as a drawn picture, an algebraic formula, or a map, but the most influential "tool of the mind" in Vygotsky's thinking is language. And, because language appears to be so intimately associated with cognition (thinking), teachers must be aware that application of reading, writing, speaking, and talking processes is basic to thinking and learning in the social studies. It is through language that we learn about, and become more capable members of, our culture.

TECHNOLOGY SAMPLER

Useful sources for related social studies topics include these Internet sites:

The Global Campfire (Children from around the world take part in constructing a "story tree" by submitting the next paragraph of an ongoing story.)
http://www.indiana.edu/~eric_rec/fl/pcto/

Web 66 (locate school web pages)
http://web66.coled.umn.edu/

Useful sources for related social studies topics include these software titles:

KidPix Studio (presentation software)
Broderbund

HyperStudio (presentation software)
Roger Wagner Publishing

PowerPoint (presentation software)
Microsoft Corporation

The Amazing Writing Machine (word processing)
Broderbund

A sophisticated writing program that is appropriate for the 6–12 year age range. An enjoyable approach to spur children's imaginations to tell stories.

Bank Street Writer (word processing)
Scholastic

Children's Writing and Publishing Center (word processing)
The Learning Company

ClarisWorks (word processing)
Claris

A basic word processing program that is excellent for designing and publishing papers, newsletters, reports, and cards.

Mavis Beacon Teaches Typing 5 (keyboarding skills)
Mindscape
Children in grades 3 and up develop keyboarding skills through arcade-style games.

Microsoft Works (word processing)
Microsoft
Another "works" package that provides the basics for processing words.

Print Shop Deluxe (word processing)
Broderbund

Type to Learn (keyboarding skills)
Sunburst
Helps children in grades 3–8 develop keyboarding skills.

Ultimate Writing & Creativity Center (word processing)
The Learning Company
Full-featured word processor with friendly drawing tools, ready-made illustrations, and helpful writing tips. Supports all phases of the writing process for children in grades 2–5. Includes story starters, dictionary, thesaurus, and spell checker.

WHAT I *NOW* KNOW

Complete these self-check items once more. Determine for yourself whether it would be useful to take a more in-depth look at any area. Use the same key as you did for the preassessment form ("+", "?", "-").

I can *now*

_____ describe how writing contributes to learning in the social studies.

_____ explain what is meant by the *writing process*.

_____ defend the place of expository writing in the social studies.

_____ discuss the value of expressive writing in the social studies.

_____ plan for appropriate imaginative writing experiences.

_____ create a classroom atmosphere that promotes productive writing in the social studies.

_____ explain how to promote the writing process in the social studies through the use of word processing programs.

_____ describe how reading and writing are interrelated processes.

REFERENCES

Applebee, A. N. (1984). Writing and reasoning. *Review of Educational Research, 54,* 577–596.

Atwell, N. (Ed.) (1990). *Coming to know: Writing to learn in the intermediate grades.* Portsmouth, NH: Heinemann.

Bangert-Drowns, R. L. (1993). The word processor as an instructional tool: A meta-analysis of word processing in writing instruction. *Review of Educational Research, 63,* 69–73.

Britton, J., Burgess, T., Martin, N., McLeod, A., & Rosen, H. (1975). *The development of writing abilities.* Schools Council Research Studies. London: Macmillan, 11–18.

Bromley, K. D. (1992). *Language arts: Exploring connections.* Boston: Allyn and Bacon.

Caprio, J. (1986). The influences of firsthand experiences on children's writing. Doctoral dissertation, University of New Jersey at New Brunswick, 1986. *Dissertation Abstracts International* 47: 02A. (University Microfilms No. 86–09, 228).

Combs, M. (1996). *Developing competent readers and writers in the primary grades.* Englewood Cliffs, NJ: Prentice-Hall.

Cooper, J. D. (1997). *Literacy: Helping children construct meaning.* Boston: Houghton Mifflin.

Cullinan, B. E., & Galda, L. (1994). *Literature and the child.* Fort Worth, TX: Harcourt Brace College Publishers.

Denman, G. A. (1988). *When you've made it your own: Teaching poetry to young people.* Portsmouth, NH: Heinemann.

Farris, P. J. (1993). *Language arts: A process approach.* Madison, WI: Brown & Benchmark.

Freedman, R. (1989). *Lincoln: A photobiography.* New York: Clarion.

Frye, N., Baker, S., & Perkins, G. (1985). *The Harper handbook to literature.* New York: Harper & Row.

Galda, L., Cullinan, B. E., & Strickland, D. S. (1993). *Language, literacy and the child.* Fort Worth, TX: Harcourt Brace Jovanovich.

Giacobbe, M. E. (1981). Who says that children can't write the first week? In Walshe, R. D. (Ed.), *Donald Graves in Australia: "Children want to write...."* Rozelle, Australia: Primary English Teaching Association.

Graves, D. H. 9 (1983). *Writing: Teachers and children at work.* Exeter, NH: Heinemann.

Haley-James, S. M., & Hobson, C. D. (1980). Interviewing: A means of encouraging the drive to communicate. *Language Arts, 57,* 497–502.

Harp, B., & Brewer, J. (1991). *Reading and writing: Teaching for the connections.* Fort Worth, TX: Harcourt Brace Jovanovich.

Hennings, D. G. (1990). *Communication in action.* Boston: Houghton Mifflin.

Hennings, D. G. (1997). *Communication in action: Teaching literature-based language arts.* Boston: Houghton Mifflin.

Keller, H. (1920). *The story of my life.* Garden City, NY: Doubleday.

Murray, D. (1979). The listening eye: Reflections on the writing conference. *College English, 41.*

Murray, D. (1980). How writing finds its own meaning. In T. R. Donovan and B. W. McClelland (Eds.), *Eight approaches to teaching composition.* Urbana, IL: National Council of Teachers of English.

Murray, D. (1987) In N. Atwell, *In the middle.* Portsmouth, NH: Heinemann/Boynton Cook.

Newby, T. J., Stepich, D. A., Lehman, J. D., & Russell, J. D. (1996). *Instructional technology for teaching and learning.* Englewood Cliffs, NJ: Merrill/Prentice Hall.

Norton, D. E. (1997). *The effective teaching of language arts.* Columbus, OH: Merrill/Prentice Hall.

O'Day, K. (1994). Using formal and informal writing in middle school social studies. *Social Education, 58,* 39–40.

Prelutsky, J. (1984). *The new kid on the block.* New York: Greenwillow Books.

Proett, J., & Gill, K. (1986). *The writing process in action: A handbook for teachers.* Urbana, IL: National Council of Teachers of English.

Salinger, T. (1988). *Language arts and literacy.* New York: Merrill/Macmillan.

Simonson, M. R., & Thompson, A. (1997). *Educational computing foundations.* Upper Saddle River, NJ: Merrill/Prentice Hall.

Templeton, S. (1997). *Teaching the integrated language arts.* Boston: Houghton Mifflin.

Tompkins, G. E., & Hoskisson, K. (1995). *Language arts: Content and teaching strategies.* Englewood Cliffs, NJ: Prentice-Hall.

Vygotsky, L. S. (1978). *Mind in society: The development of higher mental processes.* Cambridge, MA: Harvard University Press.

CHAPTER 13

WHAT I KNOW

This exercise provides a "scaffold" that will enable you to relate the chapter material to your background knowledge. Complete the form before you read the chapter and use the results to guide your reading. Use a "+" to indicate confidence, a "?" for uncertainty, and a "-" if you feel deficient in any area.

I can

_____ explain what areas are encompassed in the *expressive arts*.

_____ offer a sound rationale for utilizing the expressive arts to strengthen learning in the social studies curriculum.

_____ justify curriculum time spent on activities related to the expressive arts.

_____ explain how the expressive arts help children make sense of their world.

_____ describe how teachers aid children articulate meaning through the expressive arts.

_____ explain how teachers help students create their own expressive arts products.

_____ plan social studies experiences that involve contributions from the expressive arts.

Using the results as a guide, what questions will you seek to answer as you read?

Integrating the Expressive Arts

◆ CLASSROOM SKETCH

Mrs. Torres chose to help her students discover important cross-cultural understandings by taking them to an "Igbo Arts" exhibit at the local museum. The exhibit displayed more than 100 objects produced by the Igbo (or Ibo) people of southeastern Nigeria. The items in the exhibit included wooden totemic sculptures, pottery, textiles, examples of painting and body adornment, and a variety of masks. Though wood predominated, as it does in most African art, the exhibit also included objects fashioned from bronze, iron, and ivory.

The purpose of the visit was to stimulate interest in the Igbo through the beauty of their creative work. Mrs. Torres's goal was achieved, as the students returned full of questions ripe for research and discovery: "Why did the Igbo make the small totemic figures? What were the purposes of the elaborate masks on display?" The children ventured into the world of the Igbo through intensive reading and research in the school library, newspapers, books at home, and other references, including informational pamphlets from the exhibit.

A whole new world opened up to them through the arts—the children learned that Igbo art forms were a direct expression of their culture. For example, the small, wooden totemic figures (*ikenga*) symbolized traditionally masculine attributes such as strength, courage, and aggressiveness. These carved figures were kept in the men's meetinghouse. Among women, body jewelry such as ivory and brass anklets symbolized prestige and social satisfaction. The masks played a major role in the Igbo's masquerades, in which male performers acted out various aspects of their spiritual beliefs. Other art forms—sculpture, drama, dance, paintings, music, and costumes—were also used in masquerades.

The Igbo culture became more meaningful each day. Its rich creativity came alive in the classroom. After the children had accumulated enough information to satisfy their curiosity, they settled on ways to share what they had found out. One group recreated jewelry for a mini-display; another made a model of an Igbo mask; a third dramatized an Igbo spiritual celebration; a fourth made a model *ikenga*. Through their expressive activities, the children became creators of original art forms that communicated the discoveries they made as fascinated learners.

◆ CLASSROOM CONNECTION

Mrs. Torres capitalizes on the expressive arts produced by people around the world as she involves her students in the study of any culture. In her classroom, students reproduce the style of Mary Cassatt's paintings, perform dramatic interpretations of Greek legends, and sing folk tunes from many lands. Mrs. Torres considers social studies instruction incomplete unless students also experience the artistic expressions of cultures under study, their *music, drama, dance, literature,* and *visual arts.* Through no other source, Mrs. Torres asserts, can we as effectively communicate the values, beliefs, and character of a culture or society; artistic works or products reflect the substance and spirit of the society from which they come.

Like Mrs. Torres, teachers around the country are being encouraged to view the world from a perspective that integrates social studies with the expressive arts. (Literature was discussed separately in Chapter 11.) This larger perspective calls for joining together history and music, geography and art, creative dramatics and political science. The overall aim is to help students gain a sense of a culture's human spirit by examining the great works of art created by its people. That idea is simple, but the harsh truth is that arts education is denied to most children in our elementary school classrooms today. Eisner (Brandt, 1987/1988), a respected scholar in both the arts and education, has declared that "people in this country—educators and the public at large—[view] the arts for young children at least, as having little value other than something to put on the refrigerator door. That conception of art can never compete adequately for time in the school program" (p. 7). Egan (1997) places the blame for this state of affairs on the public's fascination with activities that seem to lead directly to skills of practical use in adulthood: "Accordingly, the 'basics' of education are usually thought to be the early development of skills that will later be useful in employment. It is becoming easier for those promoting computer literacy, for example, to argue for curriculum time on the grounds that computer skills will be useful when searching for jobs. Thus, computer literacy is rapidly becoming yet another 'basic' competing for precious teaching time" (p. 341). Schools have responded to public pressures by requiring more cumbrous academic requirements and striving for improved standardized test scores. In this quest to improve the "basics," many schools have initiated "no frills" programs that seriously neglect the expressive arts. Fowler (1989) offers this forceful reaction to our failure to tender a role for the expressive arts in our school curricula, particularly as it relates to the social studies:

> By denying children the arts, we starve our civilization. We produce children who are more fitted for an age of barbarism than the advanced civilization of the information age. . . . But equally important, we fail these children educationally by depriving them of the insights that the arts afford. The arts provide windows to other worlds. . . . The arts illuminate life in all its mystery, misery, delight, pity, and wonder. Encounters with the arts invite us to explore realms of meaning that, according to an old Persian proverb, lie next to the curtain that has never been drawn aside. (p. 62)

Years earlier, Rockefeller (1977) described a similar state, but offered his crafty support for the concept of a "basic education," suggesting that "the arts, properly taught, are basic to individual development since they more than any other subject awaken all the senses. . . . We endorse a curriculum which puts the 'basics' first, because arts are basic, right at the heart of the matter" (p. 6).

THE EXPRESSIVE ARTS

Excellent social studies programs are not limited to the singular role of "conveyor of information." They do not exist simply to create a data package that often results in a partial or shallow view of the world. Instead, the best programs offer comprehensive and interconnected experiences that enlighten students' understandings of humanity past and present. They pull from many areas of the curriculum, including the social sciences and the arts—creative writing, dance, music, drama, and visual arts—to present a cohesive, compelling impression of the world. The social sciences convey the content; the arts give us the human dimension. The arts tell us about people—how they feel and what they value. Isadora Duncan, a renowned dancer, once explained, "If I could tell you what I mean there would be no point in dancing" (McCormack, 1985, p. A15). Thus, the social sciences *inform* us while the arts *move* us. Fowler (1994) argues in support of this connected view of social studies education:

We need every possible way to represent, interpret, and convey our world for a very simple but powerful reason: No one of these ways offers a full picture. Individually . . . history [and the social sciences] convey only part of the reality of the world. Nor do the arts alone suffice. A multiplicity of symbol systems are [*sic*] required to provide a more complete picture and a more comprehensive education . . . . Both views are valid. Both contribute to understanding . . . . The British aesthetician and critic Herbert Read once said, "Art is the representation, science the explanation—of the same reality." (pp. 5–8)

The social sciences supply insight and wisdom; the arts reflect the spirit of the people who created them. People in all cultures preserve and maintain their collective existence through the observations and imaginations in their art. Horace Pippin, an African American artist born near Philadelphia, expressed his memories of war with his first painting, *End of the War: Starting Home.* In this painting, Pippin shows us a battle between German and American soldiers in World War I, when American troops were segregated into units of all black and all white men. Pippin fought in one of the all-black units, so his painting shows his unit engaged in battle with German soldiers. Similarly, songs like "When Johnny Comes Marching Home," "Over There," and "The Ballad of the Green Berets" convey strong feelings of support for those who fought in various conflicts throughout our nation's history. A wealth of expressive art is available to help children understand the human condition both intellectually and emotionally. Every child should have opportunities to explore the expressive arts as "language of civilization," for, as Fowler (1989) concludes, "the arts may well be the most telling imprints of any society" (p. 62). The National Endowment for the Arts (Hodsoll, 1988) points out the considerable merits of an integrated arts program:

1. Arts education provides students with a more complete understanding of civilizations being studied.
2. Arts education trains students to make critical assessments and evaluation.
3. Arts education offers students opportunities to express their own creativity.
4. The arts offer effective alternative means of communication—new verbal and nonverbal means of expressing thoughts and feelings.

INVOLVEMENT IN THE ARTS

For elementary school children, experiences in music, drama, dance, and the visual arts should cushion the pervasiveness of verbal instruction in the social studies classroom. The expressive arts help students heighten their awareness of civilization and inspire them to look at the world around them in different ways. The arts are a basic form of human communication that provide our most expressive outlets for thought, emotions, and aspirations.

A recent position paper by The Association for Childhood Education International (Jalongo, 1990) has encouraged schools to recognize the value of exploiting the arts throughout the curriculum. The paper describes how the arts influence children's intellect and creative imagination. The following recommendations are particularly significant for the social studies program:

Every child has a right to opportunities for imaginative expression. Imaginative expression is not the exclusive province of special programs for the gifted and talented. It is not a curricular "frill" to be deleted when time is limited. Nor is imagination synonymous with enrichment, something reserved for those children who have already completed their "work." Rather, imagination is a capacity in every child that should be nurtured.

Creative expression should permeate the entire curriculum. When we speak of basics in education, people immediately think of reading, writing, and arithmetic. But is that what is basic? If basic means something that is fundamental to the experience of all children, then other things would surely be basic. Play would certainly be "basic.". . . Telling and enacting stories would be "basic.". . . Drawing, painting and sculpture would surely be "basic" because, even before children can read, write or calculate, they are using these ways of communicating their ideas, emotions and individuality. Music and dance are "basic" because even before children can speak, they can listen and move to music.

The educated imagination is the key to equity and intercultural understanding. Creative productivity can be social rather than isolationist and its outcomes need not be money-saving, labor-saving or even artistic. Imagination dramatizes the inner workings of our minds and is the undercurrent of human interaction. . . . As we gain insight into ourselves, we can use imagination powers to identify with others. . . . We can empathize with their situations, envision possibilities and enact creative solutions to social problems. These connections with others, forged by imagination, are the basis for intercultural understanding. (pp. 195–201)

Social studies teachers may thus integrate the expressive arts and the social studies using a combination of three complementary perspectives: (1) students examine and respond to creative works already produced; (2) students reproduce the art products of a culture; and (3) students create art as an expressive or informative medium of communication. This means that, as a social studies teacher, you have the responsibility to consistently search for and put your students in contact with art products created by people of cultures under study and, while interest is high, help them become involved in related art activities.

Examining and Responding to Art

Students must be exposed to a wide range of artistic encounters. Elementary school children must experience original art (concerts, museums, and performances) and be presented opportunities to enjoy reproduced art (records or CDs, CD-ROMs, videos, posters, and the like). These valuable firsthand encounters help students understand the place of art in people's lives. However, to have the highest positive impact on learning, Nixon and Chalmers (1990) suggest that we must expand our idea of what the arts encompass if we are to meaningfully inspire the students' interest in them:

. . . many examples need to be considered, not just those we find in galleries and museums, concert halls and theaters. The popular, vernacular and folk arts are also significant. In the visual arts, we need to take into account architecture and the built environment, interior design and decoration, clothing and body ornamentation, posters, videos and films, comic books and other forms of visual imagery. In music, we should think of television themes, advertising jingles, nursery rhymes, rock songs, patriotic songs and holiday tunes. Besides theater and dance, our definition of the performing arts should include sports activities such as figure skating and gymnastics. (p. 14)

Art that is meaningful to children is not the same as "great art," but children must gain a sense of art in their own lives before they can be expected to value artistic achievements from the past or from other cultures. By appreciating the sources of expressive art most closely involved in children's lives, you can push to a wider understanding of the world of art. The arts belong in social studies programs because they make indispensable contributions to a child's total education. The arts help students improve the quality of their lives by challenging them to look at cultural beliefs, ideas, conditions, and problems in new ways. You need not be a professional musician, actor, or artist to present this segment of a culture's greatness to your students. You need only be aware of the beauty and excitement of the outside world and bring that world into your classroom. The arts belong in our schools because they are *not* frills, and you must treat them as essential parts of education.

The arts help children understand the exciting, rich customs of the people who make up our nation and world.

Reproducing Art

Exposure to the arts must not stop at examining and responding. You should give children opportunities to recreate what they observe as an extension or enrichment of the topic under study. Because the process of recreating an expressive arts product is intended to reinforce specific understandings, authenticity and accuracy of the representation are primary considerations. Few achievements of value could be expected, for example, if students learning about early dances in Colonial America were allowed to move freely to the music instead of duplicating the specific steps of a minuet. The designated purpose of the activity dictates the amount of conformity you must demand. If the purpose of an activity is to "deepen understandings of Kachina dolls as religious educational objects of the Hopis," then you must use accurate details, colors, and distinctive symbols. For example, a rain-cloud design on each cheek of the Kachina is a symbol with a specific meaning. The children should use this symbol only if they intend to communicate that meaning. Likewise, other special symbols, shapes, and colors convey specific messages to the Hopis. Experiences with Kachinas, then, must begin with research. By examining a Kachina doll (or its representation), you must determine where, why, how, and by whom it was made. Then give students the opportunity to apply what they learn to the accurate reproduction of Kachinas.

Cullum (1967) describes the excitement of reproducing great art in the social studies classroom:

> We turned our sixth-grade classroom into a Renoir Room! . . . Slowly but delightedly the students hung . . . fifty-four reproductions of Renoir paintings . . . on the four classroom walls.
>   The purpose of this project was to have students enter the world of Renoir through the beauty of his work, to engage in independent research to discover the man Renoir, and to digest and share this newly found world with the rest of the school. (pp. 52–53)

Experiences in recreating a culture's art, then, must be authentic; these projects lead children to deepened interest in academic pursuits and strengthen their understanding of culture.

Creating Art

A primary aim of the arts is to maximize children's creative potential, so the social studies should move beyond opportunities to examine and reproduce art toward providing opportunities for original self-expression. These experiences are recognized for their value in developing divergent thinking and creativity as well as cognitive enrichment. To return to the Kachina doll example, suppose that you have approached the project in a way similar to our recommendations—learning about real Kachinas followed by having students create an accurate reproduction, or model. Now you wish to elicit creative ideas through the influence of these cognitive events. You may choose to inform your students that there are over 200 actual Kachinas, and that new ones are often invented. You might approach the creative phase of the experience by furnishing a variety of materials and encouraging the children to construct Kachinas creating new symbols for whatever spirit they wish to represent.

John Dewey once made a vivid connection among all three of these complementary aspects of the arts when he said, "A beholder must create his own experience." Children must be given opportunities to enrich and express what they learn through as many expressive experiences as possible. An influential report, *Performing Together: The Arts in Education* (Alliance for Arts Education, 1985) states that "[s]tudying the arts gives all students that gift. When they study drama, they can become someone else, if only for a few minutes. When they create a painting, they can see the world with fresh eyes. Research has shown that students who study the arts are also more likely to display originality and creativity in other subjects" (p. 3).

THE VISUAL ARTS

Today's social studies teachers must help their students investigate cultures all around the world by delving into their visual arts. This can be done by bringing to class examples of the arts and crafts of people under study to help clarify their cultural distinctiveness. These materials not only arouse a great deal of interest in a topic and convey meaningful information, but they stimulate many questions, too. During a study of Puerto Rico, for example, Mr. Dean arranged a display of colorful gourds commonly used in a variety of ways by people of the Caribbean. Once dried and hollowed, gourds can be transformed into bowls for serving and eating food, different types of musical instruments, or engaging toys for children. The questions came quickly and furiously: "How are they made? What plants were used? How were they decorated?" The students' interest was high as Mr. Dean launched his sixth graders into researching the many ways gourds are used in Puerto Rico, as described in Activity 13–1.

Activity 13–1

 ## Case Study

Caribbean Crafts

Mr. Dean's students discovered that, in Puerto Rico, gourds are prepared in a very special way. First the gourds are dried, and then soaked in water so the outer skin can be peeled off. Then they are cut in half. Next, the seeds and pulp are removed and the exterior is polished with a rough herb. To decorate, a pattern is traced on the exterior and then carved with a knife, stained, burned, or painted to create exciting color combinations. The finished gourds serve as containers, bowls, toys, and musical instruments, and as decorative art objects in themselves.

After discovering this information and working in small groups, Mr. Dean's students had the opportunity to experiment with gourds and to paint designs onto their creations with tempera paint (carving and burning the designs were considered too dangerous). A few had worked with gourds before, but for most it was a new experience. The activity was enjoyed by all.

Mr. Dean's colleague, Ms. Zeller, invigorated her fifth graders' study of prehistoric life by engaging them in a study of ancient cave paintings. Displaying large study prints of actual cave paintings and art books available from the library, Ms. Zeller led the students through a discussion of what was important in the life of prehistoric humans, as depicted by their art. Then, making paint from grass and berries, and using homemade brushes of sticks and reeds, students created designs on large rocks illustrating subjects important to them.

In like manner, teachers across the country offer students the major types of visual arts experiences: (1) examining and responding to a culture through its visual art, (2) reproducing a culture's artworks, and (3) leading the children to express themselves through creative art-related projects.

Examining and Responding to the Visual Arts

There is no one correct way to use the visual arts in social studies classrooms. Regardless of the method you choose, a general rule is that students must learn about the art as it relates to a culture before being encouraged to be expressive and inventive themselves. In doing so, they require initial time to examine the art on their own, letting it soak in cognitively and emotionally without any pressure to answer questions or to discuss their impressions and feelings. The major goal is to experience the art and to form individual perceptions without the influence of a teacher's guided discussion.

Once the free observation time is complete (the time will vary from one experience to another), you may wish to promote a meaningful discussion during which each student's views are received seriously and respectfully. However, of all the things people do with art (especially for teachers with little formal training in the arts), helping students make informed judgments about what they are looking at can be the most difficult. A good rule of thumb is to allow free discussion after the children have had the opportunity to observe. Children need to talk about what they saw, how it looked, its composition, how it made them feel, what they liked best about it, and how it compared with other works of art. All children need not agree that the work of art is an excellent one; the objective is to help them recognize and react to the special qualities of art. Meek (1988) offers this example from a third-grade classroom involved in the study of folk art from America:

> Mrs. Wainner . . . moved to the comparison of *Evening at Kuemers* (Andrew Wyeth) and *The Old Oaken Bucket* (Grandma Moses). The Wyeth shows a dusky rural dwelling with a lighted window; the Moses, a cheerful primitive farmscape. Something exciting began to happen.
>
> Mrs. Wainner began by posing a question about the colors used by the two artists. "These are quiet colors," said one child, of the Wyeth.
>
> Another added, "It looks like a farm; the sun's going down."
>
> Another added, "It gives me a muddy feeling, like it's just finished raining."
>
> "There's a light on in the house," Ben observed.
>
> Mrs. Wainner moved on to the Grandma Moses farm, asking what kinds of colors these were and whether it looked like a real farm. Then Ben, his mind still on the Wyeth, told about going into his house and opening the curtains to make the house light. He was feeling emotions generated by light, the sweet security and aesthetic pleasure of coming home and letting in the light. I thought of Rembrandt's reply to the question about the most important person he had ever painted: "The most important person in any painting is light." I thought Ben had recognized intuitively the importance of the lighted window. (p. 58)

Ben offered a completely personal and honest response to the art. His candid view was natural and appropriate. You must not only provide opportunities for children to look at art, you must also encourage them to open their eyes and minds to see more in the world around them.

Reproducing Visual Arts

In elementary school classrooms where children's self-expression is valued and nurtured, you can carefully follow up exposure to the visual arts with appropriate materials that encourage students to express themselves with individuality. When elementary school youngsters are free to communicate their observations and feelings, they develop pride in what they produce and realize that their thoughts and actions have value.

As students explore the art of Africa, for example, they will be eager to try their hands at tie-dye, weaving, mask construction, or sculpture. You could enhance the study of Greece by having students create plaster reliefs or signature seals. Compare contemporary drinking vessels to recreated *amphorae* (urns) from Greece, and compare amphorae to vessels from other cultures such as the coil clay pots of some Southwest Native Americans. Enliven a lesson on medieval Europe by having children study and recreate coats of arms, stained glass, and castle designs. You can use the arts of "Gyokatu" (fish printing), block printing, kite making, batiks, and folded-paper design to introduce students to Asian cultures. Native American sand paintings, blankets, Kachina dolls, and totem poles help students learn about the earliest cultures in North America. "Pysanky" (intricately designed Easter eggs) and flax (straw) dolls bring to life important aspects of Ukrainian culture. The potential is unlimited for integrating the visual arts and social studies.

Select activities not because they appear to be "fun" or "cute," but because they contribute directly to students' understanding and appreciation of a culture. What rationale, for example, could you use to support making log cabins with pretzel sticks and peanut butter or constructing tepees with painted construction paper cones? These activities commonly appear in idea resource books, but they create a weak connection between the experience and an understanding of early colonial or Native American cultures. This word of caution is not meant to stifle your eagerness for a "hands-on" approach to social studies instruction, but rather to point out your responsibility to organize and coordinate meaningful knowledge through the visual arts to channel students' imagination and enthusiasm into creations that reflect *accurate* understandings of a culture.

To use the visual arts properly, you must research accurately the items to be recreated and carefully plan your lessons so they result in authentic learning. For example, among the settlers of the Southwest, dolls made of corn husks were especially enjoyed by the children. Do not ask your students to reproduce corn husk dolls without first examining the importance of corn in the culture of these settlers. The same is true for any topic or theme you are planning; you must not only search for expressive activities carefully, but also spend time conducting accurate library research.

Creating Visual Arts

When children become aware of art as something valuable that people do in real life, they are inspired to create their own. The social studies contribute to a child's natural inclination to create by offering countless opportunities to paint, draw, or sculpt. After a trip to a farm, for example, children's artwork often tells stories: Carol might draw the barn and silo in such detail that it would seem she could still see it before her; John might paint the farmyard full of farm machinery; Marie's picture would reflect her growing interest in farm animals; Mark's drawing might show a determined rider sitting on a large horse, with the caption, "This is me leading the cows to pasture."

Prerequisite to any art work in the social studies is a stimulating learning experience that has special meaning for the child. A significant *intake* of ideas through direct experience or intensive research must occur before ideas develop to the point where they can be expressed effectively in some art medium.

Additionally, children need an *assimilation* period before they become ready to express their thoughts. For example, one teacher asked his students to illustrate the high points of John F. Kennedy's life immediately after his biography had been read to them. The children produced inaccurate and careless drawings. After examining his strategy, the teacher realized that he did not follow up the story with a discussion of major events to help the children organize their thoughts. The original experience was good, but the teacher did not give his students a chance to sort out and put together ideas so they could then create expressively.

Students will not express themselves artistically if you simply pass out sheets of drawing paper and boxes of crayons and tell them to draw a picture of something. You must help your students think about what they want to represent by asking focusing questions: "What would be the most appropriate art medium to use for your project? Where does the event you are representing take place? When? How could you show this in your artwork? How will you depict any person or people? What are their distinguishing features?"

In subsequent discussion, when the students share their artworks, you may productively furnish guidance with follow-up questions: "Why did you choose to represent the scene as shown in your artwork? Why did you choose those specific art media? How did this artwork help you better understand what we've been studying?"

These two stages—intake and assimilation—require that you organize your art lessons related to the social studies. You may, for example, organize your lessons according to the type of product you wish the children to create. These product types include illustrations, dioramas, murals, mosaics, and collages.

Illustrations

Illustrating concepts is probably the most popular art technique used in elementary social studies classrooms. You may have children draw the details of the process involved in making linen from flax, to use crayon for indicating various areas on a state map, or to paint a picture of a landscape in the high Andes Mountains. Children like to illustrate group notebooks and decorative charts. There are literally hundreds of possibilities. For example, Mr. Tatum helped his students build a background of understandings as they located the geographic area where Native Americans of the Great Plains once lived. Mr. Tatum then organized daily learning experiences around such motivating questions as "What would it be like to eat a meal with a Cheyenne friend of the past?" (food gathering and consumption) and "What games would you play if you visited the home of a Sioux friend of long ago?" (leisure, recreation, and education). Today's question of intrigue was, "How did the Plains Indians retell their history to their children?"

Mr. Tatum selected the Sioux as the focus of exploration to answer that question. He informed the students that, like all native North Americans, the Sioux of the Great Plains had no written language. Mr. Tatum explained that stories and history were passed down from one generation to the next in the oral tradition. To set the scene, Mr. Tatum sat together with his students on the floor and read a story to them from the book *Why the Possum's Tail Is Bare: And Other North American Nature*

Tales by James E. Connolly (Stemmer). After the story, Mr. Tatum described one way that the Sioux wise men recalled the major events of passing years for their tales—the "winter count." Each year a tribal artist would depict a meaningful event that occurred that year, drawing it on bison hides that the women had stretched and dried in the sun on drying racks. Mr. Tatum showed an example of one event, a drawing of a horse. He explained that about 250 years ago the Sioux got horses from the Spanish. These horses had both positive and negative influences on the lives of the Sioux. They allowed them to hunt bison more skillfully, but they also caused them to stop growing their own food. By drawing a picture to remember one event, such as the introduction of horses to the Sioux, the wise storyteller could retell the history of the tribe.

Mr. Tatum invited his students to retell some of the important events in Sioux history as read to them earlier in the lesson by making their own "winter counts" using the following steps:

1. Cut a long sheet of brown butcher paper (8″ × 15″) or section of a grocery bag and tear it into the shape of a bison hide.
2. Crumple the sheet into a ball and dip it into a container of water until it is thoroughly soaked.
3. Press out the sheets on newspaper and let them dry.
4. Recount important events in the lives of the Sioux.
5. As the students select events to depict, draw them on the sheets with crayon (press hard with the crayon).
6. Place the sheets between two pages of newsprint and press with a warm iron. The colors will darken and the "winter count" will have a weathered appearance.

Dioramas

A *diorama* is a three-dimensional model that depicts activities performed by people, animals, or objects. A cardboard box usually encloses the representation. Cut the lid from the box and paint the exterior or cover it with colored paper. Paint background scenery or cut it from colored paper and paste it to the interior walls. Make cutouts of people, animals, and other objects with a construction paper tab at the base; fold this tab and glue or staple it to the bottom of the box to keep the figure in place.

A variation of the diorama is the "peep show." Remove the lid from a cardboard box and place a mirror on the inside wall of one end. In the opposite end, punch a small hole. Construct the rest of the interior in the same way as the diorama. When you are finished, glue a sheet of translucent paper over the top of the box, thus making the scenery on the inside indistinguishable except through the peephole. The effect is extraordinary.

Murals

In many social studies units, a mural can summarize a group's investigation or pull together the contributions of several groups into one expressive product for the entire class.

It is important that we use the energy and creativity of our youth to express their understandings and feelings through art.

Research is the first step in constructing an authentic mural, to develop the necessary background for planning a theme. Once you have chosen the theme, have the class compose a list of the significant contributing ideas. Place a large, durable piece of wrapping paper on the floor of the classroom and assign each group a section of the mural. Assign each child to a portion of the mural, making it at her or his own desk. Usually, individual contributions are made from paintings, sketches, cut paper, and similar art techniques. When the pupils finish, place the sections on the mural. When all of the pieces are in place, suggest the need for a background, usually a simple tempera-painted scene. When the background is complete, the children place their work back on the paper for gluing or pasting in final arrangement.

Mosaics

Begin a mosaic by having the children lightly draw their scenes on a 9″ × 12″ piece of construction paper. This will serve as a pattern for the mosaic work. Then paste on small pieces of colored paper, seeds, beans, rice, macaroni, eggshells, or other materials to form the mosaic pattern.

Collages

A *collage* is an arrangement of pictures or other materials. Abstract collages can be constructed by pasting pictures from newspapers or magazines within an outline in a freeform style. Realistic collages can be constructed by pasting scraps of materials in patterns. For example, a truck can be cut from construction paper, clouds can be made from chunks of cotton, foliage can be represented by green fabric, and a fence can be made from corrugated cardboard. Dried grass can be pasted in place to show a field. Encourage children to use their imaginations as much as possible while experimenting with collages, but they should not become so engrossed in novel materials that they forget the original purpose of the finished work.

MUSIC

You have heard music ever since you were a tiny baby. Like most infants, your early life contained pleasurable moments listening to lullabies—warmhearted tunes expressing love and affection. Throughout the world, lullabies are an important part of *socialization*, bringing an individual into a human group. It is through these lullabies that infants learn their first "lessons" about their culture and what is important to its people. For example, in the Middle East, where the goat is very important, babies hear the old tune "Raisins and Almonds," in which a goat ventures off to market to bring back raisins and almonds to the baby. In lullabies of North and South America, animals such as horses and lambs often appear.

As with lullabies, the folk songs of cultures around the world often vividly reflect a group's personality, expressing cultural aspects that cannot otherwise be effectively communicated. Frazier (1980) explains:

> People have sent messages across distances by pounding on drums. People have marched off to war to stirring music and down the aisle to the joyous strains of a wedding march. People—great crowds of people—have raised their voices in national anthems. People have sung work songs or chants to keep their work rhythm straight as they pulled in nets or pried rails back into line. People have sung songs of worship in camp meetings and cathedrals, and they have celebrated harvests with festive dances. People have expressed their grief in tender ballads and their love in songs and dances both tender and gay. People have delighted in playacting that brought song and dance to the stage. They have been eager everywhere to listen to good music sung and played for itself alone. Wherever and whenever possible, people have gained satisfaction and joy in making music for themselves and for others. (p. 141)

How can you help children to understand all of this? Certainly, they must have experiences with many kinds of music. Table 13–1 lists some of the different types of music and their functions. Different people and faraway places may be abstract notions for some children, but they can be made more concrete by forging an integral relationship with music and social studies.

TABLE 13–1
Functions of Music

Function	Type of Music	
	Vocal	**Instrumental**
Communication (over distance)	Yodels	Drum messages Band music (at sports events)
Marching, parading	Marching songs	Marches: military, wedding, funeral, parade
Uniting together	War songs Patriotic songs	Dance: tribal
Working	Work songs and chants	Recorded music in stores and factories
Worshiping	Masses Oratorios Hymns	Processionals
Celebrating, rejoicing	Victory hymns and chants Holiday songs	Victory dances Festival music Folk dances
Grieving	Ballads Lamentations	Funeral marches
Romancing, courting	Love songs	Dances of many kinds
Playacting	Opera Operetta Musical comedy	Incidental music for plays and background music for movies
Pleasing self and others, entertaining	Art songs, popular songs Choral works	Chamber music Ballet Symphonies Solo works of many kinds

Source: Frazier, A. (1980). *Values, curriculum, and the elementary school.* Boston: Houghton Mifflin. Copyright © 1980 Houghton Mifflin Company. Used with permission.

Examining and Responding to Music

Important concepts about people around the world may be effectively developed by sharing the music they create. Many possibilities exist for integrating music and the social studies. Exposure to folk music is, perhaps, the most fitting vehicle for teaching about the lifestyles and beliefs of various groups. *Folk music* is, generally, traditional music created by people as part of their everyday existence and handed down from one generation to another, and it reflects the cultural heritage and traditions of a group.

Ms. Faber sought to enrich her unit on the state of Hawaii by including a study of its folk music. This segment of the unit was to emphasize the idea that groups create special music to reflect the way they live. She realized that for the music to have a valuable role in the unit, she must have accurate background information. After hours of informative library research, Ms. Faber discovered that the early Hawaiians created their musical instruments from objects found in the island's natural environment—the low "wail" of the conch shell, the resonating "rattle" of hollowed-out gourds filled with pebbles, the "clack" of split bamboo, the hollow "tock" of hardwood sticks, and the "click" of smooth stones tapped lightly together. From such sounds created by common objects found in the sea, forest, garden, and river, Hawaiian music first accompanied chants called *olis* and dances called *hulas*. Since there were no written records in ancient Hawaii, the history of its people and events were often told through and passed on by olis and hulas. Some olis and hulas were used for entertainment, and others only for religious ceremonies. Ms. Faber had recently vacationed in Hawaii, so she was able to display several native instruments for the children to observe as she played recorded songs and chants for them. She was careful to use appropriate language labels as she introduced the instruments—*ili-ili* (smooth oval pebbles), *kalaau* (hardwood sticks), and *ipu* (large hollow gourds filled with pebbles). Ms. Faber emphasized that times have changed in Hawaii, as they have in any location that has been modernized. But even today, original instruments still accompany programs or other special pageantry of the islands. Ms. Faber then shared a brief video clip of a performance of the "Va Nani O Nuuanu" ("Pebble Dance").

This brief classroom example suggests how music can make valuable contributions throughout the social studies program. Because it is difficult to compartmentalize learning into neat packages throughout the elementary school program, whenever we think we are teaching something discrete (music, for example), we are always teaching much more. In like manner, you will want to use various musical activities that are integral parts of cultures around the world today and in times past. Garretson (1966) upholds this suggestion when he writes, "Music is an integral part of all cultures and the hopes, fears, aspirations and beliefs of various ethnic groups are often expressed through their folk music. Complete understanding of these peoples cannot be achieved unless all aspects of their cultures, including music, are included in the units of study taught in the schools" (p. 79).

Reproducing Music

Listening to the unique and fascinating music of the folk song tradition is an important activity while children learn social studies content, but, as we found with the visual arts, a learner's experiences in music should include opportunities to reproduce the music accurately—singing songs, moving to rhythm, or trying out musical instruments. Ms. Faber realized the value of this dimension of music integration and capitalized on it during her unit on Hawaiian customs and traditions. After her students learned of the early music of the Hawaiian people, she introduced them to "Kauiki," an old song about a dormant volcano that juts out into the sea. Background music for "Kauiki" is ukulele accompanied by *ipu* beats. Ms. Faber was able to obtain a few ukuleles on loan from parents, and brought in her own *ipu*. Volunteers strummed the ukuleles (the strings were tuned to the proper chords) and beat the *ipu* while the rest of the class sang the lyrics in both Hawaiian and English.

Like visual art, music establishes a cultural link among people, past and present. It places the child in the role of learner, producer, and creator while communicating thoughts and information difficult to express through conventional means. The following are useful guidelines for this phase of music integration:

- Be sure the students understand what the song is all about. (What is "Kauiki," for example?)
- Sing the song all the way through to the children or play a recording of it. (The children will respond much more eagerly if *you* sing it.)
- Invite the students to join you as they feel comfortable with the lyrics.
- Refrain from comments such as "Everyone sing now" or "Alex knows the words already; listen to him sing" (a sure way to quiet anyone).
- If the students have not learned the whole song by the time you've repeated it a few times, it's probably too difficult. Put it away and learn from the experience.
- Choose songs with "catchy" words or phrases. Children particularly enjoy nonsense tunes such as "Jennie Jenkins," a traditional North American folk song:

> I'll buy me a fol-de-rol-dy
> Til-dy-tol-dy seek-a-double roll
> Jennie Jenkins roll.

- Have fun! Have confidence in your musical skills, drop any musical inhibitions, and relax. Children are rarely music critics; they'll enjoy the experience if they see you are actually enjoying what you are doing.

Creating Music

Reproducing music and creating music are closely related processes. Children everywhere enjoy creating music as an expression of their own uniqueness. All children have the capacity to take planned musical experiences and to make from them something unique—something that pleases them and that they are eager to share with others. It is your task not only to involve children in reproducing music, but also to provide an open, accepting climate that stimulates further exploration and discovery. Students may create music within the context of the social studies in three primary ways: (1) through singing, (2) through playing instruments, and (3) through moving.

Singing

Singing affords students a major medium for expressing their creativity. Making up new words to songs or chants is a creative activity that comes easily to elementary school children. Countless songs and chants invite lyric substitution. For example, the Yuma Indian chant "Oh, Great Spirit," shown in Figure 13–1, may invite children to add verses or to substitute a natural condition of the environment.

FIGURE 13-1
Oh, Great Spirit

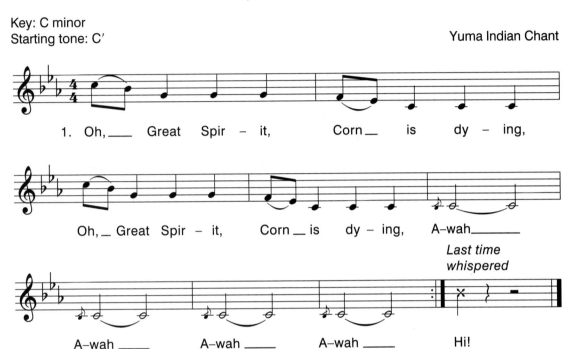

OH, GREAT SPIRIT

Key: C minor
Starting tone: C′

Yuma Indian Chant

2. Oh, Great Spirit, send us rain clouds (2)
   A-wah! (4)

3. Oh, Great Spirit, rain is falling (2)
   A-wah (4)

The old North American folk song "Skip to My Lou" is an excellent example of how you might invite children to extend particular phrases. Most of you are familiar with the tune; the words are as follows:

> Lou, Lou, skip to my Lou!
> Lou, Lou, skip to my Lou!
> Lou, Lou, skip to my Lou,
> Skip to my Lou, my darling!
> Fly's in the buttermilk, shoo, fly, shoo! (3 times)
> Skip to my Lou, my darling!

1.

2.
                                    Lost my partner, what'll I do? (3 times)
                                        Skip to my Lou, my darling!
3.
                                    Find another one, prettier than you! (3 times)
                                        Skip to my Lou, my darling!

Excitement will reign as the students think up creative verses to add to this pattern. Encourage the children to invent what might happen next; brainstorming new verses within cooperative groups will produce many good ideas.

Using music leads a child to a fuller and more enjoyable understanding of culture. One delightful musical experience is to help the children pronounce and recognize words in the culture's native language by adapting familiar tunes. Here is one teacher's use of this technique, singing "Twinkle Twinkle Little Star" in Japanese with the children:

Pi-ka, pi-ka, ho-shi-yo
A-na-ta-wa-do-na-ta
O-so-ra-ni-ta-ka-ku
Da-i-ya-no-yo-o-ni
Pi-ka, pi-ka, ho-shi-yo
A-na-ta-wa-do-na-ta.

The Japanese words, rendered phonetically above, are translated below. (Because the last two lines repeat the first two, only lines one through four are given here.) Note that Japanese word order is different from English, so although the idea in the song remains the same, the reading is not similar.

Sparkle, sparkle star
You who?
Sky in the higher
Diamond look like

Playing Musical Instruments

Musical instruments add much enjoyment to children's creative efforts. Rhythm instruments such as sticks, wood blocks, hand cymbals, maracas, or drums help children easily create rhythmic accompaniments for singing and moving. Children are able to create and improvise rhythmic patterns much earlier than they can learn to read music, so rhythmic exploration might be most appropriate for younger children. As far as improvising melodies, one easy-to-use chording instrument furnishes delightful opportunities for creativity: the autoharp. The autoharp is very simple to play; primary-grade youngsters often enjoy playing it. You only have to press down on a chord bar and strum the strings to produce the desired sound—the chord bar leaves the correct strings free while stopping all the rest. Each chord bar is marked on the autoharp.

Moving

Creative movement and dance are closely related to music making, so bodily expression should be a component of musical involvement in the social studies program.

There are a wide range of possibilities for social learnings through creative movement and dance. The following section describes the topic in detail.

CREATIVE MOVEMENT AND DANCE

Music, creative movement, and dance are integrally related. People in all cultures respond to music with their bodies. Use songs to develop a repertoire of associated dance movements, both to enhance understandings of people and for creative self-expression. Folk songs, as we saw in the discussion of Hawaii, can be used for these purposes.

Ms. Faber recognized this advantageous application of movement and dance within her unit on Hawaii. Her students made grass skirts (to represent the authentic ti-leaf skirts used on the island for performances) and leis. The girls wore the grass skirts while the boys dressed in clam diggers and colorful shirts; both boys and girls were bedecked in flowers and leis. Ms. Faber, dressed in a unique muumuu and adorned with flowers in her hair, played a recording of the traditional Hawaiian chant "Ka Hana Kamalii" ("What Children Should Do"). The chant was composed for Queen Emma of Hawaii and recited by children to demonstrate to the queen that they had learned the lessons in personal hygiene that the missionaries had taught them—to wash with soap and to use mirrors to see that they were clean. Their words were accompanied by a hula dance to show what they should do. Ms. Faber taught the chant to the children and demonstrated the hula routine. Throughout the entire experience, one child beat an *ipu* (hollow gourd) in a continuous rhythm. After the class finished the hula, they proudly demonstrated a *pau* (Hawaiian bow).

When you offer creative movement and dance experiences in the social studies, you must plan the activities very carefully so that children acquire accurate concepts of the culture. You may find the suggestions below to be of value in your planning.

- Learn the dance well before you demonstrate it to your students.
- If possible, wear garb indigenous to the culture under study. If the relevant costume is unavailable to you, invite a resource person to demonstrate the attire, show a film or videotape, or display large pictures or study prints of people dressed suitably for the dance.
- On a map or globe, locate the homeland of the people whose culture is being examined.
- Associate the characteristics of that region (or its people) with the special features of the music and dance.
- Be sure the children know what they will be singing about. In the traditional North American folk song "Paw Paw Patch," for example, how many children will actually know a what a "paw paw" is? Likewise, "Kumbaya" is another favorite folk tune; you've all probably sung it. What does *kumbaya* mean? Be sure to clarify any unknown concepts before introducing the song to the students.
- If you will be leading the singing or chanting, conduct an introductory conversation. For example, display a papaya ("paw paw") and share ideas about what it is and what its significance was to the people who created the song. Invite the

students to listen to the song or chant as you sing it all the way through. Repeat it a few times, inviting children to sing along as they are ready. You may easily adapt the same procedure to a recording of the song or chant.

- Demonstrate the dance movements associated with the music. Face away from the students so they can more easily duplicate your movements.
- Discuss the importance of the dance to the culture under study.

A folk dance is a model the children must copy, and some teachers prefer not to use a patterned experience initially. Instead, they prefer to stimulate free movement during the first creative movement activities. Middle and Far Eastern, African, and some Western classical music are outstanding motivators for individual responses. Encourage children to move according to how the music makes them feel. If they seem self-conscious at first, try using colorful scarves, streamers, or balloons to start the dance activity. These accessories divert attention from the children and help minimize self-consciousness.

Both planned dance experiences and free-movement activities are delightful exercises to draw upon. You may further enhance them by inviting resource people

Detail is an important element in creating a setting that builds understandings through dance.

into the classroom to share their talents with the children, or by allowing children to use musical instruments during the activity. Whatever the situation, exploiting the value of movement experiences in the social studies program demonstrates to children that all forms of music are integral parts of all people's lives rather than a form of expression for only a talented few.

DRAMA

Our final major arts-based approach to helping students acquire social studies understandings is that of using drama and plays. Since the dawn of civilization, people have used dramatic performance to reveal their innermost feelings of conflict, despair, truth, beauty, hope, and faith. Drama brings out the essence of a culture clearly before one's eyes and is an excellent vehicle to challenge students to think about and appreciate societies from generation to generation.

Examining and Responding to Drama

The dynamic nature of social studies is a perfect match for creative drama. Drama is a vital aspect of a society; by its very nature, drama presupposes an important kind of social communication. For primitive humans it was a ritualistic attempt at communicating with a spirit in a magical sense; through ritualistic half-acting episodes, while dressed in masks and skins, groups would try to seek cooperation with special spirits to control certain events (a good hunt, the power of thunder, fertility, and the like). As humans began to settle in regular communities and rely on agriculture, their greatest terror was bitter weather and a ruined harvest. The simple half-acting gradually evolved into a ritual of more formalized movement—a king overcomes death (winter) to bring life (spring), for example. From these early patterns, drama developed into a stylized form of communication with intricate dialogue, disguises, and symbolism. Most civilizations throughout history have used some form of drama to express their important thoughts.

Drama essentially is action; the term itself comes from the Greek word *drao*, meaning *I do*. Drama is an art that tells a story through the action and speech of its characters. Dramatic stories usually focus on the feelings caused by some type of conflict: forces in the physical environment, disputes among people, clashes of ideas or beliefs, or inner turmoil.

To fully understand any group or civilization, students must receive and respond to its created dramatic forms. Therefore, students will often assume the role of "audience" as others communicate drama to them. Whether witnessing an example of Japanese *Kabuki* theater or a puppet play about North American cowboy life, you must guide students through any quality dramatic episode as effective audience members if you wish them to achieve specific learning outcomes. The audience has the following responsibilities:

1. To understand the nature of the created dramatic form.
2. To watch and listen to the dramatic experience as it comes alive.

3. To perceive the elements of the playmaking that communicate the story.

4. To determine whether and how the conflict within the drama was resolved.

5. To evaluate the experience by giving a personal response to the playmaking.

Your primary role following the examination of the performance is to invite students to respond using both direct and open-ended questioning techniques. For example, the question "How did Theseus, the great Athenian hero, succeed in killing the Minotaur?" is a direct question because it requires students to converge their answers toward a single acceptable response. These questions help you assess whether the basic elements of the drama were perceived. On the other hand, the question "What solutions, other than the one used by Theseus, could you suggest for overcoming the Minotaur?" allows students to elaborate on or extend the content of the drama. You must not only summarize the main points and encourage divergent thinking, but must also keep the discussion purposeful and brief with deliberate, fitting questions.

Provide students with opportunities to observe quality dramatic experiences throughout the school years. These can range from professional theater groups to students in drama classes in middle or high school. Regardless of the source, however, children must have opportunities to discover for themselves the power of drama as it is used to communicate representative ideas and feelings of people around the world.

Reproducing Drama

A strong and frequently immediate consequence of a satisfying audience experience is the desire of students to participate in their own theater; young children experience theater both by taking it in and giving it out. One suitable way of providing students this experience is to have them view, and then accurately reproduce, a popular drama. In this process, your role essentially involves the following:

1. *Providing an absorbing firsthand experience.* Either through direct or second-hand experience (video, film), the students view the actual drama.

2. Stimulating a follow-up discussion. Help the students talk about the drama they witnessed.

3. *Guiding students' words and actions.* Help children recall the sequence of words and actions that accurately communicate the intended message of the original source.

4. *Helping with costumes, props, and scenery.* If appropriate to the learning experience, students create authentic scenic objects that enhance the drama.

Reproducing drama benefits the social studies program in many ways. First and foremost, students enjoy it, which enhances their interest in learning. Reproducing drama also provides a purpose for gathering information that is needed to accurately portray real-life circumstances in the dramatic representations. This spontaneous interest in new information can be exploited to expand the children's knowledge of other people's characteristics and actions. Dramatics can build their sensitivity to others' feelings. By the time players have come to know their characters, the decisions they must face, and their motivations, they have gained a great deal of insight into understanding people in unique situations. Recreating drama also provides a worthwhile experience in group cooperation. Social acceptance is often a valuable outcome, as children develop a common bond of respect for a job well done. Finally, recreated drama can be used to evaluate concept attainment. The situations children portray reflect their knowledge of related information.

Creating Drama

By nature, children are born to create. As it applies to drama, they create in a joyfully daring way. They are confident and expressive in their actions and improvise freely (make up dialogue and actions). Such informal dramatic experience is important to the social studies curriculum, for, as the Joint Committee of the National Council of Teachers of English and the Children's Theatre Association (1983) explains:

> Informal classroom drama is an activity in which students invent and enact dramatic situations for themselves, rather than for an outside audience. This activity, perhaps most widely known as creative drama, . . . is spontaneously generated by the participants who perform the dual tasks of composing and enacting their parts as the drama progresses. This form of unrehearsed drama is a process of guided discovery led by the teacher for the benefit of the participants. (pp. 370–372)

Creative drama helps students discover meaning behind the material they are studying. It can help them get a sense of the events relative to Custer's last battle, for example; students would not look at Custer from the outside (names, dates, and places removed from their own lives), but from the "inside" (deciding what to do and say when faced by the Cheyenne). Students must draw on their own knowledge of Custer, about the situation (both Custer's and the Cheyenne's view), about the terrain, and about the political climate of the country at the time. As youngsters create together, they will at times call upon these major creative dramatic arts: pantomime, improvised skits, dramatizations, and sociodrama.

Pantomime

Children of all ages enjoy using bodily expressions to convey ideas without words, and this is a good technique for introducing creative dramatics to the social studies program. Pantomime offers opportunities to characterize actions and personalities without having to furnish dialogue. Use your imagination to determine stimulating situations for pantomime in the social studies classroom. One possibility is the popular "What Am I Doing?" or "Who Am I?" game. Many social studies concepts relate to people involved in making or doing something. Children enjoy imitating others' unique movements. They can be encouraged to portray activities of people in the unit under study and to challenge their classmates to guess who they are.

Some suggestions: Pilgrims landing at Plymouth Rock, the first landing on the moon, Ben Franklin's kite-flying experience, Henry Aaron's record-breaking home run, the type of work people do at home or in the community.

Your role in guiding social studies pantomimes begins with establishing a varied background of study trips, books, magazines, films, pictures, recordings, and other sources of information on which children build their pantomimes. After they share an experience, the children should discuss its characteristics and their thoughts about the insights they gained. You may then divide the class into small groups and encourage each group to pantomime its most meaningful recollection. Each group should then share its creative expression with the others, after which you should lead a follow-up discussion: "What persons are represented in the action? What helped you recognize them? Where do you think the action took place? What helped you know this? What do you think the people were talking about? What are some of the feelings you think the characters experienced? From what you know about the actual situation, do you think the actors accurately portrayed what really happened? What feelings did you have as you watched the action? What would you have done if you were any one of the characters in the same situation? Can you predict what might happen to the people after what was shown in the pantomime?"

Improvised Skits

A charming characteristic of young children is their ability to use their creative imaginations in improvisations, unplanned situations where dialogue is necessary and characterized by scenes involving *no* learned lines, *no* costumes, and *no* sophisticated scenery. With a thorough knowledge of the story situation, however, dialogue begins to flow, and children further their understanding of a social studies condition by describing its characters more completely.

Many of the classroom situations described as pantomiming activities are also suitable for improvisation experiences. Begin the initial improvisation experiences with simple situations. As the children gain confidence, they can attempt more challenging material.

Mr. Carson, for example, was itching to try something new to enhance the study of early human life with his sixth graders, so he employed a short improvised skit to draw his students into an anthropological learning experience. To start, Mr. Carson displayed a large print of cave paintings that depicted a hunt. The students were dazzled by the lifelike images of horses, deer, and bison. Mr. Carson engaged them in a series of imaging tasks—"walking" into the dark passage, "touching" the damp walls, "listening" to the water as it dripped from the ceiling, and "smelling" the damp, stale air. Mr. Carson explained the need for rituals in the lives of early humans as the students "huddled" in the cave, and let them know that we may never understand exactly what role the paintings played in the culture of the Cro-Magnons. Mr. Carson went on to tell of several possible explanations of how the depictions of animals on cave walls might have been an important part of Cro-Magnon life.

Mr. Carson asked the students to read a short selection about Cro-Magnon culture, and then asked them to depict different scenes on a mural to describe what they had read: fishing, gathering plants, using tools, launching spears, building camps.

In drama, children examine and compare the rituals of life as they are acted out by various cultures.

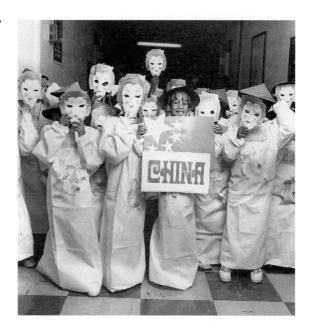

He did this by dividing the class into groups, asking each group to become familiar with its topic, and encouraging each to plan its portion of the mural, using stick figures to represent people and animal forms as depicted in the cave paintings. When they were finished, each group was to write a "site report" detailing its composition as a way to share its results with classmates.

The activity furnished Mr. Carson's students a great sense of accomplishment and generated huge interest in conducting additional research into early human life. When students become engaged in such active anthropological study, they become increasingly eager to explore all of humanity's rich heritage.

Elementary school children enjoy acting out such scenes and often repeat them to communicate different interpretations of the related information, to switch roles, or to create new endings to open-ended situations. Youngsters easily fluctuate between worlds of fantasy (witness the number of children who have "imaginary" playmates) and reality; pantomime and improvisation give them opportunities to enter and leave new and different worlds at will. Even though spontaneity appears to be strongest during kindergarten and the early primary years and tapers off as children reach the later grades, a skillful teacher can bring it to the surface again in a relaxed, developmentally appropriate setting.

By mimicking words and actions as they have experienced them in other settings, children actually *feel* how tired the mail carrier becomes, how frustrated a teacher becomes when children act rowdy, or how elated a candidate is when he wins an important election victory. It is the power to help children empathize that makes dramatic experiences so valuable; children express and experience another person's viewpoint. This creative technique helps children understand people or events more fully.

Dramatization

Older children may wish to put on a formal play with script, costumes, and scenery. If the children have had sufficient experience with pantomime and improvisation, the most effective type of formal play is one in which the children are responsible for most of the planning. Your role is to guide the students in formulating the different scenes. As the children plan their script, ask them, "What are the most important things to tell? What are the people really like? What kind of place do they live in? What do the people do to make their lives interesting? How will you stage your play?"

The dramatization can result from many of the same sources described for pantomime and improvisation. The students' concern for elaborate scenery and costumes should not take precedence over the concepts or ideas the play is designed to convey. Simple objects can effectively represent more intricate objects; for example, a mural or bulletin board design can serve as a backdrop; a branch in a big can filled with dirt makes an excellent tree or bush; your desk becomes a cave; chairs placed in a straight line can be seats on a train or airplane; a pencil can become a hand-held microphone. Activity 13–2 presents a dramatic skit composed by a group of fifth graders following a reading of *Mufaro's Beautiful Daughters* (Lothrop).

Activity 13-2

Classroom Exercise

Dramatizing an African Naming Ceremony

African villagers celebrate the birth of babies with great enjoyment. Babies are an important part of African life. The African baby belongs not only to mother and father; rather, it is everyone in the village's baby. Everyone in the village loves the baby and is responsible for giving it protection and direction in life.

SCENE:	People are milling about the village. Nyoka and Nyasha are standing and holding their baby.
Nyoka:	With pride and gladness, we announce that on this special day our child is to be named.
Nyasha:	Come be our guests at this joyous celebration.
SCENE:	Everyone comes together. All guests sit in a circle with Nyoka and Nyasha. The ceremony begins when the oldest living member of the family recites the family history.

Oldest:	Welcome to all who join us to bless and honor the child of Nyoka and Nyasha. Out of deep respect for their ancestors, we begin the ceremony with a short family history.
	The baby's mother is Nyasha, who is the most worthy and most beautiful daughter in the land. Nyasha's father is Mufaro. Mufaro is very rich because he has two most beautiful daughters, nyasha and Manyara. Mufaro is known for his great wisdom and patience. Dayo (DAH-YO) is Nyasha's mother. She can sing so sweetly about the land! It is said that she composed a song for each cow in a herd of thousand. This is Nyasha's gift from Dayo—a voice as sweet as honey.
	The baby's father is Nyoka. He has the special power to appear as all living things. Nyoka's father is Olu (OH-LOO). Olu had a large family, all of whom were fearless warriors. Olu is the one who built the great city. As an adventurous young man, Olu spent much time in the tropical forest by himself. Olu learned many new things from the beasts and serpents he befriended. Olu was a great king. He was handsome, tall, and strong. Olu had a son and named him Nyoka. Olu taught Nyoka all that he had learned in the tropical forest. That is the reason Nyoka now has the power to appear as all living things.
	Now, everyone will join together to introduce this child to the nature of life.
Friend 1:	I offer a few drops of wine to the baby because the wine ensures the child a full and fruitful life.
Friend 2:	I splash a few drops of water on the baby's forehead and put a drop or two into its mouth when it cries. This is a way of showing that water is important for all living things. It also tells me if the baby is alert. This looks like a very fine baby—alert and responsive. I now wish it a smooth sail through the sea of life.
Friend 3:	I drop a bit of honey onto the baby's tongue. This is to show the child that life is sweet.
Friend 4:	I place a pinch of pepper on the baby's lips to represent the spice of life. Although we have learned that life is sweet, we must also know that life is exciting.
Friend 5:	I lay a dab of salt on the baby's lips. The salt stands for the liveliness and zest of life.
Oldest:	The baby of Nyoka and Nyasha will be rich in its pursuit of life.

SCENE: Everyone, including Nyoka and Nyasha, must give the baby a name. Girls are named on the seventh day after birth; boys are named on the eighth.

Oldest: On this joyful _____th day after birth, all who are present are invited to offer a chosen name for the baby of Nyoka and Nyasha.

The rest of the group uses the sentence pattern shown below to offer a name for the child.

Child: I have picked the name NAYO because it means *we have joy.* This child brings much happiness to Nyoka and Nyasha.

Oldest: The ceremony is now complete. May Nyoka and Nyasha have many beautiful days with their lovely new child.

Sociodrama

Our examples of creative dramatics in the social studies classroom have dealt primarily with methods of summarizing or communicating highlights of learning experiences through pantomime, improvised skits, or dramatization. Sociodrama is a specialized use of any of these techniques in a situation characterized by an affective, or human relations, dilemma. Unrehearsed, children dramatize real problems and offer suggestions for resolution through their dramatic interpretations. The topics should be fairly simple at first—schoolroom, playground, or cafeteria conflicts, for example. Later, children can play out problems they encounter in social studies class.

Zeleny (1964) designates the following four steps for developing sociodramas in the elementary school classroom:

1. *Identify the problem.* Through discussion and observation, you and the children identify problems that may be causing difficulties. For example, one young girl had been the target of ridicule in her classroom because she had recently tried out for her elementary school football team, until then exclusively the boys' domain. However, the adults in charge of the football program would not allow a girl, however eager or talented, to participate in the traditionally male sport. The boys in the classroom were unrelenting in their demeaning comments. The teacher thought the problem had reached such proportions that sociodrama would be the best way to alleviate it. Frank discussions of the problem were then initiated, and the children were asked to share their thoughts.

2. *Assign the roles.* Tensions in social situations usually arise because people do not understand the motivations and feelings of those involved. Therefore, children should be encouraged to imagine what others facing the problem would say and do. After the problem has been discussed and the principal roles identified, volunteers

are chosen to enact it spontaneously in front of the class, acting as *they* would in the situation, *not* as they think the real characters would.

3. *Discuss the situation.* By analyzing the sociodrama, the class can easily develop a more complete understanding of the problem. The teacher should guide discussion by directing questions such as these to the players and audience: "How did each of you feel in your role? Do you think the treatment was fair? Why do you think the girl was treated as she was? Do you think people were fair to her? Why?"

4. *Replay the situation.* At this point, the children may wish to replay the situation, to depict what they consider to be proper treatment or to suggest a fair solution to the problem. Replay may be done by the same group or by several different groups who may suggest alternative solutions. The various proposals can be discussed and an optimum solution decided upon.

Because sociodrama is an effective process for understanding feelings, some teachers extend its use from illustrating issues in the classroom to studying people's feelings as they face important decisions in contemporary life and throughout history. You can glean scenarios from newspaper stories, textbook readings, photographs or study prints, films, and the like.

AFTERWORD

A strong program in the expressive arts offers many opportunities to integrate learning in a satisfying manner. The overall goal of such integration is not to fashion each child into a gifted artist, but to advocate sharing a variety of works from various people and time periods so that students are able to explore the world meaningfully and actively. As an outgrowth of sharing experiences, you must give students many opportunities to produce works of art in meaningful ways. They may then realize that their creative thoughts and actions are valued and can be used as unique ways of communicating personal ideas about the world.

By integrating the arts, the social studies classroom often looks like a large studio. The process that goes on is the artist's process, but the products that come out are children's products. The richness of cultures under study offers the substance through which children can act as real artists.

TECHNOLOGY SAMPLER

Useful sites for related social studies topics include these Internet sites:

Crayola Art Education (volumes of easily implemented art ideas)
http://www.crayola.com/art_education/

Kids' Space (artwork, stories, music, and other children's creations)
http://www.kids-space.org

One World (explore stories, photographs, and artwork from around the world)
http://www.envirolink.org/oneworld/

Free Stuff for Crafting (many freebies that you can write away for)
http://www.ppi-free.com

Library of Congress
http://lcweb.loc.gov/

Louvre Museum
http://www.paris.org/Musees/Louvre/

Museums, World Wide Arts Resources
http://wwar.com/museums.html

National Museum of the American Indian
http://www.si.edu/nmai/

Museum of Fine Arts
http://www.mfa.org/

Smithsonian Institution
http://www.si.edu/

U.S. Holocaust Museum
http://www. ushmm.org/

WHAT I *NOW* KNOW

Complete these self-check items once more. Determine for yourself whether it would be useful to take a more in-depth look at any area. Use the same key as you did for the preassessment form ("+", "?", "–").

I can *now*

_____ explain what areas are encompassed in the *expressive arts.*

_____ offer a sound rationale for utilizing the expressive arts to strengthen learning in the social studies curriculum.

_____ justify curriculum time spent on activities related to the expressive arts.

_____ explain how the expressive arts help children make sense of their world.

_____ describe how teachers aid children articulate meaning through the expressive arts.

_____ explain how teachers help students create their own expressive arts products.

_____ plan social studies experiences that involve contributions from the expressive arts.

REFERENCES

Alliance for Arts Education (1985). *Performing together: The arts in education.* Arlington, VA: Author.

Brandt, R. (1987/1988). On discipline-based art education: A conversation with Elliot Eisner. *Educational Leadership, 45,* 7.

Cullum, A. (1967). *Push back the desks.* New York: Citation Press.

Egan, K. (1997). The arts as the basics of education. *Childhood Education, 73,* 341–345.

Fowler, C. (1989). The arts are essential to education. *Educational Leadership, 47,* 62.

Fowler, C. (1994). Strong arts, strong schools. *Educational Leadership, 52,* 4–9.

Frazier, A. (1980). *Values, curriculum, and the elementary school.* Boston: Houghton Mifflin.

Garretson, R. L. (1966). *Music in childhood education.* New York: Appleton-Century-Crofts.

Hodsoll, F. (1988). *Toward civilization: A report on arts education.* Washington, DC: National Endowment for the Arts.

Jalongo, M. R. (1990). The child's right to the expressive arts: Nurturing the imagination as well as the intellect. *Childhood Education, 66,* 195–201.

Joint Committee of the National Council of Teachers of English and Children's Theatre Association (1983). Forum: Informal classroom drama. *Language Arts, 60,* 370–372.

King, E. W. (1971). *The world: Context for teaching in the elementary school.* Dubuque, IA: William C. Brown.

McCormack, P. (1985). Are school art courses a frill or a staple? West Chester, PA: *Daily Local News.*

Meek, A. (1988). An ordinary lesson. *Educational Leadership, 45,* 58.

Nixon, G. T., & Chalmers, F. G. (1990). The experience arts in education. *Childhood Education, 67,* 14.

Rockefeller, D., Jr. (1977). *Coming to our senses.* New York: McGraw Hill.

Zeleny, L. D. (1964). How to use sociodrama. *How to Do It Series,* no. 20. Washington, DC: National Council for the Social Studies.

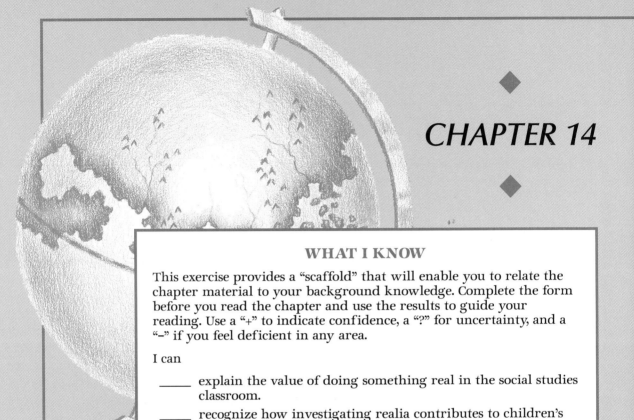

CHAPTER 14

WHAT I KNOW

This exercise provides a "scaffold" that will enable you to relate the chapter material to your background knowledge. Complete the form before you read the chapter and use the results to guide your reading. Use a "+" to indicate confidence, a "?" for uncertainty, and a "–" if you feel deficient in any area.

I can

_____ explain the value of doing something real in the social studies classroom.

_____ recognize how investigating realia contributes to children's learning.

_____ identify the characteristics of a beneficial field trip.

_____ give examples of how to use resource persons productively.

_____ design instruction that integrates computers in the social studies program.

_____ explain how to incorporate videos, slides, and filmstrips into social studies instruction.

_____ describe the teacher's role in carrying out picture discussions.

_____ develop a strategy for using simulation games in the classroom.

_____ design and demonstrate the use of learning centers in the social studies classroom.

_____ compare the advantages of using various print sources.

Using the results as a guide, what questions will you seek to answer as you read?

Selecting Instructional Resources

◆ **CLASSROOM SKETCH**

"I had an elementary school teacher, Mrs. Dunbar, who made social studies one of my favorite subjects. We learned a lot because Mrs. Dunbar always had something interesting for us to do. Once, in fifth grade, we were studying prehistoric life. Mrs. Dunbar asked us to clean off and bring in bones left over from our dinner at home. You could probably guess that the next day we had a pile of all kinds of bones—fish, chicken, steak, you name it! Our job was to clean them thoroughly with a scrubber, boil them in vinegar water, soak them in a bleach and water solution to make them white, and put them in a large box called 'the boneyard.' Mrs. Dunbar then organized us into groups and let us choose any of the bones we wanted and glue or wire them together in the general shape of the dinosaurs we were studying. We gave our 'dinosaurs' their scientific names and displayed an information card next to the models. Mrs. Dunbar called us *paleontologists*. I still remember the word because it was a real thrill to be given such an impressive-sounding title. Elementary school social studies was so much fun, at least in Mrs. Dunbar's room. As a matter of fact, she has had more influence on my choice of teaching as a career than any other single factor."

◆ CLASSROOM CONNECTION

Mrs. Dunbar was a talented fifth-grade teacher with many years of experience when I first met her during my first year of teaching. A model professional who exerted a tremendous influence on my career, this remarkable person did all she could to encourage students to be curious, active, and persistent in finding answers to life's mysteries. We all know extraordinary teachers like Mrs. Dunbar who work hard to create the conditions for children to be eager learners. They realize that the goal of social studies education is to develop informed, caring citizens who draw on meaningful knowledge and refined skills to attack important problems and issues in their world. These teachers recognize the importance of variety—reading fascinating stories of Alaska's untamed frontiers, helping the class publish a colonial-period newspaper, churning butter, creating a salt-and-flour relief map of the United States, or searching through the Internet to find information for a report on coal mining.

Unfortunately, we might also revive memories of less-rousing classroom experiences—reading pages 79 to 81 in the text and writing answers to the questions that followed (while the teacher corrected the weekly spelling tests), listening to the teacher describe how a cotton gin works (without benefit of a picture or model), or being required to memorize facts about the early explorers of North America (where they came from, when they left their homeland, the date they arrived here, and where they explored).

For good or bad, the teachers who presented these lessons did so with a proper idea of *what* they wanted to teach; however, some used effective methods and materials, while others needed reminders of how to teach the content appropriately. Throughout this text, you have read about specific instructional methods appropriate for use in elementary school social studies classrooms. In this chapter, you will read about the large variety of useful materials and resources to draw from as instructional resources.

As I remembered Mrs. Dunbar, William Webster (1993) retained vivid memories of one of his most inspiring teachers, Miss Monroe. While a little boy in Miss Monroe's room, Webster first learned about colonial America and Brazil through activities and materials that motivated real interest and curiosity.

> When we studied the Colonial era, we visited Philiplse Manor, the home of an early Dutch patroon. We danced the minuet and made candles. We also wrote stories, created plays, and learned our arithmetic by preparing Colonial food and building sets for our dramas.
>
> That year we also studied Brazil and the great Amazon River, and it sparked in me a lifelong desire to go see the river, the rubber trees, and how tapioca grew. . . . My mother came to school and helped my teacher, Miss Monroe, cook the tapioca, something we now call parental involvement. My classmates and I constructed a native village using papier-mache for the rubber trees and weeds for thatch-roofed houses. The richest girl in the class was the daughter of a ship captain who had been to Belem. Her father came and told us about the city, which we now label "using community resources." (p. 45)

As a result of his involvement in these splendid activities, Webster developed a lifelong infatuation with Brazil and the Amazon River—he had a powerful dream to travel to these places. Decades later, Webster's little-boy dream came true; he visited

Brazil and traveled the Amazon, living everything he had learned about in Miss Monroe's class. Webster was fortunate to have a teacher who brought such a high degree of life to her social studies program that she was able to inspire lifelong dreams within her students. However, Webster laments that many of today's social studies teachers are being cheated of their dream-building time by an overwhelming emphasis on meeting standards and achieving high test scores. Has the quest for inspiration been squelched by a sanitized and bland educational process?

Like all other young children, Webster constantly wondered about anything and everything, striving to figure out the answers to so many of life's mysteries. That is why it is such a pleasure to plan a social studies program for elementary schoolers. As with Webster, all we need to do is maintain their willingness to explore and support their inner drive to learn.

It is also a reason why elementary school social studies teachers must take a firm stand: They must convince administrators and parents that elementary school students cannot sit down and be quiet all day. The extensive use of endless drills and mountains of workbook pages commonly associated with test-driven programs violates the nature of young children. Instead of capitalizing on their sense of curiosity as they pass through the wondrous period of childhood, these methods and materials violate and negate the natural enthusiasm and spirit for learning youngsters bring to school.

Some children, then, like Webster, will only need to have their natural enthusiasm for learning sustained, while a number of unfortunate others will need to have it revitalized. Teachers can help both groups, however, by offering learning materials that fascinate children and capture their interest. Sometimes they will use textbooks and workbooks, but not all the time; these will be but one kind of teaching tool. A true test of a teacher's skill lies in how well he or she chooses other materials for instruction. What will work best today—tradebook, textbook, video, computer, slides, filmstrip, pictures, transparancy, cooking, singing, dancing, field trip, guest speaker? *Sometimes* the children will need to sit, but most of the time they will be up and involved, performing tasks and investigating mysteries. Activity 14–1 describes a number of activities one teacher selected for a theme dealing with Africa.

Activity 14–1

Case Study

Mrs. Lukaczyk and her second-grade children were at work investigating African cultures through interesting learning resources. Two groups donned earphones at a listening center and read along to a prerecorded version of Karen Williams's story *Galimoto* (Lothrop), enraptured by Kondi's skills in bargaining and building. Others read from multiple copies of books in a collection arranged at a learning center by Mrs. Lukaczyk. Three students were absorbed in Gerald McDermott's

Anansi the Spider: A Tale from the Ashanti (Holt). Three others selected Muriel Feelings's *Moja Means One* (Dial). Another group was engaged in a CD-ROM rainforest safari at the computer center. Their interest soared as they took simulated trips on a jeep, helicopter, and riverboat while learning about the ecology of Africa.

The motivation for this investigation grew from an earlier visit by a parent who had recently toured West Africa and returned with slides of West African life, samples of clothing and art, and money from several nations. The students emerged from this experience with a thirst for more knowledge, and Mrs. Lukaczyk scurried for resources to aid them. Working with the librarian, Mrs. Lukaczyk's goal was to help her students acquire knowledge and an appreciation of Africa's rich culture, while ensuring that they did not come to believe any ethnocentric stereotypes or other misconceptions. She therefore based her students' research on a carefully compiled collection of nonfiction and fiction books, realia, computer information sources, guest speakers, and other resources.

To pull together all the special investigations, one group decided to create a mural of the book *Why Mosquitos Buzz in People's Ears* by Verna Aardema (Dial), using a simulated woodcut design to show the way Aardema made her award-winning illustrations. Throughout the mural, the students placed Aardema's unusual animal sounds ("wasawusu, wasawusu, wasawusu," "mek, mek, mek," "krik, krik, krik") in cartoon balloons above the animal making the sound. Another group made a colorful wall display depicting East African numbers they learned about in the book *Moja Means One.* A group that selected Muriel Feelings's *Jambo Means Hello* (Dial) wanted to present the information clearly, so the students created a chart illustrating words and their definitions.

Mrs. Lukaczyk knew that her students liked to retell stories they enjoyed, so she designed a learning center containing aids to help them retell their stories, either in whole or in part. One center activity called for the students to make a story map or timeline of the sequence of events in the book *Why Mosquitos Buzz in People's Ears.* In another, students designed their own figures for a story, backed them with flannel or felt, and used them to retell the story on the flannelboard.

Throughout this study of African cultures, Mrs. Lukaczyk's second graders were immersed in quality learning experiences. Many individual or group options were open to the students so that they would be able to select and experiment with a variety of learning opportunities.

DOING SOMETHING REAL

Because children of all ages must be offered experiences in which they can actively participate, the first job of all social studies teachers is to challenge them with fascinating materials and abundant stimulation. Direct involvement in such activities as making fabric dyes from berries or building a model pyramid not only deepens their understandings, but also widens their interests. For example, Claire Boyer, a second-grade teacher at Media Elementary School, wanted to take the study of local government beyond the textbook to where the action is. Her story is described in Activity 14–2.

Activity 14–2

Case Study

For a special midyear social studies project, Ms. Boyer placed her children in the position of creating a town for themselves and running it. To begin this special project, Ms. Boyer asked her children to pretend to be adult members of families driven out of Media by severe pollution. The families, traveling together in search of a new place to settle, were led downstairs inside their school to a large, empty room made available for their project. To keep track of the victims of this unfortunate plight, the children were asked to fill out "official town survey sheets." Once this census was complete, the members of this new town (named "Newmedia" by vote) built homes for themselves from large packing boxes saved from the past summer's shipment of new furniture. They painted and pasted until the boxes took on the appearance of houses and brought a sense of reality to the empty room. Streets were laid out and named: Dunlap Street was obviously a tribute to Mr. Richard Dunlap, the principal of Media Elementary School, but no one was quite sure of the inspiration for Grape Road or Ice Road. A town newspaper was begun to chronicle the daily progress of Newmedia's citizens and to keep its populace informed. "Pollution Sends Townspeople to New Land" blared the headlines on January 7, the first day of the project. A subsequent story read "Townspeople Paint the Town," in reference to the construction of new homes.

The day after the families completed their homes, they met to discuss town problems, with Ms. Boyer presiding. As is often the case with youngsters of this age, they could foresee no problems. However, Ms. Boyer was quick to suggest potential problems—fires, crime, and what would happen if she were not available to lead future town meetings. Discussion led to the establishment of police and fire departments and an election for mayor. The children quickly set up minimum qualifications for voter registration and went about soliciting candidates for the mayoral position. Seven candidates immediately announced their intent to run, but three dropped out of the race the following day—they were too busy. Campaigning and debating began as students formed their platforms: Alex promised low taxes, and Curtis vowed gun control. Candidates then planned campaign strategies, directly learning that political make-believe can mirror political reality. There was, to be specific, the "great cookie caper," involving Alex and her closest opponent, Curtis. On the last day of campaigning, Alex distributed "Vote for Alex" pamphlets decorated with paper hands grasping real chocolate chip cookies. Curtis's followers quickly cried "Bribery!" and complained that Alex was trying to buy votes. The matter went to the election board, which found that "No influence was obtained through the distribution of the cookies."

Following her 14–2 victory, Alex immediately appointed Curtis as chief of police and presented him with his first book of tickets. Using his tickets to control the breaking of laws such as speeding (running in the halls) and loitering (watching the classroom chess game), Curtis eventually learned the powers of his position. Through it all, Alex made new friends, was subject to pressures of old ones, and generally learned that a position of authority has its rewards as well as its pitfalls. "I learned I'm never gonna be the real mayor," she reflected. "Even just pretending to by the mayor is a tough job."

Leading Newmedia through its hectic early days, Alex and her council members provided leadership as the town began to grow. Other classrooms, for example, contributed to the new town. The first grade, studying the topic "Needs of People," contributed a food store and displayed the products themselves (Aisha's California watermelon: $20 a pound). The third grade, studying "What Towns Need," built an electric power station, stringing yarn lines from one paper light pole to another. The fourth grade, not involved in a relevant social studies topic at the time, demonstrated the interrelatedness of the physical and social sciences. They wired up street lights by connecting batteries to lightbulbs, thus applying their knowledge of energy to making lives better for people. The fifth grade, anxious to contribute with the rest, made a cardboard trash truck (complete with oatmeal-box "trash cans" for the customers) and a bus from cardboard boxes. Finally, the kindergarten class spruced up the entire town with pink and red paper flowers.

The entire growing village remained on display for the remainder of the school year as the children shared their learning experiences with others. They simply served as hosts while the popularity of their venture grew.

Like Ms. Boyer, social studies teachers around the country have developed significant learning situations in which their children are actively involved:

- Planting tulip and daffodil bulbs at a homeless shelter.
- Making sod bricks (as in constructing sod houses) from mud, straw, and water while studying pioneer life.
- Designing an Egyptian-style calendar, creating numbers the ancient Egyptian way.
- Decorating Ukrainian Easter eggs, called *pysanky.*
- Preparing and eating Russian pancakes, called *bliny* (blee-NEE).
- Celebrating "Juneteenth," a slang combination of "June" and "nineteenth." Food, music, and dance commemorate the day in 1865 when the slaves discovered the Civil War had ended.
- Reciting this prayer chant, to the slow beat of a drum, that was used by the Navajo people:

> May I walk in beauty before me.
> May I walk in beauty behind me.
> May I walk in beauty below me.
> May I walk in beauty above me.
> With beauty all around me, may I walk.

- Folding paper in the Japanese origami tradition.
- Playing "Marble Bridge," a game German children like to play.
- Constructing a piñata to hang from the ceiling during the classroom celebration of *Los Pasados,* a Mexican holiday recalling the Holy Family's journey from Nazareth to Bethlehem.

REALIA

In addition to providing children opportunities to do real things, you should also arrange opportunities for them to investigate real objects whenever possible. It is fascinating for children to handle a real Akua-ba doll from Ghana as you tell the story of how it is tucked into a skirt at the waist and carried by girls who hope to have children in the future. Opening up a matryoshka (mah-tree-OSH-ka) doll from Russia to reveal smaller and smaller dolls helps the children conceptualize this favorite nesting toy in ways that words alone can never equal. A set of worry beads from Greece is the only way to meaningfully explain this great relaxation technique. And what child wouldn't enjoy twirling a cowboy lariat while studying America's Old West? Real items inspire fascination and awe in any social studies topic.

This is not meant to imply that teachers should never talk, but only to stress that they enhance learning by allowing children to interact with real things. Think about all the possibilities for bringing in realia during any unit of study:

- Clothing (cowboy chaps, Japanese happi coat, chef hat and apron).
- Money (ruble, yen, mark, peso).
- Documents (wills, letters, newspapers, court records).
- Household items (colonial butter churn, Asian wok, African calabash).
- Musical instruments (Mexican guiro, Japanese den den, Zulu marimba).
- Tools (stethoscope, mortar and pestle, fishing net).
- Food (Pueblo Feast Day cookies, Mexican wedding cakes, Nigerian peanut soup).
- Toys (Chinese kites, Colonial "buzz saw," Jewish dreidel).

Oftentimes, teachers make collections of objects related to a theme and store them in boxes so they are kept well-organized from year to year. These "prop boxes" can represent countries, cultures, community helpers, or most any other topic. In selecting items for cultural boxes, be sure that you represent "present-day" conditions whenever you include traditional items such as kimonos, kilts, or sombreros. If you want to put together a box of serapes, sombreros, and other traditional Mexican dress, for example, you will give an unfair picture of what people are like today unless you also include pictures of contemporary Mexicans.

Start by obtaining a large, sturdy cardboard carton that can be painted and easily decorated (preferably by your students). Place manipulatives inside; some can be bought, others might be donated by businesses, and parents are always willing to contribute items (if they're returned in the condition you received them). Below, you will find two suggestions for prop boxes: One is specific to community helpers, the other to a culture.

Physician's Box

Doctor's bag, stethoscope, bandages, empty pill bottles, white shirt to use as a uniform, nurse's hat, plastic digital thermometers, eye chart, pad and pencil, telephone.

China Box

Chinese tops, kite, wok, chopsticks, tea cup, dried lentils (bean sprouts), noodles, silk cloth, bamboo mat, pleated fan, lantern, calligraphy brush, abacus, tangram puzzle, and game materials for *Ti Jian Zi* (similar to *Hackey Sack* in the United States). Also, shirts with mandarin collars, farmer hats, and silk dresses may be included, along with pictures of Chinese people in modern apparel.

FIELD TRIPS

Field trips are choice learning adventures for any age—kindergartners, upper-graders, high school or college students, and adults. Who doesn't learn best when taken to a firsthand source?

Good field trips for elementary school youngsters entice them to become active participants. A trip to the automobile museum during which children are lectured by a guide or required to be mere onlookers is not as good as a trip that allows them to get into an automobile, sit in the driver's seat, talk to the owner, listen to the engine's clatter, and possibly even be taken on a short, bouncy ride. A trip to the bakery where the children can only watch something being made is not as good as a trip that allows them to measure and mix the ingredients for a batch of muffins that they will gobble down later. A good field trip must inundate elementary school children with opportunities for direct, quality involvement.

At no time was this point made more clearly for Mr. Potter than when he planned to take his class to Cooperstown, NY, a community full of exciting places to visit, and only a short trip from his school. Although there were several possible attractions, Mr. Potter divided the trip between two sites—the Baseball Hall of Fame and the Farmer's Museum. These locations seemed very appropriate because it was October (World Series time), and the class had been studying Colonial America, too. Mr. Potter realized that a good field trip should never be a last-minute inspiration, so he made certain to plan details carefully and establish the purposes for the visits, making sure his children understood them, too. The children's excitement peaked during the day before the trip; nearly everyone couldn't wait to see all the baseball memorabilia. Very little enthusiasm was evident for the Farmer's Museum, however.

The first visit was to the Hall of Fame. A tour guide escorted the children to the various exhibits, and he loved to talk! Midway through the tour, the captive audience became restless, and a several children began to show outward signs of boredom. By the time the tour was over, the children stared blankly at the displays as the guide droned on, so exhausted that they were ready to go home. A short visit to the souvenir shop revived them enough so they could savor lunch at a favorite fast-food restaurant. "Can we go home now?" the children asked wearily after they ate and boarded the bus. "No, not yet," they were informed. "Not until we go to the Farmer's Museum." Amid loud groans of displeasure, the busload of downcast youngsters ambled off to its dreaded destination.

The gloomy spirits seemed to disappear instantly as the class walked down the path connecting the parking lot to the restored colonial village called the "Farmer's Museum." Authentic in every detail, the village is an actual working farm in which people dress in period garb and use authentic implements to perform the duties of colonial farmers. About halfway down the path, the class fixed their eyes in horror as a farmer led a huge ox directly toward them. "Look at that huge thing!" shrieked Frank as the ox, oozing slobber, stopped next to him. The farmer invited Frank to pat the ox, but Frank was too intimidated to try. "I never knew an ox was so big," Lois marveled as she stepped up and patted it on its wet nose. Following Lois's lead, several classmates approached the ox, some patting it and others commenting on its size, smell, and drawing power for flies.

The farmer told the class about the importance of oxen to colonial life and they were enthralled with his story. He thanked them for stopping and advised them that his tired animal needed to go to the barn for a rest. This experience seemed to break the ice, transforming the students from audience to actors. "That was awesome," said Luke. "What else is there?" The first building the children stopped in was a

By observing this metalsmith at work, these children will learn more about Colonial America than they could through any classroom experience.

school, where a "school marm" taught them about the ABCs exactly as a teacher would have done in colonial times. Spirits soared as the children went to the barn where workers involved them in the entire process of making linen from flax. By now, it was getting late and Mr. Potter tried to get the class to move on to the tanner, wigmaker, blacksmith, gunsmith, cooper (barrel maker), and glass blower, but the children insisted on staying at the barn for the cornhusking bee and gunnysack race. At every stop, the children had an opportunity to touch, handle, and use; Mr. Potter had an equally tough time pulling them away so they could visit the next exhibit. The "exhausted" children had been miraculously transformed into a group of stimulated participants.

What lessons did Mr. Potter learn from all of this? First, it was clear that children should not be put into the role of a passive audience; they must be involved. Experiences should have a direct, personal impact. Second, Mr. Potter realized that he should go on potential field trips first—in effect, embark on a "scouting mission" to test out whether the trip is more of a stimulant or a sedative. From this point of his teaching career on, Mr. Potter always followed a set of specific guidelines whenever he planned field trips for his students. He learned that appropriate field trips include the following responsibilities:

1. Address logistical concerns associated with the trip:
   - Have you taken the trip beforehand?
   - Have you made all necessary arrangements at the field trip site—what time you will arrive, where the restrooms are located, accommodations for children with special needs, places for lunch and snack?
   - Are there any special rules or regulations that must be followed at the site?
   - Have parental permission slips been signed (even if the school uses a blanket permission form)? Do not take children who haven't returned them.
   - Has transportation been arranged? (For liability reasons, a school bus is much better than private car.)
   - If private cars are to be used, have you verified that each driver has adequate insurance and a valid driver's license? Have you provided each driver with a map and precise directions?
   - Have you planned proper supervision? (I always felt a 4:1 child-adult ratio was maximum).
   - Are chaperones informed about what you expect of them? Do they know the behaviors expected of the children?
   - Do parents understand what clothing is appropriate for their children?
   - Do the students understand the expected standards of conduct? (Children respond better when they have a voice in determining these.)

2. Establish a clear purpose for the trip; be sure the children understand clearly why they are going ("What are we looking for?" "What do we want to find out?"):
   - Read books, share brochures or posters, and talk about what to expect at the site. Give the children an idea of what to expect.
   - Involve children in planning the trip.

3. Prepare for the trip:
   - Use name tags (including the school name and teacher's name). This helps if a child gets lost, as well as assisting volunteers when they need to call a child by name.
   - Assign a partner, or buddy, for each child. Explain why it is important to stick together.
   - Divide the class into groups. Give each student a specific group responsibility (recorder, photographer or illustrator, organizer, etc.).
   - Show the students how they will record information from the trip (worksheet or guidesheet).

4. Take the trip:
   - Be sure to take roll when you leave and each time you depart or return to the bus.
   - Take along a basic first-aid kit (or nurse). Several wash cloths or paper towels will be needed if a child gets sick on the bus.
   - Arrive on time.
   - Keep the children who will need your attention close to you.
   - Introduce your class (but not each individual child) to your guide, if there is one.
   - Enjoy the experience!

5. After the trip:
   - Have the children write (or dictate) thank-you notes, or draw pictures expressing their appreciation to volunteers and field site personnel.
   - Talk with the class about what they liked best.
   - Provide enrichment activities—draw pictures, write stories or poems, create a dramatic skit, make a map, or conduct any related activity to help the children deepen their understanding of the trip. (See Figure 14–1 for a first grader's drawing and written response after a trip to the fire station.)
   - Have the students evaluate the trip: Did they accomplish the purposes identified at the beginning of the trip?

It is a fact of life that, regardless of how well you plan a trip, "surprises" will be sure to pop up: Ethan yanked on Jamielle's homemade necklace and sent beads rolling in every direction; midway through the site visit, Blaine got frightened by a goat's loud bellow and wailed, "I want my mama. I wanna go home!" After you resolved those problems, Joseph wet his pants and Carrie brought up her snack. And when you returned to school, individual letters of thanks revealed some interesting "confessions":

> Dear Sir:
>   I am sorry about the way our class acted on our trip to your park, but I did not personally curse or anything. I hope you let us come back. Our friend who pulled down his pants is sorry!

> Dear Sir:
>   I am sorry that our class was bad on its trip to the park. I apologize for exposing myself. I hope you let us come back. (P.S.—I am a boy.)

These are the moments that try teachers' souls. Perplexed, they often wonder, "What in the world am I doing here? I should have stayed back in the classroom and just read a book!" It's quite normal to have such reactions, but don't give up on field trips. Experience and good planning will help you avoid most of these disasters.

It is best, however, not to plan trips outside of school until the children have been there for at least one month. Allow them first to get used to you, other children, and

FIGURE 14-1
Drawing Made After a Field Trip

the challenges of their new learning environment. Once they have become a cohesive group and are familiar with the adults, a brief trip not far from the school might be taken first. A walk around the block or the school grounds, for example, is a good place to start. Even the most obvious things are worth pointing out, because your goal is to help the children develop an awareness of their environment and the ability to describe the things they see and hear. On trips near school, you will notice many interesting things: traffic lights, fire hydrants, mailboxes, bus stops, telephone booths, and parking meters. It is exciting to observe activities such as loading and unloading trucks and repair work on streets where the children can safely see exposed pipes, open manholes, or large cranes.

As the children become comfortable with short walking trips, trips farther away from school can be planned. There is a tremendous wealth of possibilities out there: farm, museum, supermarket, post office, airport, public library, fire station, zoo, orchard, pumpkin patch, duck pond, bakery, construction project, railroad station, library, aquarium, hospital, courthouse, airport, police station, firehouse, art gallery, shopping center, monuments, radio or television station, florist, dance studio, animal shelter, pet store, restaurant, cultural center, or factory.

RESOURCE PERSONS

Resource persons are individuals from the world outside who come into your classroom to share some expertise or knowledge with your class. They serve the same purpose as field trips, providing opportunities for direct action when the children cannot go to specific sites. As with field trips, the resource person should not be a talker putting on a demonstration while the children serve as an attentive audience. The children must be involved in the action.

Although not as intrinsically motivating as going out to field sites, children nevertheless enjoy contact with outside visitors and the contributions and interesting materials they share. You might invite people who provide goods or services in your specific location: police officers, firefighters, farmers, delivery people, construction workers, doctors, nurses, newspersons, bakers, industrial workers, store workers, craftspersons, lawyers, bankers, clergy, government officials, and so on. When introducing children to different cultures or ethnic groups, you can ask people with appropriate backgrounds to provide information and carry out demonstrations.

Visitors to the classroom provide the children with memorable experiences because they offer important adventures in a very personal way. One day, for example, Ms. Graham heard a discussion about firefighters among a small group of her first graders as they were looking at a book in the library corner. She listened as the children talked excitedly about the big rubber boots and hard red hats the firefighters wore. Seizing the moment, she suggested that it might be possible for a firefighter to visit their classroom. "Would he really come to see us?" asked Michael. "I'd like him to come here," offered Sarah, "How can we ask him?" Ms. Graham had no doubt that interest was high, so she called the fire department to ask if a firefighter could visit the children. She was informed that not only was such a visit possible, but that arrangements could be made for two firefighters to bring a small fire truck to the school.

The next day the children eagerly waited at the school parking lot for the truck to arrive. Their anticipation grew into excitement as the bright red and silver truck motored

Whether you take the children to the action or bring the action to the children, firsthand sources are packed with direct, personal learning.

up the winding entrance. Keeping the children well in control, Ms. Graham reminded them to stay behind her until the fire truck came to a halt. When it did, the children gingerly approached the vehicle. The firefighters came out to show the children all their paraphernalia and explain their jobs. "The truck is so shiny," remarked Rebecca. "Yeah, and look at all those big hoses!" shouted Ben. "One of the firemen is a lady. Wow, a lady fireman," said Denise, all agog. "Do you have to go to college to learn how to be a fireman?" asked Oren. The children watched, listened, commented, and asked questions as they tried on the hard hats and floppy boots, watched the brilliant lights, and listened to the firefighters talk. The most adventuresome youngsters even accepted an invitation to climb up into the cab and sit in the fire truck. All this wonderful activity culminated in a well-supervised short trip around the parking lot on the back of the truck. Ms. Graham was rewarded by the fact that this learning experience was thoroughly enjoyed by the children, and that they had learned a great deal about a valuable community service.

After the firefighters left the school, Ms. Graham assembled the children as a group and invited them to share their thoughts. As they spoke, Ms. Graham recorded their comments on an experience chart. Later the children dictated a thank-you note that was mailed to the firehouse.

Classroom guests are usually very willing to share their special skills or talents with children. These people might include some who can help break down stereotypes, such as senior citizens with special skills or hobbies, women carpenters, male nurses, and so on. Care must be exercised, though, in the way guests are selected. The safest approach seems to be requesting recommendations from other teachers, involved parents, and other school personnel. In this way, you will be able to select speakers who will appropriately inform and motivate your children. You and your students will benefit the most if you send your speakers a list of helpful suggestions similar to the following:

1. *Think young.* Remember that you are speaking to young children, so be especially careful of your vocabulary. Also, limit your talk to the attention level of the children—about 20 minutes for K–2 children and 40 minutes for grades 3 and up.

2. *Bring something.* Real, touchable objects that relate to your area of expertise help children understand your life and work. For example, a construction worker recently visited our class and brought along a hard hat, small tools, and a lunch box.

3. *Move around.* As you speak, try to move to various sections of the classroom so the children will feel personally involved. It helps to ask them questions once in a while, too.

4. *Share personal stories.* Is there something that happened during your childhood that motivated you to do what you're now doing?

5. *Allow time for student questions.* When students do ask you questions, repeat them back to the class so all can hear.

6. *If possible, leave the children a memento.* You might bring something small to leave with the children (a florist brought a small flower for each child, an artist left an autographed sketch, and a flight attendant gave out some "wing" pins). If you can't leave a small souvenir, you might want to create something (the construction worker helped the children build a structure with blocks).

COMPUTERS

When computers were first introduced into elementary schools during the late 1970s and early 1980s, they were used primarily as "interactive taskmasters," providing drill and practice exercises and serving as "electronic workbooks." Students were presented problems and entered their responses; the computer would send a graphic reward (smiley face or explosion, for example) for the right answer. This usage clearly concerned many educators, for they envisioned computer terminals as centers of "busy work" with the same potential for abuse as regular worksheets and workbooks.

Although software companies continue to produce "drill-and-practice" programs, educators everywhere are convinced that the singular "interactive taskmaster" role of computers is long gone. The evolution of tutorials and simulations quickly joined the drill-and-practice programs as powerful tools for teaching content and skills. Some, like *Oregon Trail* (MECC), remain among the most popular programs in elementary school social studies classrooms. As we moved into the 1990s, dramatic changes in computer technology brought word processing, CD-ROMs, and the Internet into elementary school classrooms. Now educators everywhere are trying to figure out ways to enhance learning in elementary school classrooms with computers. "I see the computer as an irreplaceable tool in my classroom," comments Mrs. Kathy Nell, a fourth-grade teacher from Philadelphia. "I don't see it as a workbook, but a sky-light—a skylight that opens up so many new opportunities for my students. The computer is pretty much my ally."

Not all teachers share Mrs. Nell's vision, however. Brandt (1995) reports that "few teachers in a relatively small number of schools possess the equipment and knowl-edge to have their students. . . send e-mail to people in other countries, consult CD-ROMs for information, and prepare multimedia reports. The vast majority do not have access to the newest technologies—and even those who do tend to use them in conventional ways" (p. 5). Indeed, merely putting a computer into a classroom and connecting it to the Internet won't guarantee improvement. If teachers are going to use technology, they will need to be as skilled in using computers as they are in reading and writing. Fortunately, "the cavalry is on the way" to help teachers get in touch with technology's promise and power; a blaring bugle call signals the "charge" of schools of education to include technology training for their undergrad-uate students. Many school districts have joined the battle by instituting technology training programs for their in-service teachers. To support their efforts, in 1997 Sen-ator Patty Murray (D–Washington) introduced the Teacher Training Technology Act, a bill that would mandate teacher training for school districts that receive federal funding.

As we said, drill-and-practice computer programs remain, but an expanded va-riety of increasingly sophisticated educational software gives more attention to higher level thinking processes. These programs can be classified within the fol-lowing functions: (1) tutorial, (2) problem-solving, (3) simulation, (4) word pro-cessing and database, (5) telecommunications, and (6) hypermedia presentations.

Tutorial Software

Computer tutorials operate much like a complex textbook; their major roles are to display information step by step and to organize questions and answers. Tutorial pro-grams focus on the presentation of new knowledge and skills, as opposed to the re-view and reinforcement of previously acquired skills and knowledge found in the outdated drill-and-practice programs. One example of a tutorial program is *Nigel's World* (Lawrence Productions), a fascinating world of adventures and learning expe-riences for children of all ages. Nigel is a fearless Scot who takes on the world, camera in hand, in search of a photograph that will earn him first place in a photog-raphy contest. As he journeys to the ends of the earth snapping pictures, Nigel calls for the help of the students to make decisions involving geography and basic map skills.

Another popular tutorial program is *Stickybear Town Builder*, for students from ages 5–10 (available from Optimum Resource–Weekly Reader Software). The pro-gram is intended to teach youngsters basic map skills in an entertaining manner. Children who are fans of previous popular *Stickybear* programs will enjoy this one.

Three open-ended activities encourage students to build their own towns while learning important map skills. In the "Build a Town" phase, students choose buildings and objects to locate in their towns, with roads automatically connecting the features. "Take a Drive" helps build directional skills as students reach certain destinations before they run out of fuel. "Find the Keys" is a searching game where students try to find the secret hiding places of 12 keys randomly scattered about the town before running out of fuel. A compass indicates to the driver which way to direct the car.

Tutorial programs are available on a variety of topics; as students learn new content and respond to questions, the programs usually assess what the students know and branch accordingly to new instructional segments. Properly formulated, these programs effectively provide information, challenge, evaluate, and remediate on an individual basis.

Problem-Solving Software

Problem-solving programs often present highly complex situations where students face a dilemma, choose from a number of possible alternatives, and arrive at a solution. The computer encourages active exploration and discovery. One extremely popular problem-solving program for children in grades 3–8 is *Where in the World Is Carmen Sandiego?* (available from Broderbund Software). Students become crime-fighters as they search the world for Carmen Sandiego (an ex-secret agent turned thief) and her gang of criminals, who are out to steal our most precious natural treasures. The venture starts with one of the 16 thieves hiding in a city and leaving a trail of clues for student "detectives" to decipher. The students read descriptions of various cities, visit clue locations, and check possible destinations, all the while using their problem-solving and analytical skills. Along the same principle, the program developer has added *Where in the USA Is Carmen Sandiego?, Where in Europe is Carmen Sandiego?*, and *Where in Time Is Carmen Sandiego?*

Simulation Software

Computerized instruction may take the form of *simulations*, or imitations of something real. Simulation programs place students into situations that are as authentic as possible. Social studies teachers employ simulations because they invite many modes of thought: conceptualization, problem solving, and varied opportunities to apply knowledge and skills. One of the most noteworthy simulations available for upper-grade elementary school classrooms is *The New Oregon Trail* (available from Minnesota Educational Computer Consortium). It presents a series of decisions that pioneers faced in 1847 as they set out in wagon trains to find new homes in the Oregon Territory. They stock up with provisions at the beginning of the five-to-six-month journey, but heavy rains, wagon breakdowns, illness, and robberies eventually deplete their supplies. Children must make decisions along the way, but if they choose to hunt for food or stop at a fort, for example, they lose precious time and could suffer starvation or illness, or fail to pass the western mountains before the freeze and the blizzards. The computer mathematically determines the outcome of the children's decisions and gives the decision makers immediate feedback about the consequences of their choices. Although most simulations involve only one user per computer, *The New Oregon Trail* may involve a small-group approach by engaging a student family of four or five children to make the difficult decisions.

SimAnt, SimCity, and *SimEarth* (available from Maxis) are simulations that place students into settings where they describe, create, and control a system. For example, in *SimAnt*, the system is an ant colony. The students must figure out how the system works and take control of it by leading their ants to food, defending their nest and queen, and destroying an enemy red ant colony. Students win when they destroy the enemy red queen, make new colonies, take over the yard, and drive the humans out of the house. However, the most important outcome is not winning; it is the knowledge and reasoning skills that grow as new ideas for adaptability are developed and tested while colonies develop and decline in response to various conditions.

Another useful simulation for students in grades 4–8 is *Galleons of Glory: The Secret Voyage of Magellan* (available from Broderbund Software). The students imagine the world of 1519 by taking the place of Magellan and trying to sail a galleon around the globe. They are confronted with problems ranging from nature's fury to shipboard politics as they react to changing circumstances that arise during the voyage. Calm seas give way to vicious storms, and a frightened crew comes close to mutiny, challenging students to make decisions in situations representative of actual historical events.

Word Processing and Database Software

Word processing systems are computer software programs designed to facilitate the efficient collecting, revising, storing, and printing of text. Word processing software has made it possible for elementary school students to type a first draft of a composition or report on a keyboard and simultaneously display it on a computer screen. By using a few quickly learned computer commands, the author can insert or delete text; combine sentences; "cut-and-paste" words, sentences, and paragraphs, moving them to new locations; change grammar and spelling errors; and print out the completed copy. In the early 1980s, word processing programs were quite cumbersome and much too difficult for most young children, but today's software is quite simple and readily available for the beginner.

One type of word processing system helps students prepare neat, well-edited written pieces; another, called desktop publishing, combines graphics and text and allows users to produce other products such as signs, banners, greeting cards, newsletters, letterheads, travel brochures, and newspapers. (To learn more about both of these word processing functions turn to Chapter 12.)

Databases are simply collections of data. All of us encounter databases each day, whether we are comparing batting averages of the players on the university baseball team, looking for a recipe, or figuring out our grades at the end of the semester. Databases have existed for quite some time—much before the advent of the computer. Throughout history, people have devised their own systems for managing data; some are very raw (throwing recipes into a desk drawer), and others are much more refined (creating a systematic filing system). Computer database programs, however, allow a level of organization never before possible. With databases, students can enter, store, and compare information about nearly any social studies topic. Then, if they want to reference somehting stored in the database (e.g., the 50 most populous cities in the world), all they would need to do is go to a file containing that information, and it will be in that database. Sunal and Haas (1993) offer their thoughts about why database activities are useful for elementary school students:

> Often when data is sorted to answer a question, new questions arise. As new questions arise students can carry out further research and add additional information to the database. Of course, sometimes the information just is not available. This teaches students that not every question can be readily answered. Making databases . . . demonstrates the power of information and also the power of cooperative effort. To construct a comprehensive database with a lot of information in it on one's own can be a daunting task, but it is one that is quite easily accomplished as a cooperative effort. (pp. 166–168)

Telecommunications

In a small but growing number of classrooms, connections to the Internet are providing access to vast outside sources of information and creating new opportunities for collaborative learning. The Internet is often designated as a *telecommunications* service because it involves two-way communication via telephone lines. You are using a form of telecommunication when you chat with someone on the phone; a person who faxes a document from one fax machine to another transmits over telephone lines, too. In much the same way, we now find it possible to transfer data from one computer to another via telephone lines with the use of *modems*. If your classroom and others have computers, it is possible to connect to one another through a modem and telephone lines and go *online*. This means that you are connected to a network of uers who can exchange files, send and receive electronic mail (*e-mail* for short), conduct joint projects, share data, and even play educational games with one another.

Of course, to accomplish this, you must subscribe to a major online service such as *America Online (AOL), CompuServe, Microsoft Network (MSN),* or *Prodigy*. The other easy way to reach the Internet is by subscribing to an Internet-only service. With the computer software provided by these services, you will gain access to all the major public areas of cyberspace:

- *The World Wide Web.* Provides access to information on the Internet in the mouse-driven, point-and-click format familiar to Macintosh or Microsoft Windows users.

- *Electronic Mail (e-mail).* Allows you to send and receive messages from someone else on the Internet. To do this, you need an address, which looks like *myname@myschool.edu.*

- *Newsgroups (Usenet) and Mailing Lists (Listservs).* Permit one person to communicate with many others—something like placing a message on a bulletin board or a bulk mailing. It is easy to send a single e-mail message about a topic of common interest (such as the Civil War) to a list of interested schools.

- *Telnet Sites.* Offer one way to retrieve information. Often located at universities or libraries, these sites let you operate distant computers from your keyboard.
- *File Libraries (FTP) and Gopher Sites.* Other sources of information or ways to retrieve information. FTP stands for *file transfer protocol*; it allows you to access file archives on the Internet and then transfer them to your computer. A software system called *Archie* allows users to search the database for information of interest. Gopher sites (designed to "go for" information) maintain collections of information and references to information.

Most of the information you need to find your way through cyberspace is found on the Internet itself. Once you access a commercial online service or a direct Internet connection, your membership will allow you to tap into *Netscape* or Microsoft *Internet Explorer,* the two major web browsers. A search for information about the White House can be initiated by typing in its web address or URL (Universal Resource Locator), usually in a format like this: *http://www.whitehouse.gov.* Your computer sends that address to the server's computer, which decodes it. With the address decoded, the server sends your request to the one computer on the Internet that you asked for—in this case, to the White House computer. Because the Internet consists of over 7 million computers linked together, your request may travel through a computer in Taiwan before making it to Washington, DC. When the destination receives your request, it first checks to see if you are allowed to have the information. If you are, it sends the information back to you.

If you do not have the URL for a site you wish to visit, the browsers can provide easy access to it through a number of search engines. Usually accessed through an icon on the browser screen, *search engines* are files of multimedia informational resources that can be text, graphics, audio, or even digital video. Yahoo!, Lycos, Excite!, AltaVista, Magellan, and Infoseek are currently the most popular search engines. (Several of these have separate search engines just for children; Yahooligans! and Magellan's Kidstuff are two examples.) Instructions for locating resources and information can be found on the search engine's homepage (the first page you'll see). To search for information on the White House, for example, simply type the words *White House* in the designated box on the homepage and a number of different information sites will be identified. Helpful links can be *bookmarked,* or stored by the browser for future use.

As fascinating as the Internet world can be, it can also confront you with a few problems. Perhaps the greatest is the availability of material not suitable for children. The Telecommunications Act requires Internet services to keep such material away from children, but nothing substitutes for careful supervision. Online services provide controls that allow you to limit what your children can access. Software such as *Cybersitter* or *Surfwatch* lets you supervise visits to the Internet.

Some teachers hail the Internet as a new era in learning. Mrs. Nell maintains that her online connection has revitalized her teaching and motivated and excited her students, who are learning much of the same information as in their textbooks, but in a more engaging way. According to Mrs. Nell, this added motivation comes from the fact that her students have an immediate, authentic audience for their work; through planning and sharing with their online peers, they find that the information they exchange has meaning—an immediate and utilitarian motive. One of the greatest benefits cited by Mrs. Nell is the capacity for collaborative research. She and her students have joined other classrooms around the country to investigate everything from the weather to prices for consumer goods. The major complaint voiced by Mrs. Nell is that there just are not enough online classrooms to make a comprehensive exchange of projects and ideas possible.

While many teachers applaud the entrance of the Internet into the elementary school classroom, implementation cost is the biggest obstacle for widespread use. For many schools still struggling to get basic computer equipment, the cost of modems, online fees, and long-distance telephone charges is too much to manage. Nevertheless, proponents are certain that, regardless of expense, this new technology is so useful that it will somehow spread, either through shrinking costs or greater willingness of school districts to spend money on computers in the classroom.

For many teachers, it's a challenge to bridge the gap bewteen traditional instruction and technology. But, as many teachers have learned, tapping into the Internet helps children benefit from a rich source of new ideas, friends, and experts. Blagojevic (1997) describes several categories of project ideas that were carried out in classrooms using the Internet:

- *To make new friends.* Using electronic mail, children from Maine exchanged letters with Icelandic children.

- *To extend the curriculum.* After listing favorite storybook characters, children from Sacramento and Baltimore initiated a "story swap." Each group created and e-mailed original stories to each other.

- *To build cross-cultural comparisons.* Children from Oregon worked with children from Florida, Arizona, Japan, Russia, and South Africa on a collaborative book. Each location responded to the question "How do you like to play?" The children assembled a *How We Play* book of stories and drawings.

- *To produce information.* After a bee stung young Ted on the leg one day, his classmates suggested they build a Web page that would educate people about bees. They researched bees and added their own drawings to the informational pages.

- *To learn more.* A week after creating their Web page, the class received an e-mail message from a bee expert. He pointed out that their bee was actually a yellowjacket wasp and explained the difference between bees and wasps. The children used this information to correct their page.

- *To meet new people.* While they were studying penguins, a group of children electronically "met" a class of second graders from Dunedin, New Zealand. They were awed to learn that their New Zealand friends could walk a half mile down the road to see penguins in the bay.

- *To explore the world.* The Internet allows children to break out of the walls of their classroom to interact with people all over the world.

To learn how you can post your students' work on a Web site, go to Web 66 at http://web66.coled.umn.edu/

Computers give children easy access to learning beyond the walls of the school.

Hypermedia

A special area of interest that has contributed greatly to social studies programs today has been the use of *hypermedia*, a communications tool that combines video, graphics, animation, and text. Known as "presentation software," hypermedia authoring programs enable students to organize and communicate information in innovative and thought-provoking ways, accessing and integrating information from such diverse sources as the Internet, sounds or clip art pulled from public domain software, photographs from a digital camera or scanner, and clips from a video camera or CD-ROM. Three widely used presentation software programs are *Hyper-Studio, ClarisWorks,* and, especially for the younger set, the *SlideShow* portion of *KidPix.* These are not the only hypermedia tools available to teachers and students, but they are excellent examples of how such programs work.

I once heard a computer expert say, "To be truly literate, one must learn to communicate in the dominant system of a culture." At no other time was this truism clearer to me than when I visited an elementary school "History Fair" and examined all of the wonderful projects. Every display attracted a great deal of attention, but one stood out above all the others. I was made aware of this special display by a neighbor who turned to me and asked, "Can you believe what Raymond did on the computer?"

I walked over to Raymond's space and was met with eye-popping graphics, clear text, dazzling animation, and breathtaking audio. Telling about the life of Harriet Tubman, Raymond's presentation gave every impression of a professional presentation. Scanned photos from literature sources, spoken text that highlighted the key events in Harriet Tubman's life, recorded spirituals, and the culminating video clip of Martin Luther King, Jr.'s, "I Have a Dream" speech made the presentation a special occasion. The "flash" was not the priority in Raymond's presentation; the message was certainly the important element. However, the presentation software added much more to Raymond's research than if he had simply put together an oral or written report.

Some presentation software systems contain special "buttons" that allow the user to immediately access another part of the presentation by clicking on a prompt. For example, Raymond's presentation included a button at the point in Harriet's life when she gave slaves secret directions on how to flee to the North. By using the mouse to click the button, the user could listen to the song "Follow the Drinking Gourd" while looking at an illustration of the Big Dipper.

Speaking of presentation software, Muir (1994) comments that

> if students find learning more interesting and engaging as a result of creating an interactive project (perhaps one that makes information pop up on the screen when you click a button), then computers have served their purpose. If students become more enthusiastic about research—because they know that their final report is going to look good and be fully interactive—then computers have made a valuable contribution to the educational process. (p. 32)

Presentation software is available, relatively inexpensive, and not difficult to use. Teachers should use this practical technology application and demonstrate modern, effective communication techniques to their students.

Evaluating Software

Computer software must be carefully evaluated before purchase. Most is somewhat expensive, and schools normally have limited software budgets. Ideally, you should preview the software with the children before purchasing it. You also should try it out several times before introducing it to your students. The software selection checklist displayed in Figure 14-2 may serve as a useful initial screening instrument for choosing computer programs for your social studies program. Any personally preferred rating system can be used.

CD-ROM (Interactive Technology)

CD-ROMs (Compact Disc–Read Only Memory) are silvery, compact storage discs that store data. The discs hold video clips, still photographs, music, and text—vast amounts of information. To operate CD-ROMs, you need a special CD-ROM drive. Most computers now have a CD-ROM drive built in; older models must be connected to one.

FIGURE 14–2
Software Selection Checklist

	Best 5	4	3	2	Worst 1
Name of Program _____ Publisher _____					
Type of Program _____ Grade Level _____					
Simple, understandable instructions					
Clearly stated program objectives					
Developmentally appropriate					
Colorful, engaging graphics and sound					
Software runs smoothly and quickly					
Features higher-order thinking and problem solving					
Easily readable screen					
Provides supportive feedback					
Program varies in complexity					
Holds child's attention					
User initiates and sets pace of program					
Manual offers teaching suggestions					
Clear of stereotypes					

The number of CD-ROMs entering the marketplace has mushroomed in recent years. Betts (1994) reports that 2 million discs were sold in 1992; by 1997, the number was expected to escalate to over 64 million discs. Despite this increasing popularity, Betts (1994) claims that most CD-ROMs are substandard; many merely repackage information from another format, usually print.

Despite this problem, good CD-ROMs offer the advantage of print, graphics, and animation all in one package and at a relatively low cost. In thinking of the type of CD-ROM to purchase for your classroom, the rule of thumb is that if you have to purchase only one kind of CD-ROM, you should probably choose an encyclopedia. Which one should you buy? The *Grolier Multimedia Encyclopedia* (Grolier Interactive), for example, offers a comprehensive source of information in a multimedia format. It contains more than 33,000 carefully researched selections, from "Art" to "World History," with over 4,000 color and black-and-white images. Video sequences bring to life such memorable events as suffragettes marching for the right to vote and U.S. soldiers raising the flag at Iwo Jima. The combination of photographs, music, maps, digital video sequences, and spoken audio makes research and learning profitable and fun for all students. And Grolier offers maps that are among the best.

Encarta (Microsoft Corporation) is frequently a popular choice among elementary school children. It comes in two versions: *Encarta* on a single disk and *Encarta Encyclopedia Deluxe*. The *Deluxe* version doubles the multimedia content of the regular version and has more interactive features. The outstanding multimedia content makes browsing for information quite interesting.

Two other CD-ROM encyclopedias to consider are *Compton's Interactive* (Compton's New Media) and *World Book Multimedia* (World Book Multimedia). Both contain excellent articles, pictures, videos, and maps.

PilgrimQuest (Decision Development Corporation) is a CD-ROM simulation based on historical research that helps students acquire a deeper understanding of colonial exploration and settlement from 1620 to 1626. Decisions begin as the Pilgrims must choose the provisions most necessary for their voyage. They continue as pirates and fierce storms complicate the trip. Challenges mount as the students must determine a location and establish a colony. Full-motion film clips, sound, and other multimedia features offer a stimulating way to learn social studies. Codeveloped with the National Geographic Society, *PilgrimQuest* helps students learn to predict outcomes and develop critical-thinking skills. The National Geographic Society has become especially active in producing CD-ROMs for educational purposes in the elementary school, having among its list such appropriate titles as *Our Earth, Picture Atlas of the World, The Presidents: It All Started with George,* and *World of Animals.*

CD-ROM technology provides students with wide access to data and offers a challenging way to learn social studies content. All users need to be able to do is to insert a disk into the CD-ROM drive and select from a multimedia presentation the data they desire. Elementary schools around the country are rapidly becoming interested in employing information services such as CD-ROM. We cannot yet imagine the untapped potential of this technological wonder as an educational tool.

VIDEOS, SLIDES, AND FILMSTRIPS

When direct experiences are not feasible, teachers often plan to share representations of reality through the use of various audiovisual materials, including videotapes, filmstrips, slides, models, posters, and other displays. In most classrooms, the television set has replaced the movie projector and screen as the most popular piece of audiovisual equipment. Videos on virtually every social studies topic can be found in school libraries. What are the benefits of these programs? First, they involve action. When action is essential to the concept being taught, a good video will get the idea across. And if stop-frame, time-lapse, or slow motion can help clarify a point, the VCR is ready to respond. Second, the video can transport students to other times and places too difficult to reach in any other way. A trip back to the Battle of Gettysburg or a voyage on the *Mayflower* is as easy as the click of a few controls. Third, the video adds interest and variety to teaching. Through music and excellent camera work, the viewer becomes immersed in the mood of educationally significant times and places.

Some videos are interesting when they are viewed a second time. The second viewing can occur the same day if the program is short, but if it is lengthy, the second viewing should be done the next day. As the video is shown the second time, you could ask the students to interpret the action as the sound is turned all the way down. The students could also be asked to narrate each scene.

The VCR, along with a video camera, makes it possible to record a variety of student activities. Recording a field trip, resource person, or student project offers endless opportunities to supplement instruction in the social studies classroom. Use audiotapes and videotapes to prepare a student program each week. The format of the show can be anything you like, but one that works especially well is the music/news/talk show format: "My name is Lisa Forrest, and this is television (or radio) station WOW right here in Cedar Elementary School." (Changing the host weekly generates more interest.) "Hope you're having a good day and are ready to listen to the top tune of the week as voted on by the fifth graders of Cedar Elementary. Here it goes!" (Once the song is over, you may wish to provide a teletype background for the news—an electric typewriter does fine. News items may range from actual current events to announcements of school events, special student accomplishments, or other local happenings.) Commercials may be interjected to promote items such as a school band concert, the school store, and so on. Some children enjoy creating parodies of actual commercials. The talk show format may conclude the broadcast as the host interviews a teacher who has taken an interesting trip, a student who has won a special prize, and so on.

Suggestions for using videotapes can be directly applied to slides and filmstrips. Filmstrips are a connected series of images on a roll of film. Audiotapes provide narration and background music. Filmstrips are relatively inexpensive; they can be purchased from many commercial instructional supply firms for almost every common social studies topic. The major benefit of filmstrips is that they offer teachers flexibility; the filmstrip can be stopped at individual frames and then discussed or analyzed. Slides are quite similar to filmstrips, except that the individual frames are not connected. Despite the ease and convenience of videotaping, slides remain quite popular with elementary school teachers. Taking along a 35mm camera on a field trip and making slides from the film is more convenient than hauling a more cumbersome video camera. And some schools have equipment to make slides from computer programs—a valuable source of in-class experience.

PICTURES

A rich storehouse of social studies information is contained in the countless pictures found in such sources as posters, literature books, textbooks, prints, newspapers, travel brochures, calendars, and magazines. Pictures help children envision people, places, events, or feelings that are difficult to imagine in other ways, proving the truth of the old expression, "One picture is worth a thousand words."

As you display and discuss pictures, remember that children vary in their ability to read and interpret them, much as they vary in their ability to read and interpret words. Some children may function only at the *literal* level, being able to simply name, list, and describe specific details about items being observed. Most, however, extend their skills to the *inferential* level, where they are able to speculate about such things as character traits, missing details or elements, or cause-and-effect relationships, and to

Social studies teachers start the wheels of learning turning with a wide array of instructional resources.

the *critical* level, where they are able to make judgments of worth or express emotional or attitudinal reactions. You should attempt to structure discussions with questions of varying degree of difficulty, giving children of different abilities the chance for success at their individual levels and exposing less mature learners to the higher-level thoughts expressed by their more mature peers. Sample questions follow.

- *Literal Questions*

  "Tell me what you see."
  "How many _____ ?"
  "Describe the _____ ."
  "What color (size, distance, etc.) is the _____ ?"
  "What is this person wearing?"

- *Inferential Questions*

  "Where (or when) does this take place?"
  "What will happen next?"
  "What are the _____ doing?"
  "How is this the same as (different from) _____ ?"
  "What kind of a person do you think _____ is?"

- *Critical Questions*

  "Why did _____ happen?"
  "Do the people like one another? How do you know?"
  "What do (don't) you like about the picture?"

"What conclusions could you make about _____ ?"
"How might the information in this picture be used?"

SIMULATION GAMES

As students progress through the elementary grades, they should continually experience developmentally appropriate activities that require them to make decisions similar to those people actually face in life. *Simulation games* place students in these kinds of situations; they involve students personally by requiring them to assume roles and seek solutions to problems. The degree to which actions and decisions meet with positive results determines the winner of a simulation game. The "Stores and Shoppers" game illustrates the major features of a simulation game designed to deepen economics concepts (see Activity 14–3). Its instructional objectives include:

1. Helping children discover that people may prefer to buy for any of several reasons—lower prices, better goods or services, convenient location, customer confidence.

2. Helping children understand that owners of stores earn income from the production and sales of services and goods, and that from income they must pay for goods and materials to replace what they have sold, wages for their workers and selves, rent and utilities, repair and replacement of tools and equipment, and taxes.

3. Helping children understand that the income left after the business owner has paid all expenses is profit. The owner earns this profit by taking risks, since she can't be sure that her customers will buy the goods and services she sells.

4. Helping children discover that business owners compete to attract customers with better goods and services or lower prices.

5. Helping children understand how stores use advertising to tell customers what they are selling and what their prices are. This helps children understand how advertising assists people in making choices.

Activity 14–3

Classroom Exercise

Stores and Shoppers

The Situation
The players are divided into two groups: shoppers and store owners. In a class of thirty, there might be four stores with three owners per store. Each store selects an owner to be the treasurer. Pupils are scorekeeper, resource keeper, and card dealer. Others are shoppers.

Resources for Players

Each shopper has some sort of medium of exchange, which can be play money or a simulated medium such as red paper circles. Each shopper receives an equal amount of "money," and all shoppers receive identical shopping lists of items to be obtained at the stores. All the stores have equal amounts of the exchange medium, but their amounts are not equal to that of the shoppers. The stores are also provided with goods for the shoppers to buy, but the quantity and prices vary among the stores. Goods are represented by different colored paper squares, triangles, and rectangles. Prices are set by the teacher; for example:

Store 1: 2 green triangles sell for 3 circles.

Store 2: 6 green triangles sell for 1 circles.

Store 3: 1 green triangle sells for 5 circles.

Store 4: 1 green triangle sells for 5 circles.

The card dealer has small cards that designate amounts of exchange medium that must be paid by store owners at different intervals. For example, "Pay rent—5 circles."

The resource keeper is only used in a more complex game for a middle grade. He sells goods to stores when they want to use their profit to buy more goods.

Goals for Actors

The shoppers try to buy all the things on their shopping lists. The shopper who completes or comes closest to completing his or her list in the given time is the winner. If two shoppers tie, the shopper with the most exchange medium left is the winner.

The store owners try to sell all their goods at the prices the teacher has set. The store with the most profit is the winner.

The scorekeeper is in charge of counting the stores' profits and determining the winner among the shoppers.

Special Rules and Limits

1. When the card dealer blows the whistle, each store treasurer must draw a card and pay what the card says to the dealer.

2. All sales are final.

3. Shoppers cannot resell goods.

4. Stores cannot trade goods; shoppers cannot trade.

5. Playing time is set by the teacher—approximately 20 to 30 minutes.

Follow-Up
The most important part of a simulation game is the follow-up. Leading questions asked by the teacher help children verbalize the objective of the game and the meaning of the game symbols. Such a question for this game might be, "Why did you buy green triangles at Store 2 instead of Store 1?" Hopefully the answer would be that the price was lower at Store 2.

Source: Tivoler, J., Montgomery, L., & Waid, J. (1970). Simulation games: How to use. *Instructor 68.* Reprinted from *Instructor,* copyright © March 1970 by The Instructor Publications, Inc. Used by permission.

Simulation games are enjoyable and easy to play. Their success or failure, however, depends on how carefully you've prepared. Sound preparation involves the following components:

1. *Preplanning.* Know the game well. Carefully examine the rules and game materials. If possible, play the game with several friends in advance. Divide and organize game materials before you give them to the children, and introduce the game by *briefly* telling the students what it's all about. Divide the players and assign roles, giving students a clear description of each role.

2. *Playing the game.* Do not help the players with their strategies, but be available to answer questions concerning rules. Keep the players informed of the scores throughout. Permit students to play the game several times, since they may be interested in trying alternate strategies or other roles.

3. *Follow-up discussion.* Discuss decisions the players faced and the strategies they chose. What were their reasons for using certain strategies? How can the decisions and strategies be applied to real life?

Because children have a natural love for games, simulation games are self-motivating. They actively involve children in social studies learning; because the game situations represent real-life circumstances, the students view them as relevant to their lives. Another advantage of simulation games is that children work cooperatively, sharing ideas and helping one another find solutions. Despite the fact that simulation games may require up to an entire class day to play, teachers have found that students' motivation remains high, and that the positive outcomes far outweigh any sacrifices made in class time.

LEARNING CENTERS

Learning center is a loose term used to describe any area of the classroom where students can work independently or with other students on varied learning activities. The center may be designed to help children practice new skills, review important content, use research materials and resources, solve arresting problems, or think critically about a variety of issues. Materials and activities should be geared to various student abilities and talents.

Educationally sound learning centers that meet the needs and interests of individual students are the product of careful planning. You should plan each center around specific program goals that will be achieved through work at the center. If your program places high priority on academic skills, then enrichment or reinforcement of content and skills receive top priority. If social skills are highly prized, projects requiring collaboration will assume greater importance.

Selecting Activities

After deciding precisely what you want your center to accomplish, you must consider the types of activities that have the most potential to help achieve your instructional objectives. For example, if your major objective is to review sources of clothing fiber, a basic "wheel" activity might be useful. Simply cut out a wheel (approximately eight to ten inches in diameter), divide it into eight segments, and print a fiber source on each segment. The student matches correct answers to the wheel by using clip-on wooden clothespins (See the example in Figure 14-3).

FIGURE 14–3
Sample Learning Center Activity—"Wheel"

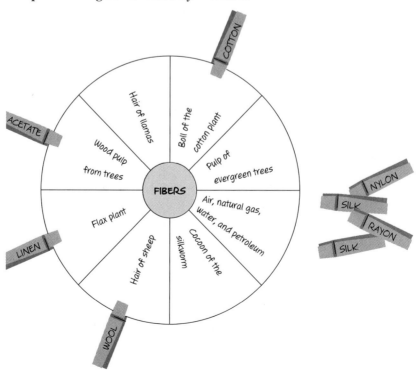

If your major goal is to help refine new skills (such as critical thinking), a reading–writing experience might be appropriate. In a learning center on the famous ship *Titanic*, for example, a teacher might ask students to read the book *The Titanic Lost . . . and Found* by Judy Donnelly (Random House). Have blank double-entry journal pages and pencils available. As the students read, they should jot down brief notes about the plot in the left-hand column. Afterward, they record their thoughts in the right-hand column (see Figure 14-4).

The scope of activities for learning centers ranges from simple to complex. The particular content of the learning center, as well as the special needs and interests of

FIGURE 14–4
Double-Entry Journal

Something Interesting	How I Felt About It
Titantic is ready to sail on its first voyage.	I would be excited.
Titantic is in icy waters off the coast of Canada.	I would feel scared in the dark.
The lookouts sees a mountain of ice. The Titantic hits the iceberg.	I would panic: "Is the ship going to hit it." It is going to sink!
People laugh and joke.	They still think they are on a ship that cannot sink.
Some people get into the lifeboats.	Women and children go first — they're lucky.
Titantic sinks into the black water.	I feel sad so many people died.
A ship called the Carpathia saves the people in the lifeboats.	I feel better that some people are saved.
Titantic lies many miles down under the atlantic.	I would love to see how beautiful the ship was.

Susanna

your students, dictates the number of activities you will want to offer at the center. Don't overwhelm the children by planning more than they can handle, and don't provide them with such unattractive or unchallenging activities that interest in the center soon wanes. Don't hesitate to change or drop an activity if it seems inappropriate or unpopular. Experience in using learning centers and observing children at work in centers will indicate what constitutes an appropriate number and variety of activities.

Writing Directions

Giving clear directions enables children to use the learning center activities independently. In addition to carefully introducing the children to each center activity and thoroughly explaining how to use it, display clear directions so the children will be constantly aware of how the center is designed to operate.

Carefully print or type the directions, and remember that brevity is important. Avoid unnecessary words; for example, don't say, "Get some crayons. Find the stack of drawing paper. Take a piece of paper and draw a winter scene." Instead, say, "Draw a winter scene." The materials should be provided right at the center. Underline or highlight key words that are essential for completing an activity; for example, "*Draw* a picture of . . ." Whenever possible, use action words to begin directions; for example, "*Look* carefully at the picture . . ."

Enumerate the directions in proper sequence; for example, "*First*, ask 15 classmates to name their favorite rock stars. *Second*, list the names of the stars in order so that the most popular star is first, etc. *Third*, compare your list with a classmate's list. Are your lists the same or different? Why do you think this is so?" Include pictures or hand-drawn illustrations to help students who may have difficulty reading printed directions. A drawing of a pencil can illustrate a writing task, or a picture of scissors a cutting task. Tape-record the learning center directions for the very young child or the child who has extreme reading difficulties.

Providing examples in the directions is helpful. Whenever possible, try to make the directions open ended; that is, encourage the child to extend the activity into a new area of interest: "How would the results be different if . . ." or "Compare your results with a friend. Why are they the same? Different?"

Explain in the directions how the finished work will be evaluated: An answer key? Answers on the reverse side of the material? Covered answers? Tell students what will be done with the finished work. Sample direction cards are illustrated in Figure 14–5.

Completing a Task

Build into the learning center some means or device so the children can tell immediately whether they have completed a task successfully. Provide a special answer key at the center for immediate reference, or place the answers on the reverse side of the activity card. Another approach to feedback is to use a code. Letters or numerals can be placed on the reverse side of the activity cards, and matching symbols can be placed on the bottoms of cans, cartons, or boxes into which the cards are to be

FIGURE 14–5
Sample Direction Cards

Reach your hand
inside this box and
pick out a surprise card.
Complete the activity.

Clip from the
magazines at this
center pictures of
people who help
meet your needs.
Write a caption that
tells what they do.

Spend one school day
observing all the people
you depend on to meet
your needs. Make a list
of these people and write
one sentence describing
each.

Write a thank-you letter
or design a thank-you
card for someone who
helps meet one of your
important needs.

sorted. You also can use symbol or color codes. Children match colors or pictures to check their answers. Some activities are self-correcting by design; for example, when puzzle pieces fit together, they show the student she is correct.

Center directors may correct the children's work, or teacher's aides, parent volunteers, older students, or classmates who have completed the activity can do it. Teacher–student conferences are often used in addition to self-evaluation. They are especially useful as feedback for creative activities that have no one correct answer, or when you want to know more about the children's attitudes toward the activities in the centers. Of course, diagnostic information about the child's growth in skill or concept development also emerges as you ask questions or observe pupil performance in activities.

Designing Attractive Backgrounds

Children respond favorably to things that come in attractive packages. Capitalize on this attribute by providing an enticing background picture accompanied by a catchy caption to attract attention. Place the directions in a strategic spot on the center background. If you are not a great artist, don't despair; you can obtain pictures for center backgrounds from several sources. Commercially prepared transparencies can be projected on a sheet of oaktag. Trace around the image with a marking pen and color in the areas with marking pens, crayons, or paint. You can also prepare your own transparencies by running a favorite picture through a thermofax machine or tracing it on a sheet of clear acetate. Use an overhead projector and follow the preceding procedure. Pictures can also be projected onto a sheet of oaktag with an opaque projector. Instead of projecting an image for tracing to create your center background, you can simply cut out illustrations from magazines and newspapers, store displays, advertising circulars, and coloring books and paste the pictures on heavy tagboard.

In addition, plan to place the centers in different spots around the classroom (see Figure 14–6). Learning centers should contain a number of activities necessary to complete an objective; when the children differ in achievement levels, multilevel activities should be provided.

FIGURE 14–6
Possible Learning Center Sites

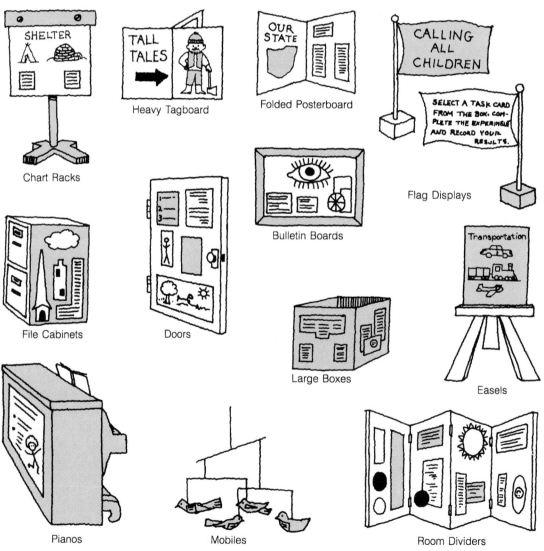

Introducing Learning Centers

Because children need careful guidance with any new classroom procedure, an introduction to learning centers is no place to hurry. Introducing children to this new classroom learning arrangement all at once by setting up a room full of centers and expecting each child to work independently with little or no introduction may be devastating to both teacher and child. The analogy of the tortoise and the hare is apropos; starting out quickly with learning centers, you may find that the children do not understand what to do with them, even though they are enthusiastic and all too willing to rush headlong into their use—just like the hare in the race. Instead, slow the children down and give them more careful guidance to introduce the new learning center environment. To introduce learning centers, it is better to adopt the tortoise's gait rather than the hare's, establishing a starting point and proceeding slowly, clearly explaining every step to the children. Gradually, you will find that your classroom is operating smoothly and efficiently, without the setbacks that befall an impulsive and hasty teacher.

Inform students about how the learning centers are to be used. Don't get involved with detailed educational jargon, but explain the following points simply:

- What kinds of activities are available at each center.
- When the centers are to be used.
- How each center is to be used.
- How the children are to be assigned to the various centers.
- What responsibilities the children who are working at the centers have.
- What is to be done with the work that has been completed.

A Sample Learning Center

Trying something new is always a bit frightening. But you will know how effective you have been when you observe whether you are more relaxed, more stimulated, and more excited about teaching, and whether your children are more interested, more involved, and happier in school.

You will know if it has been a profitable experience when you observe whether the children are developing interests and skills in subject areas and whether they seem to be gaining self-confidence, initiative, and independence. You will know by their test scores, comments from their parents, and their motivation whether their achievement is the same, poorer, or better than it had been in a more formal learning environment. You will judge the impact of this approach on individual children. You will know which ones flourish in an environment that encourages responsibility for self-learning, and which ones need more structure, more instruction, more outer controls. Eventually, you will be able to design a classroom flexible enough to meet almost all of the children's needs.

The learning center plan described in Activity 14–4 illustrates one approach to independent work in the elementary school social studies classroom.

Activity 14–4

Classroom Exercise

Learning Center: Inventors and Inventions

Background

Arrange for your students to visit the library to find information about inventions and inventors. Encourage them to ask the librarian for help in finding books and other helpful materials. Have each student pick one invention, find out about it, and share the story of the invention with the class. Then, to extend and reinforce what the students learn, plan and organize independent games and activities within an "Inventive Inventions" learning center.

Center Activities

Inventor Concentration

Write the names of the inventors studied on index cards. Write their corresponding inventions on index cards of another color. Instruct the students to combine and shuffle the cards before arranging them face down in rows on the playing area. Taking turns, one player turns over two cards (one of each color). If the "inventor card" matches the "invention card," the player keeps the cards and takes another turn. If the cards do not match, the player returns the cards to their original positions. The game is over when all the cards are taken up. Should you wish to designate a "winner," it should be the student holding the most cards.

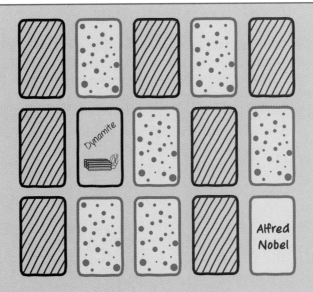

Wall of Fame

Induct noteworthy inventors into a classroom "Wall of Fame." Ask each student to pick an invention/inventor that has been most beneficial in making their lives easier. Then ask them to illustrate the invention within the frame that you predraw on a piece of drawing paper. Print the inventor's name below. Have students write two to four sentences explaining the significance of their choice to complete a "Wall of Fame" plaque. Add each plaque to a growing "Wall of Fame" display (see accompanying illustration).

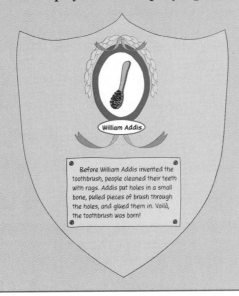

Invention Convention

Display copies of original diagrams or sketches of popular inventions at the center. Have students work in pairs to think of something not yet invented that could make their or someone else's life different. One draws a design of the idea, labeling its parts and telling how it works (see accompanying illustration).

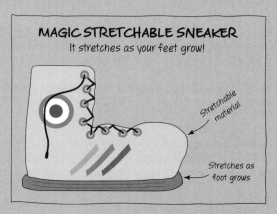

Have one member of the pair design an ad to help sell the invention. To help this student plan the ad, display some common advertising techniques.

BANDWAGON

SPECIAL OFFER

SYMBOL

IMAGE APPEAL

CATCHY PHRASE
OR JINGLE

ENDORSEMENT

Thank-You Cards

Encourage students to select an inventor's biography from a collection of books at the center and design thank-you cards containing a rhyme that highlights the contributions of the inventor. Provide a model to stimulate thinking.

To John Montagu,

The Fourth Earl of Sandwich

As every day I eat my lunch,
Upon your sandwiches I crunch.
PBJ and tuna fine,
Hot pastrami blows my mind.
Baloney, cheese, don't stop there,
Add hot peppers-they'll curl your hair.
So, thank you, thank you, day or night,
I'll think of you with every bite.

PRINT MATERIALS

Textbooks and Trade Books

Oftentimes, when teachers are asked to describe their social studies curriculum, they will tell you all about their textbooks. Principals regularly introduce new teachers to the school's social studies curriculum by informing them, "Here's the textbook. You should become familiar with it." Starr (1989) estimates that "ninety percent of all classroom activity is regulated by textbooks" (p. 106). In recent years there has been a great deal of debate about whether textbooks or trade books (stories, informational books, poetry) should be used as the major source for teaching social studies. Lapp, Flood, and Farnan (1992) advise that textbooks and trade books can coexist, and that students should read both types. Kellough (1997) agrees, suggesting however that textbooks should not dominate instructional experiences; they should be considered only one of many teaching tools, not the ultimate word.

In opposition, Goodman (1988) recommends that the instructional spotlight should be focused on trade books, characterizing textbooks as mere surveys of topics—not going into anything with any degree of depth or passion. Since charges such as Goodman's permeate the educational literature, textbook publishers have increased the number of complete stories, poems, and informational articles in their textbooks, but all too often these added features are abridged, specially adapted for the textbook, or written for the textbook.

It is my contention that using social studies textbooks as the entire instructional program is not a good idea. Children need to experience a wide variety of print sources in the social studies program. Textbooks can be used to survey a topic; trade books can add depth and passion. Beginning teachers often rely on textbooks and their accompanying teacher's guides to gain confidence in the classroom; as their teaching abilities grow, they rapidly move toward using trade books. Many experienced teachers, especially those using an integrated thematic approach to social studies instruction, incorporate reading from a variety of sources, including textbooks and the rich treasures of children's literature. In support of this idea, the authors of *Becoming a Nation of Readers* discuss the strength of the literacy–social studies connection: "[T]he most logical place for instruction in most reading and thinking strategies is in social studies . . . rather than in separate lessons about reading" (Anderson, Hiebert, Scott, and Wilkinson, 1985, p. 73). There are many opportunities to use literacy strategies in the social studies program. Teachers familiar with the concept of "literacy across the curriculum" know that they must supplement the textbook with some of the many superb trade books available today. Information books, historical fiction, folklore, biographies, and poetry collections, as well as newspapers, add depth and substance to any topic under study.

Newspapers

Amendment 1—United States Constitution

Congress shall make no law respecting an establishment of religion, or prohibiting the free exercise thereof, or abridging freedom of speech, or of the press; or the right of a free people to peaceably assemble, and to petition the Government for a redress of grievances.

People over the centuries have argued that a *free press* (not only newspapers, but all broadcast media, too) is the keystone of a democracy, and predict that without it our democratic form of government would fail. Likewise, it has been argued that a *free education* is the keystone of a democracy. Combining these two popular sentiments, we find that neither a free press nor an informed citizenry could exist without each other. The free press ensures the public's right to know; our schools have a responsibility to prepare able and interested citizens to understand the issues involved in their lives. With important issues changing as rapidly as they do in contemporary society, the matter of being well informed is now more important than ever. The foundation for developing such informed citizens should be established in the elementary grades as you establish an effective newspaper-based current affairs program.

Perhaps the best place to begin an effective current affairs program is to teach children how to read a newspaper. Children should learn to examine the various sections of the newspaper (world news, sports, community events, etc.), with special attention directed toward the sources of material for these sections—wire services, local writers, and syndicated columns. Children can understand that a good news article answers four basic questions (*who, what, where,* and *when*) in the first paragraph or two, and then should go on to state *why* and *how*. Lead the children through the literal interpretation of news articles by making copies of a news article, distributing it to each child, allowing them sufficient time to read it (for a *purpose*, of course), and then guiding their interpretation:

- "Who is the story about?"
- "What did the person do?"
- "When did the event take place?"
- "Where did the event take place?"
- "Why did the event come about?"
- "How can this event be extended (be prevented from happening again, teach us a lesson, etc.)?"

News stories are objective; they present the facts with an absence of personal reaction. Encourage the children to share their feelings regarding any particular news article with questions such as the following:

- "How did you feel about the situation?"
- "What would you have done?"
- "Would you be willing to do the same thing?"
- "Do you agree with the central character?"
- "Is there any information you can add to the article?"
- "Do you think the story was written fairly (accurately)?"

Teachers should use newspapers in creative ways. The following are some guidelines you might find helpful with your students:

- Fictionalize a story about what happened just before and just after the moment captured in a selected newspaper picture.
- Give students a newspaper headline and ask them to write their own news story based on it.
- Take a student survey to find out what part of the newspaper interests them most. Divide the class into groups, each with a variety of interests. Each week, assign a group to report to the class. Urge "reporters" to read all they can find in the newspaper each day concerning their field. Each "reporter" then reads to the class one especially interesting item each week.
- Read only the first paragraph of a news article, and then make up the rest. Be original! Compare your story with the original article if you want.
- Have each student study newspaper articles about different well-known personalities and pantomime personality sketches as other students try to guess who is being portrayed. As students become skilled in mime techniques, have them scan the newspaper for simple situations to play out in pairs or small groups. Other students will enjoy guessing the actions.

- Have a student assume the personality of a person in the news and have class-mates interview him or her. Remember, the student who assumes the character's personality must answer questions using the character's observed speech and other mannerisms.
- Have students take a favorite nursery rhyme and write it up as a news story, giving it an appropriate headline; for example, *Mr. Egg Fractures Skull.*
- Let your students be advice columnists. Have them read letters to a popular advice columnist. Pupils then write their own advice on real problems affecting playground behaviors, classroom problems, and other sources of conflict.
- Clip headlines from stories, but keep one newspaper intact. Have students read news stories and write their own headlines. Did students discover the main idea of the story expressed in the headline? Compare student headlines with the headlines in the uncut issue.
- After identifying the main topic of an editorial, scan the paper to locate stories related to the topic and read them. Study how the editorial was developed and then have students write their own editorials on the same issue.

Newspapers are an excellent classroom resource, for many reasons.

- They are an adult medium. No fifth grader with a reading problem likes to be seen carrying around "Six Ducks in a Pond," but will be proud to be seen reading the newspaper.
- They bridge the gap between the classroom and the real world.
- They contain something for every student: front-page news for those who want to read an objective account of a newsworthy event; informative and entertaining articles on a variety of subjects; comics for those who desire humor; challenging puzzles and games for personal amusement; and editorials from which students may gain insight into controversial issues.
- They contain practical vocabulary—words students will use throughout their lives.
- They can be marked, cut, pasted, or colored—important to young children who learn by doing and seeing.
- They contain in their news stories the best models for clear, concise, simple writing.
- They are the perfect model for teaching students to write for a purpose and for a particular audience.
- They are the only really up-to-date social studies text there is.
- They are the only text the majority of children will continue to read throughout their lives.
- They are an influential and integral part of our free society. Freedom of the press is guaranteed under the U.S. Constitution; some have said that this freedom is "less the right of the newspaper to print than it is the right of the citizen to read."

Current events periodicals help keep students up to date on what is going on in the world.

Electronic Newspapers

Knowing what is going on in the world creates better citizens. One of the major goals of elementary school social studies programs is to help children acquire a life-long interest in newspapers so they can keep in touch with what is going on in the world outside. However, when teachers try to interest children in current events, they often assign a child to bring in a newspaper article the next day. What normally happens is that the child realizes at 9 P.M. that she needs a current events article, and her parent frantically searches the front page to clip out something the child can take to school. Or, even worse, the child informs a parent just before he goes to sleep that he needs a current events article on Tasmania for tomorrow. The newspaper has probably been discarded, but even if it hasn't, did anything newsworthy happen in Tasmania today? The value of such hit-or-miss newspaper programs is questionable.

An option being pursued by many elementary school teachers today is online newspapers. They have selected this option for several reasons. One that stands out is immediacy—the newspaper that is discussed in school at 9:00 A.M. does not include the important stories that broke at 8:00 A.M. Online news fills the gap; keeping the class informed creates links between what is in the newspaper and what is happening right now. In addition to immediacy, the multimedia presentation of online newspapers is impressive. Video clips, sound, and full-color images accompany on-line news stories. And, should a particular story capture the interest of the class, on-line newspapers allow them to search the story by keyword and access a rich store-house of related news. Students can incorporate all of these sources into their own multimedia packages, properly cited, creating a customized newspaper.

Several online sources offer colorful, easy-to-read newspapers. *The Christian Science Monitor* is one of the most useful (http://csmonitor.com). Others include *CNN Interactive* (http://www.cnn.com), *MSNBC* (http://msnbc.com), and *USA Today Online* (http://usatoday.com). Several local newspapers have online versions, too, so check to see what is available.

None of these online newspaper sources is meant to replace the daily newspaper; newspapers are here to stay. However, online newspapers can augment the use of classroom newspapers by serving as an alternative that many people believe will be the dominant source for delivering information in the future.

Current Affairs Periodicals

Teachers often rely on commercially produced current events magazines or newspa-pers for most of their program in current affairs. This approach has both advantages and disadvantages.

Some teachers become too dependent on a formal reading–reciting technique when using periodicals, but I find them to be an important educational tool for sev-eral reasons. First, these periodicals can motivate. They are written especially for children, and even reluctant readers respond positively to the nontext format and the comfortable reading levels. Second, the periodicals select interesting, contemporary topics. This week's big news, a special TV presentation, or the latest technological breakthrough helps to make the classroom more current. Finally, periodicals are accompanied by comprehensive teacher's guides that describe creative teaching strategies. The magazines are used in thousands of schools around the country and are a valuable resource material.

AFTERWORD

The heart of successful social studies instruction is balance and proportion. These ele-ments do not normally emerge during a student's undergraduate certification program, during student teaching, or even after a year on the job. They often emerge after re-peated successes with textbook-based instruction. You will not rely on textbooks to guide you throughout your entire teaching career; a feeling of unrest and a strong desire to "spread your wings" will begin to entice you to expand your repertoire and experi-ment with varied instructional materials and activities during your earliest years of teaching. Katz (1972) describes this professional evolution as a stage-related process:

- *Stage 1*:   You are preoccupied with survival. You ask yourself questions such as, "Can I get through the day in one piece? Without losing a child? Can I make it until the end of the week? Until the next vacation? Can I really do this kind of work day after day? Will I be accepted by my colleagues?" Textbooks are useful tools that help teachers gain the confidence necessary to manage the routines causing most of the anxiety during this stage. (*First year*)

- *Stage 2*:   You decide you *can* survive. You begin to focus on individual children who pose problems and on troublesome situations, and you ask yourself these kinds of questions: "How can I help the shy child? How can I help a child who does not seem to be learning? What more can I do for children with special needs?" (*Second year*)

- *Stage 3*:   You begin to tire of doing the same things with the children. You like to meet with other teachers, scan magazines, and search through other sources of information to discover new projects and activities for the children. You ask questions about new developments in the field: "Who is doing what? Where? What are some of the new materials, techniques, approaches, and ideas? How can I make social studies (or any other subject) more powerful?" (*Third and fourth years*)

According to Katz's developmental theory, then, new teachers should not expect to move away from a deliberate textbook-based routine until sometime during the third year of teaching. At first, you will feel more comfortable teaching with the help of textbooks and with ideas learned from others. The need to grow and learn will become evident as an inner drive gives you no other choice but to branch out. You should then begin to formulate and refine a personal philosophy of instruction that will serve as a foundation to undergird all professional decisions in the future. The difference between teachers who are good "technicians" and those who are educational leaders appears to be their willingness to constantly think about and work toward methods based on a sound personalized philosophy of teaching and learning.

You will use textbooks, then, and they will contribute immeasurably to your social studies program. But the emphasis of your instruction should be on variety. Continually confront youngsters with significant experiences so they get to know our world and build the qualities that help them become constructive, active citizens. The kinds of citizens our boys and girls grow up to be is determined to a great extent by the ways they live and grow in school.

TECHNOLOGY SAMPLER

Useful sources for related social studies topics include the following Internet sites:

Cable News Network
http://www.cnn.com

The ChristianScience Monitor Electronic Edition
http://csmonitor.com

CNN Interactive
http://www.cnn.com

Family PC (reviews of children's software)
http://www.familypc.com

MSNBC
http://msnbc.com

Newsweek Parent's Guide to Children's Software (reviews of children's software)
http://www.newsweekparentsguide.com

Time Magazine
http://www.pathfinder.com/time

USA Today Online
http://usatoday.com

Sources for keeping kids safe on the Internet include:

http://www.ednet.com.au/cyber/byber/cp_safe.htm

http://www.parentsplace.com

http://www.safesurf.com/wave/sskwave.html

http://www.yahoologans.com/docs/safety/indes.html

http://www.surfwatch.com/yagoologans/purchase.html

WHAT I *NOW* KNOW

Complete these self-check items once more. Determine for yourself whether it would be useful to take a more in-depth look at any area. Use the same key as you did for the preassessment form ("+", "?", "−").

I can *now*

_____ explain the value of doing something real in the social studies classroom.

_____ recognize how investigating realia contributes to children's learning.

_____ identify the characteristics of a beneficial field trip.

_____ give examples of how to use resource persons productively.

_____ design instruction that integrates computers in the social studies program.

_____ explain how to incorporate videos, slides, and filmstrips into social studies instruction.

_____ describe the teacher's role in carrying out picture discussions.

_____ develop a strategy for using simulation games in the classroom.

_____ design and demonstrate the use of learning centers in the social studies classroom.

_____ compare the advantages of using various print sources.

REFERENCES

Anderson, R. C., Hiebert, E. H., Scott, J. A., & Wilkinson, I. A. G. (1985). *Becoming a nation of readers.* Washington, DC: National Institute of Education.

Betts, F. (1994). Making decisions about CD-ROMs. *Educational Leadership, 51,* 42.

Blagojevic, B. (1997). Internet interactions. *Scholastic Early Childhood Today, 11,* 47–48.

Brandt, R. (1995). Future shock is here. *Educational Leadership, 53,* 5.

Goodman, K. S. (1988). Look what they've done to Judy Blume!: The "bazalation" of children's literature. *The New Advocate, 1,* 29–41.

Katz, L. G. (1972). Developmental stages of preschool teachers. *Elementary School Journal, 73,* 50–54.

Kellough, R. D. (1997). *A resource guide for teaching: K–12.* Upper Saddle River, NJ: Prentice Hall.

Lapp, D., Flood, J., & Farnan, N. (1992). Basal readers and literature: A tight fit or a mismatch? In K. D. Wood & A. Moss (Eds.), *Exploring literature in the classroom: Contents and methods* (pp. 35–57). Norwood, MA: Christopher Gordon.

Muir, M. (1994). Putting computer projects at the heart of the curriculum. *Educational Leadership, 51,* 30–32.

Starr, J. (1989). The great textbook war. In H. Holz, I. Marcus, J. Dougherty, J. Michaels, & R. Peduzzi (Eds.), *Education and the American dream; Conservatives, liberals, and radicals debate the future of education.* Grandy, MA: Bergin and Garvey.

Sunal, C. S., & Haas, M. E. (1993). *Social studies and the elementary/middle school student.* Fort Worth, TX: Harcourt Brace Jovanovich.

Webster, W. (1993). Thank you, Miss Monroe. *Educational Leadership, 50,* 45.

Author Index

Subject Index

ABOUT THE AUTHOR

George W. Maxim is a professor in the teacher education program of the Department of Childhood Studies and Reading at West Chester University, where he specializes in social studies methods and early childhood education. He is an experienced classroom teacher, having held positions at both the elementary and preschool levels. As an active member of the National Council for the Social Studies (NCSS), he has served on the educational Publishing Advisory committee, and the Curriculum Committee, chaired the Early Childhood/Elementary Advisory Committee, and was a member of the Editorial Advisory Board of *Social Studies and the Young Learner.* Dr. Maxim has consulted with several school districts in the development of social studies curricula and has been a conference presenter on many occasions. His teaching and professional leadership efforts have led to numerous awards. Dr. Maxim has published articles on social studies topics in such journals as *Social Education, The Social Studies,* and *Childhood Education.* In addition to writing *Social Studies and the Elementary School Child,* Dr. Maxim has authored *The Very Young* (5th edition) and *The Sourcebook* (2nd edition) for Merrill, an imprint of Prentice Hall.